Europe at War, 1914

Situation on 30 November 1914

- Central Powers and associates
- Entente Powers
- Neutral states
- Western front
- Eastern front

ST PETERSBURG (Petrograd)

Revel

Pskov

Riga

Libau

Dvinsk

Dvina

Smolensk

Konigsberg

Vilna

Minsk

Desna

anrig

annenberg

Grodno

stula

Brest-Litovsk

Lodz

Warsaw

Vorskha

Kiev

Cracow

Lemberg

Bug

Dnieper

GALICIA

Dneister

Odessa

Pruth

BESS-ARABIA

VIENNA

Budapest

MOLDAVIA

AUSTRIA-HUNGARY

Drava

BUCHAREST

Sava

BELGRADE

WALLACHIA

Black Sea

SERBIA

Danube

BULGARIA

MONTE-NEGRO

SOPHIA

riatic Sea

CONSTANTINOPLE

Angora

ALBANIA

Dardanelles

OTTOMAN EMPIRE (TURKEY)

Brindisi

Aegean Sea

GREECE

Smyrna

Messina

ATHENS

CYPRUS

Ionian Sea

500 miles

altic Sea

THE FIRST WORLD WAR

The First World War

JOHN KEEGAN

HUTCHINSON
LONDON

© John Keegan 1998

The right of John Keegan to be
identified as the Author of this work has been asserted
by John Keegan in accordance with the
Copyright, Designs and Patents Act 1988

All rights reserved

1 3 5 7 9 10 8 6 4 2

This edition first published in 1998 by
Hutchinson

Random House (UK) Limited
20 Vauxhall Bridge Road, London SW1V 2SA

Random House Australia (Pty) Limited
20 Alfred Street, Milsons Point, Sydney,
New South Wales 2061, Australia

Random House New Zealand Limited
18 Poland Road, Glenfield,
Auckland 10, New Zealand

Random House South Africa (Pty) Ltd
Endulini, 5A Jubilee Road,
Parktown 2193, South Africa

A CiP record for this book is available
from the British Library

Papers used by Random House UK Limited are natural,
recyclable products made from wood grown in sustainable
forests. The manufacturing processes conform to the
environmental regulations of the country of origin.

ISBN 0 09 1801788

Typeset in Times New Roman by
MATS, Southend-on-Sea, Essex

Printed and bound in Great Britain by
Mackays of Chatham PLC, Chatham, Kent

To the men of Kilmington
who did not return from
the Great War 1914–18

Contents

Maps

Illustrations

Austrian 305mm howitzer (*RHPL*)
British Vickers machine-gun crew (*TRH*)
A Royal Engineers Signal Service visual signalling post (*TRH*)
German infantry with an A7V tank (*RHPL*)
German infantry in a communication trench (*AKG*)
Breaking the Hindenburg Line: British infantry (*AKG*)
Breaking the Hindenburg Line: British Mark IV tanks (*AKG*)
American infantry advancing (*AKG*)
Turkish gunners (*RHPL*)
Australians and the Royal Naval Division share a trench (*ETA*)
Wounded ANZAC coming down, replacements waiting to go
   up (*TRH*)

Third section

Von Lettow-Vorbeck (*AKG*)
SMS *Seeadler* leaving Dar-es-Salaam (*AKG*)
SMS *Blücher* sinking (*TRH*)
The Grand Fleet in the North Sea (*ETA*)
The battlecruiser *Invincible*, broken in half by internal explosion,
   Battle of Jutland; HM Destroyer *Badger* approaching to pick up
   the six survivors (*TRH*)
American armed merchant ship *Covington*, sinking off Brest (*TRH*)
The torpedo room of a U-boat (*ETA*)
Fokker triplanes (*TRH*)
Sopwith Camel (*TRH*)
A squadron equipped with the SE 5a (*TRH*)
A French soldier welcomed in the liberated war zone (*RHPL*)
A Hessian regiment marching back across the Rhine (*RHPL*)
A burial party at Windmill Cemetery (*TRH*)
Tyne Cot Cemetery, Passchendaele, today (*TRH*)

Abbreviations:
AKG – AKG, London
ETA – E.T. Archive, London
Novosti– Novosti Press Agency, London
RHPL – Robert Hunt Picture Library, London
TRH – TRH Pictures, London

ACKNOWLEDGEMENTS

I grew up with men who had fought in the First World War and with women who had waited at home for news of them. My father fought in the First World War, so did his two brothers, so did my father-in-law. All four survived. My father's and my father-in-law's carefully censored memories of their war experiences first introduced me to the war's nature. My father's sister, one of the army of spinsters the war created, told me, towards the end of her life, something of the anxieties of those left behind. To them, and to the hundreds of other veterans directly and indirectly caught up in the war's tragedy to whom I have spoken over the years, I owe the inspiration for this book.

Personal recollections suffuse what I have written. Its substance derives from the reading of many years. For access to the books I have found most useful I would like to thank the Librarians and staff of the Libraries of the Royal Military Academy Sandhurst, the Staff College, the United States Military Academy, West Point, Vassar College and *The Daily Telegraph*. I am particularly grateful to Colonel Robert Doughty, Head of the Department of History at West Point, and to his Executive Officer, Major Richard Faulkner, who arranged for me to use the magnificent West Point Library while I was Delmas Visiting Professor at Vassar in 1997. I am also grateful to the Librarian and staff of the London Library and to Tony Noyes, Chairman of the Western Front Association.

I owe important debts in the production of this book to my editor at Hutchinson, Anthony Whittome, to my editor at Knopf, Ashbel Green, to my picture editor, Anne-Marie Ehrlich, to the mapmaker, Alan Gilliland, Graphics Editor of *The Daily Telegraph*, and, as always, to my Literary Agent, Anthony Sheil. Lindsey Wood, who typed the manuscript, spotted unseen errors, deciphered hieroglyphics, checked bibliographies, reconciled inconsistencies and dealt with every sort of publishing difficulty, proved as before that she is a secretary without equal.

Among others who in various ways gave help, I would like to acknowledge the forbearance of the Editor of *The Daily Telegraph*, Charles Moore, and the assistance of my colleagues Robert Fox, Tim Butcher, Tracy Jennings, Lucy Gordon-Clarke and Sharon Martin. I owe a particular debt of gratitude to the proprietor of *The Daily Telegraph*, Conrad Black.

Friends at Kilmington who make the writing of books possible include Honor Medlam, Michael and Nesta Grey, Mick Lloyd and Eric Coombs. My love and thanks as always go to my children and to my son-in-law, Lucy and Brooks Newmark, Thomas, Matthew and Rose, and to my darling wife, Susanne.

The Manor House,
Kilmington,
23 July, 1998

ONE

A EUROPEAN
TRAGEDY

THE FIRST WORLD WAR was a tragic and unnecessary conflict. Unnecessary because the train of events that led to its outbreak might have been broken at any point during the five weeks of crisis that preceded the first clash of arms, had prudence or common goodwill found a voice; tragic because the consequences of the first clash ended the lives of ten million human beings, tortured the emotional lives of millions more, destroyed the benevolent and optimistic culture of the European continent and left, when the guns at last fell silent four years later, a legacy of political rancour and racial hatred so intense that no explanation of the causes of the Second World War can stand without reference to those roots. The Second World War, five times more destructive of human life and incalculably more costly in material terms, was the direct outcome of the First. On 18 September 1922, Adolf Hitler, the demobilised frontfighter, threw down a challenge to defeated Germany that he would realise seventeen years later: 'It cannot be that two million Germans should have fallen in vain . . . No, we do not pardon, we demand – vengeance!'[1]

The monuments to the vengeance he took stand throughout the continent he devastated, in the reconstructed centres of his own German cities, flattened by the strategic bombing campaign that he provoked, and of those – Leningrad, Stalingrad, Warsaw, Rotterdam, London – that he himself laid waste. The derelict fortifications of the Atlantic Wall, built in the vain hope of holding his enemies at bay, are monuments to his desire for vengeance; so, too, are the decaying hutments of Auschwitz and the remnants of the obliterated extermination camps at Sobibor, Belzec and Treblinka. A child's shoe in the Polish dust, a scrap of rusting barbed wire, a residue of pulverised bone near the spot where the gas chambers worked, these are as much relics of the First as of the Second World War.[2] They have their antecedents in the scraps of barbed wire that litter the fields where the trenches ran, filling the French air with the smell of rust on

3

a damp morning, in the mildewed military leather a visitor finds under a hedgerow, in the verdigrised brass of a badge or button, corroded clips of ammunition and pockmarked shards of shell. They have their antecedents also in the anonymous remains still upturned today by farmers ploughing the bloodsoaked soil of the Somme – 'I stop work at once. I have a great respect for your English dead' – just as the barely viewable film of bodies being heaped into the mass graves at Belsen in 1945 has its antecedents in the blurred footage of French soldiers stacking the cordwood of their dead comrades after the Second Battle of Champagne in 1915. The First World War inaugurated the manufacture of mass death that the Second brought to a pitiless consummation.

There are more ceremonial monuments. Few French and British communities lack a memorial to the dead of the Second World War. There is one in my West Country village, a list of names carved at the foot of the funerary crucifix that stands at the crossroads. It is, however, an addition and an afterthought. The cross itself was raised to commemorate the young men who did not return from the First World War and their number is twice that of those killed in the Second. From a population of two hundred in 1914, W. Gray, A. Lapham, W. Newton, A. Norris, C. Penn, L. Penn and W. J. White, perhaps one in four of the village's men of military age, did not come back from the front. Theirs are names found in the church registers that go back to the sixteenth century. They survive in the village today. It is not difficult to see from the evidence that the Great War brought heartbreak on a scale never known since the settlement was established by the Anglo-Saxons before the Norman Conquest and, thankfully, has not been known since. The memorial cross is, the church apart, the only public monument the village possesses. It has its counterpart in every neighbouring village, in the county's towns, where the names multiply many times, and in the cathedral of the diocese at Salisbury. It has its counterpart, too, in every cathedral in France, in each of which will be seen a tablet bearing the inscription, 'To the Glory of God and in memory of one million men of the British Empire who died in the Great War and of whom the greater number rest in France'.

Nearby, certainly, will stand a memorial to the locality's own dead, itself replicated in every surrounding town and village. France lost nearly two million in the Great War, two out of every nine men who marched away. They are often symbolised by the statue of a *poilu*, defiant in horizon blue, levelling a bayonet eastward at the German frontier. The list of names on the plinth is heartrendingly long, all the more heartrending because repetition of the same name testifies to more than one death, often several, in the same family. There are similar lists to be seen graven in stone in the towns and cities of most combatant nations of the Great War. Particularly poignant, I find, is the restrained classicism of the memorial to the cavalry division of the Veneto that stands beside the cathedral of Murano in the lagoon of Venice, bearing row after row of names of young men from the lowlands of the River Po who died in the harsh uplands of the Julian Alps. I am touched by the same emotion in the churches of Vienna where severe stone tablets recall the sacrifice of historic Habsburg regiments now almost forgotten to history.[3]

The Germans, who cannot decently mourn their four million dead of the Second World War, compromised as the Wehrmacht was by the atrocities of the Nazi state, found a materially, if not morally equivalent difficulty in arranging an appropriately symbolic expression of grief for their fallen of the First, since so many lay on foreign soil. The battlefields of the east were closed to them by the Bolshevik revolution, those of the west made at best grudgingly accessible for the retrieval and reburial of bodies. The French and the Belgians found little room in their hearts or in the national soil for the creation of German war cemeteries. While the British were accorded a *sépulture perpétuelle* for their places of burial, which ramified during the 1920s into an archipelago of gardened graveyards along the line of the Western Front breathtaking in their beauty, the Germans were obliged to excavate mass graves in obscure locations to contain the remains of their casualties. Only in East Prussia, on the site of the Tannenberg epic, did they succeed in creating a mausoleum of triumphal monumentality for the fallen. At home, far from the fronts where their young men had died, they gave form to their sorrow in church and cathedral monuments that take their inspiration chiefly from the austerity of high Gothic art, often using the image of Grünewald's *Crucifixion* or Holbein's *Christ in the Tomb* as their theme.[4]

The Christ of Grünewald and Holbein is a body that has bled, suffered and died, untended in its final agony by relative or friend. The image was appropriate to the symbolisation of the Great War's common soldier, for over half of those who died in the west, perhaps more in the east, were lost as corpses in the wilderness of the battlefield. So numerous were those missing bodies that, in the war's immediate aftermath, it was proposed, first by an Anglican clergyman who had served as a wartime chaplain, that the most fitting of all the memorials to the War dead would be a disinterment and reburial of one of those unidentified in a place of honour. A body was chosen, brought to Westminster Abbey and placed at the entrance under a tablet bearing the inscription, 'They buried him among the Kings because he had done good toward God and toward His house'. On the same day, the second anniversary of the armistice of 11 November 1918, a French Unknown Soldier was buried under the Arc de Triomphe in Paris, and unknown soldiers were later reburied in many of the victor nations' capitals.[5] When the defeated Germans attempted to create a national memorial to their dead in 1924, however, the unveiling broke down into a welter of political protest. The speech made by President Ebert, who had lost two sons, was heard out. The two minutes of silence that was supposed to follow was interrupted by the shouting of pro-war and anti-war slogans, which precipitated a riot that lasted all day.[6] The agony of a lost war continued to divide Germany, as it would until the coming of Hitler nine years later. Soon after his assumption of the Chancellorship, Nazi writers began to represent Hitler, the 'unknown corporal', as a living embodiment of the 'unknown soldier' Weimar Germany had failed as a state to honour. It was not long before Hitler, in his speeches as *Führer* of the German nation, began to refer to himself as 'an unknown soldier of the world war'. He was sowing the seed that would reap another four million German corpses.[7]

War's rancours are quick to bite and slow to heal. By the end of 1914, four months after the outbreak of the Great War, 300,000 Frenchmen had been killed, 600,000 wounded, out of a male population of twenty million, perhaps ten million of military age. By the end of the war, nearly two million Frenchmen were dead, the majority from the infantry, the major arm of service, which had lost 22 per cent of those enlisted. The heaviest casualties had been suffered by the youngest year-groups: between 27 per cent and 30 per cent of the conscript classes of 1912–15. Many of those young men were not yet married. By 1918, however, there were 630,000 war widows in France and a very large number of younger women deprived by the war of the chance of marriage. The imbalance between the sexes of those aged twenty to thirty-nine stood in 1921 at forty-five males to fifty-five females. Among the five million wounded of the war, moreover, several hundred thousand were numbered as '*grands mutilés*', soldiers who had lost limbs or eyes. Perhaps the worst afflicted were the victims of disfiguring facial wounds, some of whom were so awful to behold that secluded rural settlements were established, where they could holiday together.[8]

The suffering of the German war generation was comparable. 'Year groups 1892–1895, men who were between nineteen and twenty-two when the war broke out, were reduced by 35–37 per cent.' Overall, of the sixteen million born between 1870 and 1899, 13 per cent were killed, at the rate of 465,600 for each year the war lasted. The heaviest casualties, as in most armies, fell among the officers, of whom 23 per cent were killed – 25 per cent of regular officers – as against 14 per cent of enlisted men. The surviving German '*grands mutilés*' included 44,657 who lost a leg, 20,877 who lost an arm, 136 who lost both arms and 1,264 who lost both legs. There were also 2,547 war blind, a fraction of those seriously wounded in the head, of whom most died. In all, 2,057,000 Germans died in the war, or of wounds in its aftermath.[9]

Germany, though it lost the largest number of counted dead – those of Russia and Turkey remain uncounted with any exactitude – was not the worst proportionate sufferer. That country was Serbia, of whose pre-war population of five million, 125,000 were killed or died as soldiers but another 650,000 civilians succumbed to privation or disease, making a total of 15 per cent of the population lost, compared with something between two and three per cent of the British, French and German populations.[10]

Even those smaller proportions left terrible psychic wounds, falling as they did on the youngest and most active sections of society's males. It has, as the war recedes into history, become fashionable to decry the lament for a 'Lost Generation' as myth-making. The loss, demographers demonstrate, was swiftly made good by natural increase of population, while loss was felt, the harder-hearted sort of historian insists, by a fraction of families. At the very worst, they argue, only 20 per cent of those who went to the war did not return, while the aggregate was lower, 10 per cent or less. For the majority, the war was but a passage in their lives, an interruption of normality to which society rapidly returned as soon as the guns fell silent.

This is a complacent judgement. It is true that the Great War, by comparison with that of 1939–45, did little material damage. No large European city was destroyed or even seriously devastated during its course, as all large German cities were by aerial bombardment during the Second World War. The First World War was a rural conflict, on the Eastern as on the Western Fronts. The fields over which it was fought were swiftly returned to agriculture or pasturage and the villages ruined by bombardment – except for those around Verdun – quickly rebuilt. The war inflicted no harm to Europe's cultural heritage that was not easily repaired: the medieval Cloth Hall at Ypres stands today as it did before the bombardments of 1914–18, so do the town squares of Arras, so does the cathedral of Rouen, while the treasures of Louvain, burnt in an uncharacteristic act of vandalism in 1914, were replaced piece by piece in the war's aftermath.

Above all, the war imposed on the civilian populations involved almost none of the deliberate disruption and atrocity that was to be a feature of the Second. Except in Serbia and, at the outset, in Belgium, communities were not forced to leave their homes, land and peaceful occupations; except in Turkish Armenia, no population was subjected to genocide; and, awful though the Ottoman government's treatment of its Armenian subjects was, the forced marches organised to do them to death belong more properly to the history of Ottoman imperial policy than to that of the war itself. The First, unlike the Second World War, saw no systematic displacement of populations, no deliberate starvation, no expropriation, little massacre or atrocity. It was, despite the efforts by state propaganda machines to prove otherwise, and the cruelties of the battlefield apart, a curiously civilised war.

Yet it damaged civilisation, the rational and liberal civilisation of the European enlightenment, permanently for the worse and, through the damage done, world civilisation also. Pre-war Europe, imperial though it was in its relations with most of the world beyond the continent, offered respect to the principles of constitutionalism, the rule of law and representative government. Post-war Europe rapidly relinquished confidence in such principles. They were lost altogether in Russia after 1917, in Italy after 1922, in Germany in 1933, in Spain after 1936, and only patchily observed at any time in the young states created or enlarged by the post-war settlement in Central and Southern Europe. Within fifteen years of the war's end, totalitarianism, a new word for a system that rejected the liberalism and constitutionalism which had inspired European politics since the eclipse of monarchy in 1789, was almost everywhere on the rise. Totalitarianism was the political continuation of war by other means. It uniformed and militarised its mass electoral following, while depriving voters generally of their electoral rights, exciting their lowest political instincts and marginalising and menacing all internal opposition. Less than twenty years after the end of the Great War, the 'war to end wars' as it had come to be called at the nadir of hopes for its eventual conclusion, Europe was once again gripped by the fear of a new war, provoked by the actions and ambitions of war lords more aggressive than any known to the old world of the long nineteenth-century peace. It was also in the full flood of rearmament, with weapons – tanks, bombing aircraft, submarines – known only in embryo form in the First World War and threatening to make a Second an even greater catastrophe.

The Second World War, when it came in 1939, was unquestionably the outcome of the First, and in large measure its continuation. Its circumstances – the dissatisfaction of the German-speaking peoples with their standing among other nations – were the same, and so were its immediate causes, a dispute between a German-speaking ruler and a Slav neighbour. The personalities, though occupying different status, were also the same: Gamelin, the French commander in 1939, had been principal staff officer to Foch, the Allied Supreme Commander in 1918, Churchill, First Lord of the Admiralty in 1939, had been First Lord of the Admiralty in 1914, Hitler, 'the first soldier of the Third Reich', had been one of the first volunteers of Kaiser Wilhelm's Reich in August 1914. The battlefields were to be the same: the River Meuse, crossed with spectacular ease by the German panzer divisions in May 1940, had proved impassable at Verdun throughout 1914–18; Arras, focus of some of the British Expeditionary Force's worst trench fighting on the Western Front, was the scene of the British army's only successful counter-attack in 1940; while the River Bzura, a narrow watercourse west of Warsaw, was to be critical to the conduct of operations on the Eastern Front both in 1939 and in 1915. Many of those who marched off in 1939 were the same people who, younger in age, junior in rank, had also marched away in 1914, convinced they would be home, victorious, 'before the leaves fall'. The fortunate survivors would, however, have admitted this difference. In 1939 the apprehension of war was strong, so was its menace, so, too, was knowledge of its reality. In 1914, by contrast, war came, out of a cloudless sky, to populations which knew almost nothing of it and had been raised to doubt that it could ever again trouble their continent.

EUROPEAN HARMONY

Europe in the summer of 1914 enjoyed a peaceful productivity so dependent on international exchange and co-operation that a belief in the impossibility of general war seemed the most conventional of wisdoms. In 1910 an analysis of prevailing economic inter-dependence, *The Great Illusion*, had become a best-seller; its author Norman Angell had demonstrated, to the satisfaction of almost all informed opinion, that the disruption of international credit inevitably to be caused by war would either deter its outbreak or bring it speedily to an end. It was a message to which the industrial and commercial society of that age was keenly sympathetic. After two decades of depression, precipitated by an Austrian bank failure in 1873 but sustained by a fall in the prices to be had both for raw materials and for manufactured goods, industrial output had begun to expand again in the last years of the nineteenth century. New categories of manufactures – electrical goods, chemical dyes, internal combustion vehicles – had appeared to tempt buyers; new sources of cheaply extractable raw materials had been found; so, too, had new deposits of precious metals, above all in South Africa, to fertilise credit. Rising population – there was a 35 per cent increase in Austria-Hungary between 1880 and 1910, 43 per cent in Germany, 26 per cent in Britain, over 50 per cent in Russia – sharply enlarged the size of internal markets; emigration – twenty-six million people left Europe for the Americas and Australasia in 1880–1910 – increased demand for goods there also, while the enormous expansion of overseas empires, formal and informal, in Africa and Asia, drew millions of their inhabitants into the international market, both as suppliers of staples and consumers of finished goods. A second revolution in transport – in 1893 steamship overtook sailing-ship tonnage for the first time – had greatly accelerated and expanded the movement of commerce overseas, while the extension of the railway network (virtually complete in Western Europe and the United States by 1870) in Eastern Europe and in Russia – where it grew in length from 31,000 to 71,000 kilometres between 1890 and 1913 – added that enormous region, rich in cereals, minerals, oil and timber, to the integrated international economy. It is scarcely surprising that, by the beginning of the century, bankers had recovered their confidence, gold-based capital was circulating freely, largely from Europe to the Americas and Asia, at a rate of £350 million a year in the first decade of the

10

twentieth century, and return on overseas investment had come to form a significant element of private and corporate incomes in Britain, France, Germany, Holland and Belgium; Belgium, one of the smallest countries in Europe, had in 1914 the sixth largest economy in the world, the result of early industrialisation but also of intense activity by its banks, trading houses and industrial entrepreneurs.

Russian railways, South African gold and diamond mines, Indian textile factories, African and Malayan rubber plantations, South American cattle ranches, Australian sheep stations, Canadian wheatfields and almost every sector of the enormous economy of the United States, already by 1913 the largest in the world, producing one-third of its industrial output, devoured European capital as fast as it could be lent. The greater proportion passed through the City of London. Though its central banking reserve of gold was small – only £24 million in 1890, when the Bank of France had £95 million, the Reichsbank £40 million and the United States Federal Reserve £142 million – the worldwide connections of its private banks and discount houses, insurance and commodity companies and equity and produce exchanges made it nevertheless the principal medium of buying, selling and borrowing for all advanced countries. Its predominance fed the belief so persuasively advanced by Norman Angell that any interruption of the smooth, daily equalisation of debit and credit it masterminded must destroy not only confidence in the monetary mechanism by which the world lived, but the very system itself.

Speaking to the Institute of Bankers in London on 17 January 1912, on 'The Influence of Banking on International Relations', Angell argued that

> commercial interdependence, which is the special mark of banking as it is the mark of no other profession or trade in quite the same degree – the fact that the interest and solvency of one is bound up with the interest and solvency of many; that there must be confidence in the due fulfilment of mutual obligation, or whole sections of the edifice crumble, is surely doing a great deal to demonstrate that morality after all is not founded upon self-sacrifice, but upon enlightened self-interest, a clearer and more complete understanding of all the ties that bind us the one to the other. And such clearer understanding is bound to improve, not merely the relationship of one group to another, but the relationship of all men to all other men, to create a consciousness which

11

must make for more efficient human co-operation, a better human society.

W. R. Lawson, a former editor of the *Financial Times*, observed at the end of the speech, 'It is very evident that Mr. Norman Angell had carried this meeting almost entirely with him.'[11]

It was not only bankers – of whom many of London's foremost were German – that accepted the interdependence of nations as a condition of the world's life in the first years of the twentieth century, a necessary condition and one destined to grow in importance. The acceptance was far wider than theirs. Much of it had a purely practical basis. The revolution in communications – by railway, telegraph and stamped postage – required international co-operation to service the new technologies and bureaucracies of travel and messaging. An International Telegraph Union was established in 1865 and the International Postal Union in 1875. An International Conference for Promoting Technical Uniformity in Railways was set up in 1882 – too late to standardise gauges between Western and Eastern Europe, where Russia had already adopted the broad gauge which was to make the use of its railways by invaders so difficult both in 1914 and 1941 but which, in peace, was nothing but an impediment to commercial traffic. The International Meteorological Organisation, set up to exchange information on the world's weather movements, of critical importance to maritime transport, appeared in 1873 and the International Radiotelegraph Union, which allotted separate wavelengths for the new invention of wireless, in 1906. All these were governmental organisations whose workings enjoyed the support of treaty or statute in member states. The world of commerce was meanwhile establishing its own, equally necessary, international associations: for the Publication of Customs Tariffs in 1890, of Patents and Trademarks in 1883, for Industrial, Literary and Artistic Property in 1895, of Commercial Statistics in 1913; an Institute of Agriculture, which collected and published statistics of farming production and marketing, came into being in 1905. Particular industries and professions meanwhile set up their own international bodies: the International Congress of Chambers of Commerce was established in 1880, the Congress of Actuaries in 1895, the Association of Accountancy in 1911, the International Electrotechnical Commission in 1906, the Committee for the Unification of Maritime Law in 1897, the Baltic and White Sea Conference (which standardised maritime charter) in

1905. An International Bureau of Weights and Measures had been organised in 1875 and the first International Copyright Conventions were signed in the 1880s.

Without such bodies the network of buying and selling, collecting and distributing, insuring and discounting, lending and borrowing could not have knotted as it did in the square mile of the City of London. Internationalism, however, was not merely commercial. It was also intellectual, philanthropic and religious. The only truly transnational religious movement remained, as it had since the collapse of the Roman empire, the Catholic Church, with bishoprics throughout the world centred on that of Rome; its incumbent in midsummer 1914, Pope Pius X, was, however, a willing prisoner in the Vatican, a root-and-branch opponent of all modernising tendencies in theology and as suspicious of his own liberals as he was of Protestants. The latter were equally divided among themselves, Lutheran, Calvinist, Anabaptist and Independent of many hues. Some denominations nevertheless succeeded in co-operating in the missionary field at least. The China Inland Mission, uniting several Protestant churches, dated from 1865. A World Missionary Conference held at Edinburgh in 1910 broadened that impetus and in 1907 Christians in universities had founded the International Christian Movement at Tokyo. Little of this spirit, however, permeated Europe. There the only inter-Protestant body was the Evangelical Alliance, founded in 1846 in resistance to Catholicism.

Doctrinal differences therefore made fellowship between Christians a chancy spiritual undertaking. Common Christianity – and Europe was overwhelmingly Christian by profession in 1914 and strongly Christian in observance also – found an easier expression in philanthropy. Anti-slavery had been an early issue to white international sentiment, Christian at its root. In 1841 Britain, France, Russia, Austria and Prussia had signed a treaty that made slave-trading an act of piracy, a policy Britain was already energetically enforcing through the anti-slavery patrols of the Royal Navy off West Africa. The treaty's provisions were extended by another signed in 1889 at Brussels, ironically the capital of a king who ran a brutal slave empire in the Congo. Nevertheless the oceanic slave trade had by then been extinguished by international co-operation. The traffic in women and children for prostitution, 'White Slavery', also stimulated international action, or at least expressions of disgust. An International Abolitionist Federation Congress met at Geneva in 1877, there were other conferences in 1899 and 1904 and in 1910 a convention, subsequently signed by nine states, decreed the traffic to be a crime punishable by their domestic law wherever committed.

Conditions of labour were also a philanthropic concern. In an age of mass emigration governments neither could nor sought to regulate the welfare of those seeking a new life in distant lands. The impulse to restrict working hours and forbid the employment of children had been a major influence, however, on domestic legislation in many European states during the nineteenth century and was by some subsequently given international force. By 1914 many European states had entered into bilateral treaties protecting workers' rights to social insurance and industrial compensation, while restricting female and child labour. Most were designed to protect migrant workers in border areas; a typical treaty was that of 1904 between France and Italy, guaranteeing reciprocal insurance facilities and protection of respective labour laws to each other's citizens. They may best be seen as a state response to the activities of the international working man's movements, particularly the First International, founded by Karl Marx in London in 1864, and, the Second, Paris 1889. It was their preaching of social revolution that had driven governments, particularly Bismarck's in Germany after 1871, to enact labour welfare laws as a measure of self-protection.

Other, older measures of self-protection were present in international agreements to check the spread of disease, usually by the quarantining of ships in the distant trade and of immigrants from the Near East, identified as the main source of epidemic outbreaks in Europe. The sale of liquor and drugs was also subject to international control; an Opium Conference between twelve governments met at the Hague in 1912; inevitably it failed in its purpose, but the undertaking was evidence of a growing willingness by governments to act collectively. They had done so with success to suppress piracy. They would also co-operate to repatriate each other's criminals, though usually not if their offences could be decreed political. There was a strong objection in liberal states to supporting the rule of tyrannical governments, despite the prevailing commitment of all to the principle of absolute sovereignty. Non-intervention in the domestic affairs of other states, however, was restricted to Christendom. The Ottoman empire's treatment of its minorities had prompted international intervention in Greece in 1827, in the Lebanon in 1860, and several times later. The Chinese empire's complicity in the Boxer siege of the

Peking embassies in 1900 had prompted the despatch of a full-scale international relief expedition, mounted by British bluejackets, Russian Cossacks, French colonial infantry, Italian Bersaglieri and detachments of the German and Austro-Hungarian armies, as well as Japanese guardsmen and United States marines.

The relief expedition was a complete success, showing that Europe could act together when it chose. It could, of course, also think and feel together. Europe's educated classes held much of its culture in common, particularly through an appreciation for the art of the Italian and Flemish renaissance, for the music of Mozart and Beethoven, for grand opera, for the architecture of the Middle Ages and the classical revival, and for each other's modern literature. Tolstoy was a European figure; so, too, were other writers of Europe's present or recent past. Victor Hugo, Balzac, Zola, Dickens, Manzoni, Shakespeare, Goethe, Molière and Dante were familiar, at least as names, to every European high school child, and French, German and Italian were commonly taught them in their foreign-language classes. Despite a growing resistance to the primacy of Latin and Greek in the high schools, Homer, Thucydides, Caesar and Livy were set-books in all of them and the study of the classics remained universal. Through the teaching of the tenets of Aristotle and Plato, there was, despite the nineteenth-century turmoil of ideas stoked by Hegel and Nietzsche, even a congruence of philosophy; the classical foundations stood, perhaps more securely than the Christian. Europe's university graduates shared a corpus of thought and knowledge and, tiny minority though they were, their commonality of outlook preserved something recognisable as a single European culture.

It was enjoyed by an ever-increasing number of European cultural tourists. Ordinary people travelled little; seamen, transhumant pasturers herding their flocks across mountain frontiers, migrant workers moving to the harvest, cooks and waiters, itinerant musicians, pedlars, specialist craftsmen, the agents of foreign business, these were the only sort of aliens Europe's settled people would have met before 1914. The monied tourist was the exception. Travel had been the pastime of the rich in the eighteenth century. By the beginning of the twentieth it had become a middle-class pleasure as well, thanks to the railway revolution and the rise of the hotel industry which it fuelled. Karl Baedeker's Guides, the essential handbook for the tourist abroad, were in 1900 in their thirteenth edition for Rome, their ninth for the Eastern Alps and already their seventh for Scandinavia.

Tourism was, for the majority, channelled and unadventurous. The most visited locations were Venice and Florence, the Holy City, the castles of the Rhine, and Paris, 'City of Light'; but there were also large annual migrations to the spa towns of Central Europe, Carlsbad and Marienbad, to the French and Italian rivieras and to the Alps. Some travellers were venturing further afield. Oxford and Cambridge undergraduates, with their tutors, had already embarked on what was to become the twentieth-century institution of the Hellenic tour; and Baedeker's Guide to Austria included Bosnia, with an entry on Sarajevo: '. . . the numerous minarets and the little houses standing in gardens give the town a very picturesque appearance . . . The streets on the river-banks are chiefly occupied by the Austrian and other immigrants, while most of the Turks and the Servians have their houses on the hillsides . . . the so-called Konak is the residence of the Austrian commandant. Visitors are admitted to the garden.'[12]

The most important visitor to Sarajevo in 1914 would be Franz Ferdinand, heir to the Austrian throne. He, of course, was travelling within his own territory but the members of the royal houses of Europe were great international travellers and their acquaintanceship one of the most important of bonds between states. If international marriages were uncommon even between Europe's upper classes, between royal houses they remained an instrument of foreign relations. The offspring of Queen Victoria were married into most of the Protestant royal families of the continent; one granddaughter, Ena, had breached the religious barrier and was Queen of Spain. Grandsons of Victoria occupied the thrones of her own country and of Germany in 1914; her daughter-in-law's family, the Sonderburg-Glucksburgs of Denmark, numbered as members the Empress of Russia and the Kings of Greece and Norway. It was broadly true that all European royalty were cousins; even the Habsburgs of Austria, most imperious of sovereigns, occasionally mingled their blood with outsiders; and since every state in Europe, except France and Switzerland, was a monarchy, that made for a very dense network of inter-state connections indeed. Symbolic relationships ramified those of birth. The Kaiser was Colonel of the British 1st Dragoons and an admiral in the Royal Navy; his cousin, George V, was Colonel of the Prussian 1st Guard Dragoons. The Austrian Emperor was Colonel of the British 1st Dragoon Guards; while among foreign colonels of Austrian regiments were the Kings of Sweden, Belgium, Italy, Spain, Bavaria, Württemburg, Saxony and Montenegro and the Tsar of Russia.

Symbolic relationships were, however, not hard currency in foreign affairs, any more than were royal cousinship or marriage ties. Nineteenth-century Europe had produced no solid instruments of inter-state co-operation or of diplomatic mediation. The 'Concert of Europe', which had been Napoleon's unintended creation, had withered; so, too, had the anti-revolutionary League of the Three Emperors. It is commonplace to say that Europe in 1914 was a continent of naked nationalism: it was true all the same. The Catholic Church had long lost its pan-European authority; the idea of a secular ecumenicism had died with the Holy Roman Empire in 1804. Some effort had been made to supply the deficiency through the establishment of a code of international law. It remained a weak concept, for its most important principle, established by the Treaty of Westphalia in 1648, was that of the sovereignty of states, which left each in effect unfettered by anything but judgement of self-interest. The only area over which states had agreed to limit the operation of self-interest lay not on land but at sea, which the leading powers had agreed at Paris in 1856 should be one where neutrality was respected and private military activity outlawed. The immunity of medical personnel and of those in their care had been established by the first Geneva Convention of 1864 and some limitation of the destructiveness of weapons had been negotiated at St Petersburg in 1868. The Geneva Convention, however, was on common humanitarianism, while the St Petersburg Declaration did not inhibit the development of automatic weapons or high-explosive projectiles.

The decision of Tsar Nicholas II in 1899 to convene an international conference dedicated not only to strengthening the limitation of armaments but also to the founding of an international court for the settlement of disputes between states by arbitration was therefore a creative innovation. Historians have perceived in his summons of the powers to the Hague an admission of Russia's military weakness. Cynics said the same at the time, as did Russia's professional enemies in Germany and Austria. People of goodwill, of whom there were many, thought differently. With them the Tsar's warning that 'the accelerating arms race' – to produce ever larger armies, heavier artillery and bigger warships – was 'transforming the armed peace into a crushing burden that weighs on all nations and, if prolonged, will lead to the very cataclysm it seeks to avert' – struck a chord. It was to some degree in deference to that public opinion that the 1899 Hague Conference did consent both to a limitation of armaments, in

17

particular the banning of aerial bombardment, and to the creation of the International Court.

A EUROPE OF SOLDIERS

The flaw in the provision for an International Court was that its convening was to be voluntary. 'The greatest thing', wrote the American delegate about the conference, 'is that the Court of Arbitration . . . shall be seen by all nations [to] indicate a sincere desire to promote peace [and to] relieve the various peoples of the fear which so heavily oppresses all, the dread of a sudden outburst of war at any moment.' A German delegate more realistically noted that the Court's 'voluntary character' deprived it of 'the very last trace of any compulsion, moral or otherwise, upon any nation'.[13] The truth of Europe's situation at the turn of the century lay rather with the German than the American. There was, admittedly, a fear of war in the abstract, but it was as vague as the perception of what form modern war itself might take. Stronger by far, particularly among the political classes in every major country, was the fear of the consequences of failure to face the challenge of war itself. Each – Britain, France, Germany, Russia, Austria-Hungary – felt its position threatened in some way or other. The three great European empires, German, Austrian and Russian, felt threatened by the national dissatisfactions of their minorities, particularly in Austria-Hungary, dominated by Germans and Magyars but populated by Slav peoples who outnumbered them. All three were also troubled by demands for wider democracy – in Russia for any democracy at all – and all the more acutely when nationalism and the democratic impulse found a common voice. Democracy was not the problem in Britain or France, since their male populations exercised full electoral rights. It was the burden of a different sort of empire that weighed upon them, the administration of vast overseas dominions in Africa, India, Arabia, South-East Asia, the Americas and the Pacific, a source of enormous national pride but also a spur to aggressive jealousy among their European neighbours. The British believed that Russia had ambitions on India, which its Central Asian possessions closely abutted; the belief was probably mistaken but held nonetheless. The Germans certainly and deeply resented their lack of colonies, sought to extend the few they had acquired in Africa and the Pacific and were ever ready to quarrel, particularly with France, over influence in the few remaining areas not yet subject to European rule.

In a continent in which a handful of powers exercised control over a large cluster of subordinate peoples, and from which two, Britain and France, ruled much of the rest of the world, it was inevitable that reactions between all should be infused with suspicion and rivalry. The worst of the rivalries had been provoked by Germany, through its decision in 1900, enacted in the Second Naval Law, to build a fleet capable of engaging the Royal Navy in battle. Even though Germany's merchant fleet was by then the second largest in the world, the British rightly decided to regard the enactment of the Second Naval Law as an unjustified threat to its century-old command of the seas and reacted accordingly; by 1906 the race to outbuild Germany in modern battleships was the most important and most popular element of British public policy. There was a strong and complementary military rivalry between the continental powers, exemplified at its starkest by the decision of France, a nation of forty million people, to match the strength of Germany, with sixty million, in number of soldiers; the 'Three Year Law' of 1913, extending the service of conscripts, promised, at least in the short term, to achieve that object. There were other rivalries, not least between Britain and France which, by 1900 mutual allies in the face of Germany's rising aggressiveness, nevertheless managed to quarrel over colonial interests in Africa.

What uniformly characterised all these disputes was that none was submitted to the process of international arbitration suggested by the discussions at the Hague in 1899. When issues of potential conflict arose, as they did over the first (1905) and second (1911) Moroccan crises in Franco-German relations, turning on German resentment of the extension of French influence in North Africa, and over the First (1912) and Second (1913) Balkan Wars, the results of which disfavoured Austria, Germany's ally, the great powers involved made no effort to invoke the Hague provision for international arbitration but settled affairs, as was traditional, by ad hoc international treaty. Peace, temporarily at least, was in each case the outcome; the ideal of supranational peacemaking, towards which the Hague Conference had pointed the way, was in no case invoked.

International, which chiefly meant European, policy was indeed, in the opening years of the twentieth century, guided not by the search for a secure means of averting conflict but by the age-old quest for security in military superiority. That means, as the Tsar had so eloquently warned at the Hague in 1899, translated into the creation

19

of ever larger armies and navies, the acquisition of more and heavier guns and the building of stronger and wider belts of frontier fortification. Fortification, however, was intellectually out of fashion with Europe's advanced military thinkers, who were persuaded by the success of heavy artillery in recent attacks on masonry and concrete – as at Port Arthur, during the Russo-Japanese War of 1904–5 – that guns had achieved a decisive advantage. Power had transferred, it was believed, from static defence to the mobile offensive as represented particularly by large masses of infantry manoeuvring, with the support of mobile field guns, at speed across the face of the battlefield. There was still thought to be a role for cavalry, in which European armies abounded; the German army, in the years before 1914, added thirteen regiments of mounted riflemen (*Jäger zu Pferde*) to its order of battle, while the French, Austrian and Russian armies also expanded their horsed arm. It was on numbers of infantrymen, equipped with the new magazine-rifle, trained in close-order tactics and taught, above all, to accept that casualties would be heavy until a decision was gained that, nevertheless, the generals counted upon to achieve victory.[14] The significance of improvised fortification – the entrenchments and earthworks thrown up at speed which, defended by riflemen, had caused such loss to the attacker on the Tugela and Modder rivers during the Boer War, in Manchuria during the Russo-Japanese War and at the lines of Chatalja during the Second Balkan War – had been noted, but discounted. Given enough well-led and well-motivated infantry, the European military theorists believed, no line of trenches could be held against them.

Among the other great industrial enterprises of Europe in the first years of the twentieth century, therefore, the industry of creating soldiers flourished. Since the triumph of Prussia's army of conscripts and reservists over the Austrians in 1866 and the French in 1870, all leading European states (Britain, sea-girt and guarded by the world's largest navy, was the exception) had accepted the necessity of submitting their young men to military training in early manhood and of requiring them, once trained, to remain at the state's disposition, as reservists, into late maturity. The result of this requirement was to produce enormous armies of serving and potential soldiers. In the German army, model for all others, a conscript spent the first two years of full adulthood in uniform, effectively imprisoned in barracks which were governed by distant officers and administered by sergeants all too close at hand. During the first five years after his discharge from duty he was obliged to return to the reserve unit of his regiment for annual training. Then, until the age of thirty-nine, he was enrolled in a unit of the secondary reserve, or *Landwehr*; thereafter, until the age of forty-five, in the third-line reserve, the *Landsturm*. There were French, Austrian and Russian equivalents. The effect was to maintain inside European civil society a second, submerged and normally invisible military society, millions strong, of men who had shouldered a rifle, marched in step, borne the lash of a sergeant's tongue and learnt to obey orders.

Submerged, also, below the surface of Europe's civil geography was a secondary, military geography of corps and divisional districts. France, a country of ninety administrative departments, created by the First Republic to supplant the old royal provinces with territorial units of approximately equal size, named for the most part after the local river – Oise, Somme, Aisne, Marne, Meuse (names to which the First World War would give a doleful fame) – was also divided into twenty military districts, comprising four or five departments. Each military district was the peacetime location of a corps of the 'active' army, and the source in war of an equivalent group of divisions of the reserve; the XXI Corps had its location in French North Africa. The forty-two active divisions, comprising 600,000 men, would on mobilisation take with them into the field another twenty-five reserve divisions and ancillary reserve units, raising the war strength of the army to over three million. From the I Corps District (departments of the Nord and Pas-de-Calais) to the XVIII (Landes and Pyrenees) the military replicated the civil geography of France at every layer. So, too, did it in Germany, also divided into twenty-one Corps Districts, though there a larger population yielded both more conscripts and more reserve units.[15] The I Corps District in East Prussia was the peacetime station of the 1st and 2nd Infantry Divisions, but also of the wartime I Reserve Corps and a host of additional *Landwehr* and *Landsturm* units, dedicated to the defence of the Prussian heartland, against the danger of Russian attack. Russia's military geography resembled Germany's; so, too, did that of Austria-Hungary, whose multilingual kaleidoscope of archduchies, kingdoms, principalities and marquisates produced Europe's most complex army, comprising Hungarian hussars, Tyrolean riflemen and Bosnian infantry in the fez and baggy trousers of their former Ottoman overlords.[16]

Whatever the diversity of the European armies' component units – and that diversity embraced French *Turcos* in turban and braided waistcoats, Russian cossacks in kaftan and astrakhan hats and Scottish highlanders in kilt, sporran and doublet – there was a central uniformity to their organisation. That was provided by the core fighting organisation, the division. The division, a creation of the Napoleonic revolution in military affairs, normally comprised twelve battalions of infantry and twelve batteries of artillery, 12,000 rifles and seventy-two guns. Its firepower in attack was formidable. In a minute of activity, the division could discharge 120,000 rounds of small-arms ammunition – more if its twenty-four machine guns joined in the action – and a thousand explosive shells, a weight of fire unimaginable by any commander in any previous period of warfare. There were in Europe, in 1914, over two hundred divisions, in full existence or ready to be called into being, theoretically deploying sufficient firepower to destroy each other totally in a few minutes of mutual life-taking. The current belief in the power of the offensive was correct; whoever first brought his available firepower into action with effect would prevail.

What had not been perceived is that firepower takes effect only if it can be directed in timely and accurate fashion. That requires communication. Undirected fire is wasted effort, unless observers can correct its fall, order shifts of target, signal success, terminate failure, co-ordinate the action of infantry with its artillery support. The communication necessary to such co-ordination demands, if not instantaneity, then certainly the shortest possible interval between observation and response. Nothing in the elaborate equipment of the European armies of the early twentieth century provided such facility. Their means of communication were at worst word of mouth, at best telephone and telegraph. As telephone and telegraph depended upon preserving the integrity of fragile wires, liable to be broken as soon as action was joined, word of mouth offered the only standby in a failure of communication, consigning commanders to the delays and uncertainties of the earliest days of warfare.

Radio communication, wireless telegraphy as it was then known, offered a solution to the difficulty in theory, but not in practice. Contemporary wireless sets, dependent on sources of energy too large and heavy to be useful militarily outside warships, were not practicable tools of command in the field. Though wireless was to play a minor strategic role early in the coming war, it was to prove of no tactical significance at any time, even at the end. That was to prove true at sea also, because of the failure of navies to solve the problem of assuring radio security in the transmission of signals in action and in close proximity to the enemy.[17] In retrospect, it may be seen that a system existing in embryo, though promising to make effective all the power available to combatants in their quest for victory, lagged technically too far behind its potentiality to succeed.

If the potentiality of modern communications failed those dedicated to waging war, how much more did it fail those professionally dedicated to preserving the peace. The tragedy of the diplomatic crisis that preceded the outbreak of the fighting in August 1914, which was to swell into the four-year tragedy of the Great War, is that events successively and progressively overwhelmed the capacity of statesmen and diplomats to control and contain them. Honourable and able men though they were, the servants of the chancelleries and foreign officers of the great powers in the July crisis were bound to the wheel of the written note, the encipherment routine, the telegraph schedule. The potentialities of the telephone, which might have cut across the barriers to communication, seem to have eluded their imaginative powers. The potentialities of radio, available but unused, evaded them altogether. In the event, the states of Europe proceeded, as if in a dead march and a dialogue of the deaf, to the destruction of their continent and its civilisation.

TWO

WAR PLANS

ARMIES MAKE PLANS. Alexander the Great had a plan for the invasion of the Persian empire, which was to bring the army of the emperor Darius to battle and to kill or make him prisoner.[1] Hannibal had a plan for the second Punic War: to evade Rome's naval control of the Mediterranean by transferring the Carthaginian army via the short sea route to Spain, crossing the Alps – everyone remembers the story of his elephants – and confronting the legions in their homeland. Philip II had a plan to win a war against England in 1588: sail the Armada up the Channel, load the army which was fighting his rebellious Dutch subjects and land it in Kent. Marlborough's plan to save Holland in 1704 was to draw the French army down the Rhine and fight it when distance from its bases made its defeat probable. Napoleon made a plan almost every year of his strategic life: in 1798 to open a second front against his European enemies in Egypt, in 1800 to defeat Austria in Italy, in 1806 to blitzkrieg Prussia, in 1808 to conquer Spain, in 1812 to knock Russia out of the continuing war. The United States had a plan in 1861, the Anaconda Plan, designed to strangle the rebellious South by blockade of the coasts and seizure of the Mississippi river. Napoleon III even had a plan of sorts for his catastrophic war against Prussia in 1870: to advance into southern Germany and turn the non-Prussian kingdoms against Berlin.[2]

All these, however, were plans made on the hoof, when war threatened or had actually begun. By 1870, though Napoleon III did not appreciate it, a new era in military planning had begun; that of the making of war plans in the abstract, plans conceived at leisure, pigeonholed and pulled out when eventuality became actuality. The development had two separate, though connected, origins. The first was the building of the European rail network, begun in the 1830s. Soldiers rapidly grasped that railways would revolutionise war, by making the movement and supply of troops perhaps ten times as

27

swift as by foot and horse, but almost equally rapidly grasped that such movement would have to be meticulously planned. Long-distance campaigners had made their arrangements in the past; the idea that the armies of antiquity or the Middle Ages spurred off into the blue is a romantic illusion. Alexander the Great either marched coastwise within seventy-five miles of the ships that carried his supplies or sent agents ahead to bribe Persian officials into selling provender. Charlemagne required the counts of his kingdom to set aside as much as two-thirds of their grazing for his army if it needed to campaign in their territories.[3] The re-supply of the Third Crusade, after a disastrous start, was assured by Richard the Lionheart choosing a route that kept him in constant touch with his supporting fleet.[4] Nevertheless, pre-railway logistics had always been hit-and-miss; equally, they allowed flexibility, for livestock and draught animals could always be parked off the road when not needed, and live animals might be bought or looted to replace those eaten or killed by overwork. None of that was true of railways. Locomotives could not be picked up in farmyards, while the mismanagement of rolling stock during the Franco-Prussian War, when a tangle of empty wagons in the unloading yards blocked the arrival of full ones for miles up the line, taught the French army a lesson never to be forgotten.[5] Railways need to be timetabled quite as strictly in war as in peace; indeed more strictly, nineteenth-century soldiers learnt, for mobilisation required lines designed to carry thousands of passengers monthly to move millions in days. The writing of railway movement tables therefore became a vital peacetime task.

It was a task in which officers had to be trained; fortunately, suitable places of training already existed, in the armies' staff colleges. There lay the other root of abstract war planning. Staff colleges, like industrial and commercial schools, were a creation of the nineteenth century. Napoleon's subordinates had learnt their business from their elders and as they went along. Their practical mastery persuaded their competitors that expertise must be systematised. In 1810 Prussia established, on the same day as a University of Berlin was founded, a War Academy to train officers in staff duties.[6] There had been earlier equivalents, in Prussia itself and in other countries, but the staff work taught was narrowly interpreted: clerking, map-making, tabulation of data. The products of such colleges were destined to be minions; as late as 1854, fifty-five years after Britain had founded a staff college, the commanders of the British army going to the Crimea chose their executives by the immemorial method of nominating friends and favourites.[7] By then Prussia, under the influence of the highly intellectual Helmuth von Moltke, was about to transform its staff college into a real school of war. Its future graduates would be encouraged to think like generals, play realistic war games, study concrete military probabilities on the ground during 'staff rides' and write 'solutions' to national strategic problems. After the spectacular Prussian victories over Austria in 1866 and France in 1870, existing institutions in those countries and others were hastily modernised or new, 'higher' ones founded, the French *Ecole de Guerre* in 1880, a Centre for Higher Military Studies in Paris, 'the School for Marshals', in 1908.[8] Methods of training, through war games and staff rides, were made to imitate the Prussian; German texts were translated, recent military history was analysed; the best graduates, when appointed to the general staffs of their armies after competitive selection, were set to arranging mobilisation schedules, writing railway deployment timetables and designing plans for every eventuality in national security, often highly offensive in character. In the diplomatic world there was ironically no equivalence; the professorship of Modern History at Oxford had been established in the eighteenth century to educate future diplomats, but the British Foreign Office in 1914 was still choosing many of its entrants from the ranks of honorary attachés, young men whose fathers were friends of ambassadors, the equivalent of the favourites who had gone with Lord Raglan to the Crimea.

Diplomacy, therefore, remained an art taught in embassies. It was a benevolent education. Europe's diplomats were, before 1914, the continent's one truly international class, knowing each other as social intimates and speaking French as a common language. Though dedicated to the national interest, they shared a belief that their role was to avoid war.

The Ambassadors, for instance, of France, Russia, Germany, Austria and Italy, who under Sir Edward Gray's chairmanship, managed to settle the Balkan crisis of 1913, each represented national rivalries that were dangerous and acute. Yet they possessed complete confidence in each other's probity and discretion, had a common standard of professional conduct, and desired above all else to prevent a general conflagration. It was not the fault of the old diplomacy . . . that . . . Europe was shattered by the First World War . . . other non-diplomatic influences and interests assumed control of affairs.[9]

Thus Harold Nicolson, himself a diplomat of the old school and the son of another. Among the non-diplomatic interest he cites was, of course, that of the professional soldiers. Though no more professional warmongers than their diplomatic colleagues, they had been trained in an entirely contrary ethos to theirs: how to assure military advantage in an international crisis, not how to resolve it. What determined their outlook was the syllabus of the Staff College and what in turn determined that were the imperatives of mobilisation, concentration and deployment of troops dictated by the capacities of railways. Though A.J.P. Taylor was flippantly wrong to characterise the outbreak of 1914 as 'war by timetable', since statesmen might have averted it at any time, given goodwill, by ignoring professional military advice, the characterisation is accurate in a deeper sense. Timetabling having so demonstrably contributed to Prussia's victory of 1870 over France, timetables inevitably came to dominate thereafter the European military mind. M-Tag (mobilisation day), as the Germans called it, became a neurotic fixed point. From it, inflexible calculation prescribed how many troops could be carried at what speed to any chosen border zone, what quantity of supplies could follow and how broad would be the front on which armies could be deployed on a subsequent date against the enemy. Simultaneous equations revealed the enemy's reciprocal capability. Initial war plans thus took on mathematical rigidities, with which staff officers confronted statesmen. Joffre, chief of the French General Staff in July 1914, felt he discharged his duty in warning the government's Superior War Council that every day's delay in proclaiming general mobilisation entailed, as if by a law of nature, the surrender of twenty-five kilometres' depth of national territory to the enemy; indeed, the assumption by meteorologists of the use of the word 'front' to describe moving belts of high and low pressure derives from the strategy of the First World War and provides, reflexively, one of the more useful insights we have into the working of military mentalities in the years before its outbreak.[10]

All European armies in 1904 had long-laid military plans, notable in most cases for their inflexibility. None was integrated with what today would be called a 'national security policy', made in conclave between politicians, diplomats, intelligence directors and service chiefs, and designed to serve a country's vital interests, for such a concept of national leadership did not then exist. Military plans were held to be military secrets in the strictest sense, secret to the planners alone, scarcely communicable in peacetime to civilian heads of government, often not from one service to another.[11] The commander of the Italian navy in 1915, for example, was not told by the army of the decision to make war on Austria until the day itself; conversely, the Austrian Chief of Staff so intimidated the Foreign Minister that in July 1914 he was left uninformed of military judgements about the likelihood of Russia declaring war.[12] Only in Britain, where a Committee of Imperial Defence formed of politicians, civil servants and diplomats as well as commanders and intelligence officers had been instituted in 1902, were military plans discussed in open forum; even the CID, however, was dominated by the army, for the Royal Navy, Britain's senior service and heir of Nelson, had its own plan to win any war by fighting a second Trafalgar, and so held magnificently aloof from the committee's deliberations.[13] In Germany, where the army and the Kaiser had succeeded by 1889 in excluding both the War Ministry and parliament from military policy-making, war planning belonged exclusively to the Great General Staff; the navy's admirals were fed crumbs and even the Prime Minister, Bethmann Hollweg, was not told of the central war plan until December 1912, though it had been in preparation since 1905.

Yet that plan, the 'Schlieffen Plan', so-called after its architect, was the most important government document written in any country in the first decade of the twentieth century; it might be argued that it was to prove the most important official document of the last hundred years, for what it caused to ensue on the field of battle, the hopes it inspired, the hopes it dashed, were to have consequences that persist to this day. The effect exerted by paper plans on the unfolding of events must never be exaggerated. Plans do not determine outcomes. The happenings set in motion by a particular scheme of action will rarely be those narrowly intended, are intrinsically unpredictable and will ramify far beyond the anticipation of the instigator. So it was to prove with the Schlieffen Plan. In no sense did it precipitate the First World War; the war was the result of decisions taken, or not taken, by many men in June and July 1914, not by those of a group of officers of the German Great General Staff, or any single one of them, years beforehand. Neither did its failure, for fail it did, determine what followed; it was a plan for quick victory in a short war. The long war which followed might have been averted by a resolution of the combatants to desist after the initial, abortive clash of arms. Nevertheless, Schlieffen's plan, by his selection of place for a war's opening and proposal of action in that theatre by the German army, dictated, once it was adopted in the heat of crisis, where the war's focus would lie and, through its innate flaws, the possibility of the war's political widening and therefore the probability of its protraction. It was a plan pregnant with dangerous uncertainty: the uncertainty of the quick victory it was designed to achieve, the greater uncertainty of what would follow if it did not attain its intended object.

Schlieffen's was a pigeonholed plan par excellence. He was appointed Chief of the German Great General Staff in 1891 and began at once to consider in the abstract how best to secure his country's security in the political circumstances prevailing. The plans inherited from his predecessors, the great Moltke the Elder and Waldersee, took the predicament of Germany's interposition between France, implacably hostile since the defeat of 1870 and the loss of Alsace-Lorraine, and Russia, long France's friend, as their starting point. That presaged, in worst case, a two-front war. Both discounted the likelihood of a success against France, which was protected by a chain of fortresses, undergoing expensive modernisation, and therefore concluded that the German army should fight defensively in the west, using the Rhine as a barrier against a French offensive, and deploy its main strength in the east; even there, however, its aims should be limited to gaining a defensible line just inside the Russian frontier; to follow up a victory in the (Russian) kingdom of Poland by 'pursuit into the Russian interior', Moltke wrote in 1879, 'would be of no interest to us'. Moltke remembered the catastrophe of Napoleon's march on Moscow.[14]

So, it must be said, did Schlieffen; but he, a pupil of Moltke's system of staff education, understood only its disciplines, not its inspiration. Moltke, while insisting on rigour in military analysis, had always taken trouble to adjust his strategic ideas to the spirit of his country's diplomacy. He and Bismarck, whatever their

32

differences over policy, opened their minds to each other. Schlieffen was uninterested in foreign affairs. He believed in the primacy of force. Because of the young German Kaiser's ill-judged repudiation of Bismarck's 'reinsurance' treaty with Russia in 1890, a treaty holding Russia to neutrality with Germany unless Germany attacked France, and Germany to neutrality with Russia unless it attacked Austria-Hungary, Germany's ally, he was allowed, on succeeding as Chief of Staff, to give his preoccupation with force full rein.[15] Chess-board thinking came to possess him. The pieces he identified were few: a France weaker than Germany but protected by forts, a Russia weaker than Germany but protected by great space; a weak Austrian ally, but hostile to Russia and therefore useful as a distraction and perhaps even as a counterweight; a very weak Italy, allied to Germany and Austria, which therefore did not count; a Britain which could be ignored, for Schlieffen was so uninterested in seapower that he even despised the German navy, darling of the Kaiser though it increasingly became during his reign.[16]

Given the relativities of force, and they alone influenced his thinking, he arrived in progressive stages at a plan to commit seven-eighths of Germany's strength, in the contingency of war, to an overwhelming offensive against France, an all-or-nothing endgame that risked his own king in the event of failure. Schlieffen, however, discounted failure. Already by August 1892 he had decided that the west, not the east as in Moltke's and Waldersee's thinking, must be the centre of effort. By 1894 he was proposing a scheme for destroying the French fortresses along the Franco-German frontier. In 1897, having accepted that Germany's heavy artillery could not do sufficient damage to the forts, he began to argue to himself that the 'offensive must not shrink from violating the neutrality of Belgium and Luxembourg', in other words, neutralising the French fortresses by outflanking them. Plans written between 1899 and 1904, tested in war games and staff rides, envisaged an advance through Luxembourg and the southern tip of Belgium with more than two-thirds of the army. Finally, in the so-called 'Great Memorandum' of December 1905, completed just before his retirement after fourteen years in the highest military post, he cast moderation aside. Belgian neutrality – guaranteed jointly by Britain, France and Prussia, since 1839 – was not tepidly to be infringed but violated on the largest scale. Almost the whole of the German army, drawn up on a line hinged on the Swiss frontier and reaching nearly to the North Sea, was to march forward in a huge wheeling movement, first through Belgium, the outer wing to pass north of Brussels, then across the plains of Flanders to reach, on the twenty-second day after mobilisation, the French frontier. On the thirty-first day, the German line was to run along the Somme and Meuse rivers and from that position the right wing was to turn southwards, envelop Paris from the west and begin to drive the French army towards the left wing advancing from Alsace-Lorraine. A great semi-circular pincer, 400 miles in circumference, the jaws separated by 200 miles, would close on the French army. Under inexorable pressure the French would be pinned to the ground of a decisive battlefield, fought to a standstill and crushed. By the forty-second day from mobilisation, the war in the west would have been won and the victorious German army freed to take the railway back across Germany to the east and there inflict another crushing defeat on the Russians.[17]

Schlieffen continued to tinker with his plan, even in retirement, until his death in 1912. He had no other occupation. He was a man

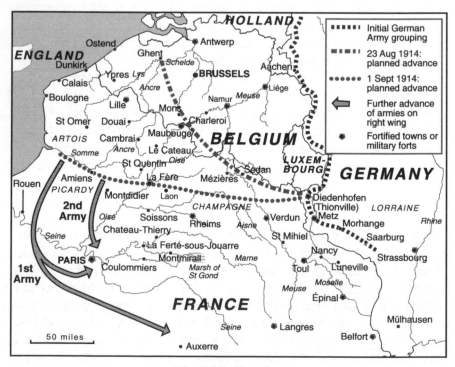

The Schlieffen Plan

without hobbies. As Chief of Staff he had often worked until midnight, then relaxing by reading military history to his daughters. Military history was a subordinate passion to writing war plans. He had been the Great General Staff's military historian before becoming its chief, but studied history in a wholly technical way. It was the dispositions of armies on a map that interested him, not the spirit of their soldiers, nor the reasoning of governments that had brought them to the clash of arms.[18] He had an obsession with Cannae, the battle in which Hannibal had encircled the Roman legions in 216 BC. Hannibal's crushing victory was a major inspiration of his Great Memorandum of 1905. In Cannae he perceived the pure essence of generalship, untainted by politics, logistics, technology or the psychology of combat. His practical service as a young officer with the Lancers of the Guard seems to have left no mark; in the wars of 1866 and 1870 he was already on the staff: by 1884 he was a professional military historian; after 1891 the routines of the map table appear to have possessed him completely. Aloof, sarcastic, intellectually arrogant, ever more olympian as his tenure of office extended to its unprecedented duration, he had by the end of his career succeeded in reducing war, at least for himself, to a pure abstraction, so many corps here, so many there. An extract from the Great Memorandum gives the flavour:

If possible, the German Army will win its battle by an envelopment with the right wing. This will therefore be made as strong as possible. For this purpose eight army corps and five cavalry divisions will cross the Meuse by five routes below Liège and advance in the direction of Brussels-Namur; a ninth army corps (XVIIIth) will join them after crossing the Meuse above Liège. The last must also neutralise the citadel of Huy within whose range it is obliged to cross the Meuse.

Odder still, given his obsession with troop movements, Schlieffen had no interest in enlarging the size of the German army so as to ensure its capacity to overwhelm the enemy. As Holger Herwig has recently argued, he shared a prevailing fear of the Prussian *Generalität* that expansion would corrupt an army of apolitical country lads with socialists from the big cities.[19] Though in 1905 he demanded the raising of thirty-three new infantry battalions, that was because he had calculated such a number to be the shortfall threatening his plan with failure. He wanted at that stage no more,

35

though Germany's large and expanding population of young men could easily have supplied it. The intellectual problem he had set himself, and believed he could solve, was how to win a short war with the resources available. His ambition was to repeat the triumphs of the great von Moltke in 1866, against Austria, and 1870, against France, wars of six and seven weeks respectively. Above all he wanted to avoid a 'wearing-out' war. 'A strategy of attrition', he wrote, 'will not do if the maintenance of millions costs billions.'[20]

He did not live to discover, as Hitler would, that brilliant schemes of aggression, if flawed, entail attrition as if by an inexorable reactive law. Yet Schlieffen was, within the circumstances his own time imposed, right to limit numerically the scope of the offensive he devised. Hitler's scheme was to fail because, after a whirlwind victory in the west, he persuaded himself that he could repeat victory in the vast spaces of the east. Schlieffen shrank from those spaces. He recognised that a marching army of foot and horse would exhaust its impetus in the limitless room of the steppe. Hence his midnight vigils over the maps of Flanders and the Ile-de-France, a corps here, a flank march there, a river bridged, a fortress masked. His midnight pettifoggery had as its object an exact adjustment not of German numbers to those that the French could deploy, but to what the Belgian and French road network could carry. Such calculations were the groundwork of staff-college training: students, transferring from prepared tables the length of a marching column – twenty-nine kilometres for a corps, for example – to a road map, could determine how many troops could be pushed through a given sector at what speed. Since thirty-two kilometres was the limit of a forced march, that would be the advance of a corps on a single road; but the tail of a column twenty-nine kilometres long would remain near or at the marching-off point at the day's end. If there were twin parallel roads, the tails would advance half the distance, if four three-quarters and so on. Ideally, the units of a corps would advance not in column but in line abreast, allowing all of it to arrive at the day's end thirty-two kilometres further on; in practice, as Schlieffen admitted in one of his amendments, parallel roads were at best to be found one to two kilometres apart. As his great wheeling movement was to sweep forward on a front of three hundred kilometres with about thirty corps, however, each would have only ten kilometres of front on which to make its advance, in which there might at best be seven parallel roads. That was not enough to allow the tails of the columns to catch up with the heads by the day's end. The drawback was serious in itself; more seriously, it absolutely forbade any attempt to crowd more troops into the radius of the wheeling movement. They would not fit; there simply was not room.[21]

Schlieffen's determination to work with the numbers he had was therefore correct; the plan derived from mathematical realities. As he recognised in his final amendment, any attempt to increase numbers on the roads, perhaps even to work with the numbers in hand, would result in a useless traffic jam: 'an unnecessary mass will be formed behind the firing-line'.[22] The plan, unfortunately for the Germans was not, however, derived purely from mathematical realities. Its ultimate wellspring was wishful thinking. Schlieffen had a dream of repeating the great victories of 1870, not as then on the Franco-German frontier, for he realised that the French were unlikely to do Germany the 'willing favour' of plunging a second time headfirst into its territory, but deep inside France itself. Yet France, as he emphasised time again and again, was a 'great fortress', fortified on its frontiers and in its interior, fortified above all at Paris, a city surrounded by modern fortifications. Belgium, though fortified also, offered a way round the French frontier forts, for its army was too small to resist German strength for any period; but to pass through Belgium towards Paris both lengthened and narrowed the front of advance. Hence the obsession with the road network, the search for a corridor through Flanders to the Ile-de-France and Paris down which the corps of the right wing could crowd fast enough to reach the field of decisive battle within the time limit of six weeks from mobilisation day; longer than that and the Russians would have emerged from their great spaces to overwhelm the exiguous forces left in the east to defend the approaches to Berlin.

The dream was of a whirlwind; the calculations warned of a dying thunderstorm. Even in the Great Memorandum of 1905 Schlieffen took counsel of his fears. 'It is therefore essential', he wrote, 'to accelerate the advance of the German right wing as much as possible' and 'the army commanders must be constantly on the alert and distribute the marching routes appropriately'; this when, by his own admission, the median marching speed of trained troops was twenty kilometres a day.[23] Orders to speed up or to switch roads could scarcely alter that. Then there was the well-known 'diminishing power of the offensive'; 'the active [peacetime] corps must be kept intact for the battle and not used for duties in the lines of communication area, siege-works, or the investing of fortresses', though, at the same time, 'the railways necessary to supply the army must also be guarded;[24] the great cities and the populous provinces of Belgium and north-western France must be occupied';[25] such duties were a sponge soaking up fighting troops. Then there were contingencies: 'should the English land and advance, the Germans will halt . . . defeat the English and continue the operations against the French'; no allowance of time made for that delay. Then, in a later amendment, there was the danger that the French, so despised after their collapse in 1870, might have found a new fighting will: 'now that they are imbued with the offensive spirit, we must assume that the part [of their army] not attacked will advance offensively'.[26] That raised the dark spectre of attrition, the long battle, to be fought out with blood and iron. The danger was there in any case: 'If the enemy stands his ground in the face of the great wheeling movement, all along the line the corps will try, as in siege-warfare, to come to grips with the enemy from position to position, day and night, advancing, digging-in, advancing'; even if such advances were possible, if the Germans averted 'a standstill as happened in the war in the Far East' (the Russo-Japanese War of 1904–5), the French might fall back further into the 'great fortress' as which 'France must be regarded';[27] 'if the French give up the Oise and the Aisne and retreat behind the Marne, Seine etc . . . the war will be endless'.[28]

This is not the only note of desperation in the Great Memorandum. There are others. Schlieffen yearns for more troops at the decisive point, the right wing of the great wheel through Belgium and northern France: 'Still greater forces must be raised . . . Eight army corps must be raised . . . We continue to boast of the density of our population, of the great manpower at our disposal; but these masses are now trained or armed to the full number of men they could yield . . . the eight army corps are most needed on or behind the right wing.' Schlieffen urges the creation of these eight corps, an addition of a full quarter to the strength of the army, from the reserves, the *Ersatz* (untrained contingents) and the *Landwehr* (over-age reservists), even though he apparently shared his brother generals' fear of enlarging the army through the enlistment of unreliable elements. The note of desperation grows stronger: 'How many [of the eight corps] can be transported [to the right wing] depends on the capacity of the railways . . . [they] are needed for the envelopment of Paris . . . How they advance and the attack on the position are shown on Map 3.'[29]

It is at this point that a careful reader of the Great Memorandum recognises a plan falling apart: Map 3 in no way shows how the new corps are to advance or to invest Paris, the central strongpoint of the 'great fortress' that was Schlieffen's France. The corps simply appear, with no indication of how they have reached Paris and its outskirts. The 'capacity of the railways' is irrelevant; railways, in Schlieffen's plan, were to carry the attackers no further than the German frontier with Belgium and France. Thereafter it was the road network that led forward, and the plodding boots of the infantry that would measure out the speed of advance. Schlieffen himself reckoned that to be only twelve miles a day. In the crisis of August and September 1914, Germans, French and British units would all exceed that, sometimes day after day – the 1st Battalion the Gloucestershire Regiment averaged sixteen and a half miles during the great retreat from Mons to the Marne, 24 August – 5 September, and covered twenty-three and twenty-one miles on 27 and 28 August respectively – but Schlieffen's mean was not far short of the mark.[30] Von Kluck's army on the outer wing of the great wheel achieved a little over thirteen miles a day between 18 August and 5 September, 1914, over a distance of 260 miles.[31] For the 'eight new corps', needed by Schlieffen as his plan's clinching device, to arrive at the decisive place of action, they would have actually needed to march not only further and faster, which defied probabilities, but to do so along the same roads as those occupied by the corps already existing, a simple impossibility.

It is not surprising, therefore, to find buried in the text of the Great Memorandum its author's admission that 'we are too weak' to bring the plan to a conclusion and, in a later amendment, 'on such an extended line we shall still need greater forces than we have so far estimated'.[32] He had run into a logical impasse. Railways would position the troops for his great wheel; the Belgian and French roads would allow them to reach the outskirts of Paris in the sixth week from mobilisation day; but they would not arrive in the strength necessary to win a decisive battle unless they were accompanied by eight corps – 200,000 men – for which there was no room. His plan for a lightning victory was flawed at its heart.

It was pigeonholed for use nonetheless. Moltke the Younger, nephew of the victor of 1866 and 1870, tinkered with it when he succeeded as Chief of the Great General Staff in 1906. Schlieffen did so himself, literally up to the eve of his death on 4 January 1913. Neither solved the inherent difficulties. Moltke is conventionally accused of compounding them, by strengthening the left wing of the planned German deployment at the expense proportionately of Schlieffen's massive right; that is scarcely the point. Moltke's staff certainly abbreviated the time needed to entrain and offload the troops at the frontier deployment points, by at least two days in some sectors and four in others.[33] That was scarcely the point either; beyond the railways, where movement could be accelerated by planning, lay the roads, where it could not. There the inflexible average of the twelve marched miles a day cramped the calculations of the finest minds. Moltke and the Great General Staff responded to the difficulty by ignoring it. The Schlieffen Plan was left to lie in its pigeonhole, to be extracted and instituted in August 1914 with calamitous results.

Yet the French war plan that lay in its pigeonhole in 1914, Plan XVII, proposed exactly that 'favour' to Germany Schlieffen had discounted France making. It was a plan for a headlong attack across the common Franco-German frontier, into Lorraine and towards the Rhine, judged by Schlieffen the least well to serve French interests. For just as France had spent time and vast quantities of money since the 1880s in improving and extending the fortifications that protected its territory, so had Germany. The provinces of Alsace and Lorraine, annexed to the new German Empire in 1871, had been heavily fortified by France in the two preceding centuries. Under German imperial government – Alsace-Lorraine was 'Reich' territory, coming directly under the administration of Berlin – the fortifications of Metz and Thionville on the River Moselle and of Strasbourg on the Rhine had been expensively modernised. Those cities were the gateways from France to Germany. Schlieffen presumed that the French high command would shrink from planning to attack them.

In the period while the Great Memorandum was in preparation, Schlieffen's presumption was correct. The French Plan XIV, completed in 1898, predicated defence of the common frontier in the event of war with Germany. A French attack was thought impossible by reason of disparity of numbers. A static French population of forty million could not challenge an expanding German population already fifty million strong, and rising fast. Moreover, the French high command was intimidated by Germany's proven ability to enlarge its army rapidly in time of crisis by incorporation of reservists. The French reserve system had failed in 1870. The French generals of 1898 did not trust that the system would work any better in the future. Plan XIV allotted no role to separate reserve formations, Plan XV of 1903 a subordinate one.

The problem of reserves was to afflict the French military mind throughout the first decade of the twentieth century. While the German generals wrestled with the difficulty of how numbers were to be transported at the greatest possible speed to the chosen field of action, the French agonised on how adequate numbers were to be found at all. The Conscription Law of 1905, imposing two years of military service on all young Frenchmen, without exemption, eased that difficulty by increasing the size of the 'active' or peacetime army; the Law actually made the French peacetime army larger than that which Germany intended to deploy into Belgium, which brought the problem of reserves back again. A peacetime army large enough to outnumber the German on the common frontier would still need to incorporate reserves rapidly if the front widened. In 1907 Plan XV *bis* allowed for a concentration of French troops against southern Belgium; two years later Plan XVI enlarged that concentration, even though the new arrangements depended on incorporating reservists whom the high command still doubted it knew how to employ carefully. By 1911 fears of a large German offensive through Belgium, reinforced by massive reserves, were becoming acute and a new French Chief of Staff, Victor Michel, proposed a radical departure from the strategies of Plans XIV–XVI: all available reserves were to be amalgamated with the active units, and the army was to be deployed on mobilisation along the whole French frontier from Switzerland to the North Sea.[34]

Michel's plan mirrored, though he could not know it, Schlieffen's; it even proposed an offensive into northern Belgium which would have met Schlieffen's 'strong right wing' head on; with what results cannot be guessed, though surely not worse than those produced by the totally different French war plan of 1914. Michel, unfortunately, was a military odd-man-out, a 'Republican' general whose politics were disliked by his fellows. He was soon ousted from office by a new right-wing government. Plan XVII, which came into force in April 1913, reversed his scheme. The amalgamation of reserve with active units was set aside. The deployment northwards to the sea was curtailed, leaving only the left-hand Fifth Army to deal with the danger of a German advance through northern Belgium from a position opposite southern Belgium. Most important, the operations on the common frontier were designed to be offensive. 'Whatever the circumstances', Plan XVII laid down, 'the intention of the commander-in-chief is to advance with all forces united to the attack on the German armies'; that meant an attack into Lorraine, the 'favour' Schlieffen doubted France would grant.[35]

There were several reasons for the adoption of Plan XVII, the brainchild of Michel's successor, Joseph Joffre. One was an absence of any firm assurance by the intelligence services that the Germans would indeed risk anything as strategically problematic and diplomatically reprehensible as a drive through northern Belgium; given the intense secrecy which surrounded all contemporary war planning – but also the blinkered refusal of the French Second (Intelligence) Bureau to recognise the clues – such intelligence was not easily to be had.[36] Another was the anxiety induced by Germany's response to the French Two-Year Law of 1905; in 1911–13 it passed conscription laws of its own which sharply increased the size of its peacetime army.[37] Those measures, and Germany's known ability to deploy reserve formations at mobilisation, put a premium on using the strength of the French peacetime army as forcefully as possible, before the reserves of either side could come into play. That meant attacking, and attacking at a point which the Germans must defend and where they could be found quickly, which was across the common frontier. Moreover, France had responded to the German conscription laws of 1911–13 by another of her own, extending service to three years; this Three-Year Law of 1913, though it could not compensate for the growing preponderance of German armies over French, did increase the size of the French peacetime army, while automatically reducing that of the reserves, thus reinforcing the argument for immediate offensive action in war. A final reason for the adoption of Plan XVII was supplied by the developing relationship between France and her associates. Since 1905 the British and French general staffs had been in active conclave. By 1911 there was between them a firm understanding that in the event of Germany's violation of the Anglo-French-Prussian treaty of 1839 guaranteeing Belgium's neutrality, a British Expeditionary Force would take its place on the French left, an understanding which palliated, if it did not solve, 'the Belgian problem'. The two countries had hoped for more: that Belgium would allow one or other or both to advance troops on to its territory if Germany threatened. Both had been rebuffed by the Belgian General Staff – the rebuff to France was an additional reason for its adoption of Plan XVII – but France could draw comfort from the British commitment of support. Though the two countries were bound by no formal treaty, the French generals had learnt that 'when [their] staffs agreed upon something, action followed'.[38]

It was precisely because 'such was not often the case when the French and Russian experts' – whose governments were indeed allied – 'settled upon a plan' that the French generals believed the Plan XVII offensive to be a necessity if Russia were to lend the help France would need at the outset of a German war.[39] Russia's strategic difficulties both resembled and differed from those of France. Like France, it would be slower than Germany to utilise its reserves in a crisis. Its initial operations would therefore also have to be mounted with the active army. Unlike France, which had simply failed to fix upon a satisfactory scheme for integrating its reserves with the peacetime army, its difficulties of reinforcement were more geographical than organisational. It was the vast distance between population centres within Russia and their remoteness from the border with Germany, which would delay deployment to the front. Yet those distances were also an advantage to Russia, since the dimension of space is also one of time amid the urgencies of war. Russia would not be pressed, in the crisis of mobilisation. It would accept an initial loss of territory while it rallied its army, something France could not afford. Of that France was acutely aware. Plan XVII was therefore justified in one sense because the great battle it was designed to provoke would buy time in the east; it was motivated, in another sense, by the need the French felt to convince the Russians at the outset that the struggle was one of life and death. The bigger and quicker the crisis, the greater the danger to France, the sooner the subsequent threat to Russia and therefore the more imperative the need for it to march rapidly to the help of France also.

Yet Russia had a reputation for dilatoriness. It rightly exasperated the French generals. Bad enough that their Russian equivalents were secretive and often unbusinesslike, in contrast to the British, who inspired confidence even though they were not formal allies; worse was Russia's evasion of fixed commitments. 'Before 1911 the Russians had, despite continual French pressure, refused to promise more than unspecified offensive action by the twentieth day of mobilisation. In late 1910 even this minimum expectation was shaken when St Petersburg withdrew several units from Russian Poland and the Tsar met with the Kaiser at Potsdam.' It took new staff talks, convoked by a thoroughly alarmed Joffre in August 1910, to win from General Sukhomlinov, the Russian War Minister, an assurance that the Russian army would 'undertake some offensive action on the sixteenth day in the hope of tying down at least five or six German corps otherwise employable on the western front'. The assurance was still only verbal. The French had no written guarantee that the Russians would do what they said, indeed no clear impression even of what action the Russians contemplated.[40]

The Russians were not wholly to be blamed. The first decade of the century was for them a time of troubles, revolution at home, defeat in war with the Japanese in the Far East. The war left the state in poverty, defeat the army in disarray. The years 1906–9 were those in which the Schlieffen Plan would have worked, for the Russians hoped at best, in the event of conflict, to stand on the strategic defensive, a posture that would have given France no help at all. By 1909 they had recovered enough to write a Mobilisation Schedule, Number 18, which at least included provision for an offensive, though only after a pause to cover the concentration of reserves and to identify whether the main threat was poised by Germany or Austria. In June 1910 the Russian staff had become more positive. Mobilisation Schedule 19 accepted that Germany would be the chief enemy; still, the plan would also have abandoned most of Russian Poland to the enemy. That prospect outraged the commanders of the western districts, whose role had long been that of engaging the Austrians. Further debate within the general staff ensued, over the relative weights of what was operationally possible, what was owed to Russia's traditional commitments in south-eastern Europe and what was due to the French alliance. The outcome was a compromise, known as Variants A and G to Schedule 19, A for a main effort against Austria, G against Germany.[41]

Variant A, had the French known of it, would have confirmed their worst fears. Fortunately for them, in the same month, August 1912, that the Russian General Staff completed the drafting of the two variants to Schedule 19, they were able to extract from General Zhilinsky, the Russian Chief of Staff, a promise that his army would attack Germany with at least 800,000 men – half its peacetime strength – 'after M + 15', fifteen days from mobilisation.[42] The promise was made specific – 'on' rather than 'after' M + 15 – in Article III of the Russo-French Military Convention of September 1913. This sudden show by the Russians of wholehearted commitment to their ally has been explained in a variety of ways. One is that by 1913 the Russian army had largely recovered from the chaos into which it had been thrown by defeat at the hands of the Japanese; a new scheme of spending, Sukhomlinov's 'Great Programme', promised positive improvement and actual expansion within four years. A second reason, it has been suggested, was misleading intelligence. In 1913 Russia had an 'agent in place', the Austrian Colonel Alfred Redl, who had sold them the plans for his army's mobilisation, plans which appeared to minimise the dangers foreseen in Variant A. 'A third explanation for Russian conduct was the weight of the [French] alliance . . . If France readily fell to the Germans, the Russians had little confidence they could hold against the combined hordes of Germany and Austria-Hungary . . . Russia and France either rose or fell together and . . . Russia should strain to the utmost in meeting its obligations, even to the point of conducting offensive operations at M + 15.' Finally, there is the suggestion that the Russian generals abruptly closed their minds to the dangers into which an offensive, rather than a self-interested but safe defensive war would lead them. In that, however, they differed from the French and the Germans only in the lateness of their decision to gamble.[43]

If Russia alarmed France by prevarication and procrastination in the years 1906–14, so did Austria her German ally. The two countries, enemies in the war of 1866 which had given Germany the leadership of central Europe, had made up their differences by 1882. The alliance then signed, however, contained no military provisions. Bismarck, Germany's Chancellor, sagely shrank from the danger of involvement in Austria's manifold internal and external difficulties, among which the antagonism with Ottoman Turkey was age-old, the quarrel with Italy over lost Venice but recently papered over, the designs of Serbia and Romania on Habsburg lands inhabited by their minorities strong and growing. There were informal explorations of respective strategies between the two general staffs, nonetheless; Austria learnt that, in the event of a two-front war, Germany intended to defend against France, attack Russia; Germany learnt with satisfaction that Austria would attack Russian

Poland. There things rested. The Austrian staff found Schlieffen, when he came into office, 'taciturn' and 'hardly forthcoming'.[44] It was not until after his retirement that productive negotiations commenced, in January 1909.

Moltke the Younger, German Chief of Staff, knew what he wanted. The Schlieffen Plan lay in its pigeonhole. It required of the Austrians the largest and speediest deployment possible against Russian Poland. The initiative for the talks, however, had come from his Austrian opposite number, Conrad von Hötzendorf, then alarmed at a threat of war not with Russia only, but her protégé, Serbia, also. There were other fears. Italy was not a reliable ally, nor was Romania. He saw a web of combinations and eventualities, none favourable to Austria. The worst eventuality was that Serbia might provoke a war with Austria-Hungary, in which Russia would intervene after the Habsburg army had deployed the weight of its forces in what would then be the wrong direction, south to the Danube instead of north to Poland. The solution he suggested was the division of his army into three at mobilisation: a *Minimalgruppe Balkan* of ten divisions, to deploy against Serbia, a *Staffel-A* of thirty divisions for the Polish theatre and a *Staffel-B* of twelve divisions, to act as a 'swing' force reinforcing either, as need be.

The scheme offered little to Moltke and on 21 January he wrote to better Conrad's terms. Dismissing Austrian fears of Italian or Romanian falseness, he assured Conrad that the war in the west would be over before Russia could fully mobilise and that Germany would by then have sent strong forces to the east; but he gave no timetable, an omission to cause Conrad anxiety, since he had a two-front war of his own to plan. On 26 January he warned Moltke that Germany could not count on the transfer of *Minimalgruppe Balkan* to Poland before fifty days from mobilisation. Could Germany guarantee to send support within forty days? If not, he had better stand on the defensive in Poland and destroy Serbia in an all-out offensive. The destruction of Serbia was Conrad's real desire; like many German-Austrians, he detested the small Slav kingdom, not merely because it failed to show due deference to Austria's unofficial imperium over the Balkans but also because it was a magnet of attraction to dissident Serbs within the Habsburg empire. A victory over Serbia looked to be the surest solution of Austria's general difficulties with its other Slav minorities.

Moltke replied with a mixture of assurances and dismissals. The

French could not delay German reinforcements more than four weeks – the Schlieffen Plan, to the details of which Austria was not privy, reckoned six weeks – so that it was perfectly safe, as well as essential, for Austria to attack Russia in Poland; and, even if Austria found itself committed to a Serbian war, it would not be let down by Germany; as to Serbia, the problem 'will solve itself for Austria as a matter of course'. Conrad noted: 'Certainly: but what am I to do if already tied down in Serbia?'[45] Since the Austrians outnumbered the Serbs by sixty divisions to ten, twice the proportion conventionally reckoned necessary for victory, Conrad might be reckoned timorous. His army could not be beaten by the Serbs, even if he committed only *Minimalgruppe Balkan* against them. Moltke, above all concerned to arrange that Russia should also have to fight on two fronts – a Polish western front where the Germans would be temporarily weak, a Polish southern front where he hoped the Austrians would be strong – stifled any irritation Conrad's prevarication provoked and he promised almost by return of post to join with Austria in an offensive: 'I will not hesitate to make the attack to support the simultaneous Austrian offensive.'[46] That was a promise he should not have given and could not certainly make good. The Schlieffen Plan, indeed, stipulated that the fraction of the German army left in East Prussia while the great western battle was fought should stand on the defensive. He apparently gave the promise in good faith, nonetheless, and the letter of 19 March 1909 in which it was offered remained the understanding between the two allies in the years that followed. Conrad, whose bellicosity brought about his removal from office in November 1910, found that it still lay on file on his reappointment a year later. When he and Moltke had their final prewar meeting at the holiday resort of Carlsbad in May 1914, the German Chief of Staff responded to the Austrian's request for the commitment of additional troops in the east, with the vague assurance, 'I will do what I can. We are not superior to the French.'[47] Schlieffen's pigeonholed plan, drawing the trace of a 'strong right wing' on the map of northern France, had insisted otherwise; but he had counted on a firmer Austrian will and feebler Russian power.

What he had not counted upon was the intervention of the British. Schlieffen's Great Memorandum alludes to the possibility; an appendix of February 1906 discusses its import, but with the presumption that they would do no more than land at Antwerp, or perhaps on Germany's North Sea coast. There was no apprehension that they would place themselves in the French line of battle at a point to impede the German advance through Belgium. Since military conversations between France and Britain, an outcome of the agreement of *entente cordiale* in April 1904, did not begin until December 1905, the month in which the Great Memorandum was finished, he had no indication that they might. Moreover, the British, even while they opened their discussions with the French, themselves remained in two minds over what they should do with their army if it were committed to the continent. There was indeed the possibility of an amphibious operation, one the Royal Navy favoured as a means of forcing out the German High Seas Fleet to give battle.[48] That, on the other hand, was a 'strategy of diversion'. The universal military mood called for a 'strategy of concentration' at the decisive point. The decisive point, in a war in which Germany was the attacker, would lie in France and it was there, in progressive stages, that the British General Staff agreed with the French an expeditionary force should be committed. In April 1906 the Committee of Imperial Defence drew up plans to send troops directly to the Low Countries. There was then a lapse of five years, brought about by Belgian unwillingness to admit a British army and by French inability to design a convincing war plan. All changed in 1911, with the appointment of Joffre as French Chief of Staff, Henry Wilson as British Director of Military Operations. Joffre was formidable, Wilson dynamic. When they met for the first time in Paris in November, Joffre unveiled the outlines of Plan XVII.[49] Wilson, in August, had already outlined to the Committee of Imperial Defence how best a British Expeditionary Force might be employed, small though it would be, for spending on the navy and the country's continued resistance to conscription allowed it to keep an army of only six divisions at home. Those six divisions, by operating against the German right wing, might tip the balance by forcing the Germans to divert strength to deal with it. 'The larger the force detached by the Germans from the decisive point', Wilson argued, 'the better it would be for France and ourselves.' He proceeded to the detailed planning of how most quickly and efficiently the expeditionary force could be transported across the Channel, with the active co-operation of the navy, which supported a speedy operation that would then leave it free to concentrate on tempting the German fleet to decisive action. The British were nevertheless cautious. Ardently Francophile though he was, Wilson succeeded in denying to the French any specific indication as to where the expeditionary force would take the field, right up to August 1914, while it was only in November 1912 that the French extracted from the Foreign Secretary, Sir Edward Grey, something like a commitment to common action.[50] 'If either government', the letter read, 'had grave reason to expect an unprovoked attack by a third Power, or something that threatened the general peace, it should immediately discuss with the other, whether both Governments should act to prevent aggression and to preserve peace, and if so what measures they should take in common. If these measures involved common action, the plans of the General Staffs would at once be taken into consideration, and the Governments should then decide what effect should be given to them.' The principle of splendid isolation, for all the dangers offered by diminishing economic power and growing German naval strength, could still cause Britain to hesitate at binding herself to an ally.

Britain, of course, enjoyed a luxury of choice the continental powers did not, the choice between 'taking as much or as little of a war' as it wanted; Bacon's summary of the advantages of sea power remained as true in the twentieth as it had been in the sixteenth century. France and Germany, Russia and Austria, did not benefit from the protection of salt-water frontiers. Separated from each other at best by river or mountain, at worst by nothing more substantial than a line on the map, their security resided in their armies. That threw them into a harsh and mutual predicament. It resembled that which would bind the nuclear superpowers sixty years later. 'Use them or lose them' became the imperative of missile strategy; for missiles not used in a crisis might become the debris of an opponent's first strike: an army which did not strike as soon as time permitted might be destroyed in mid-mobilisation; even if it completed its mobilisation but then failed to attack, it would have shown its hand and lost the advantage the war plan had been so painstakingly devised to deliver. That danger most acutely threatened Germany: if it failed to move to the offensive as soon as the troop trains disgorged their passengers at the unloading points, the unequal division of force between west and east would be pointlessly revealed and so, worse, would be the concentration against Belgium. The Schlieffen Plan would have been betrayed, France given the time to recoil from the peril of Plan XVII, Russia the incentive to invade East Prussia in overwhelming force, and

Austria the unsought and probably undischargeable burden of guaranteeing the security of Central Europe.

The existence of a permanent medium of negotiation between the European powers might have robbed the war plans that lay in their pigeonholes of their menacing instantaneity; sixty years later the suicidal risks of nuclear war planning prompted the superpowers, divided though they were by ideological differences that had no counterpart in the Europe of kings and emperors, to find such a medium, through the convocation of regular summit conferences and the installation of a 'hot line' between Moscow and Washington. Before 1914 technology could not offer the opportunity of frequent and immediate communication but more important than that lack was the absence of a mood to seek an expedient. The mood was absent not only from diplomacy, which clung to the stately rhythms of past times, but also within governments. Britain's Committee of Imperial Defence, bringing together service chiefs, diplomats and statesmen, was unique but also imperfect; the Royal Navy, insistent on its seniority, kept its own counsel. The French army behaved likewise in the much more makeshift Superior War Council. In Germany, Russia and Austria, countries of court government, where the sovereign was commander-in-chief both in name and fact, and each organ of the military system answered directly to him, communication between them was beset by secretiveness and jealousy. The system, disastrously, took its most extreme form in Germany, where

> there was no governmental process that corrected ... the concentration of the assessment [of plans and policy] in a single person, the Kaiser. Almost fifty people had direct access to him but there were no routines to discuss or co-ordinate among or between them or to share the important and discrete information each possessed. No established or regular councils existed for that purpose. Even information about the war plan was top secret and restricted to those who had a need to know; it was not shared between the Great General Staff, the War Ministry, the Military Cabinet, the Admiralty, the Naval General Staff and the Foreign Office.[51]

It was as if, sixty years later, the United States Strategic Air Command had enjoyed the freedom to write plans for nuclear war against Russia without reference to the State Department, Navy or

Army and to leave the President to circulate within government such details of it as he saw fit. An elected president, chosen by competition between veteran politicians, might nevertheless have brought order to the system; a hereditary monarch, who took increasingly less interest in military detail after 1904, was unlikely to do so.[52] The Kaiser in practice did not; in the crisis of 1914, when he alone might have put brakes to the inexorable progression of the Schlieffen Plan, he found he did not understand the machinery he was supposed to control, panicked and let a piece of paper determine events.

THREE

THE CRISIS OF 1914

SECRET PLANS DETERMINED THAT any crisis not settled by sensible diplomacy would, in the circumstances prevailing in Europe in 1914, lead to general war. Sensible diplomacy had settled crises before, notably during the powers' quarrels over position in Africa and in the disquiet raised by the Balkan Wars of 1912–13. Such crises, however, had touched matters of national interest only, not matters of national honour or prestige. In June 1914 the honour of Austria-Hungary, most sensitive because weakest of European powers, was touched to the quick by the murder of the heir to the throne at the hands of an assassin who identified himself with the monarchy's most subversive foreign neighbour. The Austro-Hungarian empire, a polity of five major religions and a dozen languages, survived in dread of ethnic subversion. The chief source of subversion was Serbia, an aggressive, backward and domestically violent Christian kingdom which had won its independence from the rule of the Muslim Ottoman empire after centuries of rebellion. Independent Serbia did not include all Serbs. Large minorities remained, by historical accident, Austrian subjects. Those who were nationalists resented rule by the Habsburgs almost as much as their free brothers had rule by the Ottomans. The most extreme among them were prepared to kill. It was the killing by one of them of the Habsburg heir that fomented the fatal crisis of the summer of 1914.

The Habsburg army's summer manoeuvres of 1914 were held in Bosnia, the former Ottoman Turkish province occupied by Austria in 1878 and annexed to the empire in 1908. Franz Ferdinand, nephew to the Emperor Franz Josef and Inspector General of the army, arrived in Bosnia on 25 June to supervise. After the manoeuvres concluded, on 27 June, he drove next morning with his wife to the provincial capital, Sarajevo, to carry out official engagements. It was an ill-chosen day: 28 June is the anniversary of the defeat of Serbia by the Turks in 1389, Vidov Dan, the event from which they date their long

55

history of suffering at the hands of foreign oppressors.[1] The role of oppressor, after the retreat of the Ottoman Turks, had been assumed, in the eyes of nationalist Serbs, by the Habsburgs, and the provincial administration had been warned that his visit was unwelcome and might be dangerous. The warnings he ignored; threats to the great were commonplace in an era which had brought the killing by fanatics or lunatics of a Tsar, an Austrian Empress and a President of the United States. In this case a murder team was in place, a group of five young Serbs and a Bosnian Muslim, he recruited by the conspirators for cosmetic purposes, all equipped with bombs and pistols.[2] On the Archduke's way to the residence of the provincial governor, one of the terrorists threw a bomb at the car carrying Franz Ferdinand and his wife but it bounced off, exploding under the car following and wounding an officer occupant. The imperial party proceeded on its way. Three-quarters of an hour later, however, en route to visit the casualty in hospital, the archducal couple's chauffeur took a wrong turning and, while reversing, came to a momentary halt. The stop brought the car opposite one of the undetected conspirators, Gavrilo Princip, who was armed with a revolver. He stepped forward and fired. The Archduke's wife died instantly, he ten minutes later. Princip was arrested on the spot.[3]

Investigation swiftly revealed that, though the terrorists were all Austrian subjects, they had been armed in Serbia and smuggled back across the Austrian border by a Serbian nationalist organisation. The Austrian investigators identified it as the *Narodna Odbrana* (National Defence), set up in 1908 to work against the incorporation of Bosnia into the Austrian empire; it was a tenet of the nationalist creed that Bosnia was historically Serb. In fact the responsible organisation was the clandestine 'Union or Death', commonly known as the Black Hand. The misapprehension was scarcely substantial, since the two shared members and the *Narodna Odbrana* in Bosnia lent help to the Black Hand.[4] The latter, more sinister, body had as its aim the 'unification of Serbdom' and administered a death oath to its initiates. More important, it lay under the control of 'Apis', as he was code-named, the colonel commanding the intelligence section of the Serbian army's General Staff.[5]

The exact degree of foreknowledge of the plot attributable to the Serbian government has never been established; intelligence is a murky world, then as now, but then more commonly one peopled by uniformed officers, as the Dreyfus affair had sensationally revealed.

Apis, properly Colonel Dragutin Dimitrijevic, was a revolutionary as well as a soldier – he had taken part in the brutal overthrow of the Obrenovic dynasty in 1903 – and may well have been living two lives. Whatever the truth, by 2 July three of the murder team had made a full confession; it disclosed that they had been supplied with weapons from a Serbian military arsenal and helped to cross the border by Serbian frontier guards. The information was sufficient to confirm Austria's rooted belief in Serbian malevolence and to arouse its equally ready desire to punish the small kingdom for its disturbance of order within the empire.

The Slav problem was the weightiest of the empire's many difficulties with its minorities but, within those difficulties, the Serb problem constituted an active and growing threat. While the problem of the Poles was diffused by the partition of their ancient kingdom with Germany and Russia, the problem of the Czechs by the heavy Germanisation of their cities and the problem of the Croats by their Catholicism, nothing, it seemed, could diffuse that of the Serbs but the use of force. Their Orthodox Christianity made them a religious as well as national minority and one which Russia's guardianship of the Orthodox Church made cocksure; their long years of guerrilla resistance to Turkish rule had rendered them headstrong and self-reliant but also, in Austrian eyes, devious and untrustworthy; their poverty kept them warlike. The small kingdom of Serbia was intensely warlike. It had won independence from the Ottomans by its own effort in 1813 and glory and territory in the Balkan Wars of 1912–13. National rebirth had raised the idea of a Greater Serbia, strong within the kingdom and a beacon to Austria's Serbs in Bosnia and Croatia. It had to be resisted, for not only were Serbs but one minority among others in those territories but neither could be surrendered. Strategy forbade it but so also did the imperial system itself, which was creakily sustained by the denial of the worth of nationality as a political idea. Concession to one nationality would soon entail concession to others and that way lay the dissolution of the empire itself.

The evidence of Serb complicity, official or not, in the assassination of Franz Ferdinand, exposed by the conspirators' confessions of 2 July, was therefore enough to persuade many in the imperial government that a war against Serbia was now a necessity. As it happened, Count Berchtold, the Austro-Hungarian Foreign Minister, had spent much of the week before the assassination preparing aggressive diplomatic measures against Serbia. His scheme was to persuade Germany to support Austria in seeking an alliance with Bulgaria and Turkey, Serbia's enemies in the Second Balkan War of 1913, which would confront the Belgrade government with a hostile encirclement: Bulgaria and Turkey to the east, Austria-Hungary to the west and north. The assassination lent urgency to Berchtold's diplomacy. An Austrian emissary was ordered to Berlin with the document in early July. On 4 July, the eve of his departure, Berchtold made radical amendments to it. The memorandum now requested the German government to recognise that the empire's differences with Serbia were 'irreconcilable' and stated the 'imperious . . . necessity for the Monarchy [Austria-Hungary] to destroy with a determined hand the net which its enemies are attempting to draw over its head'. A covering letter alleged that 'the Sarajevo affair . . . was the result of a well-organised conspiracy, the threads of which can be traced to Belgrade' and insisted that 'the pivot of the Panslavic policy' (Serbia as the protagonist of a 'Greater Serbia') 'must be eliminated as a power factor in the Balkans'.[6] Berchtold gave the emissary, Count Hoyos, verbal authority to warn the Germans that Vienna would ask Belgrade for guarantees as to its future conduct, to be followed by military action if refused. Within six days of the assassination, therefore, Austria had staked out her position. It remained to see whether the German Emperor and his government, without whose backing the Austrians dare not act, would support them.

Dare not Austria might; in retrospect it is tempting to surmise that, had she struck at once in anger, trumpeting dynastic wrath and righteous belief in Serbia's guilt, Europe might have allowed her to mount positive measures without outside interference. Russia, a great Slav brother, had tender feelings towards the Serbs but feelings are different from vital interests and certainly no motive for war. The Bulgarians were Slavs also, and they had suffered defeat and humiliation in 1913 without Russia intervening to rescue them. The Serbs, moreover, were odd-man-out even in the wild Balkans, worse than that in the eyes of civilised Europe. The 'Asiatic' behaviour of their army's officers in 1903, when they had not only killed their king and queen but then thrown the bodies from a window of the royal palace and hacked them limb from limb with their swords, had shocked sensibilities everywhere. Italy, which coveted the same Adriatic coastline towards which 'Greater Serbia' aspired, would certainly not have impeded her Triple Alliance partner if she had punished Belgrade. France, though she had supplied Serbia with weapons, had no means of lending her further support, even had she wished to do so. Britain had no involvement in the Balkans whatsoever. Had Austria moved at once, therefore, without seeking Germany's endorsement, it is possible, perhaps probable, that the Serbs would have found themselves as isolated strategically as, initially, they were morally, and so forced to capitulate to the Austrian ultimatum. It was Austria's unwillingness to act unilaterally that transformed a local into a general European crisis and her unwillingness so to act must be explained in large part by the precautionary mood of thought which decades of contingent war planning had implanted in the mind of European governments.

The net of interlocking and opposed understandings and mutual assistance treaties – France to go to war on Russia's side and vice versa if either were attacked by Germany, Britain to lend assistance to France if the vital interests of both were judged threatened, Germany, Austria-Hungary and Italy (the Triple Alliance) to go to war together if any one were attacked by two other states – is commonly held to have been the mechanism which brought the 'Allies' (France, Russia and Britain) into conflict in 1914 with the 'Central Powers' (Germany and Austria-Hungary). Legalistically that cannot be denied. It was no treaty, however, that caused Austria to go running to Berlin for guidance and support in the aftermath of the Sarajevo assassination – no treaty in any case applied – but anticipation of the military consequences that might ensue should she act alone. At their worst, those consequences would bring Russia to threaten Austria on their common border as a warning to desist from action against Serbia; Austria would then look to Germany for support; that support, if given, risked drawing France into the crisis as a counterweight against German pressure on Russia; the combination of France and Russia would supply the circumstances to activate the Triple Alliance (with or without Italy); the ingredients of a general European war would then be in place. In short, it was the calculation of presumed military response, of how it was guessed one military precaution would follow from another, that drove Austria to seek comfort in the Triple Alliance from the outset, not the Triple Alliance that set military events in train.

Those Austrians who calculated the potential consequences were not Berchtold, a suave procrastinator suddenly emboldened by the Serbian affront, so emboldened that he chose not to discriminate between Serbia itself and Serb nationalism, nor the Chief of Staff,

Conrad von Hötzendorf, who had so long been adamant for a Serbian war that he scorned to make the distinction. The cautious men were the old emperor, Franz Josef, in the sixty-sixth year of his reign in 1914, and Count Tisza, Prime Minister of Hungary. The Emperor opposed war for many reasons but ultimately because war brought change and he rightly identified change as the enemy of his empire's frail stability. Tisza also feared the changes war might bring because Hungary's equal partition with Austria of power within the empire, a share not justified by Hungarian numbers, required that the imperial system be preserved exactly as it was. The consequence of an unsuccessful war might be concessions to the Slavs, perhaps the 'trialism' which would undo Austro-Hungarian 'dualism'. The consequence of a successful war, in which the empire's Slavs made a contribution to victory, might be trialism all the same. It was those two men's prudence, dispassionate in the Emperor's case, partisan in Tisza's, on which the urge for instant action against Serbia broke. On 2 July the Emperor insisted to Berchtold that he must not move before he consulted Tisza. Tisza told Berchtold the same day that the Emperor must have time to consider Hungarian objections. Berchtold, frustrated in his desire to act alone and soon, therefore decided on the fateful step of averting the first of the two other men's fears – that Austria might find itself isolated in a crisis on which hostile, in particular Russian, war plans might impinge – by seeking assurance that Germany would stand by her.

With the arrival of Berchtold's emissary, Count Hoyos, in Berlin, on 5 July, calculations of the import of war planning switched to the German side. Berchtold's memorandum was delivered to the Kaiser by the Austrian ambassador the same day. Over lunch Wilhelm II authorised him to tell Emperor Franz Josef that Austria could 'rely on Germany's full support'.[7] The offer seemed to apply as much to the proposal for an alliance with Bulgaria as to action against Serbia; the possibility of Russian intervention was discussed but discounted. So it was also in the discussions with the Kaiser's ministers and military advisers whom the ambassador saw next. General von Falkenhayn, the Minister of War, asked if preparatory measures should be taken and was told not. Bethmann Hollweg, the Chancellor, had been independently advised by his Foreign Office that Britain would not involve herself in a Balkan crisis nor would Russia if it came to the point. The following day, Monday 6 July, after repeating his own judgement to a number of military officers that Russia, and France also, would not involve themselves and that precautionary measures were consequently not necessary, the Kaiser departed on the imperial yacht, *Hohenzollern,* for his annual cruise in the Norwegian fjords. He was to be absent for three weeks. The Chief of the Great General Staff and the Secretary of the Navy were already on leave and he left no orders for their recall.

The Kaiser had, however, insisted both to the Austrian ambassador and to his officials on one point. That was that it was for Austria to come to a firm resolution about what it wanted to do. Austrian *Schlamperei* – a mixture of prevarication and procrastination – was a constant irritant to the emphatic Germans. The young empire, the creation of an urgent nationalism and urgent in all it did, found little patience for the old empire, which thought time a solution to all problems. The first week of July 1914 therefore brought a strange reversal of attitudes. Austria was for once in a hurry. Germany went on holiday. Fundamentally, however, things remained as usual. The Kaiser's party aboard *Hohenzollern* exercised vigorously, held boat races, listened to lectures on military history. The Austrians, under pressure to make up their minds, dithered.[8]

The Imperial Council of Ministers did not meet until Tuesday 7 July, already ten days after the assassination and five after the murderers had made their confessions. Berchtold, who sensed justification and time slipping away equally rapidly, proposed military action. Austria had mobilised against Serbia twice already in recent years, in 1909 and in 1912, on both occasions without Russia responding, and the German guarantee now put her in a stronger position. Tisza held out. He insisted that the taking of military measures be preceded by the issue of a note of demands, none of them too humiliating for Serbia to accept. Only if they were rejected would he agree to an ultimatum leading to war. His opponents – three German-Austrians, a Pole and a Croat – argued but he, as Prime Minister of the Hungarian and co-equal half of the empire, could not be talked down. He won the concession that Berchtold should not present proposals to the Emperor until he had prepared his own objections in writing. That would require another day. Thus no decision could be taken until Thursday 9 July.

Franz Josef then agreed that any ultimatum be preceded by the transmission of a note, as Tisza wanted. That was not what Berchtold desired to hear. His position was steadily hardening, towards that of Field Marshal Conrad, who had wanted war from the outset. He sustained his pressure, so that by Sunday 12 July, Tisza was prepared to agree to the presentation of a note, to be followed if necessary by an ultimatum, instead of a note with a time limit for a response attached. The importance of the distinction was greater than the choice of words might seem to imply: a note did not commit a sovereign power, an ultimatum did. By Tuesday 14 July, when Tisza and Berchtold met again, the Hungarian Prime Minister won his case against an ultimatum but was forced to concede the shortest possible time limit attaching to a note. It was to be only forty-eight hours after the document was delivered. The terms of the note were drafted and so was the date of the ministerial meeting at which it would be finally approved.

That date, however, was Sunday 19 July, the twenty-first day since the assassination. Worse, Berchtold told Tisza that the note would not formally be presented for another week after that. He had a justification. The French President, Raymond Poincaré, who would leave to make a state visit to Russia on 16 July, would not, it was believed, begin his return until Saturday 25 July. The delivery of an Austrian note to Serbia in the days when the Russian and French heads of state – respectively the Serbs' protector and his chief ally – would be in intimate contact was likely to throw them into diplomatic and strategic conclave. Hopes of localising the dispute and of isolating Serbia – objectively already so much diminished by delay, as Berchtold must subjectively have recognised – would be dangerously reduced thereby. That was the explanation given to Berlin for the further postponement of the *démarche*; the Germans, Berchtold expostulated, could feel absolutely 'assured . . . that there was not a thought of hesitation or uncertainty [in Vienna]'.

The Austrian note, conclusively agreed on Sunday 19 July, met some of Tisza's objections. He had from the beginning opposed the presentation of any demands that might increase the number of Slavs within the empire and so it contained no threat of annexation nor, despite Conrad's desires, of dismemberment. Serbia, if it capitulated to the full list of Austrian demands, was to be left intact. On the other hand, the note also fulfilled Berchtold's wish that Serbia be asked for guarantees as to its future conduct. To that end, the note required first of all that the Serbian government newspaper publish on its front page a condemnation of all propaganda for the separation of any portion of imperial territory, a condemnation to be repeated by the Serbian King in an order of the day to the Serbian army. It then listed ten numbered demands, of which five were elaborations of the prohibition of propaganda or subversion and the last a demand for information that the others were being enacted. None of these points entailed any infringement of Serbian sovereignty. Points 5, 6, 7 and 8 did, since, besides stipulating the arrest, interrogation and punishment of Serbian officials implicated in the assassination, they also demanded that Austro-Hungarian officials should take part in the necessary processes on Serbian soil. Serbia, in short, was not to be trusted to police the crime itself; Austria should supervise. The time limit for an answer attached to the note was forty-eight hours from delivery. That would take place on the day Berchtold had now learnt the French President would leave Russia, Thursday 23 July. The document would reach Belgrade at six o'clock (local time) in the afternoon of that day and expire on Saturday 25 July.

It was then the twenty-fifth day since the assassination and the Serbian government had been warned that the note was on its way. Nicholas Pasic, the Serbian Prime Minister, had nevertheless decided to leave the capital for the country and, even after word reached him that the Austrian ambassador had brought the document to the foreign ministry, proceeded with his journey. Only during the night did he decide to return and it was not until ten o'clock in the morning of Friday 24 July that he met his ministers to consider what answer should be made. The Russian, German, and British governments had already received their copies of the text, and so had the French though, with the President and Foreign Minister still at sea, in Paris it was in the hands of a deputy. In Belgrade, however, the British minister was ill, the Russian minister had just died and not been replaced, while a replacement for the French minister, who had had a nervous break-down, had only just arrived. The Serbian ministry were thus deprived of experienced diplomatic advice at a moment when the need was critical. Belgrade was a small and remote city, and the government, though experienced in the rough-and-ready diplomacy of Balkan warfare, was ill-equipped to deal with a crisis likely to involve all the great powers. The Serbian ministers, moreover, had taken fright as they pored over the Austrian note in the absence of Pasic. On his return, though there was some bold, initial talk of war, the mood quickly moved towards acquiescence. Messages were received from Sir Edward Grey, the British Foreign Minister, and from Paris, both counselling acceptance of as much of the Austrian note as possible. By the following morning, Saturday 25 July, both the British and French delegations in Belgrade reported home that Belgrade would agree to the Austrian demands, excepting the condition that imperial officials be admitted on to Serbian territory to supervise the investigations.

Even on that sticking point, however, the Serbians had as yet not made up their minds. As late as the twenty-seventh day after the assassination, it therefore seemed possible that Austria would arrive at the result it might very well have achieved had it exercised its right as a sovereign power to move against Serbia from the outset. The vital interest of no other power was threatened, except by consideration of prestige, even if Serbia permitted Austrian officials to participate in judicial proceedings conducted on its territory. That would be a humiliation to the Serbs, and a violation of the idea of sovereignty by which the states of Europe conducted relations between themselves. Yet, given Serbia's semi-rogue status in the international community, it was unlikely to constitute an issue of principle for others, unless others made that choice. Even at noon on Saturday 25 July, therefore, five hours before the time limit attached to the Austrian note would expire, the crime of Sarajevo remained a matter between Austria-Hungary and Serbia, diplomatically no more than that.

Such was strictly true in the arena of diplomatic protocol. In the real world, however, the elapse of three weeks and six days since the murders had given time for fears to fester, premonitions to take form, positions to be taken in outline. Grey, on the Friday afternoon when the Serbian ministers were preparing to capitulate, had already asked the German and Austrian ambassadors in London, Prince Lichnowsky and Count Mensdorff, to consider proposing an extension of the time limit, so anticipating the possibility that the Serbs might after all jib. He also raised the question of mediation. Accepting, as the Austrians had made clear, that they would refuse any interference in their dealings with Serbia, he proposed nevertheless the idea that Germany, with France and Italy, might offer to mediate between Austria and Russia, if Russia were to mobilise, which the diplomatic community recognised to be a potential development. A Russian mobilisation would harden attitudes everywhere, even though it was not thought to entail that of other armies, and certainly not the consequence of war. Nevertheless, Mensdorff returned to the Foreign Office in the evening to reassure the officials – Grey had left for a weekend's fishing – that the note was not an ultimatum and that Austria would not necessarily declare war if a satisfactory answer had not been received when the time limit lapsed.

The night and most of Saturday remained for it to be seen what the Serbians would do. On the morning of 25 July they were still reconciled to capitulation, though reluctantly and with occasional bursts of belligerence. Then, during the afternoon, word was received from their ambassador at the Tsar's country palace that the mood there was fiercely pro-Serbian. The Tsar, though not yet ready to proclaim mobilisation, had announced the preliminary 'Period Preparatory to War' at eleven o'clock. The news reversed everything the Serbian ministers had decided. In the morning they had agreed to accept all ten Austrian demands, with the slightest reservations. Now they were emboldened to attach conditions to six and to reject absolutely the most important, that Austrian officials be allowed to take part in the investigation of the assassinations on Serbian territory. In the hurried hours that followed, the reply to the note was drafted and redrafted, lines crossed out, phrases corrected in ink. As would happen in the Japanese embassy in Washington on the night before Pearl Harbor, the typist gave way to nerves. The finished document was an undiplomatic palimpsest of revisions and afterthoughts. With a quarter of an hour in hand, however, it was finished, sealed in an envelope and taken by the Prime Minister himself, Nicholas Pasic, for delivery to the Austrian ambassador. Within an hour of its receipt, the personnel of the legation had boarded the train for the Austrian frontier and left Belgrade.

There followed a curious two-day intermission, Sunday and Monday, 26–27 July. Serbia mobilised its little army, Russia recalled the youngest reservists to the units in its western military districts, there were scenes of popular enthusiasm in Vienna over the government's rejection of the Serbian reply and similar scenes in German cities, including Berlin. On Sunday, however, the Kaiser was still at sea, while Poincaré and Viviani, the French Foreign Minister, aboard *La France*, did not receive a signal urging their immediate return until that night. Meanwhile there was much talk, reflective and anticipatory, rather than decisive or belligerent. Bethmann Hollweg instructed the German ambassadors in London and Paris to warn that the military measures Russia was taking could be judged threatening. The German ambassador in St Petersburg was told to say that the measures, unless discontinued, would force Germany to mobilise which 'would mean war'. Bethmann Hollweg learnt from him in reply that the British and French were working to restrain Russia while Sazonov, the Russian Foreign Minister, was moderating his position.

The Kaiser and the Austrian government were informed. The British Foreign Office, working from information of its own, perceived a hope that the Russians were ready to acquiesce in a mediation by the United Kingdom, France, Germany and Italy. There was, briefly, the circulation of a feeling that the crisis, like those of 1909 and 1913, might be talked out.

The weakness of that hope was the ignorance and misunderstanding among politicians and diplomats of how the mechanism of abstract war plans, once instigated, would operate. Only Sir George Buchanan, the British ambassador in St Petersburg, and Jules Cambon, the French ambassador in Berlin, fully comprehended the trigger effect exerted by one mobilisation proclamation on another and the inexorability of deployment once begun.[9] Buchanan had already warned the Russians, as he reported to the Foreign Office, that a Russian mobilisation would push the Germans not into a responsive mobilisation but to a declaration of war. Cambon had come to the same conclusion. Mere ambassadors as they were, however, and far from home in an age of formal and indirect communication, their voices lacked weight and, worse, failed to convey urgency. It was those at the point of decision – in the entourages of the Tsar and Kaiser, in Paris, in Vienna, in London – who were heard. They, moreover, though few in number – a handful of ministers, officials and soldiers in each capital – did not equally share the information available, nor understand what they did share in the same way, nor agree within each capital about what was understood. Information arrived fitfully, sometimes much, sometimes little, but was always incomplete. There was no way of correlating and displaying it, as there is in modern crisis management centres. Even had there been, it is not certain that the crisis of 1914 would have been managed any better than it was. Modern communication systems may overload those who seek to be informed through them, so consuming time necessary for thought; underload, in 1914, consumed time as men puzzled to fill in the gaps between the facts they had. Time, in all crises, is usually the ingredient missing to make a solution. It is best supplied by an agreement on a pause.

Today there are mechanisms to hand designed to negotiate pause: regional security councils, the United Nations. In 1914 there were none. Any pause would have to be arranged by men of goodwill. Grey, British Foreign Secretary, was such a man. He had raised the proposal for a four-power conference on Sunday 26 July and spent Monday trying to convene one. Had it been the only proposal in circulation he might have succeeded but others were set in motion and that deflected attention. The Russians proposed, on Monday, direct talks with the Austrians for a moderation of their demands on the Serbs; they also suggested that the great power ambassadors in Belgrade exert pressure in the opposite direction to weaken Serb resistance. To distraction was added deliberate confusion. The senior official in the German Foreign Office, Gottlieb von Jagow, verbally assured the British and French ambassadors that Germany was anxious to preserve the peace but preferred direct talks between Russia and Austria to a wider mediation; meanwhile, Germany did nothing to encourage Austria to speak to Russia. Her aim was to delay a Russian mobilisation while sustaining a process of diplomacy that would keep Britain and France – the latter agreed on Monday afternoon to join Grey's proposed four-power conference – inert. Finally, there was sabotage. When Berchtold, in Vienna, learnt of Grey's conference proposal that same Monday he informed the German ambassador that he intended 'to send official declaration of war tomorrow, at the latest the day after, in order to cut away the ground from any attempt at mediation'.[10]

In the event, Austria-Hungary declared war on Serbia on Tuesday 28 July. It was Berchtold rather than Conrad who was now in a hurry. There had already been an exchange of fire between Serbian and Austrian troops – it was one-sided, an Austrian volley at Serbs who had strayed too near the Austrian border – but Berchtold chose to regard it as an act of war. War was now what he wanted on the terms he might have had during the days immediately following the murders, a straightforward offensive against Serbia uncomplicated by a wider conflict. The month's delay had threatened that simplicity, but he retained hopes that diplomacy would delay the taking of irretrievable decisions by others while he settled the Serbian score.

His urge to act was heightened by the discovery that his own country's war plans impeded what prospect remained of a speedy resolution.[11] Conrad's tripartite division of forces – the 'minimal' concentration on the Balkan frontier, the major concentration against Russia in Poland, the 'swing' grouping to reinforce one or the other – precluded, the Field Marshal warned him, an immediate offensive against Serbia unless it could be guaranteed that Russia would not mobilise. Small though Serbia's army was, only sixteen weak divisions, it outnumbered Austria's 'minimal' group; operational prudence therefore required the commitment of the 'swing' grouping if a quick Serbian war were to be brought off. If the 'swing' grouping went south, however, the northern frontier with Poland would be left dangerously exposed. All therefore depended on what Russia would do next.

Russia had already done much. On the previous Saturday, when news of her emphatic support for Serbia had encouraged the Belgrade government to change its mind and reject the Austrian note, she had instigated the military measures known as the 'Period Preparatory to War'. Entailing in this case only the bringing to operational readiness of the peacetime army in European Russia, the procedure was precautionary and intended not to provoke an escalation to mobilisation by another power. The equivalent in Germany was the 'State of Danger of War' *(Kriegsgefahrzustand)* and in France *la couverture*, covering operations behind the frontier. The Russian measure could be justified by the fact that Serbia had mobilised and Austria mobilised against her only, a partial mobilisation, on the same day. France was informed of the measure – the Franco-Russian Convention required that Russia consult her ally before mobilisation – and the German military representative at the Russian court informed Berlin that he had 'the impression that all preparations are being made for a mobilisation against Austria'.[12] In practice, much more had been done. Under cover of the 'Period Preparatory to War', orders had been sent for the mobilisation of the military districts of Kiev, Odessa, Moscow and Kazan – half of European Russia – and were extended on Monday 27 July to the Caucasus, Turkestan, Omsk and Ipkutsk.

By the beginning of what was to prove the last week of peace, therefore, half the Russian army – though the half not stationed in the military districts adjoining Germany, those in Poland, White Russia and the Baltic provinces – was coming to a war footing. France had been informed and approved; indeed, Messimy, the Minister of War, and Joffre, the Chief of Staff, were pressing the Russians to achieve the highest possible state of readiness.[13] The Russian generals at least needed little urging. Their responsibility as they saw it – all generals in all countries in July 1914 saw their responsibility in such terms – was to prepare for the worst if the worst came. The worst for them would be that, in seeking to deter Austria from making war in Serbia, their preparations provoked Germany into full-scale mobilisation. That would come about if their partial mobilisation, already in progress, prompted a full Austrian mobilisation which, they had good reason to believe, required a full German mobilisation also. On Tuesday 28 July, therefore, the Russian Chief of Staff, Janushkevich, with his quartermaster-general, chief of mobilisation and chief of transportation, agreed that the 'Period Preparatory to War' must now be superseded by formal mobilisation announcements.[14] Privately they accepted that general war could probably not be avoided: the sequence Russian partial mobilisation against Austria = Austrian general mobilisation = German general mobilisation = war stood stark before them. They decided, however, that publicly they would announce only partial mobilisation, while preparing with the order for it another for general mobilisation, both to be set simultaneously before the Tsar for signature.

Sazonov, who had received word of Austria's declaration of war on Serbia that Tuesday morning and conferred with Paléologue, the French ambassador, in the afternoon – Albertini, the great historian of the origins of the war, concluded that Paléologue 'must now have approved of [the decision for partial mobilisation] and promised full French solidarity' – attempted to palliate the fears the proclamation would certainly arouse by telegraphing Vienna, Paris, London and Rome (though not Berlin) with the news and requesting that the German government be informed, with 'stress on the absence of any intention on the part of Russia to attack Germany'.[15] Nevertheless, that evening Janushkevich informed all military districts that '30 July will be proclaimed the first day of our general mobilisation' and on the following morning, having seen Sazonov, called on the Tsar and secured his signature to the orders for full as well as partial mobilisation.[16] In the afternoon the chief of the mobilisation section got the relevant ministers' signatures – the minister of the interior, a deeply devout Orthodox believer, signed only after making the sign of the cross – and in the evening the quartermaster-general had the orders typed up at the St Petersburg central telegraph office and prepared for despatch.

This decision to order general mobilisation 'was perhaps the most important . . . taken in the history of Imperial Russia and it effectively shattered any prospect of averting a great European war'.[17] It was also unnecessary. Sazonov's support for the soldiers seems to have been supplied by his learning of a bombardment of Belgrade by Austrian gunboats on the Danube on the night of 29 July. The attack was a pinprick; Kalimegdan, the Turkish fortress crowning the Belgrade heights at the junction of the Danube and the Save, is impervious to anything but the heaviest artillery and remains unscarred to this day. On the wider front, Russia's security was not threatened by the Austrian mobilisation. Indeed, Austria's war with Serbia precluded its fighting a larger war elsewhere. Small as Serbia's army was, its size, to say nothing of its proven fighting ability, required, even by Vienna's calculation, the commitment against it of over half the Austrian force available. The 'minimal' and 'swing' groupings totalled twenty-eight of Austria's divisions, and the twenty remaining were too few to launch an offensive into Russian Poland. The Serbian interior, moreover, was difficult campaigning country, mountainous, largely roadless and heavily forested, and therefore likely to impose serious delay on an invader seeking speedy decision: such was to prove exactly the case in 1915 when Germany, Austria and Bulgaria fell on the Serbs from several directions but took two months to conclude the campaign.[18]

Russia might, therefore, without risk to its security, threat to the general peace or abandonment of the Serbs, have confined itself to partial mobilisation deep within its own frontiers on 29 July. General mobilisation, including that of the military districts bordering Germany, would mean general war. That awful prospect was now taking shape in all the European capitals. Those who most feared the military preparations of others – Janushkevich, Moltke, Conrad, Joffre – were looking to their own lest they be taken at a disadvantage. Those who more feared war itself were scrabbling for stopgaps. Bethmann Hollweg, the German Chancellor, was one of them; he had already instructed the German ambassador in St Petersburg to warn Sazonov that 'Russian mobilisation measures would compel us to mobilise and that then European war could scarcely be prevented'.[19] The Kaiser was another. On the afternoon of 29 July, he telegraphed his cousin the Tsar, in English, urging him 'to smooth over difficulties that may still arise'. In reply the Tsar pathetically suggested, 'It would be right to give over the Austro-Servian problem to the Hague conference', that weakling brainchild of his not scheduled to meet again until 1915.[20] Later that evening a second telegram from the Kaiser reached the Tsar. 'It would be quite possible', he suggested, 'for Russia to remain a spectator of the Austro-Servian conflict without involving Europe in the most horrible war she has ever witnessed' and ended by again representing himself as a mediator. Immediately on receipt of this telegram, the Tsar telephoned the War Minister and ordered the cancellation of general mobilisation; the order was to be for partial mobilisation only after all. He intervened only just in time, for at 9.30 in the evening of 29 July the Russian quartermaster-general was actually standing over the typists at the Central Telegraph Office in St Petersburg as they tapped out the orders on to telegraph forms.[21]

The cancellation should have brought the pause which the search for peace required. At the opening of the day following, Thursday 30 July, the British – though refusing to reveal whether they would or would not intervene in a general European war – were still seeking to arrange a mediation, France had not taken any substantial precautionary measures, the Austrian troops mobilised were marching against Serbia only and Germany had mobilised no troops at all. The leaders of the German army were nevertheless in a state of acute anxiety. To General von Falkenhayn, the Minister of War, Russia's partial mobilisation had consequences as threatening as full; it gave the Russians a start that would upset the feather-balance timing of the Schlieffen Plan. He wanted to mobilise at once, Bethmann Hollweg did not. He was still hoping that Berchtold would deal directly with the Russians and succeed in persuading them to accept the offensive against Serbia as a local war. Moltke, the Chief of the Great General Staff, was less bellicose but wanted at least the proclamation of the *Kriegsgefahrzustand*, which would match Russian preparations. In order to get his way, he wished himself on a meeting Bethmann held at one o'clock with Falkenhayn and Admiral Tirpitz, the naval minister. He failed to get what he wanted; but what he learnt shortly afterwards so alarmed him that he decided he must get general mobilisation at once and by any means. The Austrian liaison officer to the Great General Staff outlined to him his army's current dispositions which, Moltke instantly grasped, would leave Germany's eastern frontier desperately exposed if war came. 'He needed forty Austro-Hungarian divisions in (Austrian Poland) ready to attack; what he was getting were twenty-five divisions standing on the defensive.'[22] He at once expressed his extreme alarm to the Austrian military attaché; later that evening he telegraphed Conrad in Vienna, as one Chief of Staff to another, 'Stand firm against Russian mobilisation. Austria-Hungary must be preserved, mobilise at once against Russia. Germany will mobilise.'

Even in militaristic Germany, Moltke thereby vastly exceeded his powers. What made his meddling even more reprehensible was that the Chancellor and the Kaiser were still seeking to persuade Austria to localise the war against Serbia and limit its objectives: 'Halt in

71

Belgrade' was the phrase in circulation. Berchtold, when he saw the telegram next morning, Friday 31 July, expressed an understandable surprise. 'How odd! Who runs the government: Moltke or Bethmann?' Nevertheless, he took his cue. Telling Conrad, 'I had the impression that Germany was beating a retreat; but now I have the most reassuring pronouncement from responsible military quarters', he arranged for the general mobilisation order to be laid before Emperor Franz Josef later that morning.[23] It was returned signed shortly after noon and published immediately.

That announcement in itself would have ensured a reconsideration of the Tsar's decision to cancel general mobilisation in the evening of 29 July. In fact, it had already been reconsidered. Throughout Thursday 30 July, Sazonov, Sukhomlinov and Janushkevich – Foreign Minister, War Minister, Chief of Staff – had badgered the Tsar with their fears. He was at his summer residence on the Baltic, swimming, playing tennis, worrying about a bleeding attack suffered by his haemophiliac son, clinging to hopes of peace and trusting in the best intentions of his cousin the Kaiser. A good but infuriatingly evasive man, he deflected their arguments during the morning; in the afternoon, Sazonov set out by train to Peterhof to confront him. Sazonov was in a state of high agitation. It was no help that Paléologue, the French ambassador, whom he had seen earlier, did nothing to deter him from heightening the crisis. Paléologue, a strident patriot, appears to have given way already to belief in the inevitability of war and to have wanted only the certainty of Russian involvement when it came.[24] Sazonov had never wanted war but his was an excitable and impressionable nature and he was keyed up by the warnings of the generals over losing advantage; moreover, he possessed in an acute form the Russian neurosis over control of the Balkans, with which went fears of a hostile power dominating the Bosphorus, Russia's Black Sea exit to the Mediterranean and wider world. Between three and four o'clock on the afternoon of Thursday 30 July he rehearsed his anxieties to the Tsar who listened, pale and tense, occasionally showing an uncharacteristic irritation. General Tatistchev, his personal representative to the Kaiser, who was present, at one point observed, 'Yes, it is hard to decide.' The Tsar replied in a rough, displeased tone, ' I will decide.'[25] Shortly he did. Sazonov left the audience chamber and telephoned Janushkevich with the order to proclaim general mobilisation. 'Now you can smash your telephone,' he concluded. Janushkevich had earlier threatened that if he got the order for general mobilisation a second time he would smash his telephone and make himself unobtainable until mobilisation was too far advanced for another cancellation to take effect.

The hour had come. That evening the posters announcing mobilisation went up in the streets of St Petersburg and of all cities in Russia. The reservists would begin reporting to their depots next day, Friday 31 July. For reasons never properly elucidated, what was necessary knowledge for every Russian failed officially to reach London and Paris until late that evening; the British ambassador was dilatory in telegraphing, Paléologue's telegram was inexplicably delayed. The Germans were not so ill-informed. They knew on Friday morning. At 10.20 a telegram arrived for Pourtalès, their ambassador in St Petersburg, 'First day of mobilisation, 31 July'.[26] It was what Moltke wanted to hear. He would now get the permission he needed to take the military precautions he believed essential. It was not what Bethmann Hollweg wanted to hear. He had retained the hopes up to the moment of the telegram's arrival that Austria could be brought directly to negotiate with Russia and that Russia could be brought to accept the war against Serbia as local and limited. Now he had to accept what seemed inevitable. News of Austria's general mobilisation arrived half an hour after noon. Germany proclaimed the 'State of Danger of War' half an hour after that.

The 'State of Danger of War' was an internal measure not entailing mobilisation. Nevertheless, with Austria and Russia mobilising, the Germans concluded that they must mobilise also unless Russian general mobilisation was reversed. An ultimatum to that effect was sent soon after three o'clock on the afternoon of 31 July to St Petersburg and another to Paris. The relevant sentence in each read: '[German] mobilisation will follow unless Russia suspends all war measures against ourselves and Austria-Hungary.' That to Russia demanded, within twelve hours, 'a definite assurance to that effect', that to France included the warning 'Mobilisation inevitably means war' and required a declaration of neutrality 'in a Russo-German war . . . within eighteen (18) hours'.[27]

The afternoon of 31 July thus brought to a crux the crisis which had begun thirty-four days earlier with the murders at Sarajevo. Its real duration had been much shorter than that. From the murders on 28 June to the conclusion of the Austrian judicial investigation and the confessions of the conspirators on 2 July was five days. It was in the period immediately following that the Austrians might have decided for unilateral action, and taken it without strong likelihood of provoking an intervention by the Serbs' protectors, the Russians. Instead, Austria had sought a German assurance of support, given on 5 July; elapsed time from the murders, eight days. There had then followed an intermission of nineteen days, while the Austrians waited for the French President to conclude his state visit on 23 July. The real inception of the crisis may thus be dated to the delivery of the Austrian 'note with a time limit' (of forty-eight hours) on 24 July. It was on its expiry on Saturday 25 July, twenty-eight days from the murders, that the diplomatic confrontation was abruptly transformed into a war crisis. It was not a crisis which the participants had expected. Austria had simply wanted to punish Serbia (though it had lacked the courage to act alone). Germany had wanted a diplomatic success that would leave its Austrian ally stronger in European eyes; it had not wanted war. The Russians had certainly not wanted war but had equally not calculated that support for Serbia would edge the danger of war forward. By 30 July, thirty-three days from the murders, the Austrians were at war with Serbia, yet were doing nothing about it, had declared general mobilisation, but were not concentrating against Russia. Russia had declared partial mobilisation but was concentrating against nobody. The German Kaiser and Chancellor still believed that Austria and Russia could be brought to negotiate their mobilisations away, even if the Chief of the Great General Staff by then wanted a mobilisation of his own. France had not mobilised but was in growing fear that Germany would mobilise against her. Britain, which had awoken to the real danger of the crisis only on Saturday 25 July, still hoped on Thursday 30 July that the Russians would tolerate an Austrian punishment of Serbia but were determined not to leave France in the lurch.

It was the events of 31 July, therefore, the dissemination of the news of Russian general mobilisation, and the German ultimata to Russia and France, which made the issue one of peace or war. The day following, 1 August, the thirty-fifth since the murders, would bring Germany's mobilisation against Russia – thus making, in the words of the German ultimatum to France, 'war inevitable' – unless Germany withdrew its ultimatum to Russia, which was incompatible with its status as a great power, or Russia accepted it, which was incompatible with such status also. German mobilisation would, under the terms of the Franco-Russian Convention of 1892, require both to mobilise and, if either were attacked by Germany, to go jointly to war against her.

As the hours drew out on 31 July – the twelve demanded for a response from Russia, the eighteen demanded from France – only a hair's breadth kept the potential combatants apart. There was still a hope. The Russo-French Convention of 1892, strictly interpreted, required that Germany actually attack one country or the other before the two went to war against her. German mobilisation entailed only their mobilisation. Even a German declaration of war, unless followed by German military action, would not bring the treaty into force. Nevertheless, the Germans had warned France that their mobilisation meant war with Russia and the outbreak of war between great powers not followed by fighting was a state of affairs without credibility in early twentieth-century Europe. The twelve hours given by Germany to Russia for acceptance of the ultimatum was, by any rational calculation, the last twelve hours of available peace. It was, in France, an inexact twelve hours. Wilhelm Freiherr Schoen, the German ambassador to Paris, who came to communicate news of the ultimatum to Russia at the French foreign ministry at six p.m. on Friday 31 July was unclear when the period began and ended – it was midnight to noon next day – but the exact delimitation was by then beside the point. War hovered half a day away.[28]

That, by 31 July, was certainly the view of the French army. News, true or exaggerated, of German military preparations, had thrown even Joffre, 'a byword for imperturbability', into a state of anxiety. The loss of advantage was a fear that now afflicted him as acutely as it had Janushkevich on 29 July and Moltke on 30 July. He foresaw the secret approach of German troops to their deployment positions while his own soldiers were still in barracks, German reservists kitting out at their depots while his were still at home. On the afternoon of Friday 31 July, he handed to Messimy, the Minister of War, a short note which epitomises, better than any other document of the crisis of July 1914, the state of mind which possessed the military professionals of the age.

It is absolutely necessary for the government to understand that, starting with this evening, any delay of twenty-four hours in calling up our reservists and issuing orders prescribing covering operations, will have as its result the withdrawal of our concentration points by from fifteen to twenty-five kilometres for each day of delay; in other words, the abandonment of just that much of our territory. The Commander-in-Chief must decline to accept this responsibility.[29]

75

That evening he formally requested the President to order general mobilisation at once. His representation was debated by the cabinet next morning and the first day of mobilisation, to be 2 August, proclaimed at four o'clock that afternoon.

The French had hoped to delay the proclamation until after the announcement of German mobilisation, in order to avoid any appearance of provocation. In practice, though the French order preceded the German, no such appearance was given, for the interval was only one of an hour. Moreover, two hours after that, the German ambassador in St Petersburg delivered to Sazonov the declaration of war on Russia. The hour was soon after seven in the evening, local time, Saturday 1 August. The exchange took place in a mood of high emotion. There were mutual recriminations, accusations against others, regrets, embraces, tears. The ambassador left Sazonov's room 'with tottering steps'.[30]

Yet the irrevocable did not yet seem done. The Tsar still hoped, on the strength of a telegram from the Kaiser begging him not to violate the German frontier, that war could be averted. The Kaiser, meanwhile, had fixed on the belief that the British would remain neutral if France were not attacked and was ordering Moltke to cancel the Schlieffen Plan and direct the army eastward. Moltke was aghast, explained that the paperwork would take a year, but was ordered to cancel the invasion of Luxembourg, which was the Schlieffen Plan's necessary preliminary.[31] In London this Sunday 1 August, the French ambassador, Paul Cambon, was thrown into despair by the British refusal to declare their position. Britain had, throughout the crisis, pursued the idea that, as so often before, direct talks between the involved parties would dissolve the difficulties. As a power apart, bound by treaties with none, it had concealed its intentions from all, including the French. Now the French demanded that the understanding between them and the British be given force. Would Britain declare outright its support for France and, if so, on what issue and when? The British themselves did not know. Throughout Saturday and Sunday 2 August, the cabinet debated its course of action. The treaty of 1839, guaranteeing Belgian neutrality, would force it to act, but that neutrality was still intact. It could give no firm answer to France, any more than it could to Germany, which had requested a clarification on 29 July. Precautionary measures had been taken; the fleet had been sent to war stations, France was even secretly assured that the Royal Navy would protect its Channel coast; but further than that the cabinet would not go. Then, on 2 August, Germany delivered the last of its ultimata, this time to Belgium, demanding the use of its territory in operations against France and threatening to treat the country as an enemy if she resisted. The ultimatum was to expire in twenty-four hours, on Monday 3 August. It was the day Germany also decided, claiming violation of its own territory by French aircraft, to present France with a declaration of war. The expiry of the ultimatum to Belgium, which the British cabinet had finally resolved would constitute a cause for war, proved the irrevocable event. On Tuesday 4 August, Britain sent an ultimatum of its own, demanding the termination of German military operations against Belgium, which had already begun, to expire at midnight. No offer of termination in reply was received. At midnight, therefore, Britain, together with France and Russia, was at war with Germany.

The First World War had still not quite begun. The Austrians succeeded in delaying their declaration of war on Russia until 5 August and were still not at war with Britain and France a week later. Those two countries were driven to make up the Austrians' mind for them by announcing hostilities on 12 August. The Italians, Triple Alliance partners to Austria-Hungary and Germany, had stood on the strict terms of the treaty and declared their neutrality. The Serbians, cause of the crisis in the first place, had been forgotten. War was not to come to their little kingdom for another fourteen months.

FOUR

THE BATTLE OF
THE FRONTIERS
AND THE MARNE

STATESMEN WERE FILLED WITH foreboding by the coming of war but its declaration was greeted with enormous popular enthusiasm in the capitals of all combatant countries. Crowds thronged the streets, shouting, cheering and singing patriotic songs. In St Petersburg the French ambassador, Maurice Paléologue, found his way into the Winter Palace Square, 'where an enormous crowd had congregated with flags, banners, icons and portraits of the Tsar. The Emperor appeared on the balcony. The entire crowd at once knelt and sang the Russian national anthem. To those thousands of men on their knees at that moment the Tsar was really the autocrat appointed of God, the military, political and religious leader of his people, the absolute master of their bodies and souls.'[1] The day was 2 August. On 1 August a similar crowd had gathered in the Odeonsplatz in Munich, capital of the German kingdom of Bavaria, to hear the proclamation of mobilisation. In it was Adolf Hitler who was 'not ashamed to acknowledge that I was carried away by the enthusiasm of the moment and . . . sank down upon my knees and thanked Heaven out of the fullness of my heart for the favour of having been permitted to live in such times'.[2] In Berlin the Kaiser appeared on his palace balcony, dressed in field-grey uniform, to address a tumultuous crowd: 'A fateful hour has fallen upon Germany. Envious people on all sides are compelling us to resort to a just defence. The sword is being forced into our hands . . . And now I command you all to go to church, kneel before God and pray to him to help our gallant army.' In the Berlin cathedral, the Kaiser's pastor led a huge congregation in the recitation of Psalm 130 and at the Oranienstrasse synagogue the rabbi conducted prayers for victory.[3]

There were to be similar scenes in London on 5 August. In Paris it was the departure of the city's mobilised regiments to the Gare de l'Est and Gare du Nord which brought forth the crowds. 'At six in the morning', an infantry officer reported,

81

without any signal, the train slowly steamed out of the station. At that moment, quite spontaneously, like a smouldering fire suddenly erupting into roaring flames, an immense clamour arose as the *Marseillaise* burst from a thousand throats. All the men were standing at the train's windows, waving their képis. From the track, quais and the neighbouring trains, the crowds waved back . . . Crowds gathered at every station, behind every barrier, and at every window along the road. Cries of 'Vive la France! Vive l'armée' could be heard every-where, while people waved handkerchiefs and hats. The women were throwing kisses and heaped flowers on our convoy. The young men were shouting: '*Au revoir! A bientôt!*'[4]

All too soon, for most of the young men, the summons to follow would come. Reservists not yet called were already putting their affairs in order; in most armies the day before the stipulated date for reporting was a 'free day' for farewells to family and employer. 'Complete strangers', recorded Richard Cobb, the great historian of France, 'could be heard addressing one another in bizarre fashion, as if Parisians had all at once become figures out of Alice [in Wonderland]: playing cards, days of the week, or dates in a new sort of calendar. "What day are you?" And, before the other could get in an answer, "I am on the first" (as if to suggest: "beat that"). "I am the ninth" ("Bad luck, you'll miss all the fun, it'll be over by then"). "I am the third, so won't have to wait *too* long." "I am the eleventh" ("You'll never make Berlin at that rate").'[5] A German officer-candidate reservist gives a more prosaic account of how the procedure swept up the individual. He was on busi-ness in Antwerp. His military document told him he had to report

to the nearest regiment of field artillery on the second day of mobilisation . . . When I reached Bremen on 3 August, my family was frantic. They thought the Belgians had arrested and shot me . . . on 4 August, I presented myself to the army as a reservist and was told I now belonged to Reserve Field Artillery Regiment No. 18, which was forming in Behrenfeld near Hamburg, about seventy-five miles [away]. Relatives were not allowed near the building where we had to assemble. As soon as I could I gave a message to a little boy so my family knew . . . Relatives were not allowed on the railway platform either, only Red Cross people who gave us free cigars, cigarettes and candy. On the troop train I was glad to see friends I knew well from my rowing and tennis clubs . . . On 6 August I was issued my field-grey uniform which

I had never worn before. The colour was grey-green with dull buttons, the helmet was covered with a grey cloth so that the ornaments would not glitter in the sun and the high riding boots were brown and very heavy . . . All soldiers and most of the officers were reservists but the commanding officer was a regular . . . Most of the NCOs were regulars. The horses were reservists, too. Owners of horses – sportsmen, businessmen and farmers – had to register them regularly and the army knew at all times where the horses were.[6]

Horses, like men, were mustering in hundreds of thousands all over Europe in the first week of August. Even Britain's little army called up 165,000, mounts for the cavalry and draught animals for the artillery and regimental transport waggons. The Austrian army mobilised 600,000, the German 715,000, the Russian – with its twenty-four cavalry divisions – over a million.[7] The armies of 1914 remained Napoleonic in their dependence on the horse; staff officers calculated the proportion between horses and men at 1:3. Walter Bloem, a reserve officer of the 12th Brandenburg Grenadiers, packed as much luggage for his two horses as himself when he mobilised at Stuttgart: 'my trunk, my brown kitbag, and two boxes of saddlery . . . with the special red labels. "War luggage. Immediate"' before sending them ahead by train to Metz on the French border.

Trains were to fill the memories of all who went to war in 1914. The railway section of the German Great General Staff timetabled the movement of 11,000 trains in the mobilisation period, and no less than 2,150 fifty-four-waggon trains crossed the Hohenzollern Bridge over the Rhine alone between 2 and 18 August.[8] The chief French railway companies, Nord, Est, Ouest, PLM, POM, had since May 1912 had a plan to concentrate 7,000 trains for mobilisation. Many had moved near the entraining centres before war began.

Travellers coming in [to Paris] from Melun brought extraordinary accounts of empty, stationary trains, engineless, and often of mixed provenance, the carriages from different companies strung up together, passenger ones mixed up with guard trucks, many with chalk marks on their sides . . . waiting on side-lines the whole way from the *chef-lieu* of the Seine-et-Marne to the approaches of the Gare de Lyon. Equally bizarre were the reports brought in by travellers to the Gare du Nord of the presence along the immense sidings of Creil of several hundred stationary locomotives, smokeless and passive.[9]

They were not long stationary. Soon they would be moving, filled with hundreds of thousands of young men making their way, at ten or twenty miles an hour and often with lengthy, unexplained waits, to the detraining points just behind the frontiers. Long prepared, many of the frontier stations were sleepy village halts, where platforms three-quarters of a mile long had not justified the trickle of peacetime comings and goings. Images of those journeys are among the strongest to come down to us from the first two weeks of August 1914: the chalk scrawls on the waggon sides – *'Ausflug nach Paris',* and *'à Berlin'* – the eager young faces above the open collars of unworn uniforms, khaki, field-grey, pike-grey, olive-green, dark blue, crowding the windows. The faces glow in the bright sun of the harvest month and there are smiles, uplifted hands, the grimace of unheard shouts, the intangible mood of holiday, release from routine. Departure had everywhere been holidaylike, with wives and sweethearts, hobble-skirted, high-waisted, marching down the road to the terminus arm-in-arm with the men in the outside ranks. The Germans marched to war with flowers in the muzzles of their rifles or stuck between the top buttons of their tunics; the French marched in close-pressed ranks, bowed under the weight of enormous packs, forcing a passage between crowds over-spilling the pavements. One photograph of Paris that first week of August catches a sergeant marching backwards before his section as they lean towards him, he like a conductor orchestrating the rhythm of their footfalls on the cobbles, they urgent with the effort of departure and the call to arms.[10] An unseen band seems to be playing 'Sambre-et-Meuse' or 'le chant du depart'. Russian soldiers paraded before their regimental icons for a blessing by the chaplain, Austrians to shouts of loyalty to Franz Joseph, symbol of unity among the dozen nationalities of his creaking empire. In whichever country, mobilisation entailed enormous upheaval, the translation of civil society into the nation in arms. The British army, all-regular as it was, stood the readiest for war; once its reservists were recalled, it was prepared to deploy. 'We found the barracks full of Reservists – many still in civilian dress – and more were flocking in by almost every train', wrote Bandsman H.V. Sawyer of the 1st Rifle Brigade at Colchester on 5 August. 'Fitting them out with uniform, boots and equipment was proceeding rapidly but in some cases was no easy job. I remember one man in particular who must have weighed eighteen stone . . . It was hard on the Reservists, leaving good jobs and comfortable homes to come back to coarse uniforms and heavy boots.'[11]

Bandsman Shaw packed his peacetime kit and sent it home by rail. 'As it turned out, I needn't have bothered. But I wasn't to know that I'd packed that lovely dark green review order tunic for the last time in my life.'[12] In Paris Lieutenant Edward Spears, 11th Hussars, on exchange from the British to the French army, changed into khaki. '"How funny you look, disguised as a dusty canary", observed the female concierge who let me in at one of the more obscure entrances to the *Ministère de la guerre*. This was disappointing, but one became used to the fact that for a long time the French thought that to go to war in a collar and tie [British officers wore an open-necked tunic in service uniform] represented an attitude of levity quite out of keeping with the seriousness of the situation.'[13] The British, as a result of the Boer War, had decided on a sartorial revolution the French had not been able to make. Despite much experiment and debate, it went garbed for war in 1914 much as it had done in 1870, almost as under Napoleon. The heavy cavalry wore brass helmets with a long horsehair plume, the light cavalry frogged jackets and scarlet trousers; some of the heavy cavalry were burdened with breastplates unchanged in pattern from Waterloo. The light cavalry of the *Armée d'Afrique* were dressed in sky-blue tunics, the *Spahis* in flowing red cloaks, the Zouaves in baggy red breeches and Turkish waistcoats. Most conspicuous of all, because of their numbers, were the infantry of the metropolitan army. Under long, turned-back blue greatcoats, their legs were encased in madder-red trousers tucked into calf-length boots.[14] All was made of heavy wool; the stifling weight of antique uniforms was to prove one of the additional ordeals of combat in the sun-drenched autumn of 1914.

The Austrian cavalry rode to war in uniforms as antiquated as the French; only the infantry had been re-equipped with service grey. The Russians were unexpectedly modern. Their service dress was a loose olive-green overshirt, the *gymnastirka* modelled on an athlete's tunic; but there were exotic exceptions, notably the Astrakhan light cavalry. Only the Germans had made as clean a sweep as the British. Their army was uniformly field-grey. With an antiquarian deference to tradition, however, each branch of the service was outfitted in a camouflage version of parade-ground finery. Uhlans wore double-breasted lancer tunics and hussars field-grey frogging, while cuirassiers, dragoons and infantrymen kept their spiked helmets, disguised with field-grey covers. Little patches of colour and braid and lace distinguished regiment from regiment in almost all armies; the

Austrians meticulously differentiated between ten shades of red, including madder, cherry, rose, amaranth, carmine, lobster, scarlet and wine, for collar patches, six shades of green and three of yellow. The Hungarian regiments of Franz Joseph's army wore braided knots on their trousers and the Bosnian-Herzogovinian infantry the red fez and baggy breeches of the Balkans. Even the British, whom Captain Walter Bloem would describe on first encounter as wearing 'a grey-brown golfing suit',[15] excepted Lowlanders and Highlanders from the uniformity of khaki. They preserved their tartan trews or sporrans and kilts.

However clothed, the infantrymen of every army were afflicted by the enormous weight of their equipment: a rifle weighing ten pounds, bayonet, entrenching tool, ammunition pouches holding a hundred rounds or more, water bottle, large pack containing spare socks and shirt, haversack with iron rations and field dressing; that was a common outfit. The British, after the experience of long marches across the veldt in the Boer War, had adopted the 'scientific' Slade-Wallace equipment of canvas webbing, designed to distribute weight as evenly as possible over the body; even so, it dragged on the shoulders and waist. The Germans clung to leather, with the greatcoat hooped outside a stiff back-pack of undressed, and so water-repellant, hide. The French piled everything into a mountainous pyramid, '*le chargement de campagne*', crowned with the individual's metal cooking pot; gleams of sunlight from such pots would allow young Lieutenant Rommel to identify and kill French soldiers in high standing corn on the French frontier later that August.[16] The Russians rolled their possessions, greatcoat and all, into a sausage slung over one shoulder and under the other arm. However arranged, no infantryman's marching load weighed less than sixty pounds; and it had to be plodded forward, mile after mile for an expected twenty miles a day, in stiff, clumsy, nailed boots – 'dice-boxes', *brodequins, Bluchers*, to the British, French and Germans – which were agony until broken to the shape of the foot.

Feet were as important as trains in August 1914, horses' feet as well as men's feet for, after detrainment in the concentration area, cavalry and infantry deployed on to the line of march. That, for the Germans, presaged days of marching west and southwards, days in which human feet would bleed and horses throw shoes. The telltale clink of a loose nail warned a cavalryman that he must find the shoeing-smith if he were to keep up next day with the column; the same sound to the senior driver of a gun-team threatened the mobility of his six harnessed animals. There were 5,000 horses in an infantry division in 1914, more than 5,000 in a cavalry division. All had to be kept shod and healthy if the twenty miles of the day were to be covered to timetable, the infantry fed, reconnaissance reports returned, small-arms combat covered by artillery fire should the enemy be encountered. Fourteen miles of road was filled by an infantry division on the march and the endurance of horses – those pulling the wheeled field-kitchens, cooking on the march, quite as much as those drawing the ammunition waggons of the artillery brigades – counted with that of the infantry in the race to drive the advance forward.[17]

The race was tripartite. For the French it was north-eastward from their detraining points at Sedan, Montmédy, Toul, Nancy and Belfort behind the 1870 frontier. For the British Expeditionary Force, which began to disembark at Boulogne on 14 August, it was south-eastward towards Le Câteau, just before the Belgian border. These were short marches. For the Germans the marches planned were long, westward first and then southward towards Châlons, Eperney, Compiègne, Abbeville and Paris. General von Kluck's First Army on the right faced a march of 200 miles from its detraining points at Aachen to the French capital.

Before Paris, however, there was Liège and Namur and the other fortresses of the Belgian rivers which impeded any easy crossing for a German army into France. Belgium, small but rich out of proportion to its size, its wealth the product of an early industrial revolution and the colonisation of the Congo, had invested heavily in fortification to protect its neutrality. The forts at Liège and Namur, guarding the crossings of the Meuse, were the most modern in Europe. Built between 1888 and 1892 to the design of General Henri Brialmont, they were constructed to resist attack by the heaviest gun then existing, the 210 mm (8.4 inch). Each consisted of a circle, twenty-five miles in circumference, of independent forts, arranged at sufficient distance to protect the city itself from attack and to lend each other the protection of their own guns. At Liège there were 400, of 6-inch calibre or less, disposed in the twelve forts of the complex, all protected by re-inforced concrcte and armour plate. The garrison of 40,000 provided the gun crews but also 'interval troops' who were supposed, at the threat of invasion, to dig trenches between the forts and hold at bay enemy infantry attempting to infiltrate through the gaps.

The strength of the Belgian forts had alarmed Schlieffen and his General Staff successors. They were, indeed, immensely strong, subterranean and self-contained, surrounded by a ditch thirty feet deep. Infantry assault upon them was certain to fail. Their thick skins would have to be broken by aimed artillery fire, and quickly, for a delay at the Meuse crossings would throw into jeopardy the smooth evolution of the Schlieffen Plan. No gun heavy enough for the work existed at the time of Schlieffen's retirement in 1906. By 1909, however, Krupp had produced a prototype of a 420 mm (16.8 inch) howitzer powerful enough to penetrate the Belgian concrete. The Austrian Skoda company was meanwhile working on a 305 mm (12.2 inch) model which was ready the following year. It had the advantage of being road-transportable, when broken down into barrel, carriage and mount, on three motor-drawn waggons. The Krupp howitzer, in its original form, had to be transported by rail and embedded for action at the end of a specially built spur track in a concrete platform. Until a road-transportable model could be perfected, Austria lent Germany several of its 305s; only five of the Krupp rail and two of the new road-transportable guns had been finished by August 1914.[18]

Yet Liège had to be taken. Such was the necessity, and such the urgency, that the German war plan provided for the detachment of a special task force from Second Army to complete the mission. Commanded by General Otto von Emmich, its start line was drawn between Aachen and Eupen, at the north of the narrow corridor of French territory lying between Holland and Luxembourg: Luxembourg, though independent and neutral, was to be overrun in the great German advance a few days after Emmich's task force struck. The time allotted for the mission was forty-eight hours. It was expected by the Germans that Belgium would either not resist an invasion of its neutral territory or, should it do so, that its resistance would be swiftly overcome.

Both expectations were to be proved wrong. One of the clauses of the oath sworn by the Belgian sovereign on accession to the throne charged him with defence of the national territory, while Article 68 of the constitution appointed him commander-in-chief in time of war; he was also constitutionally president of his own council of ministers and therefore head of government, with executive powers unusual in a democracy. Albert I, King of the Belgians, was a man to take his responsibilities to heart. Intellectual, strong-willed, high-minded, he led an exemplary private life and set an example of fine public leadership. He was aware that his uncle, the aged Leopold II, had been bullied by the Kaiser in 1904: 'You will be obliged to choose. You will be with us or against us.' He had experienced the same treatment himself at Potsdam in 1913, when his military attaché had been warned that war would be 'inevitable and soon' and that it was 'imperative for the weak to side with the strong'.[19] Albert was determined not to take sides, correctly interpreting the treaty of 1839 to mean that Belgium's right to neutrality was balanced by the requirement to avoid commitment to any foreign power.[20] It was for that reason his government had so peremptorily rejected a British offer of 1912 to lend assistance in the event of a German invasion; to have accepted it would have been to prejudice Belgium's enjoyment of the international guarantees of its independence.

The British proposition, and the knowledge that only diplomatic delicacy deterred France from duplicating it, had the effect, however, of compelling the Belgian staff to confront the realities of national defence. Any intervention by the British or French, though necessitating resistance, would be benevolent. It would not threaten Belgian independence in either the long or even short term. A German intervention, by contrast, would have as its object not only the pre-emption of Belgian territory for a wider aggression but quite possibly the requisition of Belgian resources for the German war effort, and the subjection of Belgium to German military government for the duration of hostilities. From 1911 onwards, therefore,

> Belgium's political and military leadership had undertaken a major re-evaluation of Belgian policy. Three questions in particular worried Brussels: how to devise a military strategy that would limit the destruction of Belgium, how to ensure that a guarantor nation did not force Belgium into a war against its will, and how to ensure that a protesting power, once invited, would leave. Slowly, over a period of months and after much debate, the answers emerged. Militarily the Belgian General Staff planned to oppose any violation of Belgium; at the same time they hoped to confine all the fighting to a small area, possibly to the province of Belgian Luxembourg. Simply stated, Belgium would resist, yet seek to avoid losing either its integrity or its neutrality.[21]

Easier said than done. Belgium had adopted the principle of compulsory military service only in 1912, following the strategic review, and it had taken little effect by 1914. The army was one of the most old-fashioned in Europe. The cavalry still wore early nineteenth-century uniforms, crimson trousers, fur busbies, Polish lancer caps. The infantry were in dark blue with oilskin-covered shakos, feathered bonnets or grenadier bearskins. The few machine guns were drawn, like the Flemish milk carts much photographed by tourists, behind teams of dogs. Most of the artillery was allotted to the fortresses of Liège and Namur and the older defences of Antwerp. The army was actually outnumbered by the *Garde Civique*, the top-hatted town militias which descended from the days of the Thirty Years' War. Belgium's soldiers were patriotic and to prove themselves notably brave, but their capacity to confine any fighting for possession of their country to its eastern corner was delusory.

Yet, at the outset, they made a bold stab at enacting the General Staff's strategy. The German ultimatum, fictively alleging a French intention to violate Belgian territory and asserting Germany's right to do so in anticipation, was delivered, with a twelve-hour time limit, on the evening of Sunday 2 August. King Albert, acting as president of a council of state, considered it two hours later. The meeting lasted into the early hours of the morning. There were divided counsels. The Chief of Staff, General Antonin de Selliers, confessed the weakness of the army and advocated retreat to the River Velpe, outside Brussels. The Sub-Chief, General de Ryckel, demanded a spoiling attack into Germany: 'Send them back where they belong.' This fantasy was rejected. So, too, was Sellier's defeatism. The King was most concerned that no appeal should be made to France or Britain, whose aid was assured, unless they reasserted their respect for the country's independence. Eventually a middle way was decided. Belgium would not appeal for French or British assistance until her territory was physically violated, but the German ultimatum would meanwhile be rejected. The reply, described by Albertini as 'the noblest document produced by the whole crisis', ended with the resolution 'to repel every infringement of [Belgium's] rights by all the means at its power'.[22]

It was delivered to the German Legation at seven o'clock on the morning of 3 August and received in Berlin shortly after noon. The Germans contrived to believe, nevertheless, that the Belgians would make no more than a show of force, sufficient to demonstrate their neutrality, before giving them passage. Later that evening the Kaiser sent a personal appeal to Albert – a member of the House of Hohenzollern-Sigmaringen and so a distant relative – restating his 'friendliest intentions' and claiming 'the compulsion of the hour' as justification for the invasion that was about to begin.[23] On its receipt, the Belgian King gave way to his first outburst in two nerve-racking days: 'What does he take me for?' He immediately gave orders for the destruction of the bridges over the Meuse at Liège and the railway bridges and tunnels at the Luxembourg border.[24] He also charged the commander of the Liège fortress, General Gérard Leman, 'to hold to the end with your division the position which you have been entrusted to defend'.

Leman, the King's former military tutor, was a long-service professional soldier in the nineteenth-century tradition. Thirty years of his life had been spent at the Belgian War College. He was also a man of honour and, despite his advanced age, of courage and an unyielding sense of duty. The Meuse, which he was entrusted to hold, is a mighty river. 'Sambre-et-Meuse' is a traditional marching song of the French army, for the two rivers form a barrier which the revolutionary armies had defended against their enemies in 1792. At Liège the river runs in a narrow gorge 450 feet deep. It cannot be crossed in the face of a determined defence. So Emmich was to discover. His command entered Belgium early on the morning of 4 August, the outriders distributing leaflets disclaiming aggressive intent. Soon they came under fire from Belgian cavalrymen and cyclist troops who showed a quite unexpected resolution to oppose their advance. Pressing on to Liège, they found the bridges above and below the city already blown, despite the warning given that demolitions would be regarded as 'hostile acts'. The Germans responded as threatened. Memories of 'free firing' by irregulars against the Prussian advance into France in 1870 were strong and had been re-enforced by official stricture. Despite the heroic place allotted to the *Freischütze* who had waged the War of Prussian Liberation against Napoleon in 1813–14, official Germany interpreted international law to mean that an effective occupying force had the right to treat civilian resistance as rebellion and punish resisters by summary execution and collective reprisal.[25] There were, later enquiries would reveal, few or no *franc-tireurs* in Belgium in 1914. It was an unmilitary nation, prepared for war neither in mind nor body; the loyal government, though determined on a legal defence with the inadequate means it possessed, showed itself anxious from the start to deter citizens from useless and dangerous opposition to the German invasion. It issued placards urging avoidance 'of any pretext for measures of repression resulting

91

in bloodshed or pillage or massacre of the innocent population'.[26] The government also advised civilians to lodge firearms with the authorities; in some places the Civic Guard took the warning so seriously that it deposited its government weapons at the local town hall.[27]

Non-resistance did nothing to placate the invaders. Almost from the first hours, innocent civilians were shot and villages burnt, outrages all hotly denied by the Germans as soon as the news – subsequently well attested – reached neutral newspapers. Priests were shot, too, perhaps because German officers remembered that it was the priests who had led the resistance of Catholic Brittany against the armies of the French Revolution in 1793. The 'rape of Belgium' served no military purpose whatsoever and did Germany untold harm, particularly in the United States, where the reputations of the Kaiser and his government were blackened from the outset by reports of massacre and cultural despoliation. The reputation of the German army was dishonoured also. On 4 August, the first day of the Emmich incursion against the Meuse forts, six hostages were shot at Warsage and the village of Battice burnt to the ground. 'Our advance in Belgium is certainly brutal', Moltke wrote on 5 August, 'but we are fighting for our lives and all who get in the way must take the consequences.'[28] The consequences were to get worse. Within the first three weeks, there would be large-scale massacres of civilians in small Belgian towns, at Andenne, Seilles, Tamines and Dinant. At Andenne there were 211 dead, at Tamines 384, at Dinant 612. The victims included children and women as well as men and the killing was systematic; at Tamines the hostages were massed in the square, shot down by execution squads and survivors bayoneted. The execution squads were not, as were the 'action groups' of Hitler's holocaust, specially recruited killers but ordinary German soldiers. Indeed, those who murdered at Andenne were the reservists of the most distinguished regiments of the Prussian army, the Garde-Regimenter zu Fuss.[29]

Worst of all the outrages began on 25 August at Louvain. This little university town, the 'Oxford of Belgium', was a treasure store of Flemish Gothic and Renaissance architecture, painting, manuscripts and books. Panicked allegedly by a misunderstood night-time movement of their own troops, the occupiers, 10,000 strong, began to shout 'snipers', and then to set fire to the streets and buildings where *franc-tireurs* suspectedly operated. At the end of three days of incendiarism and looting, the library of 230,000 books had been burnt out, 1,100 other buildings destroyed, 209 civilians killed and the population of 42,000 forcibly evacuated.[30] The worldwide condemnation of Germany's war against 'culture' bit deep in the homeland. There academics and intellectuals were in the vanguard of the appeal to patriotism, representing the war as an attack by barbarians, philistines and decadents – Russians, British and French respectively – on high German civilisation. On 11 August, Professor von Harnack, director of the Royal Library in Berlin, had warned that 'Mongolian Muscovite civilisation could not endure the light of the eighteenth century, still less of the nineteenth century, and now in the twentieth century, it breaks loose and threatens us.'[31] 'Light' was a cherished idea to the Germans. The eighteenth-century Enlightenment of Lessing, Kant and Goethe – who had called for 'more light' on his deathbed – had been Germany's passport into Europe's life of the mind. Enlightenment had been the inspiration of Germany's enormous contributions to philosophical, classical and historical scholarship during the nineteenth century. For Germans to be found out as book-burners cut educated Germany to the quick. Even harder to bear were the expressions of disgust from the world's great centres of learning and research; American as well as European universities denounced the atrocity and committees were formed in twenty-five countries to collect money and books for the restoration of the Louvain library.[32] Germany's scholars and writers responded by a 'Call to the World of Culture', signed by such pre-eminent scientists as Max Planck and Wilhelm Röntgen, which 'endorsed the *franc-tireur* hypothesis and the right to reprisal, and claimed that if it had not been for German soldiers, German culture would long have been swept away'.[33]

The call fell on deaf ears. The damage had been done. It had been done, ironically, by latecomers to the invasion, the 17th and 18th Reserve Divisions, which had been retained for three weeks in their home district of Schleswig-Holstein to guard against the supposed danger of amphibious attacks by the British on the North Sea coast.[34] Far from the scene of action, the divisions imbibed to the full the newspaper propaganda about *franc-tireurs*, as well as the objective reports of the Belgian army's wholly unexpected tenacity in defence of the Meuse forts. It is difficult to estimate with hindsight which more enraged the Germans. Perhaps the latter: the myth of *franc-tireurs* in rooftops and hedgerows had the force of alarming rumour; the fact of real Belgian resistance not only exploded the fictive belief in Belgian passivity but threatened the smooth unrolling of the German advance in the west at its most critical point.

Emmich's task force, composed of the 11th, 14th, 24th, 28th, 38th and 43rd Brigades, specially detached from their parent divisions, together with the 2nd, 4th and 9th Cavalry Divisions and five élite Jäger (light infantry) battalions, all drawn from the peacetime army but reinforced for the operation, crossed the Belgian frontier on 4 August. It headed straight for Liège, twenty miles to the west, along the line of what today is the Aachen-Brussels international motorway. With them the units of the task force brought two batteries of 210 mm (8.4 inch) howitzers, the heaviest available until the Austrian and Krupp monsters could be got forward. On the morning of 5 August Captain Brinckman, recently the German military attaché in Brussels, appeared in Liège to demand Leman's surrender.[35] He was sent packing. The German bombardment on the eastern forts opened shortly afterwards. When the infantry and cavalry attempted to advance, however, they found the way barred. Because of blown bridges, the 34th Brigade had to be ferried across the Meuse in pontoons. The garrisons of the forts returned fire steadily, while the 'interval troops' of the 3rd Division, manning the hastily dug entrenchments, fought manfully whenever the German advance guards tried to penetrate the line. Throughout the night of 5/6 August German casualties mounted steadily. They were particularly heavy at Fort Barchon, where the attackers 'came on, line after line, almost shoulder to shoulder, until as we shot them down the fallen were heaped on top of each other in an awful barricade of dead and wounded'.[36] There was, in the confused and bitter fighting of the night, a ghostly foretaste of what would ensue at places not yet touched by the war, at Vimy, Verdun and Thiepval.

Yet there was also opportunity for success through leadership that the barbed wire and continuous trench lines of the Western Front would deny. Early in the morning of 6 August, General Erich Ludendorff, the liaison officer between Second Army and Emmich's command, rode forward into the confusion to find that the commander of the 14th Brigade had been killed. Instantly assuming the vacancy, and ordering up a field howitzer to provide firepower at the point of assault, Ludendorff fought his new command through the straggling village of Queue-de-Bois to a high point from which he could look down, across the Meuse and the two unblown city bridges, into Liège itself. Unknown both to the Belgians and to the German high command, with which Ludendorff had lost touch, a force of 6,000 Germans had penetrated to the interior of Leman's circle of defences. From his vantage point, Ludendorff ordered forward a party under a flag of truce to demand Leman's surrender, which was again refused; a raiding force that followed was shot down at the door of Leman's headquarters.[37] Ludendorff's bold sally nevertheless prompted Leman to leave the city and take refuge in Fort Loncin on the west side of the outer ring. Leman also decided to send the infantry, the 3rd Division and its supporting 15th Brigade, back to join the field army on the River Gette outside Brussels, believing that they would be overwhelmed in a battle with what he calculated were five German corps. There he miscalculated. The German brigades merely represented the five different corps to which they belonged. In the long run, however, his decision was justified, for it spared one-sixth of the Belgian army to fight in the defence of Antwerp, which King Albert had already chosen to make his strongpoint in Belgium's last stand.

A moment of equilibrium ensued. Ludendorff was inside the ring, but without sufficient force to compel a surrender. Most of Emmich's command was outside the ring. Leman was determined to continue resistance as long as the forts remained intact, as all still did. The French government, to which Albert appealed for help, promised only to send Sordet's cavalry corps and then just to reconnoitre. The British, who had been expected to deploy their Expeditionary Force of six divisions into Belgium, now decided to retain two at home. Joffre refused to extend the mass of his army northwards, since to do so would detract from his planned offensive towards the Rhine; he actually wanted Albert to bring the Belgian army down from Brussels, away from Antwerp, to join his left wing. The situation map showed a French army aligned towards Lorraine, a German army whose weight had not yet crossed either the Belgian or French frontier, a British army still mobilising to embark, a Belgian army concentrated in the centre of its homeland and, at Liège, a small German striking force immobilised by a handful of Belgian fortress troops guarding the crossings on the possession of which the future of military events in the west turned.

The equilibrium was upset by Ludendorff. Large in physique and personality, utterly devoid of moral or physical fear, indifferent to the good opinion even of superiors, dislikeable, insensitive – he was to suffer the death of two stepsons during the coming war without faltering in his exercise of high command – Ludendorff resolved on the morning of 7 August to launch the 14th Brigade into the centre of Liège and take the chance that he would be opposed. He was not. Driving up to the gates of the old citadel, he hammered on the door with the pommel of his sword and was admitted.[38] The surrender of the garrison gave him possession of the city. His bold sortie had put the bridges into his hands. He decided to return post-haste to Aachen and urge forward Second Army to complete his success.

While he was away Emmich's task force broke the resistance of Forts Barchon and Evegnée, though more by luck than deliberate reduction. That would wait upon the appearance of the monster howitzers which General von Bülow, at Ludendorff's insistence, despatched on 10 August.[39] The first road-transportable Krupp 420, diverted by demolitions, eventually arrived within range of Fort Pontisse on 12 August. After it was emplaced, the bombardment began. The crew, wearing head-padding, lay prone 300 yards away while the gun was fired electrically. 'Sixty seconds ticked by – the time needed for the shell to traverse its 4,000 metre trajectory – and everyone listened in to the telephone report of our battery commander, who had his observation post 1,500 metres from the bombarded fort, and could watch at close range the column of smoke, earth and fire that climbed to the heavens.'[40] The first of the shells, delay-fused to explode only after penetration of the fort's protective skin, fell short. Six minutes later, the next was fired and then five more, each 'walked up' towards the target as the elevation was corrected. The relentless approaching footfall of the detonations spoke to the paralysed defenders of the devastation to come. The eighth struck home. Then the gun fell silent for the night but next morning, joined by the other which had completed the journey from Essen, the bombardment reopened. The range had been found and soon the 2,000-pound shells were 'stripping away armour plate and blocks of concrete, cracking arches and poisoning the air with heavy brown fumes'.[41] By 12.30 Fort Pontisse was a wreck, its garrison physically incapacitated, and it surrendered. Fire then shifted to Fort Embourg, which surrendered at 17.30; Fort Chaudfontaine had been destroyed by the explosion of its magazine at nine o'clock. On 14 August it was the turn of Fort Liers, 09.40 hours, and Fléron, 09.45 hours. Finally, on 15 August, the howitzers, one of which was by now emplaced in the main square of Liège, reduced Forts Boncelle, 07.30 hours, and

Lautin, 12.30 hours, before turning their fire on to Fort Loncin, to which General Leman had shifted his headquarters nine days earlier. After 140 minutes of bombardment the magazine was penetrated and the fortress destroyed in the resulting explosion.

The German pioneer troops who advanced to take possession found 'a miniature Alpine landscape with débris strewn about like pebbles in a mountain stream ... Heavy artillery and ammunition had been thrown everywhere; a cupola had been blown from its place ... and had fallen on its dome; it now looked like a monstrous tortoise, lying on its shell.' Amid the ruins General Leman was found lying insensible. To Emmich, whom he had met on manoeuvres some years previously, he said from the stretcher on which his captors placed him, 'I ask you to bear witness that you found me unconscious.'[42]

The last two forts, Hollogne and Flémelle, surrendered without further fight on 16 August and the Krupp and Skoda guns were then broken out of their emplacements and diverted towards the forts of Namur, where they would arrive on 21 August and repeat the victory of Liège after three days of bombardment on 24 August. These two 'naval battles on land', in which guns heavier than those mounted by any Dreadnought had cracked armoured targets incapable of manoeuvre, spelt the end of a three-hundred-year-old military trust in the power of fortress to oppose the advance of a hostile army without the active intervention of supporting mobile troops. That trust had never been more than conditional in any case. The Prince de Ligne, one of the leading generals of the eighteenth-century fortress age, had written, 'The more I see and the more I read, the more I am convinced that the best fortress is an army, and the best rampart a rampart of men.'[43] Forts – at Maubeuge, at Przemysl, at Lemberg, at Verdun – would form the focus of intense fighting in 1914, 1915 and 1916 – but only as fixed points of encounter around which decisive battle would be waged by fluid masses and mobile weapons. Ramparts of men, not steel or concrete, would indeed form the fronts of the First World War.

Just such a rampart was in the making far to the south of the Meuse crossings even while Emmich's task force was battering Liège and Namur into fragments. If the Emmich element in the German plan was bold, the French plan for the opening of the war was bolder in a different dimension, nothing less than a headlong offensive across the 1871 frontier into annexed Alsace-Lorraine. 'Whatever the circumstances', Plan XVII stated, 'it is the Commander-in-Chief's intention to advance with all forces united to attack the German armies.'[44] Those the French expected to find, as in 1870, deployed along the common frontier between Luxembourg and Switzerland. Joffre's scheme of operations was to throw forward his five armies in two groups, Fifth and Third on the left, Second and First on the right, with Fourth echeloned slightly in rear to cover the gap between the two masses, into which topography and fortification, the French calculated, would funnel any successful German advance.

Had the Germans not long committed themselves to an entirely different plan that made the French dispositions both irrelevant and dangerous, Plan XVII was not ill-conceived. It was well adapted to the military geography, natural and man-made, of eastern France. Germany's annexations of 1871 had robbed France of long lengths of her 'natural' frontier, including the Rhine between Strasbourg and Mulhouse. They nevertheless left strong positions in French hands, including the high ground of Côtes de Meuse between Verdun and Toul and, further south, the crests of the Vosges mountains above Nancy and Epinal.[45] The unfortified opening between, known as the Trouée de Charmes, was the trap into which the French hoped to tempt the Germans. The buttresses to left and right – Meuse heights, Vosges mountains – provided in any case firm points of departure, well furnished with road and rail heads and strongly fortified, for the two groups of armies to begin their descent into the Moselle and Rhine valleys. The two thrusts, by the Fifth and Third and the Second and First Armies respectively, were the essence of Plan XVII.

Before either could be set in motion, however, Joffre had unleashed a preliminary assault, designed, as was Emmich's into Belgium, to open the way for the larger offensive to follow. On 7 August General Bonneau's VII Corps, based at Besançon, moved forward to seize Mulhouse in Alsace and, it was hoped, raise the countryside against the Germans. Bonneau expressed reluctance and showed it in practice. He took two days to cover the fifteen miles to Mulhouse and allowed himself to be driven out within twenty-four hours when the Germans counter-attacked. Worse, he then beat a retreat to Belfort on the Swiss frontier, the only fortress to have sustained resistance to the Germans throughout the Franco-Prussian war. The humiliation, actual and symbolic, incensed Joffre. He dismissed both Bonneau and Aubier, commander of the accompanying 8th Cavalry Division, on the spot. It was a warning of a greater purge to come. Joffre was a sacker. He had removed two obviously incompetent generals after the 1913

98

manoeuvres and already seven divisional commanders who had shown themselves torpid or unfit in the period of mobilisation and *couverture*.[46] By the end of August he would have dismissed an army commander, three out of twenty-one corps commanders and thirty-one out of 103 divisional commanders. In September he was to dismiss another thirty-eight divisional commanders, in October eleven and in November twelve.[47] Others were to be transferred, from active to territorial divisions, or demoted. In some divisions generals were given only a month to show their paces, sometimes less. The inappropriately named Generals Superbie and Bataille lasted respectively five weeks and ten days at the head of the 41st Division. Bolgert, who succeeded Bataille, lasted nine days before demotion to a reserve division, and must have thought himself lucky not to disappear altogether. The majority did. Only seven of the forty-eight commanders of peacetime infantry divisions were still *en poste* in January 1915. One, Raffenet, of the 3rd Colonial, had been killed, another, Boë of the 20th, had been severely wounded. A few, Deligny, Hache, Humbert, had been advanced to command corps; so, too, had Pétain, who started the war as a mere brigadier. The rest had gone for good. 'My mind was made up on this subject', Joffre would write later. 'I would get rid of incapable generals and replace them with those who were younger and more energetic.' Right was on his side. French generals were too old – in 1903 their average age had been sixty-one against fifty-four in Germany – or, if younger, often unfit.[48] Joffre, admittedly, set no example. Heavily overweight, he was devoted to the table and allowed nothing, even at the height of the crisis in 1914, to interrupt lunch. He was, for all that, shrewd, imperturbable and a keen judge of character, the qualities that would see the French army through the coming campaign as the crisis deepened.

THE BATTLE OF THE FRONTIERS

A curious interval of calm had followed the upheaval of mobilisation and the subsequent mass migration to the areas of concentration. Both French and German divisional histories record an interlude of a week or even ten days between detraining behind the frontier and the onset of action. It was spent in distributing stores, hurried exercises and deployment on foot towards the front. There was, for some very senior officers on both sides and for others who had read their history, a certain familiarity about the preliminary events. They resembled those of the first days of the Franco-Prussian War forty-four years earlier, with the difference that everything was working with greater efficiency. Otherwise, the troop trains looked the same, the long columns of horse, foot and guns looked the same, on the French side the uniform looked the same, on both sides even the weapons looked the same; the revolutionary power of quick-firing artillery and magazine-rifles had yet to reveal itself.

The battlefront chosen by the French high command was, for much of its length, almost exactly the same also. True, in 1870, there had been no operations north of the point where the French met the Luxembourg frontier, while in 1914 the deployment areas of the French Third, Fourth and Fifth Armies reached from there towards Belgium. In Lorraine, however, the soldiers of the First Army found themselves treading the same roads as their grandfathers had done under the command of Napoleon III. The lines of departure were further to the west, transposed thence by the German seizure of territory that had been the price of defeat in 1871, but the avenues of advance were the same and so were the objectives: the line of the River Saar, Saarbrücken and the country beyond on the way to the Rhine. These had been given in Joffre's General Instruction No. 1 of 8 August.[49]

The Lorraine offensive opened on 14 August, when Dubail's First Army, with de Castelnau's Second echeloned to its left, crossed the frontier and advanced towards Sarrebourg. Bonneau's setback at Mulhouse seemed forgotten. The French advanced as liberators and conquerors, bands playing, colours unfurled. The thought that the Germans might have plans of their own for victory in the lost provinces – to them 'Reich territory' – appears to have crossed no mind in the French high command. Its intelligence underestimated the Germans' strength and its judgement was that they would stand on the defensive. In fact the German Sixth and Seventh Armies, commanded by Crown Prince Rupprecht of Bavaria and General Josias von Heeringen, a Prussian ex-War Minister, comprised eight, not six, corps and were preparing to strike the French a weighty counterblow as soon as they overreached themselves.

They were shortly to do so. For four days the Germans fell back, contesting but not firmly opposing the French advance, which in places reached twenty-five miles into Reich territory. A German regimental colour was captured and sent for presentation to Joffre at Vitry-le-François, where he had established General Headquarters

(GQG). Château-Salins was taken, then Dieuze, finally on 18 August, Sarrebourg, all places that had been French since Louis XIV's wars against the Habsburgs in the seventeenth century. Then the front lost its sponginess. The French infantry found German resistance stiffening. The small Army of Alsace, advancing continuously on the First's right, recaptured Mulhouse next day, but its success lent no support, for a wide gap yawned between it and Dubail's positions. It was not the only gap. First Army was not firmly in contact with Second; west of the Saar Valley, Dubail and Castelnau were not in operational touch at all. Dubail was conscious of the weakness and intended on 20 August to mend it by launching an attack that would both restore contact and open a way through for Conneau's Cavalry Corps (2nd, 6th and 10th Divisions) to debouch into the enemy's rear and roll up his flank; but even as he set the attack in motion on the night of 19/20 August, the Germans were preparing to unleash their planned counter-offensive.[50]

Rupprecht's and Heeringen's Armies had been temporarily subordinated to a single staff, headed by General Krafft von Delmensingen. Thus, while the French Second and First Armies co-ordinated their actions only as well as sporadic telephoning could arrange, the German Sixth and Seventh fought as a single entity. Here was the anticipation of a new trend in command, which would bring into being formations as large as existing communication systems could control. On 20 August its worth was swiftly demonstrated. Dubail's night attack was checked as soon as begun. The setback was followed by a simultaneous offensive along the whole line of battle by the eight German corps against the French six. The French VIII Corps, which had reached the Saar at Sarrebourg, was overwhelmed; its artillery was outmetalled by the heavier German guns, under the fire of which the German infantry drove the French from one position after another.

Heavy artillery did even worse damage to Second Army, which was struck by a concentrated bombardment along its whole front as day broke on 20 August. The XV and XVI Corps abandoned their positions under the infantry attacks that followed. Only the XX, on the extreme left, held firm. It was fighting on home ground and was commanded by General Ferdinand Foch, of exceptional talent and determination. While his soldiers clung on, the rest of the Army was ordered by Castelnau to break contact and retreat behind the River Meurthe, the line from which it had begun its advance six days earlier.

It had very nearly been enveloped on both flanks, which would have resulted in irretrievable disaster to the whole French army, and had completely lost touch with the First Army, which Dubail was therefore obliged to disengage from battle also. By 23 August it, too, had returned to the Meurthe and was preparing to defend the river, hinging its defence on strong positions which Foch had established on the high ground of the Grand Couronné de Nancy. There the two armies entrenched to await further German assaults. Schlieffen had warned such assaults must not be attempted if the victory he had rightly anticipated would follow a French offensive in Lorraine. The temptation to exploit the victory proved, however, too strong to resist. Von Moltke yielded to the demands of Rupprecht and Delmensingen and sanctioned their renewal of the offensive which, between 25 August and 7 September, broke on the stout defences the French unexpectedly established along the Meurthe.[51]

The significance of the French recovery on the right of their enormous front would take time to emerge. Elsewhere disaster persisted. Next above the First and Second Armies stood the Third and Fourth, given by Joffre the mission of penetrating the forest zone of the Ardennes and striking towards the towns of Arlon and Neufchâteau in southern Belgium. Their front of attack was twenty-five miles, the depth of forest to be penetrated about eight. Two considerations argued against Joffre's offensive instructions. The first was that the terrain of the Ardennes – tangled woods, steep hillsides, wet valleys – impedes military movements, confining marching troops to the infrequent roads. The second was that the German armies, Fourth, commanded by the Duke of Württemberg, and Fifth, commanded by the German Crown Prince, were deployed to attack to the east on a collision course with the approaching French, and in exactly equal strength, eight corps against eight. Of this equality Joffre's headquarters were quite unaware. The main French reconnaissance force, Sordet's Cavalry Corps, had criss-crossed the Ardennes between 6 and 15 August without detecting the enemy's presence. The troopers had ridden bare their horses' backs – French cavalry had the bad habit of not dismounting on the march – but seen neither hide nor hair of the enemy. As a result, GQG had assured both de Langle, Fourth Army, and Ruffey, Third Army, on 22 August, that 'no serious opposition need be anticipated'.[52] Reports from French aviators had confirmed this wholly false judgement throughout the previous week.[53]

The Germans were better informed than the French. Their aviators had reported significant enemy movements on the front of Fourth Army and, though what had been observed was the northward march of elements of Lanrezac's Fifth Army towards the Meuse, the mistaken interpretation alerted the Germans to Joffre's real intentions.[54] On 20 August the Crown Prince's army had remained in its positions while its heavy artillery had brought the French frontier fortresses of Montmédy and Longwy – both old and ill-defended – under bombardment, but on the morning of 22 August both it and Fourth Army were on the march.[55] Fourth Army was particularly concerned with the danger of being outflanked and its headquarters issued orders for the corps on its left to take particular care to maintain contact with its neighbour.[56]

In fact, it was the French, not the Germans, who risked being unhinged. Their formations were disposed 'en echelon', like a flight of steps descending in a shallow easterly direction from north to south, so that the flank of each corps was exposed on its left. Were the Germans to push hard against the top of the French front, there was a danger that the steps of the French line would separate in sequence, leading to the wholesale collapse of Fourth and Third Armies. That, on 22 August, was exactly what happened. In practice, it was Third Army which collapsed first. Advancing at daybreak, its vanguard ran into unexpected German resistance and, when a sudden bombardment overwhelmed its supporting artillery, the infantry were panicked into flight. The rest of the Army, with a gap yawning in its centre, was stopped in its tracks and had to fight hard to hold its position. Fourth Army, thus unsupported to its south, also failed to advance, except in the centre, a position held by the Colonial Corps. This, the only truly regular element of the French army, was composed of white regiments which in peacetime garrisoned the empire in North and West Africa and Indo-China. Its soldiers were hardened and experienced veterans. That was to be their undoing. Pressing forward with a determination the unblooded conscripts of the metropolitan army could not match, it rapidly became embedded in a far larger mass of Germans. Five of its battalions, advancing one behind the other on a front only 600 yards wide, launched repeated bayonet attacks through dense woodland, only to be thrown back by concentrated rifle and machine-gun fire. The harder the Colonials pressed, the higher their casualties mounted. By the evening of 22 August, the 3rd Colonial Division had lost 11,000 men killed or wounded, out of a strength of 15,000, the worst casualties to be suffered by any French formation in the Battle of the Frontiers.[57] Its effective destruction spelt an end to Fourth Army's efforts to take ground forward, just as V Corps' collapse had halted Third Army's offensive further to the south.

Plan XVII had thus been brought to a standstill along a crucial section of front, seventy-five miles wide, between Givet and Verdun. Joffre at first refused to credit the outcome. On the morning of 23 August he signalled de Langle de Cary to say that there were 'only . . . three [enemy] corps before [you]. Consequently you must resume your offensive as soon as possible'.[58] De Langle de Cary obediently attempted to do as ordered, but his army was only driven further back that day. Unsuccessful, too, were the Third and the recently assembled Army of Lorraine. On 24 August, the Fourth Army retired behind the protection of the River Meuse and Third Army shortly followed. Much of Maunoury's Army of Lorraine was meanwhile withdrawn to Amiens, where a new Army, the Sixth, was to be created around its complement of reserve divisions.

The Battle of the Sambre

On two sectors of the French frontier, Alsace-Lorraine and the Ardennes, the Germans had, by the end of the war's third week, achieved significant victories. The scene of action was now to shift to the only sector as yet untouched by major operations, the frontier with Belgium. It was there that Germany's offensive plan must succeed if Schlieffen's dream of a six-week war were to be realised. The seizure of Liège had laid the ground. The consequent retreat of the Belgian field army to the entrenched camp at Antwerp had opened the way. The fall of Namur, clearly imminent by 24 August, would complete the clearing of the theatre of major obstacles. Most important of all, the French high command, despite the weight of warning given by the German invasion of eastern Belgium, remained apparently and obstinately blind to the danger that threatened. Lanrezac, commander of Fifth Army deployed at the northern end of the line, had begun to warn GQG, even before war was declared, that he feared an envelopment of his left – northern – flank by a German march into Belgium. Joffre, whose thoughts were fixed on his own offensive into Germany, dismissed these anxieties. As late as 14 August, when Lanrezac brought his concerns to GQG at Vitry-le-François on the Marne, east of Paris, and soon to lie within earshot of the guns, the Commander-in-Chief continued to insist that the Germans would not deploy any major force inside Belgium north of the Meuse.

Over the next six days, Joffre began to reconsider, issuing orders that first directed Lanrezac's Fifth Army into the angle between the Meuse and the Sambre, as a precautionary measure, then that instructed Lanrezac to join with the British Expeditionary Force in operations against the left wing of the German battle line, whose appearance in great strength in Belgium could no longer be denied.[59] By that date the battle with von Kluck's, von Bülow's and von Hausen's Armies – the battle of the Sambre to the French, Mons to the British – was already about to begin. It was in its opening stages what military theorists call a 'battle of encounter', the nature of which is decided by the actions of the troops engaged rather than by orders received from the top. Orders, indeed, discouraged engagement. Lanrezac, in a conference held at Chimay on the afternoon of 21 August, told the Chiefs of Staff of his subordinate corps that the plan was for Fifth Army to hold the high ground on the south bank of the Sambre.[60] He feared that if he committed his soldiers to hold the dense belt of little industrial buildings and cottages – le Borinage – that line the bank between Charleroi and Namur, they would become involved in small-scale street fighting and be lost to his control. The Germans received similar orders from von Bülow, who was co-ordinating the movements of First and Third Armies as well as of his own Second, though given for different reasons. On 20 August Moltke had warned Bülow that the French were present in strength in front of him and the British were to his right, but in unlocated positions, and that he should in consequence attack across the Sambre only when Second and Third Armies could co-ordinate a pincer movement. On the morning of 21 August, Bülow accordingly wirelessed von Hausen that he was postponing Second Army's advance, which meant that Third was to pause also.

Events at a lower level then took charge. Rivers, unless wide, are always difficult to defend. Meanders create pockets that soak up troops and cause misunderstandings between neighbouring units as to where responsibilities start and end. Bridges are a particular problem: does a bridge which marks a boundary between units lie in one sector or another? Buildings and vegetation compound the problems, breaking lines of sight and impeding easy lateral movement along the river when local crises, requiring rapid reinforcement, arise. Long experience has taught soldiers that it is easier to defend a river on the far, rather than the near, bank but, if the near bank is to be defended, then it is better done behind it than at the water's edge.[61] All these truths were to be proved again in the battle that developed on the Sambre during 21 August.

Lanrezac, with perfect orthodoxy, had ordered the bridges to be held only by outposts, while the bulk of the Fifth Army waited on higher ground, whence it could advance to repel a German crossing or mount its own offensive across the bridges into Belgium. The outposts at the bridges, however, found themselves in a dilemma. At Auvelais, halfway between Namur and Charleroi, for example, they were overlooked from the far bank, and requested permission either to cross or to fall back. Their regimental commander, bound by Lanrezac's instructions, refused but sent more troops to support them. The reinforcements discovered more bridges than their orders indicated had to be defended. While they were making their dispositions, German patrols of Second Army appeared opposite, sensed an opportunity and requested permission to chance a crossing from corps headquarters. It was that of the Imperial Guard, which, fortuitously, Ludendorff happened to be visiting when the message arrived. Showing the same initiative as he had done fifteen days earlier at Liège, he took personal responsibility for approving the venture. The 2nd Guard Division attacked, found an undefended bridge – there were eight in a sector where the French troops had thought there was but one – and established a foothold. To the west of Auvelais, at Tergné, a patrol of the German 19th Division found another unguarded bridge and crossed without asking for orders. Responding to opportunity, the divisional commander sent a whole regiment to follow and drove the French defenders away. By the afternoon of 21 August, therefore, two large meanders of the Sambre were in German hands and a gap four miles wide had been opened across the river front.

The results were characteristic of an encounter battle and greatly to the credit of the German front-line troops and their local commanders. Yet Lanrezac might still have retrieved the situation had he stuck to his original plan of holding the high ground south of the Sambre as his main position. Inexplicably, however, he now acquiesced in the decision of his two subordinates commanding III and X Corps to counter-attack, in an attempt to retake the meanders of the Sambre already lost. They tried and on the morning of 22 August their troops were repelled with heavy loss.

The French infantry made a gallant show, advancing across the Belgian beet fields with colours unfurled and bugles sounding the shrill notes of the 'charge'. As the ranks drew near to the German lines ... rifles and machine guns pounded forth a rapid-fire of death from behind walls and hummocks and the windows of houses. Before it the attack wilted. Running, stumbling, crawling, the French sought cover as best they could, and the attack ended leaving the German Guard undisputed masters of the field.[62]

That night both corps had taken positions on Lanrezac's original and preferred line on the high ground with nothing to show for the day's brave effort but yet more casualties. They were very heavy. Of the regiments engaged, each beginning with a strength of some 2,500 men, the 24th had lost 800, the 25th, a Cherbourg regiment, 1,200, the 25th (Caen) 1,000, the 49th (Bordeaux) 700, the 74th (Rouen) 800, the 129th (le Havre) 650.[63] Strategically the result was even worse. Nine French divisions had been defeated by three German, and forced to retreat seven miles, contact with the Fourth Army, on the Meuse, had been broken, contact with the British Expeditionary Force at Mons had not been established and Sordet's Cavalry Corps, which had wholly failed in its mission of finding the Germans before they fell on the French along the Sambre, was drawing back through Fifth Army's positions, its men exhausted and its horses worn out. The situation did not improve during 23 August. Though parts of the Fifth Army tried to resume the offensive, it was the Germans who made ground, particularly on the right, where they got across the water obstacle of the Sambre-Meuse confluence in strength; that despite a counter-attack organised by General Mangin, thenceforth to be recognised as one of the French army's most ferocious warriors. An hour before midnight Lanrezac concluded he was beaten and telegraphed Joffre that as the 'enemy is threatening my right on the Meuse ... Givet is threatened, Namur taken ... I have decided to withdraw the Army tomorrow'.[64]

The Battle of Mons

Lanrezac made no mention of the situation on his left, though there his British allies had also been locked in combat with the Germans throughout 23 August, showing considerably more effectiveness in defence of a water obstacle – the Mons-Condé Canal – than his own troops had done on the Sambre. The British Expeditionary Force, of one cavalry and four infantry divisions, had begun landing at Le Havre, Boulogne and Rouen eleven days before and had arrived on the canal on 22 August. By the morning of 23 August they were deployed on a front of twenty miles, II Corps to the west, I Corps, commanded by General Douglas Haig, to the east, with the whole of von Kluck's First Army, fourteen divisions strong, bearing down on them from the north. General Sir John French, the BEF Commander, had expected to march level with Lanrezac in an advance into Belgium. News of Lanrezac's defeat on the Sambre ruled that out but, when a message arrived from French Fifth Army headquarters just before midnight on 22 August, asking for assistance, he agreed to defend the canal for twenty-four hours. It was evidence of how poorly the French grasped the nature of the German onset that the request was actually for an attack into von Kluck's flank; von Kluck's flank already extended beyond both Fifth Army's and the BEF's positions. The British, if only for a moment, were to be cast into the role of opposing both the concept and the substance of the Schlieffen Plan – 'Keep the right wing strong' were allegedly Schlieffen's dying words – at the crucial point.

The BEF was equal to the task. Alone among those of Europe, the British army was an all-regular force, composed of professional soldiers whom the small wars of empire had hardened to the realities of combat. Many of them had fought in the Boer War fifteen years earlier, against skilled marksmen who entrenched to defend their positions, and they had learnt from them the power of the magazine-rifle and the necessity of digging deep to escape its effects. Russian veterans of the war against Japan remembered those lessons. The British were the only soldiers in Western Europe who knew them by heart. Ordered to hold the Mons-Condé Canal, they began to dig at once and by the morning of 23 August were firmly entrenched along its length. At the heart of a mining area, the canal offered excellent defensive positions, mine buildings and cottages providing strong-points and the spoil heaps observation posts from which the supporting artillery could be directed onto the advancing enemy masses.[65]

The Germans, who outnumbered them by six divisions to four, were unprepared for the storm of fire that would sweep their ranks. 'The dominating German impression was of facing an invisible enemy', hidden behind freshly turned earth in trenches much deeper than the

108

inexperienced French or amateur Belgians thought to dig.[66] On the Tugela and the Modder rivers, at Spion Kop, the Boers had taught British infantry the cost of assaulting skilled riflemen in deep earthworks and on 23 August the British found the opportunity to teach the lesson themselves. The British Lee-Enfield rifle, with its ten-round magazine, was a superior weapon to the German Mauser, and the British soldier a superior shot. 'Fifteen rounds a minute' has become a catchphrase, but it was the standard most British infantry-men met, encouraged by extra pay for marksmanship and an issue of free ammunition to win the badge in their spare time.[67] A German officer of the 12th Brandenburg Grenadiers was among the first to experience the effect of long-range, well-aimed rifle fire. 'In front [of my company position] lay an extremely long, flat marshy-looking meadow. Its left side was broken into by scattered buildings and sheds, and on the right a narrow strip of wood jutted into it. At the far end, about 1,500 yards straight ahead, were more scattered groups of buildings. Between the near and far buildings a number of cows were peacefully grazing.'[68] The peace of the bucolic scene was illusory. On the day following, Captain Bloem would discover how the British 'had converted every house, every wall into a little fortress; the experience, no doubt, of old soldiers gained in a dozen colonial wars'.[69] On the morning of Mons, as his company stepped out into the void, the danger the empty vista held suddenly became reality. 'No sooner had we left the edge of the wood than a volley of bullets whistled past our noses and cracked into the trees behind. Five or six cries near me, five or six of my grey lads collapsed in the grass ... The firing seemed at long range and half-left ... Here we were as if advancing on a parade ground ... away in front a sharp, hammering sound, then a pause, then a more rapid hammering – machine guns!'[70]

The soldiers opposite the Brandenburg Grenadiers belonged to the 1st Battalion Queen's Own Royal West Kent Regiment and it was their rifles, rather than the battalion's two machine guns, that were causing the casualties. By the end of the day, Bloem's regiment was 'all to pieces'. Many of the men had lost contact with their officers during the fighting and, shamefaced and full of explanations, rejoined only in the evening; 500 had been killed or wounded, including three out of four of his battalion's company commanders. Bloem was lucky to be untouched. The results were the same in many other units, for every British battalion held its ground and the supporting artillery, including the 60-pounders of 48th and 108th Heavy Batteries, had

109

kept up a steady supporting fire throughout the action. Total British casualties were 1,600 killed, wounded and missing. German casualties, never fully disclosed, must have reached nearly 5,000; the 75th Regiment, of infantry from Bremen, lost 381 men attacking the Royal Scots and King's Royal Rifle Corps, without making any dent in their line.

That evening the Germans of von Kluck's army slept where they tumbled down, exhausted, on the north bank of the canal, with the day's work of carrying crossings over it to do all over again on the morrow; only one foothold had been gained. The British, exhausted too, prepared to fall back on positions a little to the canal's south. They were flushed with the emotion of a fight well fought; the German official historian's judgement that 'the Battle of Mons had ended in failure for the British' would not have rung true with them.[71] They expected to sustain their defence of the Allies' left flank the following day. Even as they began to retire to their night positions, however, new orders came in. They were for retreat.

Late on the evening of 23 August, the British liaison officer with the French Fifth Army, Lieutenant Edward Spears, arrived at General Sir John French's headquarters with alarming news. General Lanrezac had warned Joffre that, as a result of the German success on the Sambre, he was giving orders for Fifth Army to retreat southwards the following day. French, who had announced only a few hours before, that 'I will stand . . . on the ground now occupied' and that positions were to be strengthened 'by every possible means during the night' was forced to recognise that, as his allies intended to fall back, he must do likewise.[72] On the morning of 24 August, the BEF began a general retirement. At 9.35 Joffre explained in a message to the Minister of War why the whole front must be withdrawn.

In the north, our Army operating between the Sambre, the Meuse and the British Army, appears to have suffered checks of which I still do not know the full extent, but which have forced it to retire . . . One must face facts . . . Our army corps . . . have not shown on the battlefield those offensive qualities for which we had hoped . . . We are therefore compelled to resort to the defensive, using our fortresses and great topographical obstacles to enable us to yield as little ground as possible. Our object must be to last out, trying to wear the enemy down, and to resume the offensive when the time comes.[73]

THE GREAT RETREAT

The great retreat had begun, a retreat which would carry the French armies, and the BEF on their left, back to the outskirts of Paris during the next fourteen days. GQG, Joffre's headquarters at Vitry-le-François, would be abandoned on 21 August, first to roost at Bar-sur-Aube, then to establish itself on 5 September at Châtillon-sur-Seine, the river on which Paris itself stands. Yet Joffre's despatch, doleful as it must have read to Messimy, Minister of War, remains one of the great documents of the war. In its few sentences it sketched out a plan of recovery, even of eventual victory. The great fortresses, Verdun foremost, were indeed still in French hands. The topography which defends France against Germany from the east, the mountains of the Vosges, the waterways of the Seine river system, were unviolated. The spirit of the French army, unwisely committed in peace to a maniac offensive, survived unbroken by war. Could the army but retain its cohesion as it fell back on the capital, the opportunity for a counterstroke remained. With every mile marched, the German army's links with its base of support on and beyond the Rhine attenuated, while the French army's were shortened and strengthened. 'Future operations', Joffre wrote in his General Instruction No. 2 of 25 August, 'will have as their object to reform on our left a mass capable of resuming the offensive. This will consist of the Fourth, Fifth and British Armies, together with new forces drawn from the eastern front, while the other armies contain the enemy for as long as possible.'[74]

The location indicated by Joffre for the positioning of the 'new offensive mass' (comprising the Sixth Army, under General Maunoury, and Ninth, under General Foch) was the line of the River Somme near Amiens, seventy-five miles south-west of Mons. Thus Joffre already envisaged a long retreat before his redeployment of forces could permit a resumption of the attack. There was a grim realism to his appreciation of the French army's situation. Even in Lorraine, where it had suffered the worst of its setbacks, thirty miles was the longest retreat it had yet made. The reality of the coming retreat was to be grimmer by far than anything Joffre anticipated. The German infantry of the right wing, despite twelve days of fighting and marching through Belgium, remained fresh. Buoyed up by victories already gained, hardened by days on the road, hearts high with the expectation of final victory soon to come, they were ready to forget sore feet, lean on their chinstraps and step out with a will if the demands of distance would defeat the French army. 'This frantic, everlasting rush', Bloem's battalion commander told him on the seventh day after Mons, 'is absolutely essential . . . use all your powers to keep up spirits at any price. Make it clear that we must allow the enemy no rest until we have utterly defeated him on the whole front. Tell them that sweat is saving blood.' Bloem's Brandenburgers needed little encouragement. Despite 'inflamed heels, soles and toes . . . whole patches of skin rubbed off to the raw flesh', they kept up the pace under the grilling sun of one of the century's most brilliant summers for day after day.[75] Falling back before them, the 1st Battalion the Gloucestershire Regiment, for example, recorded a distance covered of 244 miles in thirteen days, with only one of rest (29 August) and two successive marches of over twenty miles on 27 and 28 August.[76] What the British and French endured, the Germans did likewise.

Both sides fought as well as marched, the French and British to delay the German advance or to escape from danger, the Germans to force a way through any resistance they met. The British I Corps had to fight at Landrecies and Maroilles on 26 August but, since it had suffered very little at Mons, disengaged easily and resumed its retreat; II Corps, battered by Mons, was forced to fight at Le Câteau on the same day an even bigger battle in order to get away. General Smith-Dorrien, commanding II Corps, had three infantry divisions under command, supported by the Cavalry Division. His tired men were assaulted on the morning of 26 August by three German infantry and three cavalry divisions, reinforced during the day by two more infantry divisions, a total of eight against four. Such an inequality of force offered the Germans the opportunity to overlap the ends of the British line and that, as the day developed, was what they achieved. The front ran along the ancient Roman road between Le Câteau and Cambrai where, three years and three months later, the British would launch the first massed attack with tanks, a weapon of war not then invented or even envisaged. At first the British infantry held the line by their usual outpouring of aimed and rapid rifle fire, supported by salvoes from the field artillery. Then, as enemy numbers mounted during the afternoon, the flanks began to crumble, units to break up and batteries to lose their gun crews under the weight of opposing bombardments. As evening approached, II Corps stared dismemberment in the face. It was saved partly by German mistakes but, as much as anything, by the intervention of Sordet's Cavalry Corps, which at Le Câteau retrieved much of the reputation it had lost by its failure to find the Germans in their advance through Belgium, and by one of the despised French Territorial divisions, whose over-age reservists fought valiantly outside Cambrai to delay the arrival of the German II Corps. As dusk fell, II Corps, which had lost 8,000 killed, wounded and missing during the battle – more than Wellington's army at Waterloo – summoned its reserves of strength to slip away and resume the retreat.[77] Thirty-eight guns, half a divisional artillery, were lost nonetheless, despite desperate attempts to save them. At the position of 122nd Battery, Royal Artillery, efforts at rescue by a gallant officer and his team to extricate their equipment left 'an extraordinary sight: a short wild scene of galloping and falling horses, and then four guns standing derelict, a few limbers lying about, one on the skyline with its pole vertical, and dead men and dead horses everywhere'.[78]

On the day of Le Câteau, Joffre met Sir John French, the BEF's commander, at St Quentin, together with Lanrezac and General d'Amade, Commander of the Territorial Group which had fought so unexpectedly well on the BEF's left. It was not a happy meeting. Lanrezac and French had got on badly since their first encounter ten days earlier, while Joffre was already beginning to doubt the capacities of the Fifth Army commander, who had long been his protégé. The atmosphere of the conference, held in a darkened room in a private house, was uneasy. French denied having received Joffre's General Instruction No. 2, for a future counter-offensive. All he could talk of were his own difficulties and, by implication, of Lanrezac's failure to support him. Lanrezac's manner implied that the BEF was an embarrassment rather than a support. There was a language difficulty. The French did not speak English, French scarcely any French; General Henry Wilson, Deputy Chief of Staff, translated. There were also personal differences. Joffre and Lanrezac, big, heavy men in dark blue, gold-buttoned uniforms, looked like station masters, the vulpine Wilson and the peppery French, in their whipcord breeches and glittering riding boots, like masters of foxhounds. It was also confusing to the French that the commander of the BEF was a field marshal. '*Marechale*' was, in the French army, not a rank but a 'dignity of state', conferred on victors. The republican soldiers, none of higher rank than general, looked askance at a titular superior whose successes had been won against South African farmers.

The conference came to no clear decision and, when it ended,

Lanrezac declined to lunch with French.[79] Joffre, however, accepted and, when he left, returned to GQG with the intention of stiffening Lanrezac's backbone. He perceived that the British needed a breathing space, for he was aware of the risk that a beaten BEF might disengage and head for safety in the Channel ports, and so sent orders to Lanrezac to check his retreat next day, 27 August, and counter-attack the German Second Army, treading close on his heels in its path towards Paris. Lanrezac complained but obeyed. His instructions were to align Fifth Army along the upper course of the River Oise, which Bülow's divisions would have to cross to reach their objectives, with two corps, X and III, facing north in defence and another, XVIII, to attack to the west where the river turned south to join the Seine at Pontoise above Paris. A fourth Corps, the I, commanded by the very determined Franchet d'Esperey, was to stand in reserve behind the right angle formed by Fifth Army's two wings. The battle – known to the French as Guise, to the Germans as St Quentin – opened on the morning of 29 August in thick mist. The Imperial Guard Corps and Plattenburg's X Corps stepped out with a will, their commanders believing that no serious French resistance was to be met before the River Aisne, thirty-five miles distant. They were surprised by the strength of X and III Corps' opposition, against which they began to suffer heavy casualties. Plattenburg, the Guard Corps commander, lost a son killed in the fighting and at one stage Prince Eitel Friedrich, the Kaiser's second son, had to put himself at the head of the 1st Foot Guards, Germany's premier regiment, and lead it forward beating on a drum.[80]

During the course of the day, however, the Guard and the Hanoverians of X Corps advanced some three miles and, as evening approached, were preparing to consolidate the ground won. At that moment the character of the battle was transformed. Franchet d'Esperey had been ordered shortly after noon to engage in support and at six o'clock, having spent the intervening hours positioning his artillery to achieve maximum firepower effect, he did so in person. Riding a chestnut charger at the head of regiments advancing behind their unfurled colours and the braying brass of their bands, with the corps artillery thundering overhead, he led his soldiers forward in counter-attack. The effect galvanised III and X Corps to join in and, as darkness fell, villages lost in the morning were retaken and the victorious French took up positions from which they intended to resume the counter-attack next day. Their success was all the more surprising since their orders had been merely to hold ground, while de Mas Latrie's XVIII Corps relieved pressure on the British by attacking towards St Quentin. The result of 29 August on his front was disappointing and he would shortly be relieved of command. Franchet d'Esperey, by contrast, made his reputation at Guise. 'Desperate Frankie', as his British admirers christened the fire-eater, would soon succeed Lanrezac at the head of the Fifth Army. It would be a just reward, for his spectacular intervention had halted the Germans in their tracks and won an extra day and a half for the army to reposition itself for the counterstroke which Joffre remained determined to deliver.

Whether he could or not now depended more on the movements of the German armies than his own. Were they to persist in their march south-westward, aiming to pass Paris to the right, Joffre's scheme of forming an offensive mass to drive into their flank might be defeated by distance and logistic difficulty. Were they, on the other hand, to press to the south-east, leaving Paris on the left, they would be doing the French what Schlieffen, in another context, had called a 'willing favour'. Schlieffen had, as his Great Memorandum reveals, come to fear that whichever decision was taken, it would favour the French. To aim to pass Paris to the right would expose the German outer wing to a thrust launched from the Paris fortified zone by its strong garrison; to pass Paris to the left would open a gap between the outer German force and those with which they should keep station, for Paris, like a breakwater, would then divide the tide of the German onset, open a gap in the line and expose the force the wrong side of it to an alternative thrust from Paris in the opposite direction. This 'problem of Paris' had driven Schlieffen to 'the conclusion that we are too weak to continue operations in this direction'.[81] The fault of conception Schlieffen had recognised in his study the German General Staff was now discovering in the field, as its troops marched southward, while their chiefs dithered about their eventual destination.

The difficulty of choice had revealed itself soon after the Kaiser and the Great General Staff – the Supreme Army Command, *Oberste Heersleitung* or OHL, as it became in war – had displaced from Berlin to Coblenz, on the Rhine, on 17 August (its next location would be in Luxembourg and its final station the little resort town of Spa, in Belgium). Moltke's decision to allow von Bülow, of Second Army, to oversee the operations of First and Third, understandable in the early stages of the campaign while the need to overwhelm Belgium was paramount, began to have unfortunate consequences soon after the move to Coblenz had been completed. Bülow's anxiety to assure mutual support between the armies of the right wing deprived Hausen, Third Army, of the chance to strike into Lanrezac's rear as he disengaged from the Sambre on 24 August. Then, as the line of battle descended to the River Somme, Moltke allowed anxieties of his own about the predicament of the Eighth Army, defending East Prussia against the Russians, to distort his control of the larger and more critical operations in the west. Seeing in the fall of Namur a chance to economise force, he decided to redirect the troops thus released not to their parent formations but across Germany to the eastern frontier.[82]

Eighth Army did not want the reinforcement of the Guard Reserve and XI Corps, as Ludendorff, newly appointed its Chief of Staff, told OHL on 28 August. They were sent all the same. Meanwhile the marching armies had been further weakened by the detachment of III Reserve Corps to contain the Belgian army in the Antwerp entrenched camp, of IV Reserve Corps to garrison Brussels and of VII Reserve Corps to besiege Maubeuge on the Sambre, where a large French garrison bravely held out behind enemy lines. The loss of five corps from the fighting line – one-seventh of the western army – actually eased Moltke's logistical difficulties, which grew as the armies drew further away from Germany but closer together as they approached Paris on the overcrowded road network. Nevertheless, preponderance of force at the decisive point is a key to victory and Moltke's dispersions made preponderance less rather than more likely of achievement. On 27 August, moreover, he further diminished his chance to secure a concentration of superior force by ordering the outer armies, von Kluck's First, von Bülow's Second, to fan out. First Army was to pass west of Paris, Second to aim directly for the fortified city, while Third was to pass to the east and Fourth and Fifth, still battling with the French armies defending the lower Meuse, to press westward to join them. Sixth and Seventh, operating on the front where the French had launched their opening offensive of the war, were to attempt to reach and cross the River Moselle.

The march west of Paris was the manoeuvre which Schlieffen had deemed the German army 'too weak' to realise. If attempted, it might have proved so but the practicability of Moltke's directive was not put to the test. The day after its issue, 28 August, von Kluck independently decided to change his line of march and move south-eastward, inside Paris, giving as his reasons the disappearance of any threat from the

Leaders

Right: Hindenburg, in Austrian uniform.

Below: Schlieffen.

Below right: Ludendorff, wearing the Grand Cross of the Iron Cross.

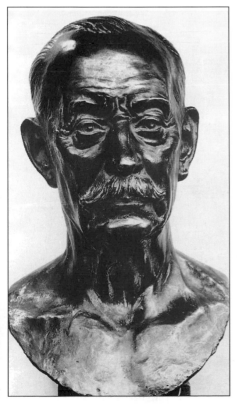

Top: The Kaiser distributing Iron Crosses, Warsaw, September 1915.

Above: Conrad von Hötzendorf.

Right: Joffre and Haig at GQG, Chantilly, 23 December 1915.

Top: Pétain; behind him Joffre, Foch, Haig and Pershing.

Above: Brusilov.

Left: Kemal Ataturk (encircled) at Gallipoli.

Mobilisation

Top: The Guard Pioneer Battalion leaves Berlin, August 1914.

Above: A Russian reservist bids farewell.

Right: French infantrymen off to the front.

The Campaign in the West, 1914

Above: Belgian infantry await the invader, Louvain, 20 August 1914.

Right: Machine-gun section of a French infantry regiment.

Left: French 75mm battery in action, Varreddes, 13 September 1914.

Top: German infantrymen of the 147th Regiment advancing in open order before Tannenberg. The regiment, later 'von Hindenburg's', was local.

Above: Russian transport on the road to Przemsyl, September 1914.

Trench Warfare

Right: Soldiers of the French 87th Regiment, 6th Division, at Côte 304, Verdun, 1916.

Below: The 1st Lancashire Fusiliers in a communication trench at Beaumont Hamel, Somme, late June 1916.

Top: A Grenadier Guards trench sentry, Somme, 1916.

Above: A working party of the Manchester Regiment going up the line, Serre, March 1917, before the battle of Arras.

BEF, seemingly incapacitated by Le Câteau, and the desirability of finally disabling Fifth Army by a drive into its flank. Moltke, despite his quite precise order of 27 August that Kluck should go west of Paris, acquiesced and on 2 September went further. In a message to First and Second Armies, wirelessed from OHL's temporary headquarters in Luxembourg, he announced that it was 'the intention of the High Command to drive the French back in a south-easterly direction, *cutting them off from Paris* [italics supplied]. The First Army will follow the Second in echelon and will also cover the right flank of the armies.' This was an acceptance of events rather than an effort to determine them. Second Army had halted to recuperate from the effects of fighting and the long march, so that for First to echelon itself with it would entail a pause also. The French Fifth Army meanwhile was slipping away to the east, thus eroding the danger of an attack into its flank and distancing itself from Paris in so doing. The BEF was not disabled but had merely disappeared into the countryside, unhampered by the German cavalry as the advancing Germans had been by the French in Belgium in the opening weeks of the campaign, while the growing assemblage of Joffre's new striking force in and around Paris remained undiscovered by the enemy altogether.[83]

Meanwhile the marching armies tramped on, fifteen and twenty miles a day in the heat of a brilliant late summer. 'Soon we were crossing the last ridge that separated us from the Marne valley', recorded Bloem. 'It was another grilling, exhausting day. Twenty-five miles up hill and down dale under a blazing sun. To our left we could hear the guns of Bülow's army with which we seemed nearly in touch again.' There were flashes of action, engagements between advance and rear guards, short, bitter little battles, such as that at Néry on 1 September, where the British 1st Cavalry Brigade and L Battery, Royal Horse Artillery, held up the progress of the German 4th Cavalry Division for a morning. L Battery's gunners won three Victoria Crosses in their unequal contest with the enemy, which ended, a German historian recorded, 'decidedly to the disadvantages of the German cavalry'.[84] There was a great deal of bridge-blowing and re-bridging, as the armies negotiated the many-branched river system of the Paris basin, of contested delays at obstacles, of artillery exchanges, of brief outbursts of rifle fire, as scouts ran into outposts or the tail of a retreating column was overtaken by pursuers. For the vast majority on both sides, however, the last week of August and the first of September was an ordeal of day-long marches, begun before the sun rose, ended in the twilight. A trooper of the 4th Dragoon Guards, Ben Clouting, recorded that his regiment was roused at 4.30 on the morning of 1 September, 2 on the morning of the 2nd, 4.20 a.m. on the 3rd and 5th and 5 a.m. on the 6th. He remembered that the horses, beside which they often walked to spare their backs, 'soon began to drop their heads and wouldn't shake themselves like they normally did . . . they fell asleep standing up, their legs buckling. As they stumbled forward . . . they lost their balance completely, falling forward and taking the skin off their knees.' For the men, 'the greatest strain . . . worse than any physical discomfort or even hunger was . . . fatigue. Pain could be endured, food scrounged, but the desire for rest was never-ending . . . I fell off my horse more than once, and watched others do the same, slowly slumping forward, grabbing for their horse's neck, in a dazed, barely conscious way. At any halt men fell asleep instantaneously.'[85]

The infantry, who got no chance to ride, dropped behind the column of route in scores and these stragglers, 'in grim determination . . . hobbled along in ones or twos . . . as [they] sought desperately to stay in touch with their regiments . . . Food came up from Army Service Corps ration dumps, which were just boxes of biscuits [and] tins of bully beef . . . Very occasionally, a chalk notice marked the food up for a particular regiment, but more often than not we just helped ourselves, stuffing what we could into every pocket.'[86] Joffre, out on inspection of the French armies on 30 August, passed 'retreating columns . . . Red trousers had faded to the colour of pale brick, coats were ragged and torn, shoes caked with mud, eyes cavernous in faces dulled by exhaustion and dark with many days' growth of beard. Twenty days of campaigning seemed to have aged the soldiers as many years.' The French and British, long though their daily marches, were at least falling back on their lines of supply. The Germans marched ahead of theirs and often went without food, though, like the British, their need was for rest rather than rations. A French witness noticed on 3 September, when a unit of the invaders reached their billets for the night, 'they fell down exhausted, muttering in a dazed way, "forty kilometres! forty kilometres!" That was all they could say.'[87]

On 3 September von Kluck's headquarters were installed in Louis XV's chateau at Compiègne. It was there that he received Moltke's wireless message of 2 September directing his First Army to follow Bülow's Second 'in echelon' to the south-east, in order to cut the

French off from Paris.[88] Kluck decided to interpret the order literally, as giving him freedom to veer further eastward still in pursuit of Lanrezac's Fifth Army, to cross the River Marne and to initiate the decisive battle that Moltke actually intended to be delivered by the armies of the centre, coming west from the Meuse. The German strategic effort, though neither Moltke nor Kluck perceived it, was beginning to fall apart. 'Moltke', a French historian comments, 'had never much believed in the possibility of manoeuvring masses . . . like his uncle [the elder Moltke], he thought it necessary to leave each army commander a wide freedom of movement.'[89] Laxity of control had not mattered in 1870, when the front of battle was narrow and the opportunity for armies to diverge from the critical axis of advance correspondingly slight. Moltke the Younger's easy reign over the far wider battlefront of 1914 had resulted in his right-hand army, the army on which all depended, first slipping to the south when it should have been marching south-westward, then turning south-eastward, at right angles to the direction which the plan of campaign laid down it must maintain for victory to be achieved.

Critics would later point out Schlieffen's own inability to decide what track the right wing should take, apologists argue that Kluck was doing the right thing by keeping on Lanrezac's heels. The truth is that he was being led by the nose. Every mile he marched in pursuit of the Fifth Army, once he had crossed the Oise and headed towards the Marne, served Joffre's purpose. The line on which Joffre wished to fight may have receded southward from the Somme to the Oise to the Marne as the situation map shifted and August drew into September, the opportunity to deliver the disabling blow improved proportionately. For the further Kluck widened the gap between army and Paris to his right, without achieving the crucial overlap which would allow him to begin an encirclement of Lanrezac from the west, the more space he created for Joffre to position the 'mass of manoeuvre' against the German flank. That mass, with the existing garrison of Paris, menaced a fiercer strike against Kluck than he could now hope to deliver at the enemy.

The creation of this 'mass of manoeuvre' had been foreshadowed in Joffre's General Instruction No. 2 of 25 August. Then he had said that it was to consist of VII Corps, of four Reserve divisions and perhaps another Active corps, which were to be transported to the west by rail. By 1 September it consisted of VII and IV Corps, taken from First and Third Armies, and the 55th, 56th, 61st and 62nd Reserve Divisions, the whole forming Sixth Army under General Maunoury; with it was associated the garrison of Paris, including the 45th Division, from Algeria, five Territorial Divisions, 83rd, 85th, 86th, 89th and 92nd, a brigade of Spahis and a brigade of *fusiliers-marins*.[90] Together they constituted the Armies of Paris, under the overall command of General Gallieni. Gallieni, a veteran of the French wars of empire, was sixty-five in 1914, Maunoury sixty-seven; even in a war of old generals – Moltke was sixty-six, Joffre sixty-two – they might have appeared too elderly to find energy sufficient to mastermind a counterstroke against the largest army ever deployed in the field. Maunoury and Gallieni, however, were men of vitality, Gallieni exceptionally so. Recalled from retirement on 25 August to replace the ineffective General Michel as Military Governor of Paris, he had at once warned Messimy, Minister of War, that the enemy would be at the gates in twelve days to lay a siege the capital could not withstand. He demanded reinforcements, which could only be got from Joffre who was unwilling to release any and, as supreme commander with war powers, could not be overruled by ministers or even the President. Gallieni's demands provoked a government crisis. Messimy, finding himself blamed for the dangers of which Gallieni was now warning, insisted on being dismissed rather than accept a new appointment and by so doing brought about the resignation of the whole ministry. Messimy was replaced by the tough and taciturn Millerand and departed to join the armies at the front as a major of reserve.[91]

The political upheaval shook Joffre's imperturbability no more than military setback. He adhered to his routine of the long lunch, of a solid dinner and regular hours of sleep. Nevertheless, unlike Moltke, who remained secluded in his Luxembourg headquarters far from the scene of action, he also visited subordinate commanders and troops almost every day. He saw Lanrezac on 26, 28 and 29 August, visited the commanders of Third and Fourth Armies on 30 August and Lanrezac again on 3 September. He also saw Sir John French on 26 August and 3 September. The British were causing anxiety. French had been shaken by the intensity of the fighting at Mons, even more by that at Le Cateau, and had convinced himself that his army needed several days of rest before it could re-enter the line. As the retreat lengthened, he and his staff officers began to consider the eventuality of retiring to base, leaving France altogether and returning only when the troops had rested and re-equipped in England. He had come to believe that the French to left and right of him were retreating without warning, leaving him exposed to attacks by the advancing Germans. He next announced his intention of retiring below the Seine, in eight days of easy marching, and of transferring his stores from Rouen and Le Havre, on the English Channel, to St Nazaire or even La Rochelle on the Atlantic coast. Kitchener, Secretary of State for War, demanded clarification in a series of telegrams. When none came, he took a destroyer to France, summoned French to the British embassy in Paris and left him in no doubt that his task was to co-operate with Joffre even at extreme risk to his own army.[92]

That meant its taking its place in the 'mass of manoeuvre' which, by 3 September, was gathered north-west and west of Paris: the new Sixth Army, the Paris garrison, the BEF, the Fifth Army and, on its right, the Ninth Army, also new and commanded by General Ferdinand Foch. Foch, promoted from command of XX Corps, was a star in the ascendant. Lanrezac's star fell on 3 September; Joffre motored to his headquarters at Sézanne that day to tell him he was replaced by Franchet d'Esperey. It was a painful meeting. They were friends and Lanrezac had been Joffre's protégé. Now he was a man worn-out by the burden of confronting the danger he, almost alone, had foreseen of the German attack through Belgium. The two generals walked around the playground of the school where Fifth Army had its headquarters while Joffre explained that he judged his subordinate to have lost the power of decision. Then Lanrezac departed, accompanied by a single non-commissioned officer, not to be seen again in uniform.[93]

Gallieni, also a star in the ascendant, was meanwhile terrorising the municipality of Paris with his orders to put the city into a state of defence. On 2 September the government had, as in 1870, transferred its seat to Bordeaux. Joffre had incorporated the capital into the Zone of the Armies, where he ruled with total power, on 31 August. With constitutional authority, therefore, the Military Governor issued instructions to prepare the Eiffel Tower for destruction (it was the transmitting station for general staff radio communications), to lay demolition charges under the Seine bridges, to send all rolling stock useful to the enemy out of the Paris rail system, to provision the 2,924 guns of the fortifications with ammunition, to clear fields of fire for the artillery of trees and houses and to conscript the labourers to do the work. Paris, in 1914, was still a fortified city, surrounded by walls and a girdle of forts. It was also, under Gallieni's command, constituted an Entrenched Camp, with improvised defences stretching out into its surrounding countryside, further to enhance the 'obstacle of Paris' which had so troubled Schlieffen in the long years while he had been devising his plan.

Yet the obstacle had already done its work. On 3 September Schlieffen's 'strong right wing' represented by Kluck's First Army, had drifted forty miles to the east of Paris and was aligned to the south, with the Sixth Army and the Paris garrison behind it, the BEF on its right flank, the Fifth Army to its front and Foch's Ninth Army menacing its left and threatening an irruption into the gap which had opened between it and Bülow's Second Army. It was the existence of Paris and Lanrezac's evasive manoeuvring that had brought about this result.

Meanwhile the French railway system was hurrying to the front the forces with which Joffre planned to deliver his counterstroke. Since it centred on Paris, its network brought troops rapidly from the increasingly stabilised eastern sector to the critical points. By 5 September the Sixth Army consisted, besides Sordet's Cavalry Corps and the 45th (Algerian) Division, of the VII Corps, brought from Alsace, and the 55th and 56th Reserve Divisions from Lorraine; the IV Corps was on route from Fourth Army. The Ninth Army, originally constituted as the Foch Detachment, comprised the IX and XI Corps transferred from Fourth Army, together with the 52nd and 60th Reserve Divisions and 9th Cavalry Division, the 42nd from Third Army and the 18th Division from Third Army. Between the Paris Entrenched Camp and the Marne, Joffre therefore disposed, at the opening of the great battle named after the river, of thirty-six divisions, including the BEF, strengthened by the arrival of four fresh brigades from England, while the German First, Second, Third, Fourth and Fifth Armies opposing totalled just under thirty. Schlieffen's 'strong right wing' was now outnumbered, the result of Moltke's failure to control his subordinates and of Joffre's refusal to be panicked by early defeat. Much else had contributed to the mismatch, notably the logistic difficulties imposed on the Germans as their lines of communication lengthened, and the consequent easing of the problems of reinforcement and supply enjoyed by the French as they fell back on the centre. Nevertheless, the opening circumstances of the Battle of the Marne betrayed a failure of German generalship. It remained to be seen whether French generalship might yet pluck victory from the jaws of defeat.

THE BATTLE OF THE MARNE

'It is the thirty-fifth day', the Kaiser exulted to a delegation of ministers to his Luxembourg headquarters on 4 September, 'we are besieging Rheims, we are thirty miles from Paris.'[94] The thirty-fifth day had an acute significance to the German General Staff of 1914. It lay halfway between the thirty-first day since mobilisation, when a map drawn by Schlieffen himself showed the German armies poised on the Somme to begin their descent on Paris, and the fortieth, when his calculations determined that there would have been a decisive battle.[95] That battle's outcome was critical. Schlieffen, and his successors, had calculated that the deficiencies of the Russian railways would ensure that not until the fortieth day would the Tsar's armies be assembled in sufficient strength to launch an offensive in the east. Between the thirty-fifth and the fortieth day, therefore, the outcome of the war was to be decided.

On 4 and 5 September, the commanders issued the orders which would set the engagement in motion. 'The enemy', von Moltke admitted, on 5 September, 'has eluded the enveloping attack of First and Second Armies and has succeeded, with part of his forces, in gaining contact with Paris.'[96] First and Second Armies were therefore to stand on the defensive outside Paris, while Third Army was to advance towards the upper Seine and Fourth and Fifth Armies were to attack to the south-east, with the object of opening a way for the Sixth and Seventh to cross the River Moselle and complete the encirclement of the enemy. This was the opposite of what Schlieffen had intended; his plan was for the First and Second Armies to drive the French into the arms of the left wing. On 4 September, Joffre had issued General Instruction No. 6 which exactly anticipated Moltke's recognition of his predicament and proposed means to exploit it. 'It is desirable to take advantage of the exposed position of the German First Army to concentrate against it the strength of the Allied armies [opposite]'.[97] Accordingly, the Sixth Army, at the outermost extremity, was to cross the Ourcq, a tributary of the Marne, and advance round the Germans' flank, while the BEF, the Fifth Army and Foch's Ninth Army were to make a fighting advance northward; effective date of the order, 6 September. The biter was to be bit. The German, not the French, army was to be the target of an encirclement.

What stood between conception of the order and its realisation were water barriers, not the Marne itself, but its tributaries, the Ourcq,

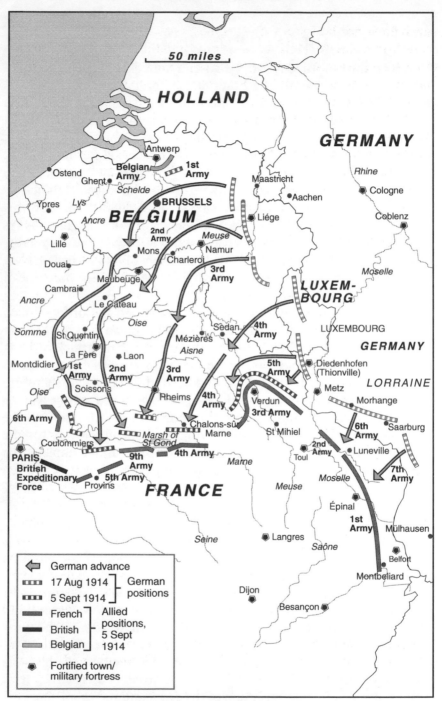

The German advance, 1914

which flows north to south athwart the line of advance of Maunoury's Sixth Army, and the Morins – the Grand and the Petit – which run east to west, and so across the front of the BEF and the Sixth and the Ninth Armies; the latter's room for manoeuvre was further impeded by the marshes of the St Gond which formed part of the riverine system. None of the waterways was a serious obstacle. They defined, nevertheless, the lines on which action was to be joined and required preparation for deliberate attack. That necessity, as it proved, was to favour the Germans rather than the French, thanks to tactical quick-thinking by a commander on the spot at a critical point. The man was General von Gronau, an artillery officer commanding IV Reserve Corps. His formation had played little part in the campaign thus far, had indeed been much weakened by transfers of units to act as flank guards for the main body of First Army. Von Gronau, nevertheless, remained alert to his responsibilities. His Corps held station on the outermost edge of the German invasive swathe and was therefore not only in a vulnerable position itself but stood security on the right for the whole offensive deployment. On the morning of 5 September, as Maunoury's Sixth Army probed forward to take up attacking positions for the following day, he was seized by disquiet at the reports sent back by his attached cavalry division. Its patrols found advancing French troops all across its front. As the IV Reserve Corps was aligned at right angles to and to the rear of von Kluck's First Army, that meant that the enemy was manoeuvring to take First Army in flank and roll it up. His response was instantaneous and courageous. He decided to attack.

As Maunoury's advance guard, the 55th and 56th Reserve Divisions and the Moroccan Brigade, breasted forward towards the Ourcq in the mid-morning of 5 September, they were suddenly brought under fire by the rifles, machine guns and artillery of Germans who were occupying terrain supposed empty. The French went to ground and a fierce firefight broke out that lasted the rest of the day. As darkness fell, von Gronau wisely judged he had won the time necessary to save First Army from surprise attack and disengaged his troops, who slipped away to the line the French had intended to assault on 6 September. In bright moonlight the French followed, launching attacks against positions the Germans had already abandoned.

The battle of the Marne had therefore opened a day earlier than Joffre had intended, and on terms dictated by the enemy. Thanks to von Gronau's independent action, the beckoning open flank which offered the opportunity for an encirclement had been covered and von Kluck given the warning necessary to hurry reinforcements from his central to his right before the danger heightened. Kluck reacted with an energy and decisiveness he had not shown during the days when he had let his army drift reactively eastward in the footsteps of Lanrezac's defeat. By the morning of 6 September, he had transferred his II Corps from south of the Marne to west of the Ourcq, to form a line north of von Gronau's position and he would successively transfer northward the IV Corps on 7 September, the III Corps on 8 September and the IX Corps on 9 September. What strategists call 'interior lines' were now working in von Kluck's favour, as they had worked for Joffre in the last week of August and first week of September, when he had brought the constituents of Sixth and Ninth Armies behind the fighting front from the armies that were holding their ground in Alsace and Lorraine.

There was this difference. It was critical. Joffre's transfers had not altered the strategic situation on the eastern front, which had stabilised as soon as the French ceased to attack and found strong defensive positions behind the Meuse and Moselle. Kluck's withdrawals, by contrast, weakened his principal front at the point where his mission was still to deliver a decisive, war-winning blow and at a moment, in the very last of the forty days which were expected to bring victory, when the French were gathering to deliver their counter-offensive over the same ground. Indeed, by 9 September, the fortieth day itself, the German First Army, instrument and hope of Schlieffen's vision, was not on the Marne at all, but had been withdrawn in its entirety to the Ourcq, where it faced not Paris, in popular imagination the object of the whole campaign, nor the mass of the French army, its strategic target, but Maunoury's detached manoeuvre force. Between the German First Army and Second an enormous gap had opened, thirty-five miles wide, which the Germans could disregard only because they believed that the enemy troops opposite, the British Expeditionary Force, lacked the strength and had demonstrated the disinclination to penetrate.[98]

The high command of the BEF, though not its brave soldiers, had given von Moltke, Kluck and Bülow reason for so believing. Sir John French, 'the little Field Marshal', stout, florid, peppery, had proved a dashing cavalry leader in the British Army's small wars. At the head of his country's only field army in the largest war ever to involve it, he displayed an increasing tendency to nerves. The losses at Mons had unsettled him, the far heavier losses at Le Cateau had shaken his resolve altogether. He feared that the BEF would fall to pieces unless given a respite to rest and re-equip. What heightened his anxieties was his fixed conviction that Lanrezac had let him down, retreating from the Sambre without warning and leaving the BEF to cover the withdrawal. Before August was out, he had come to hate Lanrezac and to distrust the French generally. For Joffre he retained a personal regard but, as he told Kitchener on 30 August, 'my confidence in the ability of the leaders of the French Army to carry this campaign to a successful conclusion is fast waning'.[99] During the next days, he spoke of transferring his base from the Channel ports to Brittany, of the impossibility of allowing the BEF to 'take up a position in the front line for at least ten days', of retiring behind the Seine by 'marching for some eight days . . . at a considerable distance from the enemy'.[100] It took Kitchener's visit to Paris on 2 September to check this defeatism but he remained unwilling to rejoin battle. As late as 5 September, when it had been made clear to him that the participation of the BEF in the counter-offensive prescribed by Joffre's General Instruction No. 6 was essential to its success, he continued to prevaricate. Only when Joffre found the time, at this moment of acute crisis, to visit his headquarters and make a personal appeal did he stiffen. French was an emotional man. Joffre's clutching of his hands and supplication in the name of 'France' set tears running down his cheeks. He tried his ally's language, fell tongue-tied, then blurted at a staff officer who spoke French better, 'Damn it, I can't explain. Tell him that all man can do our fellows will do.'[101]

Difficulties remained. The BEF had fallen too far to the rear to join at once with Sixth and Fifth Armies in the general offensive. 'Desperate Frankie', the new commander of Fifth Army whom all his British collaborators admired, fell into a rage at his ally's apparent unco-operativeness. Sixth Army, marching up in echelon to bar its advance into the German rear, but opposed progressively by the whole of Kluck's strength, faltered under one counter-attack after another. It would have been surprising if it had not. In any case an improvised force, its components – four Reserve divisions, only two Active divisions, and a collection of cavalry and Active North African formations – lacked both the quality and numbers to stand up to Kluck's First Army, which contained eight Active divisions, besides Reserve and cavalry formations. The distances over which the arriving

German divisions had to travel, compared to those Sixth Army's had covered from the eastern frontier, were quite short. The IX Corps, which appeared opposite Maunoury's left flank on the morning of 9 September, had made the longest march, but it was one of only forty miles. It deployed intact and in vigour. The corps which had arrived earlier had blunted all Maunoury's efforts to take ground, and had continually counter-attacked. One critical situation had been saved for the French only by a dashing intervention of the 45th Division's artillery, led by Colonel Nivelle, a future commander of the French army, another by the arrival from Paris of a portion of the city's garrison mounted in commandeered taxicabs, an episode of future legend. The battle of the Ourcq, between 5 and 8 September, nevertheless tended Kluck's way. On the evening of 8 September, he felt confident enough to signal his subordinates that 'the decision will be obtained tomorrow by an enveloping attack'. The Schlieffen Plan, in short, might be about to work after all.[102]

Geography spoke otherwise. The aggressiveness Kluck's army had shown against Maunoury's had actually worked to enlarge the gap that now loomed between it and Second Army, a gap too wide for the only German troops not engaged elsewhere, those of 2nd and 9th Cavalry Divisions, to fill. They were, moreover, too weak to oppose the force marching up to exploit the weakness in the German line the gap presented. True to his reluctant word, Field Marshal French started the whole of the BEF forward on 6 September and, though it had ten miles to make up before it reached Joffre's intended point of departure, it soon covered the distance, bringing with it the elements of a new, third, corps, formed in France on 21 August. The intervention of the British, who fought a sharp encounter action at Rozoy, alarmed von Kluck. Even more alarmed was von Bülow, whose Second Army was heavily engaged throughout the day against the French Fifth Army, galvanised by the leadership of its new commander, Franchet d'Esperey. On 7 September Bülow radioed the high command to warn that he was withdrawing the troops on the east of the gap, into which the BEF was marching, behind the Petit Morin river, for safety, a retreat of ten miles and more. Worse, under pressure during the day, he was obliged to swing his right wing northward, thereby further widening the gap between his army and von Kluck's and leaving the way open for a full-scale Allied advance to the Marne.

The right wing of the German army was now divided effectively into three sections, with Kluck's First Army north of the Marne, the right of von Bülow's Second Army south of the Marne but falling back towards it across the waterways of the Grand and Petit Morin, and his left, which connected only weakly with von Hausen's Third Army, positioned on the Petit Morin itself, in the Marshes of the St Gond, where that river rose. The whole region 'is a country of great open spaces; highly cultivated, dotted with woods and villages, but with no great forests, except [those to the south]. It is cut from east to west by the deep valleys, almost ravines, of the Grand Morin, Petit Morin, the Marne, the upper course of the Ourcq, the Vesle, the Aisne and the Ailette.' The Marshes of the St Gond are a topographical exception, 'a broad belt of swamp land . . . [extending] from east to west nineteen kilometres, with an average width of three kilometres . . . five lesser roads and three foot-paths cross [the marshes] from north to south, but they are otherwise impassable, forming a military obstacle of the first importance'.[103] Von Bülow's right, and the left of von Hausen's Third Army were, on 6 September, firmly embedded on the northern edge of the marshes, with Foch's new Ninth Army positioned on the other side. The mission given him by Joffre was to protect the flank of Fifth Army, battling to drive von Bülow beyond the Marne. It was in character that he chose to interpret it offensively. While his centre and right stood fast, he ordered his left, the 42nd Division, to advance, supported by the Moroccan Division and part of IX Corps. During 6 and 7 September they battled valiantly to work their way round the western end of the marshes, while the rest of Ninth Army and the Germans opposite conducted artillery duels over the sodden ground of the marshes themselves.

The battle of the marshes threatened to descend into a stalemate, as that on the eastern frontier had become. Then it was transformed by the uncharacteristic boldness of von Hausen. This Saxon general has been described as too deferential to the wishes of the Prussian Kluck and Bülow on his right, too overawed by the German Crown Prince who commanded on his left, to take forthright decisions in the handling of his own army. On 7 September he displayed an independence that contradicted both judgements. Persuading himself that the ferocity of the two previous days' fighting had blunted the enemy's alertness, he decided to launch a surprise night attack. In the moonlit early morning of 8 September, the Saxon 32nd and 23rd Reserve Divisions and the 1st and 2nd Guard Divisions advanced through the marshes and across the dry ground further east, fell on the French with the bayonet and drove them back three miles. This was a local victory that shook the confidence of Foch's Ninth Army, which lost further ground on its right during the day and merely held its own on the left.

The events of 8 September prompted Foch to draft the later legendary signal: 'My centre is giving way, my right is in retreat, situation excellent. I attack.'[104] It was probably never sent. Nevertheless, the general's actions bore out the spirit of those words. During 9 September, using reinforcements lent by Franchet d'Esperey, and in expectation of the arrival of XXI Corps from Lorraine, Foch succeeded in plugging every gap in the line opened by Hausen's continuing offensive and did, at the day's end, actually manage to organise a counter-attack at the right hand extremity of his army's position. Merely by holding his front, Foch achieved a sort of victory.

On the Ourcq, meanwhile, 9 September was also a day of crisis. Kluck's First Army was now fighting as an independent entity, separated from Bülow's Second Army by a forty-mile gap into which the BEF was pushing northward towards the Marne almost unopposed, but still formidably strong and still committed to attack. With four corps in line, it still outnumbered Maunoury's Sixth Army and, overlapping the flanks of the French to north and south, still retained the chance of winning an encirclement battle and so reversing the increasingly dangerous situation on the critical right wing. The weight of his deployment was in the north, where von Quast's IX Corps, supported by von Arnim's III, was positioned and prepared to fall on the French 61st Reserve Division, turn its flank and drive into the rear of the defenders of Paris. On the morning of 9 September von Quast began his attack opposed initially only by the weak artillery of the French 1st and 3rd Cavalry Divisions. When his troops came up against the positions of the 61st Reserve Division, they drove the French infantry to flight, so that by early afternoon they were poised to sweep forward into undefended territory. The balance of advantage on the Marne seemed once more to have tilted the Germans' way.

The Mission of Lieutenant-Colonel Hentsch

That was the local reality. Von Quast sensed no resistance to his front. His soldiers were elated by success. Paris, only thirty miles distant, beckoned. The way to the French capital seemed to lie open and victory therefore to promise. Then, at two o'clock in the afternoon, Quast received a telephone call from Kluck's headquarters. The offensive was to be discontinued. An order for retreat had been received. The First Army was to retire northward towards the Marne and it appeared not the First Army only but the whole of the right wing. Local reality was dissolved in a larger reality. The great advance, the sweep through Belgium and northern France, the master stroke that was to end the war in the west before the fortieth day, had failed. Schlieffen's vision had evaporated in the heat of battle.

Not just the heat of battle. The cool appraisal of a military technician had decided that the position of First, Second and Third German Armies was untenable. The technician was a middle-ranking officer of the General Staff, Lieutenant-Colonel Richard Hentsch, the peacetime head of the Operations Section of the Great General Staff, since mobilisation the head of the Intelligence Section at Supreme Headquarters. In the war's aftermath Allied historians expressed surprise that an officer of such junior rank should have been devolved the authority to nullify Schlieffen's great plan. The German high command itself, at Hentsch's request, held an official inquiry in 1917 to examine the probity of his intervention. Even today the scope of the powers delegated to him seems remarkably wide, and all the more so because Hentsch was a Saxon, not a Prussian officer, in an army the Prussians dominated. Moreover, he was an intelligence, not an operations, officer, on a general staff whose operations section treated the intelligence section as a handmaiden. Nevertheless, Hentsch was a considerable figure. He had shone as a student at the War Academy, won the high opinion of his contemporaries and superiors and was on intimate terms with both Moltke and Bülow.[105] He was therefore an obvious person to choose as an intermediary between Supreme Headquarters and the right wing, at a moment when the distance separating them had increased to 150 miles. Moltke felt unable to make what would be a time-consuming journey himself. He judged signal communications to be both unsatisfactory and insecure. His well-informed intelligence section chief was perfectly qualified to bridge the gap. It was unfortunate, and would continue to appear so, that Moltke wrote nothing down but despatched Hentsch on his mission with nothing more substantial to validate his plenipotentiary authority than a verbal instruction.[106]

Hentsch set off by motor car from Luxembourg at eleven o'clock on the morning of 8 September. He was accompanied by two captains, Köppen and Kochip, and visited in succession the headquarters of Fifth, Fourth and Third Armies. With each he discussed its situation and concluded that no withdrawal from its front was necessary, with the possible exception of Third Army's right wing; he nevertheless radioed Luxembourg that the 'situation and outlook entirely favourable at Third Army'.[107] In the evening he arrived at Second Army's headquarters, from which Bülow was temporarily absent. When Bülow returned, he, his two principal staff officers and the Hentsch party settled to survey the situation. The result of their discussion was to be decisive for the outcome of the campaign in the west. Bülow dominated. He represented his army's predicament as one the enemy might exploit in two ways, either by turning the right wing of his own army or by massing against the left wing of First Army. Since the gap between the two was in the hands of the French and British, they enjoyed freedom of action and could use it with 'catastrophic' results. Bülow proposed to avert disaster by a 'voluntary concentric retreat'.[108] That meant a withdrawal from the positions from which the German offensive threatened Paris to safer but defensive lines beyond the Marne. On that note, towards midnight, the meeting dispersed. Next morning, 9 September, Hentsch conferred again with Bülow's staff officers, though not the General himself, and agreed that he would visit Kluck at First Army to advise a retirement, which would close the menacing gap. He left at once. While he was covering the fifty miles to First Army headquarters, Bülow decided to act on the conclusions arrived at by his juniors. He signalled Kluck and Hausen that 'aviator reports four long columns marching towards the Marne' (the aviator was Lieutenant Berthold, the columns those of the BEF) and that consequently, 'Second Army is beginning retreat'.[109]

The retreat that followed was orderly but precipitate. Once Second moved, First and Third were obliged to conform, as by the working of interlocking parts. Mechanistically, Fourth, Fifth and Sixth fell in with the retrogression. Along a front of nearly 250 miles, the German infantry faced about and began to retrace its steps over the ground won in bitter combat during the last two weeks. Moltke gave the orders himself for the retreat of the left wing, and in person. When Hentsch at last returned to Supreme Headquarters at two in the afternoon of 10 September, bringing the first comprehensive account of the situation at the front to amplify the few brief signals Moltke had received from him and Bülow in the previous two days, the Chief of Staff decided that he must do what he might have done in the first place and visit his subordinate army commanders himself. On the morning of 11 September he departed by road from Luxembourg, first for the headquarters of Fifth Army, where he saw the Crown Prince, next to Third Army, where he found Hausen stricken with dysentery, then to Fourth Army. While there he received a message from Bülow warning of a new danger to Third Army, posed by a fresh French attack, and decided that Fourth and Fifth must follow Third, Second and First in retirement. The positions to which he directed them were those on the river system next above the Marne, that of the Aisne and its tributaries. 'The lines so reached', he stipulated 'will be fortified and defended.'[110]

Those were the last general orders he issued to the German armies; on 14 September he was relieved of command and replaced by General Erich von Falkenhayn, the Minister of War. They were also the most crucial orders to be given since those for general mobilisation and until those initiating the armistice four years and two months later. For the 'fortification and defence' of the Aisne, which the German First and Second Armies reached on 14 September, initiated trench warfare. Whatever the technical factors limiting the German army's capability to manoeuvre with flexibility and at long range from railhead in 1914 – lack of mechanical transport, rigidity of signal networks working along telephone and telegraph lines – none constrained its power to dig. It was better provided with field engineer units than any army in Europe – thirty-six battalions, against twenty-six French – and better trained in rapid entrenchment.[111] The entrenching tool had become, by 1914, part of the equipment of the infantryman in every army. However, while the British cavalry took pride in avoiding entrenchment exercises, and the French disregarded 'the most demanding notions of cover', the German soldier had been obliged to use the spade on manoeuvre since at least 1904. 'From 1906 onward, foreign observers [of German manoeuvres] noted that German defensive positions frequently consisted of several successive trench lines linked by communication saps, often with barbed wire entanglements strung in front of them.' The Germans had not only noted the significance of entrenchments in the Boer and Russo-Japanese Wars but, unlike others, had drawn the lesson.[112]

When, at the end of the second week of September, therefore, the French and British troops pursuing the enemy came up against the positions on which the Germans had halted, they found their counter-offensive halted by entrenchments which ran in a continuous line along the crest of the high ground behind the Aisne, and its tributary

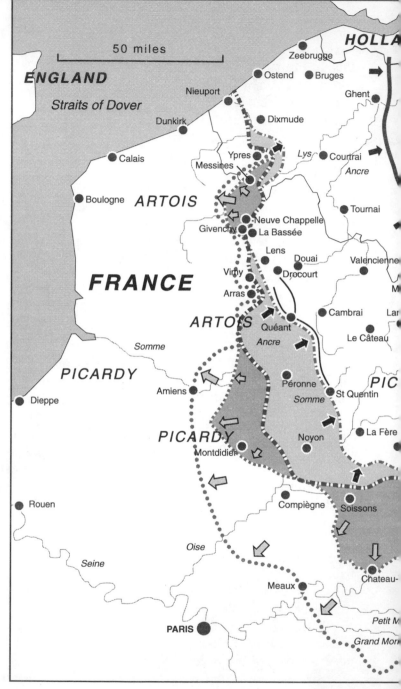

The Western Fr

the Vesle, between Noyon and Rheims. The line ran on beyond, turning south-west at Verdun and following the River Meurthe until it climbed away through the precipitate Vosges to reach the Swiss frontier near Basle. Beyond Rheims, however, the opposing armies – the German Fifth and Sixth, the French First and Second – had been so weakened by combat and by withdrawals to reinforce the crucial western sector that active operations had attenuated. The Aisne had now become the critical front and there, between 13 and 27 September, both sides mounted a succession of attacks, as troops became available, the Allies in the hope of pressing their pursuit further, the Germans with that of holding their line or even going over again to the offensive. The Allies began in optimistic mood. Wilson, British Deputy Chief of Staff, had discussed with Berthelot, his French equivalent, during the advance to the Aisne how soon their armies would be on the Belgian frontier with Germany. He thought a month, Berthelot three weeks. They were shortly to discover that the days of 'open warfare' were over.[113]

The Aisne is a deep, wide river, passable only by bridging. At the outset of the battle not all the bridges had been destroyed, while others were improvised; none was safe while within range of German artillery fire. Beyond the Aisne the ground rises some 500 feet above the valley to form a long massif, indented by re-entrants between bluffs and in places heavily wooded. The feature, some twenty-five miles long, affords excellent points of observation and dominating fire positions, while the road that traverses it, the Chemin des Dames, laid out for the daughters of Louis XV, provides easy lateral communication from left to right.[114] A British formation, the 11th Infantry Brigade, was the first to attempt an assault. It had found an unbroken bridge at Venizel and managed to establish itself on the crest on 12 September, after a thirty-mile approach march in pouring rain.[115] Thereafter the difficulties increased. The French Sixth Army tried on 13 September to get round the flank of the Chemin des Dames ridge near Compiègne but met German resistance across its whole front. The BEF was also held up under the centre of the Chemin des Dames that day and the only success was achieved on the right where the French Fifth Army found the gap that still existed between von Kluck's and von Bülow's armies and reached Berry-au-Bac on the Aisne's north bank.

The gap was rapidly being filled, however, by troops hurrying down from Maubeuge, where the valiant French garrison had at last been compelled to surrender the fortress on 8 September, and by others brought from Alsace and Lorraine to form a new German Seventh Army between First and Second. Moreover, with the Germans digging furiously – the first load of 'trench stores' to reach what was becoming the Western Front arrived from Germany on 14 September – the enemy line thickened almost by the hour.[116] The French ability to find reserves was meanwhile hindered by their need to hold Rheims, recaptured on 12 September, but subjected to devastating bombardment in the days that followed; the damage done to its famous cathedral, outside which stands the statue of Joan of Arc, would cause as much discredit to the invaders as the sack of Louvain a month earlier. What troops were available Joffre was forming into a new Second Army on his outer wing, under the fiery General de Castelnau. It was composed at the outset of corps taken from the Sixth, First and former Second Armies, most released by the stabilisation of the front in Lorraine and Alsace.

Joffre's object, not yet fully formulated, was to deploy across the rear of the Germans' thickening front on the Chemin des Dames and so to regain possession of the northern departments, rich in agriculture and industry, lost to France during August. While from 14 September Sir John French was ordering his troops to entrench wherever they occupied ground on or above the Aisne, Joffre was seeking means for this new manoeuvre. On 17 September he instructed his armies to 'keep the enemy under threat of attack and thus prevent him from disengaging and transferring portions of his forces from one point to another'.[117] Three days earlier, Falkenhayn, the new German Chief of Staff, had likewise ordered counter-attacks along the whole front with a similar object. Both commanders had grasped that opportunity in the campaign in the west now lay north of the active battlefront, in the hundred-mile sweep of territory standing, denuded of troops, between the Aisne and the sea. Whoever could find an army to operate there, without weakening his grip on the entrenched zone, might still outflank the enemy and so triumph.

There was an army in the region. It was the Belgian, hanging grimly on to the 'national redoubt' in the entrenched camp at Antwerp, to which it had retreated in the third week of August. King Albert, acting as Commander-in-Chief, was keenly aware of the damage he might do to the invader's strategic position by operating against his rear and on 24 August had mounted a large-scale sortie from Antwerp towards Malines. The scratch force, III Reserve Corps and the Naval Division, left by German Supreme Command to contain the Belgians, proved just strong enough to block their advance and turn them back on the third day. On 9 September Albert tried again and his men advanced as far as Vilvoorde, ten miles from the outer lines of the fortresses, before being halted.[118] There was a third, equally fruitless, attempt at an offensive on 27 September, which was also the last day of active operations between the Allies and Germans on the Aisne. Thereafter the German besiegers of Antwerp, who had been reinforced, were able to begin a deliberate reduction of the fortress, while the campaign between the Aisne and the sea took on the character of a frenzied search for the 'open flank' by the Allies and Germans in succession.

This passage has come to be called 'the Race for the Sea'. A race it was; not for the sea, however, but to find a gap between the sea and the Aisne position before it was exploited by the other side. Both sides, with the line stabilising along its whole length, could economise force in the burgeoning entrenchments to send formations northward. The largest was the new French Tenth Army, commanded by General de Maud'huy and comprising the X and XVI Corps, which from 25 September onwards began to deploy beyond the River Somme on the great stretch of open chalk downland that sweeps northward above the steeper countryside of the Aisne. The army arrived in the nick of time, for the only French troops thereabouts were a scattering of Territorials and cavalry. Even as it began to deploy, however, with the object of pushing south-eastward behind the German front, an equivalent German mass was marching forward to oppose it. It consisted of three corps, the IV, the Guard and the I Bavarian Reserve, which together were to compose a new Sixth Army, some of which had marched cross-country from the Aisne, other parts having been transferred by rail to Belgium first.[119] Falkenhayn's plan, agreed with Bülow, was to use Sixth Army to mount an offensive westward towards the Channel, while eight of the eleven German cavalry divisions swept the Flanders coast and the besiegers of Antwerp brought Belgian resistance to a peremptory end. The outcome Falkenhayn intended was a new drive through northern France, leaving the Germans in possession of all the territory above the Somme and thus positioned to march down towards Paris from lines that outflanked the French entrenched zone between the Aisne and Switzerland.

Part of the Falkenhayn plan succeeded. At Antwerp, General von Beseler, an engineer by training, had by 27 September devised an effective scheme to crack the entrenched camp's three lines of defences. The siege train of super-heavy guns that had reduced Liège and Namur having been transferred to his command, he began by bombarding the outermost and newest ring and then launched his infantry through the breach gained on 3 October. A British intervention temporarily stayed the crisis. On 4 October an advance guard of the Royal Naval Division, which had landed at Dunkirk on 19 September and had meanwhile roamed western Belgium, arrived in Antwerp by train.[120] In its wake appeared the First Lord of the Admiralty, Winston Churchill, thirsting for action and glory. The Royal Marines and sailors who composed the division temporarily halted the German advance. On the night of 5 October, however, Beseler's men managed to penetrate the second ring of forts at an unguarded point and advance to the first, a cordon of obsolete redoubts erected in 1859. The German artillery quickly began to break up their antiquated masonry, forcing the Royal Naval Division and what remained of the Belgian field army to evacuate towards the westernmost corner of Belgium on the River Yser. On 10 October General Deguise, the heroic Belgian commander of Antwerp, delivered up his sword to a German colonel. He was accompanied by a sergeant and a private soldier, all that remained of the garrison still under his command.[121]

The two other elements of Falkenhayn's plan foundered. Between 1 and 6 October the offensive of the new Sixth Army, whose mission was to 'break down the weakening resistance of the enemy' between the Somme and Flanders, was checked and defeated by the French Tenth Army; it was then and there that Foch, acting as Joffre's deputy on the critical front, issued the celebrated order, 'No retirement. Every man to the battle.'[122] Finally, the great sweep of the eight German cavalry divisions, the largest body of horsemen ever to be collected in Western Europe before or since, was rapidly blunted by the appearance, west of Lille, of the French XXI Corps and its own supporting cavalry.

THE FIRST BATTLE OF YPRES

Thus, by the end of the second week of October, the gap in the Western Front through which a decisive thrust might be launched by one side or the other had been reduced to a narrow corridor in Belgian Flanders. There is one of the dreariest landscapes in western Europe, a sodden plain of wide, unfenced fields, pasture and plough

139

intermixed, overlying a water table that floods on excavation more than a few spadefuls deep. There are patches of woodland scattered between the villages and isolated farmsteads and a few points of high ground that loom in the distance behind the ancient walled city of Ypres. The pervading impression, however, is of long unimpeded fields of view, too mournful to be called vistas, interrupted only by the occasional church steeple and leading in all directions to distant, hazy horizons which promise nothing but the region's copious and frequent rainfall.

It was here, between 8 and 19 October, that the five corps now comprising the British Expeditionary Force arrived by train and road to sustain the Allied defence. To the BEF's north the remnants of the Belgian army, which had managed to escape from Antwerp, had made their way along the coast to Nieuport, the town at the mouth of the Yser river that there flows into the sea; most of the marines and sailors of the Royal Naval Division had already got away to Ostend, where the British 7th Division, landed earlier, held a bridgehead until it joined the main body of the BEF near Ypres on 14 October.[123] On the Yser, a narrow but embanked river that forms a major military obstacle in the waterlogged coastal zone, the Belgians quickly erected barricades and laid plans to inundate the surrounding countryside if the river line were breached. Though they had arrived from Antwerp a broken army, their recovery was quick and their resistance on the Yser was to win the admiration of their Allies and the respect of the Germans. Their six divisions had been reduced in strength to 60,000 men, but they succeeded in garrisoning ten miles of utterly flat and featureless terrain and in holding most of their positions until, after the loss of another 20,000 men, King Albert decided, on 27 October, to open the sluices at the mouth of the Yser and let in the sea and flood the area. The resulting inundation created an impassable zone ten miles long between Nieuport and Dixmude.[124]

South of Dixmude the line of the Yser and the Ypres canal was held by a brigade of French sailors, stalwart regulars of the *Fusiliers-marins*, then by Territorials and cavalry as far as Langemarck, on the outskirts of Ypres. From Langemarck southward the arriving British had pegged out an advanced line that ran in a circle around Ypres towards the low ridge of higher ground at Passchendaele and then southward again across the River Lys to the La Bassée canal. The length of their line was thirty-five miles, to hold which Sir John French had available six infantry divisions, with one in reserve, and three cavalry divisions, unsuitable as cavalry was, given its low scales of artillery and machine-gun equipment, for defensive operations. The only reinforcements on which he could count were another infantry division, the 8th, some additional regular cavalry and volunteer horsed yeomanry and, en route from India, the advance guard of four infantry and two cavalry divisions of the Indian Army. These, composed of British and Indian units in a ratio of one to three, though they included a high proportion of hardy Gurkhas, were scarcely suitable for warfare in a European winter climate against a German army.[125] Weak in artillery and without experience of high-intensity operations, their arrival did not promise any enhancement of the BEF's offensive capacity.

Yet, at the outset of what would swell into the First Battle of Ypres – in which Indian units would fight gallantly and effectively both in defence and attack – Field-Marshal French still preserved hopes of mounting an attack that, in company with the French armies, would carry the Allies to the great industrial centre of Lille and thence to Brussels.[126] His hope was shared by Foch, who now commanded the northern wing of the French armies and had convinced himself that the enemy could not find the strength to hold what he still believed was an open front on the coastal plain. Both deluded themselves. Falkenhayn, the new head of OHL, not only disposed of the relocated Sixth Army, with its eleven regular divisions, and of Beseler's III Reserve Corps, which had conquered Antwerp, but of an entirely new collection of war-raised formations, eight divisions strong.

These belonged to a group of seven Reserve Corps, numbered XXII–XXVII, raised from volunteers who had not previously undergone military training. Because Germany had needed to conscript only 50 per cent of the annual class of men of military age to fill the ranks of the peacetime army, (France had conscripted 86 per cent), a pool of five million men aged from twenty to forty-five was available to Germany for war service.[127] Of those the best were students exempted while they pursued their studies. They had responded to the outbreak by volunteering in huge numbers, together with high-school boys preparing for university, and other young men ineligible for the draft. The later-to-be-famous writer Ernst Jünger, who had just completed his school-leaving certificate, fell into the second category; Adolf Hitler, an Austrian citizen living in Munich, into the third. Jünger, after waiting for three days at the recruiting office, managed to find a place in the 44th Reserve Division.[128] Hitler, who had written a personal appeal to the King of Bavaria, was eventually embodied in the 6th Bavarian Reserve Division.[129] The recruits received two months' training, under sergeants who were mostly schoolmasters recalled to the colours, and then left for the front.[130] Of these thirteen new divisions, two went to Russia, one to the front in Lorraine, ten to Flanders. It was those which, in the third week of October, would open the assault on the BEF between Langemarck and Ypres.

The battle that ensued raged almost continuously from early October, while the British and French were still attempting to push forward round the imagined German flank, until late November, when both sides accepted the onset of winter and their own exhaustion. Geographically it divided into four: a renewed offensive by Beseler's corps against the Belgians on the coast, nullified by the inundations; an attempt by the French under Foch to drive north of Ypres towards Ghent, deep inside Belgium, an over-optimistic project checked by the Germans' own offensive; the battle of Ypres itself, between the BEF and the German volunteers; and, to the south, a defensive battle conducted by the right wing of the BEF against the regular divisions of the German Sixth Army. Fighting on the three latter sectors merged effectively into one battle, so confused was combat and so unrelenting the German effort. British survivors were content to say they had been at 'First Ypres', a battle honour that denoted both a crucial success and the destruction of the old regular army.

Arriving in stages from the Aisne, II Corps on 10 October, III Corps on 13 October, the BEF began by pressing forward east of Ypres towards the ridges that swell some five miles beyond. The names of these low heights – Passchendaele, Broodseinde, Gheluvelt, Messines – were to recur, had the first assailants but known it, throughout the four coming years of war and to resound with menace. As the British arrived, so did fresh German corps to meet them, the XIV on 15 October, then the VII and XIX, on 19 October the XIII Corps. Under pressure, the British fell back. The British IV Corps, composed of the 7th Division and 3rd Cavalry Division, was driven close to the ancient ramparts of Ypres. The arrival of I Corps, commanded by General Douglas Haig, on 20 October secured Ypres itself, but that exhausted the army's strength on hand; reinforcements from the empire, including the Indians, were all that were promised, and they were as yet only on their way. It was on 20 October that a general German

142

offensive began against the whole front from the La Bassée canal in the south to the estuary of the Yser in the north, twenty-four divisions against nineteen, though the latter total included the six terribly weakened Belgian. The real contest was between fourteen German infantry divisions against seven British, with three British cavalry divisions fighting as infantry, and a collection of French sailors, Territorials and cavalry holding the river line between the British and the Belgians on the sea.

The line was held by the superiority of the British in rapid rifle fire. In artillery they were outgunned more than two to one, and in heavy artillery ten to one. In machine guns, two per battalion, they were equal with the enemy. In musketry, still quaintly so called in the BEF, they consistently prevailed. Trained to fire fifteen aimed rounds a minute, the British riflemen, of the infantry and cavalry alike, easily overcame the counter-fire of the attacking Germans who, coming forward in closely ranked masses, presented unmissable targets.[131] That the British were defending, the Germans attacking might be thought to explain the extraordinary disparity in casualties suffered during the October and November fighting around Ypres – 24,000 British dead to 50,000 German – but it does not. The BEF's trenches, at best hasty scratchings three feet deep, at worst field ditches, both frequently knee-deep in rain- or groundwater, were as yet unprotected by barbed wire. At the wettest places the defenders crouched behind sandbag mounds or brushwood barricades. In the absence of strong physical barriers to hold the enemy at a distance, it was the curtain of rifle bullets, crashing out in a density the Germans often mistook for machine-gun fire, that broke up attacks and drove the survivors of an assault to ground or sent them crawling back to cover on their start lines. 'Over every bush, hedge or fragment of wall floated a thin film of smoke', wrote the German official historian, 'betraying a machine gun rattling out bullets' – mistakenly.[132] The smoke was the signature of individual British soldier's marksmanship.

By the end of October the wider German offensive had failed, at enormous cost, particularly to the German volunteer corps. At their cemetery at Langemarck today, beyond a gateway decorated with the insignia of every German university, the bodies of 25,000 student soldiers lie in a mass grave; others lie in threes and fours under headstones inscribed to Volunteer Schmidt and Musketeer Braun. Dominating the hecatomb are sculptures by Käthe Kollwitz, herself a bereaved parent of 1914, of a mother and father mourning their lost son.[133] They represent tens of thousands of bourgeois Germans whom this phase of the battle, the '*Kindermord bei Ypern*', the Massacre of the Innocents at Ypres, disabused of the belief that the war would be short or cheap or glorious, and introduced to the reality of attrition, of mass death and of receding hope of victory.

This brutal disillusionment was the work of the last Tommy Atkinses, working-class, long-service regulars, shilling-a-day men of no birth and scanty education. They shared nothing of the mystical patriotism of their German enemies who 'had left lecture rooms and school benches [to be] melted into a great inspired body, [longing] for the unusual, for great danger ... [and] gripped [by war] like an intoxicant'.[134] Their patriotism was to the little homeland of the regiment, their first loyalty to barrack-room friends. 'After a while', recalled Corporal William Holbrook of the Royal Fusiliers, separated from his platoon during confused fighting, 'I came across some more of our fellows and one officer ... Once we'd got together and were deciding what to do, a German officer came crawling through the bushes. When he saw us he said, "I am wounded" – perfect English ... [our officer] said to him, "You shouldn't make those bloody attacks, then you wouldn't get wounded." It gave us a laugh! Anyway we bandaged him up, waited on there and shortly afterwards [our officer] was killed by a stray bullet, so we had no officers then. All you could hear was some firing going on, but I didn't know where the devil I was really.' Holbrook found a friend, 'name of Cainici, he was a London Italian, he was a real Cockney he was, I used to like him', took shelter with him from shelling, dug a shrapnel ball out of his friend's knee when he was hit, saw him off to the rear, then crawled off to look for 'a better place', found a dying German, tended him, saw him die, 'covered him over with leaves and twigs, anything I could scoop up just there' until, eventually, when he could 'hear where the firing was [and] knew which direction [to go], crawled back' to rejoin his unit.[135] Holbrook's Cockney matter-of-factness – the Royal Fusiliers was a London regiment – epitomises the spirit of the old British Expeditionary Force, whose soldiers died in their thousands at Ypres not because of an ideal of self-sacrifice but because it was expected of them and, in any case, there was no alternative.

On 31 October Falkenhayn renewed the offensive on a narrower front, astride the road that leads from Menin, on the higher ground the Germans occupied, to Ypres. The attack was mounted by the specially assembled Group Fabeck, named after its commander, which consisted of a mixture of regular and volunteer corps, six divisions in all. Pressing down into the low ground, through a belt of vegetation the British would continue to call 'woods' – Polygon, Shrewsbury, Nuns' Wood – long after the trees had disappeared, the Germans secured territory everywhere, and at the height of the attack broke through at Gheluvelt. Their thrust was repelled by the hasty assembly of bits and pieces of broken and exhausted battalions, Worcesters, Gloucestershires, Welch, Queen's, 60th Rifles, Loyals, Sussex, Northamptonshires, Gordon Highlanders, Oxfordshire and Buckinghamshire Light Infantrymen, and some Royal Dragoons fighting on foot. The German history speaks of 'the enemy reserves being too strong' and of the British 'bringing up two new divisions'.[136] The reality was of tiny parcels of tired men stopping gaps in the line, stuffing fresh clips into their Lee-Enfields and firing 'mad minutes' at the onpressing field-grey ranks. The arrival of some French units, begged by French from Foch, thickened the defence, but the crucial sector was held by British rifle fire.

The Germans renewed their offensive on 11 November, by their calculation the twenty-second day of a battle 'in which death had become a familiar comrade'.[137] The point of pressure was Nuns' Wood (Nonnenboschen), just north of the Menin road and only four miles from Ypres itself. Already the magnificent Gothic buildings of the ancient wool town, the Cloth Hall, the Cathedral, the merchant weavers' houses, were falling into ruin under the weight of heavy German artillery fire. The outlying country, too, was taking on the pockmarked, denuded look that would characterise its landscape for years to come. Its villages and farmsteads were broken by shelling, the little chateaux of the Flemish nobility already stood roofless and forlorn; a direct hit on Hooge chateau, two miles from Ypres, had killed many of the staff of the British 1st and 2nd Divisions on 31 October.[138] Hooge was the target of a concerted attack by the Prussian Guard and the German 4th Division on 11 November and the battle raged all day. The initial assault by the 1st Foot Guards, premier regiment of the German army, was stemmed by a collection of cooks and officers' servants from the 5th Field Company, Royal Engineers. Later part of the 2nd Battalion Oxfordshire and Buckinghamshire Light Infantry, a few dozen strong, counter-attacked and drove the 1st and 3rd Foot Guards back whence they came.

Fighting around Ypres would flicker on until 22 November, the date chosen by the official historians to denote the First Battle's termination. The British survivors, whose unwounded numbers were less than half of the 160,000 which the BEF had sent to France, were by then stolidly digging and embanking to solidify the line their desperate resistance over the preceding five weeks had established in the face of the enemy. The French, too, were digging in to secure the territory for which they had fought both north and south of the city. At best the line ran a little more than five miles to the eastward; elsewhere it stood much closer. Everywhere the Germans held the high ground, dominating the shallow crescent of trenches the British, who were to be its guardians for most of the coming war of attack and defence, would call 'the Salient'. Its winning had cost uncountable lives, French as well as British. The Germans, 'whose vanguards had known in the plains of Flanders life and purpose for the last time', had lost even more heavily.[139] At least 41,000 of the German volunteers, the Innocents of Ypres, had fallen outside its walls.

They represented but a fraction of all the dead of the Battles of the Frontiers, of the Great Retreat, of the Marne, of the Aisne, of the 'Race to the Sea' and of First Ypres itself. The French army, with a mobilised strength of two million, had suffered by far the worst. Its losses in September, killed, wounded, missing and prisoners, exceeded 200,000, in October 80,000 and in November 70,000; the August losses, never officially revealed, may have exceeded 160,000. Fatalities reached the extraordinary total of 306,000, representing a tenfold increase in normal mortality among those aged between twenty and thirty; 45,000 of those under twenty had died, 92,000 of those between twenty and twenty-four, 70,000 of those between twenty-five and twenty-nine.[140] Among those in their thirties, the death toll exceeded 80,000. All deaths had fallen on a male population of twenty million and more particularly on the ten million of military age. Germany had lost 241,000, including 99,000 in the 20–24 age group, out of a male population of thirty-two million.[141] Belgium, out of 1,800,000 men of military age, had suffered 30,000 dead, a figure that was to recur with gruesome consistency in each succeeding year of the war.[142] The total was the same as that for British deaths, with the difference that the British dead had almost all belonged to the regular army and its reserve of time-expired volunteer soldiers; those outside its ranks who had died, citizen soldiers of the few Territorial Force regiments, such as the London Scottish, which had reached Ypres before the end of the battle, and sepoys of the Lahore and Meerut Divisions, were few in number.[143] Their casualties would soon rise grievously, for the Indians held long stretches of the line throughout the coming winter, suffering casualties of a hundred per cent in some battalions before the year of 1915 was out, while it was the arrival of the Territorial Force in strength in 1915 that alone allowed the British army to sustain its share of the war effort in France and to participate in the offensives mounted by Joffre in the Artois and Champagne sectors of the Western Front.[144]

The prospect of any offensive, either by the Allies or the Germans, looked far away as winter fell in France at the end of 1914. A continuous line of trenches, 475 miles long, ran from the North Sea to the mountain frontier of neutral Switzerland. Behind it the opposing combatants, equally exhausted by human loss, equally bereft of re-supplies to replace the peacetime stocks of munitions they had expended in the previous four months of violent and extravagant fighting, crouched in confrontation across a narrow and empty zone of no man's land. The room for manoeuvre each had sought in order to deliver a decisive attack at the enemy's vulnerable flank had disappeared, as flanks themselves had been eaten away by digging and inundation. The hope of success in frontal attack had temporarily disappeared also. The experience of the French in Alsace and Lorraine in August, of the British in the Aisne in September, of the Germans in Flanders in October and November had persuaded even the most bellicose commanders that offensives unsupported by preponderant artillery would not overcome and, for the meanwhile, the artillery of all armies was short of guns and almost wholly without ammunition; at the end of the First Battle of Ypres British batteries were limited to firing six rounds per gun per day, scarcely enough to disturb the parapets of trenches opposite and wholly inadequate to support infantry in an advance against machine guns.[145] A sort of peace prevailed.

The war in the west had come full circle. In the four months between mobilisation and the stabilisation of the front, it had moved from hostility without action to hostility with quietus, with an intervening passage of intense aggression. Hindsight supplies a strong sense of similarity between the campaign of 1914 and that of 1870. Both had begun with French attacks in Lorraine towards the Rhine. Both had developed as German counter-offensives which resulted in grievous French defeats. Both had continued with a German advance to the outskirts of Paris, which failed to secure victory in the face of revived French resistance. Both had culminated in each side constructing

147

entrenched positions too strong to be carried by sudden assault and in the attacker's decision to wait out events until the defender's powers were overcome by the pressure of events. The comparison fails beyond that point. In 1870 the Germans succeeded in surrounding the capital and consigning the French field armies of the interior to haphazard and uncoordinated local operations. In 1914 the French army had ridden out defeat in the field, sustained its cohesion, driven the invader from the environs of the capital, won a sensational defensive victory and dictated that a war of entrenchment would be fought not in the heart of the country but at the periphery of the national territory. In 1870 German armies roamed northern, central and western France at will. At the end of 1914 the French army still controlled seventy-seven of the republic's ninety departments, remained firm in spirit, potentially strong in material force, and was supported by a great imperial and maritime power determined to see through the ordeal of an alliance war until the invader was defeated. These were the conditions that would assure Germany would enjoy no repetition of the quick and easy victory it had won forty-three years earlier.

FIVE

VICTORY AND DEFEAT IN THE EAST

'IN MILITARY OPERATIONS, time is everything', wrote Wellington, in 1800, and it was to his perfect judgement of timing that he owed, among his other victories, those of Salamanca and Waterloo.[1] Time had also oppressed Schlieffen: time to mobilise, time to concentrate, time to deploy, time to march to the crucial objective. It was his calculations of timing that had persuaded him, and those who inherited his posthumous plans, to wager almost all the force Germany commanded in the west and to let the east wait upon victory over France. Russia's known weaknesses had convinced Schlieffen and Moltke, his successor, that forty days would elapse before the Tsar's armies could appear in strength on Germany's eastern border and so to place their trust in gaining a victory against the clock.

Time is not the only dimension in which war is waged. Space is a strategic dimension also. It had served Russia well in the past, above all in 1812 when Napoleon had led the Grand Army on the long march to Moscow, but Schlieffen and the officers of the Great General Staff had argued themselves into believing in the first decade of the twentieth century that space in the east now worked on their side. The immense distances within the Russian empire, particularly those separating centres of population at which reservists must mobilise, and the relative sparsity of rail connections between such centres and the frontier, suggested to the military technocrats of Germany, and Austria, that tables of mobilisation measured in days by them would take weeks to complete by their Russian equivalents.[2]

It seemed that space might also be made to work for Germany on its side of the frontier. The division of territories between the three empires of Germany, Austria and Russia, the outcome of the partition of Poland a century earlier, might superficially be regarded to favour the latter in war, for Russian Poland, centred on Warsaw, thrust forward in a great salient between the Carpathian Mountains in Austria to the south and East Prussia to the north, threatening

German Silesia and opposed by no serious water obstacle such as those of the River Vistula or the Pripet Marshes that protected Russia's heartland from invasion. The Polish salient, however, might also be regarded as a region of operational exposure rather than of offensive opportunity, since its flanks were overlapped on either side by difficult terrain. The Carpathians form not only a defensive wall but a chain of dominating sally-ports against invaders from the northeast, while East Prussia, flat though it is as a collectivity, confronts any advancing army with a jumble of lakes and forest that defies the maintenance of order and easy intercommunication among its component units. The Masurian lakeland, home of the sprightly *Mazurka*, was a region of small communities largely isolated from the outside world, connecting with it by sandy tracks which threatened to reduce the progress of a marching army to a snail's pace. Beyond Masuria, moreover, lay a chain of German fortresses protecting the populated regions of East Prussia, at Thorn, Graudenz and Marienburg on the River Vistula, matching the Austrian Carpathian fortresses at Cracow, Przemysl and Lemberg (Lvov).[3] The Russian high command had long recognised the ambiguous strategic character of the Polish salient, where a bold offensive that threatened Berlin also risked catastrophe should the enemy co-ordinate a scissors movement in the rear, and it had accordingly starved the region of railway and road building that might aid an enemy counter-offensive. It had also cautiously designed two westward strategies, Plan G, that held a strong force in reserve, as well as Plan A, which thrust it forward.

Under French pressure, and out of a genuine desire to do its best by the western ally against the common German enemy, the Russian high command in 1914 was committed to Plan A. Two-fifths of the peacetime army was in any case stationed around the great military centre of Warsaw, from which its strategic deployment against East Prussia and the Carpathians and towards which its reinforcement by the reserves mobilised in the interior might easily be achieved.[4] Common sense and intelligence alike dictated that the bulk of Russia's western forces would have to go south, towards the Carpathians, for Austria-Hungary, unlike Germany, could count on waging a one-front war – the Serbian army appearing at the outset to be of no account – and so deploy its main strength there. Nevertheless, given Germany's anticipated weakness in the east, sufficient force could be found, by Russian staff calculations, to mount an offensive on the East Prussian frontier that would, while leaving the Austrians with their hands full, assure a crisis for Berlin in its backyard. Since that backyard was also the historic homeland of the German officer corps, dominated as it was by East Elbian landowners, an attack through Masuria towards Königsberg and the other strongholds of the Teutonic Knights from which they sprang would be certain to create in the German high command both material and psychological anxiety in acute degree.

Germany had indeed little left over from the great western *Aufsmarsch* with which to hold the Prussian heartland. Its war plan allotted only one of its eight armies to the eastern front, the Eighth Army, commanded by General Max von Prittwitz und Gaffron, a Prussian of Prussians, and consisting of the I, XVII and XX Corps, the I Reserve Corps, and the 1st Cavalry Division. All were Prussian-based, the I and I Reserve at Königsberg, seat of the Teutonic Knights, the XVII at Danzig, the XX at Allenstein, the 1st Cavalry Division at Königsberg, Insterburg and Deutsche-Eylau. To the Eighth Army was added on mobilisation a collection of reserve, *Ersatz* and *Landwehr* formations, raised from younger and older reservists, which added to it perhaps the strength of a whole corps. The army's soldiers, many of them recruits or reservists from the threatened area, could be counted upon to fight with tenacity against any invasion of their homeland.

They were, nevertheless, outnumbered by the force the Russian high command had earmarked to mount the East Prussian operations, the First and Second Armies of the North-Western Front. Together these opposed nine corps to Prittwitz's four, and seven cavalry divisions, including two of the Imperial Guard, to his one. Rennenkampf, commanding First Army, and Samsonov, commanding Second, were moreover both veterans of the Russo-Japanese War, in which each had commanded a division, while Prittwitz had no experience of war at all. Their formations were very big, divisions having sixteen instead of twelve battalions, with large masses of – admittedly often untrained – men to make up losses.[5] Though they were weaker in artillery, particularly heavy artillery, than their German equivalents, it is untrue that they were much less well provided with shells; all armies had grossly underestimated the expenditure that modern battle would demand and, at an allowance of 700 shells per gun, the Russians were not much worse off than the French fighting on the Marne.[6] Moreover, the Russian munitions industry would respond to the requirements of war with remarkable success. Nevertheless, Russia's forces were beset by serious defects. The proportion of cavalry, so much greater than that in any other army, laid a burden of need for fodder on the transport service, itself inferior to the German, which the value given by mounted troops could not justify; forty trains were needed to supply both the four thousand men of a cavalry division and the sixteen thousand of an infantry division.[7]

There were human defects also. Russian regimental officers were unmonied by definition and often poorly educated; any aspiring young officer whose parents could support the cost went to the staff academy and was lost to regimental duty, without necessarily becoming thereby efficient at staff work. As Tolstoy so memorably depicts in his account of Borodino, the Russian officer corps united two classes which scarcely knew each other, a broad mass of company and battalion commanders that took orders from a narrow upper crust of aristocratic placemen.[8] The qualities of the peasant soldier – brave, loyal and obedient – had traditionally compensated for the mistakes and omissions of his superiors but, face to face with the armies of countries from which illiteracy had disappeared, as in Russia it was far from doing, the Russian infantryman was at an increasing disadvantage. He was easily disheartened by setback, particularly in the face of superior artillery, and would surrender easily and without shame, en masse, if he felt abandoned or betrayed.[9] The trinity of Tsar, Church, country still had power to evoke unthinking courage; but defeat, and drink, could rapidly rot devotion to the regiment's colours and icons.

Still, they were splendid regiments that marched and rode out in mid-August to invade East Prussia – the Vladimir, Suzdal, Uglich and Kazan Regiments of the 16th Infantry Division, the Lithuanian, Volhynian and Grenadier Regiments of the 3rd Guard Division, the Guard Lancers and Hussars, the Cossacks of the Black Sea – with regimental singers at the head of the column and the regimental kitchens rolling at the rear.[10] War had been a tearful wrench, few of the men on the march comprehended why they were marching westward, but the regiment was a sort of village, the officer a sort of squire, and while the decencies of mealtimes and Sunday mass were observed, with the chance of vodka and a village tryst thrown in – Solzhenitsyn's *August 1914* captures unforgettably the mood of the Russian mobilisation – the Tsar's soldiers moved with a will towards the threat of gunfire.[11]

They might well have felt confidence. The enormous preponderance of Russian strength – ninety-eight mobilised infantry divisions, thirty-seven cavalry divisions – should have ensured the *Stavka*, the Russian high command, an overwhelming majority over the German Eighth Army, even after provision had been made to match the forty Austro-Hungarian divisions to the south.[12] Or it should, had Rennenkampf and Samsonov been able to move together and keep together. The wings of their armies, aligned respectively to face westward towards Königsberg and northward towards Graudenz, should, with proper handling, have passed deftly inside those two fortress towns and completed a pincer movement that surrounded Eighth Army and secured either its destruction or its precipitate flight to the rear, thus opening West Prussia and Silesia to a deeper Russian invasion.

Geography was to disrupt the smooth onset of the Russian combined offensive in space. Less excusably, timidity and incompetence were to disjoint it in time. In short, the Russians repeated the mistake, so often made before by armies apparently enjoying an incontestable superiority in numbers, the mistake made by the Spartans at Leuctra, by Darius at Gaugamela, by Hooker at Chancellorsville, of exposing themselves to defeat in detail: that is, of allowing a weaker enemy to concentrate at first against one part of the army, then against the other, and so beat both. The way in which geography worked to favour the German's detailed achievement is the more easily explained. Though eastern East Prussia does indeed offer a relatively level path of advance to an invader from Russia, the chain of lakes that feeds the River Angerapp also poses a significant barrier. There are ways through, particularly at Lötzen, but that place was fortified in 1914. As a result, a water barrier nearly fifty miles long from north to south confronted the inner wings of First and Second Army, so tending to drive them apart. Strategically, the easier option was to pass north and south of the Angerapp position rather than to force it frontally and that was what the commander of the North-Western Front, General Y. Zhilinsky, decided to direct Rennenkampf and Samsonov to do.[13]

He was aware of the opportunity such a separation offered to the Germans and accordingly took care to provide for the protection of his two armies' flanks. However the measures taken enlarged the danger, since he allowed Rennenkampf to strengthen his flank on the Baltic coast, which was not at risk, and Samsonov to detach troops to protect his connections with Warsaw, equally not threatened, while arranging for one corps of Second Army to stand immobile in the gap

The Eastern Front in outline, 1914–18

separating it from First. The result of these dispositions was a diversion of effort which left both armies considerably weakened to undertake the main task.[14] Having commenced the deployment with a superiority of nineteen divisions against nine, Rennenkampf and Samsonov actually marched to the attack with only sixteen between them.

Worse, critically worse, the two armies arrived on their start lines five days apart in time. First Army crossed the East Prussian frontier on 15 August, a very creditable achievement given that the French and Germans were then still completing their concentration in the west, but Second not until 20 August. As the two were separated in space by fifty miles of lakeland, three days in marching time, neither would be able to come rapidly to the other's assistance if it ran into trouble which, unbeknownst either to Rennenkampf or Samsonov, was the way they were heading.

The superiority of German over Russian intelligence-gathering clinched the issue. Though the Russians knew that they outnumbered the Germans, their means of identifying the enemy's location were defective. The Russian cavalry, despite its large numbers, did not seek to penetrate deep into the enemy positions, but preferred to dismount and form a firing line when it encountered resistance; and, while the aviation service of the Russian army, with 244 aircraft, was the second largest in Europe, aerial reconnaissance failed to detect German movements altogether.[15] The German 2nd Aircraft Battalion, however, and the two airships based at Posen and Königsberg, began to report both the strength and march direction of the Russian columns as early as 9 August, a week before they began to cross the frontier.[16] Aircraft and airships would continue to provide vital information throughout the campaign.[17]

It was the initial intelligence, however, that was decisive. Armed with the knowledge that Rennenkampf led Samsonov by several days – the interval would increase as Samsonov, struggling across the grain of the country and the many small tributaries feeding the Vistula, fell behind schedule – Prittwitz could decide to deploy the bulk of Eighth Army north of the Masurian lakes without undue anxiety. When the Russians opened their offensive with a probing attack at Stallupönen on 17 August, they were driven back. When their main body arrived in strength, at Gumbinnen three days later, the German I Corps was actually advancing to attack them under cover of darkness. The commander, von François, one of the many German officers of

Huguenot descent, was as aggressive as he looked, and his troops took their spirit from him. They belonged to some of the most famous of Prussian regiments, the 1st, 3rd and 4th Grenadiers, the 33rd Fusiliers, and fell fiercely on the Russians they found opposite. However, the enemy had prepared overnight trenches and fortified farm buildings and houses. The harder the Germans pressed forward, the higher rose their casualties. The Russian artillery, traditionally the best-trained arm of the Tsar's army, was well positioned and, firing at close range, added to the carnage. To add to the slaughter, the German batteries of 2nd Division mistakenly but effectively fired on their own infantry. Many sought escape by precipitate retreat and, though eventually rallied, were too shaken to be sent back into the firing line. By mid-afternoon, I Corps had come to a halt. Its neighbouring corps, XVII, commanded by the famous Life Guard Hussar, von Mackensen, who was encouraged by early reports of its success, was meanwhile attacking north-eastward into the Russians' flank. It did so without reconnaissance which would have revealed that, on its front as on that of von François, the Russians were entrenched. From their positions they poured a devastating fire into the advancing German infantry who, when also bombarded in error by their own artillery, broke and ran to the rear. By late afternoon the situation on the front of XVII Corps was even worse than that on the front of I Corps and the battle of Gumbinnen was threatening to turn from a tactical reverse to a strategic catastrophe. To the right of XVII Corps, I Reserve, under von Below, counter-attacked to protect Mackensen's flank against a Russian advance. At Eighth Army headquarters, however, even the news of that success could not stay the onset of panic. There Prittwitz was yielding to the belief that East Prussia must be abandoned and the whole of his army retreat beyond the Vistula.

At OHL, Moltke was appalled by the reports of Eighth Army's sudden predicament, which undermined the whole substance of belief in the possibility of postponing crisis in the east while victory was gained in the west. Only twenty of the vital forty days had elapsed, and Schlieffen's timetable threatened to crumble before OHL's eyes. Moreover, the apparent disaster in East Prussia aroused personal anxieties there. It was from its small estates that the army's inner circle sprang, and Prittwitz's loss of nerve exposed not just the nation at large but officers' wives, children and old retainers to the mercies of the enemy. Prittwitz's staff officers, Hoffman and von Waldersee, succeeded somewhat in stiffening his nerve on 21 August. Moltke, however, had lost confidence in him. Moltke decided first that a director of operations of the first quality must be sent instantly to the east to take charge. He chose Ludendorff, who had twice so brilliantly resolved crises in Belgium. He next determined to dispose of Prittwitz altogether, judging his declared intention to retire behind the Vistula, even if subsequently reconsidered, to be evidence of broken will. In his place he promoted Paul von Beneckendorf und Hindenburg, a retired officer noted for his steadiness of character if not brilliance of mind. As a lieutenant in the 3rd Foot Guards, Hindenburg had been wounded at Königsgrätz in 1866 and fought in the Franco-Prussian War. He claimed kinsmen among the Teutonic Knights who had won East Prussia from the heathen in the northern crusades, had served on the Great General Staff and eventually commanded a corps. He had left the army in 1911, aged sixty-four, but applied for reappointment at the war's outbreak. When the call from Moltke came, he had been out of service so long that he was obliged to report for duty in the old blue uniform that had preceded the issue of field-grey. He and Ludendorff, unalike as they were, the one a backswood worthy, the other a bourgeois technocrat, were to unite from the start in what Hindenburg himself called 'a happy marriage'.[18] Their qualities, natural authority in Hindenburg, ruthless intellect in Ludendorff, complemented each other's perfectly and were to make them one of the most effective military partnerships in history.

It was, nevertheless, to Ludendorff that Hindenburg looked for an initiative when the two arrived at Eighth Army on 23 August. Its headquarters had moved from Marienburg, ancient commandery of the Teutonic Knights, to Rastenburg, future location of Hitler's *Wolf's Lair*, the day before. On 24 August, the two generals went forward to confer with Scholtz, commanding XX Corps opposite Samsonov's Second Army, which was advancing to contact after its long flank march but was not yet engaged. Scholtz was nervous, expecting an offensive against him in strength but doubting his troops' ability to withstand it. He wanted to withdraw. Ludendorff was adamant that he must hold his ground. Assistance would reach him, but not if he retreated away from it. He must stand and fight.

The help on its way had been started forward not by Hindenburg or Ludendorff, but by the superseded Prittwitz who, after recovering from the shock of Gumbinnen, had grasped that François, despite losing 8,000 casualties, had halted Rennenkampff and so freed forces

159

to be used elsewhere. Old war games, some played by Schlieffen himself, had taught Prittwitz's generation of officers that the correct strategy for defending the East Prussian frontier was to defeat one Russian army one side of the lakes, then use the north-south railway lines to send forces behind them to the other side and repeat the process. With remarkable moral courage and wise advice from his Chief of Staff, Max Hoffmann, he decided that Rennenkampf could be counted as beaten, or at least checked, and, before Hindenburg's arrival, had already initiated the movement of I and XVII Corps to meet Samsonov on the southern front. Ludendorff did not, therefore, have to devise a plan – though he had already come to the same conclusions as Prittwitz – but merely to endorse one already in execution.

On the Russian side, Rennenkampf correctly sensed that the German forces in front of him were thinning out but inferred that François and Mackensen were withdrawing to the Königsberg fortress on the Baltic coast. That they had departed in haste, loading their troops into rail waggons and leaving only a screen of cavalry and local *Landwehr* to hold François's former positions, he did not guess. He believed he was faced with the burden of a deliberate siege of Königsberg, requiring much infantry and a reinforcement of heavy artillery, all taking time to assemble. As to urgent action, he and Zhilinsky, at North-West Front headquarters, had formed the conclusion that the task lay with Samsonov, now breasting up to contact with the Germans south of the lakes, who must be cut off by him from escape across the lower Vistula. To ensure the necessary encircling movement, he was ordered to swing his left wing even further away from Rennenkampf, who was meanwhile probing forward slowly with cavalry and transmitting orders for the planned siege of Königsberg by radio.[19]

Russian radio insecurity has become part of the legend of the Tannenberg campaign, as the sequence of battles came to be named. In its most sensational form, the story has the radio sections of Rennenkampf's and Samsonov's headquarters signalling detailed reports of the two armies' movements and intentions to each other *en clair*, to be intercepted and acted upon with deadly effect by their German opposite numbers. The reality is less simple and more mundane. There was a good deal of Russian signalling *en clair,* but it was a fault of which the Germans were guilty also. The reason, on the Russian side, was not Oblomovian laziness but difficulty in distribution of code books, on the German side lack of time. German operators were pressed and often transmitted uncoded messages on the calculation that they would be missed by listeners, just as they knew their own listeners missed so many Russian messages. 'Neither instruments nor operators could be spared to scan empty air', and there was also a shortage of interpreters.[20] The East Prussian ether, in late August 1914, therefore crackled with messages of which neither enemy could make use.

On the morning of 25 August, however, Hindenburg had a stroke of luck. Just before his departure from Eighth Army headquarters, he was passed the transcript of a complete Russian First Army order for an advance to the siege of Königsberg which revealed that it would halt some distance from the city on 26 August, well short of any position from which it could come to Second Army's assistance in the battle he planned to unleash.[21] Furnished with this assurance, he met von François, whose corps was just beginning to arrive on Samsonov's flank, in confident mood. Distance was working for him, the distance separating Samsonov and Rennenkampf's armies, and so now too was time, the self-imposed delay in Rennenkampf's advance which, had it been pressed, would have put the First Army well behind the lakeland zone in positions from which it could have marched south to Samsonov's assistance.

Then François, whose stubborn aggressiveness could take a wilfully unco-operative form, interrupted the smooth unrolling of a plan that should have brought his I corps, XVII and XX successively into action against Samsonov's flanks. Claiming that he was awaiting the arrival of his artillery by train, he was slow off the mark to attack on 25 August, and slow again the next day. Ludendorff arrived to energise the offensive, with characteristic effect, but François's hesitation had meanwhile had a desirable if unintended result. Unopposed in force to his front, Samsonov had thrust his centre forward, towards the Vistula against which he hoped to pin the Germans, thus exposing lengthening flanks both to François, now to his south, and to Mackensen and Scholtz, who were marching XVII and XX Corps down from the north. On 27 August François rediscovered his bite and pushed his men on. Samsonov, disregarding the danger to his rear, pressed on also. On 28 August his leading troops savaged a miscellaneous collection of German troops they found in their path and broke through almost to open country, with the Vistula beyond. Ludendorff, seized by a fit of the nerves his stolid appearance belied, ordered

François to detach a division to the broken units' assistance. François, creatively unco-operative on this occasion, did not obey but drove every battalion he had eastward at best speed. With the weight of Samsonov's army moving westward by different routes, there was little to oppose them. On the morning of 29 August, his leading infantry reached Willenberg, just inside East Prussia from Russian territory, and met German troops coming the other way. They belonged to Mackensen's XVII Corps, veterans of the fighting south of the Masurian Lakes, who had been attacking southward since the previous day. Contact between the claws of the two pincers – the units were the 151st Ermland Infantry of I Corps and the 5th Blücher Hussars of XVII – announced that Samsonov was surrounded.[22]

'Cauldron' battles were to be a repeated feature of the fighting in the Second World War, particularly in the east, where in 1941 the German army time and again surrounded Russians by the hundreds of thousands. Victories of encirclement were almost never to be achieved in the First. That was one reason which made Tannenberg – as Hindenburg decided to call the battle, in vindication of the defeat in 1410 of the Teutonic Knights by the Slavs at a place on the 1914 battlefield – so singular. The Germans counted 92,000 Russian prisoners, beside 50,000 enemy killed and wounded. The casualty list, already greatly exceeded in the west, was unremarkable by the standards of campaigns yet to come. The total of prisoners taken would rarely be exceeded in any comparable episode of the war or indeed approached. Tannenberg, as a result, became for the Germans their outstanding victory of the conflict. Not only had it saved the Prussian heartland from occupation by an enemy the German propagandists increasingly chose to depict as 'barbarian' – quite unfairly, for the Russian commanders, numbers of whom were Baltic Germans with family connections in East Prussia, had maintained high standards of behaviour among their soldiers – but it had also averted the danger of a deeper advance into industrial Silesia and towards Berlin.[23] Tannenberg was a deliverance, and celebrated as such. After the war the colours of the regiments that fought there were displayed in a monumental Tannenberg memorial, modelled on Stonehenge, in which the body of Hindenburg was interred after his death as President. In 1945, when the Russians reappeared in East Prussia in irresistible force, it was disinterred and the monument dynamited. The Tannenberg regiments' colours now hang in the Hamburg officer cadet school while Hindenburg's body has been given a final resting place at Schloss Hohenzollern, the seat of the imperial dynasty.[24]

Tannenberg had a military importance different from its symbolic significance, and far greater. It reversed the timetable of Germany's war plan. Before the triumph, victory was expected in the west, while the front in the east was to be held as best it might be. After Tannenberg, disaster in the east no longer threatened, while victory in the west continued to elude week after week. Tannenberg temporarily devastated the Russians. Poor Samsonov, overcome by the catastrophe, barely escaped with his life from the battle of encirclement. He did not keep it long. Riding with his officers, he repeatedly expressed despair: 'The Emperor trusted me. How can I face him again?'[25] Finding a means to be alone for a few moments, he shot himself. His body was later recovered, and buried on the family estate. It was a kinder ending than that met by so many of his soldiers, who died anonymously in the undergrowth of the Prussian forests, untended in their last hours, undiscovered in death. Their bones lie there to this day and the news of their passing was communicated to their families only by the expiry of hope. Tannenberg was the beginning of the long agony of the Tsar's armies which would culminate in their collapse in 1917.

Yet, for all the incompetence of their commanders and inadequacy of their means to fight, the Russians retained resilience, as they were to show time and again in the campaigns of 1915 and 1916. They were to show it immediately in 1914. Despite Samsonov's collapse, Rennenkampf refused in the aftermath of Tannenberg to accept defeat. When Hindenburg turned against him the whole weight of Eighth Army, now reinforced by the IX and Guard Reserve Corps from the west, he handled his troops with dexterity. It was they who were now outnumbered, despite the arrival of Tenth Army from the rear. First Army, Hindenburg's target, still only counted nine divisions, against the Germans' eighteen, but in what came to be called the battle of the Masurian Lakes, launched on 7 September, the same day as the opening of the battle of the Marne, it evaded all Hindenburg's efforts to organise an encirclement. François, directing the first stage, succeeded in cutting off some units at Lötzen in the heart of the lakeland. Thereafter Rennenkampf conducted a fighting retreat, in and above the lakes, switching units from one flank to another as need arose. On 13 September he crossed back into Russian territory, having extricated his whole army, drawing the Germans behind him. By 25 September delaying actions had allowed him the time and room to organise his own and Tenth Army for a counter-attack and on that day he unleashed it, driving the Germans from their positions, recapturing much of the ground lost and in places returning to the lines reached on the Angerrap during the August invasion.

GALICIA AND SERBIA

The high point of the Masurian Lakes counter-offensive, however, was a tactical rather than a strategic success, for it engaged only a fraction of Russia's forces. The majority were deployed across the southern face of the Polish salient, forcing the Austrians, whose main line of resistance ran along the crests of the Carpathians, through which the strategic passes led down to the Hungarian plain, to the Danube and towards the Austrian heartland. This was an enormous front, 300 miles in length from the junction of the Austrian and Russian borders with neutral Romania to Cracow in Austrian Poland, and defended by large fortifications, of which those at Lemberg (Lvov) and Przemysl had recently been modernised. The Russian war plan required the concentration on this sector of four armies, Third, Fourth, Fifth and Eighth, forming the South-Western Front under General Nikolai Ivanov, on mobilisation. They were to attack as soon as deployed. The Austrians, too, intended to attack as soon as mobilisation was completed. Because of confusion over choice of priorities between the fronts in Galicia and Serbia, however, the Austrians were slower to concentrate their force against Russia than they should have been, while the Russians, defying the German and Austrian staff appreciations, were quicker; their enemies had not made allowance for the fact that two-fifths of Russia's peacetime strength was stationed in the Polish salient, or for the eventuality that the *Stavka* would start the troops in Poland forward before general mobilisation had been completed. It was a crucial difference in attitude. The Teutonic general staffs, which had last gone to war over forty years earlier, could not conceive of large-scale operations beginning before everything their war plans stipulated was in place. The less programmatic Russians, with the Japanese War only recently over and the experience before that of decades of frontier fighting in Central Asia, were much readier to improvise. The result was that, by the end of August, the Russians had fifty-three infantry and eighteen cavalry divisions in place on the Austrian front, while the Austrians had only thirty-seven infantry and ten cavalry divisions to oppose them. The Russian formations, moreover, were larger than the Austrian; and while Russia was under pressure from France to mount operations that would divert German forces from the western front to the east, Austria was under even heavier pressure to act in relief of the outnumbered German Eighth Army in East Prussia.

Austria's principal emotional, if not rational, war aim, however, remained the punishment of Serbia, which had precipitated the July crisis by its involvement in the Sarajevo assassinations. Sense would have argued that Austria deployed its whole strength forward of the Carpathians to engage the Russians, the Serbs' protectors and great Slav brothers. Outrage, and decades of provocation, demanded the defeat of the Belgrade government and the upstart Karageorgevic dynasty. Conrad von Hötzendorf, the Austrian Chief of Staff, had long had prepared a plan to deal with Serbia alone, a situation known as 'War Case B'. During 1912–13, however, increasing consideration was given to the likelihood that a crisis with Serbia would precipitate a Russian war, 'War Case R', demanding that the Balkan army be reduced to strengthen that in Galicia.[26] The General Staff tinkered with the deployment of three groups: the 'A-Staffel' that would go to Galicia in the event of a Russian war, the 'Balkan Group' that would attack Serbia, and the 'B-Staffel' that would participate in either campaign, depending on the promptness of Russian mobilisation. The railway planning section prepared timetables accordingly.

In the event, the Austrians muddled. Conrad, whose hatred of the Serbs was almost pathological, claimed as mobilisation began that Russia's military intentions were not clear and that it was safe to send B-Staffel to join the Balkan group, which he did. When it became clear that Russia intended to attack in Galicia, which was not only Austria's strategy also but a solemn duty owed to the Germans, he decided, as he had to, that B-Staffel must go north; but as it was on its way south, and re-timetabling would present difficulties, he allowed it on 1 August to proceed after all and to take part in the attack on Serbia before re-entraining to the Galician front. It was given the mission of making a 'demonstration', to draw Serbian forces away from the main axis of the Austrian invasion.

The idea of a demonstration revealed how little the Austrians understood the Serbs' military qualities. In Vienna they were thought of as backward semi-barbarians. The Serbian officer corps' participation in the murder and mutilation of the Obrenovic King and Queen in 1903, and the widely reported practice of mutilation of corpses during the Balkan Wars, had led the Austrian army to imagine that a campaign in the Balkans would present little more difficulty than the British or French commonly encountered in their colonial campaigns in Africa or Asia. True, the Serbs had participated in the successful defeat of the Turks in 1912 but the Turks, too, were thought to be backward barbarians. The Austrians, despite the known impassability of Serbia's terrain, high, forested mountains cut by deep river valleys, with few roads and almost no railways, expected a walkover.

In fact the Serbs, if barbarian in the cruelty with which they waged war, were not militarily backward at all. Their system of conscription mobilised, even if by informal means, a higher proportion of the male population than in any other European country and their soldiers, from boys to old men, were naturally warlike as well as fiercely patriotic. They were also frugal and hardy. Their arms were varied; but every man had a weapon and the first-line units retained most of the modern weapons acquired during the Balkan Wars, including a hundred batteries of artillery and four machine guns per infantry regiment. With a third-line reserve of men aged forty to forty-five and 'capable soldiers of sixty and seventy, affectionately known as "uncles"' joining the first and second lines *(poziv),* Serbia could put 400,000 men into the field, almost as many as those in the Sixth, Fifth and Second Armies of Austria's B-Staffel.[27]

The Austrians nevertheless began with an advantage, for the Serbian commander, the *voivode* (war leader) Radomir Putnik, expected an attack from the north out of Hungary across the Danube towards Belgrade. Instead, Conrad's plan was for an attack from the west, out of Bosnia, into the salient of Serbian territory enclosed by the Drina and Sava rivers. There was sense in it, for the salient is one of the few areas of level terrain in the whole of the country, and at first the advance, begun on 12 August, went well, benefiting from the Austrians' ability to attack concentrically, south across the Sava, east across the Drina. Had Putnik hurried his troops forward, they might have been encircled and trapped. The canny veteran – *voivode* is an honorific given only to generals who have won a victory, as Putnik had spectacularly done against the Turks – declined the risk. Instead he organised his main line of resistance behind the plain, along the River Vardar and the high ground beyond. The defenders did not arrive until the night of 14 August, having force-marched sixty miles in forty-eight hours, but, once in place, brought devastating fire to bear on the attackers at close range. Potiorek, the Austrian commander, signalled Conrad to request the intervention of Second Army, the 'swing' formation of the R and B Plans, in order to take pressure off. Conrad refused, despite Potiorek's report of a 'frightful heat' in the fighting.[28] He appealed again on 16 August, as the fighting intensified, and a third time on 17 August, when the request was granted, on condition that the 'swing' formation's departure for Galicia was not delayed. The battle on the Drina and Sava now involved the Austrian Fifth and Sixth Armies, part of the Second and the whole of the Serbian, which, driven back and forward by the weight of Austrian artillery fire, always returned to the attack and gradually overbore the Austrians by its persistence. On 19 August the commander of the Austrian Fifth Army had withdrawn it across the Sava. The Second Army made a final, ineffective intervention on 20 August, before departing to join the A-Staffel in Galicia, as it should have done at the start. The Sixth Army had never been properly engaged and joined the general withdrawal. By 24 August the Serbs had expelled the enemy from the whole of their territory.

That was not the end of the fighting in Serbia in 1914. On 6 September the Serbs followed up the victory they had won, and crossed into Austrian territory. It was an unwise manoeuvre and they lost nearly 5,000 casualties when forced to withdraw across the Sava. Later in the month, however, the Serbs found a weak spot in Potiorek's defences on the Drina, crossed into Bosnia and raced towards Sarajevo, panicking the prison officials there into transferring Gavrilo Princip and his accomplices to the fortress of Theresienstadt in Bohemia. The murderer of the Archduke would die of tuberculosis in April 1918 at Theresienstadt which, in the Second World War, became infamous as 'the model ghetto' for elderly, uprooted German Jews, later to be exterminated in the Final Solution. The Serbian occupation of eastern Bosnia lasted only forty days. On 6 November, Potiorek, whose peacetime command Franz Ferdinand had visited Sarajevo to inspect, opened a general offensive with strong reinforcements behind a heavy artillery preparation and, by concentric attack, drove the Serbs back from one line to another in north-eastern Serbia as far as the line of the Morava, eighty miles from the Bosnian frontier. Twice Putnik ordered a general disengagement and retreat, through a worsening winter that covered the hills with three feet of snow. On 2 December the capital, Belgrade, fell and King Peter released his soldiers from their oaths, to go home without dishonour if they chose.[29] He announced that he intended to continue the fight and appeared in the front line, carrying a rifle. His example may have marked a turning point. Putnik, believing the Austrians overextended, launched a new offensive on 3 December which broke the Austrian line and in twelve days of fighting drove the enemy clear of Serbian territory. Over 40,000 out of the 200,000 who had campaigned against Serbia since November were lost. The *Shvaba*, as the Serbs contemptuously nicknamed the Austrians and Germans, would not resume their effort to conquer the kingdom until the autumn of 1915. Then the Serbian epic would take a grimmer turn.

The Battles of Lemberg

The Serbian campaign, however, had never been more than a sideshow to Austria's great battle on its northern frontier with Russian Poland. There operations had begun with an encounter battle. Both the Austrians and Russians had pre-war plans to attack as soon as deployment was completed. Both marched to the offensive, with varying results. Conrad's plan was to strengthen his left and attempt an encirclement of the Russian flank in the great Polish plain south of Warsaw, while conducting an 'active defence' on his right, in eastern Galicia, where he could use the great fortresses of Lemberg and Przemysl as a buttress. The Russian plan was also for an encirclement in western Galicia but for rather more than active defence in the east. There had been divided counsels on the Russian side, Alexeyev, Chief of Staff of the South-Western Front, favouring the western effort, Danisov, the guiding light of the *Stavka*, the eastern. A sort of compromise plan for a 'double envelopment' was devised, but the Russians, though stronger than the Austrians, lacked the strength to impose equal pressure in both sectors. The opening phase of the Galician battle was, in consequence, to be confused and indecisive.

Yet physical circumstances favoured the Russians. The terrain suited their enormous formations of hard-marching infantry and their plentiful cavalry. So did the geographical features defining the boundaries of the theatre of operations. The Austrian positions on the forward slope of the Carpathians formed a salient, which projected between the River Vistula and its tributary, the San, on the left and the River Dniester on the right. The Vistula, running north, boxed in the Austrians on the left; the Dniester, running south-east, gave the

168

Russians a strong support to any thrust they might make against the Carpathian salient from the right. Geography thus forced the Austrians to advance into a pocket, which the Russians threatened to dominate on two sides while being able to ignore the third.

A major additional disadvantage to the Austrians was the unreliability of parts of its army. This is a much debated matter, over which opinion has swung backwards and forwards ever since the war years. During the war, Allied publicists made much of the disaffection of Franz Josef's Slav soldiers and of their sense of brotherhood with the Russians on the other side. The readiness of some Slav contingents, particularly Czech and Austrian Serb, to surrender at will was widely reported and the collapse of the Austrian army at the end of 1918 was taken to confirm the truth of Allied propaganda about the intrinsically unstable nature of the empire. There were post-war revisions, arguing that desertions were the exception and that the army as a whole had remained remarkably *Kaisertreu*; with reason, for no Austrian defeat can be attributed to large-scale disloyalty. Today, opinion seems to have moved to the centre. Of the nine language groups of the army, of which 44 per cent was Slav (Czech, Slovak, Croatian, Serb, Slovene, Ruthenian, Polish and Bosnian Muslim), 28 per cent German, 18 per cent Hungarian, 8 per cent Romanian and 2 per cent Italian, the Germans were always dependable, if some never wholly enthusiastic; the Hungarians, non-Slavs and privileged co-equals, remained reliable until defeat stared them in the face at the end; the Catholic Croats had a long record of loyalty to the empire, which many of them maintained; the Poles, hating the Russians, distrusting the Germans and enjoying large electoral and social privileges under the Habsburgs, were *Kaisertreu*; the Bosnian Muslims, sequestered in special, semi-sepoy regiments, were dependable; the Italians and the rest of the Slavs, particularly the Czechs and Serbs, lost the enthusiasm of mobilisation quickly.[30] Once war ceased to be a brief adventure, the army became for them 'a prison of the nations', with the ubiquitous German superiors acting as gaolers.

This was an unhappy destiny for an army which, for much of Franz Josef's reign, had been a successful and even popular multi-ethnic organisation. Commanded in their own languages, spared the brutal discipline of the Kaiser's army, prettily uniformed, well-fed, loaded with traditions and honours that ascended to the seventeenth-century Turkish siege of Vienna and beyond, the regiments of the imperial army – Tyrolean Rifles, Hungarian Hussars, Dalmatian Light Horse

– made a kaleidoscope of the empire's diversity and, for three years of a young conscript's life, provided an enjoyable diversion from the routine of workshop or plough. Annual manoeuvres were a pleasurable summer holiday.[31] Regimental anniversaries, when the band played, wine flowed, and the honorary colonel, an archduke, a prince, perhaps the Emperor himself, came to visit, were joyous feasts. The return home, time expired, brought more celebration and adult respect. The reality of war was a distant eventuality.

Reality intruded rapidly and cruelly on the Carpathian front in August 1914. At the first encounter, the Austrians prevailed. They deployed thirty-seven infantry divisions, organised from left to right on a front of 250 miles, into the First, Fourth and Third Armies, with detachments on either flank, and a screen of ten cavalry divisions spread out ahead. The Russians, moving forward in an arc opposite, deployed the Fourth, Fifth, Third and Eighth Armies, comprising in all fifty-three divisions of infantry and eighteen of cavalry. Despite the Russians' superiority in numbers, Conrad's first thrust succeeded. His left wing ran into the Russian right at Krasnik, just across the River San inside Russian territory on 23 August, and attacked.[32] The leading Austrian formation was the First Army, largely composed of Slovaks from Pressburg (Bratislava) and Poles from Cracow; both Catholic, the Slovaks as yet unpoliticised, the Poles anti-Russian, they fought fiercely for their Catholic Emperor in a three-day battle against the Russian Fourth Army which had come forward without waiting for its reserves.[33] The Russian General Staff recorded that, at the opening, 'the 18th Division fell under violent enemy fire, which obliged the Riazan and Riaysk Regiments to retreat ... while the 5th Light Infantry were almost encircled'.[34] Things went from bad to worse. By 26 August, the Russians had retired twenty miles towards Lublin (where Stalin would establish his puppet Polish government in 1945). On the same day the Austrian Fourth Army encountered the advancing Russian Third at Komarov, just short of the River Bug; again, the Russians were unlucky in the racial composition of the enemy they met: the Austrian II Corps was formed of Vienna regiments, including the capital's Hoch and Deutschmeister, whose colonel was always the Emperor, in tribute to the dynasty's association with the Grand Master of the Teutonic Knights; the IX Corps was raised from Sudetenland Germans and the XVI from Hungarian Magyars. No more solidly imperial foundation for an Austrian victory could have been assembled and, after a week of fighting, it had been gained. By the conclusion, the Russians were almost surrounded.

Then the geographical insecurity of the Austrian position began to assert itself. East of Komarov, the frontier with Russia made a sharp turn to run south-eastward towards the border with neutral Romania. Superficially, this flank offered was easily defensible, since a succession of river lines, the Bug, the Dniester and its tributaries, the two Lipas and the Wereszyca, ran behind it at intervals of twenty or thirty miles; the headwaters of the Bug, moreover, were protected by the great fortress of Lemberg (Lvov), with a second even stronger fortress at Przemysl not far in its rear. The Austrian Third Army should, in such terrain, have easily been able to present a strong resistance to the Russians, since the Second Army in Serbia was now sending back to it the divisions attached to the Balkan Group, while the heart of the army itself was the famous XIV Innsbruck Corps, containing the four regiments of Tyrolean *Kaiserjäger* and their *Kaiserschützen* reserve battalions. These eagle-feathered mountain sharpshooters were the truest of the true, bearing a particular loyalty to the Emperor, who was colonel-in-chief to all four regiments.

Third Army, however, had been disfavoured by Conrad's decision to give it an 'active defensive' role, while First and Fourth attempted the encirclement of the Russian flank in western Galicia. As a result, it was deployed well inside Austrian territory, some sixty miles behind the frontier, standing on the River Gnita Lipa. There it should have been safe, had it stayed put. On 25 August, however, Brudermann, its commander, learning of the advance of 'five or six Russian divisions' westward from Tarnopol, decided to act offensively and moved forward.[35] It was the day, moreover, when he lost XIV Corps, called northward to Second Army. By transfers and movements of formational boundaries, his army now consisted largely of Romanians (XII Corps), Slovenes and Italians (III Corps) and local Ruthenian-speaking Ukrainians (XI Corps), more akin to Russians than any nationality within the Habsburg empire.[36] Not only was the ethnic mix almost the least *Kaisertreu* in Franz Josef's army, the Third Army was also to find itself grossly outnumbered by the Russian Third Army it was advancing to meet. When the encounter came, less than a hundred Austrian infantry battalions, supported by 300 guns, ran headlong into nearly two hundred Russian, supported by 685.[37] In three days of fighting in the broken country between the two Lipa rivers, the Austrians were first defeated at Zlotchow, twenty-five miles short of Tarnopol, and then driven back in confusion, sometimes panic; some of the defeated Austrians fled as far as Lemberg.

Had the Russians followed up their victory, the whole of the insecure Austrian wing might have been overwhelmed. Ruzski, the responsible general, did not follow up and Brudermann's Third Army survived. It was an odd situation, though not unprecedented in war before or since. Each side misappreciated the extent of its own achievements. Ruzski believed he had won no more than 'a fine defensive success', and paused to regroup his forces.[38] Conrad believed he had won a great victory on the other side of the theatre of operations, that the reverse on Third Army's front was local and temporary and that, if he reinforced Brudermann, he could further the double envelopment which was the basis of his war plan. By 30 August he had increased Austrian strength opposite Ruzski to a hundred and fifty battalions, supported by 828 guns, largely through the return of most of the Balkan Group to Second Army. Since Ruzski was not advancing, he judged the moment ripe to reopen the offensive, largely with Second Army fighting on Third's right, the two forming an army group under the successful commander of Second Army, Eduard von Böhm-Ermolli, brought down to energise activity. Under Conrad's orders, Second Army attacked again on 29 August between the Lipa rivers, this time with results even more disastrous than at first. Russian strength opposite now exceeded three hundred and fifty battalions, supported by 1,304 guns, and, in the ensuing maelstrom, 20,000 Austrians were captured and thousands more killed and wounded.

In the face of all the evidence, Conrad continued to believe he was winning. His local successes on the left wing, the dilatory Russian movement on the right, persuaded him that he could allow Third and Second Armies to make a deep withdrawal behind Lemberg, drawing the Russians after them and then bring Fourth Army down from the north to attack the enemy in flank. The main line of resistance was to be the River Wereszyca, a tributary of the Dniester running southward between Lemberg and Przemysl. He was motivated in part towards this doomed enterprise by a desire to emulate the success of Hindenburg and Ludendorff in East Prussia and by the apparent success of the German armies in the west; the decision for the Lemberg operation was taken before the opening of the battle of the Marne. He was also driven by the growing impatience of his allies with the Austrians' failure to pull their weight. 'Our small army in East Prussia', Kaiser Wilhelm remarked acidly in early September to

Conrad's representative at OHL, 'has drawn twelve enemy corps against it and destroyed one-half and engaged one half . . . more than this could not be demanded.' The Kaiser exaggerated; but, since Conrad was opposed at most by fifteen corps, the taunt stung. He was determined to drive his tired and battered armies to victory.[39]

In the event, the plan nearly worked. The Russians were slow to follow up the abandonment of Lemberg, which they did not enter until 3 September, thus allowing time for the Austrian Fourth Army, exhausted and depleted by losses as it was, to make its advance across the front of the Russian Third Army towards Lemberg. The Third and Second Armies actually won some success on the Wereszyca position, thus delaying for a few days the closure of the Russian encirclement of the Austrian centre, the imminent danger of which was becoming even more evident. The Russians perceived it; on 5 September Alexeyev communicated to Davidov, 'the vigorous Austrian effort to break our dispositions [north of Lemberg] may be regarded as in paralysis. The moment for announcing our counter-offensive is at hand.'[40] Conrad continued to ignore the threat. The Fourth Army marched on until, at Rava Russka, thirty miles north of Lemberg, it fell on 6 September into heavy combat with a concentration of the Russian Third Army and was halted.

Conrad's efforts to outflank with a weaker force a stronger force that was attempting to outflank him now threatened catastrophe. A huge gap had opened between his First Army still battling against the Russians in the north and his other three, locked in conflict behind Lemberg. He had no reserves of his own and the detachment of a third-line German reserve formation to assist resulted only in severe mauling. The Russians, gathering reinforcements daily, including the Ninth Army which had been assembling near Warsaw, stood with open jaws ready to close on the Austrian Fourth, Third and Second Armies. Sixteen Russian corps now faced eleven Austrian, most of which were bunched in a narrow pocket which the enemy dominated from both sides. First Army, moreover, was suffering a battering it could not resist in its isolated situation to the north, despite the efforts of the alpine troops of XIV Corps, which was fighting as a link formation between the two halves of the Austrian front into which Conrad's concentration had now been divided. He appealed to the Germans for help; the Kaiser replied 'Surely you cannot ask any more of [Hindenburg and Ludendorff] them than [they] have already achieved.'[41] He forced Second and Third Armies into a renewed offensive in the Wereszyca. When that failed, and with Russian cavalry raiding through the gaps in his line of resistance into the Austrian rear, he had no recourse but to order a general retreat, first to the River San, then to the Dunajec, a tributary of the Vistula only thirty miles east of Cracow, the capital of Habsburg Poland and the greatest city of Catholic Eastern Europe between Vienna and Warsaw. Przemysl, the huge fortress guarding the gaps in the Carpathian chain where the Rivers San and Dniester rise to flow into the Polish plain, had been abandoned, leaving its garrison of 150,000 soldiers surrounded behind Russian lines. Austrian territory to a depth of a hundred and fifty miles had been surrendered. The Habsburg Emperor had lost 400,000 men out of the 1,800,000 mobilised, including 300,000 as prisoners.[42] Among the heaviest of the casualties were those that had fallen on the 50,000 men of the XIV Tyrolean Corps, formed of Franz Josef's four treasured *Kaiserjäger* regiments, their *Kaiserschützen* reservists, the 6th Mounted Rifle Regiment and the corps mountain artillery batteries.[43] No less than 40,000 had become casualties, a loss that deprived the Austrian army of its best and bravest element, never to be replaced.[44] They had paid the price of acting as Conrad's task force in the crucial effort to hold its front together during the climactic battle around Lemberg.

WARFARE IN THE EAST

The nature of these titanic battles on the Eastern Front is difficult to represent at a human or individual level. The Russian army, 80 per cent peasant when a majority of Russian peasants were still illiterate, left no literature to compare with that of the Western Front. 'Personal reminiscences are very rare. Nobody collected them'; without amanuenses, the voice of the Russian peasant soldier could not speak to posterity.[45] The better-educated Austrians have left equally few recollections of service in the ranks, probably because the disaster of the war was overtaken in personal experiences by the even greater upheaval of the Habsburg empire's collapse. Intellectuals and artists – Wittgenstein, Rilke, Kokoschka – have bequeathed letters and diaries and at least one classic novel, Hasek's *The Good Soldier Svejk,* which is not to be taken as representative of all Habsburg soldiers' attitude; but they are isolated memorials. Some sense of the imperial army's ordeal may be caught in the sombre regimental tablets in Viennese churches, still today decorated on regimental anniversaries with ribbons and wreaths. For the most part, however, the experience of the Tsar's and Austrian Kaiser's armies in the vast campaigns of movement in 1914 has passed out of memory. Can it be reconstructed?

Photographs help, even if of pre-war manoeuvres; the rarer wartime photographs are more valuable still.[46] All show men ranked in deep masses, often shoulder to shoulder. Perhaps they are seeking, in the German phrase, 'the feel of cloth', one way men find courage in the face of fire. Long bayonets are fixed to rifles, pouches and accoutrements encumber their movements, thick clothing bulks out their bodies. To bullets it offers no protection. Within a few months, most armies will have adopted the steel helmet, the first reversion to the use of armour since its disappearance in the seventeenth century. The opening months of the First World War marked the termination of two hundred years of a style of infantry fighting which, with decreasing logic, taught that drill and discipline was the best defence against missile weapons, however much improved. Such photographs demonstrate large-scale disobedience of tactical regulations, which in all armies laid down rules of dispersion. In the Russian army, the regulations of 1912 laid down that the lowest unit, the platoon of fifty men, should extend over a hundred paces, that is, with a yard between each soldier.[47] At the same time, it prescribed a front of attack for a battalion of 500 yards, which meant that the commander should rank it in four lines of four platoons each. Since those forward would then mask the fire of those behind, it is understandable that regulations should have been discarded and the bulk of the battalion massed in the front line. Such practice obeyed, if not the letter, then the spirit of regulations, which required attacking infantry to build up a 'superiority of fire' with an advanced skirmishing line, and its supports then to rush the enemy from a distance of a hundred yards or so. The Austrian army had a similar doctrine.[48] The regulations of 1911 insisted that the riflemen of the infantry could 'without the support of the other arms, even in inferior numbers, gain victory as long as [they] were tough and brave'. This was a view common to the continental armies, German, Austrian and Russian as well as French, the most ideological exponent of the 'spirit of the offensive', and was based not merely on affirmation but on an analysis of the nature of recent combat in, particularly, the Russo-Japanese War. It was accepted that high levels of firepower entailed high casualty rates; it was still believed that a determination to accept heavy casualties would bring victory.[49]

At Tannenberg and Lemberg, therefore, we must imagine the

attacking infantry moving, in dense masses, to assault enemy positions held by infantry also densely massed, if behind improvised defences, with the field artillery, deployed in the open at close range behind the firing line, delivering salvoes in direct support. In the Russian army, the 1912 regulations 'prescribed that fire be delivered in short, rapid bursts, with field guns firing over the heads of advancing infantry'.[50] No army had procedures, or indeed the equipment, to correct aim. Telephones were few (Samsonov's whole army had only twenty-five) and telephone lines were almost automatically broken as soon as combat commenced; communication was by flag or hand signal, or by rumour; regulation of artillery fire was most often effected along human line of sight.[51]

The 1914 battles in the Eastern Front therefore closely resembled those fought by Napoleon a hundred years earlier, as indeed did those of the Marne campaign, with the difference that infantry lay down rather than stood up to fire and that the fronts of engagement extended to widths a hundred times greater. The duration of battles extended also, from a day to a week or more. The outcomes, nevertheless, were gruesomely similar: huge casualties, both absolutely and as a proportion of numbers engaged, and dramatic results. After Borodino in 1812, a battle of almost unprecedented length and intensity, Napoleon advanced a hundred miles to Moscow; after Lemberg, Conrad retreated a hundred and fifty miles to the outskirts of Cracow.

THE BATTLES FOR WARSAW

The Austrian collapse on the Carpathian front precipitated one of the first great strategic crises of the war. Not only was the Hungarian half of the Austrian empire, beyond the mountain chain, threatened with invasion – the Russian generals were even jauntily discussing among themselves the capture of Budapest, Hungary's capital – but the territory of heartland Germany suddenly lay under threat of a Russian drive into Silesia, towards the great cities of Breslau and Posen. East Prussia was not out of danger, while at the far southern end of the front, Brusilov, best of the Russian generals, was menacing the Carpathian passes. Even Moltke, worn down as he was by the evident failure of the Schlieffen Plan, could find time to turn his attention from the battle of the Aisne to the affairs of the Eastern Front, and on his last day as Chief of Staff, before his supersession by Falkenhayn on 15

September, he telephoned Ludendorff to order the formation of a new 'southern' army, southern because it was to concentrate south of East Prussia, to fill the gap between the victorious Eighth Army and the crumbling Austrians. Ludendorff, who was as alarmed as Moltke by the worsening situation, made the counter-proposal that the new army incorporate most of Eighth Army's troops, but that was a step Moltke lacked the energy to take. His successor did not hesitate. As incisive in mind as he was imposing in appearance, Falkenhayn, on 16 September, announced that most of Eighth Army would leave East Prussia to join the new army, numbered the Ninth, with Ludendorff as Chief of Staff and Hindenburg as commander; Hoffman, their operations officer during the Tannenberg battle, would join in that post. On 18 September Ludendorff motored to meet Conrad and agree with him a new plan to avert the danger under which the Austro-German front lay. The Ninth Army, instead of standing to await a Russian offensive into Silesia, would attack across the upper Vistula and drive towards Warsaw, the Russian centre of operations on the Polish front.[52]

The Russians, however, had plans of their own. During September, in fact, they had too many plans, the supreme command, the *Stavka*, having one, and the North-Western and South-Western Fronts others. The Russian General Staff reports record 'dissension between [them], resulting in different directives'.[53] The North-Western Front, now commanded by Ruzski, was, by his estimation, dangerously exposed as a result of the German successes in East Prussia and must retreat a long way, perhaps as far as the River Niemen, a hundred miles east of the Masurian Lakes; if necessary, Warsaw itself must be abandoned. The South-Western Front, by contrast, wanted to press its victorious pursuit of the Austrians westward towards Cracow. The *Stavka* had a radical alternative: the bulk of the Russian force on the Eastern Front would disengage, concentrate around Warsaw and the great fortress of Ivangorod, upstream on the Vistula, and then launch a concerted offensive towards Silesia, with the purpose of taking the war directly into Germany.

All these plans, though particularly those of Ruzski and the *Stavka*, characterise a distinctively Russian style of warmaking, that of using space rather than force as a medium of strategy. No French general would have proposed surrendering the cherished soil of his country to gain military advantage; the German generals in East Prussia had taken the defence of its frontier to be a sacred duty. To the Russians, by contrast, inhabitants of an empire that stretched nearly 6000 miles from the ploughland of western Poland to the ice of the Bering Straits, a hundred miles here or there was a trifle of military manoeuvre. In their wars with the Turks, the Swedes, above all with Napoleon, whole provinces had been lost, only to be regained when distance and the durability of the peasant soldier defeated the invader. As in 1812, so in 1914; to give ground now would be to repossess it later, and all to the enemy's disadvantage. By 23 September, the *Stavka* had acquired clear intelligence that the German Ninth Army was concentrated in Silesia and was advancing towards Warsaw. The Grand Duke Nicholas, who had now taken control of the *Stavka*, accordingly decided to withdraw most of his forces from contact and await the German advance. Meanwhile, Brusilov would be left to menace the eastern Carpathians, while the Tenth Army would be despatched to mount a new offensive against East Prussia. When Hindenburg's and Ludendorff's Ninth Army appeared in the centre, the Russian Fourth and Ninth Armies would advance from Warsaw to oppose it, while the remainder of the *Stavka*'s strategic mass, Second, Fifth and First Armies, would sweep down to take it in flank.

This was war on a titanic scale, as large in numbers committed as in the west and larger by far in terms of space and depth of movement than in any of the operations in that comparatively constricted theatre. The Russians, who were beginning to receive important reinforcements from distant Siberian military districts, successfully transferred most of their units engaged in the Carpathians to the Warsaw area in late September, without attracting the enemy's attention; the Austrians, finding their front had been thinned out, followed, but to their eventual disadvantage. All they gained thereby was the chance to relieve the garrison of Przemysl on 9 October, soon to be surrounded again when they paid the penalty of joining the Germans in Ludendorff's ill-conceived offensive towards Warsaw. The *Stavka* also enjoyed the satisfaction of watching the Russian Tenth Army return to the fray on the East Prussian frontier. Though, in the battle of Augustow (29 September – 5 October), its attack was held, its intervention caused Hindenburg and Ludendorff considerable alarm. Eighth Army, overconfident after the glory of Tannenberg, had not bothered to entrench its positions and the Russians achieved some easy tactical successes before they were checked.

By early October there were really four fronts in the east: from north to south, a German-Russian front on the eastern border of East Prussia; an Austro-German-Russian front on the Vistula; a Russian-Austrian front on the San; and a Russian-Austrian front in the eastern Carpathians. The whole extent, from the Baltic to the Romanian border, was nearly 500 miles, though with a gap of 100 miles in the north between Warsaw and East Prussia, thinly screened by cavalry. It was in the centre, however, where the Vistula flows northward from Ivangorod to Warsaw that the drama of a true war of movement, greater than any seen in Europe since the campaign of Austerlitz, was unfolding. There two complementary outflanking offensives were in motion: the German Ninth Army was marching down the west bank of the Vistula, Hindenburg and Ludendorff believing that the Russians were not in strength near Warsaw and could be encircled from the north; the Russians were preparing to cross the Vistula from the east below Ivangorod, to which the Austrians had imprudently advanced, and to march up above Warsaw, there to launch their own outflanking movement against Hindenburg and Ludendorff.

Had the Germans had any better means of mobility than the feet of their soldiers and horses they might have pulled off the manoeuvre: Hitler's eastern marshals, twenty-five years later, would have thought the circumstances ideal for an armoured encirclement; but the Kaiser's generals had no such means. Worse, the Russians had superiority of numbers: from Warsaw to Przemysl they deployed fifty-five infantry divisions against thirty-one Austrian and thirteen German.[54] When Ludendorff appreciated, on 18 October, that the Ninth Army was in imminent danger of defeat if he pushed it on towards Warsaw, he decided to withdraw it. Conrad, who had followed the Russians' deliberate retreat from Przemysl to the San, was less prudent. He tried to attack towards Ivangorod on 22 October, was defeated and on 26 October was forced to retreat; Przemysl, with its garrison of 150,000 men, was left surrounded for a second time, an Austrian island in a sea of Russians, while 40,000 soldiers of Conrad's First Army were killed, wounded or captured. The Austrians ended up near Cracow, whither they had been pushed after their defeat in the Galician battles of August, the Germans only fifty miles from Breslau in Silesia, near their starting point for the march on Warsaw.

WINTER BATTLES IN GALICIA AND THE CARPATHIANS

The battle of Warsaw was an undoubted Russian victory. Though it had not resulted in the encirclement the *Stavka* sought, it demonstrated the Russians' superiority in the warfare of manoeuvre and even in the strategy of deception. Despite an alleged German advantage in radio interception, it was Ludendorff who had been surprised by the Russian redeployment along the Vistula from Ivangorod to Warsaw, which had been carried out with speed and in secrecy. The question remained for the Russians: what to do next? The *Stavka* was not in doubt. It would resume its planned offensive, delayed by the German Ninth Army's thrust towards Warsaw, and on 2 November issued the necessary directive.[55] The continuing arrival of reinforcements from the Siberian, Central Asian and Caucasian military districts supplied the necessary force. As soon as dispositions had been made, the central mass, consisting of the Second and Fifth Armies, would press forward through Breslau and Posen towards Berlin. Meanwhile the southern armies would also go over to the offensive between Cracow and Przemysl, with the aim of 'completing' the destruction of the Austrian forces in Galicia and the Carpathians.[56]

There were two impediments to this plan, particularly as they affected the central offensive. The first was the doubtful ability of the Russians to move their troops at the required speed to the point of encounter with the enemy. During the manoeuvre which had brought the Russian mass so skilfully to Warsaw and Ivangorod in October, the *Stavka* had been able to utilise the comparatively extensive rail network of central Poland. Western Poland, however, had deliberately been deprived of railways as a defensive measure; there were only four east-west lines and only two rail crossings over the Vistula.[57] Moreover, during their retreat from Warsaw the previous month, the Germans had destroyed the rail network behind them for a depth of a hundred miles. The second impediment was positive rather than negative. Ludendorff was himself planning a resumption of the offensive, this time from bases further to the rear than in October, but with the same object: to take the Russians in flank in the plains of western Poland and cut them off from their Warsaw base. Making use of the undamaged rail link between Silesia and Thorn, the old fortress city standing on the Vistula at the point it entered German territory in West Prussia, he relocated thither the whole of Ninth Army by 10

November. It consisted of eleven divisions, including reinforcements brought urgently from the Western Front at the demand of Hindenburg who, on 1 November, had become Commander-in-Chief in the east.[58]

Ninth Army attacked on 11 November, hitting V Siberian Corps in its over-extended and unfortified positions with a great weight of artillery. A gap of thirty miles was quickly opened between the Siberians and the rest of the army to which it belonged, Second, which had already advanced some distance towards the German frontier.[59] Although the Germans were outnumbered by the Russians on this front, by twenty-four divisions to fifteen, they had the advantage and pressed on. It was only on the fourth day of their offensive, sometimes called the Second Battle of Warsaw, that the *Stavka* realised it had a crisis on its hands; fortunately, it recognised almost simultaneously that the situation could be saved only by precipitate retreat. It ordered a disengagement, which was carried out with great efficiency. In two days of forced march, the Russian Second Army fell back on the great cotton-weaving town of Lodz, a railway centre stuffed with supplies. It was now the Germans' turn to be on the wrong foot. Russian outflanking forces appeared from north and south and three German reserve divisions were for a time surrounded.[60] They were extricated with difficulty; so confident was the *Stavka* of collaring them that trains had been sent to Lodz to take their soldiers into captivity.

The battle of Lodz ended on 23 November neither as a Russian defeat nor as a German victory. Ludendorff managed to represent it as a victory all the same and so extract from Falkenhayn the transfer of four German Corps from west to east, the II, III Reserve, XII and XXI Reserve, for use on the northern sector of operations as the Tenth Army; another corps, XXIV Reserve, arrived from France to join the Austrians on the southern sector. The reinforcements deployed in the north were misused. During December they were committed to a series of frontal assaults which achieved the fall of Lodz on 6 December but then petered out after an advance of some thirty miles to the rivers Rawka and Bzura, little tributaries of the Vistula south-west of Warsaw. There the terrain is excellent for offensive operations, wide, unobstructed farming land where, in 1939, the Polish army would achieve its only successful counter-attack against Hitler's Blitzkrieg.[61] It is also well-suited to defence, if troops will dig, and the Russians were excellent at digging. Confronted by their trenches, the Germans dug also, so that the coming of winter found the central sector of the

Eastern Front completely immobilised. It would remain frozen, militarily as well as physically, until the following summer.

In the south the arrival of the German reinforcements, particularly the 47th Reserve Division of XXIV Reserve Corps, was to achieve quite different results. During November the Austrians had rallied, despite their earlier setbacks and the terrible losses those entailed, and had staged a series of counter-attacks around Cracow. Joined by the right wing of the German Ninth Army, now commanded by Mackensen in place of the promoted Hindenburg (his and Ludendorff's theatre headquarters was known as OberOst), and reinforced by Böhm-Ermolli's Second Army from the Carpathians, they succeeded, in confused fighting and at great cost, in gaining ground north of the Vistula between Cracow and Czestochowa, holy city of the Polish people. The Russian South-Western Front Armies – Second, Fifth, Fourth, Ninth, Third and Eleventh – were present in greater strength, however, and were able to bring up reinforcements. After ten days of fighting, which began on 16 November, Conrad had to accept defeat and draw his troops back to positions closer to the German border than those from which he had started. South of Cracow things ended worse. Because the front in the Carpathians had been stripped of troops for the Cracow-Czestochowa offensive, the five main passes through the mountains stood exposed to a Russian advance. Brusilov captured the Lupkow pass on 20 November and by 29 November Boroevic, his Austrian opponent, faced the prospect of an enemy offensive against Budapest.

Then the Austrians' fortunes quite unexpectedly changed for the better, the result of their taking a well-judged initiative at a moment when material circumstances particularly disfavoured the enemy. Indecision, to which the Russian high command was so prone, further aided the Austrian initiative. On 29 November the Grand Duke Nicholas summoned Ruzski and Ivanov, the two Front commanders, to the *Stavka*'s headquarters at Siedlce, to discuss future operations. They disagreed, as they had done so often before. Ruzski wanted to withdraw the North-Western Front, because of the losses it had suffered at Lodz, to Warsaw. Ivanov, by contrast, scenting opportunity in the setbacks he had inflicted on the Austrians on the Cracow-Czestochowa line, wanted to regroup his forces and return to the offensive. 'The way to Berlin lies though Austria-Hungary', he argued.[62] He got his way; but his freedom of action depended not upon the permission of the Grand Duke but on availability of supplies and reinforcements. Reinforcements were plentiful, as many as 1,400,000 recruits having been inducted between October and November, but they were untrained and many lacked weapons. Munitions were severely deficient. Russian factories had not yet achieved the levels of output they would in 1915 and, with the White Sea closed by ice, and the Baltic and Black Seas by the enemy navies, there were no imports. The artillery was rationed to ten rounds per gun per day.

Conrad struck while these circumstances prevailed. He had perceived a weak point at the junction of the Russian Third Army, south of Cracow, with Brusilov's Eighth Army in the Carpathians where, between the towns of Limanowa and Lapanow, a gap of nearly twenty miles yawned. Opposite he assembled the best of the troops available to him, the German 43rd Division and the Austrian XIV Corps. The German division was fresh, the XIV Corps was not. Thousands of its Tyrolean riflemen had been killed in the September fighting near Lemberg and the reserves to replace the losses had been hard to find. Surprise, nevertheless, was on the side of the task force and on 3 December it struck. In four days of fighting the Russians were pushed back forty miles. Then enemy reinforcements began to appear and on 10 December Conrad's drive was halted. It had, nevertheless, allowed Boroevic to go over to the offensive in the Carpathians and to secure new and stronger positions on the forward mountain slopes. As a result, the battle of Limanowa-Lapanow not only blocked Ivanov's plan to thrust past Cracow towards Germany but also punctured the Russian dream of an advance on Budapest. It was therefore in its effects a double victory, nullifying the strategies both of a direct invasion of German territory and of an indirect victory over Germany through the defeat of Austria-Hungary.

Yet, though a victory, Limanowa-Lapanow was also a last gasp. Never again would the Imperial and Royal Army unilaterally initiate a decisive operation or deliver a conclusion an Austrian commander could claim as his own. Thereafter, whether in the conflict with Russia or in the coming war with Italy, its victories – Gorlice, Caporetto – would be won only because of German help and under German supervision. As it was, the army's victory at Limanowa owed much to the loan of German troops. Henceforward it would always fight as the German army's junior and increasingly failing partner. That was in large measure the result of its having entered the conflict with insufficient numbers to engage in mass warfare and of then suffering disproportionate losses. All the combatant armies had by December lost numbers that would have seemed unimaginable in July 1914. The Russian field army had been reduced from 3,500,000 men on mobilisation to two million; but it had perhaps ten million unconscripted men yet to call to the colours.[63] Austria-Hungary, by contrast, had lost 1,268,000 men out of 3,350,000 mobilised but had less than a third as many potential replacements; the official figure put the number at 1,916,000.[64] Many, moreover, were reluctant servants of empire and would prove growingly so as the war prolonged. The valiant mountain men of the Tyrol and Vorarlberg had given almost their all before the end of 1914; the Germans of Austria proper had also suffered heavily, as had the warlike Magyars of the Kingdom of Hungary; the Emperor's Slavs would prove an increasingly doubtful quantity. The original setback in Serbia had been blamed on the half-heartedness of the VII Corps and its 21st Division, almost wholly Czech, in particular. During the fighting with the Russians, the Czechs of IX Corps were suspected of large-scale desertion to the enemy. The steadfastness of the army was further undermined by the very heavy losses suffered at the outset among its regular officers and long-service NCOs. It was on its way towards becoming what the Austrian official history would itself call 'a *Landsturm* [second-line] and militia army'.

What that presaged was revealed when, the month after Limanowa-Lapanow, Conrad attempted to repeat the success further east in the Carpathians. He did so in concert with the Germans, who were meanwhile preparing an offensive of their own in Masuria to quash for good the Russian threat to East Prussia, and was lent three German divisions – 3rd Guard, 48th Reserve and 5th Cavalry – for his effort. The plan was to attack in the lower Beskid range, where the German formations were to break through and then wheel outwards in both directions, assisted by Austrian divisions on the flanks. Conditions did not favour success. The Beskids rise to 8,000 feet, then had few roads and are covered by deep snow in winter. The Germans, moreover, were ill-equipped for mountain operations. It was not surprising that the offensive, which began on 23 January, made little headway. What was surprising was the early success of the Austrians who, in the battle of Kolomea, drove the Russians down the eastern slopes of the Carpathians and reached Czernowitz at the junction of the Austrian-Russian-Romanian border. The territorial gains made were shallow, however, and a renewal of the offensive on 27 February was rapidly checked by Russian resistance. The Austrians lost over 90,000 men in these operations, without blunting Russian effectiveness.[65] During March the Russians counter-attacked whenever opportunity offered, against an enemy worn down by the harshness of the elements and the fruitlessness of its own efforts. General von Kralowitz, Chief of Staff of the Austrian X Corps, reported 'men already cut to pieces and defenceless . . . Every day hundreds froze to death; the wounded who could not drag themselves off were bound to die . . . there was no combating the apathy and indifference that gripped the men.'[66]

With the failure of these winter counter-offensives in the Carpathians, the morale of the enormous Austrian garrison of Przemysl, surrounded since October for the second time, collapsed. Its relief had been a primary object of the January operation. When that and its renewal in February failed, the commander of the fortress, after attempting a sortie that a British officer attached to the Russians described as a 'burlesque', demolished as much of the fortifications as had survived Russian bombardment, blew up his artillery and munitions, burnt his supplies and, on 22 March, surrendered.[67] Two thousand five hundred officers and 117,000 soldiers passed into Russian captivity.[68] The officers, whom the British observer described as having 'a prosperous and well-fed look', at first suffered little thereby; an artist of the *Illustrated London News* depicted them sharing the cafés of the city with the conquerors, sitting at separate tables but exchanging salutes on entry and departure as if by the protocols of eighteenth-century warfare.[69]

In Masuria neither the Russians nor the Germans were in a mood for civilities. There the Russian Tenth Army still occupied the strip of East Prussia taken in the battle of Augustow at the end of September and the Germans were determined to retake it. There was more to their plan, however, than a hope of local success. It had two larger objects. The first was an encirclement of the Russian Tenth Army between Masuria and the forest of Augustow, last of Europe's primeval wildernesses; the second was a wider encirclement of the whole Russian position in Poland, in concert with the Austrians' offensive in the Carpathians. Falkenhayn had wanted neither operation, since both required reinforcements he preferred to husband for his continued effort in the west, but he was overborne by Hindenburg who, though his subordinate, enjoyed direct access to the Kaiser since his Tannenberg triumph. The troops were found, largely because of the German army's superior ability to create new formations from its existing structures. While the Russians and the

185

Austrians merely made good losses as best they could with often untrained recruits, the Germans subdivided first-line divisions, upgraded second-line formations and organised new divisions out of reserves and fresh classes of conscripts. In this way, during November 1914, it created eight new divisions for the Eastern Front from the replacement battalions of the military districts, numbered 75–82; though they had a strength of only nine rather than the standard twelve infantry battalions, these new divisions were as strong in artillery as the old and actually anticipated the nine-battalion organisation which would become the norm throughout the army later in the war.[70]

The 'Winter Battle in Masuria', with the 75th, 76th, 77th, 78th, 79th and 80th Divisions in the vanguard, opened on 9 February 1915. Two armies, the old Eighth which had won Tannenberg and a new Tenth, attacked from north and south of the lake belt, broke through in terrible weather – snow, fog and bitter cold – and quickly threatened the Russians with encirclement. The Russian infantry, whose entrenchments were primitive and who were, as was common practice, badly supported by artillery commanders more concerned to save their guns than stand by the 'cattle' at the front, fought back but were progressively encircled.[71] Russian intelligence was poor, consistently underestimating the strength of the Germans; the high command, which had provided the isolated Tenth Army with no reserves, complacently assured Sievers, its commander, that the Twelfth Army, far to its south, would solve its problems. He had warned, before the storm broke, that 'nothing can prevent [my army] from being exposed to the same fate as [Rennenkampf's] in September'.[72] No notice was taken by his superiors, so that, by 16 February, another Tannenberg did indeed threaten. Bulgakov's XX Corps found itself penned into an increasingly constricted sector of the Augustow forest, by attacks so fierce that a principal casualty was the surviving stock of auroch, Europe's last wild bison.[73] The German pincers closed on 21 February, when Bulgakov surrendered with 12,000 men. The Germans claimed over 90,000, but the majority of Tenth Army's soldiers not killed or wounded in the fighting had in fact escaped through the forest. There had not been a second Tannenberg but East Prussia had been liberated from the danger of Russian invasion for good – at least in this war.

The winter battle in the Carpathians promised no such clear-cut result. There, in continuance of the efforts at Limanowa in December and in the Beskid mountains in January, the Austrians and their German loan troops renewed the attack in February, only to find the Russians respond with unexpected energy. Conrad, the Austrian Chief of Staff, began the offensive with the twin aims of relieving pressure on the surrounded Przemysl garrison and of winning a success that might deter Italy, increasingly emboldened by Austrian setbacks, entering the war on the Allies' side. The terrain and the weather in the Carpathians inflicted setbacks and terrible suffering on Conrad's soldiers, who froze and starved amid the steep valleys and forests. The Russian formations, which included a corps of Finns, perhaps the hardiest soldiers in Europe, were less affected. They answered Conrad's effort at an offensive with a counter-offensive of their own in late March which, despite the arrival of three German divisions, 4th, 28th Reserve and 35th Reserve, to the Austrians' aid, pressed forward. By the beginning of April, the Russians dominated the Carpathian front and, despite losses throughout their army totalling nearly two million since the war's outbreak, were again contemplating a breakthrough over the crests to the Hungarian plains, with results decisive for the whole eastern campaign, as soon as better weather came. The Austrians, whose losses in the first three months of 1915 added 800,000 to the 1,200,000 already suffered in 1914, were at their last gasp.[74] Without massive German help, whatever price was to be paid for that by way of political dependency and national prestige, the Habsburg empire faced a culminating crisis.

SIX

STALEMATE

THE EXHAUSTION OF ALL the combatant armies' offensive force during the winter of 1914, in the east only a little later than in the west, brought Europe by the spring of 1915 a new frontier. It was quite different in character from the old, lazy, permeable frontiers of pre-war days, crossed without passports at the infrequent customs posts and without formality elsewhere. The new frontier resembled the *limes* of the Roman legions, an earthwork barrier separating a vast military empire from the outside world. Nothing, indeed, had been seen like it in Europe since Rome – not under Charlemagne, not under Louis XIV, not under Napoleon – nor would be again until the outbreak of the Cold War thirty years into the future.

Unlike the *limes* and the Iron Curtain, however, the new frontier marked neither a social nor an ideological border. It was quite simply a fortification, as much offensive as defensive, separating warring states. Such fortifications had been dug before, notably in Virginia and Maryland during the American Civil War, in Portugal by Wellington during the Peninsular War, at Chatalja outside Istanbul during the Balkan Wars and by the Tsars on the Steppe (the Cherta lines) during the seventeenth and eighteenth century. None compared in length, depth or elaboration with Europe's new frontier of 1915. Measured from Memel on the Baltic to Czernowitz in the Carpathians and from Nieuport in Belgium to the Swiss border near Freiburg, the line of earthworks stretched for nearly 1,300 miles. Barbed wire, an invention of American cattle ranchers in the 1870s, had begun to appear, strung in belts between the opposing trenches by the spring. So, too, had underground shelters, 'dugouts' to the British, and support and reserve lines to the rear of the front. In essence, however, the new frontier was a ditch, dug deep enough to shelter a man, narrow enough to present a difficult target to plunging artillery fire and kinked at intervals into 'traverses', to diffuse blast, splinters or shrapnel and prevent attackers who entered a trench from commanding more than

191

a short stretch with rifle fire. In wet or stony ground, trenches were shallow, with a higher parapet to the front, built of earth, usually sandbagged. The drier and more workable the soil, the less need for supporting 'revetments' of timber or wattle along the internal trench walls, and the deeper the dugouts; these, which began as 'scrapes' in the side of the trench nearest the enemy, excavated thus to protect the entrance from incoming shells, developed quite soon into deep shelters, approached down staircases; the '*stollen*', thirty feet or more deep, eventually excavated by the Germans into the chalk of Artois and the Somme, would prove impervious to the heaviest bombardment.

Yet there was no standard trench system. The pattern varied from place to place, front to front, the design depending upon the nature of the terrain, the ratio of troops to space – high in the west, low in the east – tactical doctrine and the course of the fighting which had caused the line to rest where it did. On wide sectors of the Eastern Front in the spring of 1915 no man's land, the space separating the contestants' front lines, might be three to four thousand yards wide. Between Gorlice and Tarnow, south of Cracow, scene of the great Austro-German breakthrough to come, 'there was not much more than a thin, ill-connected ditch with a strand or two of barbed wire before it, and communications to the rear often ran over open ground . . . There was almost no reserve position either.'[1] In the west, by contrast, no man's land was usually two to three hundred yards wide, often less, in places only twenty-five. Intense trench fighting could even produce an 'international' barbed wire barrier, mended by both sides. Barbed wire had become plentiful by the spring of 1915, though entanglements, strung on wooden posts, later on screw pickets which could be fixed without noisy hammering, were still quite narrow. The dense belts fifty yards deep were a development of later years. To the rear of the front line, the British made a practice of digging a 'support' line, separated from the first by two hundred yards and usually a sketchier 'reserve' line four hundred yards further back. Connecting these lines, and kinked also by traverses, ran 'communication' trenches which allowed reliefs and ration parties to reach the front under cover, all the way from the rear. Diagrammatically, the layout would have appeared quite familiar to any siege engineer of the eighteenth century: 'parallels', connected by saps.[2] Any diagrammatic neatness, however, quickly disappeared, as trenches were abandoned because of flooding, exposure to enemy view, or loss to the enemy in combat. New trenches were always being dug to 'improve' the line or make good stretches lost in fighting: old support or communication trenches became new front lines: a successful advance would leave a whole trench system behind, perhaps only to be taken over again as the balance of local advantage swung the other way. The Western Front, as the first air photographs taken would shortly reveal, rapidly became a maze of duplicates and dead ends, in which soldiers, sometimes whole units, easily lost their way. Guides who knew the trench geography were an essential accompaniment in unit reliefs, when one battalion took the place of another at the end of a front-line stint. So, too, were signboards pointing to the more enduring trenches and the ruined remains of human habitation; in the Ypres salient in the winter of 1914–15, there were still traces of the buildings the Tommies had named Tram Car Cottage, Battersea Farm, Beggar's Rest, Apple Villa, White Horse Cellars, Kansas Cross, Doll's House.[3]

The British, hurried to Ypres in October 1914 to stop the open gap in the Western Front, had got below ground level wherever and as best they could. Shelter pits, which one man could dig at the rate of one cubic foot of earth removed in three minutes, or enough to give him cover in half an hour, became trenches when joined up.[4] More often, the first shelter was an existing ditch or field drain; when deepened, or as rain fell, these ready-made refuges filled with water and proved habitable only at the expense of great labour or not habitable at all, as the 2nd Royal Welch Fusiliers discovered south of Ypres in October 1914. 'The roads and many of the fields are bordered by deep ditches . . . the soil is clay, mostly, and sand . . . The Company Commanders set their men to dig behind covering parties [holding the front from the Germans opposite] . . . C and D [Companies] dug regulation traversed trenches by sections. A [Company] dug by platoons . . . B Company dug a support trench . . . and left one platoon to man it. The other three platoons went to a willow-lined dry ditch behind Cellar Farm . . . and improved it with their trenching tools.'[5] In December, on a nearby sector, they took over a similar sector, 'Within twenty-four hours it was "rain, rain, rain". The winter floods had come, the ditch turned out to be a stream which opened into the river; it was one of the main drains in this much-drained low country. The parapet fell in right and left; the ditch-trench ran with a rapid current and had to be abandoned by day.' With the help of the Royal Engineers and timber from a local sawmill, the trench was eventually revetted and built up above water level. '[The timber] had to be driven into a moving mass

193

of mud . . . by men working in two feet . . . of water, within shouting distance of the enemy . . . Two weeks of hard labour produced a dry trench with a floor above the ordinary flood-water level . . . In 1917 it was still the driest trench in the sector.'[6]

The longevity of this trench was unusual; static though the Western Front was to become, few stretches endured in their original state from 1914 until 1917. The Fusiliers' experience in January 1915 in a position near the River Lys, south of Ypres, explains why:

the Lys was still rising, so it was decided to let the trenches go and build a breastwork. Work began today [January 25] . . . On land where water lay so near the surface it was often difficult to find earth solid enough to fill sand-bags, so during the following weeks the battalion toiled building breastworks out of liquid mud. The wooden frames for the parapet were made in sections by the [Royal] Engineers. These sections, large brushwood hurdles, sheets of corrugated iron, and innumerable sand-bags, formed the load of the nightly carrying-parties . . . On the left of the Battalion front a gap was found through which much of the trench there could be drained for occupation . . . While breastwork and trench were in the making the company wiring sections worked in rivalry . . . in time, belts of barbed wire several yards across, fixed on stakes, stretched across the entire front. Until the line was completed, and that was not for weeks, it remained disconnected. To get along a company front, parts had to be taken at the double or by a flying leap, running the gauntlet of German snipers, who accounted for most of the casualties during the first months of the year.[7]

Bit by bit, battalions like the 2nd Royal Welch Fusiliers turned the British sector of the front into a defensible and moderately habitable line. The Germans, whose decision to retreat from the Marne to ground of their own choosing allowed them to avoid the wet, low-lying, overlooked sectors they left to their enemies, were better established. Theirs had been a deliberate strategy of entrenchment, as reported by the commanders of the pursuing French formations which were stopped in sequence as they advanced from the Marne. On 13 September, Franchet d'Esperey signalled in his evening report to Joffre at GQG that Fifth Army had encountered a new phenomenon, an organised trench system extending beyond the city of Rheims on both sides, which his advance guards could neither turn nor penetrate. In the few days following, each of the other army commanders transmitted similar intelligence. On 15 September, Foch reported from Ninth Army that he had been stopped by an entrenched line stretching eastward from Fifth Army's flank. On 16 September Sarrail, from Third Army, signalled that it was in continuous contact with the enemy who had 'surrounded Verdun with a network of trenches' which he could not carry by infantry assault. Castelnau, on his right, found the same day that his Sixth Army was faced by a continuous trench line he could not outflank, while on 17 September Dubail, First Army, reported that his front was crossed by a continuous line of trenches thrown up by labourers the Germans had impressed from the local population.[8] From Rheims to the Swiss frontier, therefore, the Germans had already succeeded in carrying out Moltke's order of 10 September to 'entrench and hold' the positions reached after the retreat from the Marne, while from the Aisne northwards towards the English Channel a line of entrenchments was being dug piecemeal as the series of short-range outflanking movements failed one after the other. The last of these stages of the 'Race to the Sea' ended in episodes of ditch-deepening, scraping, scrabbling, pumping and rough field-carpentry, as described by the officers of the 2nd Royal Welch Fusiliers, all under the fire of an enemy dug into higher, drier ground on the ridges that overlook Ypres and its surroundings from the east.

The British, who had learnt recent and important lessons in South Africa, where the Boers had taught them at the Modder and Tugela rivers the value of complicating any trench system, compensated for the inferiority of their overlooked positions in Flanders by digging in duplicate and triplicate, an insurance both against sudden infantry assault and artillery damage. The Germans, who had last dug earthworks around Paris in 1871 and otherwise derived their knowledge of trench warfare from indirect studies of the Russo-Japanese War, had a different doctrine. In two instructions, issued on 7 and 25 January 1915, Falkenhayn ordered that the western armies were to fortify the front in a strength sufficient to assure that it could be held with small numbers against attack by superior forces for a long time.[9] Falkenhayn's insistence on this point derived from his pressing need to find reinforcements from France and Belgium for the campaign in the east, where the demands of the fighting in Masuria and the battles on the Vistula, together with the necessity to prop up the Austrians in Galicia, exerted a growing drain on his resources. He had already sent thither thirteen divisions, and another seven, excluding locally raised formations, would go before the crisis in the east would pass. Those transferred, moreover, were among his best, including the 3rd Guard and six other peacetime divisions and four first-line reserve divisions, including the 1st Guard Reserve. They represented over one-tenth of his western field army and a third of its peacetime Prussian formations, those most counted upon for their offensive qualities.

The army in the east was growing into a formidable striking force. That remaining in the west, though continuing to include an elite, thenceforth comprised a disproportionate number of non-Prussian formations, Bavarians, Saxons and Hessians, of weaker Reserve and of undertrained war-raised divisions. It is not surprising, in the circumstances, that the doctrine of defence Falkenhayn laid down was draconian. The front line was to be the main line of resistance, built in great strength, to be held at all costs and retaken by immediate counter-attacks if lost. Secondary positions were to be dug only as a precaution. Some German generals, including Prince Rupprecht, commanding Sixth Army opposite the British in Flanders, objected even so to the digging of a second line, believing that the front troops would hold less firmly if they knew there was a fall-back behind them. Not until 6 May 1915 was a binding order issued by OHL for the whole of the German front to be reinforced by a second line of trenches, two to three thousand yards to the rear.[10] By then, however, the main line of resistance was becoming a formidable fortification. In the chalk of Artois and the Somme, on the heights of the Aisne and the Meuse, the German infantry were burrowing deep beneath the surface to construct shell-proof shelters. Concrete machine-gun posts were appearing behind the trenches, which were heavily walled with timber and iron. Parapets were thick and high, trench interiors floored with wooden walkways. Militarily, the German front grew in strength week by week. Domestically, it was even becoming comfortable. Electric light was appearing in the deeper dugouts, together with fixed bedsteads, planked floors, panelled walls, even carpets and pictures. Rearward from their underground command posts ran telephone lines to their supporting artillery batteries. The Germans were settling in for the long stay.

The French permitted themselves no such comforts. The occupation of France by the enemy – the departments of Nord, Pas-de-Calais, Somme, Oise, Aisne, Marne, Ardennes, Meuse, Meurthe-et-Moselle and Vosges lay partly or wholly under his hand by October 1914 – was an intrusion to be reversed at the earliest moment. Occupation was worse, moreover, than a violation of the national territory. It was a grave disruption of French economic life. The eighty French departments not directly touched by the war were largely agricultural. The ten occupied by the Germans contained much of French manufacturing industry and most of the country's coal and iron ores. If only to prosecute the war, it was urgent that they be recovered. Joffre therefore deprecated the construction of an impermeable front line on the German model, since he wanted to use the positions his soldiers held as a base for decisive offensives across no man's land. In a sense, however, he was bound with Falkenhayn by the imperative to economise forces. Whereas his German opponent, however, wanted to turn the whole of the Western Front into a passive sector, so as to find troops for the east, Joffre wanted to subdivide it into passive and active sectors, the former providing attack forces for the latter. Geography dictated where the subdivisions should fall. The wet and the hilly sectors – Flanders in the north, the heights of the Meuse and the Vosges in the south – should be passive. The active sectors should be those intervening, particularly those shouldering the great German salient in the Somme chalklands at Arras and in the Champagne near Rheims.

Two offensives in those sectors in December proved premature. The First Battle of Artois, 14–24 December, ended without any result. The Winter Battle in Champagne, which began on 20 December, dragged on, with long pauses, until 17 March, costing the French 90,000 casualties and bringing them no gain in territory at all. There was also local and quite inconclusive fighting further south, in the Argonne, near Verdun, in the St Mihiel salient, and around Hartmann-weilerkopf in the Vosges, a dominant point to which both sides sent their specialised mountain troops, *Jäger* and *Chasseurs Alpins*, to engage in fruitless assaults against each other; '*le vieil Armand*', as the French called it, was to be the grave of many of their finest soldiers. Joffre, brought to recognise that the French army was as yet too ill-equipped, the German trenches too strong, for any decisive result to be gained, reconstituted his plans. During January he issued two instructions laying down how the front was to be organised. In the first, he ordered that the active sectors were to consist of strongpoints sited to cover the ground to the front and to the flanks with fire. The passive zones in between were to be garrisoned only with lookouts, and to be heavily wired but held by fire from the active zones. Across the whole front, active and passive, two belts of wire were to be constructed, twenty yards or so apart and about ten yards deep, with gaps for patrols to pass through. Behind the line of strongpoints there were to be secondary positions with shell-proof shelter for counter-attack companies.[11] A survey of the fronts of the eight French armies revealed that most of the work Joffre required had already been done. In his second January letter he therefore stipulated that the front be strengthened by the digging of a second line some two miles to the rear, resembling the first, as a precaution against local break-ins. Such work had already been completed in the Verdun and Rheims sectors. Joffre added the general instruction that fronts were to be held as thinly as possible, to economise manpower and avoid casualties, and that local commanders should avoid pushing outposts too close to the enemy's positions, a practice he thought wasteful of lives.

That was the exact opposite of developing British policy, which was to 'dominate no man's land' by redigging trenches closer to the enemy's and staging frequent trench raids. The first trench raid appears to have been mounted on the night of 9/10 November 1914 near Ypres by the 39th Garwhal Rifles of the Indian Corps.[12] Fierce irruptions into enemy positions under cover of darkness was a traditional feature of Indian frontier fighting and this first murderous little action may have represented an introduction of tribal military practice into the 'civilised' warfare of western armies. The event set a precedent of which the British were to make a habit and which the Germans were to copy. The French, despite their long experience of tribal warfare in North Africa, never found a similar enthusiasm for these barbaric flurries of slash and stab. Disposing of many more field guns in their corps reserves than either the British or Germans did, they preferred to dominate their defensive fronts from a distance with artillery fire, for which, after the solution of the shell shortage of the winter of 1914–15, they were amply supplied.

These three different methods of holding the Western Front, along the line on which it had settled in November, would not have been much apparent to an overflying observer in the following spring. From the air it had a drably uniform appearance, a belt of disturbed earth, ravaged vegetation and devastated buildings some four miles across. Later, as the power of artillery increased and local infantry fighting conferred advantage on one side or the other, the zone of destruction would widen. What would scarcely change for the next twenty-seven months was the length of the front or the geographical trace which it followed. That remained apparently unalterable by the effort of the armies on either side until, in March 1917, the Germans voluntarily surrendered the central Somme sector and retired to shorter, stronger, previously prepared lines twenty miles to the rear. Until then the Western Front stood the same, month after month, for almost every yard of its length, running in a reversed S shape for 475 miles from the North Sea to the Swiss border. It began at Nieuport in Belgium, where the sluggish Yser discharges seaward between high concrete embankments thirty yards apart. The eastern bank was held by the Germans, the western – since Joffre could not bring himself to entrust this critical hinge to the Belgians, even as defenders of their own territory – to the French. Below Nieuport's complex of locks, and behind its high rampart of holiday hotels that front the coastal dunes, in 1914 quickly gapped and broken by artillery exchanges, the front followed the line of the Yser southward through a perfectly flat landscape of beetfields and irrigation channels, above which the roads run on causeways, as far as Dixmude, where a spur of slightly higher ground runs out from the Flemish ridges towards the sea. After November 1914, much of this territory was under water, the inundations forming a barrier impassable to the German naval troops who held the breastworked trenches on the eastern side.

Below Dixmude the line again ran just above sea level to Ypres, which it skirted in a shallow loop – 'the Salient' – overlooked from November 1914 until October 1918 by the German trenches on the higher ground at Passchendaele and Gheluvelt. The medieval wool trade had brought wealth to Ypres, displayed by a fine cathedral and a magnificent cloth hall. Both were far advanced in ruin by the spring of 1915, together with the seventeenth-century ramparts and nineteenth-century barracks at the rear of the town, past which so many thousands of British troops were to march southwards, along a route best judged to spare them from shelling on their way to and from the trenches. Behind Ypres the ground rises towards 'Flemish Switzerland', Kemmel, Cassel and the Mont des Cats, where British generals had their headquarters and troops released from duty in the line found recreation in the little towns of Poperinge – 'Pop' – and Bailleul. 'Pop' became a place of mixed attractions to the BEF: the famous Talbot House, Toc H, run by the Reverend Tubby Clayton for the high-minded and churchy who were prepared, as he insisted, to shed rank once inside its doors; the infamous Skindles for officers who wanted a good meal and the company of loose women. Skindles today is scarcely identifiable, but Toc H survives, its attic chapel, 'the Upper Room' breathing the Anglican religiosity of suburban volunteer soldiers pitched headlong into the hell of early twentieth-century warfare. The dim, stark chapel under the eaves remains a deeply moving way-station to any pilgrim to the Western Front.

South of Ypres the geographical advantages enjoyed by the Germans become more evident in the ridges of Aubers and Messines, frequent objectives of British offensives, and in the coalfields around Lens, where spoilheaps provided vantage points and pitheads, too, until they were destroyed by shelling. Nearby, at la Bassée, the line entered France and began to ascend the chalk ridges of Artois. Here early hydraulic engineers, seeking the aquifers that lie deep beneath the surface, had first developed the artesian well – the well of Artois – and here the soil provided for the German defenders the best conditions for defensive positions they were to find on the Western Front. The chalk belt extends southwards, through the Somme, into the Champagne but nowhere did the Germans better dominate their enemies than at Vimy, where to the east the dip slope of the ridge falls suddenly and dramatically into the plain of Douai, which thence runs towards the great north-south strategic railway, the *'ligne de rocade'*, linking Lille with Metz. Because the division between upland and plain at Vimy is so radical, it was a feature which the Germans had to hold and they were to do so against repeated Allied assaults until it was taken in an epic Canadian assault in 1917.

Below Vimy the line passed slightly east of Arras, another treasury of medieval wool wealth architecture, battered flat during the war, now restored from cellars upward – cellars that sheltered Allied troops in tens of thousands during the war – to the downlands of the Somme. The Somme is an unappealing river, marshy and meandering, but the countryside that surrounds it appears fondly familiar to an English eye, rising and falling in long, green swells and hollows reminiscent of Salisbury Plain or the Sussex Downs. The British would come to know it well, for by 1916 their length of line, progressively extended southward as their numbers grew, reached almost to the valley of the River Somme at Péronne, which would form their new boundary with the French for the rest of the war.

The French share of the line, even after their transfer of the portions north of the Somme to the British, was always the longer. Immediately south of the Somme it ran through countryside closer and more wooded than that to the north until it reached Noyon on the Oise, its nearest approach to Paris, which lies only fifty-five miles distant; for most of the war the masthead of the newspaper edited by the great radical politician, Georges Clemenceau, would carry the words, '*Les allemands sont à Noyon*.' There it turned sharply eastward to follow the slope of the ridge between the Aisne and the Ailette rivers – this was the section first entrenched by the Germans after the battle of the Marne and so the original part of the Western Front – a ridge known as the Chemin des Dames after the pleasure path constructed on its crest for the daughters of Louis XV.

East of the Chemin des Dames, the abortive assault on which in 1917 was to precipitate the 'mutinies' of the French army, the line followed the heights above Rheims, which was to lie within range of German artillery for most of the war. Onward again, still drawing out to the east, the trenches crossed the dry, stony plateau of the *Champagne pouilleuse*, ironically one of the French army's largest peacetime training areas. The absence there of hedges or trees suited the manoeuvre of large bodies of troops and the practice of artillery, in pre-war rehearsals of mobile warfare that the Western Front's coming into being had wholly frustrated.

At the eastern edge of the Champagne, near Ste Menehoud, the line entered the forest of the Argonne, a tangled wilderness of trees, streams and small hills, in which neither side could mount major operations but where both, nevertheless, kept up a constant bickering. Above the Argonne rise the heights of the Meuse, crowned by the fortifications of Verdun and encircled to the east by German trenches which then dropped down into the plain of the Woevre. The Woevre was critically important to the Germans, for it gave an easy approach to their own great fortress of Metz, and they had fought hard in the opening battles of 1914 to retain it. In late September they had actually secured the advantage of gaining a foothold across the Meuse at St Mihiel, a salient that provided a bridgehead beyond the most important water obstacle on the Western Front and caused the French endless trouble. It would remain in German hands until retaken by the Americans in September 1918.

Below St Mihiel the advantage lay with the French. During the battle of the Frontiers they had succeeded in retaining the city of Nancy and such high points nearby as the Ballon d'Alsace, from which commanding views stretch in all directions. Possession of the crests of the Vosges and of the line of the Meurthe river, which makes its way through those mountains, guaranteed to the French the security of the eastern end of the Western Front.[13] Over its last fifty miles the front ran generally within German territory – though French before 1871 – through the high Vosges, across the Belfort gap until it reached the Swiss frontier near the village of Bonfol. There the Swiss militia army, fully mobilised for war, surveyed the termini of the opposed trench barriers from neutral territory.[14]

THE STRATEGY OF THE WESTERN FRONT

The strategic geography of the Western Front is easy to read now, was easy to read then and largely dictated the plans made by each side at the start of trench warfare and in the years that followed. Much of the front was unsuitable for the style of major operations both sides envisaged, in which the power of artillery would prepare the way for large-scale infantry assaults, to be followed by cavalry exploitation into open country. The Vosges was such a front, and was accepted to be so by both French and Germans, who held it with second-rate divisions, reinforced by mountain infantry who occasionally disputed possession of the high points. Indeed, south of Verdun, neither side was to make any major effort between September 1914 and September 1918 and this stretch, 160 miles long, became 'inactive'. Elsewhere, the Argonne proved unsuited to offensives as, for different reasons, did the Flemish coastal zone. The former was too broken, stream-cut and tree-choked, the latter too waterlogged for the delivery of attacks that required firm, unobstructed avenues of advance for a successful conclusion. Shelling into the Argonne threw the woodland into a jungle of broken vegetation; in the sea-level fens of Flanders, shelling quickly reduced the soil to quagmire. In the centre, the heights of the Aisne and the Meuse, though they were both to be contested in great battles, too much favoured the defender for offensive effort to be profitable. It was therefore only on the dry chalklands of the Somme and the Champagne that attacks offered the promise of decisive success. The former stood below the wet Flemish country, the latter above the mountainous forest zone of the Meurthe and Moselle. They were separated from each other by the high ground of the Aisne and Meuse, the bulge in the front to which they formed the shoulders. Military logic therefore required that it was at those shoulders that the attackers should make their major efforts and defenders be best prepared to withstand an assault.

Who would be attackers and who defenders? In August 1914 it was the Germans who had attacked; Schlieffen's maps showing the 'line of the 31st day' coincide in eerie accuracy with the early Western Front. In September the French counter-attacked; the engagements during the 'Race to the Sea' follow the course of the stabilised line in Artois, Picardy and Flanders with an equivalent precision. The trace of the railway network explains how these outcomes came about. Early in the campaign of 1914 the Germans took possession of the Metz–Lille line, running north-south within their area of conquest. The French, on the other hand, retained control of the Nancy–Paris–Arras line facing it. The latter is closer to the line of engagement than the former, and that proximity explains why the French were better able than their enemy to deliver reserves to the crucial point in time to win one battle after another.

The 'Race to the Sea' is thus best understood as a series of stalemated collisions along the successive rungs of a ladder whose uprights were formed by those vital parallel railways. Amiens, Arras and Lille, near which the principal engagements of the 'Race to the Sea' were fought are, as a glance at the railway map shows, all located on cross-country lines linking the two great north-south routes. Since the physical and human geography remained unaltered by the course of the fighting, the strategic advantage rested with the French, though the tactical advantage rested with the Germans, who had chosen the pick of the ground at the final points of contact.[15]

Since strategic geography is a major determinant of strategic choice, the geographical advantage enjoyed by the French disposed them to attack. Geography did not, however, supply the only argument for such a decision, nor for the complementary German decision to await attack on the Western Front. The real reasons were quite different. France, as the victim of Germany's offensive of August 1914, and the major territorial loser in the outcome of the campaign, was bound to attack. National pride and national economic necessity required it. Germany, by contrast, was bound to stand on the defensive, since the setbacks she had suffered in the east, in its two-front war, demanded that troops be sent from France to Poland for an offensive in that region. The security of the empire was at stake; so, too, was the survival of Germany's Austrian ally. The Habsburg army had been grievously damaged by the battles in Galicia and the Carpathians, its ethnic balance disturbed, its human and material reserves almost exhausted. A renewed Russian effort might push it over the edge. The real outcome of 1914 was not the frustration of the Schlieffen Plan but the danger of a collapse of the Central Powers' position in Eastern Europe.

A piecemeal adjustment against that risk had been made as early as the last week of August, when the 3rd Guard and 38th Divisions had been transferred from Namur to East Prussia, as a result of the Tannenberg crisis. They had been followed by ten more between September and December. Moltke had not wanted to let any go. His successor, Falkenhayn, resented the transfer of every one. He believed that the war had to be won by making the major effort in the west. There the French army was recovering from its losses of the opening campaign – thirty-three new divisions were forming – while French industry was gearing up for a war of material. The British were creating a whole new army of volunteers, while training their peacetime militia, the Territorial Force, for active service; together these would produce nearly sixty divisions, besides those from Canada and Australia which were hastening across the Atlantic and Pacific to the motherland's aid. Of these figures Falkenhayn did not have exact intelligence but his impression of the gathering of a huge reinforcement was accurate enough. It would shortly double the force opposing the Germans on the Western Front, while they were already reaching the limits of expansion open to them from their manpower potential. The number of their divisions could be increased by reducing the infantry strength of each, counting on artillery and machine guns to make good the consequent diminution of firepower, a measure already in hand. The absolute limit of troop availability already stood, nevertheless, in sight.

In the circumstances, Falkenhayn had convinced himself that 1915 must be a year of offence in the west and defence in the east, within the larger policy of bringing Russia to make a separate peace. He lacked, however, the authority to carry his case. Though the Kaiser, as Supreme War Lord, had confirmed him in the appointment of Chief of Staff in January 1915, when he gave up the post of Minister of War, he was acutely aware that the real prestige of office attached to Hindenburg, as victor of Tannenberg, and his chief of the eastern staff (OberOst), Ludendorff. What they did not want, he could not insist upon; conversely, what they wanted he was increasingly obliged to concede. Moreover, Ludendorff was waging an active campaign to undercut his primacy, which the German system in any case did not clearly define. Whereas Joffre exercised the powers of government within the Zone of the Armies, and Kitchener, appointed Secretary of State of War at the outbreak, effectively acted as Commander-in-Chief also, Falkenhayn was neither supreme commander, since that dignity belonged to the Kaiser, nor his immediate subordinate, since between him and Wilhelm II stood the Military Cabinet, a body without executive authority but ample influence.[16] It was through the Military Cabinet that Ludendorff began his intrigue. He was assisted by the Chancellor, Bethmann Hollweg, who shared the German people's admiration for Hindenburg in full measure. During January 1915, the Chancellor approached the Military Cabinet with the proposition that Falkenhayn should be replaced by Hindenburg, so that a major offensive could be opened in the east. When the senior officers of the Military Cabinet pointed out that the Kaiser liked and trusted Falkenhayn, a friend of his youth, and disliked Ludendorff, whom he thought overambitious, the Chancellor withdrew. Shortly thereafter, however, he came into contact with Ludendorff's agent inside Supreme Headquarters, Major von Haeften, who suggested he approach the Kaiser direct. Bethmann Hollweg did not only that but enlisted the help of both the Empress and the Crown Prince to argue for Hindenburg and Ludendorff's eastern strategy. Falkenhayn fought back, first confronting Hindenburg with the demand that he resign his post, though that was impossible in the face of German public opinion, then securing Ludendorff's transfer from eastern headquarters to that of the Austro-German army in Galicia.

When Hindenburg appealed to the Kaiser for his return, he found he had gone too far. Wilhelm II decided that the hero of the day was challenging the authority of the supreme command. He could not, however, find the will to impose his own. Lobbied by his wife and son, the Chancellor, even the superseded von Moltke, he clung to Falkenhayn, while knowing that he must also keep Hindenburg and grant him much of what he wanted. The result was a compromise. Falkenhayn, though affronted, decided not to make the thwarting of his strategy a resigning issue, came to a personal accommodation with Hindenburg and acquiesced in the return of Ludendorff to the *OberOst* headquarters. Hindenburg, perceiving that Falkenhayn could not be displaced, contented himself with the token of the transfer of troops from west to east that he had already received, and the freedom of action thus granted him to pursue the chance of further victories over the Russians. He had hopes that more troops could be extracted if he could make a convincing case for mounting an offensive that would cripple the Russian army and stabilise the still fluid Eastern Front. In those hopes lay the germ of the plan for a renewal of battle east of Cracow which would result in the great breakthrough at Gorlice-Tarnow in the coming May. Meanwhile the debate between Germany's 'westerners' and 'easterners' would rumble on unresolved.[17]

There was as yet no such division of opinion on the Allied side. Despite the absence of any supranational command organisation, akin to the Combined Chiefs of Staff Committee which so successfully co-ordinated Anglo-American strategy during the Second World War, the informal understanding between the British and French general staffs was working well. The Russian view was also represented through their liaison officers at both French and British headquarters. Field Marshal French was, in any case, of one mind with General Joffre. Joffre had but one thought: to drive the invader from the national territory. French shared it, if for reasons less burningly patriotic, more calculatedly strategic than those of his brother commander. Curiously, he believed, like Hindenburg, that the war would be settled on the Eastern Front. Nevertheless, 'until the Russians [could] finish the business', he was certain that the right policy for Britain was to commit all the troops available to Western Front operations.[18] They were growing rapidly in number. By early 1915 the BEF was large enough to be divided into two Armies, First and Second, the Territorials were reaching France in strength and the first of the volunteer divisions of Kitchener's New Armies were beginning to appear also. Soon the British would be able to take over stretches of the line from their ally and find a striking force to mount offensives on their own initiative.

The question was, where? An early plan to make a major effort on the Belgian coast, with the Royal Navy supporting a combined Anglo-Belgian army, foundered on Admiralty warnings that its light ships could not stand up to German coastal artillery and that its battleships could not be risked in such confined waters.[19] Plans to use troops against the Austrians were shown to be equally unrealistic. Militarily weak though Austria-Hungary was, geographically it was almost unapproachable by a maritime power. The Adriatic was an Austrian lake, denied to the Royal and French Navies by Austrian submarines and its recently built Dreadnoughts. Gallant Serbia could be supported only by use of routes through Bulgaria which, though as yet non-belligerent, was hostile, or Greece, which was prudently preserving her neutrality. If Italy were to enter the war on the Allied side, which seemed increasingly likely, that would heighten the pressure on Austria, but would bring no direct assistance to Serbia nor open the Adriatic, since the Italian Dreadnought bases were in the Mediterranean. Romania, friendly to the Allies, could not risk entering the war unless and until Russia achieved the upper hand on the Eastern Front. The only other region beyond the Western Front where Britain might use its growing strength in independent action was therefore in Turkey, which had joined Germany and Austria as a belligerent ally on 31 October. The only active front Turkey had opened, however, was against Russia in the Caucasus, which lay too far from any centre of British power for an intervention to be contemplated there. Moreover the British government was as yet unwilling to divert troops from France, though it was prepared to consider deploying naval forces, as long as its preponderance in the North Sea was not diminished, if a promising use for them could be found. In January the British War Council began to consider the preparation of a naval expedition to the Turkish Dardanelles, with the object of opening a way to Russia's Black Sea ports. The mission was to be strictly naval, however; Britain's commitment to France remained, in every sense, complete.[20]

Yet the Western Front presented not only militarily but also geographically a strategic conundrum. There was the initial difficulty of how to break the trench line; beyond that lay the difficulty of choosing lines of advance that would bring about a large-scale German withdrawal. During January the French operations staff at GQG, now located at Chantilly, the great horse-racing centre near Paris, began to analyse the problem. It turned on the rail communications which supported the German armies in the field. There were three systems that led back across the Rhine into Germany. The southernmost was short and easily defended. That left the two systems that supplied the Germans holding the great salient between Flanders and Verdun. If either, or preferably both, could be cut, the Germans within the salient would be obliged to fall back, perhaps creating once again those conditions of 'open warfare' which, it was believed, alone offered the chance of decisive victory. The French at Chantilly, the British at GHQ at St Omer, therefore agreed during January that the correct strategy during 1915 was for offensives to be mounted at the 'shoulders' of the salient, in the north against the Aubers and Vimy

Ridges which stood between the Allies and the German railways in the Douai plain behind, in the south against the Champagne heights which protected the Mezières-Hirson rail line. The attacks would, in theory, converge, thus threatening the Germans in the great salient with encirclement as well as disruption of their supplies.

It was thus agreed between the French and British. There was to be a spring offensive, jointly British and French in Flanders and Artois, French alone in Champagne.[21] Indeed, this first agreement was to set the pattern for much of the Allied effort on the Western Front throughout the war. The pattern was to be repeated in the coming autumn, during 1917 and, finally with success, in 1918. Only in 1916 would the Allies attempt something different, in the offensive against the centre of the great German salient to be known as the battle of the Somme.

This, however, is to anticipate the failure of the spring offensive of 1915. Fail it did, however, for reasons to become tragically familiar with every renewal of the French and British efforts. There was, indeed, warning of failure before the spring offensive ever began, in the miscarriage of a minor and preliminary attack by the British at Neuve Chapelle in March. All the contributing factors that were to bedevil success in trench offensives for much of the war were present, both the functional and structural. The functional were to be cured, in time, the structural persisted, even after the development and large-scale deployment of the tank in 1917. Among the functional were inadequacy of artillery support, rigidity of planning, mispositioning of reserves and lack of delegation in command. Among the structural were the relative immobility and total vulnerability to fire of advancing infantry and absence of means of speedy communication between front and rear, between infantry and artillery and between neighbouring units. The unfolding of action at Neuve Chapelle demonstrates the operation of all these factors as if in a military laboratory.

THE WESTERN FRONT BATTLES OF 1915

Neuve Chapelle was launched partly because Sir John French was unable to comply with Joffre's request that the BEF assist the preparation of the coming Artois offensive by taking over more of the French line, partly, it seems though never stated, because the Field Marshal was anxious to restore his army's reputation, damaged in

French eyes by its failure to win ground during the December fighting. The plan was simple. Neuve Chapelle, a ruined village, twenty miles south of Ypres in the Artois sector into which the British had been extending their position as fresh troops arrived in France during the winter, was to be attacked on 10 March by the British 7th and 8th Divisions and the Meerut and Lahore Divisions of the Indian Corps. The front of attack was about 8,000 yards, behind which 500 guns had been assembled, to fire a stock of 200,000 shells, mainly light-calibre, into the enemy trenches, the barbed wire protecting them and certain strongpoints in the rear.[22] There was also to be a 'barrage' – the term was French, meaning a dam or a barrier – of bursting shells fired behind the German trenches, parallel to the front of attack once it was under way, to prevent German reinforcements reaching their stricken comrades. The British and Indians, as they advanced, would be supported by reserves moving forward to take further objectives, but only on the receipt of orders from General Sir Douglas Haig, at First Army, through the subordinate corps, divisional, brigade and battalion headquarters.

The bombardment, which opened at seven o'clock in the morning, took the Germans by complete surprise. That was an achievement, rarely to be repeated; even more of an achievement was First Army's success in having assembled the leading waves of an attack force of sixty thousand men within a hundred yards of the enemy in complete secrecy, a fact scarcely ever to occur again. The defenders, belonging to two infantry regiments and a Jäger battalion, about one-seventh in strength to their assailants, were overwhelmed. Their wire had been extensively cut, their front trench destroyed. When the British infantry assaulted at five past eight, they were not opposed and within twenty minutes a breach 1,600 yards wide had been opened in the German line. The makings of a victory, local but significant, had been won.

Then the functional factors making for failure started to set in. The British plan stipulated that, after the first objective 200 yards inside the German wire was taken, the infantry was to pause for fifteen minutes while the artillery shelled the ruins of Neuve Chapelle village in front of them. The intention was to disable any remaining defenders waiting there. In fact there were none. Those that had escaped the initial bombardment were hurrying rearward towards the strongpoints which had been built precisely to check such a break-in as the British had now made. After this second bombardment the British followed fast, into open country beyond the bombardment zone and scenting triumph. Orders, however, now required that they should wait for a second time. The commander of the battalion in the centre, 2nd Rifle Brigade, managed to send back a message requesting permission to disregard the order and continue the advance. Surprisingly – there were no telephone lines and this was the pre-radio age – it was received; even more surprisingly an answer was returned from brigade headquarters speedily enough to affect the situation, wholly for the worse. Permission to move forward was refused.

It was now about half past nine and the Germans were recovering their wits. Falkenhayn's tactical instruction of 25 January had laid down that, in the event of an enemy break-in, the flanks of the gap were to be held and immediately reinforced, while reserves were to hurry forward and fill the hole. That was what was beginning to happen. On the British left, where the bombardment had left the German positions intact, two machine guns were brought into action, by the 11th Jäger Battalion, killing hundreds of soldiers of the 2nd Scottish Rifles and 2nd Middlesex; on the right, the attackers had lost their way, an all too common occurrence in the broken ground of the trench zone, and stopped to get their bearings. During the delay, the Germans there hastily organised the defence of that flank. Meanwhile, according to plan, fresh British battalions were crowding into the gap opened by the leading waves. By ten o'clock, 'roughly nine thousand men [were squeezed] into the narrow space between Neuve Chapelle village and the original British breastwork [where] they lay, sat, or stood uselessly in the mud, packed like salmon in the bridge pool at Galway, waiting patiently to go forward'. Fortunately, the German artillery batteries within range had little ammunition available.[23]

The British artillery, which had ample stocks, could not rapidly be informed of the deteriorating situation, one of the structural defects contributing to failure. Without radio, communication depended on flag signals or runners, the first usually obscured, the second slow and vulnerable. At half past eleven a bombardment was organised against the 11th Jäger's machine-gun positions, and an officer and sixty-three men came out to surrender, having killed about a thousand British soldiers. Precise and timely bombardment of their and other strongpoints could not be attempted because the gunners could not be informed. All the while the local German commanders, junior but determined and well-trained officers, were hurrying reserves to the flanks by bicycle or on foot. By contrast, and here the functional contribution to failure was at work, the British junior officers were passing their observations of the local situation, as the plan required, back up the chain of command so that authority could be granted for any alteration of the all-defining plan they requested. Behind the battle zone, telephone lines speeded communications but it was still painfully, indeed lethally, slow. 'The Corps commander in some room five miles or more from the battle had to make a decision on the flimsiest and often false information, and the necessary orders had then to travel back, along the same chain, to be considered and written out in greater detail at each stage (divisional headquarters, brigade headquarters, battalion headquarters), till finally they reached the front-line companies.'[24] What all this meant, in terms of the actual rather than planned timetable in this particular trench battle, was that between nine o'clock in the morning, when the German line had been broken and a way forward lay open for the taking, and the writing of firm orders to exploit the success at ten to three in the afternoon, nearly six hours elapsed. By the time those written orders had filtered down, via telephone and runner, another three hours were lost. The time the advance was resumed on the ground was between half past five and six.[25]

Dark was drawing in and so were the German reserves. The flanks of the break-in had been secured before midday. By nightfall fresh German troops, hurried forward from battalions in rearward support, were filling the open gap and bending their flanks forward to join up with the positions at the edges which had never been lost. Next morning the British renewed the offensive but thick mist prevented their artillery from locating targets and the attack soon stopped. It was now the turn of the Germans to discover that structural defects could impede the operation of a well-laid plan. On the day of the original attack, 10 March, a fresh division, the 6th Bavarian Reserve (in which Adolf Hitler was serving as a battalion runner) had been ordered forward to deliver a counter-attack in the early morning of 11 March. On a dark night and across country, however, the troops simply could not march fast enough to reach their designated jumping-off positions. The attack was therefore postponed for a day, at the order of Prince Rupprecht, commanding Sixth Army in whose sector Neuve Chapelle lay, after he had come to see the situation for himself. When, on the morning of 12 March, the attack did go in, it was immediately stopped with heavy German losses. The British front-line commanders had used the pause imposed by the mist the day before to consolidate their foothold and site twenty machine guns in commanding positions.

As a result, the 'exchange ratio' of casualties, as it would now be termed, at Neuve Chapelle, was eventually almost equal: 11,652 British killed, wounded, missing and prisoners to about 8,600 German.[26] That was to become a familiar outcome of trench-to-trench offensives, large and small, throughout the course of the war, whenever an initial assault was followed by an enemy counter-attack. The reasons, in retrospect, are easy to identify. At the outset, the advantage lay with the attackers, as long as they could preserve a measure of secrecy, a diminishing possibility as the war prolonged and defenders learnt how greatly survival depended upon surveillance and alertness. Almost as soon as the attackers entered the enemy's positions, however, the advantage tended to move towards the defenders, who knew the ground, which the attackers did not, had prepared fall-back positions, and were retreating towards their own artillery along, if lucky, intact telephone lines. The attackers found themselves in exactly the opposite situation, moving into unknown and confusing surroundings, and away from their supporting artillery the further they advanced, thus progressively losing contact with it as telephone lines were broken or left behind. Then, when the defenders counter-attacked, the advantage reversed. The attackers had familiarised themselves with the ground taken, organised its defences, to their advantage but the enemy's confusion, and re-established telephonic communication with their artillery. In this see-saw, functional and structural weaknesses disfavoured first one side, then the other, to the eventual frustration of all effort to break through to open country or break back to the original line of defence. The physical product of offence and counter-offence was an ever thicker and more confused trench line, resembling a layer of scar tissue, picked at and irritated, over the site of an unsuccessful surgical operation.

The British nevertheless judged Neuve Chapelle a partial success, if only because it restored the fighting reputation of their army in French eyes. It was unfair that it should ever have been doubted. What was at issue was not the combativeness of the British soldier but the still colonial outlook of their commanders, who expected decisive results for a comparatively small outlay of force and shrank from casualties. French generals, from a different tradition, expected large casualties, which their soldiers still seemed ready to suffer with patriotic fatalism. The British soldier, regular, Territorial, wartime volunteer, was learning a similar abnegation, while their leaders were coming to accept that operations in the new conditions of trench warfare could

212

succeed only with the most methodical preparation. The qualities of dash and improvisation that had brought victory in mountain and desert for a hundred years would not serve in France. The only dissentients from this new and harsher mood were the Indians, for whom Neuve Chapelle marked their swansong on the Western Front. They would fight again, in the coming battles of Festubert and Loos, but not as a striking force. Losses already suffered had crippled many battalions and the sepoy, raised in a tradition of warrior honour quite different from the European, could not understand that a wound did not exempt the recipient from a return to the trenches. 'We are as grain that is flung a second time into the oven', wrote a Sikh soldier to his father the week after Neuve Chapelle, 'and life does not come out of it.' A wounded Rajput had written home a little earlier, 'This is not war, it is the ending of the world.'[27] By the end of the year the two Indian infantry divisions would have been transferred from France to Mesopotamia where, in a desert campaign against the Turks, they rediscovered a more familiar style of warmaking.

Neuve Chapelle was significant also because it anticipated in miniature both the character and course of the spring offensive in Artois, to which it was a preliminary, as well as its renewal in Artois and Champagne in the autumn. For a moment, indeed, during Neuve Chapelle, the leading waves of British and Indian troops had glimpsed the way open to the crest of Aubers Ridge, which was to be the British objective during their part of the Artois attack. Before that could be launched, however, the British had undergone an offensive in the reverse direction, in Flanders, which came to be known as the Second Battle of Ypres. The First, which had secured the 'Salient' at the end of 1914, had petered out in confused and ineffective fighting, largely conducted by the French, in December. By the beginning of April, however, Falkenhayn had decided, in order partly to disguise the transfer of troops to the Eastern Front for the forthcoming offensive at Gorlice-Tarnow, partly to experiment with the new gas weapon, to renew pressure on the Ypres salient. The attack was to be a limited offensive, since Falkenhayn's hopes of achieving decision in the west had, he knew, to be postponed as long as Hindenburg and Ludendorff could effectively divert the movement of strategic reserves to the Eastern Front; nevertheless, he hoped to gain ground and secure a more commanding position on the Channel coast.

Gas had been used by the Germans already, on the Eastern Front, at Bolimov, on 3 January, when gas-filled shells had been fired into the

Russian positions on the River Rawka west of Warsaw. The chemical agent, known to the Germans as *T-Stoff* (xylyl bromide), was lachrymatory (tear-producing), not lethal. It appears to have troubled the Russians not at all; prevailing temperatures were so low that the chemical froze instead of vaporising.[28] By April, however, the Germans had a killing agent available in quantity, in the form of chlorine. A 'vesicant', which causes death by stimulating over-production of fluid in the lungs, leading to drowning, the material was a by-product of the German dye-stuff industry, controlled by IG Farben, which commanded a virtual world monopoly in those products. Carl Duisberg, head of IG Farben, had already rescued the German war effort from collapse by his successful drive to synthesise nitrates, an essential component of high-explosive obtainable organically only from sources under Allied control. Simultaneously he was co-operating with Germany's leading industrial chemist, Fritz Haber, head of the Kaiser Wilhelm Institute in Berlin, to devise a means of discharging chlorine in quantity against enemy trenches. Experiments with gas-filled shells had failed (though, with a different filling, gas shells would later be widely employed). The direct release of chlorine, from pressurised cylinders, down a favourable wind, promised better. By 22 April, 6,000 cylinders, containing 160 tons of gas, had been emplaced opposite Langemarck, north of Ypres, where the trenches were held by the French 87th Territorial and 45th Divisions, the latter composed of white Zouave regiments from Algeria, African Light Infantry (white punishment battalions) and native Algerian riflemen. Next to them was the Canadian Division, first of the imperial divisions to reach the Western Front; the rest of the Ypres salient was held by three British regular divisions, the 5th, 27th and 28th.

The afternoon of 22 April was sunny, with a light east-west breeze. At five o'clock a greyish-green cloud began to drift across from the German towards the French trenches, following a heavy bombardment, and soon thousands of Zouaves and Algerian Riflemen were streaming to the rear, clutching their throats, coughing, stumbling and turning blue in the face. Within the hour, the front line had been abandoned and a gap 8,000 yards wide had been opened in the Ypres defences. Some of the gas drifted into the Canadian positions but their line was held and reinforcements found to stem the advance of the German infantry who, in many places, dug in instead of pressing forward. Next day, on the Allied side, there were hasty improvisations.

The gas was quickly identified for what it was and, as chlorine is soluble, Lieutenant Colonel Ferguson, of the 28th Division, proposed that cloths soaked in water be tied round the mouth as a protection. The Germans attacked the Canadians with gas again on 24 April, but the effect was less than on the first day and more reinforcements were at hand. Efforts at counter-attack were made both by the French and British. On 1 May there was another gas attack in the jumble of broken ground known to the British as Hill 60, the Dump and the Caterpillar, south of Ypres, where a railway line runs through the spoil heaps of the cutting near Zillibeke. Today the pockmarks and tumuli of this tiny battlezone still exude an atmosphere of morbidity sinister even among the relics of the Western Front. On 1 May, when the soldiers of the 1st Battalion the Dorset Regiment clung to the firestep of their trenches as gas seized their throats and the German infantry pounded towards them across no man's land, the scene must have been as near to hell as this earth can show. The situation was saved by a young officer, Second Lieutenant Kestell-Cornish, who seized a rifle and, with the four men remaining from his platoon of forty, fired into the gas cloud to hold the Germans at bay.[29] Another officer who devoted himself to those gassed reported that 'quite 200 men passed through my hands . . . some died with me, others on the way down . . . I had to argue with many of them as to whether they were dead or not.' In fact, '90 men died from gas poisoning in the trenches; [and] of the 207 brought to the nearest [dressing] stations, 46 died almost immediately and 12 after long suffering.'[30]

The line was held, nevertheless, by the Dorsets' almost inhuman devotion to duty and the Ypres Salient, though pushed back to within two miles of the city, was thereafter never dented. Gas in a variety of forms, the more deadly asphyxiant phosgene, and the blistering 'mustard', would continue in use throughout the war, and chlorine would kill thousands of Russian troops in German offensives west of Warsaw in May. Its intrinsic limitations as a weapon, dependent as it was on wind direction, and the rapid development of effective respirators, ensured, however, that it would never prove decisive, as it might have done if large reserves had been at hand to exploit the initial surprise achieved by the Germans in the Second Battle of Ypres.

The Allies had no technological surprise with which to inaugurate either of their offensives on the Western Front in 1915, and both failed, with heavy loss of life, for little or no gain of ground. In May, the French and British attacked in Artois, against the high ground from which the Germans dominated their positions, the British against Aubers Ridge on 9 May, the French against Vimy Ridge a week later. Although the French had artillery and ammunition available in quantity – 1,200 guns, 200,000 shells – while the British had not, the difference between their achievements was negligible. Haig's First Army was simply stopped in its tracks. The French, spearheaded by Pétain's XXXIII Corps, gained the summit of Vimy Ridge, to look down into the Douai plain through which the crucial rail tracks in enemy hands ran, only to be decisively counter-attacked by reserves reaching the summit before their own, positioned six miles in the rear, could join them. It was another example of the structural factors making for failure in trench warfare actually bringing it about.[31]

When the offensive was renewed in September, this time in Champagne as well as Artois, the results were scarcely different, though both armies had considerably larger numbers of divisions to deploy than in the spring. Their number had been increased on the French side by reorganisation, which had produced another twelve (numbered 120–132), on the British by further transfers of Territorial divisions to France, and the first appearance there in number of the 'New Army' or 'Kitchener' divisions of wartime volunteers. The plan of attack had been proposed to Sir John French by Joffre on 4 June. It required as a preliminary that the British take over more of the French line, to free the Second Army, which Pétain had been appointed to command, for the Champagne phase of the offensive. Haig had already in May taken over part of the French front in Flanders; now, in response to Joffre's request, the new British Third Army moved south to the Somme to relieve Pétain's army. The British now held most of the line from Ypres to the Somme, leaving a short length near Vimy from which the French Tenth Army would attack as soon as preparations for Joffre's plan were completed.

That took time. The will was present – on 7 July, at the first interallied conference of the war, held at Chantilly, the French, British, Belgians, Serbs, Russians and Italians, who had joined the alliance in May, pledged themselves to common action – but the means were not. In late June the French and British munitions ministers had met, when David Lloyd George told Albert Thomas, his opposite number, that both guns and shells were lacking for a major effort by the BEF in France. He wished to postpone the joint offensive until the following spring. Joffre resisted; he wanted urgent action, both to sustain pressure on the Germans and deter the diversion of troops to other theatres. The British government, in which the Conservatives had joined the Liberals to form a coalition ministry on 26 May, recognised that the autumn offensive was a test of confidence and withdrew its opposition. Practical difficulties nevertheless persisted. The British takeover on the Somme took time; so did the preparation of the Champagne battlefield. Both allies were learning that a large-scale attack against trenches could not be launched extempore; roads had to be built, stores dumped, battery positions dug. The date of the opening of what would be called the Second Battle of Champagne was postponed from the end of August to 8 September, then, because Pétain demanded time for a lengthy bombardment, until 25 September.

The Germans profited from the delay, and the undisguisable signs of impending attack, to strengthen the portions of their line against which they detected the offensive was preparing. Falkenhayn's instructions of January had laid down that a second position was to be constructed behind the first, with concrete machine-gun posts in between. Despite the enormous labour entailed, the system was complete by the autumn, forming a defensive belt up to three miles deep.[32] As experience was already demonstrating that a forward movement of three miles against enemy fire tested an individual burdened with battle-gear to the limit of his physical, let alone moral powers, the German positions in the Western Front were becoming impregnable, certainly against an offensive planned to achieve breakthrough on the first day. Worse still for the attacker, German defensive doctrine required that the second position be constructed on the reverse slope of any height occupied – and the Germans, by careful choice during the retreat of 1914, occupied the high ground – so that it was protected from the Allied artillery fire designed to destroy it. The role of the German artillery was, by contrast, not to bombard trenches but to attack the enemy infantrymen as they assembled and then to lay a barrage in no man's land once they moved forward; those who penetrated that barrier of fire were to be left to the machine gunners who, experience was showing, could stop an attack at ranges as close as 200 yards or less.[33]

The effectiveness of the Germans' preparations was proved all too painfully on 25 September 1915, at Loos, the site of the BEF's offensive in Artois, at nearby Souchez, where the French renewed their assault on Vimy Ridge, and at Tahure, la Folie and la Main de Massige in distant Champagne, where the French attacked alone. In both sectors the offensives were preceded by a discharge of chlorine gas. At Loos, the gas hung about in no man's land or even drifted back into the British trenches, hindering rather than helping the advance. In any case the six British divisions engaged – three regular, 1st, 2nd, 7th, two 'New Army', 9th and 15th Scottish, one Territorial, the 47th – were quickly stopped by machine guns; when two reserve divisions, both New Army, 21st and 24th, were started forward in support, it was from a position so far to the rear that they did not reach the original British front line until dark. They were ordered to resume the advance next morning, which they spent marshalling for the attack. In early afternoon they moved forward in ten columns 'each [of] about a thousand men, all advancing as if carrying out a parade-ground drill'. The German defenders were astounded by the sight of an 'entire front covered with the enemy's infantry'. They stood up, some even on the parapet of the trench, and fired triumphantly into the mass of men advancing across the open grassland. The machine gunners had opened fire at 1,500 yards' range. 'Never had machine guns had such straightforward work to do ... with barrels becoming hot and swimming in oil, they traversed to and fro along the enemy's ranks; one machine gun alone fired 12,500 rounds that afternoon. The effect was devastating. The enemy could be seen falling literally in hundreds, but they continued their march in good order and without interruption' until they reached the unbroken wire of the Germans' second position: 'Confronted by this impenetrable obstacle the survivors turned and began to retire.'

The survivors were a bare majority of those who had come forward. Of the 15,000 infantry of the 21st and 24th Divisions, over 8,000 had been killed or wounded. Their German enemies, nauseated by the spectacle of the 'corpse field of Loos', held their fire as the British turned in retreat, 'so great was the feeling of compassion and mercy after such a victory'.[34] A German victory Loos was; though the British persisted with attacks for another three weeks, they gained nothing but a narrow salient two miles deep, in which 16,000 British soldiers had lost their lives and nearly 25,000 had been wounded. The battle had been a terrible and frustrating initiation to combat for the soldiers of the New Armies, though the Scots of the 9th and 15th Divisions, in particular, seem to have shrugged off casualties and taken setback only as a stimulus to renewed aggression. Major John Stewart, of the 9th Black Watch, wrote to his wife after the battle, 'the main thing is to kill plenty of Huns with as little loss to oneself as possible; it's a great game and our allies are playing it top hole'.[35] His was not a lone voice. The new British volunteer divisions yearned to prove their soldierly qualities and the patriotism of the French still burnt strong. It would be a year or more before the ardour of either army was quenched by the deluge of pointless losses.

Yet Loos, in strategic terms, was pointless and so, too, were the efforts of Pétain's Second Army and de Langle's Fourth in the offensive in Champagne that opened the same day. There twenty divisions attacked side by side on a front of twenty miles, supported by a thousand heavy guns and behind a gas cloud similar to that launched at Loos. The results were equally unavailing. Some French regiments attacked with colours unfurled and the brass and drums of their bands in the front trench. Others, when the advance faltered, found senior officers urging them forward. One of them, the famous colonial general, Charles Mangin, was shot through the chest as he organised an assault, though he returned to duty ten days later. For all his efforts and those of others like him, for all the continuing bravery of the French common soldier, the attempts on the Champagne heights nowhere gained more than two miles of ground. The Germans' second line was not penetrated and, when the fighting ended on 31 October, their positions remained intact, though 143,567 French soldiers had become casualties.[36]

It had been a doleful year for the Allies on the Western Front, much blood spilt for little gain and any prospect of success postponed until 1916. The Germans had shown that they had learnt much about the methods of defending an entrenched front, the Allies that they had learnt nothing about means of breaking through. It was a bitter lesson for the French, all the more so because, in a widening war, their allies seemed bent on seeking solutions elsewhere, leaving the main body of the enemy implanted in their territory. Yet the defeat of the enemy through victories outside France looked no closer a prospect than breakthrough towards the Rhine. In Russia, where German intervention had rescued Austria from collapse, on the new Italian front which had opened in May, in the Balkans, on the Turkish battlegrounds, the course of events favoured the enemy. Only at sea and in Germany's distant colonies had the Allies established an advantage, and, as they knew, in neither the naval nor the colonial theatres could success bring them victory.

SEVEN

THE WAR BEYOND THE WESTERN FRONT

BY THE END OF 1915, none of the original combatants was fighting the war that had been wanted or expected. Hopes of quick victory had been dashed, new enemies had appeared, new fronts had opened. France had the war that most nearly conformed to its General Staff's peacetime appreciation of strategic contingency, a war against Germany on its north-eastern frontier. Both timetable and costs had gone disastrously wrong, however, and it had unexpectedly found itself involved in subsidiary campaigns in the Balkans and eastern Mediterranean, as a result of Turkey's unanticipated intervention in November 1914. Turkey's entry had also upset Russia's calculation that it would have to deal with the Germans and Austrians alone; it was now also fighting a bitter and difficult campaign in the Caucasus. Germany had expected a one-front war fought in two stages: first against France, while a token force held its eastern front, then another victorious campaign against Russia. Instead, it was heavily engaged on both the Western and the Eastern Front, on the latter sustaining substantial forces on Austrian territory to prop up its Habsburg ally. Austria, which had thought the war might be limited to a punitive expedition against Serbia, had reaped the whirlwind of its folly, and found itself locked in combat not only with Russia but Italy as well. Serbia had reaped the whirlwind of its intransigence and found extinction as a state. Britain, which had committed itself at the outset only to providing an expeditionary force to widen the French left in Flanders, found itself assuming responsibility for ever longer stretches of the Western Front, while simultaneously finding men to fight the Turks at Gallipoli, in Egypt and in Mesopotamia, to assist the Serbs and to reduce the garrisons of Germany's African colonies; men had also to be found to reinforce the crews of ships denying the North Sea to the German High Seas Fleet, dominating the Mediterranean, chasing the enemy's surface commerce raiders to destruction and defending merchant shipping against U-boat attack. The war that men were already beginning to call the Great War was becoming a world war and its bounds were being set wider with every month that passed.

THE WAR IN THE GERMAN COLONIES

Germany had had to become an empire itself, the Second Reich, proclaimed in the Hall of Mirrors at Versailles in January 1871, before it could join Europe's great powers in the competition for empire. Their extensive conquests left the new state few pickings. North Africa was by then French, Central Asia and Siberia Russian, India British. Heinrick von Treitschke, the ideologist of German nationalism, announced that 'colonisation was a matter of life and death'.[1] Even so, there was little popular enthusiasm for the acquisition of colonies, perhaps because the only areas still available for exploitation were in the less favoured parts of Africa. It was German traders who supplied the impulse to enter the continent. Between 1884 and 1914, they had established commercial enclaves in Kamerun, Togo, and South-West Africa (Namibia) on the west coast, and what is now Tanzania on the east coast, which the imperial government had then consolidated. Purchase (from Spain) and deliberate imperial effort had meanwhile secured Papua, Samoa and the Caroline, Marshall, Solomon, Mariana and Bismarck Islands in the south and central Pacific. The coastal region of Kiaochow, and its port of Tsingtao, had been seized from China in 1897.

On the outbreak of war, the British and French at once took action to reduce the garrisons of Germany's colonies; the Japanese, who had entered the war (on 23 August) on a narrow interpetration of their obligations under the Anglo-Japanese Treaty of 1911, but in practice to improve their strategic position in the Pacific at Germany's expense, likewise moved against Tsingtao and the central Pacific islands. Japan occupied the Marianas, Marshalls and Carolines during October. Transferred to her by mandate after 1918, they were to form the outer perimeter of her island stronghold in the war against the United States twenty-five years later. Samoa fell to a New Zealand force on 29 August. German New Guinea (Papua) was surrendered uncon- ditionally to an Australian expedition on 17 September, together with the Solomons and the Bismarcks. The reduction of Tsingtao took longer. Heavily fortified, and defended by 3,000 German marines, it presented a formidable military obstacle to any attacker. The

Japanese, taking no chances, landed 50,000 men and commenced a deliberate siege. They were later joined by the 2nd South Wales Borderers and the 36th Sikhs from the British treaty part of Tientsin.[2] Three lines of defence confronted the attackers. The first two were abandoned by the Germans without resistance. Against the third, the Japanese dug parallels in regulation siege-warfare style and opened a bombardment with 11-inch howitzers, like those which had reduced the Russian defences of nearby Port Arthur ten years earlier. On the night of 6/7 November an infantry assault was delivered, across a no man's land which had been reduced to 300 yards in width, and the following morning Captain Meyer Waldeck, the naval officer serving as governor, surrendered his force. His marines had lost 200 men killed, against 1,455 Japanese fatal casualties. It had been a brave, if purely symbolic resistance.

In Africa, the tiny territory of Togo, sandwiched between the British Gold Coast (now Ghana) and French Dahomey (now Benin) was quickly overrun (27 August) by troops of the West African Rifles and the *Tirailleurs sénégalais*. Kamerun (now Cameroon), a much larger territory, equal in size to Germany and France combined, proved more difficult to conquer. The garrison numbered about a thousand Europeans and three thousand Africans. The Allied force included troops of the Nigeria, Gold Coast and Sierra Leone Regiments under British command, French African infantry and a Belgian contingent brought up from the Congo. Together with tens of thousands of carriers, essential support to any campaign in African forest or bush, the army eventually rose to a strength of 25,000. Despite its preponderance of numbers, distance, climate and topography blunted its early efforts. Three British columns were in motion across the Nigerian border by the end of August, each separated from the other by 250 miles of roadless terrain. Near Lake Chad, on the old Central African slave-trading route only recently conquered by the French, one was advancing towards Mora; a second was approaching Yarua, 500 miles from the sea; a third, near the coast itself, was directed at Nsanakang. All three encountered strong resistance and were turned back with heavy losses. The French did better, seizing a coastal bridgehead and winning a small battle at Kusseri, just south of Lake Chad. The arrival of reinforcements then gave the British the advantage and, with the assistance of four British and French cruisers and a fleet of small craft, they secured the coast, captured Douala, the colonial capital and wireless station, on 27

September and started inland up the rivers and the two short colonial railways. The objective was Yaounda, 140 miles inland, where the enemy had an ordnance depot. Skilful German resistance, sustained during the torrential rainy season, delayed the renewal of the advance until October 1915; in the interval, the African soldiers cultivated gardens to supplement their intermittent ration supply.[3] Finally, as the dry season opened in November, the Allies pushed forward into the central mountainous region and forced most of the Germans to seek internment in the neutral enclave of Spanish Guinea. The last German post of Mora, where the campaign had opened in the far north eighteen months earlier, surrendered in February 1916.[4]

The Cameroon campaign differed little in character from those by which the British and French had subdued the warrior tribes during the original conquests. That which opened in German South-West Africa in September 1914 was of a different quality altogether. 'German South-West', now Namibia, is an enormous territory, six times the size of England, arid, infertile and populated then by only 80,000 Africans. Mostly Herero tribesmen, whose rebellion in 1904 had been put down with ruthlessness by the Governor, the future Reichsmarschal Hermann Goering's father, they were kept under close control by the German garrison of 3,000 and the 7,000 German male settlers. The German government had hoped, as elsewhere in its African possessions, to avoid a conflict in 'South-West'; they put their trust in a vague, mutual, pre-war commitment to neutrality in Africa between the colonial powers. The British, however, were determined otherwise and, despite the fact that the withdrawal of their garrison from the neighbouring Union of South Africa on the outbreak of war left them dependent on its Defence Force, of which their former opponents in the Boer War of 1899–1902 formed a large proportion, they embarked at once on an expedition by sea and land against the German colony. Some 60,000 troops were available. A few, the South African Permanent Force, were regulars, wholly loyal to Britain, from which many came. The Citizen Force was divided; some of its units, the Durban Light Infantry, the Imperial Light Horse, were Anglo-South African and loyal to the crown, as were the contingents of white Rhodesians (one of whom was the future Air Marshal 'Bomber' Harris) who arrived from East Africa to take part. Others were a touchier proposition. Of the leading commanders of the Boer War now in British service, General Louis Botha had made his peace and would not shift; he had a personal commitment to Jan Smuts, one of

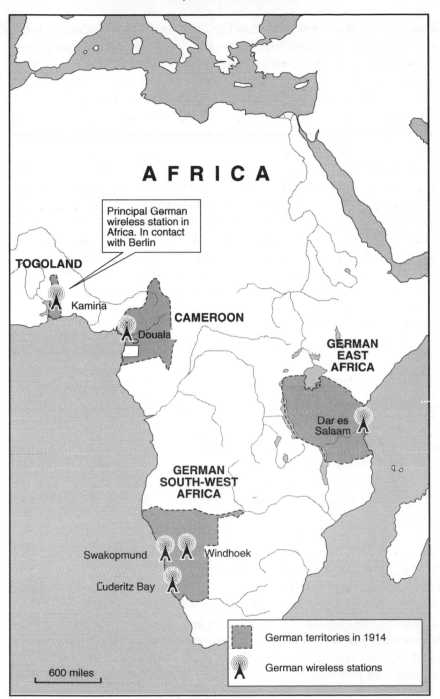

AFRICA

Principal German wireless station in Africa. In contact with Berlin

TOGOLAND

Kamina

CAMEROON

Douala

GERMAN EAST AFRICA

Dar es Salaam

GERMAN SOUTH-WEST AFRICA

Swakopmund   Windhoek

Luderitz Bay

German territories in 1914

German wireless stations

600 miles

Germany's African Territories

the most dashing ex-Boer generals but now Prime Minister of the Union. Christiaan de Wet, a Boer hero, and Christiaan Beyers, who held post as commander of the Defence Force, went into active rebellion. So, too, did General Jan Kemp and Colonel Soloman Maritz; the former resigned his commission, the latter refused to obey orders. At the very beginning, therefore, Britain found itself engaged both in a colonial campaign against the German enemy and in a Boer rebellion.[5]

The rebellion, fortunately for the British, did not take fire. About 11,000 Afrikaners joined in but, opposed by 30,000 loyalists, Boer and British, they had all been forced into surrender or, a few, into German territory by January 1915. The war against the Germans then began in earnest. The army was formed into four columns. Mainly mounted, many of the soldiers Boer 'burghers', some of whom had fought the British at Majuba in 1881, they converged on the German centres of resistance from the coast, from the Orange River and from Bechuanaland, the enormous protectorate (now Botswana) to the north of the Union. The objective was Windhoek, the German colonial capital, on which the Germans fell back in a fighting retreat. Resistance continued after its capture on 12 May 1915, though with the exchange of courtesies on both sides. The Germans were in a hopeless position. Outnumbered many times, and forced to campaign in one of the most desolate regions of the world, without any prospect of resupply from outside, they eventually surrendered unconditionally on 9 July 1915. The German officers were allowed to retain their swords, the German settler reservists to return to their farms with arms and ammunition to protect themselves, their families and their properties.[6] Windhoek remains today the only distinctively German city in the southern hemisphere.

By 1916, the last centre of German resistance to the British and French forces in the colonial empires was in 'German East', today Tanzania. The war in that enormous colony, almost exactly the size of France, had begun on 8 August, when the British cruiser *Astraea* had bombarded its port of Dar-es-Salaam. Hostilities then lapsed. When resumed, they were to last until after the negotiation of the European armistice in November 1918, testimony to the extraordinary tenacity and prowess in leadership of Colonel Paul von Lettow-Vorbeck, commander of the colony's *Schutztruppe*. Lettow-Vorbeck, aged forty-four in 1914, was an experienced imperial campaigner; he had served previously in the German contingent sent to suppress the Boxer

Rising in China and in German South-West. Appointment to German East Africa was a denomination of his standing; Baroness Karen Blixen, author of *Out of Africa*, who sailed with him on the boat out, remembered that no other German had given her 'so strong an impression of what Imperial Germany was and stood for'.[7] This colony was, indeed, the pearl of the Second Reich's overseas possessions. Togo was a trifle, Kamerun an unpeopled land of fever, 'South West' a beautiful but empty desert. German East Africa, bounded by British Uganda and Kenya to the north, the Belgian Congo and Rhodesia to the west, British Nyasaland and Portuguese Mozambique to the south, straddled the Great Lakes region, the most romantic and potentially productive part of the continent. Its boundaries were crossed or formed by Lakes Victoria, Tanganyika and Nyasa, and Mount Kilimanjaro stood within its territory.

At the outset it seemed that the pre-war understanding between the powers to exempt black Africa from hostilities might prevail. The German governor, Schnee, forbade offensive operations; the Governor of British Kenya declared his colony had no 'interest in the present war'. Moreover, neither governor disposed of any force with which to fight. They reckoned without the aggressiveness of the young men on both sides. Lettow-Vorbeck simply ignored Schnee and began assembling his forces, few though they were, about 2,500 askaris and 200 white officers. Nairobi, capital of Kenya, meanwhile began filling up with bellicose young settlers and white hunters, all bearing arms and demanding uniforms and a mission. Like the Confederate bloods and dandies of April 1861, they formed military units of their own, with outlandish names – Bowker's Horse, the Legion of Frontiersmen – and marched out to repel Lettow-Vorbeck as he made his first move. In September the war was under way, whatever the governors' wishes.

The home governments wanted war also. A German cruiser, the *Königsberg,* was operating off East Africa before the war began and opened hostilities by sinking a British warship, HMS *Pegasus.* Small though she was, her loss drove the admiral commanding the South African station to concentrate all his force, of three cruisers, against *Königsberg.* She was soon driven into the swampy depth of the Rufiji river, where her captain conducted a brilliant exercise in evasion that lasted 255 days. The cruiser was eventually sunk only after the Admiralty had sent out two shallow-draft monitors, the *Severn* and *Mersey,* from Britain to nail her in her lair. Even as a hulk, however, she continued to contribute to the campaign. Many of her crew went ashore to serve with Lettow-Vorbeck's askaris and some of her guns were dismounted and used as field artillery.

Lettow's aggressiveness had by then caused Britain to prepare a full-scale military expedition against him. He was not only raiding into Uganda and Kenya, where he raised the German flag on British territory under Mount Kilimanjaro, but conducting inland naval operations on the Great Lakes; prefabricated gun boats were eventually sent out from Britain to regain control of those inland waters. The most important reinforcement, however, was two brigades of British and Indian troops from India. The Indian regiments were second-rate but the British regulars should have compensated for that. They did not; the expedition's first landing at Tanga on 2 November 1914 ended in humiliation. The Indians ran away, the British got lost; though outnumbered eight to one, the Germans easily drove their enemies back to the beaches, where they re-embarked on 5 November, leaving sixteen machine guns, hundreds of rifles and 600,000 rounds of ammunition behind.

These supplies would help to sustain von Lettow's campaign throughout 1915, a slack period in which the British built up their strength and he learnt the essentials of the war he was going to fight. Better British troops arrived; he won a small victory at Jassin. The cost in German lives there and in ammunition – his askaris had fired off 200,000 rounds – taught Lettow that 'we had to economise our forces to last out a long war . . . the need to restrict myself to guerrilla warfare was evidently imperative'. That, thereafter, would be his strategy.[8] In March 1916, Jan Smuts arrived from South Africa, bringing the Defence Force troops released by the conquest of German South-West. He began to plan a convergent offensive, from Kenya, Nyasaland, the Belgian Congo and Portuguese Mozambique, designed to crush Lettow's little army in the interior. Lettow had no intention of being caught. Instead he would resist the British as fiercely as he could, springing savage ambushes as they pushed forward; then, before they could bring superior numbers against him, he would slip away, destroying anything of value as he retreated. Since his soldiers could live off the land, and resupply themselves with ammunition by capture from the enemy, his capacity to evade defeat in the enormous spaces of the bush was almost limitless, as he would demonstrate throughout 1916, 1917 and 1918.

CRUISER WAR

Before Lettow set off on his extraordinary venture into the vastness of the African interior, while indeed he was still conducting his opening border skirmishes, another, briefer but dramatic campaign had been mounted by the overseas squadrons of the Imperial German Navy in the depths of the Atlantic and Pacific oceans. Germany's main fleet, built to confront Britain with 'risk' to its dominant maritime position, was deliberately concentrated in Germany's North Sea ports. It was from those places that it could menace the Royal Navy with the threat of a break-out on to the high seas and with the danger of a surprise encounter in which Britain's superior numbers might be outbalanced by the vagaries of weather or chance. Germany also maintained, however, small forces in the Pacific, at Tsingtao and in the islands. In August, the cruisers *Scharnhorst* and *Gneisenau* were in the Carolines, *Emden* was at Tsingtao, *Dresden* and *Karlsruhe* were in the Caribbean, *Leipzig* was off the Pacific coast of Mexico and *Nürnberg* was en route to relieve her; the *Königsberg*, already mentioned, was on a lone mission off East Africa. Though few in number, these eight ships represented a major threat to Allied shipping, particularly to convoys bringing Australian and New Zealand troops to European waters, for they were of recent construction, fast, well-armed and commanded by officers of ability, notably Admiral Maximilian von Spee, who led the *Scharnhorst* and *Gneisenau* squadron. It was a major weakness of British naval planning that its own cruiser fleet consisted either of old, so-called 'armoured' ships too slow to catch their German equivalents, and too poorly protected and armed to harm them if taken at a disadvantage, or of light cruisers which had speed to match that of the Germans but lacked the firepower to fight. The technological gap was supposed to be filled by the newly fashionable battlecruisers, fast, lightly armoured Dreadnoughts, but their high construction costs had kept their numbers small while absorbing the funds which might have gone to modernising the conventional cruiser fleet. This unintended consequence would, in the first months of the war, cause the Royal Navy heavy loss of life and ships and grave damage to its prestige.

The navy lacked, moreover, any concerted plan to deal with an aggressive German cruising campaign. Its vast network of coaling stations diminished the incentive to plan for resupplying a pursuit across oceanic distances; the Germans, by contrast, had a train of colliers and began at once to capture prizes as a source of coal, food and water. They also sailed victualling ships from home waters to rendezvous with the raiders, and to act independently as armed merchant cruisers. If there was a weakness in the German arrangements, it was that meetings had to be arranged by wireless, in a code which the British quickly broke.

Two of the raiders were swiftly run down. *Königsberg*, the least well-handled, ceased to count after she was driven into the Rufiji delta. *Emden*, under an energetic captain, Karl von Müller, caused havoc in the Pacific and Indian oceans, though pursued at times not only by British but also French, Russian and Japanese ships. She was eventually intercepted and sunk by the Australian cruiser *Sydney* at Direction Island in the Cocos and Keeling group on 9 November 1914, after the local wireless station managed to get off a signal before the German landing party destroyed the transmitter. *Sydney* had been detached from one of the large escorted convoys bringing Australian troops to the Mediterranean. That was not quite the end of *Emden*'s remarkable cruise. The commander of the landing party on Direction Island evaded the Australians, appropriated a schooner, sailed it to the Dutch East Indies, got passage aboard a German steamer to Yemen in Arabia, fought off Bedouin attacks, reached the Hejaz railway built to bring pilgrims to Mecca and eventually arrived to a justifiably extravagant welcome in Constantinople in June 1915.[9]

Karlsruhe was destroyed by a mysterious internal explosion off Barbados on 4 November, after sinking sixteen merchant ships. *Leipzig* and *Dresden*, with varied adventures behind them, rendezvoused with Admiral von Spee in South American waters in October; *Nürnberg* had joined him earlier. These five ships then formed the most formidable threat to Allied control of the seas outside the North Sea. Spee exploited his advantage. Deterred from operating in the northern Pacific by the menace of the large Japanese fleet which cruised widely and aggressively in the early months of the war, mopping up many of the German island possessions it would use so successfully in 1941–4, Spee acted against the French possessions in Tahiti and the Marquesas but met resistance and found coaling difficult. With bold strategic sweep, he therefore decided to transfer from the Pacific to the South Atlantic, signalling *Dresden, Leipzig* and his colliers to meet him near Easter Island, the most remote inhabited spot on the globe.[10]

Interception of his insecure signals alerted the British admiral commanding the South American station, Christopher Cradock, of

232

his intentions. Passing through the Straits of Magellan, Cradock brought his squadron into Chilean waters. The light cruiser *Glasgow* went ahead; Cradock followed with the cruisers *Monmouth* and *Good Hope* and the battleship *Canopus*, so old (1896) and slow that it was left to escort the accompanying colliers. *Monmouth* and *Good Hope* were almost as old, not much faster and poorly armed. They steamed to join *Glasgow*, which had put into the little Chilean port of Coronel. Intercepted intelligence then gave Spee the advantage. Hearing that *Glasgow* was at Coronel, he waited outside for the old cruisers to appear. When they did, on the evening of 1 November, he kept out of range until darkness fell, then opened fire in the gloaming. *Monmouth* and *Good Hope* were quickly sunk, not one of the 1,600 sailors aboard surviving. *Glasgow* escaped to warn *Canopus* and save her from a similar fate.

Coronel was the first British defeat at sea for a hundred years. The outrage it caused was enormous, far exceeding that following the loss of *Hogue, Cressy* and *Aboukir,* three other old cruisers sunk by submarine U-9 off Holland on 22 September. Admiral Sir John Fisher, who had become First Sea Lord on 31 October, at once set in motion a pan-oceanic redeployment of forces designed to intercept Spee wherever he moved. The Cape, South American and West African stations were reinforced, while the Japanese navy also repositioned units, so threatening Spee's freedom of action in the Indian, Atlantic and Pacific Oceans.[11] Most dangerously for Spee, Fisher decided to detach two of his precious battlecruisers, *Invincible* and *Inflexible*, from the Grand Fleet and send them to the South Atlantic. Spee might still have remained free to cruise for a long time, losing himself in the vast expanses of the southern oceans and coaling from prizes and remote neutral ports, had he not decided to act aggressively and attack the British Falkland Islands in the South Atlantic. Having left the Pacific after Coronel, he arrived off Port Stanley on 8 December. Fatally for the Germans, Admiral Sir Doveton Sturdee, commanding the battlecruiser squadron, had also decided to visit Port Stanley and was coaling his squadron when the Germans appeared. Making steam in haste, Sturdee left harbour and worked up speed to run the five German ships down. None was a match, for the battlecruisers were both faster than *Scharnhorst* and *Gneisenau,* his strongest ships, and far more heavily gunned. Bravely, Spee turned them to cover the escape of the others but was overwhelmed by salvoes of 12-inch shells at ranges his 8.2-inch guns could not match. Two of his light cruisers were also run down by Sturdee's light cruisers. Only *Dresden* got away, to skulk for three months in the sub-Arctic inlets around Cape Horn, until cornered and forced to scuttle on 14 March 1915, by a British squadron that included the only survivor of the Coronel disaster, HMS *Glasgow*.

The victory of the Falklands terminated the high seas activity of the German navy. A few armed merchant ships would subsequently manage to slip through the North Sea into great waters and raid the shipping lanes, but the navy's regular units were not risked in such adventures. After the Falklands, indeed, the oceans belonged to the Allies and the only persistent naval surface fighting, pending a clash of the capital fleets in the North Sea, took place in landlocked waters, the Black Sea, the Baltic and the Adriatic. The Mediterranean was wholly controlled by the Royal and French Navies, assisted by the Italian after Italy's entry, and their command of it was to be disturbed only by the appearance of German U-boats there in October 1915. Inside the Adriatic, cordoned at its bottom end by an Italian mine barrier anchored on Otranto, the Austrians waged a tit-for-tat war with the Italians, of which the only strategic point was to deny the Allies more direct amphibious access to the Balkan war zone than the Mediterranean coast allowed. A similar war was waged in the Baltic between Germany's light forces and pre-Dreadnoughts and Russia's Baltic fleet. There was much mine-laying, which deterred the Russians risking their Dreadnoughts far from Finnish ports, coastal bombardment and, eventually, some daring British submarine operations. Russia's beautiful British-built *Rurik* (1906), model of the cruisers Britain should have been building for herself, was frequently and effectively engaged until badly damaged by a mine in November 1916.[12] From a naval point of view, the war in the Baltic was most notable for what did not happen there. Fisher, as ready with bad as with good ideas, had advocated a large-scale naval penetration of the Baltic as early as 1908. In 1914 he converted Churchill, equally undiscriminating if a strategic project were grand enough, and even secured funds to build three huge shallow-draft battlecruisers to make the attempt. Fortunately better sense prevailed and the monsters, which could outrun destroyers at speed, were spared inevitable destruction in the Baltic's narrow waters to become post-war aircraft carriers.[13]

In the Black Sea, where Russia maintained the second of her three fleets – the third, in the Pacific, played a minor part in the conquest of Germany's possessions there and the destruction of her raiding cruisers – her command was complete. The Turks, after their declaration of hostilities in November 1914, had neither sufficient nor good enough ships to challenge, and the Russians, if sporadically and inefficiently, mined Turkish waters and attacked Turkish ports and shipping at will. Such operations, however, were peripheral. Turkey did not depend on sea lines of communication to sustain her war effort nor could Russia project military power through her fleet; a project to land the V Caucasian Corps near Constantinople in 1916 was abandoned after the difficulties became apparent.[14]

Yet Turkey's navy was, nevertheless, to prove, even if indirectly, one of the most significant instruments in the widening of the world crisis. The Ottoman government, under the control of the 'Young Turk' nationalists since 1908, had spent the years since taking power in modernising the empire's institutions. That was a recurrent enterprise. Attempts to modernise in the first years of the nineteenth century had resulted in the murder of the Sultan, a second attempt in 1826, apparently successful, had foundered on the profound conservatism of courtiers and religious leaders. All Europeans who dealt with the Turks – and Germans, including Moltke the Elder, were prominent among them – recorded their frustration and contempt at the Ottomans' seemingly incurable indolence. The Germans nevertheless persisted with eventual success. The Young Turks, who included numbers of Balkan Muslims, seemed different from the old, welcoming German military advice and commercial investment. The railway system benefited from German money, the Ottoman army was re-equipped with Mauser rifles and Krupp guns. The Young Turks nevertheless looked to Britain, as all emergent powers of the period did, for naval armament and in 1914 were about to take delivery from British yards of two magnificent Dreadnoughts, the *Reshadieh* and the *Sultan Osman*, the latter the most heavily armed ship in the world, with fourteen 12-inch guns. On the outbreak of war with Germany, Britain peremptorily purchased both. Two days earlier, however, on 2 August, Turkey had concluded with Germany an alliance against Russia, her neighbour, oldest enemy, protector of her ex-Balkan subject peoples and conqueror of vast swathes of former Ottoman territory.[15] Germany at once sailed its Mediterranean squadron, comprising the battlecruiser *Goeben* and light cruiser *Breslau*, into Turkish waters, evading a mismanaged British effort to head them off. On arrival at Constantinople, they hoisted the Turkish flag and changed their names to *Sultan Selim* and *Midillu*: Souchon, the squadron commander, became a Turkish admiral. British protests were met with the riposte that the ships had been 'purchased' as necessary replacements for the two Dreadnoughts commandeered by Britain which, as *Erin* and *Agincourt*, now formed part of the Grand Fleet.

For the next three months, *Goeben* and *Breslau* remained peacefully at anchor off Constantinople. The conditions for Turkey's entry into the war were, however, already in place, for the treaty pledged her to assist Germany in the event of the latter having to support Austria-Hungary against Russia, a diplomatic circumstance already in force when it was signed. Enver Pasha, the leading Young Turk and Minister of War, was meanwhile completing his military preparations. Liman von Sanders, his senior German military adviser, expected him to open hostilities by an expedition into the great plains of the Russian Ukraine. Instead, Enver chose to make his attack into the wild mountains of the Caucasus, where terrain and the Muslim loyalties of the population would, he believed, work to Turkey's advantage. As a public signal of precipitation of the new war, however, he sent Souchon, *Goeben, Breslau* and some of Turkey's own raggle-taggle warships to engage the Russian fleet 'wherever it was found'.[16] Souchon, interpreting his orders broadly, divided his force and, on 29 October, attacked the Russian ports of Odessa, Sebastopol, Novorossisk and Feodosia. Three days later, Russia declared war on Turkey and by 5 November Turkey was at war with France and Britain also.

THE WAR IN THE SOUTH AND EAST

Turkey's entry did not merely add another member to the alliance of the Central Powers or another enemy to those the Allies were fighting already. It created a whole new theatre of war, actual and potential, drawn in several dimensions, religious and insurrectionary as well as purely military. Turkey was the seat of the Muslim Caliphate and, as the successor of Mahomet, Sultan Mehmed V declared 'holy war' on 11 November and called on all Muslims in British, French and Russian territory to rise in arms. The effect was negligible. Though the British felt concern that the Muslim soldiers of their Indian Army might be swayed, few were, and those mainly Pathans of the North-West Frontier, natural rebels who 'would probably be sniping at British troops within a year or two of going on pension and at home in their tribe . . . [they] owed allegiance to no man, living in an anarchic paradise ruled by the bullet and the blood feud'.[17] The troopers of the 15th Lancers who mutinied at Basra in February 1915 were Pathans, as were the sepoys of the 130th Baluchis who had mutinied at Rangoon in January. Both episodes were explicable in terms of unwillingness to serve outside India, a repetitive occurrence in the Indian Army. The mutiny of the 5th Light Infantry at Singapore on 15 February 1915 was more serious, since the sepoys were not Pathans but Punjabi Muslims, the backbone of the Indian Army, who did not merely disobey orders but murdered thirty-two Europeans and released some interned Germans, whom they hailed as fellow-combatants in the holy war.[18] Most of the Germans, putting loyalty to colour above country, rejected liberation and the mutiny was swiftly crushed. The loyal half of the regiment was, however, judged too untrustworthy to commit to any regular theatre of war and was sent to fight in the Kamerun campaign.[19] In four other cases the British decided not to risk using battalions largely Muslim in composition against the Turks; yet large numbers of Muslims did fight against the Sultan-Caliph's soldiers without demur. The numerous Muslim regiments of the French army fought the Germans without paying the Sultan's call to *jihad* any attention whatsoever.

Mehmed V's holy war was therefore a flop. The engagement of his empire, by contrast, was a strategic event of the greatest importance, for so wide was its geographical extent that its territory touched that of his enemies at many points, so ensuring the opening of new fronts wherever it did. In the Persian Gulf it formally did not, but the effect was the same, for Britain regarded the Gulf and its coastline as a British lake. The 'Trucial' Sheikhs of the Arabian coast had been bound by treaty since 1853 to refer disputes between them to the Government of India, whose power to maintain peace and punish its breach the same treaty established. The Viceroy's political officers acted as residents, in effect overseers, at the sheikhs' courts and, on the Persian side, as consuls with wide executive powers; since 1907 Persia had been divided into northern, Russian, and south-western, British, spheres of influence, an arrangement the feeble Persian government had no means to resist.[20] The discovery of oil had further strengthened Britain's interest in the Gulf and the Anglo-Persian Oil Company's refinery on the Persian island of Abadan at the head of the Gulf was by 1914 an imperial outpost in all but name. As the main supplier of fuel for the latest generation of oil-burning Dreadnoughts (the *Royal*

237

Sovereign and *Queen Elizabeth* classes), the company was judged a vital strategic asset and a controlling interest in its shares had been bought by Britain, at Winston Churchill's instigation, in 1913.[21]

Turkey's undisguised inclination towards Germany from August 1914 onwards decided Britain to secure its position at the head of the Gulf, which was Turkish territory, by military occupation. The obvious source of troops for the operation was India and in September part of the 6th Indian Division was shipped to Bahrein, then the most important of the Gulf sheikhdoms. On Turkey's declaration, the British government also took the opportunity to recognise the separate sovereignty of Kuwait, while the convoy carrying the division proceeded to the mouth of the Shatt el-Arab, the confluence of the Tigris and Euphrates rivers in Turkish Mesopotamia, bombarded the Turkish port and landed troops on 7 November. The expeditionary force then marched inland and by 9 December had occupied Basra, the chief city of southern Mesopotamia, and advanced to Qurna, where the two rivers join. There it paused, while decisions were taken about its future employment. They were to prove among the most ill-judged of the war.

Meanwhile the Turks had taken an initiative of their own in another corner of their enormous empire. Egypt remained legally part of it but, since 1882, had been under the administration of a British 'Agent' with powers of government. The higher tax officials were British and so were the senior officers of the police and army; Kitchener, British Minister of War, had first made his name as Sirdar of the Egyptian army. One of the few positive results of Mehmed V's call to holy war was to prompt his nominal viceroy of Egypt, the Khedive, to reaffirm his loyalty.[22] The British instantly abolished his office and declared a protectorate. That was resented by the Egyptian upper classes but, in a country where all power rested with the new protector and most of the commercial life was in the hands of expatriates, British but also French, Italian and Greek, their objections were wholly ineffective. Moreover, Egypt was filling up with troops, Territorials sent from Britain to replace the regular British garrison of the Suez Canal, recalled to France, and Indians, Australians and New Zealanders staging to Europe. By January 1915 their numbers had risen to 70,000.

It was this moment that the Turks, at German prompting, chose to attack the Suez Canal, which Britain had illegally closed to enemy belligerents at the outbreak of war. The conception was faultless, for the Canal was the most important line of strategic communication in the Allies' war zone, through which passed not only much essential supply but, at that moment, the convoys bringing the 'imperial' contingents from India and Australasia to Europe. The difficulty was in execution, for the Turkish approaches to the Canal lay across the hundred waterless miles of the Sinai desert. Nevertheless, careful preparations had been made. Pontoons for a water crossing were prefabricated in Germany and smuggled, through pro-German Bulgaria, to Turkey and then sent by rail across Syria to Palestine. In November the Ottoman Fourth Army was concentrated at Damascus, under the command of General Ahmed Cemal, with a German officer, Colonel Franz Kress von Kressenstein, as his Chief of Staff. Both hoped there would be an Egyptian rising once the attack was

The war in the Middle East

launched: even more wishfully, they expected to 'be joined by 70,000 Arab nomads'.[23] The approach chosen promised well, a direct march across the sands rather than down the traditional coastal route. Nevertheless, even in this very early age of aerial surveillance, a large army could not hope to pass unnoticed in terrain totally without cover during a journey of several days. It was, indeed, detected by a French aircraft before it reached the Canal, near Ismailia above the central Great Bitter Lake, on 3 February. The British were well prepared and, though fighting lasted a week, only a single Turkish platoon managed to drop its pontoon, so laboriously transported from Central Europe, into the Canal's waters. Cemal, frustrated by British resistance and the failure of the Arab tribes to ride to his support – Hussein, Sherif of Mecca, was already in revolt – turned his troops away and retreated.

The only outcome of the campaign was to keep in Egypt a larger British garrison than necessity dictated during 1915. Kress, however, remained in place and would cause the British trouble later; and there was one flicker of activity by the Arabs. In Libya, taken by Italy from Turkey in 1911, the fundamentalist Senussi sect embarked on a tiny holy war of raids against the western Egyptian border, the Italian occupiers, French North Africa and the Darfur province of the Anglo-Egyptian Sudan. Some of the veiled Tuareg warrior tribe joined them and the Senussi leader, Sidi Ahmad, found a secure base in the Siwa oasis, ancient seat of the oracle to which Alexander the Great made his pilgrimage in 331 BC before setting out on the conquest of the Persian empire. Sidi Ahmad appears to have been inspired by the hope that his display of loyalty to the Caliph would win him the guardianship of Mecca in place of the rebellious Hussein. In the event, his Ottoman liaison officer, Jaafar Pasha, after being wounded and captured by South African troops at Aqqaqia on 26 February 1916, defected to the Allies and became commander of Hussein's northern army in the later stages of the successful Arab Revolt against Ottoman rule in 1916–18.

The third front opened by Turkey's entry into the war, that in the Caucasus, was by far the most important, both for the scale of the fighting it precipitated and because of that fighting's consequences. The Ottoman advance into Russian Caucasia so alarmed the Tsarist high command that it prompted an appeal to Britain and France for diversionary assistance, and so led to the campaign of Gallipoli, one of the Great War's most terrible battles but also its only epic.

Enver, whose conception the Caucasus campaign was, chose the theatre for a variety of reasons. It was far from the main areas of deployment of the Russian army in Poland, therefore difficult to reinforce and already stripped of troops to fight the Germans and Austrians. It was of emotional importance to the Turks, as a homeland of fellow Muslims, many speaking tribal languages related to their own. It was, Enver believed, a potential centre of revolt against Russian rule, which had been imposed by brutal military action in the first half of the nineteenth century. To the Russians the wars in Caucasia had been a romantic epic, celebrated in the writings of Pushkin, Lermontov and the young Tolstoy, in which heroes of the times had battled in chivalrous combat against noble savage chieftains; Shamil, the most famous of them, had won the admiration even of his enemies.[24] To the mountaineers themselves, the Russian conquest had been the bitterest of oppressions, marked by massacre and deportation. 'By 1864', one contemporary calculated, '450,000 mountaineers had been forced to resettle ... entire tribes were decimated and relocated to assure Russian control of key areas, routes and coastlines.'[25] Enver counted on the memories of these atrocities to bring the 'Outside Turks', as Turkish nationalists liked to call all Muslims residing on territory once or potentially Ottoman, to Turkey's side. His plans, indeed, went wider, envisaging a dual-pronged offensive – of which the advance to the Suez Canal was one, that into the Caucasus the other – that would result in the raising of revolt in Egypt, Libya and the Sudan and in Persia, Afghanistan and Central Asia.

Enver's grand design was flawed on two counts. The first was that the non-Turkish peoples of the Ottoman empire, who formed the majority of the Sultan's subjects, were already awakening to their own nationalisms; they included not only the Arabs, who outnumbered the Turks, but such important minorities as the Muslim Kurds.[26] During his preparations for the advances on the Suez Canal, Cemal Pasha had found time to execute a number of Syrian Arab nationalists, who would become the original martyrs of the Arab renaissance, while many Kurds, oppressed by Ottoman officialdom for years past, took the opportunity the war presented to desert with their arms to the Russians as soon as mobilised.[27] In the circumstances, 'Outside Turks', whatever their historical associations with the Ottoman caliphate, were unlikely to respond to his appeal to holy war. The second flaw in Enver's plan was graver still, being unalterably geographical. 'The Caucasus', the Russian General Veliaminov had written in 1825, 'may be likened to a mighty fortress, marvellously strong by nature . . . only a thoughtless man would attempt to escalade such a stronghold.'

Enver was worse than thoughtless. His decision to attack the Caucasus at the beginning of winter, during which temperatures descend to twenty degrees of frost even in the lower passes and snow lies for six months, was foolhardy. He had superior numbers, about 150,000 in the Third Army, to the Russians' 100,000, but his line of supply was defective since, beyond the single railway, the troops depended on the roads, which were too few and snowbound to bear the weight of necessary traffic. His plan was to draw the Russians forward and then strike behind to cut them off from their bases. The first stage of the scheme succeeded, for the Russians favoured him by advancing during November as far as the great fortress of Erzerum and to Lake Van. This was the territory where the Seljuk ancestors of the Ottomans had won their victory of Manzikert against the Byzantines in 1071, the 'dreadful day' from which their decline to extinction at Constantinople in 1453 dated. The Turks then had been free-ranging horse nomads, unencumbered by heavy equipment. The Ottoman Third Army brought with it 271 pieces of artillery and proceeded ponderously. The weather, too, slowed its advance and caused much suffering and death; one division lost 4,000 of its 8,000 men to frostbite in four days of advance. On 29 December 1914 the Russian commander, General Mishlaevski, counter-attacked at Sarikamis, near Kars, on the railway between Lake Van and Erzerum, and triumphed. The victory was complete by 2 January, when the whole of the Turkish IX Corps surrendered, and in mid-month no more than 18,000 of the 95,000 Turks who had fought the campaign survived. Thirty thousand are said to have died of cold, an entirely plausible outcome of a campaign fought in winter at a mean elevation of 6,500 feet. Much of the credit for the victory belonged to Mishlaevski's Chief of Staff, General Nikolai Yudenich, who subsequently held command in the Caucasus with great success until the end of Russia's part in the war. The victory was, however, to have one lamentable local outcome. Among the troops the Russians had employed was a division of Christian Armenians, many of them disaffected Ottoman subjects, who took the opportunity offered by Russian sponsorship to commit massacre inside Turkish territory. Their participation in the campaign, and the declaration in April 1915 of a provisional Armenian government by nationalists on Russian-held territory, underlay the Ottoman government's undeclared campaign of genocide against their Armenian subjects which, between June 1915 and late 1917, led to the deaths of nearly 700,000 men, women and children, force-marched into the desert to die of starvation and thirst.

Despite its initial failure in the Caucasus, which the Ottoman government took care to conceal at home, Turkey's influence on the war continued to ramify. For all its long decline, which had begun with the Treaty of Carlowitz in 1699 and persisted until the conclusion of the Second Balkan War in 1913, Turkey remained, in the memory of its neighbours, particularly its European neighbours, a menacing military presence. For much of the preceding six centuries, ever since the Ottoman Turks had established their first foothold on the continent at Gallipoli in 1354, the Turks had been on the offensive against Christian Europe and, in the Balkans, had long been entrenched as occupiers and overlords. Greece, the first of the southern European Christian countries to win full independence from the Sultan, had done so only in 1832. Serbia, Bulgaria, Romania and Albania had achieved freedom much later, and the presence of Muslim minorities on their borders or within their territories was a constant reminder of former Ottoman overlordship. Italians, too, kept the memory of Ottoman power strongly in mind. Venice had waged centuries of war against Turkey and the loss to the Turks of the Venetian island empire in the Aegean rankled with them almost as much as did the more recent loss of the ports across the Adriatic to Austria. Turkey, weak though it had become, remained the only great power in the eastern Mediterranean. Its revival under the Young Turks had awoken ancient south European fears, which its defeat in the Balkan Wars had not quelled. Its alliance with Germany and Austria and its entry into the war had reinforced them.

Moreover, the reputation of the Turk as a fighting man had never dulled. Pony-riding nomad he might no longer be, farmer he might have become, but the hardiness of the Anatolian peasant, indifferent to cold, heat, privation and apparently danger also, was known to all his neighbours. The Ottoman forces, under the Young Turks, had undergone a programme of modernisation that promised to make better use of his soldierly qualities. The army, organised into four Armies, based at Istanbul, Baghdad, Damascus and Erzinjan, could put thirty-six divisions into the field. Divisions were weaker in artillery than their European equivalents, with only 24–36 guns, but the material was modern, and there were sixty-four machine-gun companies.[28] The supply and administration of the army, despite the efforts of the German military mission, led by General Liman von Sanders, remained dilatory, but the Turkish, if not the Arab, component of the army made up for shortcomings by its ability to live on very little and to march great distances without complaint. The Ottoman style of warfare had also traditionally laid great emphasis on digging. Behind earthworks, as at Plevna in 1877, the Turkish soldier fought with endurance and tenacity.

Turkey's decision to attack Russia in the Caucasus, however, its attempt against Egypt and its need to find forces to oppose the British expedition to the Tigris and Euphrates, appeared to create a military vacuum in the eastern Mediterranean that could be exploited by those with ambitions on its territory. Greece had such ambitions and, under its great nationalist leader, Venizelos, tilted towards joining the Allies. It was deterred by its military weakness and its common border with pro-German Bulgaria. Italy's territorial ambitions lay towards Austria first, from which it had failed to 'redeem' the Italian-speaking parts of the Tyrol and Slovenia in the last Austro-Italian War of 1866, but also towards the Turkish Dodecanese islands (of which she had been in occupation since 1912) and part of Turkish Syria. Diplomatically, Italy was still a party to the Triple Alliance of 1906, binding her to Germany as well as Austria, but had wriggled out of its provisions in August by a narrow interpretation of its terms, recognising that it was not strong enough to fight France by land or Britain and France by sea. The Italian navy, though recently modernised, was outgunned by their Mediterranean fleets.[29] Moreover, while Austria proved unwilling to offer any transfer of territory as a bribe to bring Italy in on her side, the Russians had made free with promises of Austrian territory if she joined the Allies, and their readiness to alter boundaries in the event of an Allied victory aroused hopes that the other Allies might do likewise. In March the Italian ambassador in London began negotiations with Sir Edward Grey, the British Foreign Secretary, about what Italy might be offered if she came over to the Allies, and the talks proceeded into April.[30] With Germany heavily engaged in France and Russia, Austria in the throes of a military crisis and Turkey overcommitted at the Asiatic borders of her empire, the reversion of alliance appeared not only risk-free but potentially highly profitable.

Moreover, Britain was already undertaking operations in the eastern Mediterranean which gave assurance that Italy would not be

Passchendaele

Top: A water cart bogged beside a brushwood track, St Eloi, 11 August 1917.

Above: Australians on a duckboard track, Chateau Wood, Ypres, 29 October 1917.

Serbia and Italy

Left: Serbian headquarters crossing the Sizir bridge, Albania, October, 1915.

Below left: Austrian mountain gunners firing a 70mm M8 howitzer.

Below: Austrian mountain machine-gun section, Italy, 1917.

French 75mm field gun
with limber and team.

Right: Austrian 305mm
howitzer at
Siemakowce, Galicia,
1915.

British Vickers
machine-gun crew.

A Royal Engineers
Signal Service visual
signalling post, at
Neuville-Vitasse,
Battle of Arras, 29
April 1917.

German infantry
training with an A7V
tank, 15 April 1918.

The Western Front, 1918

Top left: German infantry in a communications trench, Third German Offensive, May 1918.

Left: Breaking the Hindenburg Line: British infantry moving up, 29 September 1918

Top right: Breaking the Hindenburg Line: British Mark IV tanks going forward, 29 September 1918.

Above: American infantry advancing, autumn 1918.

Gallipoli

Turkish gunners
in action with
Krupp 77mm gun

Australians and the
Royal Naval Division
share a trench.

Wounded ANZAC
coming down,
relacements
waiting to go up, a
repeated Gallipoli
scene.

fighting alone in that theatre. Russia's appeal for assistance against Turkey, following the attack into the Caucasus, had had its effect. On 16 February part of the British Mediterranean fleet had entered the mouth of the Dardanelles, the waterway between the Mediterranean and the Black Sea, and bombarded the Turkish forts. The Italians had done likewise during their war with Turkey in 1911–12 and had sent light forces as far as the channel's narrows before they were turned back. Italy's purpose then had been to bring pressure on Turkey from Russia, by interfering with the economic life of Russia's Black Sea provinces, dependent as they were on the Dardenelles for access to the Mediterranean and Atlantic. Britain's purpose in 1915 was wider by far: to open a supply route to Russia through the Dardanelles and, in so doing, to 'knock Turkey out of the war' by bombarding Istanbul. An indirect effect of Britain's naval action against Turkey-in-Europe, however, was to buttress Italian resolution, promising as it did to sustain Serbia's continued resistance to Austria, thereby weakening the Austrians' ability to deploy troops on the Austro-Italian border, to deter Bulgaria from hostilities and eventually to bring arms and war supplies to Russia in quantities large enough to arm its unequipped millions and to reverse the balance of advantage on the Eastern Front.

Territorial avarice and strategic calculation prodded Italy towards a declaration of war throughout March and April. The German ambassador, Prince Bernhard Bülow, laboured to check the momentum, even offering Italy the Austrian territory Vienna had previously been unwilling to give. The majority of Italians, people and parliamentarians alike, had no enthusiasm for the dangerous adventure. The impetus came from Salandra, the Prime Minister, Sonnino, the Foreign Minister, the King, Victor Emmanuel III, and a collection of political and cultural revolutionaries, including Mussolini, then a socialist, the poet D'Annunzio and the artist Marinetti, inventor of Futurism.[31] The last, in particular, saw war as a means of dragging a backward Italy into the present and modernising it even against its will. The final stages of war preparations were conducted as a virtual conspiracy between Salandra, Sonnino and the King. On 26 April a Treaty of London was signed in secret with Britain, France and Russia, committing Italy to go to war within one month (in return for most of the Austrian territory it wanted, together with the Dodecanese islands in the eastern Mediterranean). On 23 May she declared war on Austria, though not yet against Germany.

From the beginning things went badly, as any realistic appreciation of the state of the Italian army and the nature of the terrain in which it would have to operate should have warned. The whole of the Italian frontier with Austria rested against the outworks of the highest mountains in Europe, from the Tyrol in the west to the Julian Alps in the east, forming a semi-circle of often precipitous crags 375 miles in extent, along which the enemy everywhere held the crests. At the western end, the Trentino, nine routes led through passes into the mountains; at the eastern end, where the Isonzo river cuts through the curtain, there is an avenue of advance. The Trentino, however, was a detached pocket of Austrian territory and so an unprofitable objective, while beyond the Isonzo valley the ground rises to form two desolate plateaux, the Bainsizza and the Carso, 'enormous natural fortresses towering two thousand feet or more above the surrounding lowlands'. The former is broken by a succession of steep ridges, the latter has been described as a 'howling wilderness of stones sharp as knives'.[32]

The terrain would have tried the skills of the best mountain troops. Italy possessed such soldiers, recruited from its own alpine districts, but they were few in number, forming only two brigades equipped with their own mountain artillery.[33] The majority of the army came from towns and farms, a quarter from the south and Sicily. The southerners had been subjects of the Kingdom of Italy for less than fifty years, had a low military reputation and looked to America rather than the cold and distant north as a point of emigration from their poor villages and overworked fields. The army as a whole was undertrained, it having no dedicated manoeuvre areas equivalent to those of France or Germany, was deficient in modern artillery, had only 120 heavy guns and had generally not made good its losses in all forms of equipment suffered during the Turkish War in Libya of 1911–12. Though able to put twenty-five infantry divisions into the field at the outbreak, it would remain the weakest among those of the major combatants throughout the war.

Its main strength was the officer corps it had inherited from the Kingdom of Savoy, whose army had been the instrument of the unification of Italy in 1870. Patriotic, professional and well-educated – the King of Savoy's army was the only one in Europe in which Jews enlisted freely and rose to high rank – the northern officers knew their business and had a mission to teach it to others. The Chief of Staff, Luigi Cadorna, was a martinet. He not only stood on his constitutional rights of supreme authority – independent of King and

Prime Minister – over the army once war began; he exercised that authority with a brutality not shown by any other general of the First World War. During its course, he dismissed 217 generals from duty and, in the crisis of 1917, ordered the summary shooting of officers of retreating units with pitiless inflexibility.[34] This style of command, as opposed to leadership, had its effect on the Italian army at the outset. Hopeless attacks were renewed, heavy losses accepted with an abnegation as remarkable as that of the British on the Somme or the French at Verdun. Indeed, given the uniquely impenetrable nature of the front the Italian army was set to attack, its early display of self-sacrifice may be thought unparalleled by any other. The price was paid later, in its moral collapse at Caporetto in October 1917.

Cadorna's plan for the opening of the war promised a rapid breakthrough that would avert losses. Choosing the Isonzo as the front of attack, he foresaw an advance, once the mountain barrier was broken, through the gateways cut by the rivers Drava and Sava to Klagenfurt and Agram (Zagreb) and thence into the heartland of the Austrian empire. His hopes resembled those of the Russians who, earlier in 1915, had believed that, once the crestline of the Carpathians could be taken, they would descend victorious into the Hungarian plain and capture Budapest. Cadorna's were even more misplaced. The land beyond the Isonzo is not a proper plain and the Julian Alps are an obstacle far more formidable than the Carpathians. When the Italian army attacked in what would become known as the First – of twelve, though the future kindly hid that from those involved – Battle of the Isonzo, beginning on 23 June 1915, its advanced guards did little more than establish contact with the enemy front line. That consisted of a single entrenchment, weakly manned. The Austrian army, already fighting a two-front war, in Poland and Serbia, had been holding the Italian border before the outbreak of hostilities with local militia battalions. In February some of these had been organised into two divisions. Early in May another division was detached from Serbia and later in the month three more sent from Poland.[35] By 23 May, the day of Italy's entry, General Boroevic, the Austrian commander of the Isonzo sector, had scraped together seven divisions in total, to form the Fifth Army, but they were heavily outnumbered. Had the precaution not been taken to dynamite shelters in the rock of the Carso and Bainsizza, and had the Italians been able to deploy more than 212 guns, Cadorna's hopes of a breakthrough might have been achieved. As it was, the Italian infantry, moving forward with great bravery but little tactical skill, were stopped in no man's land. Nearly 2,000 were killed and 12,000 wounded. The very high proportion of wounded was to prove a recurrent feature of the campaign, rock splintered by exploding shells becoming secondary projectiles which caused frequent injury, particularly to the head, and eyes.

There were to be three more battles of the Isonzo in 1915, in July, October and November, each incurring a heavier toll of killed and wounded, 6,287, 10,733, 7,498 dead respectively, for almost no gain of ground at all. The Austrians also suffered heavily, since artillery had the same effect on defenders in their rock-cut trenches as on attackers in the open, and by the end of the Fourth Battle they counted 120,000 killed, wounded and missing.[36] Nevertheless, they had held their positions and were beginning to receive reinforcements to strengthen the overpressed trench garrisons which had borne the brunt of the first months of fighting. By the end of 1915 the Isonzo front had been stabilised and no longer posed a major hazard to the strategic provisions of the Central Powers.

Italy's decision to go to war had, in truth, been ill-timed. If taken earlier, during the desperate battles around Lemberg, which tried the Austrians so hard, or later, when the British army had developed its full fighting strength and the Russians had staged their military recovery, an Italian initiative might have precipitated a real crisis for the German and Austrian general staffs. As events fell out, the First Battle of the Isonzo was narrowly preceded by a genuine German-Austrian victory, the breakthrough at Gorlice-Tarnow, which devastated the Russian position on the Eastern Front, saved the Austrian army from impending collapse and won the breathing space for Germany in its two-front war that would allow it to mount the Verdun offensive against France in 1916.

Gorlice-Tarnow was to be a second Limanowa-Lapanow, the battle that had saved Austria-Hungary from disaster in December 1914, but on a larger scale and with far more dramatic consequences. Like Limanowa, Gorlice was launched on a narrow front, in the gap between the River Vistula and the Carpathian Mountains; unlike Limanowa, it was to be a German rather than an Austrian victory for, though Conrad von Hötzendorf contributed sizeable numbers to the striking force, its cutting edge was German and so was its direction. The plan was Austrian, nevertheless, in its conception. Conrad was aware that the Russian army, for all its superiority of numbers, was in severe material difficulty. Between January and April, its divisions on the Eastern Front, excepting the small number in the Caucasus, received from the factories only two million shells, at a time when preparatory bombardments with several hundred thousand shells were becoming the norm; worse, the output of the Russian arsenals was insufficient to provide soldiers with the most essential tool of warfare, a personal weapon.[37] About 200,000 rifles were needed each month, to equip the new intakes of recruits, but only 50,000 were being produced. The stories of Russian infantrymen waiting unarmed to inherit the rifle of another killed or wounded were not tittle-tattle; they were nothing less than the truth.[38] Shell shortages, admittedly, were the common experience of all armies in 1914–15. All had myopically underestimated shell expenditure in intensive fighting, despite the evidence from the Russo-Japanese War that daily rates consistently exceeded factory output, with the result that production often lagged behind use by a factor of ten or more. In April 1915, for example, the field artillery of the BEF was receiving ten rounds of 18-pounder ammunition per gun per day, when ten rounds was easily shot off in a minute of bombardment.[39] Britain managed to increase its production of field-artillery ammunition from 3,000 rounds per month at the outbreak to 225,000 rounds by April 1915, and acquired other stocks by placing purchasing orders in America, but was still obliged to adjust demand to supply by limiting expenditure to a fixed number of rounds per day. The French and Germans were similarly obliged, though industrial mobilisation would dramatically increase output during 1915.[40] Russia would also, by 1916, secure adequate, if not ample, supplies of shell, much of it from British and American sources. In 1915, however, Russia's deficiency was serious, and compounded by inefficiency in distribution. For the Gorlice-Tarnow offensive, the Germans accumulated a stock of a million shells, a quantity available to the Russians only in a few fortified sectors, such as Novogeorgevisk and Kovno, where shells were stockpiled in quantities not disclosed by the fortress commanders to the General Staff.[41]

The covert concentration of men, shells and guns on the Gorlice-Tarnow sector during April 1915 therefore predisposed towards a victory. The front was short, only thirty miles. On the Russian side, it was defended by the fourteen infantry and five cavalry divisions of General Radko-Dmitriev's Third Army; opposite the assault sector, between Gorlice and Tarnow, the front was held by only two divisions, the 9th and 31st. Against them the Germans had positioned some of the best of their troops, including the 1st and 2nd Guard Divisions and the 19th and 20th (Hanoverian) Divisions. On the whole attack front, the Germans and Austrians had a superiority of over three to two in men and a very large superiority in guns, generously supplied with ammunition; their total artillery strength was 2,228 guns, heavy and light. The Russian entrenchments were sketchy and the no man's land separating them from the enemy's was wide, enabling the Germans and Austrians to push their outposts forward and dig new positions, close to the Russian wire, in the days before the attack, without being detected.

The plan for the offensive was Falkenhayn's, who entrusted its execution to Mackensen, victor in the East Prussian battles of 1914. Ludendorff and Hindenburg would have preferred not to prepare a breakthrough in the centre but to launch a double envelopment of the Russians from the Baltic and Carpathian fronts; like Schlieffen, they disfavoured 'ordinary victories', which led only to Russian withdrawal to lines further east, and argued for cutting off the enemy from the great spaces of the Tsar's empire by a manoeuvre of encirclement. Though exercising command in the east, they were, however, subordinate to Falkenhayn, whose fear was that their encirclement plans would require withdrawals of troops from the west on a scale dangerously weakening the German front there, and so overruled them. Moreover, the Ludendorff-Hindenburg plan placed a reliance upon Austrian participation which the continuing decline in quality of the Habsburg forces, Falkenhayn believed, made unrealistic.[42]

Mackensen's operation order stressed the importance of a break-in rapid and deep enough to prevent the Russians bringing forward reserves to stem the flow. 'The attack of Eleventh Army must, if its mission is to be fulfilled, be pushed forward fast . . . only through rapidity will the danger of the enemy renewing his resistance in the rearward positions be averted . . . Two methods are essential: deep penetration by the infantry and a rapid follow-up by the artillery.'[43] These orders anticipated the tactics which would be employed with such success against the British and French in 1918. The Germans were as yet insufficiently skilled to make them work against the densely defended trench fronts in the west. Against the Russians in Poland, where barbed-wire barriers were thin, entrenched zones shallow and supporting artillery short of shell, they were to prove decisive. The preparatory bombardment, which began on the evening of 1 May, devastated the Russian front line. On the morning of May 2 the attacking German infantry stormed forward to meet little resistance. Soon waves of Russian infantrymen were stumbling rearward, casting away their weapons and equipment and abandoning not only the first but also the second and third lines of trenches. By 4 May the German Eleventh Army had reached open country and was pressing forward, while 140,000 Russian prisoners marched in long columns to the rear. As the break-in widened, so did it deepen. By 13 May the German-Austrian front had reached the outskirts of Przemysl in the south and Lodz in central Poland. On 4 August the Germans entered Warsaw and between 17 August and 4 September the four historic Russian frontier fortresses of Kovno, Novogeorgievsk, Brest Litovsk and Grodno were surrendered to the enemy. The number of Russian prisoners taken had risen to 325,000 and 3,000 guns had also been lost.

The scale of the Austro-German victory had encouraged Ludendorff during June to press for a favourable reconsideration of his two-prong plan by Falkenhayn and the Kaiser. At a meeting, under the Kaiser's chairmanship, with Falkenhayn, Mackensen and Conrad, at Pless on 3 June, he requested reinforcements that would enable him to mount a wide sweeping movement from the Baltic coast southwards, cutting off the Russian armies as they retreated eastward and so, he argued, bringing the war in the east to an end. Falkenhayn, concerned as ever for the security of the Western Front, disagreed, demanding a net withdrawal of divisions from Poland to France. Conrad, who was incensed by Italy's entry into the war, wanted to send troops to the Isonzo front. Mackensen was for persisting in his demonstrably successful offensive in the centre. He, with Falkenhayn's consent, got his way.[44] As the advance continued, however, Ludendorff returned to the issue. Meeting the Kaiser and Falkenhayn again, at Posen on 30 June, he outlined an even more ambitious plan which would carry the German armies in the north from the mouth of the River Niemen on the Baltic as far as the Pripet marshes in the centre of the Eastern Front in a manoeuvre designed to cut the Russians off from their heartland and force a capitulation. Once again he was overruled and though he was permitted to stage an offensive in the Baltic sector, it was to take a frontal form as a subsidiary effort to Mackensen's continuing push eastward.

Outraged though Ludendorff was by what he saw as the supreme command's timid refusal to embrace the grand solution, Falkenhayn was reading the strategic situation more accurately than he. The Russians had been hard hit at Gorlice-Tarnow and had surrendered more ground than they would have freely chosen to do. By late July, however, they had accepted that the state of their army and its shortage of weapons and ammunition left them no recourse but retreat. The Germans had the impression of breasting forward against an undefended front. The Russians knew that they were deliberately retreating, shortening their front by withdrawal from the great bulge in central Poland and consequently lengthening the enemy lines of communication as the Germans struggled to follow, across country deficient in railways and roads, particularly all-weather roads. The heavy vehicles of the German supply columns were rattled to pieces by the rutted surface of the Polish farmers' byways, and units got forward only by requisitioning the rattle-trap *panje* waggons of the rural population. 'Every day the Russians would retreat three miles or so, construct a new line and wait for the Germans to stumble up towards it . . . In time the Germans came up to primaeval forest . . . and the great marshes of the Pripet. The railway lines stopped on the Vistula [in the German rear]; even field-railways came only to . . . the Narev [river] and supplies had to be dragged forward for the next forty or fifty miles.'[45]

By September the Russians had, by abandoning the Polish salient, shortened their front by nearly half, from a thousand to six hundred miles, an economy in space which produced a major economy in force, releasing reserves to oppose the German advance along the Baltic coast and in the centre, and even to counter-attack in the south against the Austrians at Lutsk in September. Ludendorff achieved a final success of his own in September, when he took Vilna in Russian Lithuania; but he did so at heavy cost. As the autumn *rasputitsa*, the liquefying of the surface under seasonal rain, set in, the advance came to a halt on a line that ran almost perpendicularly north-south from the Gulf of Riga on the Baltic to Czernowitz in the Carpathians. Most of Russian Poland had been lost but the territory of historic Russia remained intact and so, too, did the substance of the Tsar's army. It had suffered great losses, nearly a million dead, wounded and missing, while three-quarters of a million prisoners had been captured by the enemy. It had unwisely defended the fortresses of Novogeorgevisk west of Warsaw in late August, where huge quantities of equipment passed into German hands, and it had also lost the fortresses of Ivangorod on the Vistula, Brest-Litovsk on the Bug and Grodno and Kovno on the Niemen, all defending crossings over river lines that formed traditional lines of resistance in the otherwise featureless

Polish plain. Generals had been sacked by the score, some imprisoned for dereliction of duty in the face of the enemy.[46] On 1 September the Tsar had taken the grave step of assuming executive Supreme Command himself, with Alexeyev as his Chief of Staff, the Grand Duke Nicholas being transferred to the Caucasus. All these outcomes of the German advance and the Russian retreat brought disadvantage to Russia's military situation, or threatened to do so in the future. Nevertheless, the Russian army remained undefeated. Shell output was increasing – to 220,000 rounds a month in September – and its reserves of manpower still amounted to tens of millions. Four million men would be called up in 1916–17, against the eleven million already in the ranks, or lost by death, wounds and capture, but the real reserve, reckoning 10 per cent of the population as available for military service, approached eighteen million.[47] Russia would be able to fight on.

What it needed was a breathing space, while its armies reorganised and re-equipped. The Italian intervention had failed to divert significant numbers of Austrian troops from Galicia and the Carpathians and, though the quality of the Austrian army was in progressive decline, German assistance kept it in the field. Serbia, whose unexpectedly successful resistance in 1914 had disrupted the Austrian mobilisation, could help no further. French and British plans for a great offensive on the Western Front could not be realised until 1916. Throughout the travails of 1915, Russian hopes for a strategic reversal, which would deter Turkey from further offensives and perhaps destroy her as a combatant, had therefore turned on the faraway campaign in the Dardanelles where, in April, Britain and France had opened an amphibious operation designed to break through to Istanbul and seize the direct passage to the Black Sea and Russia's southern seaports.

GALLIPOLI

The Dardanelles, which separates Europe from Asia, is a passage thirty miles long, at its narrowest less than a mile wide, leading from the Mediterranean into the landlocked Sea of Marmara. On its north-east coast Istanbul, or Constantinople (formerly the capital of Byzantium, in 1915 that of the Ottoman empire) guards the entrance to the Bosphorus, a waterway narrower than the Dardanelles, which gives on to the Black Sea. The European shore of the Dardanelles, Sea

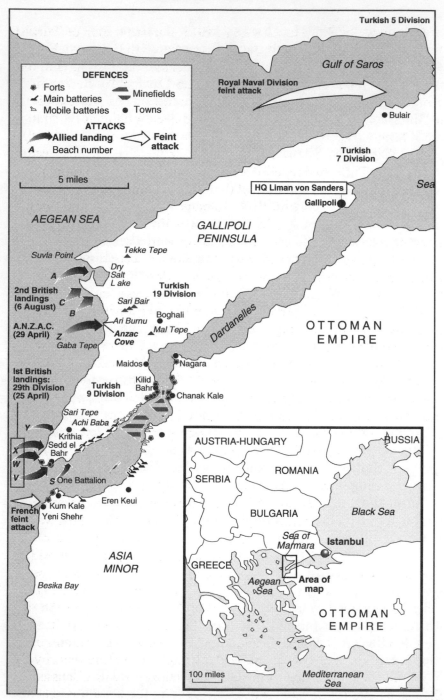

Gallipoli

of Marmara and Bosphorus was, in 1915, a narrow strip of Turkish territory. From the Asiatic shore, the expanses of the Ottoman Empire stretched north, east and south to the Caucasus, the Persian Gulf and the Red Sea. The strategic location of the Dardanelles had brought armies, and navies, to it scores of times in history. At Adrianople, in its hinterland, fifteen recorded battles had been fought; at the first, in AD 378, the Emperor Valens was killed by the Goths, a disaster that caused the collapse of Rome's empire in the west; at the most recent, in 1913, the Turks had repelled a Bulgarian attempt on Istanbul itself.

It had long been an ambition of the Tsars to complete their centuries of counter-offensive against the Ottomans by seizing Constantinople, thus recovering the seat of Orthodox Christianity from Islam and securing a permanent southward access to warm water; it stood high among Russia's current war aims. The French were disinclined, the British even more so, to concede such a dramatic enlargement of Russian power in southern Europe. Nevertheless, in the crisis of 1914–15, they were prepared to consider opening a new front there as a means both of bringing relief to their ally and of breaking the impasse on the Western Front. An attack on the Dardanelles, by sea or land, or both, appeared to be one promising version of such an initiative and, during the spring of 1915, it gathered support.

The first proposal was French. In November 1914 Aristide Briand, the Minister of Justice, raised the idea of sending an Anglo-French expedition of 400,000 troops to the Greek port of Salonika, with the object of assisting Serbia, persuading neighbouring Romania and Bulgaria, old enemies of Turkey, to join the Allies and developing an attack through the Balkans on Austria-Hungary. Joffre, whose constitutional powers as Commander-in-Chief were paramount, refused to countenance any diminution of his effort to win the war on the Western Front. Nevertheless, Franchet d'Esperey, one of his subordinates, then took the liberty of suggesting it to President Poincaré who, with Briand and Viviani, the Prime Minister, put it again to Joffre at a meeting at the Elysée palace on 7 January 1915.[48]

Joffre remained adamantly opposed. Meanwhile however the idea was attracting attention in Britain. On 2 January, the Russian Commander-in-Chief, the Grand Duke Nicholas, had sent an appeal to London for help against the Turks' attack in the Caucasus by the mounting of a diversion elsewhere. His telegram was discussed by the First Lord of the Admiralty, Winston Churchill, with Kitchener, the Secretary of State for War. Later the same day, Kitchener wrote to

255

Churchill, 'We have no troops to land anywhere . . . The only place a demonstration might have some effect would be the Dardanelles.'[49] Kitchener struck a chord. On 3 November Churchill had, in response to Turkey's declaration of war and on his own initiative, sent the British Aegean squadron to bombard the forts at the mouth of the Dardanelles. A magazine had exploded, disabling most of the heavy guns on the European point.[50] Though the ships then sailed away, without attempting to penetrate further, the success had kindled a belief in Churchill that naval power might be used against the Dardanelles with strategic rather than tactical effect.

He raised the suggestion at the first meeting of the new War Council, military sub-committee of the British cabinet, on 25 November 1914 and, though it was rejected, it was not forgotten. The consolidation of the trench line in France and Belgium, the disappearance of 'flanks' around which decisive results were traditionally achieved by manoeuvre, had persuaded Lloyd George, the Chancellor of the Exchequer, and Sir Maurice Hankey, Secretary of the Committee of Imperial Defence and effectively the executive officer of Britain's war government, as well as Churchill, that flanks must be found beyond the Western Front. They were supported by Kitchener, who was as depressed as they by the prospect of persisting in the frontal attacks in France favoured by Joffre and Sir John French, and they soon engaged the interest of the First Sea Lord, Admiral Fisher, who on 3 January urged a joint military and naval attack on Turkey, with the stipulation that it should be immediate and that only old battleships should be used.

The Fisher plan might have worked, for the Turks were only slowly repairing and strengthening the Dardanelles defences, had the War Council acted immediately, as he urged. It did not, instead falling into a consideration of alternative strategies. While it did so, Churchill took his own line. Having secured Fisher's agreement to consult Admiral Carden, commanding the British Mediterranean fleet, about practicalities, he extracted from him the admission that while it would be impossible to 'rush the Dardanelles . . . they might be forced by extended operations with large numbers of ships'.[51] That was all the encouragement Churchill needed. A romantic in strategy, an enthusiast for military adventures, of which his raising of the Royal Naval Division and its commitment to the Antwerp operation had been one, he proceeded to organise the fleet of old battleships Fisher was prepared to release and to direct it against the Dardanelles in an enlarged attempt to reduce its fortifications by naval bombardment.

Fisher accepted Churchill's forcing of the issue with 'reluctant responsibility' and as an 'experiment'; his heart, if there were to be adventures, was in a Baltic expedition; his head told him that there should be no diversion of attention from the confrontation in the North Sea.[52] He had, nevertheless, allowed Churchill the leeway he needed to proceed with his Dardanelles project. Not only was a fleet of old battleships, French as well as British, to be assembled, the brand-new *Queen Elizabeth*, prototype of the super-Dreadnought class, was to be detached to the Mediterranean fleet also, to use her 15-inch guns against the Dardanelles fortifications, and a base on the Greek island of Lemnos was to be prepared for a landing force, if it was decided to commit troops ashore. Kitchener made the 29th Division, composed of regular soldiers of the imperial overseas garrison, available. Churchill had the Royal Naval Division at his disposal, and the Australian and New Zealand Army Corps (ANZAC), awaiting onward movement from Egypt to France, was also on hand.

Whether the troops would be committed depended on the success of the naval bombardment. At the outset it was expected that the ships would prevail. The Turkish defences were antiquated, those at Cape Helles, on the European point, at Kum Kale on the Asiatic shore opposite and at Gallipoli, guarding the Narrows, medieval or older. There were known to be batteries of mobile howitzers present and the Turks had also laid minefields in the channel of the Dardanelles itself. It was believed, nevertheless, that a systematic advance of the battleships, working up-channel with minesweepers clearing a way ahead, would overcome the Turkish guns, open the Narrows and drive a way through to the Sea of Marmara and Istanbul.

The naval operation began on 19 February, with sensational political, if not military, effect. Greece offered troops to join the campaign, the Bulgarians broke off negotiations with Germany, the Russians indicated an intention to attack Istanbul from the Bosphorus, the Italians, not yet in the war, suddenly seemed readier to join the Allied side. All those who believed that an initiative against Turkey would alter the situation in southern Europe to the Allies' advantage seemed proved right in their judgement. In practice, the bombardment had done little damage and landings by Royal Marines at the end of February, though scarcely opposed by the Turks, were equally ineffective. On 25 February, Admiral Carden had renewed the bombardment but got no further than the Dardanelles' mouth. By 4 March, when a party of Royal Marines attacking the old fort at Kum Kale suffered heavy casualties, it had become obvious that the enthusiasts' early optimism had been misplaced. The Turkish garrison was more determined than had been thought, its guns either too well-protected or too mobile to be easily knocked out and the minefields too dense to be swept by the haphazard efforts of the fleet of hastily assembled trawlers. 'Forcing the Narrows' would require a carefully co-ordinated advance of all the ships available, with the trawlers working under the protection of the guns of big ships, which would suppress the fire from the shore as they moved forward.

The grand advance began on 18 March, with sixteen battleships, twelve British, four French, mostly pre-Dreadnoughts, but including the battlecruiser *Inflexible* and the almost irreplaceable super-Dreadnought *Queen Elizabeth,* arrayed in three lines abreast. They were preceded by a swarm of minesweepers and accompanied by flotillas of cruisers and destroyers. Even in the long naval history of the Dardanelles, such an armada had never been seen there before. At first the armada made apparently irresistible progress. Between 11.30 in the morning and two in the afternoon it advanced nearly a mile, overcoming each fixed and mobile battery as it moved forward. 'By 2 p.m. the situation had become very critical', the Turkish General Staff account reports. 'All telephone wires were cut . . . some of the guns were knocked out, others were left buried . . . in consequence the fire of the defence had slackened considerably.'[53] Then, suddenly, at two o'clock, the balance of the battle swung the other way. The old French battleship *Bouvet,* falling back to allow the minesweepers to go forward, suddenly suffered an internal explosion and sank with all hands. A torpedo fired from a fixed tube ashore seemed to the worried fleet commander, Admiral de Robeck, to be the cause.[54] Later it became known that, on the night of 7 March , a line of mines had been laid by a small Turkish steamer parallel to the shore and had remained undetected. In the confusion that followed, the minesweepers, manned by civilian crews, began to fall back through the fleet and, as it manoeuvred, the old battleship *Irresistible* was damaged also and fell out of the line. Next *Ocean*, another old battleship, also suffered an internal explosion and soon afterwards the French pre-Dreadnought *Suffren* was severely damaged by a plunging shell. As *Gaulois* and *Inflexible*, the modern battlecruiser, had been damaged earlier, de Robeck now found himself with a third of his battle fleet out of action.

By the end of the day, *Ocean* and *Irresistible* had, like *Bouvet*, sunk. *Inflexible, Suffren* and *Gaulois* were out of action and *Albion, Agamemnon, Lord Nelson* and *Charlemagne* had suffered damage. As darkness fell, de Robeck drew his fleet away. The ten lines of mines laid across the Narrows, numbering 373 in all, remained unswept and most of the shore batteries, though they had shot off all their heavy shell, preserved their guns.[55]

By 22 March, when Admiral de Robeck met General Sir Ian Hamilton, the nominated commander of the military force-in-waiting, aboard *Queen Elizabeth*, to discuss whether the naval advance towards the Narrows should be resumed, it was quickly agreed that it could not, without the assistance of strong landing parties. The combination of numerous moored mines and heavy fire from the shore was deadly. While the bigger Turkish guns in fixed positions could be targeted, the mobile batteries could move, as soon as they had been identified, to new positions, from which they could resume fire against the fragile minesweepers, thus preventing the clearing of the lines of mines running between the European and Asiatic shores and so denying the battleships the chance to get forward. The only solution to the conundrum was to land troops capable of tackling the mobile batteries and putting them out of action, so that the minesweepers could proceed with their work and the battleships follow in the swept channels.

Bold spirits, who included Commodore Roger Keyes, commanding the minesweepers, were for pressing on regardless of loss. Keyes believed the Turks were demoralised and out of ammunition. The more cautious officers thought more risk-taking must lead to more losses and the intelligence that came later to light revealed that to be certain. The cautious party in any case prevailed. By the end of March, the decision for landings had been taken – by de Robeck and Hamilton, independent of the Cabinet – and the only question remaining to be settled was where the landings should take place and in what strength. Raids by Royal Marines would not suffice. The intelligence service of the Mediterranean Expeditionary Force, as Hamilton's command was now known, estimated that the Turks had 170,000 men available. That was an exaggerated guess; Liman von Sanders, their German commander, had six weak divisions with 84,000 men to guard 150 miles of coastline. As, however, there were only five Allied divisions in the Mediterranean Expeditionary Force – the 29th, Royal Naval, 1st Australian and Australian and New

Zealand Divisions, and the *Corps expéditionnaire d'Orient,* of divisional strength provided by the French – every one would have been needed to secure beachheads, even had the Turks been weaker than they actually were. In practice, the decision to use all five divisions was taken at the start. From a hastily established base in Mudros Bay on the nearby Greek island of Lemnos, they would be embarked as soon as possible and got ashore. In the month between the naval defeat of 22 March and the eventual D-Day of 25 April, an extraordinary improvisation was carried forward. Mudros was filled with stores, a fleet of transports assembled and a collection of boats and improvised landing-craft got together to transship the troops to the beaches.

Nothing was more improvised than the plan. In the absence of firm intelligence about Turkish dispositions, it had to be based on guesses as to where landings would be least opposed and do most good. The Asiatic shore was tempting, for there the shore is level – Troy's windy plain leads inland nearby – but Kitchener had forbidden it to Hamilton, for the excellent reason that a force as small as his could all too easily be swallowed up in the vastness of the Turkish hinterland. Kitchener's diktat determined that the European peninsula, known as Gallipoli from the tiny town at the Narrows, must be the choice, but its topography presented difficulties. The narrow waist at Bulair, forty miles from the point of Cape Helles, offered level beaches on the Mediterranean side and the chance to cut off all the Turkish forces below. They, however, had covered the Bulair foreshore with barbed wire that looked impenetrable. Along much of the rest of the seaward side of the peninsula, steep cliffs descend to the water. Only at one place was there a practicable beach, which was allotted to ANZAC. The only other possibilities were at Cape Helles itself, where there is a chain of small, if narrow, beaches giving by reasonable gradients to the summit of the headland. As it could be covered all round by fire from the fleet standing offshore, Helles was chosen as the objective of the 29th Division. The Royal Naval Division was not to land at once, but make a demonstration at Bulair, designed to draw Turkish reinforcements away from Cape Helles, and the French were to do likewise on the Asiatic shore, at Kum Kale near Troy, before landing later alongside the 29th Division. Five beaches at Helles were selected, lettered, Y, X, W, V and S, Y lying three miles from the point on the Mediterranean side, S within the Dardanelles, and X, W and V under the Cape itself.

In retrospect, it is possible to see that Hamilton's plan could not work, nor could any other have done with the size of the force made available to him. Seizing the tip of the peninsula, below the minefields, still left them covered by Turkish artillery. An Asiatic landing would have proved equally ineffectual, and very exposed, while even a successful landing at Suvla Bay, below Bulair, would have left the Turkish forces between it and Helles not only intact but easily to be re-supplied and reinforced across the Narrows. The only certainly successful scheme would have required the deployment of a force large enough to land at and hold Bulair, Helles and the Asiatic shore simultaneously. Such a force was not available nor could it have been assembled speedily enough to bring urgent aid to the Russians. A large commitment of troops was, in any case, outside the spirit of the enterprise, which was designed to achieve large results without dissipating the force engaged on the Western Front. Hamilton's only hope of achieving success in the essentially diversionary mission he had been given, therefore, lay in the Turks mismanaging their response to the landings. Surprise there could not be. The naval offensive had alerted them to the Allies' interest in Gallipoli and they had used the month following the fleet's withdrawal to dig trenches above all the threatened beaches. Only if the Turks failed to counter-attack quickly could the Allies secure footholds deep enough from which to threaten their possession of the Gallipoli peninsula.

The soldiers of the 29th Division and ANZAC, dissimilar as they were, expected to succeed. Those of the 29th Division were regulars of the pre-war army, sunburnt Tommy Atkinses of the type Kipling knew, collected from the overseas garrisons for service in France but then brought to Egypt in case troops were needed at Gallipoli. The ANZACs, staging through Egypt to Europe, were citizen soldiers, products of the most comprehensive militia system in the world, which trained every male from early school age upwards for military service and enrolled all fit men in their local regiments. A comparable military obligation, accepted in Australia, was taken with deep seriousness by the tiny colonial community of New Zealand, strategically the least vulnerable settled place on earth. 'To be a New Zealander in 1914 was to be taught that: "The Empire looks to you to be ready in time of need, to think, to labour and to bear hardships on its behalf." '[56] More practically, when the call came, 'university classes emptied . . . sports fixtures were abandoned. To be left behind was unthinkable. If your mate was going, then somehow you had to get away too.'[57] Out of a male population of half a million, New Zealand could provide 50,000 trained soldiers aged under twenty-five. Australia furnished proportionate numbers. Fewer of the Australians were countrymen than the New Zealanders, whose settler independence and skills with rifle and spade would win them a reputation as the best soldiers in the world during the twentieth century, but Australian dash and individualism, combined with an intense spirit of comradeship, were to create units of formidable offensive power, as the Germans would later acknowledge and the Turks were soon to discover.

Before dawn on 25 April, 200 merchant ships, of every variety from liners to tramp steamers, supported by most of the bombardment fleet that had been turned back from the Narrows on 18 March, stood in towards ANZAC cove – as the Australians' and New Zealanders' landing place was soon to be known – and Cape Helles. *Queen Elizabeth* was flagship and headquarters, though its 15-inch guns were also to join in the preliminary bombardment by the older battleships. They were also troop carriers, however; from them, and other warships, the landing parties were to move to the beaches in 'tows', lines of rowing boats pulled in column behind steam pinnaces commanded by junior officers; two of those were thirteen-year-old first-term Royal Naval College cadets. As the shore shelved, the tows were to be cast off and the boats rowed ashore by bluejackets. Only one specialised landing ship had been included, the collier *River Clyde*, which was to be grounded off V Beach, alongside the old Byzantine fortress of Sedd el-Bahr. Holes had been cut in its bow through which the soldiers of the Royal Munster Fusiliers and the Hampshire Regiment were to run down gangplanks on to lighters, positioned between ship and shore, and so onto the beaches, under the covering fire of machine guns positioned behind sandbags on the forecastle.

The bombardment began about five o'clock, as day dawned, and soon the tows for all beaches were moving inshore. What lay ahead was largely unknown, for the Mediterranean Expeditionary Force intelligence service was deficient not only of information about Turkish strength and dispositions but even lacked maps of the area to be assaulted. It was believed, for example, that the ground behind Cape Helles, in fact broken by numerous gullies, formed 'a ... uniform and [un] accidented slope'.[58] The terrain behind ANZAC cove was known to be dominated by ridges but the chosen landing place was to their south, from which routes opened to a central crest where, it was intended, observation posts could be established to direct naval gunfire against the batteries at the Narrows.

That might or might not have been possible. In the event, and for reasons never satisfactorily explained, perhaps human error, perhaps a last-minute but inadequately communicated change of plan, the forty-eight boats of the ANZAC tows touched ground a mile north of the beach originally selected, under steep slopes that give onto a succession of ridges, rising in three jumbled steps above the cove. To north and south, high ground comes down to the sea, so that ANZAC takes the form of a tiny amphitheatre – the smallness of the Gallipoli battlegrounds is the most striking impression left on the visitor – dominated on three sides by high ground. Unless the Australians and New Zealanders could reach the crests before the enemy, all their positions, including the beach, would be overlooked, with calamitous effect on subsequent operations.

The ANZACs knew the importance of getting high quickly and, after an almost unopposed landing, began climbing the ridges in front of them as fast as their feet could take them. The reason their landing had been unopposed soon, however, became apparent. The enemy were few because the Turks had dismissed the likelihood of a landing in such an inhospitable spot and the landing parties rapidly found that the terrain was as hostile as any defending force. One crest was succeeded by another even higher, gullies were closed by dead ends and the way to the highest point was lost time and again in the difficulty of route-finding. Organisation dissolved in the thick scrub and steep ravines, which separated group from group and prevented a co-ordinated sweep to the top. If even some of the 12,000 ashore could have reached the summits of the Sari Bair ridge, two and a half miles above ANZAC cove, they would have been able to look down on the Narrows, and the beginnings of a victory would have been under their hands.[59] Their maximum depth of penetration by early afternoon, however, was only a mile and a half and, at that precipitous point, they began to come under counter-attack by the assembling Turkish defenders. The ANZACs, clinging lost and leaderless to the hillsides, began, as the hot afternoon gave way to grey drizzle, to experience their martyrdom.

Ten miles south, at Cape Helles, day had also broken to the crash of heavy naval gunfire, under which the ninety-six boats of the tows and the crammed *River Clyde* moved shoreward. On the flanks, at Y and X Beaches in the Mediterranean and at S Beach within the Dardanelles, the attackers met little or no opposition and soon established themselves ashore. Across the water, at Kum Kale on the Asiatic shore, the French also found their landings unopposed and, after early delays, took possession of the old Byzantine fort, the village under its walls and the cemetery on the outskirts. The Turks in the vicinity were disorganised and badly led. At Y, X and S Beaches on the peninsula the British experience was similar: the enemy was either not present or else stunned by the explosion of 12-inch shells around their positions. The landing parties sunned themselves, made tea, humped stores up from the shore and wandered about in the pretty countryside, as if the war was miles away. At W and V Beaches, just down the coast, the Lancashire Fusiliers and the Dublins, Munsters and Hampshires were fighting for their lives and dying in hundreds. The two beaches are separated by the headland of Cape Helles itself. To the west, on W Beach, ever afterwards known as Lancashire Landing, the Lancashire Fusiliers were struck by a hail of rifle and machine-gun fire a hundred yards from the shore. Most of the boats beached, nevertheless, only to find themselves in front of barbed wire at the water's edge, behind which Turks in trenches were shooting every man who rose from the sea. Major Shaw, of the Lancashire Fusiliers, recalled that 'the sea behind was absolutely crimson, and you could hear the groans through the rattle of musketry. A few were firing. I signalled to them to advance . . . I then perceived they were all hit.'

Amid these ghastly scenes, a few Lancashire Fusiliers managed to struggle through the wire and find a way round, reorganise and advance. Out of the 950 who landed, over 500 were killed or wounded but the survivors pressed inland, chasing the Turks before them and by evening had consolidated a foothold. On the other side of the headland, at V Beach, the scenes were even worse. The Dublin Fusiliers, landing from tows, thought themselves unopposed until, as the boats touched bottom, they fell under a hail of bullets. As the *River Clyde* grounded and the Hampshires and Munster Fusiliers struggled to find a way out of the ship and on to the gangplanks that were to lead them ashore, four Turkish machine guns opened fire. They had already raked the tows which beached first. The columns on the gangplanks, packed like cattle ranked for slaughter in an abattoir, tumbled one after another to fall bleeding into the sea, there to drown at once or struggle to their death in the shallows. Yet some survived, found shelter under the lip of the beach, gathered their force and drove the Turks from their trenches.

At Lancashire Landing and V Beaches many Victoria Crosses, Britain's highest award for bravery, were won that morning, six by Lancashire Fusiliers, two by sailors who struggled in the sea to hold steady the lighters bridging the gap between *River Clyde* and the shore. There were numerous other, unrecorded, feats of courage, inexplicable to a later, more timorous age. By evening, above beaches choked with bodies and a shoreline still red with blood, Lancashire Landing had been consolidated with X Beach, and V, Y and S were secure. There had been 2,000 casualties at ANZAC, at least 2,000 at Cape Helles, out of 30,000 men landed, and the number was rising by the hour, as the Turks gathered to counter-attack. The question remained whether beachheads gained at such cost could be held on the morrow.

What should have alarmed the British commanders – Hamilton of the Mediterranean Expeditionary Force (MEF), Hunter-Weston of the 29th Division, Birdwood of ANZAC – was that the injuries done to their brave and determined soldiers had been the work of so few of the enemy. MEF's estimate of the Turkish strength committed to the defence of the Dardanelles had been a gross exaggeration. The number of troops deployed by Liman von Sanders on the Gallipoli peninsula was only a fraction of his force, the rest being dispersed between Bulair and Kum Kale, between Europe and Asia. The assault area was held by a single division, the 9th, with its infantry deployed in companies all the way down the coast from ANZAC to Cape Helles and beyond. In places there were single platoons of fifty men, in some places fewer men or none: at Y Beach none, at X twelve men, at S a single platoon. Even at ANZAC there was only one company of 200 men, while V and W Beaches were defended by single platoons.[60] The massacre of the Lancashire, Dublin and Munster Fusiliers and the Hampshires had been inflicted by fewer than a hundred desperate men, survivors of the naval bombardment, and killing so that they should not be killed.

Some of the Turks, nevertheless, had run away; those at Kum Kale surrendered to the French in hundreds before the withdrawal on 26 April. More might have turned tail on the peninsula had not reserves been close at hand and under the command of an officer of outstanding ability and determination. Mustapha Kemal had been one of the earliest Young Turks but his career had not followed that of the leaders. In April 1915, he was, aged thirty-four, only a divisional commander. Fate decreed, however, that his division, the 19th, stood at the critical place at the critical moment. Massed on the peninsula just opposite the Narrows, it was only four miles from ANZAC and, though high ground lay in between, could by forced marching intervene against the landings even while they were in progress. Kemal, reacting instantly to the sound of the naval bombardment, forced the march, himself at the head. Having reached the crest of Sari Bair, the dominating ground that was the ANZAC objective, 'the scene which met our eyes was a most interesting one. To my mind it was the vital moment of the [campaign]'. He could see warships offshore and, in the foreground, a party of Turks of the 9th Division running towards him. They told him that they were out of ammunition and he ordered them to lie down and fix bayonets. 'At the same time I sent [my] orderly officer . . . off to the rear to bring up to where I was at the double those men of the [57th Regiment] who were advancing [behind me] . . . When the men fixed their bayonets and lay down . . . the enemy lay down also . . . It was about 10.00 hours when the 57th Regiment began its attack.'

The Australians had seen Kemal on the crest and fired at him, without effect. Their failure to hit him and to push forward to the top in those minutes may indeed be judged 'the vital moment of the campaign', for Kemal, as soon as his troops were to hand, began a series of counter-attacks against the Australian bridgehead that lasted until nightfall. Several high points taken earlier in the day were lost and from little of the line held did the ANZAC positions dominate the Turks. Almost everywhere they were overlooked, and a constant rain of enemy bullets sent a steady stream of wounded back to the narrow beach, passing, as they limped or were carried down, an only slightly more numerous stream of reinforcements coming up to replace them. That scene, wounded down, fresh troops up, was to be repeated every day the campaign lasted and remained every ANZAC's most abiding memory of those precipitous hillsides.

By 4 May both sides at ANZAC were exhausted. The Turks had lost 14,000 men, ANZAC nearly 10,000. After a final attack on 4 May, Kemal recognised that the enemy was too tenacious to be driven into the sea, and ordered his men to dig in. The line when finished enclosed an area a thousand yards deep, a mile and a half around the perimeter, the whole canted upwards at an angle of forty-five degrees, where the surface was not actually perpendicular. The scene reminded ANZAC's chief cipher officer, 'of the cave dwellings of a tribe of large and prosperous savages who live on the extremely steep slopes of broken sandy bluffs covered with scrub'.

On the lower ground at Cape Helles, the days after the landing had also been filled with savage fighting, as the 29th Division, and the French withdrawn from Kum Kale, struggled to connect the beachheads and push the line inland. On 26 April, the castle and village of Sedd el-Bahr were captured and next afternoon there was a general advance, the Turks locally having retreated exhausted from the scene. The objective was the village of Krithia, four miles inland. A deliberate assault was made on 28 April, known as the First Battle of Krithia, and another on 6 May. Neither reached the village, despite the arrival of an Indian brigade from Egypt and parts of the Royal Naval Division. By 8 May the British were stuck just short of Krithia, on a line that ran from Y Beach to a little north of S Beach, three miles from Cape Helles.

There it remained throughout an unbearably hot summer, balmy autumn and freezing early winter. The War Council, despite opposition from the French and within its own ranks, sent more troops to Egypt and the base on Lemnos, first one and then three more Territorial Divisions, then three Kitchener divisions. The French also added, reluctantly, to the expeditionary corps, and in August the 2nd Australian Division and 2nd Mounted Division were sent to Lemnos. To break the stalemate, General Sir Ian Hamilton decided on a fresh amphibious assault north of ANZAC at Suvla Bay. It took place on 7 August and a bridgehead was quickly seized. Mustapha Kemal, now appointed to command all Turkish troops in the northern sector, was soon on the scene, however, rushing reinforcements to the heights with the same determination to pen the Allies close to the sea as he had shown three months earlier at ANZAC. By 9 August he had succeeded and no addition of force by the British – the hard-tried 29th Division was brought up by sea from Helles – could gain ground. The attackers and defenders dug in and Suvla Bay became simply the third shallow and static enclave maintained by the Allies on the Gallipoli peninsula. The Turks now had fourteen divisions in place against an exactly equal number of Allied which were more and more obviously doing no good at great cost. There had been calls within the Dardanelles Committee of the War Council for evacuation earlier. In November they became overwhelming. Kitchener, arriving on a personal reconnaissance, was persuaded by General Sir Charles Monro, who had succeeded the discredited Hamilton, that evacuation was inevitable, and a freak storm, which drowned soldiers in their trenches and wrecked many of the beach facilities, concluded the arguments. Between 28 December and 8 January 1916, the garrison began to slip away, little troubled by the Turks who had failed to detect that a complete evacuation was in progress. By 9 January, ANZAC, Suvla and Cape Helles were empty. The great adventure was over.

The Turks, who bothered neither to bury nor count their dead, had probably lost 300,000 men killed, wounded and missing.[61] The Allies had lost 265,000. The 29th Division had lost its strength twice over, while the New Zealanders, of whom 8,566 served on the peninsula, recorded 14,720 casualties, including wounded who returned two or three times.[62] Yet of all the contingents which went to Gallipoli, it was the Australians who were most marked by the experience and who remembered it most deeply, remember it indeed to this day. Citizens of an only recently federated country in 1915, they went as soldiers of the forces of six separate states. They came back, it is so often said, members of one nation. The ANZAC ordeal began to be commemorated at home in the following year. Today the dawn ceremony on 25 April has became a sacred event, observed by all Australians of every age and ANZAC cove has become a shrine. The Gallipoli peninsula, now preserved as a Turkish national park, in which a memorial erected by Mustapha Kemal Ataturk, as President of post-imperial Turkey, magnanimously recalls the sufferings of both sides, has reverted to nature, a beautiful but deserted remoteness on the Mediterranean shore. Yet not deserted by Australians. Few British make the journey; those who do, and find their way to ANZAC's tiny and terrible battlegrounds at Lone Pine, Russell's Top and Steele's Post, never fail to be moved by the appearance of young Australians, men and women, who have trekked across Europe to see where their grandfathers and great-grandfathers fought and often died. Two-thirds of the Australians who went to the Great War became casualties and the first of the nation's Great War heroes won their medals in the two square miles above ANZAC cove. Their grandchildren and great-grandchildren often bring those medals back with them to Gallipoli on their pilgrimage, as if to reconsecrate the symbols of the ANZAC spirit, a metaphor for that of the nation itself, on sacred soil.

Yet nothing at Gallipoli can fail to touch the emotions of those who descend from the soldiers of any nation that struggled there. The village of Kum Kale, under the walls of the medieval fortress, has disappeared but the overgrown cemetery of Muslim headstones remains to mark the furthest limit of the French advance of 25 April. The war cemetery above W Beach is full of the dead of Lancashire Landing, while at Sedd el-Bahr the Dublin and Munster Fusiliers lie in graves only a few yards above the water's edge where they gave their lives for a state many of their countrymen, at Easter 1916, would confront with rebellion. Most poignant of all Gallipoli memorials, perhaps, is that of the white marble column on the Cape Helles headland, glimpsed across the water from the walls of Troy on a bright April morning. Troy and Gallipoli make two separate but connected epics, as so many of the classically educated volunteer officers of the Mediterranean Expeditionary Force – Patrick Shaw-Stewart, Arthur Asquith, the Prime Minister's son, and the poet, Rupert Brooke, dead of blood-poisoning before the landing – had recognised and recorded. It is difficult to say which epic Homer might have thought the more heroic.

SERBIA AND SALONIKA

Gallipoli, though it succeeded eventually in attracting fourteen of Turkey's thirty-six *Nizam* (first-line) divisions away from potential deployment to the Mesopotamian, Egyptian and Caucasian fronts, had failed as a military campaign. It had failed to open a supply route through the Black Sea to Russia's southern ports. It had also failed in its secondary purpose, the bringing of relief to Serbia. That beleaguered country's survival, always conditional upon its enemies' preoccupations elsewhere, had been prolonged by the opening of the Gallipoli campaign and by the entry of Italy into the war, itself hastened by the landings at the Dardanelles. As the Gallipoli vision faded, however, so too had the hopes pinned on its expected subsidiary effects, including encouraging Greece to join the Allies and deterring Bulgaria from joining the Central Powers. The Turks' containment of the Suvla Bay landing in August swung neutral opinion decisively the other way in each case. Bulgaria had a strong local interest in siding with Germany, since the Macedonian territory it had lost, after the briefest possession, at the end of the Second Balkan War in 1913 had gone to Greece and Serbia. The Allies, as suitors and protectors respectively of those two countries, would not, Bulgaria recognised, assist in its return. The Germans, on the other hand, could. The magnitude of their victory at Gorlice-Tarnow in May impressed the Bulgarians, moreover, and a month later they entered into negotiations.[63] The Allies suddenly forgot their commitment to Serbia and on 3 August offered Bulgaria its desired share of Macedonia after all. The offer, however, came too late. The dual stalemate on the Italian and Gallipoli fronts convinced the King and political leadership of Bulgaria that their best interests lay in alliance with the Central Powers rather than Britain, France and Russia – warm though Russia's patronage of Bulgaria had traditionally been – and on 6 September 1915 four treaties were signed. The terms included financial subsidy and future transfer of territory at Serbia's expense; more critically and immediately, Bulgaria undertook to go to war against Serbia within thirty days. The purpose of the campaign, in concert with Germany and Austria, was 'decisively to defeat the Serbian army and to open communications with Istanbul via Belgrade [the capital of Serbia] and Sofia [the capital of Bulgaria]'. It was at once transmitted by Falkenhayn to Mackensen, the victor of Gorlice-Tarnow, who proceeded to assemble an army. Serbia ordered general mobilisation on 22 September. A fruitless effort was made to draw Romania into the war but, unlike Bulgaria, its sympathies lay with the Allies. Meanwhile, Colonel Hentsch, whose report from the Marne battlefield had brought about the entrenchment of the Western Front a year earlier, made a survey of the Serbian theatre as a preliminary to drawing up invasion plans.

Since the failure of the second Austrian offensive in December 1914, the Serbian army had remained deployed on the northern and eastern frontiers. Mackensen's plan was to extend the front of attack far south, where Bulgaria could force the Serbs to dissipate their numbers in the defence of Macedonia. The Serbs had only eleven weak divisions, particularly weak in artillery. Against them the Bulgarians could deploy six divisions, the Austrians seven, and the Germans ten, twenty-three in all. All but one of the German divisions were regular formations, belonging to the Eleventh Army, which had led the Gorlice-Tarnow breakthrough and would be brought down to the Danube, under the command of von Gallwitz, initiator of the Namur operation, by rail.[64]

The odds overwhelmingly disfavoured the Serbs, fighting though they would be in the difficult terrain of their own country and behind wide and unbridged rivers – the Sava, the Danube, the latter a mile wide – at the frontiers. Voivode Putnik disposed of 200,000 men, of very varying quality, Mackensen of 330,000, with 1,200 guns to the Serbs' 300. Serbia's only hope of altering the balance lay in attracting Allied troops into the Balkans, via the Greek port of Salonika. That project had recommended itself to the French as early as November 1914 and actually underlay the inter-Allied discussions which resulted

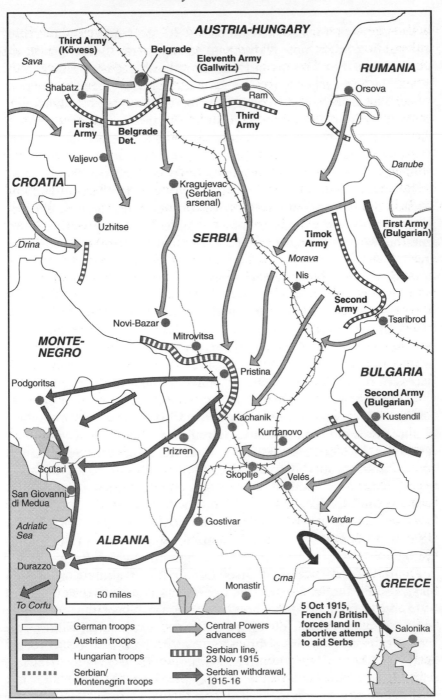

AUSTRIA-HUNGARY

Third Army
(Kövess)

Belgrade

Eleventh Army
(Gallwitz)

RUMANIA

Sava

Shabatz

Ram

Orsova

First
Army

Belgrade
Det.

Third
Army

Valjevo

Danube

CROATIA

Drina

Kragujevac
(Serbian
arsenal)

First Army
(Bulgarian)

Uzhitse

SERBIA

Timok
Army

Morava

Nis

Second
Army

Tsaribrod

Novi-Bazar

Mitrovitsa

MONTE-
NEGRO

Pristina

BULGARIA

Podgoritsa

Kachanik

Second Army
(Bulgarian)

Kurnanovo

Kustendil

Scutari

Prizren

San Giovanni
di Medua

Skoplije

Velés

*Adriatic
Sea*

Gostivar

Vardar

ALBANIA

Durazzo

Crna

Monastir

GREECE

To Corfu

50 miles

5 Oct 1915,
French / British
forces land in
abortive attempt
to aid Serbs

Salonika

	German troops	Central Powers advances
	Austrian troops	
	Hungarian troops	Serbian line, 23 Nov 1915
	Serbian/ Montenegrin troops	Serbian withdrawal, 1915-16

The campaign in Serbia, 1915

271

in the decision to land at Gallipoli.[65] In the hope that an Allied intervention might now allow them to defeat the Bulgarians in the south before the Germans and Austrians developed their attack in the north, the Serbs made a plea to the Allies to review the initiative once more. The British, still hoping to bribe the Bulgars into inactivity, declined to do so, urging Serbia to surrender the Macedonian territory they coveted. That price was one too high for Serbia to pay, even though disaster stared it in the face. An inducement to undertake the Salonika project now came from an unexpected direction. On the day Bulgaria mobilised, the Greek Prime Minister, Eleutherios Venizelos, advised the British and French governments that if they would send 150,000 troops to Salonika, he was confident of bringing his country into the war on their side, under the terms of an existing Serbo-Greek treaty.

Venizelos, 'the lion of Crete', who had won the independence of his island from Turkey in 1905, would have been a large man in any country and absolutely dominated the politics of the small Greek kingdom. He was the standard bearer of the 'Great Idea' – the national reunion of the Greek-speaking communities of the Aegean and its hinterland at Turkey's expense – and believed equally in the necessity of the Allies' support to achieve it and in the likelihood of their eventual victory. He therefore viewed the organisation of aid to Serbia as both realistic and essential. At his persuasion, Britain and France agreed to send troops to Salonika at once, first a token force, later the 150,000 troops that, by his interpretation of the Serbo-Greek treaty, would justify Greece ending its neutrality. He had, however, overestimated the strength of his position at home. King Constantine was not only the Kaiser's brother-in-law but believed his kingdom's interests best served by preserving its neutrality. On 5 October he dismissed Venizelos from office. Venizelos would return to politics in October 1916, form a government at Salonika which Britain would recognise as legitimate and, after Constantine's abdication in June 1917, resume the premiership with popular support. In the autumn of 1915, however, none of that could be foreseen. Meanwhile, the Allies took matters into their own hands. Greece, as a neutral without the means to resist, was obliged to acquiesce in the arrival of a Franco-British (and later also Russian) expeditionary force, formed in part by withdrawals from Gallipoli, in the transformation of Salonika into a vast Allied base and in the despatch in October of an Allied advance guard into Serbian Macedonia.

Its arrival came too late to assist the Serbs. On 5 October the Germans and Austrians began a bombardment across the Sava and Danube, followed by the bridging of both rivers on 7 October. Rough weather and Serbian fire destroyed some pontoons but the Austrian Third and German Eleventh Armies managed to secure footholds nonetheless and on 9 October entered Belgrade. Mackensen's plan, after gaining his lodgement, was to envelop the Serbs by driving them southward into the centre of their country. As agreed a month earlier, the Bulgarians crossed the frontier from the east on 11 October, simultaneously sending troops south to oppose the British and French in Macedonia, while the Germans and Austrians pressed down from the north. The plan, logical on paper, took insufficient account of the terrain, the climate of the approaching Balkan winter or of the Serbs' pre-modern capacity to endure hardship. The inhabitants of the central Balkans, materially the most backward region in Europe in 1915, were accustomed to seasonal privation, roadless habitat and extremes of temperature; to the hardihood that the snows and shortages of winter taught, their long history of insubmission to the Turks, and prosecution of the blood feud, added fierce tribal comradeship and contempt for danger. Hard as the Germans and Austrians pressed their pursuit after the fall of Belgrade, they found it impossible to corner the Serbs against any obstacle. Thrice they seemed to have succeeded, notably at Kosovo, the battlefield where the Turks had extinguished Serbian independence in 1389, but the Serbs, encumbered as they were by tens of thousands of refugees and the train of only symbolically useful artillery they insisted on dragging behind them, disengaged and slipped away, towards the brother-Serb principality of Montenegro, Albania and the sea. Their old King Peter marched in the centre of the columns struggling towards the coast, while the enfeebled Voivode Putnik was carried by his devoted soldiers in a closed sedan chair along the snowbound tracks and over the mountain passes. Only an army of natural mountaineers could have survived the passage through Montenegro, and many did not, dying of disease, starvation or cold as they fell out of the line by the wayside. Of the 200,000 who had set out, however, no less than 140,000 survived to cross in early December the frontier of Albania, independent since 1913 and still a neutral, and descend into the gentler temperatures of the Albanian Adriatic ports. Thence by ship, mostly Italian, the survivors, with thousands of miserable Austrian prisoners forced to accompany them in the retreat, were transferred to Corfu. In their wake the Austrian Third Army took possession of Montenegro, while the Bulgarians, whom neither the Germans nor Austrians wished to see established on the Adriatic, turned back from the border to join in the counter-offensive against the Allied invasion of Macedonia.

Other Bulgarian troops had already blunted the French and British effort to relieve pressure on the Serbs in Macedonia and by 12 December the two Allied divisions – the French 156th, the British 10th, both transferred from Gallipoli – that had crossed the Serbian frontier in October were back again on Greek territory. The British government, correctly judging that the Salonika project could serve no useful further purpose, now pressed the French to agree to the withdrawal of the Allied troops altogether. The French, in the grip of a domestic political crisis, demurred. Briand, who had replaced Viviani as premier in October, had been pro-Salonika from the start and made support for the project a test of loyalty to himself and his government. Moreover, he drew parliamentary support from the Radical Socialists, whose military favourite, Sarrail, commanded the Salonika army. To withdraw from Salonika would be to leave Sarrail without a command and unlikely to be given another, since Joffre feared and detested him. Briand therefore resuscitated his original arguments for the expedition: that it kept Greece and Romania neutral and that it posed a threat to the Austrian flank in the Balkans, which might be enlarged as later circumstances allowed. To those he added the argument that the Serbian army had not been destroyed and could, once reformed as a fighting force, be used (as it would be) on the Balkan front. As bait to Joffre, he elevated him to the command of French armies everywhere, not just in France alone; as bait to the Radical Socialists, he pointed out that Joffre must now support Sarrail because his elevation made his rival his subordinate. Between 1 and 6 December, at Calais, at GQG at Chantilly, and in London, the British and French political and military leaders took decisions for and against Salonika in rapid succession. The British nearly prevailed. Eventually, however, they were persuaded, by fear of provoking a collapse of Briand's government and by the heartfelt plea of the Russians to sustain a western pressure in the eastern theatre of operations, to leave their troops in Salonika after all.[66]

It was an odd outcome, both politically and strategically. The British and French, whose efforts in the struggle for the Greeks' liberty had been the chief cause of their winning of independence from the Turks in 1832, and who had championed independent Greece in every subsequent international crisis, now began to behave as if its sovereignty was entirely secondary to their convenience. They had already requisitioned Greek Lemnos, largest island of the northern Aegean, as a base for the Dardanelles campaign. Their landing at Salonika, the kingdom's second city, had been made without a by-your-leave. Once the Anglo-French decision had been taken to remain in Greece, the Allies proceeded to transform their Salonika base into an extraterritorial military settlement. King Constantine, at one point, protested feebly, 'I will not be treated like a native chieftain' but the Allies did so nonetheless.[67] The Greek army maintained a nominal presence at the settlement's perimeter. Within, in an area 200 miles square, the French encamped three and the British five divisions, and together created an enormous stockpile of stores and war material. Strategically, their presence exerted no pressure at all on either the Bulgarians or the Germans, who maintained a scratch force on the frontier. It drew no enemy force away from the Western Front, brought no aid to the Russians and posed no threat to the Turks. The Salonika divisions suffered, nonetheless; malaria, endemic in northern Greece, caused ten casualties for every one inflicted by the enemy, and from the mosquito, as long as the Allies remained in the disease zone, there was no escape. German journalists contemptuously described Salonika in 1915 as 'the greatest internment camp in the world'. It was worse than that. As numbers grew, and malaria rampaged, it became a great military hospital, where casualties from disease sometimes exceeded one hundred per cent of the strength of some units present.[68]

The year of 1915 thus ended on an inconclusive note. In the external theatres of war, the Western Allies had prevailed. Germany's colonies had been occupied, its colonial forces largely overcome and its cruising squadrons destroyed. Its Turkish ally had won a great, if local, victory at Gallipoli but had failed in its attempts to make either British Egypt or the Russian Caucasus diversionary fronts and was itself threatened by the British penetration of its Arab possessions in Mesopotamia. In southern Europe, Serbia had been overwhelmed and Bulgaria drawn into the Central alliance but Greece had been appropriated as an Anglo-French base and Italy persuaded to open an anti-Austrian front at its head of the Adriatic. On the two great fronts, Western and Eastern, the balance of success appeared to lie with the Central Powers. In France, the Germans had repelled every attempt by the French and British to break the trench line and had inflicted heavy losses on their enemies as the price of their efforts. On the Eastern Front, they had won a spectacular victory, at Gorlice-Tarnow, and pressed the Tsar's armies back to and, in some places, beyond the frontiers of old Russia. Poland and the Baltic coastline were theirs and the danger of a Russian invasion of Austria-Hungary across the crests of the Carpathians had been averted, apparently permanently. On the other hand, the fighting power of the Russian army had not been destroyed, the French army had sustained its aggressive spirit and the British army was transforming itself from a maritime expeditionary force of marginal significance into an instrument of continental offensive power. Germany's success in the seventeen months of fighting since the war had begun had been to survive the defeat of its plan to win quickly on two fronts, to rescue its weak Austrian ally from the collapse threatened by the prolongation of hostilities, to acquire secondary allies in the Balkans and Near East and to create a central strategic position, rich in industrial resources and raw materials, that extended from the Aisne in the west to the Drina, the Pripet and the Dniester rivers in the east. It had failed, however, to defeat any of its major enemies by land, to destroy the capacity of the Franco-British or Russian armies to return to the offensive, or to find means of breaking the maritime stronghold that was tightening about the perimeter of its landlocked base of operations. The coming year of 1916, all parties to the war recognised, would bring crisis on land, east and west, and at sea also. It would be a year of great battles between armies and fleets.

EIGHT

THE YEAR OF
BATTLES

WAR AT SEA

IF THE WAR OF 1914 was not a war which the armies of Europe were ready to fight, that was not so with Europe's great navies. The armies, as the opening campaigns had proved, were technically equipped to solve certain easily perceived problems, in particular how to overcome the defences of modern fortresses, how to move vast numbers of men from home bases to the frontiers and how to create impassable storms of rifle and field-artillery fire when those masses came into contact with each other. They were quite unequipped to deal with the unperceived and much more critical problems of how to protect soldiers from such fire storms, how to move them, under protection, about the battlefield, indeed how to move them at all beyond railhead unless on their feet, and how to signal quickly and unambiguously between headquarters and units, between unit and unit, between infantry and artillery, between ground and the aircraft with which, almost fortuitously, the armies had so recently provided themselves.

The failure of the generals of 1914 had largely been a pre-war failure. They had had the wit to adapt the technologies ready to hand, particularly that of Europe's many-branched rail network, to their purposes. They had lacked the wit to perceive the importance or potentialities of new technologies, among which the internal combustion engine and wireless-telegraphy, as radio was then called, would prove the most important; they had, indeed, lacked altogether the wit to perceive the problems to which such new technologies would be the solution. No such charge could be laid against the admirals of the years before 1914. With foresight they had divined the significance of the developing technologies likely to affect their service and had applied them to it with exactitude. Admirals have traditionally had a reputation as seadogs and salthorses, with little ability to see far beyond the bulwarks of their ships and little desire to change anything within them. Nineteenth-century admirals are commonly thought to

279

have opposed transition from sail to steam as fiercely as generals opposed the abolition of scarlet coats. Nothing could be further from the truth. When the admirals of the Royal Navy were persuaded that sail had had its day, they displayed a ruthless lack of sentimentality for the beauty of pyramids of canvas. The sailing navy was abolished almost overnight after the Crimean War, in which steam gunboats had devastated wooden walls. *Warrior*, the Royal Navy's first steam ironclad of 1861, was not an experimental but a revolutionary ship, which surpassed several intermediate stages of naval design in a single leap.[1] Palmerston, seeing her at anchor among the old men-of-war in Portsmouth harbour, described her as a 'snake among the rabbits' and the successors of the admirals who had commissioned her would build new snakes whenever they judged the old had lapsed into rabbit status. Naval design changed with almost bewildering rapidity between 1860 and 1914, from broadside to central battery to turret arrangement of guns, from all-round to 'citadel' to 'armoured deck' arrangement of protection, from wrought-iron to case-hardened to composite quality of armour, from piston to turbine engine power, from coal propulsion to oil.

The changes came faster and faster, as admirals accepted the significance of the new technologies civilian industry was creating and took stock of the evidence presented by the clash of such technologies in engagements between navies in non-European waters: the Spanish-American War of 1898, the Russo-Japanese War of 1904. In 1896 the Royal Navy, still the world leader, was launching battleships of 13,000 tons, armed with four 12-inch guns and capable of a speed of eighteen knots from piston engines fired by coal. By 1913 its most modern battleships, of the *Queen Elizabeth* class, displaced 26,000 tons, mounted eight 15-inch guns and achieved speeds of twenty-five knots from turbine engines fired by oil.[2] The key intermediate ship between these two designs had been the *Dreadnought* of 1906, which gave its name to all subsequent classes of 'all-big-gun-ships', so called because they dispensed with the previous clutter of secondary, small-calibre weapons and concentrated their armour around the ship-killing main armament, their magazines and their turbine engines. *Dreadnought*, the brainchild of Admiral Sir John Fisher, was as revolutionary as *Warrior* had been and the decision to build her as brave, for, like *Warrior*, she made all contemporary battleships obsolete, including the Royal Navy's own. Only a nation as rich, as fiscally efficient and as committed to its maintenance of maritime predominance as Britain could have taken such a risk and only a navy as technically adaptable as the Royal Navy could have seen the need to do so. The inspiration was not wholly British. Italian naval architects, always at the forefront of their profession, had anticipated the conception of the all-big-gun-ship. They did not nerve themselves to put conception into practice. The appearance of *Dreadnought*, and of a stream of similar and improved sister-ships appearing in rapid succession after her launch, forced all advanced navies – the French, the Italian, the Austrian, the Russian, the United States, the Japanese, the German – to do so. Between 1906 and 1914, Dreadnoughts went down the ways of the world's shipyards in ever-increasing numbers, to fly the flags of every major country, and of many which had not before aspired to maritime position. Turkey placed orders for Dreadnoughts in Britain and a Latin American naval race broke out between Argentina, Brazil and Chile which, lacking the resources to build large warships themselves, distributed their commissions between American and British yards. The Dreadnought in those years became a symbol of a state's international standing, whether or not it served an objective national purpose.

Competition – and competition was fierce between the British and American yards, which operated in the free market and sold abroad whenever they could – ensured that design met the highest standards and followed the most recent innovation. The ships building in Britain for foreign navies in 1914 – *Almirante Latorre* for Chile, *Reshedieh* for Turkey, *Rio de Janeiro* for Brazil – were of the most advanced class. The Admiralty had no hesitation in buying all three into British service in August 1914, when, as *Canada, Erin* and *Agincourt*, they immediately joined the Grand Fleet. *Agincourt,* which mounted twelve 14-inch guns, was the most heavily armed ship in any European navy. German Dreadnoughts were better protected than their British equivalents, having thicker armour and more elaborate internal division into small, water-tight spaces, which limited the danger of flooding, but mounted guns of smaller calibre. The latest class of the neutral United States' Dreadnoughts, *Oklahoma* and *Nevada*, achieved a remarkable compromise between speed, hitting-power and protection, while Britain's two *Queen Elizabeth* class (three more were building) clearly represented the newer generation of even faster, better armed and armoured battleships.

Marginal differences in design between Dreadnoughts would prove significant in battle, often startlingly so, for a chink in the armour might be lethal. Modern naval warfare was unforgiving. Steel ships, unlike wooden walls, could not be repaired in action (trivial damage excepted), while the huge loads of volatile high-explosive they carried in their magazines threatened them with disintegration if they received a deep hit. What, nevertheless, is striking about the Dreadnoughts is, first, their similarity to each other, second, their 'state-of-the-art' modernity. Admirals supported naval architects in striving to provide their ships with the very latest equipment on offer, from range-finding equipment (in which the German optical industry gave the High Seas Fleet a distinct advantage) to mechanical computers for calculating bearing and elevation in directing guns.[3] The armies of 1914 may not have been very efficient battle-winning organisations; the Dreadnought fleets were as efficient as they could be made within the constraints of available technology.

If there were any major technical deficiency in the equipment of fleets, it lay in their signalling arrangements.[4] Navies had enthusiastically embraced the new science of wireless-telegraphy (radio) and its introduction had enormously enhanced their ability to communicate, both strategically and tactically. It allowed the disposition of fleets to be altered over very long distances and, by radio direction-finding, for the position of enemy ships which broke wireless silence to be established with a high degree of accuracy. It also revolutionised the business of scouting and reconnaissance, by a battlefleet's attendant minor warships. Before the advent of wireless, signalling between scouts and scouts, and scouts and fleet, was limited by the height of masts above the visual horizon and by conditions of visibility within the radius thus defined, in practice twenty miles at most. After the introduction of wireless, scouts could communicate for hundreds, sometimes thousands of miles, and flagships directly and instantaneously with the humblest reconnaissance vessel and vice versa. It was the light cruiser *Glasgow*, the only survivor of the disaster of Coronel, that saved the latecomer *Canopus* from destruction and it was its wireless transmissions that set in motion the trans-equatorial chase which eventually brought Spee's squadron to defeat at the Falklands.

Naval wireless telegraphy in 1914 had, however, one critical drawback. It as yet did not transmit voice signals, only morse code. As a result, there was 'a period which includes the time taken to write out the [message], to transmit it to the wireless office, to code it, to signal it, de-code it aboard the receiving ship, write it out and transmit it to the bridge', a period estimated by Admiral Jellicoe, commanding the

Grand Fleet, to be 'ten minutes to a quarter of an hour'.[5] This lapse in 'real time' was unimportant when strategic signals were being transmitted and received. It was crucial in action, when densely ranked fleets had to manoeuvre simultaneously at the admiral's command. Wireless was therefore judged to be ineffective as a means of tactical signalling, which continued to be done, just as in Nelson's time, by flag hoist. An admiral, wishing to turn his battleline towards or away from the enemy, would instruct the flag lieutenant to 'make' the appropriate flag hoist, which the yeomen of signals on the bridge of each of his subordinate ships was expected to identify by naked eye or telescope and announce to the captain. The procedure required first the hoist, perhaps copied by a 'repeater' ship nearer the front or rear of the line, and then the display of an 'executive' flag, which ordered the manoeuvre the hoist specified when dropped. The system had worked admirably at Trafalgar, when the speed of the British approach towards the Franco-Spanish line was five knots and the distance between the leading and last ship of a formation was two miles at most. Dreadnought fleets, manoeuvring at twenty knots in formations six miles long, were controlled by flag hoist only with great difficulty, as signallers struggled to identify tiny squares of coloured cloth, obscured by the smoke of funnels and guns, at distances of a thousand yards or more.

In retrospect, it seems that it might have been possible to simplify wireless-telegraphic procedure, by dispensing with encoding and by locating a receiver on the bridge, to be used in tactical circumstances when the dangers stemming from interception, since they must occur in 'real time', would be minimised. It was not done, perhaps because, through one of those lapses into 'backwardness' so characteristic of the armies of 1914, the 'culture' of the signal flag had fleets in its grip. The lapse was common to all navies. Unfortunately for the Royal Navy, the High Seas Fleet had overcome the signalling difficulty to a degree by simplifying its system of manoeuvre, allowing large changes of direction and alignment to be achieved by fewer hoists than the Grand Fleet employed. That would prove greatly to its advantage during the battle of Jutland.

Otherwise, in technical circumstances as remarkable for their modernity as for their similarity, only one shortcoming was notable, and that affected both the navies locked in the war's critical confrontation, the British and the German. Neither had adequate reconnaissance resources. Traditionally, fleets had deployed, forward of what were now known as their 'capital' units, the battleships, and their attendant light craft, a screen of intermediate ships fast enough to find the enemy and strong enough then to disengage before suffering crippling damage. In the decades before the First World War, they had acquired the name of 'cruisers'. Admiral Fisher, the sponsor of the Dreadnought concept, had conceived the idea that the function of the cruiser would in future best be served by a vessel as large as the battleship and as well armed, but faster, its superior speed being achieved by dispensing with much of the battleship's armour. By 1916 the Grand Fleet included nine of these 'battlecruisers' and the High Seas Fleet, since the Germans had followed the British initiative, five. Of traditional cruisers neither had any number and those in service were old, slow and weak in armament and armour. That would not have mattered had the admirals restricted their employment to the appropriate reconnaissance role and deterred the battlecruiser squadron commanders from exposing their ships to punishment they were not built to withstand. Unfortunately for both navies, the belief had arisen that battlecruisers should, in extension of their scouting function, engage in action with the enemy's battleships when found, using their main armament to 'fix' them while their own supporting battleships came up, and trusting to their superior speed to escape damage in the interim. 'Speed is protection', Fisher had argued. His battlecruisers were indeed faster than any battleship then afloat by a margin of as much as ten knots (British battlecruiser *Queen Mary* = 33 knots, German battleship *Kaiser* = 23.6 knots). As battle would prove, however, speed was not protection against modern naval guns, firing 12-inch or heavier shells out to ranges of 17,000 yards. The illusion that it might prove so had caused navies to spend the money that could have bought dozens of smaller but effective cruisers on a handful of battlecruisers no better at doing their work and wholly unsuitable to challenge battleships even in the preliminaries of fleet action. The Royal Navy went into battle at Jutland in 1916 with but a handful of traditional cruisers, none up to their work, swarms of light cruisers too weak even to show themselves to the enemy's heavier ships and an advanced guard of battlecruisers which would suffer terrible and pointless loss before the main action was joined.

The clash of battlefleets at Jutland took place on 31 May 1916 and the following night. There had been two earlier engagements, near Heligoland and the Dogger Bank in August 1914 and January 1915, but neither had engaged the main battlefleets against each other. The battle of the Heligoland Bight, at the entrance to Germany's North Sea naval bases, came about through the determination of the commanders of the destroyers and submarines at Harwich, the British port nearest the German bases, to intercept the enemy's offshore patrols and inflict damage. Tyrwhitt, commanding what came to be called Harwich Force, and Keyes, commanding the Eighth Submarine Flotilla, were aggressive officers whose thirst for action won the support of Churchill, First Lord of the Admiralty, and, through him, the promise of intervention by three of Admiral Sir David Beatty's battlecruisers if opportunity for success offered. In a confused daylight encounter on 28 August, a misty day in the Heligoland Bight, the British at first succeeded in sinking only one destroyer. When German reinforcements appeared, however, Beatty's battlecruisers came forward and sank three enemy cruisers before safely disengaging.[6]

This small victory greatly heartened the British but, while prompting the Germans to thicken the defences of the Heligoland Bight with minefields and standing patrols of heavy and light vessels, including submarines, it did not deter them from further action. In an effort to treat the British as they had been treated themselves, they sent fast ships to bombard the North Sea port of Yarmouth on 3 November and, on 16 December, Scarborough, Whitby and Hartlepool, on this second occasion with most of the High Seas Fleet's Dreadnoughts following. The Grand Fleet sent a squadron to intercept but failure of intelligence prevented it making contact, fortunately, for it would have been outnumbered. In the second of the early naval encounters of the war, at the Dogger Bank, intelligence served the Royal Navy better. Its interception and cryptologic services, the latter accommodated in the Admiralty Old Building (Room 40 or 40 OB), was far superior to the German and those who worked there had benefited at the war's outset from three extraordinary pieces of luck. In August the German light cruiser *Magdeburg* grounded in Russian waters and its signal books, with the current key, were recovered and sent to England. In October, the merchantman code, seized from a German steamer interned in Australia, also reached London. Later the same month a third codebook, used by German admirals at sea and jettisoned by the senior officer of a group of German destroyers recently sunk in a small action off the Dutch coast, was dredged up accidentally in the nets of a British fishing boat and brought to the Admiralty.[7] These three documents opened the secrets of most German naval signalling to the officers of 40 OB, allowing them to read enemy transmissions often in 'real time', that is, as quickly as they were decoded by the intended recipients. In an uncanny fore-shadowing of the cryptological history of the Second World War, the German naval staff swiftly recognised that the movements of their ships were becoming known to the enemy but ascribed that intelligence success not to signal insecurity but to espionage. Their suspicions fixed on the Dutch fishing boats trawling the shallow waters of the Dogger Bank, in the central North Sea, which they decided were British-manned, flying false flags and wirelessing their observations to the Admiralty.

Believing that they could turn such reports to their advantage while revenging themselves for the Heligoland defeat, the German naval staff decided to sail the battlecruisers of the High Seas Fleet to the Dogger Bank and lay a trap for their opposite numbers. On 23 January, the First and Second Scouting Groups sortied, only to encounter heavy opposition as they approached the Dogger Bank at dawn next morning. Beatty's battlecruiser squadrons, alerted by 40 OB, were in position and, as the weaker and less numerous German formations emerged into visibility, they found themselves assailed by armour-piercing salvoes. The semi-battlecruiser *Blücher* was over-whelmed and capsized, the *Seydlitz* almost suffered a fatal internal explosion, averted only by flooding the magazines, and the two scouting groups, turning tail, escaped by the skin of their teeth. Examination of the damage caused to *Seydlitz* after she limped home revealed that far too much high-explosive, in the form of bags of propellant for the main armament, had been taken out of its flash-proof cases in the ammunition-handling chambers under the turret than was safe or necessary. Damage to the turret had ignited the charges there and the flash, travelling down the turret-trunk, detonated the loose charges below and started a fire next to the magazine. Warned in time of the dangers of bad practice, the German navy instituted much stricter procedures for the handling of its propellant, which was in any case more stable than the British equivalent. Beatty's Battle Cruiser Fleet, as it became known immediately after the Dogger Bank, continued to keep loose pro-pellant ready in quantity between magazine and turret, with results that would prove disastrous at Jutland.[8]

After January 1915, the High Seas Fleet kept close to its home bases for most of the next eighteen months and pondered its strategy. The Fleet's submarine operations could bring returns, and so could minelaying, by U-boat or surface ship. The sinking of HMS *Audacious*, a brand-new Dreadnought, by a mine laid by an armed merchant cruiser in October 1914, caused the British Admiralty even greater anguish than the torpedoing of the ancient cruisers, *Aboukir, Hogue* and *Cressy* by U-9 in the 'Broad Fourteens' off Holland in September. Submarine warfare, however, by the rules of commerce-raiding, which stipulated that an attacker must give a merchant ship warning before sinking and make provision for the escape of the crew and passengers, could cause little interruption to trade, while exposing U-boats to rapid retaliation; 'unrestricted' submarine warfare, on the other hand, when U-boats torpedoed without surfacing, could all too easily lead to diplomatic incidents, through the sinking of wrongly identified neutrals, or to diplomatic disaster, as it did in May 1915, when U-20 sank the *Lusitania*. The loss of this huge British liner, and that of the lives of 1,201 passengers, of whom 128 were American, almost caused the United States to break off relations with Germany. Negotiations smoothed over the repercussions of the atrocity but the German naval staff imposed strict limitation on the operations of its submarines in the aftermath. The British merchant fleet continued to lose between fifty and a hundred ships a month to submarine attack during 1915 but could maintain supply to the home country none-theless.[9] Meanwhile, the Grand Fleet and its subordinate squadrons and flotillas of cruisers, destroyers and submarines sustained a blockade of Germany that denied it all trade with the world beyond Europe and which was extended, by British, French and Italian naval dominance in the Mediterranean, against Austria and Turkey. The 'central position' of the Central Powers, a strategic posture ordained by military theorists to be one of great strength, had been reduced to one of infirmity, perhaps disabling weakness, by the constriction of an all-encircling blockade. Germany's sailors, during 1915, racked their brains to think of a way out.

They had brought their predicament upon themselves, aided and abetted by political and dynastic leaders who should have known better. The geography of the German-speaking lands, however con-figured into states, denies the Germans maritime power. The geo-graphy of the German empire of 1914 narrowed its access to the high seas to the short North Sea coastline between Denmark and Holland. From it, the way to the nearest ocean, the Atlantic, lay through waters easily choked by an enemy. Westward, the English Channel, only nineteen miles across at the narrows, had long lain under threat of closure by the Royal Navy; in more recent years the threat of closure by mine-barriers, though the British did not densely mine the Channel narrows until 1916, promised to render the western route impermeable. Northward, from the estuaries of the Ems, Jade, Weser and Elbe, the High Seas Fleet had a clear run into the North Sea from ports easily protected against a close British blockade. Once at sea, however, it faced a passage of 600 miles up the North Sea, between Great Britain and Norway, before it could break out into the ocean, and then only through a series of gaps, between the Faroes, Iceland and Greenland, easily kept under surveillance by light cruiser squadrons. The likelihood of the High Seas Fleet clearing the North Sea undetected or unassailed diminished, moreover, with every mile it steamed, because early in the century it had become the Royal Navy's war plan to transfer its capital units on mobilisation from its English to the Scottish ports, Rosyth near Edinburgh and Scapa Flow in the Orkney Islands, leaving its light units of cruisers, destroyers and submarines to maintain an intermediate blockade off the Heligoland Bight, which would give early warning of a German sortie. On that warning the Grand Fleet would sail south at speed, making it an operational probability that a major fleet action would be joined long before the enemy had neared the waters from which it could stage an oceanic break-out. Admiral Fisher summed up the German predicament in an exultant epitome of the critical maritime geography to King George V: 'with the great harbour of Scapa Flow in the North and the narrow straits of Dover in the south, there is no doubt, Sir, that we are God's chosen people'.[10]

The Germans had never blinded themselves to the intrinsic geographical weakness of their position or the strengths of the British. They had toyed unrealistically with means of widening their access to the North Sea, by persuading or forcing their Dutch, Danish and Norwegian neighbours to grant them bases, and continued to consider means of doing so even after the war had begun; during 1915, Commander Wolfgang Wegoner of the German naval staff wrote a series of papers advocating the occupation of Denmark, the establishment of a protectorate over Norway and, at some future date, the acquisition of ports in France and Portugal.[11] Perception of the value of the submarine, as a carrier either of mines or torpedoes, was also amplified after the war's outbreak, by the success of the very small U-boat force against both warships and merchantmen. In the main, however, the German Admiralty, having early taken a view of the nature of the fleet it should build and operate best to serve its maritime purpose, persisted with its long-laid strategic policy. That is simply stated. Germany, within the fiscal limits imposed by the maintenance of a very large army, could not outbuild Britain in capital ships. It should, therefore, confine itself to confronting the Royal Navy with 'risk' – the risk that its traditional determination to command the seas might lead to a wearing down of its preponderant strength through small actions, and by mine and submarine, which would heighten the danger that, in unforeseeable conditions, the Grand Fleet might find itself at a disadvantage to the High Seas Fleet during one of its offensive sorties. After much debate about 'risk' strategy, the Kaiser issued a final war directive to the German navy on 3 December 1912, which stipulated that its 'chief war task' should be 'to damage the blockading forces of the enemy as far as possible through numerous and repeated attacks day and night, and *under favourable circumstances* to give battle with all the forces at your disposal'.[12]

German naval operations in home waters during 1914 and 1915 had adhered strictly to the 1912 directive, and achieved some of its purposes. Heligoland and the Dogger Bank had been defeats but had indeed damaged the blockading force, since *Tiger* and *Lion* were hit at the Dogger Bank, *Lion* hard enough to have to be towed back to harbour. The sinking of *Audacious* had been achieved at the cost of a single mine. The potentiality of the U-boat in fleet warfare had also been demonstrated by the sinking of the pre-Dreadnought *Formidable* in the Channel on 1 January 1915 by U-24. In early 1915 Sir John Jellicoe, commanding the Grand Fleet, was seriously concerned that German *Kleinkrieg* (small war) successes, combined with the need to disperse units of the Grand Fleet to secondary theatres, was whittling away its superiority. In November the ratio of British to German Dreadnoughts had fallen to 17:15 (it had been 20:13 in August) and of battlecruisers to 5:4.[13] Germany was continuing to launch capital ships, moreover, and though Britain was doing likewise, it had calls on its resources, particularly in the Mediterranean, that Germany did not have to meet.

By the spring of 1916, the balance had swung back in Britain's favour. The situation in distant waters, thanks to the destruction of the German raiding cruisers, the termination of the Gallipoli campaign and the addition of the Italian to the Franco-British fleet in the Mediterranean, no longer exerted a drain on the forces at home. New classes of Dreadnoughts had come into service, particularly the fast

Queen Elizabeths and, while Germany had also added to the High Seas Fleet, the Grand Fleet had recovered a clear superiority. In April 1916 it comprised thirty-one Dreadnoughts and ten battlecruisers, the High Seas Fleet only eighteen Dreadnoughts and five battlecruisers. British superiority in light cruisers and destroyers was also large (113:72) and, while the Grand Fleet's lack of effective heavy cruisers persisted, it was unencumbered with any of the pre-Dreadnoughts which, for want of weight in the battle line, the Germans continued to count as part of their capital strength.[14]

On paper, therefore, the risk in an active implementation of Germany's 'risk' strategy was too large to be accepted; prudence counselled passivity and a reversion to traditional 'fleet in being' policy, by which a navy justified its existence simply by causing an opponent to watch its harbours. German naval pride forbade such inactivity. The navy was in Germany the junior, not, as in Britain, the senior service, and many of its officers felt it had to fight whatever the odds, if it were to keep the esteem of the German people, particularly at a time when the German army was pouring out its blood for the nation. A new and aggressive admiral, Reinhard Scheer, had taken command of the High Seas Fleet in January 1916 and a memorandum written to him by one of his captains, Adolf von Trotha, epitomises the attitude of the offensive school to which both belonged: there can be, he wrote, 'no faith in a fleet which has been brought through the war intact . . . we are at present fighting for our existence . . . In this life and death struggle, I cannot understand how anyone can think of allowing any weapon which could be used against the enemy to rust in its sheath.'[15]

Scheer quickly resumed the policy of taking the fleet to sea in the search for action. He made two sorties in February and March 1916 and four in April and May; in the April sortie he succeeded in reaching the English east coast and, in a repetition of the raids of 1914, bombarding Lowestoft. The demonstration, timed to coincide with the Irish nationalist Easter Rising, of which Germany had foreknowledge, caused dismay in Britain but emphasised once again that, while the Grand Fleet at Scapa Flow closed the exit from the North Sea, High Seas Fleet operations must be limited to tip-and-run against targets close enough to home for it to beat a retreat before the Royal Navy's heavy units could steam south and intervene. Even the Battle Cruiser Fleet, which was now located at Rosyth, one of the ports of Edinburgh, was anchored too far north to catch German raiders without considerable forewarning.

At the end of May, however, such forewarning it and Jellicoe's battleship squadrons got. Scheer had been preparing another sortie for some time, on a scale elaborate enough to surprise Beatty's battlecruisers if they came sufficiently far south. An encounter with the British Dreadnoughts he did not plan. Room 40's decryption of his signals, however, gave Jellicoe word of his movements, so that, by the time Scheer had cleared the Heligoland Bight, not only were Beatty's battlecruisers at sea and heading south from Rosyth, so too were the Scapa Flow battleships. On the morning of 31 May, over 250 British and German warships were steaming on convergent courses to a rendezvous, unanticipated by the Germans, off the Jutland coast of Denmark. Among the host of light cruisers, destroyers and submarines which made up the bulk of each side's forces, it was the presence of the big ships which promised decision. They included, on the British side, twenty-eight Dreadnoughts and nine battlecruisers, on the German sixteen Dreadnoughts and five battlecruisers. Jellicoe's arrangement of his fleet attached his four newest battleships, of the fast *Queen Elizabeth* class, to the six battlecruisers of Beatty's Battle Cruiser Fleet, deployed ahead of the Grand Fleet's Dreadnoughts as an advance guard, with orders to bring the Germans to action. Scheer's fleet, advancing fifty miles behind the First Scouting Group of five battlecruisers, included six *Deutschland*-class pre-Dreadnoughts, which he appears to have brought with him for sentimental rather than military reasons.[16] Their lack of speed, five knots less than that of his *Kaiser*-class battleships, made them a liability in a contest of rapid closing and opening of the range at which main armament took effect.

Scheer's decision to take the whole of the High Seas Fleet into the North Sea, something never ventured before, was predicated on the belief that the British would not have foreknowledge of his movements. Room 40's success in penetrating his signals therefore laid the basis for a great victory, since, with Jellicoe's and Beatty's ships advancing to an encounter likely to occur too far from port for Scheer to escape to safety during daylight hours, he risked the danger of being overwhelmed, or cut off from his line of retreat by superior force. Jellicoe's initial advantage was compromised at an early stage, however, by a procedural failure at the Admiralty in London. Mistrusting Room 40's ability to make operational judgements, the responsible staff officer asked a veiled question and concluded from the answer that Scheer's battleships were still in harbour. He transmitted that false information to Jellicoe who, in consequence, and in order to conserve fuel, limited his speed southward while allowing Beatty and the battlecruisers to forge ahead. Room 40 had correctly informed the naval staff that Scheer's wireless call sign could still be located in his home port; since the question had not been asked, however, the intelligence officers did not say that, on going to sea, it left its harbour call sign behind and adopted another. At the critical stage of the preliminaries of what would prove the largest naval encounter of the war, therefore, Jellicoe was making less than best speed to a junction with the enemy, while his reconnaissance fleet of battlecruisers was hurtling to an early and potentially disastrous encounter with a superior force.

Jutland, as the impending battle would be called (by the British; to the Germans it would, contentiously, be known as 'the victory of the Skaggerak') promised not only to be the largest naval encounter of the war but of naval history thus far. No sea had ever seen such a large concentration of ships or of ships so large, so fast and so heavily armoured. The High Seas Fleet, which had cleared the Heligoland Bight in the early morning of 31 May, consisted of sixteen Dreadnoughts, six pre-Dreadnoughts, five battlecruisers, eleven light cruisers and sixty-one destroyers. The Grand Fleet and the Battle Cruiser Fleet, which had left Scapa Flow and Rosyth the previous evening, included twenty-eight Dreadnoughts, nine battlecruisers, eight armoured cruisers, twenty-six light cruisers, seventy-eight destroyers, a seaplane-carrier and a minesweeper.[17] Both sides also had submarines at sea, in the hope that the enemy might present a target to a lucky shot. Scheer's plan, indeed, was predicated on the chance of drawing the British into a U-boat trap by showing his battlecruisers off Jutland. No such chance came, however, nor were any of the navies' associated aircraft or airships able to play a role.[18] Jutland, in consequence, was to be both the biggest and the last purely surface encounter of main fleets in naval history. The spectacle they presented never left the memory of those who took part, the densely ranked columns of battleships, grey against the grey water and sky of the North Sea, belching clouds of grey smoke from their coal-stoked boilers, the flash of white from the bows of the faster light cruisers and destroyers in attendance, as all pressed onward to action. So large was the number of ships hurrying forward that the more distant formations blurred into the horizon or were lost to sight in the play of cloud and rain squall on the observer's field of vision.

Jutland and the war in the North Sea

Jutland is the most written about battle of naval history and the most disputed between scholars. Each segment, almost every minute of the two fleets' engagement have been described and analysed by historians, official and unofficial, without any reaching agreement about exactly what happened or why, or whether, indeed, the outcome was a British or a German victory. That it was a British victory of some sort is not now denied. That it was less than a decisive victory is not denied either. It was the disparity between British expectations of victory and the success actually achieved that led to the detailed dissection of the battle's events and the controversy that persists to this day. The Royal Navy, undefeated in a major fleet action since Trafalgar, sailed for Jutland in the sure belief that, should a junction of battlefleets ensue, another Trafalgar would occur. The inconclusiveness of the event has continued to haunt the mind of the Royal Navy ever since.

Yet Jutland is not, in outline, complex at all. It falls into five phases: in the first Beatty's Battle Cruiser Fleet made a 'run to the south' on encountering the weaker German battlecruiser force; then a 'run to the north' when, on meeting the German Dreadnoughts, it turned back to draw them into Jellicoe's Grand Fleet; then two encounters between the Dreadnoughts, broken by a German 'turning away' as heavier British firepower told; and finally, after the German Dreadnoughts had sought escape from destruction, a night action in which the light forces of both sides sought to inflict crippling damage by torpedo attack.[19]

In the first phase Beatty's Battle Cruiser Fleet passed through Scheer's patrol line of U-boats without loss to arrive within fifty miles of his opposite number Hipper's First Scouting Group, undetected. Chance then directed them towards each other. Their light forces diverted to investigate a neutral merchant ship, found each other and brought the two groups of battlecruisers into contact. Fire was opened and, because of bad British signalling, the German told more heavily. It fell, moreover, on ships defective in armoured protection and in prudent ammunition-handling. First *Indefatigable,* then *Queen Mary* suffered penetrations, which set off fires in handling-rooms where too many intrinsically unstable propellant charges were lying ready to be sent into the turrets. Both blew up and sank. Beatty's superiority in numbers was suddenly reduced from seven to five.

The appearance of his supporting fast battleships reversed the imbalance but then they and the surviving battlecruisers of the Battle Cruiser Fleet found that they had run down on to the main body of German Dreadnoughts. When they turned back towards Jellicoe's

Grand Fleet, the 'run to the north' began. During it the 15-inch gunfire of the fast battleships inflicted heavy damage on the following Germans – the unlucky *Seydlitz*, so heavily hit at the Dogger Bank, was hit again – so that Scheer's battleline was in disarray when his Dreadnoughts unwittingly fell under the fire of Jellicoe's a little after six o'clock in the evening. They were to inflict one more act of destruction, when *Invincible* was blown up, through the same causes that had devastated *Indefatigable* and *Queen Mary*. Then the concentration of British superior weight of shell proved so overwhelming that Scheer hastily ordered a retreat and disappeared into the gathering gloom of a misty North Sea evening.

There might have ended, inconclusively, an already unsatisfactory encounter. Scheer, however, then decided to turn back, perhaps to come to the assistance of the damaged light cruiser *Wiesbaden* which had been left behind, perhaps because he judged that he could pass astern of Jellicoe's fleet as it continued its advance towards the Heligoland Bight, while he made his escape through the Skaggerak into the Baltic. Jellicoe, however, once again reduced speed, with the result that the German Dreadnoughts, heading north-east, encountered the British heading south-east, and steering to pass their rear so as to cut them off from safety. At the moment of encounter moreover, the British were deployed in line abreast, the Germans in line ahead, a relative position, known as 'crossing the enemy's T', that greatly favoured the British. More of their guns could be brought to bear than could those of the German fleet, ranked one ship behind the other, which thus also presented an easier target. Ten minutes of gunnery, in which the Germans suffered twenty-seven hits by large-calibre shells, the British only two, persuaded Scheer to turn away again into the dark eastern horizon, leaving his battlecruisers and lighter ships to cover his retreat in a 'death ride'. The torpedo threat they presented caused Jellicoe to turn away also – for which he has ever afterwards been reproached – and, by the time he turned back, Scheer had put ten miles between his Dreadnoughts and the pursuit. Many German ships remained to cover Scheer's flight, including his squadron of vulnerable pre-Dreadnoughts, and in a series of dusk and night actions they suffered losses. So, too, did the British cruisers and destroyers that remained in contact. By the morning of 1 June, when Scheer had his fleet home, he had lost a battlecruiser, a pre-Dreadnought, four light cruisers and five destroyers. Jellicoe, though remaining in command of the North Sea, had lost three battlecruisers, four armoured cruisers and eight destroyers; 6,094 British sailors had died, 2,551 German.

The disparity in losses caused the Kaiser to claim a victory. Scheer, his sailors and ships had undoubtedly acquitted themselves well, while the battle had revealed serious defects in British ship design and tactical practice, particularly in inter-ship and inter-squadron signalling. Beatty had failed to report promptly and accurately in the encounter stage, gunnery had not been directed effectively during the Dreadnought engagements.[20] Nevertheless, Jutland was not a German victory. Though the High Seas Fleet had lost fewer ships than the Grand Fleet, it had suffered more damage to those that survived, so that in the aftermath its relative strength in heavy units fell from 16:28 to 10:24. In those circumstances it could not risk challenging the Grand Fleet for several months nor, when it resumed its sallies from port, dared it venture outside coastal waters.[21] Contrary to conventional belief, Jutland was not the German fleet's last sortie, nor its last action. There was an encounter between German Dreadnoughts and British battlecruisers near Heligoland on 17 November 1917, while the High Seas Fleet steamed as far as southern Norway on 24 April 1918. It had accepted the verdict of Jutland nevertheless, pithily summarised by a German journalist as an assault on the gaoler, followed by a return to gaol.[22] Inactivity and discontent would eventually lead to serious disorder among the crews of Scheer's surface ships, beginning in August 1917 and culminating in full-scale mutiny in the last November of the war. After 1 June 1916, Germany's attempt to win a decision at sea would be conducted exclusively through the submarine arm.

OFFENSIVES ON THREE FRONTS

In the early summer of 1916, Germany saw as yet no need to reverse the policy of restricting U-boat operations it had adopted, for diplomatic reasons, the previous year, nor did the Allies apprehend the deadly danger that such a reversal would bring. Their thoughts were concentrated on the great offensives they jointly planned to deliver in the west and east, offensives which they believed would, after eighteen months of stalemate in France and Belgium, a year of defeats in Poland, and six months of frustration in Italy, bring them decisive victories. On 6 December 1915, representatives of the Allied powers met at French headquarters at Chantilly to agree plans. Joffre presided but had no power to impose a single strategy, only to encourage co-ordination. In that he succeeded. It was easily decided that the minor fronts, in Salonika, Egypt and Mesopotamia (though there events were suddenly to take a turn for the worse), should not be reinforced. On the major fronts, by contrast, the Russians, the Italians and the British and French bound themselves to mount attacks so timed as to prevent the Central Powers from transferring reserves between theatres and with all the forces available to each army.

The Allied forces had grown considerably since the beginning of trench warfare. Italy, industrially and demographically the weakest of the major allies, had succeeded by early 1916 in raising its number of infantry battalions from 560 to 693 and of field artillery pieces from 1,788 to 2,068; the army in the zone of combat had grown in strength since 1915 from a million to a million and a half.[23] Russia, despite the terrible fatalities of 1914–15 and the large loss of soldiers to captivity after Gorlice-Tarnow, had been able to fill the gaps with new conscripts, so that by the spring of 1916 it would have two million men in the field army. Almost all, moreover, would be properly equipped, thanks to a striking expansion of Russian industry. Engineering output increased fourfold between the last year of peace and 1916, chemical output, essential to shell-filling, doubled. As a result there was a 2,000 per cent increase in the production of shells, 1,000 per cent in that of artillery, 1,100 per cent in that of rifles. Output of the standard field-artillery shell had risen from 358,000 per month in January 1915 to 1,512,000 in November. The Russian armies would in future attack with a thousand rounds of shell available per gun, a stock equivalent to that current in the German and French armies, and its formations were acquiring plentiful quantities of all the other equipment – trucks, telephones and aircraft (as many as 222 per month) – essential to modern armies.[24]

In France, too, there had been a war-industrial revolution. Thanks in part to the mobilisation of women for factory work – the number employed in the metal industries rose from 17,731 in 1914 to 104,641 in July 1916 – shell output reached 100,000 per day in the autumn of 1915. Between August and December 1915, production of field guns rose from 300 to 600, while daily production of rifles in that month totalled 1,500; output of explosive had increased sixfold since the beginning of the war.[25] There had not been a comparable expansion of the fighting force. Because of the small size of the national demographic base, relative to Germany's, and high proportion of men conscripted and held in the reserve in peacetime, over 80 per cent of those of military age, France lacked the capacity to expand its field army to the extent possible in Germany or Russia, where the pre-war military intake was less than half the age group. Nevertheless, by skilful reorganisation and redeployment of soldiers to the front from employment in the rear, twenty-five new infantry divisions were formed between February 1915 and the spring of 1916. The French army of 1916 was stronger than that of 1914 by more than 25 per cent.[26]

The major addition to the fighting strength of the Allies, however, was British. On 7 August 1914, Lord Kitchener, on appointment as Secretary of State for War, had issued an appeal for a hundred thousand men to enlist for three years, or the duration of the war, which he believed would be long. Further appeals for 'hundred thousands' followed, and were met with an overwhelmingly enthusiastic response, in part because the promise was given that 'those who joined together would serve together'. As a result men from the same small locality, workplace or trade went to the recruiting offices in groups, were attested and then went forward to training and eventually active service in the same unit.[27] Many called themselves 'Chums' or 'Pals' battalions, among which the largest group was the Liverpool Pals of four battalions, largely raised from the shipping and broking offices of the city. Smaller towns supplied single battalions, like the Accrington Pals, the Grimsby Chums and the Oldham Comrades; others were raised by occupation, the Glasgow Tramways Battalion, or nationality; Newcastle-on-Tyne, the English industrial city, produced four battalions each of Tyneside Scottish and Tyneside Irish. The 'first hundred thousand' had included many of the pre-war unemployed. Subsequent hundred thousands – there were to be five altogether – were formed of genuine volunteers including, by January 1915, 10,000 skilled engineers, and over 100,000 each from the coal mining and the building trades. From this magnificent human resource, Kitchener was able eventually to form six 'New' or 'Kitchener' Armies, each five divisions strong, to join the army's eleven regular divisions and the twenty-eight infantry divisions of the part-time, voluntary Territorial Force. By the spring of 1916, Britain had seventy divisions under arms, a tenfold expansion since peace, and of those twenty-four were New Army divisions on or waiting to go to the Western Front.[28]

It was this enormous increment in the striking power of the Anglo-

French concentration in France and Belgium that allowed the French and British to promise their allies at Chantilly a continuation of their joint offensive efforts in 1916. It would, Joffre agreed on 29 December with General Sir Douglas Haig, the new commander of the BEF, take the form of a combined offensive in the centre of the Western Front. Joffre argued initially for mounting a series of preliminary assaults, in continuation of his policy of attrition. Haig, who feared that forces would be frittered away in such operations, counter-proposed an attack by the British in Flanders, to be matched by a French offensive further south, as had been tried in 1915. As a compromise, Joffre secured his agreement to a drive along the line of the River Somme, to which the British were to extend their line. As the movement would allow the French units north of the Somme to rejoin the main concentration of Joffre's armies to the south, the two armies would then share a clear-cut boundary which, Joffre argued, should be the axis of their great offensive in the coming year. Haig, who doubted the military logic of an operation that seemed likely at best to dent the huge salient left by the failed German advance on Paris in 1914, demurred but, in the interests of Anglo-French harmony, eventually concurred.

Plans made without allowance for the intentions of the enemy are liable to miscarry. So it was to prove in 1916. While Joffre and Haig were making their dispositions for the Somme, the Italians preparing to persist in the struggle for the heights above the Isonzo and the Russians contemplating retaliation for the loss of Poland, Conrad von Hötzendorf was laying the basis for an Austrian 'punishment expedition' against the hated Italians from the unexpected direction of the Trentino, while Falkenhayn, who had wrongly concluded that the Russians had been beaten into submission by the series of victories beginning with Tannenberg and culminating in Gorlice-Tarnow, was devising a vast punishment expedition of his own against the French at Verdun.

Falkenhayn outlined his reasoning in a letter written to the Kaiser on Christmas Day 1915. Germany's object, he insisted, must be to dishearten Britain on whose industrial and maritime power the Alliance rested. He therefore argued for a resumption of the unrestricted U-boat campaign. At the same time – he perhaps and rightly surmised that his call for a U-boat offensive would be refused – Britain's continental partners should be destroyed. Italy was too unimportant to deserve a major effort against her. Russia, on the other hand, tied up German troops which could be better used elsewhere, without presenting the opportunity to strike against her a success decisive to the outcome of the war. His assessment was that, 'Even if we cannot perhaps expect a revolution in the grand style, we are entitled to believe that Russia's internal troubles will compel her to give in within a relatively short period. In this connection it may be granted she will not revive her military reputation meanwhile.' What made even a weakened Russia too difficult to knock out of the war was the lack of a strategic objective: the capture of St Petersburg would have merely symbolic results; an advance on Moscow led towards the vast emptiness of the interior; while the Ukraine, though a prize of great value, was inaccessible except through Romania, whose neutrality Germany would be ill-advised to violate. Dismissing involvement in the Egyptian, Mesopotamian and Salonika fronts as irrelevancies, and accepting the British portion of the Western Front as too strong to attack, he therefore concluded that, since an offensive somewhere was necessary, because 'Germany and her allies could not hold out indefinitely', it must be made against France. 'The strain on France', he wrote, 'has reached breaking point – though it is certainly borne with the most remarkable devotion. If we succeed in opening the eyes of her people to the fact that in a military sense they have nothing more to hope for, that breaking point would be reached and England's best sword knocked out of her hand.' The operational solution to his analysis was for a limited offensive at a vital point that would 'compel the French to throw in every man they have. If they do so the forces of France will bleed to death.'[29]

He already had 'the vital point' in mind, the fortress of Verdun in a loop of the Meuse, isolated during the operations of 1914, exposed to attack from three sides, badly provided with communications to the French rear area but lying only twelve miles from a major railhead in German hands. He quickly secured the Kaiser's agreement to what would be called Operation *Gericht* (Judgement) and, while a dissenting Hötzendorf proceeded to prepare his own offensive against the Italians, began to mass the divisions that would try 'the remarkable devotion' of the French to its limit.

1. Offensive at Verdun

Verdun had been a fortress in Roman times and its defences had been renewed many times, by Vauban in the seventeenth century, by

Napoleon III and most recently in 1885, when its circle of detached forts had been duplicated with another at five miles' distance from the small city's centre. The new forts had subsequently been strengthened with concrete and armour but, following the collapse of Liège and Namur to German heavy artillery in August 1914, the French had lost faith in all fortifications and Verdun's fortress guns had been dismounted and sent away for use in the field. The battle of 1914 had flowed around it but its value as a point of pivot had been forgotten in the aftermath. Verdun had become a 'quiet sector' and its garrison had been whittled down until, in February 1916, it consisted of only the three divisions of XXX Corps, the 72nd, a local reserve division, the 51st, also a reserve division, from Lille, and the 14th, a regular division from Besançon; the 37th Division, from Algeria, lay in reserve. Among the units of the divisions that formed the garrison the most notable were the 56th and 59th Battalions of *Chasseurs à pied*, notable because they had cleared the Bois des Caures north of Verdun of Germans in 1914 and had been there ever since and because they were commanded by Lieutenant Colonel Emile Driant, a local member of parliament, a constitutionally insubordinate soldier and the author of numerous sensationalist books on future warfare, of which the best known, *The War of Tomorrow*, foretold a great victory by France over

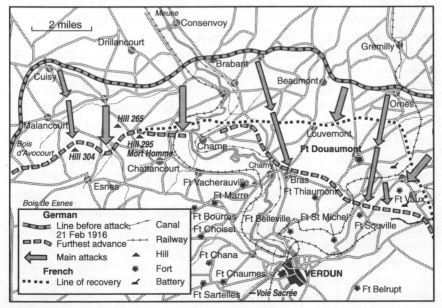

The battle of Verdun

301

Germany and had been crowned by the French Academy. Driant, in the Bois des Caures, commanded the foremost sector of Verdun's defences on the east bank of the Meuse.[30]

Opposite his and its neighbouring positions, Falkenhayn had assembled, during January and February 1916, a reinforcement to Fifth Army, the German Crown Prince's, of ten divisions, including six regular, supported by an enormous concentration of artillery. Among the 542 heavy guns were thirteen of the 420 mm and seventeen of the 305 mm howitzers that had devastated the Belgian forts eighteen months earlier, and to supply them and the field and medium artillery a stock of two and a half million shells had been accumulated. The whole of the French defensive zone on a front of eight miles – one German division and 150 guns to each mile – was to be deluged with preparatory fire, so that 'no line is to remain unbombarded, no possibilities of supply unmolested, nowhere should the enemy feel himself safe'. Falkenhayn's plan was brutally simple. The French, forced to fight in a crucial but narrowly constricted corner of the Western Front, would be compelled to feed reinforcements into a battle of attrition where the material circumstances so favoured the Germans that defeat was inevitable. If the French gave up the struggle, they would lose Verdun; if they persisted, they would lose their army.

Operation Judgement was scheduled to begin on 10 February. Bad weather postponed it from day to day, during which growing intelligence of an impending German attack gradually brought the defenders to a better state of readiness, insufficient, nevertheless, without substantial reinforcements of guns and men, to guarantee successful resistance. On 19 February the rains stopped, next day a warm sun dried the ground, and early in the morning of 21 February the bombardment opened. All morning it raged and on into the afternoon; in the Bois des Caures, 500 by 1,000 yards square, it is estimated that 80,000 shells fell before the German infantry appeared. Only Driant's meticulous preparation of his position left any of his men alive to fight.[31]

Had the Germans attacked in strength they must have overrun the devastated enemy positions on the eight-mile front, but they did not. The philosophy of the operation was that artillery would destroy the French defences, which would then be occupied by the infantry in follow-up. Driant and half of his soldiers survived until the next day, when stronger waves of Germany infantry appeared to overwhelm them. There were equivalent advances either side of the Bois des

Caures. The French outer trench lines were crumbling and the defenders began to fall back, overwhelmed by fire and numbers, towards the old forts of Vaux and Douaumont. On 23 February a surviving lieutenant of the 72nd Division signalled to higher command, 'The commanding officer and all company commanders have been killed. My battalion is reduced to approximately 180 men (from 600). I have neither ammunition nor food. What am I to do?'[32] There was little that could be done in the absence of reinforcements. On 24 February, the whole of the outer trench zone was overrun, many of the defenders abandoning their positions in terror and fleeing to the rear. Only Forts Vaux and Douaumont stood as points of resistance on the forward slopes of the heights above the Meuse which, if taken, would allow German artillery observers to direct fire on to Verdun itself and the bridges across the Meuse which sustained the resistance. Then, on 25 February, Douaumont fell, taken by a lone German sergeant of the 24th Brandenburg Regiment who, blown into the fort's moat by a near-miss, decided to explore the interior, found it occupied by only a handful of French troops and bluffed them into surrender. The news of the fort's capture spread panic among the troops in Verdun and even the first of the reinforcements arriving to strengthen the front. Depots of food were pillaged on the word that the Meuse bridges had been prepared for demolition and retreat was imminent. Verdun seemed on the point of falling.

Had it fallen the results might have been beneficial to the French conduct of the war, for it was indeed a death trap, while the broken and wooded terrain to its rear was perfectly defensible at a cost in life much lower than the French were to suffer in and around the sacrificial city in the months to come. On the morning of 25 February, however, Joffre's deputy, de Castelnau, who had commanded the Second Army at the Marne, arrived at Verdun, assessed the situation, and decided that the forward positions must be held. A 'fighting general', a romantic, a devout Catholic and a member of an ancient French military family, de Castelnau saw the fight for Verdun as a test of his country's capacity to sustain the defence of the national territory and keep alive the hope of ultimate victory. The decision he took on 25 February was the one for which Falkenhayn might have hoped and the soldier chosen to implement it, Philippe Pétain, the opponent Falkenhayn might himself have chosen. Pétain was not a man for giving up. Taciturn and charmless, his disbelief in the doctrine of the offensive had denied him promotion in the pre-war army. At the war's outbreak, however, his refusal to be deterred by losses had won him rapid advancement, from the colonelcy of the 33rd Regiment, in which Charles de Gaulle served as a subaltern, to, by 1916, command of Second Army. On his arrival at Verdun he telephoned the commander of XX Corps, newly arrived in reinforcement, to say, 'I have taken command. Tell your troops. Hold fast.'

Pétain at once identified two essentials for the defence: to co-ordinate the artillery, of which he took personal control, and to open a line of supply. Henceforth it would be the Germans on whom fell a constant deluge of shells as they clung to the front line or made their way forward to battle through the narrow valleys beyond the Meuse. Behind Verdun, the single road that led to Bar-le-Duc fifty miles away was designated a supply route for trucks alone; 3,500 were assembled to bring forward the 2,000 tons of stores the garrison needed daily, the troops being ordered to march up and down the roadside fields. Any truck that broke down was pushed off the road, lest it interrupt the day-and-night flow of traffic. A whole division of Territorials was employed in road repairs and France was scoured for additional transport. Eventually 12,000 trucks would be used on what became known as the *Voie sacrée*.

A sanctified battle was what Falkenhayn had wanted France to fight. He had not counted upon the fervour the French would show. Already on 27 February, the Germans recorded 'no success anywhere'.[33] The XX 'Iron' Corps had come into line and its soldiers were sacrificing themselves in a desperate effort to defend every foot of ground held; among those of XX Corps wounded – and captured – that day was Charles de Gaulle. The Germans sought to overcome the resistance of the French infantry by pushing their artillery ever closer to the front, through saturated ground that demanded ever larger teams of horses to move a single gun. An immediate result was appalling casualties among the gun-teams – 7,000 horses are said to have been killed in one day – yet, despite the growing weight of bombardment, the French line would not shift. By 27 February, the Germans had advanced four miles and were within four miles of the city but no increase in offensive effort could push their front forward.

On the last day of February, Falkenhayn and the Crown Prince conferred and agreed on a new strategy. Since the narrow-front attack on the east bank of the Meuse had not achieved success, the offensive must be broadened to the west bank where, behind the heights of the Mort Homme and Côte 304, the French were hiding the artillery that flailed the German infantry struggling to reach the positions from which they could look down into Verdun itself. The terrain on the west bank was different from that on the east, open and rolling instead of broken and wooded. Falkenhayn had been advised to include it in his original assault plan, for the reason that advances there could be easily gained. So they were on the first day of the assault, 6 March, when the French 67th Division collapsed. The Germans were swiftly counter-attacked, however, the ground was regained and once again the line stuck fast. Simultaneous efforts on the east bank, in the direction of Fort Vaux, Douaumont's neighbour, were equally ineffectual. The ruins of the village of Vaux changed hands thirteen times during March, and yet the fort itself still lay tantalisingly beyond German reach. It was, moreover, defending itself resolutely. Both the French and Germans were learning that the lessons of Liège and Namur were not as conclusive as had seemed. Fortifications, even quite antiquated fortifications, could stand up to intense and prolonged artillery bombardment and buttress trench lines, if occupied by garrisons prepared to sit out heavy shellfire and wait for assault by unprotected infantry. It was inexperience that had caused the Belgians, whom the Germans later came to respect as dogged defenders of any position they occupied, to give in; by 1916, the French had discovered that shellfire often sounded much worse than it was, had nerved themselves to sit it out and to repay the infantry attacks that followed with murderous small-arms fire.

By the beginning of April, Falkenhayn's belief that he could win a victory of attrition without exposing his own army to comparable loss was failing. The opening attack on the narrow front east of the Meuse had been checked at the outer line of fortification. The second offensive on the west bank had faltered under fire from the heights of the Mort Homme and Côte 304. At the beginning of April it was decided to abandon the strategy of limited offensive and attack across the extent of the whole front, now nearly twenty miles wide. The operation began on 9 April and lasted four days, until the descent of drenching rain stalled all activity for the rest of the month. On the first day the Germans reached what they thought was the crest of the Mort Homme, only to find that the real summit lay just beyond their reach. The fight for the feature then resolved itself into an artillery combat. An officer of the French 146th Regiment, Augustin Cochin, spent from 9–14 April in the Mort Homme trenches without seeing a single German, 'the last two days soaked in icy mud, under terrible

305

bombardment, without any shelter other than the narrowness of the trench . . . The Boche did not attack, naturally, it would have been too stupid . . . result: I arrived there with 175 men, I returned with 34, several half mad . . . not replying any more when I spoke to them.'[34]

During May, after the bad weather relented, it was the Mort Homme that absorbed German efforts. On 8 May the French lost the true crest but clung on to the neighbouring slopes, against which the Germans picked step by step throughout the rest of the month. The final line of resistance delineated by Pétain on taking command was breached as they continued their advance but their progress was too slow to threaten the integrity of the Verdun position. Their casualties had now exceeded 100,000, killed and wounded and, though the French had suffered equally, most of the losses borne by the Germans had fallen on the same formations. While the French rotated divisions through Verdun, the Germans kept divisions in the line, making good casualties with replacements. By the end of April, forty-two French divisions had already passed through the Verdun sector, but only thirty German, and the disparity would persist.[35] The German 5th Division, which attacked on the first day, was in line until the end of February, returned between 8 and 15 March and then again from 22 April until the end of May. The 25th Division was engaged from 27 February to 16 March, from 10 to 25 April and then again until 19 May. Between March and May the casualties in its infantry regiments amounted to 8,549, or over a hundred per cent of their strength.

A high proportion of losses on both sides was the result of the French policy of conducting an 'active defence', counter-attacking whenever possible. One opportunity that offered was at Douaumont, where carelessness detonated a German ammunition store inside the captured fort on 8 May. The vast explosion persuaded the French to venture an attempt at recapture on 22 May, and the assaulting parties succeeded in storming the fort's outworks and scaling the exterior before they were repulsed a day later. The initiative, nevertheless, rested with the Germans who continued to attack wherever they could and at the beginning of June gathered forces for a decisive effort. They consisted of the divisions of I Bavarian, X Reserve and XV Corps, attacking side by side on a front of three miles, with one man per yard of front, supported by 600 guns. The objective was Fort Vaux, which between 1 and 7 June, the Germans first surrounded, cutting off the garrison from contact with the French rear area, and then blew up section by section. Ultimately the commander of the garrison, Major

Raynal, was forced to surrender for lack of water. The attackers paid this man the honours of war and the German Crown Prince, to whom Raynal was taken, presented him with a sword to replace the one he had left behind.[36]

Direct command of the Verdun sector had now passed from Pétain, whose disregard for casualties troubled even Joffre, to Nivelle, an artillery expert, fluent and persuasive in manner, who had risen rapidly since the beginning of the war, due to his perfect English and winning ways with politicians. He was already improving control of the French guns, which were beginning to achieve dominance over those of the enemy and eventually swung the balance of advantage in the French favour. Meanwhile, however, the Germans sustained the offensive, gaining pockets of ground on the east bank and pushing forward to the surviving French forts of Souville and Tavannes. From Souville, 'it was downhill all the way to Verdun, less than two and a half miles away . . . and once the fort fell into enemy hands it would be but a matter of time before the city fell into enemy hands'.[37] German pressure continued unrelentingly after the fall of Vaux until on 22 June a new assault was preceded by a bombardment of 'Green Cross' gas – an improved form of chlorine – on the French artillery lines, which contained 600 of the 1,800 French guns at Verdun. Temporarily robbed of artillery protection, the French defence faltered before an attack by the *Alpenkorps*, an élite mountain division of Bavarian guard and German light infantry; among the light infantry officers was Lieutenant Paulus, the future commander of Sixth Army at Stalingrad.[38] A soldier of the *Alpenkorps* recorded that, during the course of the successful advance that followed the bombardment, he glimpsed the roofs of Verdun from the Souville heights. He was, however, probably mistaken. In the afternoon, the German advance petered out in the broken ground around the fort and, in the summer heat, thirst attacked the soldiers in the foremost positions gained. No water could be got up from the rear and, as night fell, the *Alpenkorps* gave up its effort to press onward.

That day, 23 June, marked both the high point and crisis of the Verdun offensive. About twenty million shells had been fired into the battle zone since 21 February, the shape of the landscape had been permanently altered, forests had been reduced to splinters, villages had disappeared, the surface of the ground had been so pockmarked by explosion that shell hole overlapped shell hole and had been overlapped again. Worse by far was the destruction of human life. By the end of June over 200,000 men had been killed and wounded on each side. The losses had fallen more heavily on the French, since they had begun the war with a third fewer men than the Germans, but to both armies Verdun had become a place of terror and death that could not yield victory. The Germans made a final effort on 11 July, which reached Fort Souville, but it was beaten off. Thereafter the Germans ceased their attempt to destroy the French army at Verdun and relapsed into the defensive. For a while it became a quiet sector until, in October, the French moved to recover the ground lost. On 24 October Douaumont was recaptured, on 15 December a wider offensive regained much of the ground lost on the east bank since the beginning of the battle. By then, however, another battle altogether, raging since 1 July, had shifted the crux of the Western Front from Verdun to the Somme.

2. Offensive on the Somme

Verdun had been planned by Falkenhayn as an operation to 'bleed white' the French army and knock Britain's 'best sword' out of her hand. Even by June, when the battle still had six months to run, it had failed in both its purposes and, as it failed, Falkenhayn's credibility as Chief of Staff had waned also. Dominating though he was in personality and intellect, handsome and forthright, self-assured to the point of arrogance and of proven ability as a staff officer and Minister of War, he suffered from the disadvantage of association, in the popular mind, with defeat rather than victory.[39] Responsibility for the failure of the Schlieffen Plan – intrinsic though failure was in the plan's defects – and for the entrenchment of the Western Front, though it properly lay in both cases at Moltke's door, nevertheless attached in practice to him as Moltke's immediate successor. The victories of the Eastern Front, Tannenberg, even Gorlice-Tarnow, seemed the achievement of Hindenburg, and of his alter ego, Ludendorff. Falkenhayn's confederality with the Austrian Chief of Staff, Conrad von Hötzendorf, landed him with shared culpability for the poor showing of the Austro-Hungarian army against the Serbs and Russians and even for the entry of Italy into the war, since Italy's motivation was essentially anti-Austrian. The only initiative undoubtedly his own, and for which he might have taken credit were it a success, was Verdun, which, by midsummer, was palpably a terrible failure. Even before the great bombardment that would usher in the

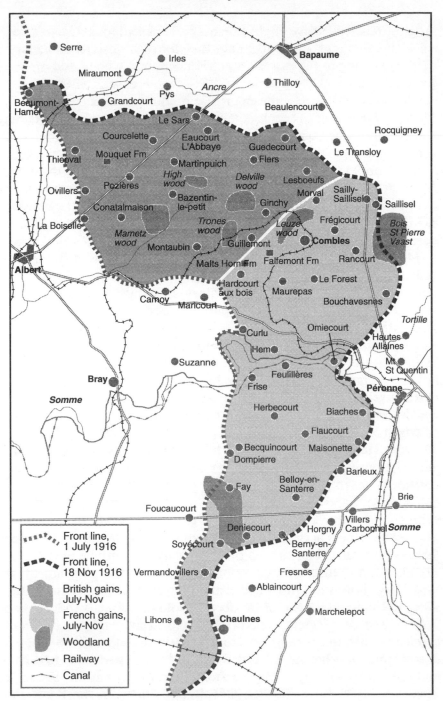

The battle of the Somme

Legend:
- Front line, 1 July 1916
- Front line, 18 Nov 1916
- British gains, July–Nov
- French gains, July–Nov
- Woodland
- Railway
- Canal

309

Anglo-French offensive on the Somme had opened, Falkenhayn's grip on high command was weakening, the star of his ascent and zenith already passing to the eastern titan, Hindenburg, who would replace him in August.

The Somme was to be the enterprise of another ascendant general, Douglas Haig. John French, 'the little field marshal' who had taken the BEF to France, had been worn down by the attrition of his beloved army of regulars, the old sweats of his Boer War glory days, the keen young troopers of the cavalry in which he had been raised, the eager Sandhurst subulterns, the generation of decent, dutiful majors and colonels who had been his companions on the veldt and in the hunting field.[40] The death of so many of them – there had been 90,000 casualties among the original seven infantry divisions by November 1914, rather more than a hundred per cent of mobilised strength – afflicted him, and he added to the pain he felt by his apparently compulsive need to tour the military hospitals and talk to the wounded. 'Horribly sad and very pathetic to see how good and cheery and patient the dear fellows are . . . I hate it all so! . . . such horrible sadness and depression.'[41] French was not made for modern war or for the politics of a national conflict. He could not feel for the citizen soldiers coming forward in their hundreds of thousands as he did instinctively for the vanishing seven-year men of the feudal order he had known as a young officer, nor could he play the ministerial game at which his War Office equals and younger subordinates were adept. Douglas Haig, commander of the BEF's First Army, was sinuous in his relationships with the great, particularly at court. He had pre-cipitately married a royal lady-in-waiting after the briefest of introductions and had accepted an invitation to correspond privately with King George V soon after the Western Front had relapsed into stalemate. Others in the BEF hierarchy shared by the end of 1915 the belief that French had proved his incapacity to continue in supreme command, and their views were made known to the government. It was Haig, however, who wielded the dagger. During a visit by the King to France at the end of October, he told him directly that French was 'a source of great weakness to the army, and no one had confidence in him any more'. All that was true, but it would have come better from Haig had he not added that he himself was ready to do his duty in any capacity. 'Any capacity' clearly meant as French's successor which, after further consultations between the King, the Prime Minister and Kitchener, still Secretary of State for War, though his perch was creaking also, he became on 16 December 1915.[42]

Haig, whom his contemporaries found difficult to know, has become today an enigma. The successful generals of the First World War, those who did not crack outright or decline gradually into pessimism, were a hard lot, as they had to be with the casualty figures accumulating on their desks. Some, nevertheless, managed to combine toughness of mind with some striking human characteristic: Joffre, imperturbability; Hindenburg, gravity; Foch, fire; Kemal, certainty. Haig, in whose public manner and private diaries no concern for human suffering was or is discernible, compensated for his aloofness with nothing whatsoever of the common touch. He seemed to move through the horrors of the First World War as if guided by some inner voice, speaking of a higher purpose and a personal destiny. That, we now know, was not just appearance. Haig was a devotee both of spiritualist practices and of fundamentalist religion.[43] As a young officer he had taken to attending seances, where a medium put him in touch with Napoleon; as Commander-in-Chief he fell under the influence of a Presbyterian chaplain whose sermons confirmed him in his belief that he was in direct communication with God and had a major part to play in a divine plan for the world. His own simple religion, he was convinced, was shared by his soldiers, who were inspired thereby to bear the dangers and sufferings which were their part of the war he was directing.[44]

Despite his strangeness, Haig was an efficient soldier, the superior to French in every branch of modern military practice, and his skills were not better shown than in his preparations for the Somme. That high and empty battlefield had not been contested since the first weeks of the war. On the enemy side, the Germans had profited from the peace in which they had been left since 1914 to construct the strongest position on the Western Front. The hard, dry, chalky soil was easily mined and they had driven dugouts thirty feet below ground, impervious to artillery fire, provisioned to withstand siege and linked to the rear by buried telephone cable and deep communication trenches. On the surface they had constructed a network of machine-gun posts, covering all angles of approach across the treeless downs, and in front of their fire trenches laid dense entanglements of barbed wire. They had time to do so. Among the half-dozen divisions garrisoning the Somme sector, the 52nd had been there since April 1915, the 12th since October and the 26th and 28th Reserve Divisions since September 1914. They had made themselves secure.[45]

On the other side of no man's land, little had been done since 1914. The French, who had occupied the sector until the extension of the British line southward in August 1915, held it as a 'quiet front', defended by artillery with few infantry in the front line. The British had introduced a more aggressive mood but the infrastructure for a great offensive was still not in place when Haig took command. Under his direction, the back area of the Somme, from the little market town of Albert to the departmental capital of Amiens twenty-five miles behind, was transformed into an enormous military encampment, cut by new roads leading towards the front and covered with shell dumps, gun positions and encampments for the army that would launch the attack. As a military technician, Haig could not be faulted. His talents as a tactician remained to be proved.

The army assembling on the Somme had no doubts in the high command or in itself. It consisted of twenty divisions, most grouped, under the command of General Sir Henry Rawlinson, in the new Fourth Army. The majority of the divisions were new to the war also. A handful were old regular formations, the 4th, 7th and 8th, and the 29th, all greatly changed since their ordeals in the original BEF and at Gallipoli. Four were Territorial, the 46th, 56th, 48th and 49th, which had been in France since the spring of 1915. The rest were 'Kitchener' formations of citizen volunteers, many organised round 'Pals' or 'Chums' battalions, for which the Somme would be their first battle. There were ten of these Kitchener divisions, of which the senior, the 9th Scottish, had arrived in France in May 1915 but the 34th only in January 1916.[46] Perhaps the most unusual was the 36th (Ulster) Division, a wholesale embodiment in khaki of the Ulster Volunteer Force of Irish Protestants opposed to Irish Home Rule who, on the outbreak of war, had collectively volunteered. The Ulstermen differed from their other Kitchener comrades only in their pre-war experience of military drill. With the reality of battle they had no more familiarity than the rest. Their infantry battalions were wholly inexperienced; so, too, and more critically, were their batteries of supporting artillery, on whose accurate shooting and prompt changing of target the success of the coming offensive depended.

Haig's plan for the Somme was simple, akin in outline to Falkenhayn's for Verdun, with the difference that he hoped to break the enemy's line rather than force him to stand and fight for it in a struggle of attrition. An enormous bombardment, to last a week and consume a million shells, was to precede the attack. As it died away on the date chosen for assault, 1 July, nineteen British divisions and, south of the River Somme, three French, all that could be spared while Verdun still raged, were to move forward across no man's land and, in the expectation that the enemy surviving the shelling would have been stunned into inactivity, pass through the broken wire entanglements, enter the trenches, take possession and move on to the open country in the rear. So certain were Haig and most of his subordinates of the crushing effect the artillery would produce, that they had decided not to allow the inexperienced infantry to advance by the tried and tested means of 'fire and movement', when some lay down to cover with rifle volleys the advance of the rest, but to keep them moving forward upright and in straight lines. At the battle of Loos the preoccupation of the General Staff had been to 'keep the troops in hand', with the result that the reserves had been kept too far behind the lines and, when sent forward too late, deployed in dense masses.[47] The preoccupation before the Somme was with the danger of the troops taking cover and not restarting the advance once they had lain down. The tactical instruction for the battle, 'Training Divisions for Offensive Action' (SS 109), and the associated instruction issued by Fourth Army, 'Tactical Notes', both prescribe an advance by successive waves or lines of troops and a continuous movement forward by all involved. 'The assaulting troops must push forward at a steady pace in successive lines, each line adding fresh impetus to the preceding line.'[48]

Haig, as Commander-in-Chief, and Rawlinson, commanding the attacking troops, though agreeing on the tactics to be followed, differed over the offensive's objects. Haig expected a breakthrough, to as far as Bapaume, the little market town on the far side of the Somme uplands seven miles from the start line. Rawlinson foresaw a more limited result, a 'bite' into the German trench system, to be followed by further bites to gain more territory. Rawlinson, as events would prove, was the more realistic. Both generals, however, were equally unrealistic in their expectations of what the preliminaries would achieve. Nearly three million shells had been dumped forward for the preparatory bombardment, to feed 1,000 field guns, 180 heavy guns and 245 heavy howitzers, giving a density of one field gun per twenty yards of front and one heavy gun or howitzer to fifty-eight yards.[49] The artillery plan was for the field guns to concentrate, before the battle, on cutting the enemy's wire in front of his trenches, while the heavy guns were to attack the enemy's artillery with 'counter-battery' fire and destroy his trenches and strongpoints. At the moment of assault, as the British infantry left their trenches to advance across no man's land, the field artillery was to lay a 'creeping barrage' ahead of the leading wave, which was intended to prevent the German defenders from manning the parapet opposite so that, in theory, the German trenches would be empty when the British arrived.

Almost everything that Haig and Rawlinson expected of the enormous artillery effort they had prepared was not to occur. The German position, for one thing, was far stronger than British intelligence had estimated. The thirty-foot dugouts in which the German front-line garrison sheltered were almost impervious to any shell the British could fire and had survived intact right up to the last days before the attack. A trench raid launched on the night of 26/27 June revealed, for example, that 'the dugouts are still good. The [Germans] appear to remain in these dugouts all the time and are completely sheltered.'[50] So it was to prove on the day. Even more ominous was the failure to cut wire. Later in the war a sensitive 'graze' fuse would come into use, which exploded a shell when it touched something as slender even as a single wire strand. In 1916 shells only detonated on hitting the ground and bombardments fired at wire entanglements therefore merely tossed them about, creating a barrier yet more dense than that laid by the enemy in the first place. The general commanding the British VIII Corps, Hunter-Weston, who had been at Gallipoli and should have known how tough wire was, reported before 1 July that the enemy wire on his front was blown away and 'the troops could walk in' but one of his junior officers 'could see it standing strong and well'.[51] Since uncut wire in front of defended trenches was death to attacking infantry, this complacent misappreciation by the staff was literally lethal.

Finally, the confidence shown in the artillery to lay a creeping barrage was misplaced. The movement of a line of exploding shells just in front of a line of advancing infantry, ideally fifty yards in front or less, was a new technique and demanded high gunnery skills. Without communication between infantry battalions and artillery batteries – and there could be none without tactical radio, a development of the future – the artillery had to fire by timetable, calculated by the speed at which the infantry was expected to advance, roughly fifty yards a minute. The guns would lay a barrage on an identified trench line, then 'lift' to the next at a moment when the infantry was deemed to have arrived. In practice, because the artillery feared killing its own

314

infantry, the intervals in distance between 'lifts' was made too long, in time too short, with the result that the experience of attacking waves would be, too often, to see the barrage creeping away in front of them, beyond trenches still strongly held by the enemy, without any means of recalling it. The corrective, to be adopted by some corps, of bringing the barrage back and then forward, would not work either, since its return frightened the infantry into taking cover from 'friendly fire', the protection being lost when the barrage crept off again without warning. The worst feature of artillery precaution was to be the lifting of the barrage from the enemy's front line too soon before the assault, while the infantry was still in no man's land and the wrong side of often uncut wire. A veteran of Gallipoli, commanding a heavy battery in Hunter-Weston's III Corps 'knew that the attack . . . in his sector was doomed when [the corps commander] ordered the heavy artillery to lift off the enemy front line trenches ten minutes before zero, and the field artillery two minutes before zero hour'.[52] It was not only in his sector that the barrage was to lift too soon. Almost everywhere on the front of Fourth Army on 1 July the artillery fire was to depart prematurely from the infantry, who were to advance against wire badly cut or not cut at all, against trenches filled with Germans fighting for their lives.

What the infantry should have done in such circumstances has generated an enormous literature, much of it quite recent. A new generation of young military historians has taken to re-fighting the battles of the British Expeditionary Force with a passion more understandable in survivors of the trench warfare disasters than in posthumous academic analysts. An underlying theme is that, dreadful as the experience of the early offensives was, it provided a learning process through which the survivors and their successors won the eventual victories of 1918, an argument akin to the thought that Dunkirk was a valuable rehearsal in amphibious operations for D-Day. At a more detailed technical level, the new Western Front historians explore such issues as what was the proper relationship between rifleman, light-machine gunners and grenadiers, how the potentialities of improved infantry weapons might have best been exploited and which was the ideal infantry formation, column, line or infiltrating 'blob'.[53] The energy expended in such reconsiderations seems, to this author at any rate, a pointless waste. The simple truth of 1914–18 trench warfare is that the massing of large numbers of soldiers unprotected by anything but cloth uniforms, however they were trained, however equipped, against large masses of other soldiers, protected by earthworks and barbed wire and provided with rapid-fire weapons, was bound to result in very heavy casualties among the attackers. That was proved to be the case, whatever the variation in tactics and equipment, and there was much variation, from the beginning on the Aisne in 1914 to the end on the Sambre and Meuse in 1918. The effect of artillery added to the slaughter, as did that of bayonets and grenades when fighting came to close quarters in the trench labyrinths. The basic and stark fact, nevertheless, was that the conditions of warfare between 1914 and 1918 predisposed towards slaughter and that only an entirely different technology, one not available until a generation later, could have averted such an outcome.

The first day of the battle of the Somme, 1 July 1916, was to be an awful demonstration of that truth. Its reality remains evident even today to anyone who returns to the centre of the Somme battlefield at Thiepval, near the memorial to the 36th Ulster Division, and glances north and south down the old front line. The view northward is particularly poignant. Along it, at intervals of a few hundred yards, run a line of the Commonwealth War Grave Commission's beautiful garden cemeteries, ablaze near the anniversary of the battle with rose and wisteria blossom, the white Portland stone of headstones and memorial crosses gleaming in the sun. The farthest, on the ridge near Beaumont Hamel, contains graves of the regular 4th Division, the nearest, in the valley of the Ancre, the Somme's little tributary, those of the Kitchener 32nd Division. A few, like those of the Ulster Division, stand a little forward of the rest, and mark the furthest limit of advance. The majority stand on the front line or in no man's land just outside the German wire. The soldiers who died there were later buried where they had fallen. Thus the cemeteries are a map of the battle. The map tells a simple and terrible story. The men of the Fourth Army, the majority citizen volunteers going into action for the first time, rose from their trenches at zero hour, advanced in steady formation, were almost everywhere checked by uncut barbed wire and were shot down. Five divisions of the seventeen attacking entered the German positions. The infantry of the remainder were stopped in no man's land.

Descriptions of zero hour on 1 July abound, of the long lines of young men, burdened by the sixty pounds of equipment judged necessary to sustain them in a long struggle inside the German trenches, plodding off almost shoulder to shoulder; of their good cheer and certainty of success; of individual displays of bravado, as in the battalions which kicked a football ahead of the ranks; of the bright sunshine breaking through the thin morning mist; of the illusion of an empty battlefield, denuded of opponents by the weight of the bombardment and the explosion of twenty-one mine chambers, laboriously driven under the German front lines, as the attack began. Descriptions of what followed zero hour abound also: of the discovery of uncut wire, of the appearance of the German defenders, manning the parapet at the moment the British creeping barrage passed beyond, to fire frenziedly into the approaching ranks, of the opening of gaps in the attacking waves, of massacre in the wire entanglements, of the advance checked, halted and eventually stopped literally dead.

The Germans (who were fighting for their lives) had practised bringing their machine guns up the steps from their deep dugouts hundreds of times. F. L. Cassell, a German survivor, recalled 'the shout of the sentry, "They are coming" . . . Helmet, belt and rifle and up the steps . . . in the trench a headless body. The sentry had lost his life to a last shell . . . there they come, the khaki-yellows, they are not twenty metres in front of our trench . . . They advance slowly fully equipped . . . machine-gun fire tears holes in their ranks.'[54] The machine guns reached even inside the British front line in places, to hit troops who had not reached no man's land. A sergeant of the 3rd Tyneside Irish recalled seeing 'away to my left and right, long lines of men. Then I heard the "patter, patter" of machine guns in the distance. By the time I'd gone another ten yards there seemed to be only a few men left around me; by the time I had gone twenty yards, I seemed to be on my own. Then I was hit myself.'[55] The whole of the Tyneside Irish Brigade, of four battalions, nearly three thousand men, was brought to a halt inside British lines, with appalling loss of life. One of its battalions lost 500 men killed or wounded, another 600. In offensive terms, the advance had achieved nothing. Most of the dead were killed on ground the British held before the advance began.

Appalling loss of life was the result of the first day of the Somme along the whole front of the attack. When, in the days that followed, the 200 British battalions that had attacked began to count the gaps in their ranks, the realisation came that, of the 100,000 men who had entered no man's land, 20,000 had not returned; another 40,000 who had been got back were wounded. In summary, a fifth of the attacking force was dead, and some battalions, such as the 1st Newfoundland Regiment, had ceased to exist. The magnitude of the catastrophe, the greatest loss of life in British military history, took time to sink in. The day following the opening of the attack, Haig, conferring with Rawlinson and his staff at Fourth Army headquarters, was clearly still uninformed of how great the casualties had been and discussed, as a serious proposition, how the offensive was to be continued, as if it were a possibility for the morrow or the day after. He believed that the enemy 'has undoubtedly been severely shaken and he has few reserves in hand'.[56] In fact, the Germans had brought up several reserve divisions during the day, while the losses suffered by their troops in line – about six thousand altogether – were a tenth of those of the British. The German 180th Regiment, for example, lost only 180 men out of 3,000 on 1 July; the British 4th Division, which attacked it, lost 5,121 out of 12,000. If the Germans had been shaken, it was by the 'amazing spectacle of unexampled gallantry courage and bulldog determination' and by their eventual revulsion from the slaughter inflicted; in many places, when they realised their own lives were no longer at risk, they ceased firing, so that the more lightly British wounded could make their way back as best they could to their own front line. There was, for the worse wounded, no early rescue. Some were not got in until 4 July, some never. A young British officer, Gerald Brenan, crossing subsequently captured ground in the fourth week of July, found the bodies of soldiers wounded on 1 July who had 'crawled into shell holes, wrapped their waterproof sheets round them, taken out their bibles and died like that'. They were among thousands whose bullet-riddled bodies gave up life that day or afterwards, beyond the reach of stretcher bearers or simply lost in the wilderness of no man's land. Even among those found and carried back, many died as they lay waiting for treatment outside the field hospitals, which were overwhelmed by the flood of cases.

If there were any exception to the unrelievedly disastrous results of 1 July, it was that the German high command, as opposed to their front-line troops, had been gravely alarmed by the scale of the British attack, particularly because in one sector, astride the River Somme itself, ground had been lost. Unknown, naturally, to Haig and Rawlinson, Falkenhayn reacted to that loss in peremptory fashion, relieving the Chief of Staff of Second Army, in whose sector it had occurred, and replacing him with his own operations officer, Colonel von Lossberg, the main architect of German defensive methods on the Western Front.[57] Von Lossberg imposed the condition, on accepting the appointment, that the attacks at Verdun be given up at once, which they were not. Falkenhayn broke his undertaking and the offensive continued until his own dismissal at the end of August. Lossberg's arrival was nevertheless significant, for his reorganisation of the Somme front ensured that the results of the first day, the outcome of British over-optimism and German hyper-readiness, would be sustained in the later stages of a battle which blunted the German edge relentlessly even as it taught the British a realism their inexperienced soldiers lacked at the outset. Lossberg's intervention caused the defenders to abandon the practice of concentrating on the defence of the front line and to construct a 'defence in depth', based not on trenches but on lines of shell holes, which the British artillery created in profusion. The forward zone was to be thinly held, to minimise casualties, but ground lost was to be speedily retaken by deliberate counter-attacks launched by organised reserves held in the rear.[58]

This German technique defied all Haig's efforts to exploit such success as had been achieved on 1 July. Not until 14 July, in the sector astride the Somme where the more experienced French had assisted the British to make a clear break-in to the German positions, was further ground gained. Haig's suspicion of night attacks was overcome by his subordinates and, in an attack at half-light, four British divisions rolled forward to take Bazentin Ridge, Mametz Wood and Contalmaison. On the map the advance looks impressive; on the ground, where the visitor covers the distance in a few minutes of motoring, less so, though the atmosphere of menace clinging to the sector's small valleys and re-entrants oppresses. Some of the BEF's cavalry, still Haig's preferred arm of decision, was brought up during the day but, after a skirmishing near High Wood at one of the Somme battlefield's most commanding points, was forced to withdraw. Imperial troops, the 1st and 2nd Australian Divisions, veterans of Gallipoli, and the South African Brigade, renewed the advance during the second half of the month, taking Pozières and Delville Wood, the latter the site of a South African epic, but no opportunity for the cavalry to intervene recurred. Like Verdun, the Somme was becoming an arena of attrition, to which fresh divisions were sent in monotonous succession – forty-two by the Germans during July and August – only to waste their energy in bloody struggles for tiny patches of ground, at Guillemont, Ginchy, Morval, Flers, Martinpuich. By 31 July, the Germans on the Somme had lost 160,000, the British and French over 200,000, yet the line had moved scarcely three miles since 1 July. North of the Ancre, or along half the original front, it had scarcely moved at all.

The offensive on the Somme might have been doomed to drift away into an autumn of frustration and a winter of stalemate had it not been for the appearance in mid-September of a new weapon, the tank. As early as December 1914 a visionary young officer of the Royal Engineers, Ernest Swinton, having recognised that only a revolutionary means could break what was already the stalemate of barbed wire and trench on the Western Front, had proposed the construction of a cross-country vehicle, armoured against bullets, that could bring firepower to the point of assault. The idea was not wholly new – it had been anticipated, for example, in H.G. Wells's short story *The Land Ironclads* of 1903, and in an imprecise form by Leonardo da Vinci – nor was the technology: an all-terrain vehicle, using a 'footed wheel', had been built in 1899 and by 1905 caterpillar track vehicles were in agricultural use.[59] It was the crisis of war that brought together technology and vision and, through that of Swinton and collaborators, Albert Stern, Murray Sueter, backed by the enthusiasm of Winston Churchill, whose Royal Naval Division's armoured cars had cut a dash in Belgium in 1914, bore fruit in the tank's prototype, 'Little Willie' of December 1915. In January 1916 a larger and gun-equipped development, 'Mother', had been produced and by September a fleet of forty-nine similar Mark I 'Tanks', as they had been named for deceptive purposes, were in France and ready to enter battle.[60]

The tanks were assigned to the Heavy Branch of the Machine Gun Corps, a war-raised formation controlling the BEF's medium machine guns. Following the attrition battles of August, a new effort was planned to open up the Somme front and the tanks, some armed with machine guns, some with 6-pounder cannon, were allotted to the Fourth and Reserve (future Fifth) Armies, to lead an assault along the line of the old Roman road that leads from Albert to Bapaume between the villages of Flers and Courcelette. The appearance of the tanks terrified the German infantry defending the sector and the armoured monsters led the British infantry onward for 3,500 yards before mechanical breakdowns and ditchings in rough ground brought the advance to a halt; a number, caught in artillery fire, were knocked out. The event brought one of the cheapest and most spectacular local victories of the war on the Western Front thus far, but its efforts were to be frustrated immediately by the disablement of almost all the thirty-six tanks that had crossed the start line. Though the infantry plugged away at the gains the tanks had made, the usual German stubbornness in manning shell holes and reserve lines blocked the potential avenue of advance and restored the stalemate.

October and November brought no change. Both the British and French attacked repetitively, at Thiepval, Transloy and in the sodden valley of the Ancre, in increasingly wet weather that turned the chalky surface of the Somme battlefield into glutinous slime. By 19 November, when the Allied offensive was brought officially to a halt, the furthest line of advance, at Les Boeufs, lay only seven miles forward of the front attacked on 1 July. The Germans may have lost over 600,000 killed and wounded in their effort to keep their Somme positions. The Allies had certainly lost over 600,000, the French casualty figure being 194,451, the British 419,654. The holocaust of the Somme was subsumed for the French in that of Verdun. To the British, it was and would remain their greatest military tragedy of the twentieth century, indeed of their national military history. A nation that goes to war must expect deaths among the young men it sends and there was a willingness for sacrifice before and during the Somme that explains, in part at least, its horror. The sacrificial impulse cannot, however, alleviate its outcome. The regiments of Pals and Chums which had their first experience of war on the Somme have been called an army of innocents and that, in their readiness to offer up their lives in circumstances none anticipated in the heady days of volunteering, it undoubtedly was. Whatever harm Kitchener's volunteers wished the Germans, it is the harm they thereby suffered that remains in British memory, collectively but also among the families of those who did not return. There is nothing more poignant in British life than to visit the ribbon of cemeteries that marks the front line of 1 July 1916 and to find, on gravestone after gravestone, the fresh wreath, the face of a Pal or Chum above a khaki serge collar staring gravely back from a dim photograph, the pinned poppy and the inscription to 'a father, a grandfather and a great-grandfather'. The Somme marked the end of an age of vital optimism in British life that has never been recovered.[61]

3. The Wider War and the Brusilov Offensive

While the great dramas of Verdun and the Somme were being played out in France, the war on the fronts elsewhere took a very varied form. In German East Africa, where Jan Smuts, the brilliant guerrilla opponent of the British during the Boer War, had arrived to take command in 1915, four columns set out in 1916 – two British from Kenya and Nyasaland respectively, one Portuguese from Mozambique, one Belgian from the Congo – to make a concentric advance on von Lettow-Vorbeck's black army, encircle it and bring the campaign to a close. The Allied fighting troops numbered nearly 40,000, Lettow's about 16,000. Dividing his force, he had no difficulty in eluding Smuts with his main body and in beating a fighting retreat southward from Mount Kilimanjaro towards Tanga and Dar es-Salaam, keeping parallel to the coast and retreating slowly southward across the grain of the country. He fought when obliged to do so but always disengaged before defeat and, destroying bridges and railway lines behind him, evaded encirclement and kept his force intact. His African askaris, moreover, were resistant to most of the parasitic diseases that attack humans in the interior. His enemies, who included large numbers of Europeans and Indians, were not. Their enormously high toll of sickness – thirty-one non-battle casualties to one battle casualty – was the real cause of their failure to run Lettow to earth. At the end of 1916 his little army was as fit, capable and elusive as at the start of the war.[62]

The Turks, so underestimated by the Allies at the outset, sustained the success they had achieved at Gallipoli. Though their efforts to revive their offensive against the Suez Canal were repulsed, in a limited campaign that took British forces to the Sinai border of Palestine, and though their army in the Caucasus suffered further defeats at the hands of the Russians, who pushed forward a perimeter from Lake Van to Trebizond on the Black Sea coast by August, in Mesopotamia they inflicted a wholly humiliating defeat on the Anglo-Indian force that had landed at the mouth of the Shatt el-Arab in 1914. During 1915 Expeditionary Force D, as it was known, pushed up the River Tigris towards Baghdad, part of the force moving by land, part by water, until in November 1915 its advance guard was at Ctesiphon. Its situation looked promising, since it was established in the heart of the Ottoman empire at a moment when the nearest Turkish reserves, according to British intelligence, were 400 miles distant in the Caucasus or 350 miles away at Aleppo in Syria. Somehow, however, the Turks managed to scrape together enough reinforcements to send troops down the Tigris and confront the Expeditionary Force. Its commander, Major General Townshend, decided, though he had not been defeated, that he was overextended and accordingly ordered a retreat to Kut al-Amara, a hundred miles down river. There the Force entrenched itself in a loop of the Tigris to await support and the recovery of its soldiers from their ordeal of the long advance and retreat.

Townshend had supplies for two months and personal experience of conducting defence; in 1896 he had successfully commanded the little North-West Frontier fort at Chitral during a siege that became celebrated throughout the empire.[63] The Turks, masters of entrenchment warfare, proved far more dangerous opponents than the Chitrali tribesmen. Having encircled Townshend's encampment with earthworks, they settled down to repel attacks both by the garrison and by the relieving force which, between January and March, four times attempted to break through their lines. Each effort was unsuccessful and the last, known as the battle of the Dujaila Redoubt, left a thousand dead at the scene of action. Townshend's headquarters was only seven miles distant from the furthest advance but, immediately after the defeat, the annual floods, fed from the snow-melt off the Zagros Mountains, swelled the rivers and put the surface of the Mesopotamian plain under water. Kut was completely cut off from outside help and on 29 April surrendered. Townshend and 10,000 survivors of the Expeditionary Force went into captivity, harsh for the common soldiers, 4,000 of whom died in enemy hands. Kut was not retaken until the end of the year, when nearly 200,000 British and Indian troops and followers had been assembled, to oppose 10,000 Turks and a handful of Germans. Like Salonika, where the Allies continued to wage an unsuccessful campaign against very inferior forces throughout 1916, Mesopotamia had become a drain on resources instead of a threat to the enemy.

On the Italian front, though there the defenders were also heavily outnumbered by the attackers, the disparity was not so great. The strength of the Italian army was increasing, and would eventually almost double, from thirty-six peacetime divisions to sixty-five, and during 1916 the Italians would attract thirty-five of the sixty-five mobilised Austrian divisions to their mountains. The consequent weakening of Austria's capacity to bear a fair share of the burden in the east would largely facilitate Russia's successful resumption of the offensive in this year. Outnumbered though they were, however, the Austrians both frustrated Italy's continuing attempts to break into the Austro-Hungarian heartland via the Isonzo route and launched a counter-offensive of their own directed towards the rich industrial and agricultural region in the plains of River Po. Conrad, the Habsburg

Chief of Staff, nurtured an almost personal animus against Austria's former partner in the Triple Alliance and had fallen out with Falkenhayn over his determination to punish them at the expense of sustaining the joint Austro-German success against the Tsar's armies which had begun at Gorlice-Tarnow. On 15 May 1916, almost on the anniversary of that victory, Conrad unleashed his own 'punishment expedition' (*Strafexpedition*) from the northern mountain chain of the Trentino, between Lake Garda, the Alpine beauty resort, and the headwaters of the River Brenta, which leads towards the lagoons of Venice. The preliminary bombardment, which opposed 2,000 Austrian guns to 850 Italian, was powerful, but the defenders were forewarned by the evidence of Austrian preparations and then fought with heroic self-sacrifice to hold the invaders at bay. The Rome Brigade was almost wiped out in its defence of Piazza. As a result, the Austrians nowhere advanced more than ten miles and, though their losses were fewer than the Italian – 80,000 to 147,000 – the punishment expedition neither threatened a breakthrough nor deflected Cadorna, the Italian Commander-in-Chief, from pursuing his relentless offensive on the Isonzo. The Sixth Battle opened in August and secured the frontier town of Gorizia, the Seventh, Eighth and Ninth followed in September, October and November. The bridgehead across the Isonzo at Gorizia was enlarged and a foothold on the harsh Carso upland secured. The Italian infantry, despite heavy losses and the frustration of their offensive efforts, still seemed ready to return to the attack, even under Cadorna's aloof and heartless direction of the war.

The course of operations in Italy during 1916 had one positive result: by attracting Austrian divisions from the Russians' southern front, it allowed the Tsar's armies to organise a successful counter-offensive against their weakened enemy. The Russians were committed to such an offensive by the Chantilly agreement of December 1915, while intelligence of Conrad's punishment expedition had caused Cadorna to request its mounting as a matter of urgency. Its results exceeded what had been promised or expected, most of all by the *Stavka*, whose plans for 1916 were for a resumption of an offensive against the Germans on Russia's northern front rather than the Austrians in the south. The German advanced positions in the north threatened Petrograd, the capital, and had brought under enemy occupation the productive Baltic States, where Ludendorff had created a full-blown occupation economy. In an anticipation of what

Hitler would less imaginatively attempt after 1941, he divided the region into six administrative areas, under a German military governor, and set about harnessing its agricultural and industrial resources to the German war effort. Ludendorff's plans went beyond the purely economic. 'I determined to resume in the occupied territory that work of civilisation at which German hands had laboured in those lands for many centuries. The population, made up as it is of such a mixture of races, has never produced a culture of its own and, left to itself, would succumb to Polish domination.' Ludendorff foresaw the transformation of Poland into 'a more or less independent state under German sovereignty' and by the spring of 1916 was planning to settle much of the Baltic States with Germans, who would take the land of the expropriated inhabitants. They did not include the Jews who, being often German-speakers, were regarded as useful instruments of occupation policy.[64]

Ludendorff's scheme to Germanise the Tsar's possessions in Poland and the Baltic regions was one reason for the *Stavka* to choose a resumption of the offensive in the north as its main strategy for 1916. It began, in response to a French appeal to relieve the pressure at Verdun, with an attack on each side of Lake Naroch, aimed at Vilna, the chief town of eastern Poland, on 18 March. Thanks to the mobilisation of Russia's industry for war, and to the call-up of new classes of conscripts, the Russian armies now outnumbered their opponents, by 300,000 to 180,000 in the north and 700,000 to 360,000 in the centre; only in the southern sector, commanded by Brusilov, did numbers remain equal at about half a million men on each side. In the north the Russians for the first time had a large superiority in guns and stocks of shell, with 5,000 guns and a thousand rounds per gun, considerably more than assembled by the Germans for the Gorlice-Tarnow breakthrough.[65]

Somehow, however, the advantage was cast away. The artillery preparation was not co-ordinated with the assault by the infantry of Second Army which, attacking on a very narrow front, ran into its own fire and then, in the salient it had won, came under bombardment by German guns from three sides. Three-quarters of the infantry, 15,000 men, were lost in the first eight hours; yet 350,000 men were theoretically available for the offensive, had it been launched on a wider front. Reinforcement merely increased the casualty list without the gain of more ground. By 31 March, when the offensive ended, Russian losses totalled 100,000, including 12,000 men who had died of exposure in the harsh late-winter weather. In April a counter-attack by the Germans, who had lost 20,000, recovered all the ground the Russians had gained.[66]

Prospects for the general offensive promised in June did not therefore augur well, since the *Stavka* again wished to attack in the north, above the Pripet Marshes that divided the front into two. In fact, Evert, commander of the army group that had failed at Lake Naroch, did not want to attack at all. Alexeyev, the Chief of Staff, was nevertheless insistent and secured the reluctant co-operation of Evert and Kuropatkin, the other army group commander on the northern sector, on the understanding that there would be copious reinforcements of men and material. To the surprise of those present at the conference on 14 April, the new commander of the southern front, Alexei Brusilov, who had succeeded Ivanov in March, was not reluctant at all. He believed victory was possible, by careful preparation, against the weakened Austrians and, as he requested no reinforcements, he was given permission to make his attempt. He had proved his ability at lower levels of command and he had also found the time to consider the problems of attacking entrenched positions covered by defending artillery with reserves in rear ready to stem a break-in. The solution, he had concluded, was to attack on a wide front, thus depriving the enemy of the chance to mass reserves at a predeterminably critical point, to protect the assaulting infantry in deep dugouts while they were waiting to jump off, and to advance the line as near as possible to the Austrian, by digging saps forward as close as seventy-five yards to the enemy trenches. These were great improvements. In the past the Russians had often left no man's land a mile or more wide, thus condemning the attacking infantry to heavy casualties during the approach, following equally heavy casualties suffered in trenches unprotected against enemy bombardment before the attack began.

Brusilov's preparations worked admirably. Though his superiority of numbers over the Austrians on the twenty miles of chosen front was only 200,000 to 150,000, with 904 to 600 guns, the enemy was genuinely surprised when the attack opened on 4 June. The Russian Eighth Army overwhelmed the Austrian Fourth and pushed on to take the communication centre of Lutsk, and to advance forty miles beyond the start line. Huge numbers of prisoners were taken, as the shaken Austrians surrendered to anyone who would take them prisoner. Eighth Army's neighbours also advanced but the greatest

AUSTRIA-HUNGARY

Pripet Marshes

Abortive attacks, June / July

Russian Third Army (Lesh)

Pripet

50 miles

Stokhod

Goryn

RUSSIA

ARMY GROUP LINSINGEN (Forces at 4th June: 38 divisions)

Kovel

Austrian Fourth Army (Archduke Joseph Ferdinand)

Krilov

Lutsk

Sluch

Rovno

Russian Eighth Army (Kaledin) 11 Inf + 4 Cav divisions

Brusilov's GHQ

Austrian First Army (Pulhallo von Briog)

Austrian Second Army (Böhm-Ermolli)

Lemberg

'German' Southern Army (von Bothmer)

Brzezany

Ternopol

Volochisk

Russian Eleventh Army (Sakharov) 8 Inf + 1 Cav divisions

RUSSIAN SOUTH-WEST ARMY GROUP (Forces at 4th June)

Gusyatin

Russian Seventh Army (Shcherbachev) 7 Inf + 3.5 Cav divisions

Stanislau

Austrian Seventh Army (Pflanzer-Baltin)

Kolomea

Kuty

Kamenets-Podolski

Russian Ninth Army (Lechitsky) 10 Inf + 4 Cav divisions

Czernowitz

Pruth

Dniester

Carpathian Mountains

Kimpolung

Sereth

Russian front line, 4 June

Railways

Russian front line, 10 October

Marshes

Main Russian attacks

Russian gains

Russian HQ / GHQ

The Brusilov Offensive

success was achieved in the south, between the River Dniester and the Carpathians, where the Austrian Seventh Army was split in two, lost 100,000 men, mainly taken prisoner, and by mid-June was in full retreat.

At the beginning of July the Russian armies north of the Pripet Marshes also went on to the offensive, profiting from Brusilov's success and the confusion reigning in the Austro-German high command as to where best to deploy its very scanty reserves, to press forward towards Baronovitchi, the old Russian headquarters town. Evert's offensive, opposed by German troops, was soon stopped but Brusilov's army group sustained its success over the Austrians throughout July and August and into September, by which time it had taken 400,000 Austrians prisoner and inflicted losses of 600,000. The German forces involved in opposing the Russian advance had lost 350,000, and a belt of Russian territory sixty miles deep had been taken back from the invaders. Had Brusilov possessed the means to follow up his victory and to bring reserves and supplies forward at speed, he might have recovered more of the ground lost in the great retreat of 1915, perhaps even to reach Lemberg and Przemysl once again. He possessed no such means. The rail system, which in any case favoured the Austrians rather than the Russians, could not provide tactical transport across the battle zone, while the roads, even had he had adequate motor transport, were unsuitable for heavy traffic. Nevertheless, the Brusilov offensive was, on the scale by which success was measured in the foot-by-foot fighting of the First World War, the greatest victory seen on any front since the trench lines had been dug on the Aisne two years before.[67]

The Russian victory, though it also cost a million casualties, sealed the fate of Falkenhayn, whose security of tenure as Chief of Staff had been weakening as the battle for Verdun protracted. His dismissal, and replacement by Hindenburg, was disguised by appointing him to command in the new campaign against Romania. Romania, long courted by both the Allies and the Central Powers, had thus far prudently avoided choosing sides. Its neighbour, Bulgaria, had thrown in its lot with Germany and Austria in October 1915 but Romania, which had acquired Bulgarian territory at the end of the Second Balkan War in 1913, continued to hold aloof. Its chief national interest was in the addition to its territory of Transylvania, where three million ethnic Romanians lived under Austro-Hungarian rule. As Brusilov's advance pushed westward, widening the common border of military contact between Russia and Romania and apparently promising not only Russian support but Austrian collapse, the Romanian government's indecision diminished. The Allies had long been offering an enlargement of Romania's territory at Austrian expense, following Allied victory, and Romania, unwisely, now decided to take the plunge. On 17 August, a convention was signed by which France and Russia bound themselves to reward Romania, at the peace, with Transylvania, the Bukovina, the southern tail of Galicia, and the Banat, the south-west corner of Hungary; in secret, the two great powers had previously agreed not to honour the convention when the time came. That the Romanians could not have known the treaty was made in bad faith does not excuse their entering into it. Good sense should have told them that their strategic situation, pinioned between a hostile Bulgaria to the south and a hostile Austria-Hungary to their west and north, was too precarious to be offset by the putative support of a Russian army which had only belatedly returned to the offensive. It was Brusilov's success that had persuaded the Romanians to take the plunge from neutrality into war, but his success was not great enough to guarantee the security of their flanks against a German intervention or an Austrian repositioning of divisions; against a Bulgarian attack it could offer no assistance at all.

The Romanians nevertheless went to war on 27 August in apparent high confidence in their army of twenty-three divisions, formed from their stolid peasantry, and in the belief that the Russian offensive north of the Pripet Marshes, towards Kovel, would prevent the transfer of German reserves towards Hungary, while Brusilov's continuing offensive would hold the Austrians in place. They appear to have made little allowance for the eventuality of Bulgarian or, as came to pass, Turkish intervention and they overestimated the military potentiality of their armed forces, which were poorly equipped and owed their reputation for fighting power to their success in the Second Balkan War at a moment when Bulgaria was hard pressed also by the Serbs, Greeks and Turks. Alexeyev, the Russian Commander-in-Chief, in a rare flash of realism, actively discounted the value of the Romanians as allies, rightly reckoning that they would drain rather than add to Russian reserves. He certainly did little to assist them. Nor did the French and British at Salonika, whose undertaking to mount a diversionary offensive had been a major consideration in bringing Romania to declare war. In the event their attack was pre-empted by the Bulgarians who, forewarned by evidence of Allied preparations and with the assistance of the German and the Turkish divisions, took the Allies by surprise, on 17 August, defeated the refugee Serbian army at Florina and succeeded in postponing the main Franco-British offensive until mid-September.

The Romanians, in these deteriorating circumstances, opened an offensive all the same, not, as the commanders in Salonika had expected, against Bulgaria, where it might have lent support to and been supported by their own, but into Hungary through the passes of the Transylvanian Alps. Retribution was quick to come. The Austrians quickly organised the local defence forces into a First Army, under General Arz von Straussenberg, while the Germans found the troops, some Bulgarian, to position two armies, the Ninth, under the ex-Chief of Staff, Falkenhayn, and the Eleventh, under the old Eastern Front veteran, Mackensen, in Transylvania and Bulgaria. While the Romanians, having occupied eastern Transylvania, then did nothing, their enemies made their preparations and struck. On 2 September the Bulgarians invaded the Dobruja, the Romanian province lying south of the Danube delta. On 25 September Falkenhayn, whose troops included the formidable mountain division known as the *Alpenkorps*, in which the young Rommel was serving, made his move in Transylvania and began to push the Romanians back through the passes towards the central plain and the capital, Bucharest, which fell on 5 December. By then Mackensen's army had crossed the Danube and was approaching Bucharest also. Assailed on three sides by four enemies, for the Turks had sent the 15th and 25th Divisions by sea to the Dobruja, the Romanians had been thrown into full retreat towards their remote eastern province of Moldavia, between the Sereth river and the Russian border. There, as winter closed in, and with support from the Russian Fourth and Sixth Armies, they entrenched themselves on the Sereth to sit out the bad weather.

Their decision for war had been disastrous. They had lost 310,000 men, nearly half as prisoners, and almost the whole of their country. Their most important material asset, the Ploesti oilfields, at the time the only significant source of oil in Europe west of the Black Sea, had been extensively sabotaged by British demolition teams before they were abandoned to the enemy. The Allies' decision to entice Romania into the war had been ill-judged also. The addition of the nominal fighting power of lesser states – Portugal (which became a combatant in March 1916), Romania and even Italy – did not enhance the strength of the Allies but, on the contrary, diminished it, once the inevitable setbacks they underwent came to require the diversion of resources to shore them up. The defeat of Romania not only necessitated, as Alexeyev had foreseen, the commitment of the Russian armies to rescue them from total collapse. It also delivered into German hands, over the next eighteen months, a million tons of oil and two million tons of grain, the resources that 'made possible the . . . continuation of the war into 1918'.[68] The accession of Greece to the Allied side, through a coup stage-managed by Venizelos but engineered by the Allies in June 1917, equally brought the Allies no advantage at all and, by its installation of a violently nationalist and anti-Turkish government in Athens, led to Greek mobilisation in the cause of the 'Great Idea' – the recovery of the Greek empire in the east – which would complicate the Allied effort to resettle the peace of Europe for years after the war had ended.

331

NINE

THE BREAKING OF ARMIES

THE FACE OF THE war at the beginning of 1917 was little altered from that it had shown to the world at the beginning of 1915, after the shutter of the trench lines had descended to divide Europe into two armed camps. In the east the course of the trench line had moved 300 miles and its southern shoulder now rested on the Black Sea instead of the Carpathians but in the north it still touched the Baltic. There was a new entrenched front on Italy's border with Austria and on the Greek border with Bulgaria, while the entrenchments at Gallipoli and Kut had come and gone. In Caucasia a front of outposts and strongpoints straggled between the Black Sea and northern Persia and in Sinai an uneasy no man's land divided the British defenders of the Suez Canal from the Turkish garrison of Palestine. That showed little change from 1915. In France there had been no change whatsoever. The geographical features on which the fighting armies had expended their final energies in the offensives of 1914 – the Yser, the low Flemish heights, Vimy Ridge, the chalk uplands of the Somme, the Aisne and the Chemin des Dames, the River Meuse at Verdun, the forests of the Argonne, the mountains of Alsace – remained the buttresses of the trench line, now greatly thickened, though over the narrowest of areas, by digging, wiring and excavation. Much digging and wiring had been deliberate, particularly on the German side where the defenders had sought to secure trenches against assault by the elaboration of their positions, by 1917 usually three belts deep and reinforced by concrete pillboxes; but a great deal of digging had also been hasty and improvised, done to incorporate stretches of trench won from the enemy into an existing system.

The thicker the trench system grew, the less likelihood was there of its course being altered even by the weightiest of offensive effort. The chief effect of two years of bombardment and trench-to-trench fighting across no man's land was to have created a zone of devastation of immense length, more than 400 miles between the North Sea and Switzerland, but of narrow depth: defoliation for a mile or two on each side of no man's land, heavy destruction of buildings for a mile or two more, scattered demolition beyond that. At Verdun, on the Somme and in the Ypres salient whole villages had disappeared, leaving a smear of brick-dust or pile of stones on the upturned soil. Ypres and Albert, sizeable small towns, were in ruins, Arras and Noyon badly damaged, the city of Rheims had suffered heavy destruction and so had villages up and down the line. Beyond the range of the heavy artillery, 10,000 yards at most, town and countryside lay untouched.

The transition from normality to the place of death was abrupt, all the more so because prosperity reigned in the 'rear area'; the armies had brought money, and shops, cafés and restaurants flourished, at least on the Allied side of the line. In the zone of German occupation, the military government ran an austere economic regime, driving the coal mines, cloth mills and iron works at full speed, requisitioning labour for land and industry and commandeering agricultural produce for export to the Reich. For the women of the north, lost for news of husbands and sons away at the war on the wrong side of the line, managing by themselves, the war brought hard years.[1] Only a few miles distant, in the French 'Zone of the Armies', a war economy boomed. Outside the ribbon of destruction, the roads were full of traffic, long lines of horsed and motor transport going to and fro, and in the fields, ploughed by farmers right up to the line where shells fell, new towns of tents and hutments had sprung up to accommodate the millions who went up and down, almost as if on factory shift, to the trenches. Four days in the front line, four in support, four at rest; on their days off, young officers, like John Glubb, might take a horse and ride 'down old neglected rides, while all round my head was a dazzling bower of light emerald green. Underfoot crunched the beech nuts, while the ground was everywhere carpeted with anemones and cowslips. Pulling up and sitting quietly on my horse in the heart of the forest, it was impossible to catch a sound of the outside world, except the jingling of my own bit and the murmuring of the trees.'[2]

If the front did not change, either in its course, its routine, or its strange intermingling of the everyday and the abnormal, the end of the first full two years of war brought great changes in its management. The year of 1917 would begin with new directors at the head of the British, French and German armies. In Russia, soon to be shaken by revolution, prestige, if not authority, had moved from the *Stavka* to

General Brusilov, the Tsar's only successful general. Change of command in Britain had been brought about by an accident of war. On 5 June 1916, Kitchener, Secretary of State for War, en route to Russia on an official visit, was drowned when the cruiser *Hampshire* struck a mine north of Scotland. He was succeeded by Lloyd George who, becoming Prime Minister on 7 December, appointed Lord Derby to replace himself. In France the long reign of Joffre also came to an end in December and he was replaced by Nivelle, the fluent expositor of new tactics; the dignity of Marshal of France was revived to spare Joffre humiliation. Since August 1916, the German armies had been under the control of the Hindenburg-Ludendorff partnership, the combination that had proved so successful on the Eastern Front. Their reputation undimmed by the setback of the Brusilov offensive, they, or more particularly Ludendorff as effective head of operations, would bring to high command a genuinely new strategy: the rationalisation of the Western Front, to economise troop numbers for action elsewhere, the mobilisation of the German economy for total war and a determination, through the politically contentious strategy of an unrestricted submarine offensive, to carry blockade to the enemy.

Would changes in command, however, change anything? The generalship of the First World War is one of the most contested issues of its historiography. Good generals and bad generals abound in the war's telling and so do critics and champions of this man or that among the ranks of its historians. In their time, almost all the leading commanders of the war were seen as great men, the imperturbable Joffre, the fiery Foch, the titanic Hindenburg, the olympian Haig. Between the wars their reputations crumbled, largely at the hands of memoirists and novelists – Sassoon, Remarque, Barbusse – whose depiction of the realities of 'war from below' relentlessly undermined the standing of those who had dominated from above. After the Second World War the assault on reputation was sustained, in that era by historians, popular and academic, particularly in Britain, who continued to portray the British generals as 'donkeys leading lions', as flinthearts bleeding the tender flesh of a generation to death in Flanders fields, or as psychological misfits.[3] There were counter-attacks, particularly to salvage the reputation of Haig, who had become an Aunt Sally to playwrights, film directors and television documentary makers committed to the view that the First World War exposed the oppressiveness of the British class structure. Little ground, however, was won back.[4] By the end of the century the

337

generals, who had stood so high at the end of its Great War, had been brought, it appeared, irredeemably low by a concerted offensive against their names and their works.

It is difficult today not to sympathise with the condemnations, worse or better informed as they have been, of the generals of the First World War. In no way – appearances, attitude, spoken pronouncement, written legacy – do they commend themselves to modern opinion or emotion. The impassive expressions that stare back at us from contemporary photographs do not speak of consciences or feelings troubled by the slaughter over which those men presided, nor do the circumstances in which they chose to live: the distant chateau, the well-polished entourage, the glittering motor cars, the cavalry escorts, the regular routine, the heavy dinners, the uninterrupted hours of sleep. Joffre's two-hour lunch, Hindenburg's ten-hour night, Haig's therapeutic daily equitation along roads sanded lest his horse slip, the *Stavka*'s diet of champagne and court gossip, seem and were a world away from the cold rations, wet boots, sodden uniforms, flooded trenches, ruined billets and plague of lice on, in and among which, in winter at least, their subordinates lived. Lloyd George, admittedly a radical and certainly no lover of his own high command, seemed to strike a just contrast when he wrote that 'the solicitude with which most generals in high places (there were honourable exceptions) avoided personal jeopardy is one of the debatable novelties of modern warfare'.[5]

There are three grounds on which Lloyd George's and, by extension, all criticism of the war's generals may be held unfair. The first is that many generals did expose themselves to risk, which it was not necessarily or even properly their duty to accept. Among British generals, thirty-four were killed by artillery and twenty-two by small-arms fire; the comparable figure for the Second World War is twenty-one killed in action.[6] The second is that, though the practice of establishing headquarters well behind the lines was indeed a 'novelty' in warfare – Wellington had ridden the front at Waterloo in full view of the enemy all day, while several hundred generals were killed in the American Civil War – it was one justified, indeed necessitated by the vast widening and deepening of fronts, which put the scene of action in its entirety far beyond the field of vision of any commander; indeed, the nearer a general was to the battle, the worse placed was he to gather information and to issue orders. Only at the point of junction of telephone lines, necessarily located behind the front, could he hope to gather intelligence of events and transmit a considered response to them. Thirdly, however, the system of communication itself denied any rapidity, let alone instantaneity, of communication when it was most needed, which was in the heat of action. The most important of the novelties of modern warfare in our own time has been the development of surveillance, targeting and intercommunication in 'real time', which is to say at the speed at which events unroll. Thanks to radar, television, other forms of sensoring and, above all, radio, commanders in the most recent large war of the twentieth century, the Gulf War, were kept in instant communication with the front, receiving and transmitting word-of-mouth information and instruction with the immediacy of person-to-person telephone conversation, while simultaneously orchestrating fire support for their troops by similarily rapid means against targets that could be observed in 'virtual reality'.

Absolutely none of these means, including radio, was available to a Great War commander. He depended, instead, once the trench lines had been dug, on a fixed and inflexible grid of telephone cables leading back through the chain of intermediate headquarters – battalion, brigade, division, corps, army – to the high command. Further from the front, the cable could be strung above ground; in the 'beaten zone' where shells fell, it had to be buried. Experience proved that a 'bury' of less than six feet was broken by bombardment, so trench floors were laboriously excavated to provide the necessary protection. By 1916 the British army had developed a sophisticated system of branching at each intermediate command level, so that headquarters could communicate in three directions – forwards, rearward, and laterally, to neighbouring headquarters – from the same exchange.[7]

All worked excellently, until fighting began. Then the system broke down, almost as a matter of routine, at the point that mattered most, the front. In defence, under the enemy's bombardment, the points of transmission were smashed up and the key personnel, forward artillery observers, were killed trying to do their job. In offence, as the troops moved forward from the heads of the cable grid, they automatically lost contact with the rear. Unwound telephone cable broke as a matter of course and expedients – signal lamps, carrier pigeons – were haphazard. To the unsatisfactory outcome in either situation there is ample and repetitive testimony. In defence on the Somme in 1916, for example, it was found by Colonel von Lossberg, OHL's tactical technician, that eight to ten hours were needed on average for a message to reach the front from divisional headquarters and so, reciprocally, to pass in the opposite direction.[8] In offence, communication could break down completely, as the reports at five levels of command – battalion, brigade, division, army and general headquarters – during the first day of the battle of the Somme, 1 July 1916, reveal.

The reports from one battalion, the 11th East Lancashire, the unit actually in contact with the enemy, begin with the commanding officer writing at 7.20 a.m. that 'the first wave crossed into no man's land'. At 7.42 he 'reported by runner [NB not telephone] intense fire of all descriptions'. At 7.50, 'I sent Lt. Macalpine to establish telephone communication . . . [he] returned and informed me all communication was cut . . . it was not re-established all day.' At 8.22 a.m. 'no information from my waves; at 9 a.m. 'saw no sign of 3rd or 4th wave'; at 10.01 a.m. 'no report from my waves'; at 11.25 a.m. 'no information from my waves'; at 11.50 a.m. 'no reports from my waves except statements of wounded men'; at 3.10 p.m. '[neighbouring unit] not in touch with any of their waves'; at 3.50 p.m. 'urgently require more men'; at 9.20 p.m. 'I have no rockets . . . or any Verey Lights [the only emergency means of communicating with the supporting artillery]'; at 9.40 this commanding officer himself was 'knocked out by a shell'.

The brigadier, at the next level of command upward, 94 Brigade, watched the battalions advancing but then lost word of them; 'the telephone wires up to his Headquarters remained working well throughout, but from his Headquarters forward they were all cut, although the line was buried six feet deep'. He reported that a runner from a battalion 'was buried three times on the way back and yet successfully delivered his message', presumably one of few, if not the only one, the brigadier received during the day. The headquarters of the 31st Division, to which the brigadier was reporting, recorded at 8.40 a.m. that he 'had telephoned that his line got across German front trenches but it is very difficult to see what is going on. He has no definite information'; at 6 p.m., nearly eleven hours after the attack had begun, the divisional commander was reporting to the level above, VIII Corps, 'I have had my signalling people trying to get into communication [with the troops] but cannot get any sign at all.' Nevertheless, at the level above VIII Corps, at Fourth Army head-quarters, the Chief of Staff that evening confidently wrote out an operation order for the morrow, prefixed by the statement that 'a large part of the German Reserves have now been drawn in and it is essential to keep up the pressure and wear out the defence', while, at more or less the same time, Douglas Haig was recording that the VIII Corps 'said they began well, but as the day progressed their troops were forced back . . . I am inclined to believe from further reports that few of VIII Corps left their trenches!!' Two hours later the War Diary of the 31st Division records that the 11th East Lancashire Regiment, whose wounded commander had seen 'my waves' depart into no man's land and enter the enemy positions before eight o'clock in the morning, had '30 all ranks available for holding front line tonight'. Complete casualty returns, taken later, would establish that the 11th East Lancs, the 'Accrington Pals', had lost 234 killed that day, of whom 131 found 'no known grave', and 360 wounded, leaving only 135 survivors.[9]

It is easy to rail against the apparent heartlessness of Haig's diary entry, written in the comfort of his chateau at Beaurepaire after a day spent in the ordered routine of his Montreuil headquarters or on chauffeured drives around the safe rear area of the battlefield. While 20,000 soldiers died, or awaited death from wounds in overwhelmed hospitals or the loneliness of a battlefield shell crater, their supreme commander worked at his desk, lunched, paid calls on his subordinates, dined and prepared for a comfortable bed. The contrast can be made to seem truly shocking, particularly if it is remembered that Wellington, after a day at Waterloo in which he had shared every risk, rode home on a weary horse to a makeshift billet and there gave up his bed to a wounded brother officer.

Yet the contrasts are unfair. Wellington had seen every episode of the battle with his own eyes and precisely directed its stages. Haig had not even been a spectator. He had seen nothing, heard nothing, except the distant roar of the bombardments and barrage, and done nothing. There was nothing for him to do, any more than there was anything for him to see; even one of his most junior subordinate commanders, Lieutenant Colonel Rickman, saw no more of his Accrington Pals once they had entered the German trenches than 'sun glinting on their triangles', the metal plates fixed to their packs as an identification mark. The iron curtain of war had descended between all commanders, low and high alike, and their men, cutting them off from each other as if they had been on different continents. High commanders, of course, had the material with which to bridge the gap, the vast numbers of guns arrayed behind the lines. What they lacked was the means to direct the fire of the artillery on to the positions of the enemy who was killing their soldiers. In an earlier war, the gunners would have seen the targets with the naked eye; in a later war, artillery observers, equipped with radio and moving with the infantry, would have directed the fire of the guns by word of mouth and map reference. In the First World War, though the front was mapped in the closest detail, almost daily updated, the radio that might have called down the fire of the guns in 'real time', in real need, did not exist. A 'trench set' was under development but it required twelve men to carry the apparatus, largely heavy batteries, and, while spotter aircraft could correct by radio the artillery's fall of shot, they could not communicate with the infantry who alone could indicate where fire was really needed.[10] Since the only method of making rapid progress through a trench system, before the appearance of the tank, was by closely and continuously co-ordinating infantry assault and fire support, it is no wonder at all that the battle of the Somme, like the battles that had preceded it and most that would follow, did not work as a military operation.

Most of the accusations laid against the generals of the Great War – incompetence and incomprehension foremost among them – may therefore be seen to be misplaced. The generals, once those truly incompetent, uncomprehending and physically or emotionally unfit had been discarded, which they were at the outset, came in the main to understand the war's nature and to apply solutions as rational as was possible within the means to hand. Robbed of the ability to communicate once action was joined, they sought to overcome the obstacles and accidents that would inevitably arise in the unfolding of battle by ever more elaborate anticipation and predisposition. Plans were drawn which laid down minute-by-minute manoeuvre by the infantry and almost yard-by-yard concentration of artillery fire, in an attempt not so much to determine as to predestine the outcome. The attempt was, of course, vain. Nothing in human affairs is pre-destinable, least of all in an exchange of energy as fluid and dynamic as a battle. While battle-altering resources – reliable armoured, cross-country vehicles, portable two-way radio – lay beyond their grasp (and they did so, tantalisingly, only in a development time to be measured in a few years), the generals were trapped within the iron fetters of a technology all too adequate for mass destruction of life but quite inadequate to restore to them the flexibilities of control that would have kept destruction of life within bearable limits.

The Mood of the Combatants

Is destruction of life ever bearable? By the beginning of 1917, this was a question that lurked beneath the surface in every combatant country. Soldiers at the front, subject to discipline, bound together by the comradeship of combat, had means of their own to resist the relentless erosion. Whatever else, they were paid, if badly, and fed, often amply. Behind the lines, the ordeal of war attacked senses and sensibilities in a different way, through anxiety and deprivation. The individual soldier knows, from day to day, often minute to minute, whether he is in danger or not. Those he leaves behind – wife and mother above all – bear a burden of anxious uncertainty he does not. Waiting for the telegram, the telegram by which ministries of war communicated to families word of the wounding or death of a relative at the front, had become by 1917 a never-absent element of consciousness. All too often, the telegram had already come. By the end of 1914, 300,000 Frenchmen had been killed, 600,000 wounded, and the total continued to mount; by the end of the war, 17 per cent of those mobilised would be dead, who included nearly a quarter of the infantrymen, drawn in the majority from the rural population, who suffered a third of the war's losses. By 1918, there would be 630,000 war widows in France, the majority in the prime of life and without hope of remarriage.[11]

The worst of the French losses had been suffered in 1914–16, years in which the novelty of cash allowances paid direct to the dependants of soldiers had palliated anxiety; the allowances were described by an official opinion-taker as 'the main cause of domestic peace and public calm'.[12] The good wages paid in the emergent war industries helped, also, to suppress anti-war feeling, as did the satisfaction of responsibility for tilling the land assumed by wives, suddenly become heads of families, or resumed by grandfathers with sons at the front. France was still overwhelmingly an agricultural country in 1914. Its communities adapted to the absence of the young men and food was nowhere short. In 1917, nevertheless, the accumulated strains were starting to become apparent to those whose duty it was to monitor the public mood, mayors, prefects, censors: in the towns, where many male workers were exempt or had actually been recalled from military service to do factory work, morale was satisfactory; but 'morale has fallen considerably in the countryside, where the original fortitude and resolution are no longer evident'.[13] Loss of fortitude and resolution by

June 1917, when this report was returned, was already widespread in the French army.

In Germany the resolution of the army and the people remained strong. Although over a million soldiers had been killed by the end of 1916 – 241,000 in 1914, 434,000 in 1915, 340,000 in 1916 – the successes at the front, which had brought the occupation of Belgium, northern France and Russian Poland and the defeat of Serbia and Romania, showed a return on sacrifice. The economic cost of waging what appeared to be a successful war was becoming however, hard to support. Female mortality, for example, increased by 11.5 per cent in 1916, 30.4 per cent in 1917 above pre-war rates, a rise attributable to diseases of malnutrition.[14] While France fed well on home-grown produce, and Britain maintained peacetime levels of food imports until mid-1917, when the German U-boat campaign began to bite hard, Germany, and Austria also, had felt the privations of blockade from 1916 onwards. During 1917 the consumption of fish and eggs was halved, so was that of sugar, while supplies of potatoes, butter and vegetables declined steeply. The winter of 1916/17 became the 'turnip winter', when that tasteless and unnutritious root appeared as a substitute or an additive at most meals. Luxuries, particularly coffee, which had become a German necessity, disappeared from the tables of all but the rich, and real necessities, like soap and fuel, were strictly rationed. 'By the end of 1916, life . . . for most citizens . . . became a time of eating meals never entirely filling, living in underheated homes, wearing clothing that proved difficult to replace and walking with leaky shoes. It meant starting and ending the day with substitutes for nearly everything.'[15] In Vienna, largest city of the Habsburg empire, hardship was even more severe. Real wages had halved in 1916 and would halve again in 1917, when the poorer in the population would begin to starve. Worse, with 60 per cent of men of breadwinning age at the front, families were dependent on a state allowance that in no way substituted for a father's income; by the end of the war, it bought less than two loaves of bread a day.[16]

The mood of all subjects of the Habsburg empire, moreover, had been altered by the death of Franz Josef, Emperor since 1848, in November 1916. Even among the least imperial of his peoples, Czechs and Serbs, many had held him in personal reverence. To the *Kaisertreu* Croats, to the Germans and to the Hungarians, whose King he was, he had stood as a symbol of stability in their increasingly ramshackle polity. His departure loosened such bonds as still held the ten main language groups – German, Magyar, Serbo-Croat, Slovenian, Czech, Slovak, Polish, Ruthenian, Italian and Romanian – in Austria-Hungary together. Though his successor, Karl I, brought youth to the imperial throne, he could not begin, in the circumstances of war, to establish a strong imperial authority of his own. His own instincts, indeed, like those of his Foreign Minister, Count Czernin, were for peace and one of his first acts as Emperor was to announce that he would seek urgently to bring it about. In March 1917, through the agency of his wife's brother, Prince Sixtus of Bourbon, he opened indirect negotiations with the French government, to identify the terms under which a general settlement might be achieved. As his principal motive, however, was to preserve his empire intact, and he was prepared to offer much German but little Austrian territory to achieve his object, his diplomatic initiative quickly foundered. The 'Sixtus affair', besides infuriating Germany, merely exposed Austria's war weariness to the Allies, without inducing them in any way to moderate their policy of fighting for a final victory.

They, moreover, had already rejected a disinterested attempt to mediate peace made by President Wilson of the United States on 18 December 1916, by which, as a preliminary, he asked each side to set out the terms necessary to its future security. Germany replied in anticipation, making no concessions at all and emphasising its belief in impending victory; the tone of the reply was much influenced by the recent capture of Bucharest and the collapse of the Romanian army. The Allied response was equally uncompromising but precisely detailed. It demanded the evacuation of Belgium, Serbia and Montenegro and of the occupied territory in France, Russia and Romania, independence for the Italian, and Romanian, and Czechoslovak and other Slav subjects of the Austrian and German empires, the ending of Ottoman rule in southern Europe and the liberation of the Turks' other subjects. It was, in short, a programme for the dismemberment of the three empires which constituted most of the Central Powers' alliance.[17]

Only states that retained a high degree of political unity could have responded with such confidence to a call for an end to hostilities in the twenty-eighth month of a terrible war. Such unity prevailed, in France and Britain alike, despite radical changes of personnel in both their governments. At the outbreak, the French assembly had renounced pursuit of party difference in a *Union sacrée* dedicated to national survival and eventual victory. The Union, despite a change of ministry, had been preserved. The Viviani administration had resigned in October 1915 but the new Prime Minister, Briand, had held office in the old government and sustained the coalition. The parties in the British parliament had also entered into coalition in May 1915, following criticism of the Liberal cabinet's capacity to ensure an adequate supply of munitions to the front in France, but Asquith remained Prime Minister and succeeded in maintaining an outward show of unity for the next year. In Lloyd George, the Minister of munitions, he had, however, a colleague relentlessly and rightly dissatisfied with his undynamic style of leadership and, at the beginning of December 1916, he found himself outmanoeuvred in a scheme to rearrange the war's higher direction. Agreeing at first to his own exclusion from a War Committee which would have draconian powers, he then declined to accept the new arrangement and forced Lloyd George's resignation. In the fracas that followed he offered his own, mistakenly expecting it to be rejected by a majority in parliament. Recognising Lloyd George's superior ability at a time of national crisis, his leading colleagues, Liberal and Conservative alike, overcame their dislike of his egotistic and devious personality and agreed to serve in a new coalition government over which the War Committee would rule with almost unlimited authority. Lloyd George's government would remain in office until the end of the war.

If these political changes sustained the coalition process in both countries, they did not, however, solve the difficulty which lay at the root of the dissatisfactions with the Viviani and Asquith ministries: their relationship with the supreme command. In Germany, command could be altered at the word of the Kaiser, who, as supreme commander, had all military posts in his gift. He had already, by the end of 1916, removed Moltke and Falkenhayn. In Britain, too, a change of command required in theory only a decision by the responsible authority, though there it lay with government rather than monarchy. In practice, however, concern for public confidence made such changes difficult, as evidenced by the failure to relieve Sir John French long after his unsuitability for the direction of operations in France had become obvious to the cabinet. In France the situation was complex and more difficult still. Joffre, as Commander-in-Chief, exercised powers within the Zone of the Armies that had constitutional force. Even parliamentary deputies lacked the right to enter the Zone without his permission, while he had authority not only over the armies on French soil but had been given similar powers over those in the 'theatres of exterior operations' as well. As a result, commanders in France and Britain and, as would soon appear, Italy also, enjoyed a security of tenure to be shaken neither by casualty lists nor lack of success at the battlefronts.

In Britain, Haig would survive in high command to the very end of the war, despite a loss of confidence in him by Lloyd George that, by the end of 1917, was almost total. In France, loss of confidence in Joffre, which had been growing since the beginning of the Verdun battle, did lead to his elevation to empty grandeur in December 1916. No satisfactory readjustment, however, of the relationship between political and military authority was devised – General Lyautey, the Moroccan proconsul appointed Minister of War at the time of Joffre's removal, was given enlarged administrative powers without rights of command in France – neither could a satisfactory substitute for Joffre be found. The politicians' choice, Nivelle, was intelligent and persuasive and had transformed the situation at Verdun, once the Germans had desisted from the offensive, his recapture of Fort Douaumont crowning with success two years of rapid ascent from colonel's rank. As events would shortly prove, however, the confidence he had in his own capacities was exaggerated, while that placed in him by the government was misjudged. How easy it is, in retrospect, to see that that was so, how difficult at the time to accept the fallibility of governments and general staffs. The fundamental truth underlying dissatisfaction with systems and with personalities in all countries was that the search for anything or anyone better was vain. The problem of command in the circumstances of the First World War was insoluble. Generals were like men without eyes, without ears and without voices, unable to watch the operations they set in progress, unable to hear reports of their development and unable to speak to those whom they had originally given orders once action was joined. The war had become bigger than those who fought it.

In Germany, in Britain and even in France, so grievously wounded by loss of life in defence of the homeland, the popular will nevertheless remained intact. *Durchhalten,* 'see it through', had become the watchword of the Germans. Terrible though the nation's sufferings were, there was still no thought of accepting an unsatisfactory outcome.[18] Belief in glorious victory might have gone; concessions remained as unthinkable as defeat. In Britain, which had begun to suffer mass loss of life only in 1916, the determination to see it through held even stronger. The year of 1916 had seen the voluntary impulse, which had brought millions into the ranks, attenuate and conscription laws passed which, for the first time in British history, compelled civilians into the army. Nevertheless, as the *Annual Register* recorded with apparent accuracy, 'The prospect of . . . sacrifices . . . appeared to be quite powerless in effecting any modification of the national resolution to prosecute the war to a successful conclusion.'[19] Even in France, the idea of the 'sacred union' as a bond not only between politicians but between classes and sections also persisted until the end of 1916, on the basis that 'France had been the target of foreign aggression and had therefore to be defended'.[20] Illogically, the belief that the war might be ended quickly, by a German collapse or a brilliant French victory, persisted as well. The hope in success of a French victory was about to be brutally shattered.

THE FRENCH MUTINIES

A great offensive had been planned for 1917 at the meeting of Allied military representatives at Chantilly, French general headquarters, in November 1916, a repetition of the Chantilly conference of the previous December which had led to the battle of the Somme and to the Brusilov offensive. As before, the Italians were to resume their offensives against the Austrians on the Isonzo and the Russians promised a spring offensive also; they were imprecise about details, although enthusiastic about its potentiality, for Russian industry was now fully mobilised for war and producing large quantities of weapons and munitions.[21] The great effort, however, was to be made in the centre of the Western Front, on the old Somme battlefield, by the French and British, to be followed by an offensive in Flanders aimed at 'clearing' the Belgian coast and recapturing the bases of the U-boats which were operating with increasing effect against Allied shipping.

Two events supervened to overtake these plans. The first was the replacement of Joffre by Nivelle, whose operational philosophy did not marry with a scheme for the resumption of the Somme battle. The Somme had degenerated into a struggle of attrition and the landscape bore the scars; broken roads, long stretches of broken ground, shattered woods, flooded valley bottoms, and labyrinths of abandoned trenches, dugouts and strongpoints. The Somme offered no terrain suitable for an abrupt breakthrough, of which Nivelle believed he had the secret. Nivelle was an officer of artillery, by 1917 the premier arm of trench warfare, and he had convinced himself that new artillery tactics would produce *'rupture'*. Under his control, a vast mass of artillery would drench the German defences with fire 'across the whole depth of the enemy position', destroying the trenches and stunning the defenders, so that the attackers, advancing under a continuous barrage and by-passing surviving pockets of resistance, would pass unopposed into open country and the enemy rear area.[22] Since the Somme was unsuitable for such tactics, Nivelle proposed to return to the terrain and the plan of 1915. He would attack at the 'shoulders' of the great German salient on either side of the Somme. The French would take the southern Aisne sector, the Chemin des Dames, as their front of assault, while the British, by inter-Allied agreement, would reopen an offensive on the northern shoulder of the Somme salient, at Arras and against Vimy Ridge.

Had Nivelle not changed the plan for 1917, a German decision would in any case have nullified the Allied intention to resume the Somme offensive. On 15 March it was noticed that the enemy were beginning to withdraw from his positions along the whole front between Arras and the Aisne. This was the second eventuality unforeseen when Joffre had convened the Chantilly conference in November. Plans in war rarely coincide. While the Allies were agreeing to reopen the offensive on ground already fought across, the Germans were making the necessary preparations to give up that ground altogether. In September 1916 work had been set in hand to construct a 'final' position behind the Somme battlefield, with the object of shortening the line and economising force, to the extent of ten divisions, for use elsewhere.[23] By January the new line, consisting of stretches named after the saga heroes, Wotan, Siegfried, Hunding and Michel and collectively known as the Hindenburg Line, was complete and by 18 March it was fully occupied. Once the British and French realised that the countryside in front of them was empty, they followed up, through a devastated landscape, and by early April were digging their own trenches opposite defences more formidable than any yet encountered.

Fortunately for Nivelle's plan, the Hindenburg Line stopped just short of the Chemin des Dames, where he planned to deliver the blow, as it did also of the Arras-Vimy Ridge sector where the British and Canadians were to attack a little earlier; the Hindenburg Line exactly bisected the base of the salient between them. Unfortunately for the French, the defences of the Chemin des Dames, built up over the previous three years, since it was first entrenched during the German retreat from the Marne in September 1914, were among the strongest on the Western Front and, from the crest line, the Germans commanded long views into the French rear area. German artillery observers could overlook the positions in which the French infantry were to form up for the assault, as well as those of their supporting artillery. Moreover, a new German defensive doctrine, introduced as a result of Nivelle's own success in recapturing ground at Verdun in December 1916, ensured that the front line would be held in minimum strength, but with counter-attack (*Eingreif* or 'intervention') divisions held just beyond the range of the enemy's artillery, so as to be able to 'lock in' (another meaning of *eingreifen*) as soon as the leading waves of the enemy's attacking infantry had 'lost' their own artillery's fire.[24] As Nivelle's plan foresaw a 'hard' and 'brutal' offensive, lasting not more than forty-eight hours, during which the whole of the German positions would be overwhelmed in three successive advances 2–3,000 yards deep, close co-operation between infantry and artillery was necessary for success.[25] Nivelle's plan, however, made no provision for the rapid pushing forward of the French artillery, which, on the steep and broken terrain of the battlefield and in the circumstances likely to prevail, was in any case infeasible.

While the French Sixth, Tenth and Fifth Armies, together constituting the Group of Armies of Reserve and including some of the most successful formations in the army, with the I, XX and II Colonial Corps in the front line, awaited the day of attack, eventually fixed for 16 April, the BEF prepared for its own supporting offensive, due to begin a week earlier. Its particular objective was the crest of Vimy Ridge, to be attacked by the Canadian Corps, from which the way led down into the Douai plain and thence, it was hoped, into the un-entrenched German rear area across which a rapid advance by cavalry could link up with Nivelle's vanguards once they had cleared the Aisne heights at the Chemin des Dames eighty miles to the south. An enormous weight of artillery and stock of munitions – 2,879 guns, one for each nine yards of front, and 2,687,000 shells – had been assembled, to prepare an assault shorter in duration but double in weight to that delivered before the Somme the previous July. Forty tanks had also been got together, while the VI Corps of Third Army, the formation making the main assault, was able to shelter its infantry in the great subterranean quarries at Arras and bring them under cover to the front line through tunnels dug by the Army's tunnelling companies. Similar tunnels had been dug opposite Vimy Ridge for the infantry of the Canadian Corps, four divisions strong, which was there to make the first major offensive effort by a Dominion contingent on the Western Front.

The April weather at Arras was atrocious, rain alternating with snow and sleet, the temperatures relentlessly low; wet and shelling had turned the chalky surface of the attack zone into gluey mud, everywhere ankle-deep, in places deeper. For once, however, the long period of preparation did not arouse fierce German counter-measures. The commander of the Sixth Army, occupying the Vimy-Arras sector, von Falkenhausen, kept his counter-attack divisions fifteen miles behind the front, apparently believing that the seven in line – 16th Bavarian, 79th Reserve, 1st Bavarian, 14th Bavarian, 11th and 17th and 18th Reserve – had sufficient strength to resist the assault.[26] That was a mistake. Allenby and Horne, commanding Third and First Armies, had eighteen attack divisions, and a vast artillery superiority, while the local German commanders, knowing that Falkenhausen was holding his strategic reserves far away, also held their tactical reserves to the rear, with the intention of committing them only if the front broke.

These dispositions proved calamitous for the Germans. Their unfortunate infantry were pinned in their deep dugouts by the weight of the British bombardment, which had also torn their protective wire entanglements to shreds. Though their sentries heard the sounds of the impending assault two hours before it began, the cutting of their telephone lines meant that they could not communicate with their artillery, which had in any case been overwhelmed by British counter-battery fire.[27] When the British and Canadians appeared, plodding behind their creeping barrage, the defenders were either killed or captured below ground or, if they were lucky, had just enough time to run to the rear. Michael Volkheimer, in the 3rd Bavarian Reserve Regiment at the southern end of Vimy Ridge, saw the advancing waves almost on top of his trench, shouted to a comrade, 'Get out! The English are coming!' and then ran to warn his regimental commander that 'unless strong reinforcements were available to be thrown in from our side, the entire regiment would be taken prisoner . . . no such reinforcements were available, so the entire Ridge . . . fell into the hands of the enemy and of our regiment [of 3,000] only some 200 men managed to get away.'[28]

The first day of the battle of Arras was a British triumph. In a few hours the German front was penetrated to a depth of between one and three miles, 9,000 prisoners were taken, few casualties suffered and a way apparently cleared towards open country. The success of the Canadians was sensational. In a single bound the awful bare, broken slopes of Vimy Ridge, on which the French had bled to death in thousands in 1915, was taken, the summit gained and, down the precipitous eastern reverse slope, the whole Douai plain, crammed with German artillery and reserves, laid open to the victors' gaze. 'We could see the German gunners working their guns, then limbering up and moving back. Transport waggons were in full retreat with hundreds of fugitives from the Ridge. There appeared to be nothing at all to prevent our breaking through', wrote a Canadian lieutenant, 'nothing except the weather.'[29] In practice, it was not the weather but the usual inflexibility of the plan that deterred progress. A predicated pause of two hours, after the objectives had been gained, prevented the leading troops from continuing the advance. When they did so, the day was shortening and impetus ran out. On 10 April the first German reserves began to appear to stop the gap and when, on 11 April, an attempt was made to widen the break-in by an attack on the right at Bullecourt, an Australian division found uncut wire which the handful of accompanying tanks could not break. An intermission was then ordered, to allow casualties to be replaced and the troops to recover. Losses by then totalled nearly 20,000, one-third of those suffered on the first day of the Somme, but the divisions engaged were exhausted. When the battle was resumed on 23 April, the Germans had re-organised and reinforced and were ready to counter-attack on every sector. As a result, attrition set in, dragging on for a month, and bringing another 130,000 casualties for no appreciable gain of ground. The Germans suffered equally but, after the humiliation at Vimy, quickly rebuilt their positions and were in no danger of undergoing a further defeat on the Arras front.

They had meanwhile inflicted a catastrophic defeat on the French. Their setback at Vimy had had two causes: first, an expectation that the British bombardment would last longer than it did, and a consequent failure to bring their counter-attack divisions forward in sufficient time to intervene, but second, an absolute deficiency in divisions on the Vimy-Arras sector. The compensation for that was to be felt by the French at the Chemin des Dames, where fifteen German counter-attack divisions had been assembled behind the twenty-one in line. If the Germans had been surprised at Vimy-Arras, it was to be the other way about on the Aisne, where evidence of a great offensive in preparation had alerted the Germans to what Nivelle intended.[30] Then, too, there had been failures of security. Documents had been captured and there had been loose talk behind the lines. Nivelle, son of an English mother, spoke the language fluently and as early as January 1917, on a visit to London, 'explained his methods in the most enchanting way across the dinner-table to enthralled and enraptured women who dashed off to tell their friends as much of the talk as they had understood'.[31]

One way or another, the Germans had got ample warning of Nivelle's plan for *'rupture'*. They had also put in place their own new scheme for 'defence in depth', devised by Colonel von Lossberg, which left the front line almost empty, except for observers, while the 'intermediate zone' behind was held by machine gunners dispersed either in strongpoints or improvised shell hole positions. The supporting artillery, meanwhile, was deployed not in lines but in a haphazard pattern to the rear, while the real strength of the defence lay in the reserves deployed outside artillery range 10,000 and 20,000 yards from the front. The arrangement spelled doom to Nivelle's plan, which required the French infantry to cross the first 3,000 yards of the Chemin des Dames front, a steep, wooded slope, pitted by natural cave openings, in three hours, the next 3,000 yards, on the reverse slope, where they would pass out of sight of their supporting artillery, in the next three hours, and the final 2,000 yards in two hours. Quite apart from the difficulties to be encountered in contesting those 8,000 yards – initial German resistance, wire entanglements, by-passed machine guns, local counter-attacks – the intrinsic weakness of Nivelle's plan was that the energy of its initial stage was to be expended in an area that stopped 2,000 yards short of the real German defences. However successful, therefore, the French assault, and that was problematical, the attackers, when and if they achieved their final objectives, would immediately confront fresh troops whom, in their exhausted state, they would be hard-pressed to resist.

Nevertheless, something of Nivelle's confidence in *'rupture'* had communicated itself to his soldiers. General E.L. Spears, a British liaison officer, described the scene at dawn on 16 April on the start line, 'A thrill of something like pleasure, excited sanguine expectation, ran through the troops. I was surrounded by the grinning faces of men whose eyes shone. Seeing my uniform, some soldiers came up to me eagerly. "The Germans won't stand here . . . any more than they did before you at Arras. They fairly ran away there, didn't they?" The effect of the cheerful voices was enhanced by the sparkles of light dancing on thousands of blue steel helmets'. As zero hour approached, the waiting infantry fell silent, while the artillery, which was to jump its barrage forward in enormous leaps, purportedly to carry the infantry onward, crashed into action. 'The start seemed good', Spears thought. 'The German barrage gave the impression of being ragged and irregular. Hundreds of golden flares went up from the enemy lines. They had seen the French assaulting-waves and were calling their guns to the rescue . . . Almost at once, or so it seemed, the immense mass of troops within sight began to move. Long, thin columns were swarming towards the Aisne. Suddenly some 75s appeared from nowhere, galloping forward, horses stretched out, drivers looking as if they were riding a finish. "The Germans are on the run, the guns are advancing," shouted the infantry jubilantly. Then it began to rain and it became impossible to tell how the assault was progressing.'[32]

It was not only the rain – and sleet, snow and mist, weather as bad and cold as on the first day of the battle of Arras – that made it impossible to chart the progress of the assault. The line of battle itself was disintegrating as the German defence sprang into action. 'The headlong pace of the advance was nowhere long maintained. There was a perceptible slowing down, followed by a general halt of the supporting troops which had been pressing steadily forward since zero hour. German machine guns, scattered in shell holes, concentrated in nests, or appearing suddenly at the mouths of deep dugouts or caves, took fearful toll of the troops now labouring up the rugged slopes of the hills.'[33]

The over-rapid pace of the barrage, by which the infantry should have been protected, was leaving the foot soldiers behind. 'Everywhere the story was the same. The attack gained at most points, then slowed down, unable to follow the barrage which, progressing at the rate of a hundred yards in three minutes, was in many cases soon out of sight. As soon as the infantry and the barrage became disassociated, German machine guns . . . opened fire, in many cases from both front and flanks, and sometimes from the rear as well . . . On the steep slopes of the Aisne the troops, even unopposed, could only progress very slowly. The ground, churned up by the shelling, was a series of slimy slides with little or no foothold. The men, pulling themselves up by clinging to the stumps of trees, were impeded by wire obstacles of every conceivable kind. Meanwhile the supporting troops were accumulating in the assault trenches at the rate of a fresh battalion every quarter of an hour. As the leading waves were held up, in some cases a few hundred yards and seldom as much as half to three-quarters of a mile ahead, this led to congestion . . . Had the German guns been as active as their machine guns, the massacre that was going on in the front line would have been duplicated upon the helpless men in the crowded trenches and on the tracks to the rear.'[34]

The massacre was comprehensive enough. Mangin, the hard colonial soldier commanding Sixth Army assaulting the left-hand end of the ridge, on hearing that his troops, who included his own colonials and the veterans of the XX 'Iron' Corps, were held up, ordered that 'where the wire is not cut by the artillery, it must be cut by the infantry. Ground must be gained.' The order was entirely pointless. Tanks might have broken the wire but none of the 128 little two-man Renault tanks, the first to be used by the French in battle, reached the German front line, almost all bogging in the churned-up approaches. The infantry by themselves could but struggle forward as long as they survived. On the first day they penetrated no more than 600 yards; on the third day the Chemin des Dames road, crossing the ridge, was reached; on the fifth day, when 130,000 casualties had been suffered, the offensive was effectively abandoned. There had been compensatory gains, including 28,815 prisoners, and a penetration of four miles on a sixteen-mile front, but the deep German defences remained intact. There had been no breakthrough, no realisation of Nivelle's promise of *'rupture'*. On 29 April he was removed and replaced by Pétain. The French losses, which included 29,000 killed, could not be replaced.[35]

Nor could, for a time at least, the fighting spirit of the French army. Almost immediately after the failure of the offensive of 16 April, there began what its commanders would admit to be 'acts of collective indiscipline' and what historians have called 'the mutinies of 1917'. Neither form of words exactly defines the nature of the breakdown, which is better identified as a sort of military strike. 'Indiscipline' implies a collapse of order. 'Mutiny' usually entails violence against superiors. Yet order, in the larger sense, remained intact and there was no violence by the 'mutineers' against their officers. On the contrary, a strange mutual respect characterised relations between private soldiers and the commissioned ranks during the 'mutinies', as if both sides recognised themselves to be mutual victims of a terrible ordeal, which was simply no longer bearable by those at the bottom of the heap. Soldiers lived worse than officers, ate inferior food, got less leave. Nevertheless, they knew that the officers shared their hardships

355

and, indeed, suffered higher casualties. Even in units where there was direct confrontation, as in the 74th Infantry Regiment, the 'mutineers' made it clear that they wished their officers 'no harm'. They simply refused to 'return to the trenches'.[36] That was an extreme manifestation of dissent. The general mood of those involved – and they comprised soldiers in fifty-four divisions, almost half the army – was one of reluctance, if not refusal, to take part in fresh attacks but also of patriotic willingness to hold the line against attacks by the enemy. There were also specific demands: more leave, better food, better treatment for soldiers' families, an end to 'injustice' and 'butchery', and 'peace'. The demands were often linked to those of participants in civilian strikes, of which there was a wave in the spring of 1917, caused by high prices, resentment at war profiteering and the dwindling prospect of peace.[37] Civilian protesters were certainly not demanding peace at any price, let alone that of a German victory, but they complained that 'while the people have to work themselves to death to scrape a living, the bosses and the big industrialists are growing fat'.[38]

Civilian discontent fed military discontent, just as the soldiers' anxieties for their families were reinforced by the worries of wives and parents for husbands and sons at the front. The French crisis of 1917 was national. It was for that reason that the government took it so seriously, as did its nominee to replace Nivelle, Philippe Pétain. For all his outward abruptness, Pétain understood his countrymen. As the crisis deepened – and five phases have been identified, from scattered outbreaks in April to mass meetings in May, and hostile encounters in June, followed by an attenuation of dissent during the rest of the year – he set in train a series of measures designed to contain it and return the army to moral well-being. He promised ampler and more regular leave. He also implicitly promised an end, for a time at least, to attacks, not in so many words, for that would have spelled an end to the status of France as a war-waging power, but by emphasising that the troops would be rested and retrained.[39] Since retraining would take divisions away from the front, he also introduced a new doctrine, akin to that already in force on the German side of the line, of 'defence in depth'. Instructions he issued on 4 June were to avoid 'the tendency to pack together the infantry in the front lines, which only augments casualties'. Instead, the first line was to be held only in strength enough to keep the enemy at bay and provide artillery observation.[40] The majority of the infantry was to be kept in the second line, with a reserve in the third to mount counter-attacks. These instructions were strictly defensive in purpose. While the front was being reorganised for these new tactics, the army's officers, with Pétain's approval, were attempting to win back the men's obedience by argument and encouragement. 'No rigorous measures must be taken', wrote the commander of the 5th Division's infantry. 'We must do our best to dilute the movement by persuasion, by calm and by the authority of the officers known by the men, and acting above all on the good ones to bring the strikers to the best sentiments.' His divisional commander agreed: 'we cannot think of reducing the movement by rigour, which would certainly bring about the irreparable'.[41]

Nevertheless, the 'movement' – indiscipline, strike or mutiny – was not put down without resort to force. Both high command and government, obsessed by a belief that there had been 'subversion' of the army by civilian anti-war agitators, devoted a great deal of effort to identifying ringleaders, to bringing them to trial and to punishing them. There were 3,427 courts-martial, by which 554 soldiers were condemned to death and forty-nine actually shot.[42] Hundreds of others, though reprieved, were sentenced to life imprisonment. A particular feature of the legal process was that those sent for trial were selected by their own officers and NCOs, with the implicit consent of the rank and file.

Superficially, order was restored within the French army with relative speed. By August, Pétain felt sufficient confidence in its spirit to launch a limited operation at Verdun, which restored the front there to the line held before the German offensive of February 1916, and in October another operation on the Aisne drove the Germans back beyond the Ailette, the first-day objective of Nivelle's ill-fated offensive. In general, however, the objects of the mutinies had been achieved. The French army did not attack anywhere on the Western Front, of which it held two-thirds, between June 1917 and July 1918, nor did it conduct an 'active' defence of its sectors. The Germans, who had inexplicably failed to detect the crisis of discipline on the other side of no man's land, were content to accept their enemy's passivity, having business of their own elsewhere, in Russia, in Italy and against the British.

'Live and let live' was not a new phenomenon, either of the First World War or any other. It had prevailed in the Crimea and in the trenches between Petersburg and Richmond in 1864–5, in the Boer War, where the siege of Mafeking stopped on Sundays, and on wide stretches of the Eastern Front in 1915–16. Soldiers, unless harried by their officers, have always been ready to fall into a mutual accommodation in static positions, often to trade gossip and small necessities, and even to arrange local truces. There had been a famous truce between the British and the Germans at Christmas, 1914, in Flanders, repeated on a small scale in 1915, while the Russians had organised Easter as well as Christmas truces as late as 1916. More generally, both sides on the Western Front, once they had properly dug themselves in, were content on those sectors unsuitable for major offensives – and they included the flooded zone in Flanders, the Belgian coal-mining area, the Argonne forest, the Vosges mountains – to fall into an unoffensive routine. In places the proximity of the enemy made anything but 'live and let live' intolerable; legend describes a sector of 'international wire', defending trenches so close that each side allowed the other to repair the barrier separating them. Even in places where no man's land was wide, opposing units might unspokenly agree not to disturb the peace. The British high command fiercely disapproved of 'live and let live' and sought by many means – the ordering of trench raids, the despatch of trench-mortar units to particular sectors, the organisation of short artillery bombardments – to keep sectors 'active', with tangible results.[43] The Germans found trench duty opposite British units, which consistently accepted casualty rates in trench warfare of several dozen a month, unsettling. The French, by contrast, were less committed to raiding than the British, rewarding those who took part in 'patrols' with leave (whereas the British regarded raiding as a normal duty), and generally preferred to reserve their manpower for formal offensives. After the Nivelle offensive, though divisions which had been affected by indiscipline took trouble to organise raids and report their activity to higher headquarters, the majority in practice relapsed on to the defensive.[44] The cost of their effort to win the war – 306,000 dead in 1914, 334,000 dead in 1915, 217,000 dead in 1916, 121,000 dead in 1917, mostly before the mutinies, altogether a million fatalities out of a male population of twenty million – had deadened the French will to fight. Defend the homeland the soldiers of France would; attack they would not. Their mood would not change for nearly a year.

REVOLT IN RUSSIA

It was not only the French army that recoiled from the mounting cost of the war in 1917. The Russian army too, never as cohesive or as 'national' as the French, was creaking at the joints, even before its high command began to organise the spring offensives its representatives had promised at the inter-Allied Chantilly conference in December 1916.[45] Its complaints mirrored those to be heard from the French after the Nivelle offensive: bad food, irregular leave, concern for the welfare of families at home, rancour against profiteers, landlords and 'shirkers', those who avoided conscription and earned good wages by so doing, and, more ominously, disbelief in the usefulness of attacks.[46] The military postal censorship, which had warned the French government so accurately of discontent in the ranks, intercepted at the end of 1916 evidence of 'an overwhelming desire for peace whatever the consequences'.[47] It was fortunate for the Russian high command that the winter of 1916–17 was exceptionally severe, preventing any large-scale German offensive which, in the prevailing mood of the Tsar's army, might have achieved decisive results.

Yet the situations in France and Russia were not comparable. Even during the worst of its troubles, at the front and at home during 1917, France continued to function as a state and an economy. In Russia the economy was breaking down and thereby threatening the survival of the state. The economic problem, however, was not, as in Germany or Austria, one of direct shortage, brought about by blockade and the diversion of resources to war production. It was, on the contrary, one of uncontrolled boom. Industrial mobilisation in Russia, financed by an enormous expansion of paper credit and abandonment of budgeting balanced by gold, had created a relentless demand for labour, met by releasing skilled workers from the ranks – hence so much of the discontent among peasant soldiers who did not qualify for a return to civilian life – and by a migration of exempt peasants, those who could show family responsibilities, from the land to the cities, where cash incomes were far higher than those won, often by barter, on the farm. Migrant peasants also found work in the mines, where employment doubled between 1914 and 1917, on the railways, in the oilfields, in building and, above all, in factories; state factories more than tripled their work force during the war.[48]

Higher wages and paper money brought rapid inflation, inevitable in a country with an unsophisticated treasury and banking system, and inflation had a particularly disruptive effect on agricultural output. Large landowners took land out of production because they could not afford the threefold increase in wages, while peasants, unwilling or unable to pay high prices for trade goods, withdrew from the grain market and reverted to self-subsistence. At the same time the railways, though employing 1,200,000 men in 1917, against 700,000 in 1914, actually delivered less produce to the cities, partly because of the demands made on them by the armies, partly because the influx of unskilled labour led to a decline in maintenance standards.[49] By the beginning of 1917, at a time when exceptionally low temperatures had increased demand, supplies of fuel and food to the cities had almost broken down. In March, the capital, Petrograd, had only a few days' supply of grain in its warehouses.

It was the shortage of food which provoked what would come to be known as the February Revolution (Russia, working by the old Julian calendar, calculated dates thirteen days behind the Gregorian calendar used in the west). The February Revolution was not political in origin or direction. It was initially a protest against material deprivation and became a revolution only because the military garrison of Petrograd refused to join in the repression of the demonstrators and then took their side against the gendarmerie and the Cossacks, the state's traditional agencies of police action. The revolution began as a series of strikes, first staged to commemorate the 'Bloody Sunday' of 9 January, when the Cossacks had put down the 1905 revolt, widening in February (March) to large-scale and repetitive demands for 'Bread'. The size of the demonstrations was swelled by a sudden rise in temperatures, which brought the discontented out into winter sunshine, at first to search for food, then to join the activists in the streets. On 25 February, 200,000 workers were crowding the centre of Petrograd, smashing shops and fighting the outnumbered and demoralised police.[50]

The Tsar's government was used to civil disorder and had always before found means to put it down. In the last resort, as in 1905, it called out the army to shoot the crowds. In February 1917 ample military force was to hand, 180,000 soldiers in the capital, 152,000 nearby. They belonged, moreover, to the Tsar's most dependable regiments, the Guards – Preobrazhensky, Semenovsky, Ismailovsky, Pavlosky, fourteen in all – which had served the dynasty since the raising of the most senior by Peter the Great. The Preobrazhensky, which wore the mitre caps of the wars against Charles XII of Sweden, and into which the Tsarevitch was traditionally commissioned as a boy-officer, were the guards of guards. The Tsar himself chose its soldiers from the annual recruit contingent, chalking 'P' on the clothes of those he selected, and he counted on them to defend him to the death.

By 1917, however, the infantry of the guards had been used up several times over. Those stationed at Petrograd belonged to the reserve battalions and were either new recruits or wounded veterans, 'very reluctant to be returned to duty'.[51] Their officers were for the most part 'raw youths', recent products of the cadet schools, while some of the soldiers were of a type – educated townsmen – whom care had been taken to exclude in times of peace.[52] One of them, Fedor Linde, recorded his reaction to the first attempts at repression of the demonstrations near the Tauride Palace. 'I saw a young girl trying to evade the galloping horse of a Cossack officer. She was too slow. A severe blow on the head brought her down under the horse's feet. She screamed. It was her inhuman, penetrating scream that caused something in me to snap. [I] cried out wildly: "Fiends! Fiends! Long live the revolution. To arms! To arms! They are killing innocent people, our brothers and sisters!"' Linde, a sergeant of the Finland Guards, was billeted in the barracks of the Preobrazhensky who, though not knowing him, followed his call, took to the streets, and began to battle with gendarmes, Cossacks, officers and such troops – the Ismailovsky and Rifle Guards held firm – as remained loyal.[53]

The main outbreak of violent demonstrations was on 27 February. By 28 February strikers and the whole of the Petrograd garrison had joined forces and revolution was in full swing. Tsar Nicholas, isolated at headquarters at Mogilev, preserved a characteristic unconcern. He seems to have believed, like Louis XVI in July 1789, that his throne was threatened by nothing more than a rebellion from below. He did not grasp that the army of the capital, the chief prop of his authority, was, like the *Gardes françaises* in Paris in 1789, in revolt against his rule and that the political class was following its lead. Russia's parliament, the Duma, was discussing its mandate in the Tauride Palace, while Soviets, committees of the common people formed spontaneously not only in factories and workshops but in military units also, were meeting, sometimes in almost permanent session, passing resolutions and appointing representatives to supervise or even replace those in established authority. In Petrograd, the chief Soviet had nominated an executive committee, the Ispolkom, which was acting as the representative body of all political parties, including the Marxist Mensheviks and Bolsheviks as well as moderates, while on 27 February the Duma had formed a Provisional Committee which anticipated the creation of a new government. At the front, the officers of the General Staff recognised the force of irresistible events. A proposal to despatch a punitive expedition to Petrograd under the command of General Ivanov was cancelled by the Tsar himself when he conferred with his military advisers at Pskov, en route to his country palace of Tsarskoe Selo, on 1 March. There he also conceded permission for the Duma to form a cabinet. There, finally, on the afternoon of 2 March, he agreed to abdicate. The decisive influence upon him during those two days had been the advice of his Chief of Staff, Alexeyev, who on 1 March had cabled him in the following terms:

> A revolution in Russia . . . will mean a disgraceful termination of the war . . . The army is most intimately connected with the life of the rear. It may be confidently stated that disorders in the rear will produce the same result among the armed forces. It is impossible to ask the army calmly to wage war while a revolution is in progress in the rear. The youthful makeup of the present army and its officer staff, among whom a very high proportion consists of reservists and commissioned university students, gives no grounds for assuming that the army will not react to events occurring in Russia.[54]

The Tsar's abdication left Russia without a head of state, since the succession was refused by his nominee, the Grand Duke Michael, while the Duma would not accept that of the Tsarevitch. The revolution also shortly left Russia without the apparatus of government, since by an agreement signed between the Duma cabinet and the Ispolkom of the Petrograd Soviet, on 3 March, all provincial governors, the agents of administrative power, were dismissed and the police and gendarmerie, the instruments of their authority, disbanded. All that was left in place outside the capital were the district councils, the *zemstva*, boards of local worthies without the experience or means to carry out the orders of the Provisional Government. Its orders were, in any case, subject to the veto of the Ispolkom, which arrogated to itself responsibility for military, diplomatic and most economic affairs, leaving the government to do little more than pass legislation guaranteeing rights and liberties to the population.[55]

Yet the two bodies at least agreed on one thing: that the war must be fought. They did so from different motives, the Provisional Government for broadly nationalist reasons, the Ispolkom, and the Soviets it represented, to defend the revolution. While they continued to denounce the war as 'imperialist' and 'monstrous', the Soviets nevertheless feared that defeat by Germany would bring counter-revolution. Thus their 'Appeal to the Peoples of the World' of 15 March, called on them to join Russia in action for 'peace' against their ruling classes, but at the same time they were urging the army, through the Soviets of soldiers, to continue the struggle against 'the bayonets of conquerors' and 'foreign military might'.[56]

The soldiers, with a popular revolution to defend, rediscovered an enthusiasm for the war they seemed to have lost altogether in the winter of 1916. 'In the first weeks of the [February Revolution], the soldiers massed in Petrograd not only would not listen to talk of peace, but would not allow it to be uttered'; the petitions of soldiers to the Provisional Government and Petrograd Soviet indicated that they 'were likely to treat proponents of immediate peace as supporters of the Kaiser'.[57] The only supporters of immediate peace among all the socialist groups represented on the Ispolkom, the Bolsheviks, were careful not to demand it and, with all their leaders – Trotsky, Bukharin and Lenin – currently in exile, were in no position to do so.

A renewed war effort needed leadership of its own, however, and neither the Ispolkom nor the original Provisional Government was headed by figures of inspiration. The Ispolkom's members were socialist intellectuals, the Prime Minister, Prince Lvov, a benevolent populist. The socialists, obsessed with abstract political ideas, had no understanding of practicalities, nor did they wish for any. Lvov had a high-minded but hopelessly unrealistic belief in the capacity of 'the people' to settle the direction of their own future. The Bolsheviks, who knew what they wanted, were excluded from influence by the people's reborn bellicosity. In the circumstances it was to be expected that leadership should pass to a man of dynamism. He appeared in the person of Alexander Kerensky, whose unsocialist instinct for power but impeccable socialist credentials allowed him to combine member-ship of the Ispolkom with ministerial office, and to enjoy the strong support of ordinary members of the Soviet. First appointed Minister of Justice, he became Minister of War, in May (April under the Julian calendar, which the Provisional Government had dropped), and at once set about a purge of the high command, which he regarded as defeatist. Brusilov, the army's most successful commander, became Chief of Staff, while Kerensky's own commissars were sent to the front with the mission of encouraging an offensive spirit among the common soldiers.

Those in the Petrograd garrison may have been adamant for war in the immediate aftermath of the February Revolution. They petitioned, and sometimes demonstrated – 'War for Freedom until Victory' – safe in the knowledge that they would not be called upon to risk their lives; the seventh of the eight points of the Ispolkom's notorious Order No. 1, abolishing governorship and police, stipulated that 'military units that had participated in the Revolution . . . would not be sent to the front'. Troops at the front, though they treated Kerensky as a popular idol on his tours of inspection, proved less enthusiastic for what has come to be called the 'Kerensky offensive', of June 1917, launched to bring about the defeat of 'foreign military might' for which there was so much verbal enthusiasm in the rear. General Dragomirov, commanding the Fifth Army, reported the warning signs: 'in reserve, regiments declare their readiness to fight on to full victory, but then baulk at the demand to go into the trenches'.[58] On 18 June, nevertheless, Kerensky's offensive opened, after a two-day preparatory bombardment, against the Austrians in the south, directed once again against Lemberg, pivot of the fighting in 1914–15, and target of Brusilov's offensive the previous summer; subsidiary offensives were launched in the centre and the north. For two days the attack went well and several miles of ground were gained. Then the leading units, feeling they had done their bit, refused to persist, while those behind refused to take their place. Desertion set in, and worse. Fugitives from the front, in thousands, looted and raped in the rear. When the Germans, who were forewarned, counter-attacked with divisions already brought from the west, they and the Austrians simply recovered the ground lost and captured more themselves, driving the Russians back to the line of the River Zbrucz on the Romanian border. The Romanians, who attempted to join the Russians in the offensive from their remaining enclave north of the Danube, were also defeated.

While calamity overtook the Revolution's forces at the front, the Revolution itself was coming under attack in the rear. Those who had overthrown the monarchy were not, in Russian political terms, extremists. That title belonged to the Majority (Bolshevik) wing of the Social Democrat Party whose leaders – Lenin, Bukharin – were in February either absent from Petrograd or in exile abroad. Lenin was in Zurich, Bukharin and Trotsky, the latter not yet a member of the Bolsheviks, in New York. By April, however, all had returned, Lenin through the good offices of the German government which, scenting the opportunity to undermine Russia's continuing if faltering will to war by implanting the leaders of the peace movement in its faction-ridden capital, had transported him and his entourage from Switzerland aboard the famous 'sealed train' towards Sweden. From Stockholm the party proceeded to Petrograd, where it was welcomed not only by the local Bolsheviks but also by representatives of the Ispolkom and the Petrograd Soviet. Immediately after his arrival he addressed a Bolshevik meeting where he outlined his programme: non-co-operation with the Provisional Government; nationalisation of banks and property, including land; abolition of the army in favour of a people's militia; an end to the war; and 'all power to the Soviets', which he already had plans to bring under Bolshevik control.[59]

These 'April Theses' failed to win support even from his Bolshevik followers, to whom they seemed premature, and his first effort to put them into practice justified their misgivings. When in July some of the more dissident units of the Petrograd garrison took to the streets, with Bolshevik connivance, in protest at an order to go to the front, an order designed to get them out of the capital, Kerensky was able to find enough loyal troops to put their rebellion down. The 'July Events' gave Lenin a serious fright, not least because, in the aftermath, it was revealed that he was receiving financial support from the German government. Time, nevertheless, was on his side, time measured not in the 'inevitability' of the 'second revolution' for which he was working, but in the increasingly limited willingness of the field army to remain at the front. The collapse of the Kerensky offensive had dispirited even those soldiers who resisted the increasingly easy opportunities to desert. Their lapse of will allowed the Germans in August to launch a successful offensive on the northern front which resulted in the capture of Riga, the most important harbour city on the Baltic coast. Militarily, the Riga offensive was significant because it demonstrated to the Germans the effectiveness of a new system of breakthrough tactics, designed by the artillery expert, Bruchmüller, which they were perfecting with the thought of applying it on the Western Front.[60] Politically, it was yet more significant, since it prompted a military intervention which, though designed to reinforce the authority of the Provisional Government, would shortly result in its collapse.

The 'July Events' had caused Kerensky, the government's only effective leader, to supersede Lvov as premier, while retaining the ministries of war and the navy. As Prime Minister, he also decided to replace Brusilov, though he had appointed him Commander-in-Chief, with an outspoken proponent of the anti-German war effort, General

Lavr Kornilov. Kornilov was a man of the people, the son of Siberian Cossacks. For that reason he believed he would be followed, even by war-weary soldiers, in a personal campaign first against the defeatist Bolsheviks, then against his country's enemies. On 25 August he ordered reliable troops to occupy Petrograd, with further orders to disperse the Soviet and disarm the regiments there should the Bolsheviks seek to take power, as seemed to be and was in fact their intention. Even before the fall of Riga, he had confronted Kerensky with demands for a programme of reform: an end to the Soldiers' Soviets, the disbanding of politicised regiments.[61] Militarily, his programme was entirely sensible. It was the only basis for continuing the war and for saving a government which, in a sea of defeatism, supported that policy. Politically however, Kornilov's programme confronted Kerensky with a challenge to his authority, since its institution would inevitably entail conflict with the Soviets, the war-shy Petrograd garrison and the Bolsheviks, with all of whom the Provisional Government was living in uneasy equilibrium. As Kornilov's popularity grew among moderates, Kerensky's authority dwindled, until a challenge became unavoidable. Kerensky could not throw in his lot with Kornilov, since he correctly doubted whether the general commanded sufficient force to do down the extremists. Equally, he could not turn to the extremists, since to do so would be to subordinate the Provisional Government to their power, which the most extreme among them, the Bolsheviks, would then be certain to wrest into their own hands. He could only await events. Should Kornilov succeed, the Provisional Government would survive. Should he fail, Kerensky could resume the political struggle in Petrograd in the hope of playing the factions off against each other. In the event, Kornilov was manoeuvred by others into staging a coup he had not planned, which failed through the refusal of his soldiers to join in, and so was removed from command.

His fall ended any chance of sustaining the fiction that Russia was still fighting a war. The Provisional Government lost what remained of its authority in the aftermath, since Kerensky's dismissal of Kornilov lost him what support he retained among moderates and senior officers without winning him any from the forces of the left. The Bolsheviks were, indeed, now determined to mount the 'second revolution' and Lenin, who had now established his absolute leadership over the party, was looking only for a pretext. It was given him by the Germans who, during September, enlarged their success at Riga by gaining positions in the northern Baltic from which they could directly threaten Petrograd. The Provisional Government reacted by proposing to transfer the capital to Moscow.[62] The Bolsheviks, who represented the proposal as a counter-revolutionary move to consign the seat of the people's power to the Kaiser, won wide support for the creation of a defence committee with authority to defend Petrograd by every means. As they now controlled their own disciplined force of Red Guards and could count on their own ability to manipulate the sentiments of the Petrograd garrison to their advantage, it merely remained to choose a date for a coup. Kerensky, aware that a coup was in the offing, took half-hearted measures to defend government offices during 24 October. His orders, which were ineffectively implemented by officers who no longer gave him their trust, tipped Lenin into decision. On the night of 24/25 October, his Red Guards seized the most important places in Petrograd – post offices, telephone exchanges, railway stations, bridges and banks – so that by next morning the Bolsheviks were in control. The Provisional Government put up a feeble resistance which was quickly overwhelmed. On 26 October Lenin announced the formation of a new government, the Council of People's Commissars, whose first acts were to proclaim the 'socialisation' of land and an appeal for peace, to begin with a three-month armistice.

The three-month armistice effectively ended Russia's part in the First World War. The army at once began to melt away, as soldiers left the front to return to what they believed would be land for the taking in their villages. The Germans and Austrians, nervous at first of dealing with revolutionaries, who were simultaneously calling for the workers of all lands to rise against the ruling classes as a means of everywhere bringing the war to a close, were slow to react to Lenin's Peace Decree of 26 October. When world revolution – to the Bolsheviks' surprise – failed to erupt and the appeal to peace was repeated by them on 15 November, the Germans decided to respond. On 3 December, their delegation, and those of Austria, Turkey and Bulgaria, met the Soviet representatives at Brest-Litovsk, the Polish fortress town on the River Bug lost by the Russians in 1915. Discussions, frequently adjourned, dragged on into 1918. The three-month armistice, tacitly accepted by the Germans, was rapidly running out, but the Bolsheviks, with no hand to play, continued to resist the enemy's terms, which were for the separation of Poland from Russia and wide annexations of territory further east. Lenin protracted the negotiations, in part because he thought that, if peace were signed, Germany and its enemies would combine against the Soviet government in order to put down the general revolution he continued to believe was about to break out in Western Europe.[63] In the end, the Germans lost patience and announced that they would terminate the armistice unless their terms were accepted and take as much of Russia as they wanted. On 17 February, their invasion began. Within a week they had advanced 150 miles, meeting no resistance, and seemed prepared to go further. Panic-struck, the Soviet government ordered its delegation to Brest-Litovsk to sign at Germany's dictation. The resulting treaty ceded to the enemy 750,000 square kilometres, an area three times the size of Germany and containing a quarter of Russia's population and industrial resources and a third of its agricultural land.

The Eastern Front, 1917–18

Germany had already transferred the best of its eastern army to the Western Front, in preparation for what it planned to be the war-winning offensives against the French and British, leaving only skeleton formations to occupy and exploit its new empire in the Ukraine. The Russian army had disappeared, its soldiers, in Lenin's memorable phrase, having 'voted for peace with their feet'. Hundreds of thousands had walked away from the war even before the October Revolution, into enemy captivity; 'in 1915, while retreating from Galicia, about a million Russian soldiers became prisoners-of-war, three-quarters of them freely'.[64] By the end of 1917 nearly four million Russians were in German or Austrian hands, so that the old imperial army's prisoner losses eventually exceeded battlefield casualties by three to one; the most recent estimate of Russian battlefield deaths is 1.3 million, or about the same as the French, whose loss of prisoners to the Germans was trifling.[65] The Russian peasant soldier simply lacked the attitude that bound his German, French and British equivalent to comrades, unit and national cause. He 'found the psychology of professional soldiers unfathomable, [regarding his] new duty as temporary and pointless'.[66] Defeat rapidly brought demoralisation, so that even soldiers decorated for bravery found little shame in giving themselves up to an enemy who at least promised food and shelter. It is greatly to the credit of Russia's enemies in the First World War that they showed a duty of care to their myriads of prisoners not felt in the Second, when three of the five million Soviet soldiers captured on the battlefield died of starvation, disease and mistreatment. Perhaps because captivity did not threaten hardship, the Russian army had begun to disintegrate even before the collapse at the rear. Once the Bolsheviks began to sue for peace, disintegration became terminal.

By the spring of 1918, after the German occupation of the Ukraine, the revolutionary government found that it lacked the force to defend the power it had nominally seized. The only disciplined unit at its disposal was a band of Latvian volunteers, more committed to the cause of Latvia's national independence than Bolshevik ideology. The peasant mass had returned to the land, leaving in uniform only a residue of the rootless, the lawless and the orphaned, ready to follow the flag of any leadership which could provide food and strong drink. Some of those leaders were ex-Tsarist officers, who, as opponents of Bolshevism, would raise 'White' armies, others Commissars who wanted a Red Army, but in either case desperate to find men, weapons to arm them, money to pay them. The Russian civil war was about to begin.

ROUT ON THE ITALIAN FRONT

In Italy, too, there was to be a breaking of armies in 1917, to follow that of the French and the Russian, though as the result of a great defeat, rather than a failed offensive or a social revolution. In October, at Caporetto, a small frontier town on the River Isonzo, the Germans and their Austrian allies would achieve a dramatic breakthrough of the positions the Italians had so painfully won in the thirty preceding months and dash the fragments of their army down into the plains.

The Caporetto disaster lost the Italian army its reputation, which it failed to regain during the Second World War. Gibes at the military qualities of the Italians have been commonly and cheaply made ever since. Unfairly; the Italians of the Renaissance city states had been notable soldiers, the Venetians an imperial people whose galleys and fortresses had defied the Ottoman Turks for 300 years. The Kingdom of Savoy had fought doughtily for national independence and unification against Habsburg power and battled as equals beside the French and British in the Crimea. It was only after unification that Italy's military troubles began. Then, on to the hardy stem of the army of Savoy, recruited among the mountaineers of the Italian Alps and the industrious peasants and townspeople of the northern plains, were grafted the

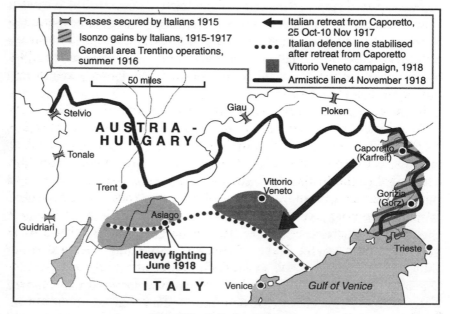

The War in Italy, 1915–18

remnants of the papal and Bourbon armies of the south, toy armies without loyalty to their dynastic rulers or any sense of military purpose. 'Dress them in red or blue or green', the indolent King 'Bomba' of Naples had once observed to his military counsellors during a debate on new uniforms, 'they'll run away just the same.' Bomba was a realist. He knew that, in a state where the landowners who should have supplied officers were principally concerned to wring the last ounce of rent or labour from the poor or landless peasants who supplied the rank and file, there could be no willingness to lay down life.

The professionals of the army of Savoy, an army notable for its skills in artillery practice and fortress engineering, skills the Italians of the Renaissance had largely invented, did their best to transform the old and new elements into a national force, and with high intelligence; one of the distinctive features of the Savoyard officer corps was that, alone among those of Europe, it offered Jews a career open to talents. The disparity in quality between the recruits of north and south largely defeated their efforts. It is now disputed that the southerners made notably worse soldiers than northerners during the war.[67] Some southern units certainly fought well. Nevertheless, it seems indisputable that, while the better-educated and more skilled recruits from the northern industrial cities went to the artillery and engineers, the infantry was disproportionately filled from the agricultural south. 'The north-south division within the Kingdom was thus perpetuated by these wartime developments', with the poor southerners bearing an unfair share of the human cost of a war which had been initiated by the kingdom's northern dynasty and was directed, harshly and inflexibly, by northern generals.[68]

In the circumstances it was highly creditable that the Italian army had persisted in eleven costly and fruitless assaults on Austria's mountain borderland. The incidence of an offensive every three months, between May 1915 and August 1917, was higher than that demanded of the British or French armies on the Western Front and the contingencies more wearing; shellfire in the rocky terrain caused 70 per cent more casualties per rounds expended than on the soft ground in France and Belgium.[69] Italian discipline was harsher also. It may have been, as the Italian Commander-in-Chief, General Luigi Cadorna believed, that the social frailty of his army required punishments for infractions of duty of a severity not known in the German army or the BEF: summary execution and the choosing of victims by lot.[70] Nevertheless, it is unlikely that the British or Germans would

371

THE FIRST WORLD WAR

have stood for such 'normal persuasion' and it is a tribute to Italy's sorely tried and dumbly uncomplaining peasant infantrymen that they did.[71]

All armies, however, have a breaking point. It may come when those in the fighting units are brought to calculate, accurately or not, that the odds of survival have passed the dividing line between possibility and probability, between the random chance of death and its apparently statistical likelihood. That dividing line had been crossed for the French at the beginning of 1917, when the number of deaths suffered already equalled that of the infantry in the front-line divisions: the million and more French deaths exceeded the infantry strength of the army's 135 divisions. A survivor might therefore compute that chance – the 'stochastic' factor – had turned against him and that, in the British Tommy's phrase, his 'number was up'. By the autumn of 1917 the Italian army, with sixty-five infantry divisions, or about 600,000 infantrymen in fighting units, had suffered most of the 571,000 deaths to be incurred during the war, and the sense of 'one's number being up' may have become collective. 'Incredibly, morale still remained high on the eve of the Eleventh Battle of the Isonzo fought on the Bainsizza Plateau from 19 August to 12 September. The basic reason for this was rather ominous; everyone expected this to be the 1st, decisive battle of the war'.[72] The outcome, however, was deeply dispiriting. 'The army suffered 100,000 losses and the gains left the Italian front line more vulnerable than before. Fifty-one divisions . . . had been thrown into this massive struggle but by the second week of September the end of the war seemed as far away as ever.'

Not to the Austrians. Just as, in the spring of 1915, the Russian successes in Galicia that had led to the fall of Przemysl and Lemberg caused Austria to ask the Germans for help, now the weight of the Italian attack in the Eleventh Battle prompted a similar appeal. On 25 August, the Emperor Karl wrote to the Kaiser in the following terms: 'The experience we have acquired in the eleventh battle has led me to believe that we should fare far worse in a twelfth. My commanders and brave troops have decided that such an unfortunate situation might be anticipated by an offensive. We have not the necessary means as regards troops.' His request was for Germans to replace Austrians on the Eastern Front, so that the divisions thus released could be brought to the Isonzo. Eventually, however, he was persuaded that German substitutes would be better employed against the Italians directly, a judgement Ludendorff endorsed, and, after a scheme to mount a

The War in Africa

Von Lettow-Vorbeck.

Below: SMS *Seeadler* leaving
Dar-es-Salaam for Germany, 1914;
the band of the *Schutztruppen* in the
foreground.

Left: The Grand Fleet in the North Sea, 4th Battle Squadron (*Iron Duke*, *Royal Oak*, *Superb*, *Canada*) in the foreground.

Below: The torpedo room of a U–boat.

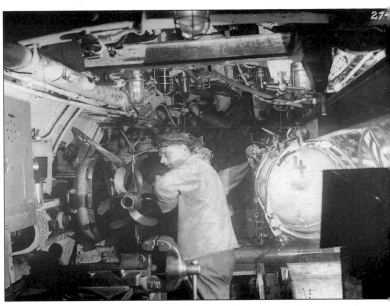

Left: SMS *Blücher* sinking at the Battle of Dogger Bank, 24 January 1915.

Right: American armed merchant ship *Covington*, sinking off Brest, 2 July 1918, after torpedoing by U–86.

Left: The battlecruiser *Invincible*, broken in half by internal explosion, Battle of Jutland, May 1916; H.M. Destroyer *Badger* approaching to pick up the six survivors.

The War in the Air

Right: Fokker triplanes; Richthofen, Germany's leading ace, scored many of his victories in this machine.

Below: A Sopwith Camel, Noyelles-sur-l'Escaut, 8 October 1918; a highly manoeuvrable fighter, its rotary engine made it difficult to handle on take-off and landing.

A squadron equipped with the SE 5a, the most successful British fighter of the final period of air fighting.

A French soldier welcomed in the liberated zone.

Below: A Hessian regiment marching back across the Rhine at Coblenz, November 1918, displaying the Grand Ducal instead of Imperial colours.

A burial party at Windmill Cemetery, Monchy-le-Preux, begun for soldiers killed in the Battle of Arras, April 1917.

Tyne Cot Cemetery, Passchendaele, today. The largest of the Commonwealth war cemeteries, it contains the bodies of 12,000 soldiers killed in the Third Battle of Ypres and commemorates 35,000 whose bodies were not found.

diversionary offensive from the Tirol had been considered and rejected, it was decided to commit seven German divisions, formed with six Austrian into a new Fourteenth Army, in a direct counter-offensive on the Isonzo. The German divisions were specially selected. They included the 117th, which had had a long spell of mountain warfare experience in the Carpathians, the 200th, which included ski troops, and the illustrious *Alpenkorps,* a Bavarian mountain division, in one of whose units, the Württemberg Mountain Battalion, the young Erwin Rommel was serving as a company commander.[73]

Altogether the Austro-German force assembled for the 'twelfth battle' numbered thirty-five divisions against the Italians' thirty-four, with 2,430 guns against 2,485. That was certainly not enough to achieve a breakthrough or even, by conventional reckoning, to mount an offensive at all. Cadorna, the Italian commander, had, however, as a result of his repetitive attacks, both come to disregard the eventuality of an enemy counter-measure and, at the same time, created conditions that promised to facilitate an enemy success. By his capture of much of the valley of the Isonzo, a mountain river running through a deep-cut valley, he had unwittingly created a trap in his own rear. By pushing across the river, but not far enough, he had left two bridgeheads in the enemy's hands, which offered them the opportunity to drive down and up the valley from north and south and join hands behind the whole of the Italian Second Army.

Such was the Austro-German plan. Cadorna had done much to assist its realisation, by keeping the front line full of troops, where they were most likely to be cut off, and positioning his reserves far too near the rear, whence they would have difficulty arriving at the front in the event of a crisis.[74] The intermediate lines were scarcely manned at all; all this, despite clear signs during October that an enemy operation was pending. Cadorna, however, could not clearly identify where it would fall and, because his staff lived in fear of his domineering personality, he received no advice that more prudent dispositions of his forces should be made on the most vulnerable sector. The only subordinate to differ from his view that the ground gained in the Eleventh Battle must be held with every man available – General Capello, a corps commander in Second Army – actually wanted to return to the offensive.

Objectively, there was no question of returning to the offensive. The enemy was already too strongly reinforced. Moving under cover of darkness over several nights, in the deep valleys beyond the Isonzo, the German and Austrian attack divisions had no difficulty in evading detection by Italian air patrols and in arriving in their jump-off positions on the evening of 23 October.[75] Next morning the bombardment opened early, first with gas against the Italian artillery positions – Hugh Dalton, a future British Chancellor of the Exchequer, then a young artillery officer whose battery was on loan to the Italian front, recorded that Italian gas masks were ineffective – later switching to high explosive. By seven o'clock the Italian trenches were devastated and the assault began.

The point divisions were the Austrian 22nd, locally recruited in Slovenia, followed by the 8th 'Edelweiss' Division, largely composed of the élite Tirol *Kaiserjäger*. Attacking from Flitsch downstream, they were to follow the valley of the Isonzo towards Caporetto (called Karfreit by the Austrians), to meet the other point division, the *Alpenkorps,* attacking upstream from Tolmino (Tolmein). In the vanguard of the *Alpenkorps* marched the Bavarian *Leibregiment* (Body Guards), supported by the Württemburg Mountain Battalion. Rommel, commanding a group of the Würrtemberg Mountain Battalion's companies, was no more content as a lieutenant with a supporting role than he would be a panzer general in the 1940 blitzkrieg. He soon found himself separated from the Body Guards and out in front. There was little sign of the enemy and no resistance. 'I then had to decide whether I should roll up the hostile position or break through in the direction of the Hevnik peak [a key height in the Italian rear]. I chose the latter. The elimination of the Italian positions followed once we had possession of the peak. The further we penetrated into the hostile positions, the less prepared were the garrisons for our arrival, and the easier the fighting. I did not worry about contact right and left.'[76] Rommel was, in fact, practising 'infiltration' tactics, a manoeuvre with infantry that, in the Second World war, he would repeat with tanks, driving deep, narrow corridors into the lines of the enemy, with the object of collapsing both their means and will to resist by a combination of material and psychological shock.

What Rommel was achieving on his tiny but critical sector was being repeated elsewhere. The Germans and Austrians, penetrating the steep defile of the Isonzo valley, by-passing Italian strongpoints and striking for the high ground, were biting out an enormous gap in the Italian front, fifteen miles wide, leaving behind them four Italian divisions isolated and surrounded. Moreover, the deeper the Austro-

German Fourteenth Army advanced, the more they threatened the flanks of the larger concentrations of Italian troops to north and south, menacing the whole of Cadorna's eastern front with the collapse of its rear area. The rational alarm of the high command was reinforced by panic in the ranks. Rumour of enemy breakthrough undermined the will of the common soldiers to resist, just as it would twenty-three years later when Rommel's tanks would romp unchecked through the demoralised French army behind the Meuse. Lieutenant Rommel began to take prisoners in increasing numbers, first a few dozen, then hundreds, eventually a whole regiment 1,500 strong who, after hesitating to surrender to a single officer waving a white handkerchief as a signal of what he wanted – Rommel, always the individualist, had gone forward alone – suddenly threw down their arms, rushed forward to raise him to their shoulders and burst into shouts of *'Evviva Germania'*.[77]

The capitulation of this regiment, the 1st of the Salerno Brigade, came on the third day of the Caporetto battle. By then the whole Italian front on the Isonzo had fallen into collapse, the army was no longer obeying orders or even making a show of attempting to do so and hundreds of thousands of soldiers were streaming down from the mountains to the plains. There was worse; 'reserves moving up prepared to do their duty were greeted with yells of "Blacklegs". [Austrian] troops encountered Italian units in formed bodies marching into captivity, calling out *"Evviva la Austria"*.'[78] On 26 October Cadorna, a man beset by nightmare, realised that a general retreat to the Tagliamento, the next large river west of the Isonzo, was inevitable. The enemy, rampaging forward, did not allow him to rest there. Though the Italians blew the bridges behind them, their pursuers got across and by 3 November had pressed them back to the River Piave, a major obstacle not to be crossed except by a deliberate assault of which the exultant victors, who had outrun their lines of supply, were not capable. Nevertheless, their achievement had been extraordinary. In eleven days they had advanced eighty miles, to within striking distance of Venice, forced the retreat of the Italians from the whole length of their mountain frontier between the Tirol and its hinge on the sea, and captured 275,000 prisoners; Italian battle casualties amounted to the comparatively small total, by First World War standards, of 10,000 dead.

Cadorna did his best to increase the number, by a ruthless and characteristic institution of the summary execution of stragglers, an episode unforgettably described by Ernest Hemingway, an ambulance volunteer with the Italians, in *A Farewell to Arms;* he was not actually present but that does not detract from the veracity of his account, one of the greatest literary evocations of military disaster. Cadorna's judicial savagery could not halt the rout nor did it save his neck. He had never trusted his fellow-countrymen; they, in return, had never found it in their hearts to like him or even to respect him, unless out of fear. When, in the aftermath of Caporetto, he attempted to cast responsibility for the army's collapse on to defeatism in the rear – there had been an outbreak of strikes in August and sporadic effusions of enthusiasm for 'Lenin' and 'revolution' – he lost the government's support. On 3 November, echoing sentiments expressed in France after the Nivelle offensive, he referred to the Caporetto retreat as 'a kind of military strike'. Five days later he had been removed from command, to be replaced by General Armando Diaz who, like Pétain after the Nivelle catastrophe, would offer the common soldier a more indulgent regime of leave and comforts as an inducement to sustain the fight.[79]

In practice, the Italian army, like the French, would not resume the offensive until the following year. When it did so, it would be in the company of a far stronger foreign contingent, largely British, than any offered as a buttress to the French in 1918. Caporetto, one of the few clear-cut victories of the First World War, was a triumph for the Germans, a vindication of the military qualities of their faltering Austrian allies, and a major defeat for the Allies at the end of a year which had brought disabling setbacks to their cause. If it had one positive effect, it was to force Britain and France to recognise that their haphazard system of directing their war effort, through informal liaison and intermittently convened conferences, could not continue if the war was to be brought to a conclusion in their favour. On 5 November, an inter-Allied meeting was convened at the Italian city of Rapallo, at which it was decided to establish a permanent Supreme War Council, with responsibility to co-ordinate the Allies' strategy, to sit at Versailles under the aegis of the British, French and Italian prime ministers and the President of the United States.

AMERICA, SUBMARINES AND PASSCHENDAELE

President Woodrow Wilson had said America was 'too proud to fight', a sentiment that mirrored his own distaste for war. High-minded, idealistic, academic, he had formed the belief that plain dealing between nations in open diplomacy was the secret of averting and evading conflict. During 1916 he had, through his emissary, Colonel Edward House, made a determined effort to bring the combatants to negotiation on terms he regarded as fair to all and he had been dispirited by its failure. He was not, however, unrealistic about the place of force in international affairs nor was he unwilling to use force if necessary. In 1915 he had brought Germany's campaign of 'unrestricted' submarine warfare to a close by a threat to use American naval power to preserve the freedom of the seas and he authorised Colonel House to promise to the Allies an American military intervention if they would accept his conditions for a peace conference and the Germans would not. As late as the spring of 1917, nevertheless, he had no intention of bringing his country to join the war, nor was there enthusiasm for entry among his fellow citizens. Among the large proportion of German descent were activists who, through the German-American Bund, campaigned against it.

Two events changed America's outlook. The first was a clumsy German approach to Mexico, proposing an alliance, baited with the offer to return Texas, Arizona and New Mexico, if America went to war against Germany; this 'Zimmermann telegram' was transmitted to the American government by British naval intelligence – though the US State Department had intercepted it independently – and caused outrage when it was published on 1 March 1917. The second was Germany's decision to resume the unrestricted U-boat campaign: sinking merchant shipping without warning in international waters.[80] A return to the policy of 1915 had been debated in Germany since August 1916. The breach of maritime law, and its possible repercussions, was recognised. The prevailing code required commerce raiders, whether surface or submarine, to stop merchant ships, allow the crew to take to the boats, provide them with food and water and assist their passage to the nearest landfall before destroying their vessel. The unrestricted policy allowed U-boat captains to sink by gunfire or torpedo at will. The proponent of the policy was Admiral Henning von Holtzendorff, chief of the German naval staff, whose argument was that only through an all-out attack on British maritime supply could the war be brought to a favourable conclusion before blockade by sea and attrition on land had exhausted Germany's capacity to continue the war. He demonstrated by statistical calculation that a rate of sinking of 600,000 tons of Allied, but largely British, shipping a month would, within five months, bring Britain to the brink of starvation, meanwhile also depriving France and Italy of the supply of British coal essential to the working of their economies. A similar argument was to be used by the German navy during the Second World War, when it instituted an unrestricted sinking policy from the start. In the spring of 1917, the German navy, with about a hundred submarines available for operations in the North Sea, Atlantic, Baltic and Mediterranean, was ordered to open unrestricted attack against the twenty million tons of British shipping, out of a total of thirty million worldwide, on which the British homeland depended for survival.[81]

Hindenburg and Ludendorff, though opposed by the Chancellor, Bethmann Hollweg, responded enthusiastically to Holtzendorff's memorandum of 22 December 1916, urging the institution of unrestricted sinkings, and it was decided to take the risk – 'fear of a break' (with the United States), Holtzendorff had argued, 'must not hinder us from using this weapon that promises success' – at an imperial conference on 9 January 1917.[82] The campaign, in the seas around the British Isles, on the west coast of France and in the Mediterranean, began on 1 February. The political effect in the United States was felt immediately and the severity of American reaction vastly exceeded German expectation. On 26 February, President Wilson asked Congress for permission to arm American merchant ships, the same day that two American women were drowned in the sinking of the Cunard liner *Laconia* by a German submarine. On 15 March German submarines made direct attacks on American merchant ships, sinking three. That was a direct challenge to the dignity of the United States as a sovereign power, one which Wilson reluctantly decided he could not ignore. On 2 April, before a special session of Congress, he reviewed the development of the German submarine campaign, declared it to be a 'war against all nations' and asked Congress 'to accept the status of a belligerent which has thus been thrust upon it'. Four days later Congress resolved that war against Germany should be formally declared. Declarations against Austria-Hungary, Turkey and Bulgaria followed, selective military conscription was enacted (18 May 1917) and the armed forces of the United States began at once to prepare for operations in Europe.

The mobilisation of the United States Navy, with the second largest fleet of modern battleships in the world after Britain's, immediately altered the balance of naval power in the Atlantic and North Sea unchallengeably in the Allies' favour; after December 1917, when five American Dreadnoughts joined the Grand Fleet, the High Seas Fleet, outnumbered by thirty-five to fifteen, could not hope to stand against it in battle.[83] The United States Army, by contrast, was in April 1917 only 108,000 strong and in no condition to take the field; the federalisation of the National Guard, of 130,000 part-time soldiers, scarcely added to its effectiveness. The best American units belonged to the Marine Corps, but numbered only 15,000. Nevertheless, it was decided to form an expeditionary force of one division and two Marine brigades and send it to France immediately. Meanwhile, conscription would produce a first contingent of a million recruits, with another million to follow. It was expected that two million men would arrive in France during 1918.

The spectre of America's gathering millions lent even greater urgency to Germany's attempt to starve out its European enemies by U-boat action. The first months of unrestricted sinkings suggested that it might succeed. During 1915 the U-boats had sunk 227 British ships (855,721 gross tons), the majority in the first unrestricted campaign. During the first half of 1916 they sank 610,000 tons of shipping of all flags, but sinkings then declined sharply when, after May 1916, the German Admiralty reverted to stricter observance of maritime law. By the beginning of 1917, when an accelerated building programme had raised the total of U-boats to 148, sinkings rose proportionately, to 195 ships (328,391 tons).[84] From February, when unrestricted sinkings began, the totals rose month by month to terrifying levels: 520,412 tons in February, 564,497 tons in March and 860,334 tons in April. Holtzendorff's target of the 600,000 tons of monthly sinkings necessary to win the war had been exceeded, threatened to increase and bring Allied defeat.

The Admiralty could see no means to avert disaster. Arming merchant ships was pointless when U-boats attacked submerged with torpedoes. Mining the exits from the U-boat bases was ineffective, since British mines were unreliable and the bases too many and too inaccessible to be stopped up. Hunting U-boats, though tried, was like looking for a needle in a haystack, even on the shipping routes. Trapping U-boats with apparently harmless decoys not worth a torpedo, the celebrated 'Q' ships disguised as small merchantmen but heavily armed, worked on odd occasions until the German captains got canny. Diversion of shipping away from identified danger areas reduced losses only until the U-boats tried elsewhere. Meanwhile the haemorrhage continued apparently unquenchably. U-boat losses were negligible: ten in October to December 1916, only nine in February–April 1917, two of which were to German mines. The Allies' only anti-submarine weapon, the depth charge, was useless unless U-boats could be found, and the hydrophone, the only detection device, could not find U-boats beyond a few hundred yards.

There was a solution available – convoy – but the Admiralty resisted it. Sailing ships in groups, even under escort, seemed merely to offer a larger group of targets. As the Admiralty's Operational Division wrote in January 1917: 'it is evident that the larger the number of ships forming the convoy, the greater is the chance of a submarine being able to attack successfully'. The paper concluded by arguing that sailing 'independently' was the safer procedure.[85] The analysis was, of course, wrong. In the spaces of the sea, a group of ships is little more conspicuous than a single ship, and, if not found by a U-boat, all would escape attack. Single ships sailing in succession, by contrast, presented the U-boat with a higher chance of making a sighting and so a sinking. Moreover, the Admiralty had been deluded by another mathematical misperception. In attempting to estimate the number of escorts it would have to find if it adopted convoy, it counted all sailings, which amounted to 2,500 weekly from British ports, and concluded it had insufficient warships. It was only under closer analysis by the new Minister for Shipping, Norman Leslie, and a junior naval officer, Commander R.G.A. Henderson, that a more manageable picture was revealed. The number of weekly arrivals of ocean-going merchant ships, those that actually sustained the war, was only 120–140 a week, and for those sufficient escorts could easily be found.[86]

By 27 April the senior admirals were convinced of the need to adopt convoying – apparently not at Lloyd George's prompting, as is usually stated – and on 28 April the first convoy was sailed. It reached Britain without loss on 10 May. Thenceforward convoy was progressively introduced for all oceanic sailings and losses began to decline. Even in August they were still running at 511,730 tons, and they stood at 399,110 as late as December. Not until the second quarter of 1918 would they drop below 300,000 tons monthly, by which time nearly four million of the world's thirty million tons of shipping would have been sunk in a little over a year. It was convoy that had reversed the fatal trend; but, as in the second U-boat war of 1939–43, it was not any one measure that brought about the U-boat's defeat. Important subsidiary measures included the systematic laying of mine barriers (70,000 in the Northern Barrier between Scotland and Norway), the dedication of large numbers of aircraft and airships to anti-submarine patrols in narrow waters (685 aircraft, 103 airships) and the multi-plication of escorts (195 in April 1918).[87]

An important indirect effect of convoy was to draw the U-boats into coastal waters, to hunt unescorted small vessels, where air patrol, hydrophone and depth charge could more easily find them, and minefields claim victims. Of the 178 U-boats lost during the war, out of 390 built, 41 were mined, only 30 depth-charged. Direct attack on U-boat bases, as on the famous Zeebrugge raid of 23 April 1918, interrupted submarine operations not at all. Nevertheless, however uncertain and halting the anti-submarine campaign, Holtzendorff's war-winning total of sinkings was never achieved. If the British did not exactly win the U-boat war, the Germans still managed to lose it.

The unrestricted campaign nevertheless had the effect of driving Britain to undertake what would become its most notorious land campaign of the war, the Third Battle of Ypres, or Passchendaele, so-called after the village, destroyed in the course of the offensive, which became its ultimate objective. At the First Battle of Ypres in October–November 1914, the old BEF had succeeded in closing the gap between the open wing of the French army and the Flemish coast, so completing the Western Front. In the Second, in April 1915, the BEF had sustained the first gas attack of the war in the Western Front and, though surrendering critical ground in front of the city of Ypres, had held the line. In 1917, the military situation in the British army's sector was a novel one. The Germans, despite their success against the French and the Romanians, and despite the progressive enfeeblement of the Russian army, were no longer in a position, as they had been in the year of Verdun, to undertake offensive operations. Their armies were overstretched and Hindenburg and Ludendorff awaited a strategic shift of balance, perhaps to be brought by a U-boat victory, perhaps by a final Russian collapse, before they could realign their forces for a new and decisive effort. In the meantime the British, on whom Nivelle's aborted campaign had cast the burden of carrying on the war in the west, considered their position.

Douglas Haig, the hero of the First Battle, the defender of Ypres in the Second, had long nurtured plans to make the Ypres salient the starting point for a counter-offensive that would break the German line, while an amphibious attack cleared the coast, depriving the

Germans of their naval bases at Blankenberghe and Ostend, and thus also dealing, it was hoped, a deadly blow to the U-boats. Haig had first proposed the scheme on 7 January 1916, soon after he succeeded French, in command of the BEF. He reworked it for consideration at the Chantilly conference in November, only to see it set aside in favour of Nivelle's project for breakthrough on the Chemin des Dames. With that devastated, Haig's Flanders plan took on a certain inevitability. It was discussed at an Anglo-French conference held in Paris on 4–5 May, when Pétain, Nivelle's successor, gave assurances that the French would support it with up to four attacks of their own. By June the French could no longer conceal from their British allies that such attacks could not be delivered. On 7 June, Haig met Pétain at Cassel, near Ypres, to be told that 'two French Divisions had refused to go and relieve two Divisions in the front line'; the true figure was over fifty and Pétain's assurance that 'the situation in the French army was serious at the moment but is now more satisfactory' was wholly meretricious.[88] Lloyd George had, at Paris, guessed at the truth when he had challenged Pétain to deny that 'for some reason or other you won't fight'.[89] Pétain had then merely smiled and said nothing. By June, with the truth of the French mutinies no longer deniable, it was clear that the British would have to fight alone. The matter of moment was to find a justification for them doing so.

Haig was adamant that they should and believed they would win a victory, the best of all reasons for fighting a battle. Local events in June, south of the Ypres salient, lent credence to his case. There on 7 June, the day he heard from Pétain the first admission of the French army's troubles, Plumer's Second Army had mounted a long-prepared assault on Messines Ridge with complete success. Messines continues the line of the Flemish heights east of Ypres, held by the Germans since the First Battle of October 1914, southward towards the valley of the Lys, which divides the plains of Belgium from those of France. So gradual are the gradients that, to the eye of the casual visitor, no commanding ground presents itself to view. More careful observation reveals that the positions occupied by the Germans dominated those of the British all the way to the only true high ground in Flanders, Mount Kemmel and the Mont des Cats, while denying the British observation into the German rear areas between Ypres and Lille. It had long been an ambition of the British commanders of the Ypres salient to take possession of the Messines crest and during 1917 their tunnelling companies had driven forward nineteen galleries, culminating in mine chambers packed with a million pounds of explosives. Just before dawn on 7 June 1917, the mines were detonated, with a noise heard in England, and nine divisions, including the 3rd Australian, the New Zealand and, veterans of the first day of the Somme, the 16th Irish and 36th Ulster, moved forward. Nearly three weeks of bombardment, during which three and a half million shells had been fired, had preceded the attack. When the assault waves arrived on the Messines crest, permanently altered by the devastations, they found such defenders as survived unable to offer resistance and took possession of what remained of the German trenches with negligible casualties. At a blow the British had driven the enemy from the southern wing of the Ypres salient. Haig's ambition to drive in the centre and thence advance to the Flemish coast was greatly enhanced thereby.

The obstacle to a second major Western Front offensive, to follow the Somme the previous year, remained the hesitation of the Prime Minister. David Lloyd George was oppressed by the rising tide of British casualties, already a quarter of a million dead, and the paltry military return gained by the sacrifice. He looked for alternatives, in Italy against the Austrians, even against the Turks in the Middle East, policies that came to be known as 'knocking away the props' of Germany's central military position. None commended themselves and Haig's insistent demand for permission to launch a great Flanders offensive gained strength. Haig's belief in its promise was not shared by Lloyd George's principal military adviser, General Sir William Robertson, the ex-cavalry trooper whose innate intelligence and strength of character had carried him to the British army's highest position. Yet he, despite his doubts, preferred Haig's military single-mindedness to the Prime Minister's political evasions and, when required to throw his weight one way or the other, threw it behind Haig.

In June Lloyd George formed yet another inner committee of the Cabinet, in succession to the Dardanelles Committee and the War Council, to assume the higher direction of the war. The Committee on War Policy, which included Lords Curzon and Milner and the South African, Jan Smuts, first met on 11 June. Its most important sessions, however, took place on 19–21 June, when Haig outlined his plans and asked for their endorsement. Lloyd George was relentless in his interrogation and criticism. He expressed doubts all too accurate about Haig's belief in the importance of the Kerensky offensive, questioned the likelihood of capturing the U-boat ports and enquired how the offensive was to be made to succeed with a bare superiority, at best, in infantry and nothing more than equality in artillery. Haig was unshaken throughout two days of debate. Despite Lloyd George's fears about casualties, compounded by the difficulties in finding any more men from civil life to replace those lost, Haig insisted that 'it was necessary for us to go on engaging the enemy . . . and he was quite confident, he could reach the first objective', which was the crest of the Ypres ridges.[90]

This was the nub of the difference: Haig wanted to fight, Lloyd George did not. The Prime Minister could see good reasons for avoiding a battle: that it would lose many men for little material gain, that it would not win the war – though Haig at times spoke of 'great results this year', that neither the French nor the Russians would help, that the Americans were coming and that, in consequence, the best strategy was for a succession of small attacks ('Pétain tactics'), rather than a repetition of the Somme. He weakened his case by urging help to Italy as a means of driving Austria out of the war but his chief failing, unexpected in a man who so easily dominated his party and parliamentary colleagues, was a lack of will to talk Haig, and his loyal supporter, Robertson, down. At the end, he felt unable, as a civilian Prime Minister, 'to impose my strategical views on my military advisers' and was therefore obliged to accept theirs.[91]

The consequences would be heavy. The 'Flanders Position', as the Germans called it, was one of the strongest on the Western Front, both geographically and militarily. From the low heights of Passchendaele, Broodseinde and Gheluvelt, the enemy front line looked down on an almost level plain from which three years of constant shelling had removed every trace of vegetation; it had also destroyed the field drainage system, elaborated over centuries, so that the onset of rain, frequent in that coastal region, rapidly flooded the battlefield's surface and soon returned it to swamp. To quagmire and absence of concealment the Germans had added to the BEF's difficulties by extending the depth of their trench system and its wire entanglements and by building a network of concrete pillboxes and bunkers, often constructed inside ruined buildings, which offered concealment to the construction teams and camouflage to the finished work.[92] The completed Flanders Position was actually nine layers deep: in front, a line of listening posts in shell holes, covering three lines of breastworks or trenches in which the defending division's front-line battalions sheltered; next a battle zone consisting of machine-gun posts, supported by a line of pillboxes; finally, in the rearward battle zone, the counter-attack units of the division sheltered in concrete bunkers interspersed between the positions of the supporting artillery batteries.[93] As important as the physical layout of the defences was the formational; the German army had, by the fourth summer of the war, recognised that the defence of a position required two separate formations and reorganised their divisions accordingly. The trench garrison, which was expected to bear the initial assault, had been thinned out, to comprise only the companies and battalions of the division in line. Behind it, in the rearward battle zone, were disposed the counter-attack divisions, whose mission was to move forward once the enemy assault had been stopped by the fixed defences and local ripostes of the troops in front.[94]

The defenders of the Flanders Position belonged, in July 1917, to ten divisions, including such solid and well-tried formations as the 3rd Guard Division and the 111th, in which Ernst Jünger was serving with the 73rd Hanoverian Fusiliers. On the main line of defence, that to be attacked by the British Fifth Army, 1,556 field and heavy guns were deployed on seven miles of front. The British had concentrated 2,299 guns, or one to five yards, ten times the density on the Somme fourteen months earlier. Fifth Army, commanded by the impetuous cavalry-man, Hubert Gough, also deployed over a division to each mile; they included the Guards Division, the 15th Scottish and the Highland Divisions, arrayed shoulder to shoulder between Pilckem, where the British Guards faced the German Guards north of Ypres, to the torn stumps of Sanctuary Wood, south of the city, which had given shelter to the original BEF in 1914.

The Fifth Army had also been allotted 180 aircraft, out of a total of 508 in the battle area; their role was to achieve air superiority above the front to a depth of five miles, where the German observation-balloon line began.[95] Visibility, in good conditions, from the basket of a captive balloon, was as much as sixty miles, allowing the observer, via the telephone wire attached to the tethering cable, to correct the artillery's fall of shot with a high degree of accuracy and at speed. Improvements in wireless were also allowing two-seater observation aircraft to direct artillery fire, though laboriously, for two-way voice transmission was not yet technically possible. The war in the air, which in 1918 would take a dramatic leap forward into the fields of ground attack and long-range strategic bombing, remained during 1917

385

largely stuck at the level of artillery observation, 'balloon busting' and dogfighting to gain or retain air superiority.

The French air service, though a branch of the army, was unaffected by the disorders which paralysed the ground formations during 1917. It operated effectively against the German air raids over the Aisne in April and May and lent important support to the Royal Flying Corps during the Third Battle of Ypres. Its best aircraft, the Spad 12 and 13, were superior to most of those flown by the Germans at the beginning of the year and it produced a succession of aces, Georges Guynemer and René Fonck the most celebrated, whose air-fighting skills were deadly. When Guynemer was killed during Third Ypres on 11 September, the French Senate ceremonially enshrined the victor of fifty-three aerial combats in the Pantheon.[96] The year was also to see, however, the emergence of the most famous German aces, including Werner Voss (48 victories) and the legendary 'Red Baron', Manfred von Richthofen (80 eventual victories), whose achievements were owed not just to their airmanship and aggressiveness but also to the delivery to the German air service of new types of aircraft, particularly the manoeuvrable Fokker Triplane, which displayed a significant edge in aerial combat over the British and French equivalents. Aeronautical technology, during the First World War, permitted very rapid swings in superiority between one side and the other. 'Lead times' in the development of aircraft, now measured in decades, then lasted months, sometimes only weeks; a slightly more powerful engine – when power output ranged between 200 and 300 h.p. at most – or a minor refinement of airframe could confer a startling advantage. During 1917 the Royal Flying Corps received three rapidly developed and advanced aircraft, the single-seater Sopwith Camel and S.E.5 and the two-seater Bristol Fighter, which provided the material to make its numbers, inexperienced as many of its pilots were, tell against the German veterans.[97] It began also to produce its own aces to match those of the French and German air forces, the most famous being Edward Mannock, James McCudden and Albert Ball. McCudden, an ex-private soldier, and Mannock, a convinced Socialist, were cold-hearted technicians of dogfighting from backgrounds wholly at variance with the majority of public school pilots whom Albert Ball typified.[98] Of whatever class or nation, however, all successful participants in the repetitive and unrelenting stress of aerial fighting came eventually to display its characteristic physiognomy: 'skeletal hands, sharpened noses, tight-drawn cheek bones, the bared teeth of a rictus smile and the fixed, narrowed gaze of men in a state of controlled fear'.[99]

The outcome of the Third Battle of Ypres would be decided, however, on the ground, not in the skies above it. As at Verdun, and the Somme, the key questions at the outset were: could the weight of artillery preparation crush the enemy's defences and defenders sufficiently quickly and completely for the attackers to seize positions within his lines from which counter-attack would not expel them? There was to be no initial attempt, as Nivelle had desired on the Aisne, for an immediate breakthrough. Instead, the first objectives had been fixed 6,000 yards away from the British start line, within supporting field-gun range. Once those had been taken, the artillery was to be moved forward and the process recommenced, until, bite by bite, the German defences had been chewed through, the enemy's reserves destroyed and a way opened to the undefended rear area. The key feature to be taken in the first stage was the 'Gheluvelt plateau' south-east of Ypres and two miles distant from the British front line, whose slight elevation above the surrounding lowland conferred important advantages of observation.

The bombardment, which had begun fifteen days earlier and expended over four million shells – a million had been fired before the Somme – reached its crescendo just before four o'clock in the morning of 31 July. At 3.50 a.m., the assaulting troops of the Second and Fifth Armies, with a portion of the French First Army lending support on the left, moved forward, accompanied by 136 tanks. Though the ground was churned and pock-marked by years of shelling, the surface was dry and only two tanks bogged – though many more ditched later – and the infantry also managed to make steady progress. Progress on the left, towards the summit of Pilckem Ridge, was rapid, at Gheluvelt less so. By late morning, moreover, the familiar breakdown of communication between infantry and guns had occurred; cables were everywhere cut, low cloud prevented aerial observation, 'some pigeons got through but the only news from the assault was by runners, who sometimes took hours to get back, if indeed they ever did'.[100] Then at two in the afternoon the German counter-attack scheme was unleashed. An intense bombardment fell on the soldiers of XVIII and XIX Corps as they struggled towards Gheluvelt, so heavy that the leading troops were driven to flight. To the rain of German shells was added a torrential downpour which soon turned the broken battlefield to soupy mud. The rain persisted during the next three days, as the

British infantry renewed their assaults and their artillery was dragged forward to new positions to support them. On 4 August a British battery commander, the future Lord Belhaven, wrote of 'simply awful [mud], worse I think than winter. The ground is churned up to a depth of ten feet and is the consistency of porridge . . . the middle of the shell craters are so soft that one might sink out of sight . . . there must be hundreds of German dead buried here and now their own shells are re-ploughing the area and turning them up'.[101]

Rain and lack of progress prompted Sir Douglas Haig to call a halt to the offensive on 4 August until the position could be consolidated. He insisted to the War Cabinet in London, nevertheless, that the attack had been 'highly satisfactory and the losses slight'. By comparison with the Somme, when 20,000 men had died on the opening day, losses seemed bearable: between 31 July and 3 August the Fifth Army reported 7,800 dead and missing, Second Army rather more than a thousand. Wounded included, total casualties, with those of the French First Army, numbered about 35,000, and the Germans had suffered similarly.[107] The Germans however, remained in command of the vital ground and had committed none of their counter-attack divisions. Crown Prince Rupprecht, on the evening of 31 July, had recorded in his diary that he was 'very satisfied with the results'.

The battle, however, had only just begun. Rupprecht could not reckon with Haig's determination to persist however high losses mounted or wet the battlefield became. On 16 August he committed the Fifth Army to an attack against Langemarck, scene of the BEF's encounter with the German volunteer divisions in October 1914, where 500 yards of ground was gained, and the Canadian Corps to a diversionary offensive in the coalfields around Lens, that awful wasteland of smashed villages and mine spoilheaps where the BEF had suffered so pointlessly during the winter and spring of 1915. He also continued a series of fruitless assaults on the Gheluvelt Plateau, from which the Germans dominated all action on the lower ground. Little ground was gained, much life lost.

On 24 August, after the failure of a third attack on Gheluvelt, Haig decided to transfer responsibility for the main effort at Ypres from Gough's Fifth Army to Plumer's Second. Gough, a young general by the war's gerontocratic standards, had recommended himself to Haig as a fellow-cavalryman, noted for his 'dash' and impatience with obstacles. His troops had already learnt reasons to feel less confidence in his generalship than his superior held. Plumer, by contrast, was not only older than Gough but looked older than he was and had an elderly caution and concern for those in his charge. He had commanded the Ypres sector for two years, knew all its dangerous corners and had endeared himself to his soldiers, in so far as any general of the First World War could, by his concern for their well-being. He now decided that there must be a pause, to allow careful preparation for the next phase which would take the form of a succession of thrusts into the German line even shallower than Gough had attempted.

There was to be one last action before the pause, on 27 August, to attempt the capture of two long vanished woods, Glencorse Wood and Inverness Copse, just north of the remains of Gheluvelt village. The official history admits that the ground was 'so slippery from the rain and so broken by the water-filled shell holes that the pace was slow and the protection of the creeping barrage was soon lost' by soldiers who had been marched up during the night and kept waiting ten hours for the battle to start. When it did, just before two in the afternoon, the advance was soon held up by impassable ground and heavy German fire. Edwin Vaughan, a wartime officer of the 1st/8th Warwickshire Regiment, describes the effort of his unit to get forward:

Up the road we staggered, shells bursting around us. A man stopped dead in front of me, and exasperated I cursed him and butted him with my knee. Very gently he said, 'I'm blind, Sir', and turned to show me his eyes and nose torn away by a piece of shell. 'Oh God! I'm sorry, sonny', I said. 'Keep going on the hard part', and left him staggering back in his darkness . . . A tank had churned its way slowly behind Springfield and opened fire; a moment later I looked and nothing remained of it but a crumpled heap of iron; it had been hit by a large shell. It was now almost dark and there was no firing from the enemy; ploughing across the final stretch of mud, I saw grenades bursting around the pillbox and a party of British rushed in from the other side. As we all closed in, the Boche garrison ran out with their hands up . . . we sent the 16 prisoners back across the open but they had only gone a hundred yards when a German machine gun mowed them down.

Inside the pillbox Vaughan found a wounded German officer. A stretcher bearer party appeared with a wounded British officer 'who greeted me cheerily. "Where are you hit?" I asked. "In the back near the spine. Could you shift my gas helmet from under me?" I cut away the satchel and dragged it out; then he asked for a cigarette. Dunham produced one and he put it between his lips; I struck a match and held it across, but the cigarette had fallen on to his chest and he was dead.' Outside the pillbox he came across a party of Germans eager to surrender.

> The prisoners clustered around me, bedraggled and heartbroken, telling me of the terrible time they had been having, '*Nichts essen, Nichts trinken*', always, shells, shells, shells . . . I could not spare a man to take them back, so I put them into shell holes with my men who made a great fuss of them, sharing their scanty rations with them.
>
> From other shell holes from the darkness on all sides came the groans and wails of wounded men; faint, long, sobbing moans of agony, and despairing shrieks. It was too horribly obvious that dozens of men with serious wounds must have crawled for safety into new shell holes, and now the water was rising about them and, powerless to move, they were slowly drowning. Horrible visions came to me with those cries, [of men] lying maimed out there trusting that their pals would find them, and now dying terribly, alone amongst the dead in the inky darkness. And we could do nothing to help them; Dunham was crying quietly beside me, and all the men were affected by the piteous cries.

This was almost the end of Lieutenant Vaughan's experience of 27 August. Just before midnight his unit was relieved by another, and he led his survivors back to the lines they had left on 25 August.

> The cries of the wounded had much diminished now, and as we staggered down the road, the reason was only too apparent, for the water was right over the tops of the shell holes . . . I hardly recognised [the headquarters pillbox], for it had been hit by shell after shell and its entrance was a long mound of bodies. Crowds [of soldiers] had run there for cover and had been wiped out by shrapnel. I had to climb over them to enter HQ and as I did so a hand stretched out and clung to my equipment. Horrified I dragged a living man from amongst the corpses.

Next morning, when he awoke to take a muster parade,

> my worst fears were realised. Standing near the cookers were four small groups of bedraggled, unshaven men from whom the quartermaster

sergeants were gathering information concerning any of their pals they
had seen killed or wounded. It was a terrible list . . . out of our happy
little band of 90 men, only 15 remained.[103]

Vaughan's experience was typical of what the Third Battle of Ypres
was becoming. Despite losses lighter than those suffered on the
Somme in a comparable period, 18,000 killed and missing (the dead
drowned in shell holes accounting for many of the missing), and
50,000 wounded since 31 July, the fighting was assuming for those
caught up in it a relentlessly baleful character: constant exposure to
enemy view in a landscape swept bare of buildings and vegetation,
sodden with rain and in wide areas actually under water, on to which
well-aimed shellfire fell almost without pause and was concentrated in
lethal torrents whenever an assault was attempted against objectives
which, nearby in distance, came to seem unattainably remote as failure
succeeded failure. On 4 September, Haig was summoned to London to
justify the continuation of the offensive, even in the limited form
proposed by the prudent Plumer. Lloyd George, reviewing the whole
state of the war, argued that, with Russia no longer a combatant and
France barely so, strategic wisdom lay in husbanding British resources
until the Americans arrived in force in 1918. Haig, supported by
Robertson, insisted that, precisely because of the other Allies'
weakness, Third Ypres must continue. His case was bad – Ludendorff
was actually withdrawing divisions from the Western Front to assist
the Austrians – but because Lloyd George advanced worse arguments
of his own, in particular that there were decisions to be won against
the Turks and on the Italian front, Haig got his way. Henry Wilson,
the superseded sub-chief of the General Staff and a fanatical
'Westerner', commented with characteristic cynicism to his diary that
Lloyd George's scheme was to give Haig enough rope to hang himself.
The assessment that the Prime Minister wished to relieve his principal
military subordinate, but dared not until he was compromised by
overt failure, was probably accurate.[104] There was, however, no
obvious successor to Haig and so, however ill-judged his strategy and
harmful its effect on his long-suffering army, it was to be continued for
want of a better man or plan.

Plumer's 'step-by-step' scheme, for which the pause in early
September was the preparation, was conceived in three stages. In each,
a long bombardment was to precede a short advance of 1,500 yards,
mounted by divisions on a frontage of 1,000 yards, or ten infantrymen

for each yard of front. After three weeks of bombardment, the 1st and 2nd Australian Divisions, with the 23rd and 41st British, attacked up the Menin Road east of Ypres. The accompanying barrage fell on a belt a thousand yards deep and, under that devastating weight of fire, the Germans fell back. The same results were achieved in the battle of Polygon Wood, 26 September, and of Broodseinde, 4 October. 'Bite and hold', Plumer's tactics had been successful. The Gheluvelt Plateau had at last been taken, and the immediate area in front of Ypres put out of German observation (troops, nevertheless, continued to march out of the ruined town through its western end and circle back to reach the battlefield, as they had done since the Salient had been drawn tight around it in 1915, to escape long-range shelling on the only roads that rose above the waterlogged plain). The question was whether the next series of 'bite and hold' attacks could be justified. The first three, particularly that on Broodseinde, had hit the enemy hard. Plumer's massed artillery had caught the German counter-attack divisions massed too far forward on 4 October and had caused heavy casualties, particularly in the 4th Guard Division.[105] As a result, the Germans once again decided to refine their system of holding the front. Before Broodseinde they had brought their counter-attack divisions close up into the battle zone, to catch the British infantry as they emerged from their protective barrage. As the result had been merely to expose them to the ever heavier weight and deeper thrust of the British artillery, Ludendorff now ordered a reversal: the front was to be thinned out again and the counter-attack divisions held further to the rear, in positions from which they were not to move until a deliberate riposte, supported by a weighty bombardment and barrage, could be organised.[106]

In essence, British and German tactics for the conduct of operations on the awful, blighted, blasted and half-drowned surface of the Ypres battlefield had now been brought, as if by consultation, to resemble each other exactly. The attackers were to shatter the defenders with a monstrous weight of shellfire and occupy the narrow belt of ground on which it had fallen. The defenders were then to repeat the process in the opposite direction, hoping to regain the ground lost. It was, if decisive victory were the object, a wholly futile exercise, and Haig might, from the evidence with which events almost daily confronted him, have declined to join the enemy in prolonging the agony the struggle inflicted on both sides.

Even the most enthusiastic technical historians of the Great War, ever ready to highlight the overlooked significance of an improvement in the fusing of field-artillery shells or range of trench-mortars, concede that Haig should have stopped after Broodseinde.[107] He determined adamantly otherwise. Before Broodseinde he told his army commanders, 'the Enemy is faltering and . . . a good decisive blow might lead to decisive results'.[108] Immediately after, at a time when Lloyd George was surreptitiously trying to limit the number of reinforcements sent to France to make good losses suffered at Ypres, he wrote to Robertson, the Chief of the Imperial General Staff, 'the British Armies alone can be made capable of a great offensive effort [so that] it is beyond argument that everything should be done . . . to make that effort as strong as possible'.[109]

The battle of the mud at Ypres – Passchendaele, as it would become known, after the smear of brick that represented all that remained of the village which was its final objective – would therefore continue. Not, however, with British soldiers in the vanguard. Some of the best divisions in the BEF, the Guards, the 8th, one of the old regular divisions, the 15th Scottish, the 16th Irish, the 38th Welsh, the 56th London, had fought themselves out in August and early September. The only reliable assault divisions Haig had left were in his ANZAC and Canadian Corps, which had been spared both the first stages of the battle and the worst of the Somme a year earlier. In what was called the 'First Battle of Passchendaele', the New Zealand and 3rd Australian Divisions tried on 12 October to reach the remains of the village on the highest point of ground east of Ypres, 150 feet above sea level, where the Germans' Second Flanders Position of trenches and pillboxes marked the last obstacle between the BEF and the enemy's rear area. 'We are practically through the enemy's defences', Haig told a meeting of war correspondents on 9 October, 'the enemy has only flesh and blood against us.' Flesh and blood, in the circumstances, proved sufficient. Caught in front and flank by machine-gun fire, the ANZACs eventually retreated to the positions from which they had started their advance on that sodden day. So wet was the ground that shells from their supporting artillery buried themselves in the mud without exploding and the New Zealanders alone suffered nearly 3000 casualties in attempting to pass through uncut wire.

Having consigned the II ANZAC Corps to a pointless sacrifice, Haig then turned to the Canadians. General Sir Arthur Currie, commanding the Canadian Corps, had known the Ypres Salient since 1915; he did not want to lose any more of his soldiers there and his precise, schoolmaster's mind forecast that the assault Haig requested would cost '16,000 casualties'. Though he had means of recourse to his own government, and might have declined, he nevertheless, after protest, complied with Haig's order. The early winter had brought almost continuous rain and the only way forward towards the top of the ridge was along two narrow causeways surrounded by bogs and streams.[110] On 26 October, the first day of the 'Second Battle of Passchendaele', the Canadians broke the First Flanders position and, at heavy cost in lives, advanced about 500 yards. The 11th Bavarian Division, defending the sector, also lost heavily and was taken out of the line. On 30 October the battle was resumed, and a little more ground taken, three soldiers of the 3rd and 4th Canadian Divisions winning the Victoria Cross. The 1st and 2nd Canadian Divisions took over the front of attack for a fresh assault on 6 November, which captured what was left of Passchendaele village, and a final assault was made on 10 November, when the line was consolidated. The 'Second Battle of Passchendaele' had cost the four divisions of the Canadian Corps 15,634 killed and wounded, almost exactly the figure Currie had predicted in October.[111]

The point of Passchendaele, as the Third Battle of Ypres has come to be known, defies explanation. It may have relieved pressure on the French, in the aftermath of the mutinies, though there is no evidence that Hindenburg and Ludendorff knew enough of Pétain's troubles to plan to profit by them. They had too much trouble of their own, in propping up their Austrian allies and in settling the chaos of the Russian front, to mount another Verdun; moreover, by the autumn of 1917, Pétain's programme of rehabilitation was having its effect on the French army, which staged an attack near the Chemin des Dames, on 23 October, that recaptured over seven miles of front, to a depth of three miles, in four days, a result equivalent to that achieved with such effort and suffering at Ypres in ninety-nine. Edmonds, the official British historian, justifies Haig's constant renewal of the Passchendaele battle with the argument that it attracted eighty-eight divisions to the Ypres front, while 'the total Allied force engaged was only 6 French divisions and 43 British and Dominion [Australian, New Zealand and Canadian] divisions'.[112] Context puts his judgement in perspective: eighty-eight divisions represented only a third of the German army, while Haig's forty-three were more than half of his. What is unarguable is that nearly 70,000 of his soldiers had been killed in the muddy wastes of the Ypres battlefield and over 170,000 wounded. The Germans may have suffered worse – statistical disputes make the argument profitless – but, while the British had given of their all, Hindenburg and Ludendorff had another army in Russia with which to begin the war in the west all over again. Britain had no other army. Like France, though it had adopted conscription later and as an exigency of war, not as a principle of national policy, it had by the end of 1917 enlisted every man that could be spared from farm and factory and had begun to compel into the ranks recruits whom the New Armies in the heyday of volunteering of 1914–15 would have rejected on sight: the hollow-chested, the round-shouldered, the stunted, the myopic, the over-age. Their physical deficiencies were evidence of Britain's desperation for soldiers and Haig's profligacy with men. On the Somme he had sent the flower of British youth to death or mutilation; at Passchendaele he had tipped the survivors into the slough of despond.

THE BATTLE OF CAMBRAI

There remained one means of offence against the Germans that the mud of Flanders had denied its potentiality: machine warfare. The main reserve of the Tank Corps, built up incrementally during 1917, therefore remained intact. Its commander, Brigadier General H. Elles, had been seeking an opportunity to use it in a profitable way during the summer and had interested General Sir Julian Byng, commanding Third Army, in the idea of making a surprise attack with tanks on his front, which ran across dry, chalky ground on which tanks would not bog. One of Byng's artillery officers, Brigadier General H.H. Tudor, of the 9th Scottish Division, had meanwhile been devising a plan of his own to support tanks with a surprise bombardment, thus denying the enemy forewarning of an attack. Byng accepted both Elles's and Tudor's plans in August and Haig's headquarters approved them on 13 October, in principle at least. By early November, with the battle at Passchendaele lapsing into futility, Haig was anxious for a compensatory success of any sort and on 10 November, at Byng's urging, gave his consent to the Elles-Tudor scheme.

The offensive was to be launched at the earliest possible moment at Cambrai with over 300 tanks. They were to be followed by eight infantry divisions and supported by a thousand guns. The nature of the artillery plan was crucial to success. Conventionally, artillery bombardments and barrages commenced only after all the batteries had 'registered', that is, established the accuracy of their fire by observing their fall of shot, a lengthy process which always alerted the enemy to what portended and allowed them to call reserves to the threatened sector. Tudor had devised a method of registering guns by calculating the deviation of each from a norm by electrical means; when the deviations were transferred mathematically to a comprehensive map grid, the artillery commander could be confident that his batteries would hit their designated targets without any of the preliminary registration which had always hitherto given offensive plans away.[113]

The tanks, massed on a front of 10,000 yards, were to advance in dense formation, with the infantry following close behind to take prisoners, capture guns and consolidate the ground conquered. The way into the enemy positions would be secured by the tanks crushing lanes through the wire – in the Hindenburg position at Cambrai several hundred yards deep – while the tanks would find a way across the trenches by dropping into them 'fascines' – bundles of brushwood – as bridges. There were three successive German lines, 7,000 yards – nearly four miles – deep, and it was intended to break through all in a single bound on the first day. Because the Cambrai front had long been quiet, it was garrisoned by only two divisions, the 20th *Landwehr* and the 54th Reserve, supported by no more than 150 guns.[114] The 20th *Landwehr* was classified 'fourth-rate' by Allied intelligence. Unfortunately, the 54th Reserve, a better formation, was commanded by an officer, General von Walter, an artilleryman, who had, unusually among German soldiers, taken account of the tanks' potentiality, and trained his gunners to engage moving targets from protected positions.[115]

Walter's keen interest in tank operations – at a time when the German army had no tanks – was to be of the greatest influence on the outcome of the battle. So, too, was the failure of comprehension of the tank's potential on the part of General G.M. Harper, commanding the 51st Highland Division, the infantry formation at the centre of the front of attack. Harper, brave but conventional, did not like tanks but loved his Highland soldiers. He had formed the view that tanks would attract German artillery fire on to his infantry and so, instead of insisting that they follow closely, ordered them to keep 150–200 yards behind.[116] The resulting separation was to spell doom to the British attack at the now critical moment of the battle.

All began well. The unfortunate German soldiers garrisoning the

Cambrai sector were unprepared for the hurricane bombardment that descended upon them at 6.20 on the morning of 20 November and the appearance of dense columns of tanks, 324 in all, rolling forward with infantry following. Within four hours the attackers had advanced in many places to a depth of four miles, at almost no cost in casualties: in the 20th Light Division, the 2nd Durham Light Infantry lost four men killed, the 14th Durham Light Infantry only seven men wounded.[117]

The difference was in the centre. There the 51st Highland Division, gingerly following the tanks at some hundred yards' distance, entered the defended zone of the German 54th Reserve. Its gunners, trained by General von Walter, began to engage the British tanks as they appeared, unsupported by infantry, over the crest near Flesquières village, and knocked them out one by one.[118] Soon eleven were out of action, five destroyed by a single German sergeant, Kurt Kruger, who was killed by a Highlander when the 51st Division's infantry at last got up with the tanks. By then, however, it was too late for the division to reach the objective set for it for the day, so that, while on the left and right of the Cambrai battlefield, the whole German position had been broken, in the centre a salient bulged towards British lines, denying General Byng the clear-cut breakthrough espousal of Elles's and Tudor's revolutionary plan should have brought him.

In England the bells rang out for a victory, the first time they had sounded since the beginning of the war. The celebration was premature. Byng's cavalry, which had picked its way across the battlefield in the wake of the tanks in the twilight of 20 November, was held up by wire they had not cut and turned back. His infantry nudged their way forward on 21 November and the days that followed. Then, on 30 November, the German army demonstrated once again its formidable counter-attack power. In the ten days since the attack had been unleashed, twenty divisions had been assembled by Crown Prince Rupprecht, the local commander, and in a morning attack they took back not only much of the ground lost to the tanks on 20 November but another portion, which the British had held beforehand. The Cambrai battle, which should have yielded a deep pocket driven into the German front, ended on ambiguous terms along the line of the 'Drocourt-Quéant Switch', a sinuous double salient which gave both the British and the Germans some of each other's long-held territory. It was an appropriate symbol of the precarious balance of power on the Western Front at the end of 1917.

TEN

AMERICA AND ARMAGEDDON

'THEY WILL NOT EVEN COME', Admiral Capelle, the Secretary of State for the Navy, had assured the budgetary committee of the German parliament on 31 January 1917, 'because our submarines will sink them. Thus America from a military point of view means nothing, and again nothing and for a third time nothing.'[1] At the beginning of 1917, four months before the United States entered the war on the side of the Allies, its army – as opposed to its large and modern navy – might indeed have meant nothing. It ranked in size – 107,641 men – seventeenth in the world.[2] It had no experience of large-scale operations since the armistice at Appomattox fifty-one years earlier, and possessed no modern equipment heavier than its medium machine guns. Its reserve, the National Guard, though larger, with 132,000 men, was the part-time militia of the individual forty-eight states, poorly trained even in the richer states and subject to the sketchiest Federal supervision. The only first-class American force, the United States Marine Corps, 15,500 strong, was scattered in America's overseas possessions and areas of intervention, including several Central American republics which the United States had decided to police in the aftermath of the Spanish-American War of 1898.

Yet, by June 1917, the commander of an American Expeditionary Force, General John J. Pershing, had arrived in France and on 4 July, American Independence Day, elements of his 1st Division paraded in Paris. Throughout the following months, fresh units of an army planned to reach a strength of eighty divisions – nearly three million men, for American divisions were twice the size of French, British or German – continued to arrive. By March 1918, 318,000 men had reached France, the vanguard of 1,300,000 to be deployed by August, and not one had been lost to the action of the enemy in oceanic transport.[3]

Rare are the times in a great war when the fortunes of one side or the other are transformed by the sudden accretion of a disequilibriating reinforcement. Those of Napoleon's enemies were so transformed in 1813, when the failure of his Moscow campaign brought the Russian army to the side of Britain and Austria. Those of the United States against the Confederacy were transformed in 1863 when the adoption of conscription brought the North's millions into play against the South's hundreds of thousands. Those of an isolated Britain and an almost defeated Soviet Union would be transformed in 1941, when Hitler's intemperate declaration of war against America brought the power of the world's leading state to stand against that of Nazi Germany as well as Imperial Japan. By 1918, President Wilson's decision to declare war on Germany and its allies had brought such an accretion to the Allied side. Capelle's 'they will never come' had been trumped in six months by America's melodramatic 'Lafayette, I am here.'

The United States had not wanted to enter the war. America, its President Woodrow Wilson had said, was 'too proud to fight' and it had sustained a succession of diplomatic affronts, from the sinking of the *Lusitania* and its American passengers to the German attempt to foment a diversionary war in Mexico, without responding to provocation by material means. Once committed to hostilities, America's extraordinary capacity for industrial production and human organisation took possession of the nation's energies. It was decided at the outset to raise the army to be sent to France by conscription, overseen by local civilian registration boards. Over 24 million men were registered in 1917–18 and those deemed most eligible – young and unmarried males without dependants – formed the first contingent of 2,810,000 draftees. Together with those already enrolled in the regular army, the National Guard and the Marines, they raised the enlisted strength of the United States ground forces to nearly four million men by the war's end.

Many Americans were already fighting. Some, as individuals, had joined the British or Canadian armies. Others had enlisted in the French Foreign Legion. A large group of American pilots was already serving in the French air force, where they formed the Lafayette Escadrille, one of the leading air-fighting units on the Western Front. Its veterans would bring invaluable experience to the American Expeditionary Force's Air Corps once it crossed the Atlantic. Though forced to adopt foreign equipment – the American industrial effort failed to supply tanks, artillery or aircraft to the expeditionary force, which depended for supplies of those items largely on the French

402

(3,100 field guns, 1,200 howitzers, 4,800 aircraft) – American pilots rapidly established a reputation for skill and dash. Eddie Ricken-backer, America's leading ace, was as much a hero in France as in his home country.

A blind spot in America's mobilisation lay over its response to its black population's willingness to serve. W. E. B. DuBois, one of the most important champions of black America in the early twentieth century, argued that, 'if this is our country, then this is our war'. White America, particularly the white military establishment, continued to believe that blacks lacked military spirit and were suitable for use only as labour or service troops. That despite the fact that the 'buffalo soldiers', the four regular regiments of black infantry and cavalry, had always performed well in the wars on the Indian frontier and that black regiments had fought with tenacity in the Civil War. Reluctantly a black division, the 92nd, was raised, with some black officers, none holding higher rank than captain, commanding sub-units. It did not do well in action. Its failure – 'Poor Negroes – They are hopelessly inferior', wrote the commander of the corps in which the 92nd Division served – was ascribed throughout the army to racial incapacities. No professional American officer seems to have taken note of the reliance the French were already placing on the black contingents of *Tirailleurs sénégalais*, who showed a readiness to fight in the second half of 1917 that native white Frenchmen had, at least temporarily, lost. The racially supercilious American officers of the AEF may be forgiven for failing to anticipate the outstanding performance of black combat troops in America's wars of the later twentieth century. The poor record of black American troops on the Western Front in 1918 bears the classic signs nevertheless of self-fulfilling prophecy; little being expected of them, little was given.

The ordinary soldier of the Allied armies, British or French, remained unaware of a racial problem that proved a solely domestic concern. To the battered armies that had attacked and defended throughout 1914 to 1917, the appearance of the doughboys, as the American conscripts of the last year of the war were universally known, brought nothing but renewed hope. Their personal popularity was everywhere noted. The Americans were light-hearted, cheerful, enthusiastic, dismissive of difficulties. 'We'll soon settle this,' was the doughboy attitude. The French and British military professionals, alarmed by the AEF's deficiency in technical military skills, par-ticularly in artillery method and inter-arm cooperation, propagated the message that the Americans were suitable only as replacements or subordinate units. Pershing was to have none of it, insisting that a united American army, under American command, was the only force that would do justice to his country's involvement. The point of principle on which he stood was to be justified by the American Expeditionary Force's contribution to victory.

The arrival of Lafayette's expeditionary force to the aid of the colonists in 1781 at the crisis of the American War of Independence had confronted their British enemies with an alteration of force they could not match. The arrival of the Americans created no such unalterable imbalance in 1917. By the end of the year, the Germans, too, overstretched as they had been throughout 1915–16 by the need to prop up their Austrian allies, by the losses incurred at Verdun and on the Somme, and by the unanticipated recovery of the Russians in 1916, had turned a corner. The political collapse of Russia had released from the Eastern Front fifty divisions of infantry which could be brought to the west to attempt a final, war-winning offensive. Not indifferent divisions either; the total collapse of Russia's military power at the end of 1917 allowed the German high command to leave in the east no more force than was needed to maintain order and collect produce inside the German-occupied area. It consisted chiefly of overage *Landwehr* and skeleton cavalry formations. The shock troops that had sealed the Kerensky army's fate – Guard and Guard Reserve Divisions, Prussian and north German divisions of the pre-war active army – had been successively disengaged during the winter and brought westward by rail to form, with others already on the Western Front, an attacking mass of sixty divisions.[4]

The German high command, which had for so long been compelled to sustain defensive strategy in the west, had given great thought and preparation to perfecting the offensive methods to be employed by the attack force, the last reserve it could hope to assemble.[5] It was a grave deficiency that the German army had no tanks. A clumsy prototype was under development, and British tanks captured during 1917 were being pressed into service, but no concentration of tanks such as was already available to the British and French stood to hand. Hindenburg and Ludendorff counted, in its absence, on a refinement of artillery and infantry tactics, practised in the last stages of the Russian campaign, to compensate for German weakness at the technical level. The infantry had been re-equipped with large numbers of stripped-down machine guns (the 08/15), rough if not wholly adequate

404

equivalents of the British and French light machine guns, the Lewis and Chauchat, and had been trained to 'infiltrate' enemy positions, by-passing centres of resistance, rather than stopping to fight when held up directly to their front. These tactics anticipated blitzkrieg, which the German army would apply so successfully in mechanised operations in a later war. Each attacking division, in addition, had been ordered to form specialised 'storm' battalions of lightly equipped infantry which, with grenade and carbine, were to drive deep but narrow cavities through the crust of the enemy positions, breaking it into isolated sections to be overcome by the following waves of conventional infantry at a slower pace.

The emphasis of the German attack plan, however, was on speed. Nivelle had hoped, unrealistically, to overcome the German position on the Chemin des Dames the previous year in a few hours. He had lacked the trained troops and weight of artillery to bring his hope to realisation. Ludendorff now had the necessary troops and guns and a realistic plan. The enemy was to be attacked both on a broad front – fifty miles – and in depth, the depth of the attack to be achieved by concentrating an enormous weight of artillery firing the heaviest possible bombardment at short, medium and long range in a brief but crushing deluge of shells, lasting five hours. Ludendorff's bombardment force amounted to 6,473 field, medium and heavy guns and 3,532 mortars of varying calibre, for which over a million rounds of ammunition were assembled.[6] All the guns, many of which had been brought from the east, were 'registered' beforehand at a specially constructed firing range, producing data of each gun's variance from a theoretical norm which, when combined with detailed meteorological allowance for barometric pressure and wind speed and direction, would ensure, as far as was humanly possible, that all would hit their designated targets, whether enemy trenches or battery positions. Explosive shell was also to be intermixed with varieties of gas projectiles, lachrymatory and asphyxiating phosgene, in a combination calculated to outwit the protection offered by enemy gas masks. Lachrymatory or tear gas was designed to make the enemy infantry take off their gas masks, in a relief reflex, when phosgene would disable them.

Some combination of all these measures had been tried in the last offensive against the Russians at Riga in September 1917, when the German artillery had fired without preliminary registration on the Russian positions and created the conditions for a breakthrough.[7]

Bruchmüller, Ludendorff's artillery supremo, there proved to his satisfaction that the firing of guns previously registered behind the front, and so not needing to betray their positions by ranging on enemy targets until the moment of attack, could create the circumstances in which an infantry assault would lead to victory.[8]

It was with Bruchmüller's verified experiment in mind that Hindenburg had, at Mons on 11 November 1917, come to the decision to launch an all-or-nothing offensive in the west in the coming year.[9] The expectations pinned to its outcome were far-reaching. As Ludendorff expressed the mind of the high command in a letter to Hindenburg on 7 January 1918, 'the proposed new offensive, should . . . lead to the decisive success for which we hope . . . We shall [then] be in a position to lay down such conditions for peace with the Western Powers as are required by the security of our frontiers, our economic interests and our international position after the war.'[10] Eventual victory might bring rewards in the west, notably control of Belgium's industrial economy and the incorporation of the French coal and iron basin of Longwy-Briey within the wider German Ruhr industrial area.[11] Belgium's Flemish-speaking region, traditionally hostile to French-speaking Wallonia, was not immune to German seductions. In February 1917, a Council of Flanders had been set up in Brussels, under the patronage of the German military government, and in the following months had bargained autonomy for itself under German patronage. Flemish expectations of what autonomy would bring were, however, not what Germany intended to concede. Flanders wanted democracy and true independence; Germany required subordination. Its external policy, in the Belgian direction, thus foundered during 1918 on the stubborn liberalism of a people whose pan-Teutonic feelings did not extend to the surrender of their national rights.[12]

THE WAR IN THE EAST CONTINUES

Despite the weight of Germany's military preoccupation with preparation for the coming offensive in the west, its political concerns for the future remained concentrated in the east, where national sentiment was less self-assured and independent identities weaker. Germany correctly calculated that its opportunity to impose subordinate relationships on the peoples who had only just escaped from domination by the old Russian empire was altogether more promising. The Baltic peoples – Lithuanian, Latvian, Estonian – had retained their sense of association with the German-speaking lands for centuries; much of the land-owning class was German by origin. Finland, though it had enjoyed a degree of autonomy inside the Tsarist empire, was anxious to regain full independence and ready to accept German help to do so. Lenin's early policy was to allow the non-Russian peoples of the empire to secede if they chose, while encouraging the local left, with the support of any remaining Russian soldiers, to stage pro-Soviet revolutions. In the Baltic lands, already under German occupation as a result of the successful offensives of 1916–17, revolution was swiftly put down and semi-independent pro-German regimes were established, though not without protest in Lithuania, which sought but failed to achieve full sovereignty.[13] In Finland, where power in parliament, an institution of the old Tsarist constitution, was fairly evenly divided between left and right, the issue of what relationship with Germany the country should establish provoked civil war. The right had been pro-German throughout the European conflict and an all-Finnish volunteer unit, the 27th Jäger Battalion, had fought with the German army on the Baltic front since 1916. The right's readiness to form a German alliance, after independence was declared in December 1917, provoked the left into forming a worker militia of its own; in January 1918 fighting broke out, the left seizing Helsinki, the capital, the right retiring into the northern provinces. The Germans sent arms, 70,000 rifles, 150 machine guns and twelve field guns, all of Russian origin; also from Russia came the commander who was to lead the right-wing forces, Gustav Mannerheim, a Baltic nobleman and ex-Tsarist officer, of formidable personal and military capacities.

Mannerheim had been commissioned into the Chevalier Guards, grandest of the Tsar's cavalry regiments, and had served under Brusilov in the Model Cavalry Squadron; his career testified to his outstanding qualities. The war had brought him command of the VI Cavalry Corps, which he succeeded in keeping intact while the rest of the imperial army disintegrated after the failure of the Kerensky offensive.[14] After the October Revolution, he decided, however, that he must transfer his loyalty to his homeland; he made his way to Finland and secured appointment as the Commander-in-Chief of the anti-Bolshevik army. The Petrograd Bolsheviks had, under German pressure, recognised the independence of Finland on 31 December 1918; but four days later, Stalin had persuaded the Petrograd Soviet to alter the terms on which independence was granted and then offered the Finnish socialists Russian help to establish 'socialist power'. Its basis was already present on Finnish soil in the form of Russian units not yet repatriated, and in the Finnish Red Guards. While Mannerheim consolidated his base in the western region of Ostrobothnia, the left took possession of the industrial towns.

During January and February 1918, both sides prepared for the offensive. The Reds had about 90,000 men at their disposal, Mannerheim only 40,000.[15] His troops, however, were under the command of professional officers and stiffened by cadres of the 27th Jägers. The Red forces lacked trained leadership. Moreover, while Germany was preparing to send an experienced expeditionary force, largely comprising General von der Goltz's Baltic Division, to the Finns' assistance, Lenin was increasingly nervous of taking any action that would provoke a German landing in an area adjacent to the revolution's centre at Petrograd, where the military force at his disposal was scarcely adequate to protect the Bolshevik leadership from its enemies, let alone repel an organised foreign expeditionary force. After the signing of the treaty of Brest-Litovsk, which formally ended war between Russia and Germany, the Soviet actually began withdrawing what troops it had left in Finland, though it continued surreptitiously to support and supply the native Red forces.

Mannerheim seized the opportunity to push forward. The leader of the Finnish nationalists, Svinhufvud, was too pro-German for his taste, prepared to acquiesce in the German plan to make his country an economic and political dependency of the German empire for the sake of comfort, while he, as he would shortly proclaim, wanted no 'part of another empire but . . . a great, free, independent Finland'.[16] In early March the Red advance into Mannerheim's area of control in Ostrobothnia petered out and he went over to the offensive. His enemy, though controlling the capital, was menaced by another nationalist force to the rear, operating on the isthmus of Karelia between the Baltic and Lake Ladoga, through which the Red lines of communication led to Petrograd. Mannerheim's plan was to organise a concentric advance which would simultaneously cut those lines of communication and squeeze the Reds between two convergent attacks.

Before he could consummate his plan, von der Goltz's Baltic Division, which had been detained on the southern Baltic coast by ice, appeared at the port of Hangö, formerly the Tsarist navy's forward base, and advanced on Helsinki, which it entered on 13 April. On 6 April, however, Mannerheim had taken Tampere, the Reds' main stronghold in the south, a victory which allowed him to transfer forces south-eastward towards Karelia. At his approach, the remaining Red forces beat a hasty retreat across the border into Russia and on 2 May all resistance to Mannerheim's armies came to an end. Finland was free, both of a foreign imperialism and of the foreign ideology which had succeeded it. It was not, however, yet independent. The Germans had extracted a high price for their support and for their intervention. The treaty signed between the two countries on 2 March gave Germany rights of free trade with Finland but not Finland with Germany, and bound Finland not to make any foreign alliance without German consent.[17] The Svinhufrud government was content to accept diplomatic and economic client status, even a German prince as regent of a restored Grand Duchy, if that would guarantee German protection against the threat of renewed social revolution or Russian aggression.[18] Mannerheim was not. His fervent nationalism and justified pride in his army's victory stiffened his resolve to submit to no foreign authority; moreover, his firm belief that Germany could not win the world war caused him to reject any policy identifying Finland with its strategic interests. On 30 May he resigned his command and retired to Sweden, from which he would return at the war's end to negotiate an honourable settlement of his country's differences with the victors.

Finland, though compromised by the German alliance, had had a swift and comparatively painless exit from the chaos of Russian collapse. Total casualties in the war numbered 30,000 and, though that was a large figure in a population of three million, it would pale into insignificance, relatively as well as absolutely, beside the terrible toll of the civil war which was beginning to spread throughout Russia proper.[19] That war would last until 1921 and take the lives, directly or indirectly, of at least seven and perhaps ten million people, five times as many as had been killed in the fighting of 1914–17.[20]

There need have been no civil war in Russia had the Bolsheviks not thrown away the advantages they had gained in the first months of revolution, advantages lost by mismanagement of their diplomacy and through a hopelessly unrealistic confidence placed in the power of the revolutionary impulse to undermine the 'capitalist' states from below. Between November 1917 and March 1918 the Bolsheviks had won a great internal victory in most of the seventy-five provinces and regions into which the old Tsarist empire had been divided. During the so-called 'railway' (*eshelonaia*) war, picked bands of armed revolutionaries had fanned out from Petrograd down the empire's railway system to make contact with the 900 Soviets that had replaced the official organs of administration in Russia's cities and towns and to put down the resistance of groups opposed to the October Revolution. The Russian railways, during this brief but brilliant revolutionary episode, worked for Lenin as the German railways had not for Moltke in 1914. Decisive force had been delivered to key points in the nick of time, and a succession of crucial local successes had been achieved that, in sum, brought revolutionary triumph.

Then, with Russia in their hands, the Bolsheviks had prevaricated with the Germans over the terms of the peace settlement that would have confirmed their victory. Brest-Litovsk was a harsh peace. It required the Bolsheviks to accept that Russian Poland and most of the Baltic lands should cease to be part of Russia proper, that Russian troops should be withdrawn from Finland and Transcaucasia and that peace should be made with the nationalists of the Ukraine, who had declared their independence.[21] Since Poland and the Baltic lands had already been lost to Russia, Finland was about to fall to Mannerheim's nationalists, and Bolshevik power in the Ukraine and Transcaucasia was everywhere fragile and in places non-existent, the harshness of the Brest-Litovsk terms lay in the letter of the treaty rather than in fact. The Bolsheviks might well have signed without damage to their objective circumstances, making the mental reservation that the seceding territories could be reintegrated when Germany's fortunes worsened and theirs improved. The Bolsheviks were, however, possessed by the illusion that the menace of world revolution, which they had made a reality in their homeland, threatened all 'imperialist' powers and that, by defying the Germans to do their worst, they would provoke Germany's workers to rise against their masters in solidarity with the Bolshevik cause.

Their illusions were fed by a wave of strikes that broke out in Germany on 28 January 1918, involving a million industrial workers, whose leaders called for 'peace without annexations', the core policy of the Bolsheviks, and in some towns set up workers' councils.[22] The strikes, however, were rapidly put down; moreover, as with similar strikes in France during 1917, the impetus came not from revolutionary enthusiasm but from weariness with the war and its hardships, psychological as well as material. Their effect on the Bolshevik leadership was nevertheless calamitous. While Lenin, with his usual hardheadedness, urged caution, in effect arguing that the time offered by accepting Germany's terms must be used to strengthen the revolution's hand against enemies within and without, Trotsky, now Commissar for Foreign Affairs, succumbed to a romantic ideological urge and carried with him the majority in the Bolshevik Central Committee. To challenge the Germans to do their worst, a worst which would bring down the wrath of world revolution on the imperialists' heads, first in Germany itself, then elsewhere in the capitalist lands, there was to be 'neither peace nor war'.[23] Russia would not sign; neither would it fight. In earnest of this extraordinary decision, an abdication of material power in expectation of a spiritual engulfment of the revolution's enemies, the total demobilisation of the Russian army was announced on 29 January.[24] At Brest-Litovsk, Trotsky continued to fence with the Germans for another ten days. Then, on 9 February, the Germans made a separate peace with the Ukraine, simultaneously issuing to the Bolsheviks an ultimatum requiring them to sign the treaty by the following day or else acquiesce in the termination of the armistice of the previous December and the occupation by the German army, together with Austrian and Turkish contingents, of the territories scheduled at Brest-Litovsk for separation from old Russia.

In the next eleven days, the Germans swept forward to what the ultimatum had called 'the designated line'.[25] Operation *Faustschlag* (Thunderbolt) overwhelmed the Bolshevik forces in White Russia (Belarus), in the western Ukraine, in the Crimea, in the industrial Donetz basin and eventually, on 8 May, on the Don. In less than two months, 130,000 square miles of territory, an area the size of France, containing Russia's best agricultural land, many of its raw materials and much of its industry, had been appropriated by the enemy. 'It is the most comical war I have ever known', wrote General Max Hoffmann, who had served Hindenburg as Chief of Staff at Tannenberg. 'We put a handful of infantrymen with machine guns and one gun on to a train and rush them off to the next station; they take it, make prisoners of the Bolsheviks, pick up a few more troops and so on. This proceeding has, at any rate, the charm of novelty.' It was the novelty of lightning victory, dreamed of by Schlieffen, not achieved by any German army since the beginning of the war.

Lightning victories, experience tells, store up evil consequences, usually for the victors. Operation Thunderbolt had consequences but, to add to the many inequities produced by the Russian revolution, the evil was suffered not by the Germans but by the defeated Bolsheviks. The results of their defeat were threefold. First, a number of Russia's minorities seized the opportunity offered to throw off control by Petrograd and establish their own governments. Second, the failure of the Bolsheviks to resist the German irruption, followed by their precipitate agreement to sign a dictated peace, confirmed the Western Allies – France and Britain, but also the United States and Japan – in their tentative resolve to establish a military presence on Russian soil, with the purpose of subjecting the German forces of occupation to a continued military threat. Finally, the collapse of Bolshevik armed force, such as it was, provided the opponents of revolution inside Russia with the circumstances in which they could stage a counter-revolution that swiftly became a civil war.

Finland had been the first of the 'nationalities' to strike for its freedom. The ethnic Romanians of the provinces of Bessarabia and Moldavia were next; with the remnant of the Romanian army close at hand, they declared a Moldavian People's Republic in January 1918, which in April became part of Romania proper. Despite the presence of a sizeable Russian minority, it would remain Romanian until 1940. In Transcaucasia, which had fallen under Tsarist rule only during the nineteenth century, ethnic Russians were altogether fewer, being for the most part town-dwellers, railway workers, government officials or soldiers.[26] The dominant nationalities, Christian Georgians and Armenians, Muslim and Turkic-speaking Azeris, were granted the right to make their own arrangements for self-government by the Petrograd Bolsheviks in November 1917 and in April 1918 declared a Federative Democratic Republic.[27]

Federation lasted only a month, brought to an end by the revival of historic hostilities between the three ethnicities. The independence of Armenia and Azerbaijan would last, however, until 1920, when the Bolsheviks decided to go back on their concession of political freedoms, that of Georgia until 1921. In the interim, all three independent states had been drawn into the culminating stage of the Great War by the intervention, direct or indirect, of the major combatants.

Transcaucasia and Transcaspia, to its south-east, might have remained backwaters had not both contained resources of the greatest strategic value – Caucasian oil, refined at the port of Baku on the Caspian Sea, the cotton crop of Turkestan in Transcaspia – and been served by railways that allowed their extraction. Under the terms of the Treaty of Brest-Litovsk, Bolshevik Russia was obliged to supply a proportion of both to Germany. The Bolsheviks naturally wanted some for themselves. So did the Turks, who also cherished ambitions of incorporating the Turkic-speaking Transcaspians into the Ottoman empire. In the spring of 1918, the German forces positioned in the eastern Ukraine and Donetz basin by Operation Thunderbolt began to push columns eastward towards Baku; so did the Turks across their Caucasian border. At the same time, the British, from their imperial base in India and from the sphere of influence established in southern Persia by great-power agreement with Tsarist Russia in 1907, advanced their own troops into the region.[28]

In the early stages of the Great War, British-Indian forces had fortified their presence in the region by creating the so-called East Persian Cordon with the object of interdicting efforts by German, Austrian and Turkish agents to foment trouble on the Indian empire's North-West Frontier through Afghanistan. The Indian 28th Cavalry had been transferred for extended duty to the East Persian Cordon,[29] while a local force, the South Persian Rifles, had been raised to patrol the border of Indian Baluchistan with the Persian empire.[30] At word of the German-Turkish advance towards Transcaucasia and Transcaspia in the spring of 1918, the British presence had been reinforced. A column of British armoured cars under General Dunsterville ('Dunsterforce') had been started forward from Mesopotamia to the Caspian, with Baku as its objective, in January. It was followed in June by a force of Indian troops, commanded by General Malleson, which crossed the North-West Frontier to establish a base in the Persian city of Meshed, south of the Caspian, with the object of preventing German or Turkish penetration of Russian Central Asia.

These were tiny forces in a vast area, but the 'Great Game' played by the British and Russians for influence over Central Asia since the early nineteenth century had never involved more than a handful of men on either side. With the incorporation during the 1880s of the Central Asian khanates and emirates into the Russian empire, Britain's opportunity to play tribal politics had been curtailed. It was extinguished altogether, as was Russia's in the opposite direction, by the Anglo-Russian Convention of 1907 'defining their respective interests in relation to Afghanistan, Persia and Tibet'.[31] Revolution revived the Great Game all over again, and multiplied the number of players. To the local tribal leaders who, at Lenin's subsequently

413

regretted encouragement, had established agencies of self-government and organised a Central Caspian Directorate, were added bodies of German and Austro-Hungarian prisoners-of-war, 35,000 in number, whose services as soldiers were eagerly solicited by all parties, though those still ready to fight inclined towards the Bolsheviks. The others included the Bolsheviks themselves, based on Astrakhan at the head of the Caspian Sea and at Tashkent on the Central Asian Railway, and the German and Turkish armies which, from their respective bases in the eastern Ukraine and the Caucasus, pushed forward soldiers and diplomatic missions, towards Baku and beyond. Finally there were British, with Dunsterville – schoolmate of Rudyard Kipling and the subject of his Stalky stories – who was principally concerned to deny Baku's oil both to the Germans and Turks and assist Malleson in interdicting Turkey's access to the Turkic-speaking peoples of Central Asia, its use of the Central Asian Railway and its desire to incite trouble inside Afghanistan on India's North-West Frontier.

The drama of the Great War in Central Asia, sensational though it potentially was, had an anti-climactic conclusion. Dunsterville was driven from Baku in September by a Turkish advance, which resulted in a massacre of Baku's Armenians by their Azeri enemies. Malleson's penetration of Central Asia was swiftly reversed, but not before the murder of twenty-six Bolshevik commissars, abducted from Baku, also in September, by his Turkic confederates, had provided the Soviet government with the raw material to damn the British as 'imperialists' to Central Asians for as long as Russian Communism would last.[32] Neither the German nor Turkish interventions in the Caspian region would endure; Germany's would be ended by its defeat on the Western Front, Turkey's by the collapse of its imperial system after the armistice of 31 October 1918.

In the long run, victory in Central Asia went to the Bolsheviks, though their war of second thoughts against the peoples of the Caucasus would last until 1921, and the struggle against the Turkic 'Basmachi' insurrectionists in Central Asia, among whom the young Turk Enver Pasha made a brief but tragic firebrand appearance after the Ottoman defeat, would persist for years after that.[33] The Central Asian episode, nevertheless, has its significance, for the British tentatives were elements in a wider scheme of foreign interference in Russian affairs that, besides poisoning relations between the West and the Soviet government for decades to come, also illuminate the diplomacy of the closing stages of the Great War in arresting focus.

The Western Allies – the French and British but also the Americans and Japanese – all sent troops to Russia during 1918. None, however, despite the version of events later constructed by Soviet historians, did so, initially, with the purpose of reversing the October Revolution. Indeed, the first troops to set foot ashore, a party of 170 British marines, who landed at the north Russian part of Murmansk on 4 March 1918, the day after the Bolsheviks at last signed the Treaty of Brest-Litovsk, arrived with the encouragement of Trotsky, who two days earlier had telegraphed the Murmansk Soviet with instructions to accept 'all and any assistance' from the Allies.[34] Trotsky and the British had a common interest. Murmansk, which had been developed as a major port of entry for British war supplies to the Russian army between 1914 and 1917, was crammed with weapons and munitions. Following the victory of the anti-Bolshevik Finns in their civil war, both Trotsky and Britain had reason to fear that the Finns and their German allies would advance to seize the material. The White Finns, who also had territorial ambitions in the region, were keen to do so; it was Mannerheim's disapproval of such a blatant and ill-judged anti-Allied initiative that, among other reasons, had caused him to give up command and retire to Sweden. Trotsky's particular anxiety was that the Finns, once rearmed, would, with German assistance, march on Petrograd, while the British were alarmed by the prospect of the Germans turning Murmansk into a naval base, north of their mine barriers, from which U-boats could roam the North Atlantic.[35]

Trotsky also wanted the store of British weapons for his own Red Army which, following the precipitate dissolution of the old Russian army on 29 January 1918, had effectively been brought into being by a decree creating a Red Army high command on 3 February; a conscription decree would shortly follow.[36] The function of the Red Army would be to defend the revolution against its real enemies, whom Trotsky identified, in a speech to the Central Committee in April 1918, not as 'our *internal* class enemies, who are pitiful', but as 'the all-powerful *external* enemies, who utilise a huge centralised machine for their mass murder and extermination'.[37] By 'external' enemies he meant those of the British, French and Americans: that is to say the Germans, Austrians and Turks, who were not only established on Russian soil but were actually extending their area of control over Russia's richest agricultural and resource-yielding regions in the Ukraine, Donetz and Caucasus. Thus, even as late as April 1918, despite the signing of the Brest-Litovsk treaty which had made a theoretical peace between the Bolsheviks and Russia's enemies, despite the ideological hostility of the Bolsheviks to the capitalist system that Britain, France and the United States represented, they and the Bolsheviks still retained a common interest, the defeat of the Central Powers.

Pursuit of the common interest had faltered in November 1917, when the Bolsheviks had proclaimed an armistice and called on the Allies to initiate peace negotiations with the Germans, Austrians and Turks.[38] It had been seriously set back in December, when France and Britain had been encouraged by the appearance of anti-Bolshevik resistance within Russia to send representatives to the counter-revolutionaries, in the hope that they would sustain the Russian war effort that Lenin and Trotsky seemed bent on terminating.[39] It had been revived in January, to such effect that in February the Bolsheviks were using the Allies' offer of assistance as an instrument to win better terms from the Germans at Brest-Litovsk. After the German imposition of the treaty, and its ratification won with difficulty by Lenin from the Fourth Soviet Congress on 15 March, it seemed fated for extinction.[40] Yet, thanks to the heavy-handidness of German occupation policy in the Ukraine and beyond, it might still have survived, had not haphazard and unforeseen events supervened to set the Bolsheviks and the West irredeemably at odds.

In the summer of 1918, the Western Allies became inextricably entangled with the Bolsheviks' Russian enemies. That had not been the Allies' intention. Calamitous though the October Revolution had been to their cause and repugnant though the Bolshevik programme was to their governments, sufficient realism prevailed in their policy-making to deter them from opening an irreparable breach with the regime that controlled Russia's capital city and what survived, even in an unfamiliar form, of its administrative system. The Bolsheviks' domestic enemies, though patriotic, anti-German and supporters of the traditional order, were disorganised, disunited and dispersed around the margins of Russia's heartland. The most important grouping, known as the Volunteer Army, had actually come into being through the flight in November 1917 of two of the Tsar's leading generals, Alexeyev, his Chief of Staff, and Kornilov, who had led the August attempt to restore his authority, from their badly guarded prison at Bykhov, near the former supreme headquarters at Mogilev, to the distant Don region in South Russia.[41] The Don had been chosen as their destination because it was the homeland of the largest of the

Cossack hosts, whose fierce personal loyalty to the Tsar made them seem the most promising confederates in raising the standard of counter-revolution against the Petrograd Bolsheviks. Neither the Don Cossacks, nor those of the more remote Kuban steppe, were, however, sufficiently numerous or well-organised to prove a real threat to Soviet power, as the leaders of the Volunteer Army swiftly found. Don Cossack resistance collapsed in February 1918, under the weight of a Soviet counter-attack, and when Kornilov withdrew the tiny Volunteer Army across the steppe towards the Kuban, disaster ensued. Kornilov was killed by a chance shell and, although he was replaced by the energetic Denikin, the new leader could not find a secure base for his refugee force.[42] Only 4,000 strong, it seemed fated in April to disintegrate under Bolshevik pressure and the pitilessness of Russia's vast space.

What changed everything – for the Bolsheviks, for their Russian enemies and for the Western Allies – in the unfolding of the struggle for power within Russia was the emergence to importance of a force none of them had taken into account, the body of Czechoslovak prisoners of war released by the November armistice from captivity in the Ukraine. In April they began to make their way out of Russia to join the armies of the Allies in the Western Front. The Ukraine in 1918 was full of prisoners of war, German as well as Austro-Hungarian, but, while the Germans awaited liberation at the hands of the advancing German army, the two largest Austro-Hungarian contingents, Poles and Czechs, were determined not to be repatriated. Their hopes were that, by changing sides, they might advance the liberation of their homelands from imperial rule. The Poles made the mistake of throwing in their lot with the separatist Ukrainians and were overwhelmed in February by the Germans when the Rada, the Ukrainian nationalist committee, signed its own peace at Brest-Litovsk. The cannier Czechs put no trust in the Rada, insisted on being allowed to leave Russia for France via the Trans-Siberian Railway, secured Bolshevik agreement to their demand in March and by May were on their way.[43] Their journey pleased neither the British, who had hoped the Czechs would go north to assist in the defence of Murmansk, nor the French, who wanted the Czechs to remain in the Ukraine and fight the Germans. The Czechs, who were in direct contact with the foreign-based leaders of their provisional government, Masaryk and Benes, were adamant. Their objective was the Pacific terminal of the Trans-Siberian at Vladivostok, from which they expected to take ship to France. They intended that nothing should interrupt their transit.

It was nevertheless interrupted on 14 May 1918 when, at Cheliabinsk in western Siberia, an altercation broke out between the eastward-bound Czechs and some Hungarian prisoners being returned westward to the Habsburg army.[44] Two patriotisms were involved: that of the Czechs for an independent Czechoslovakia, that of the Hungarians for their privileged place in the Habsburg system. A Czech was wounded, his Hungarian assailant was lynched and, when the local Bolsheviks intervened to restore order, the Czechs rose in arms to put them down and assert their right to use the Trans-Siberian Railway for their exclusive purposes. As they numbered 40,000, strung out in organised units along the whole length of the railway from the Volga to Vladivostok, suspected correctly that the Bolsheviks desired to disarm them and dismember their organisation, and were under the influence of an aggressively anti-Bolshevik officer, Rudolph Gajda, they were both in a position and soon in a mood to deny the use of the railway to anyone else.[45] The loss of the Trans-Siberian was a serious setback to the Bolsheviks, since their seizure and retention of power was railway-based. Worse was to follow. The Czechs, originally neutral between the Bolsheviks and their Russian enemies, embarked on a series of sharp local operations eastward along the railway which had the indirect effect of overturning Soviet power in Siberia; 'by midsummer 1918, both Siberia and the Urals [territorially the greater area of Russia] had been lost to the Bolsheviks'.[46]

Meanwhile the Western Allies, committed as they were to the extraction of the Czech Corps for service on the Western Front, began to channel direct aid, in the form of money and weapons as well as encouragement, to the Czechs, who found a sudden enthusiasm not to leave Russia before they had dealt the Bolsheviks a death blow. At the same time, the Russian anti-Bolsheviks, including both the forces of a self-proclaimed Supreme Ruler, Admiral Kolchak, in Siberia and the original standard-bearers of revolt in South Russia, the Volunteer Army of Denikin, as well as the Don and Kuban Cossack Hosts, were heartened by the Czech success to return to the fray with renewed confidence. The apparent commonality of cause between them and the Czechs thus came to qualify them for Allied support also. It had not at the outset been the Allies' intention to make the Bolsheviks their enemies and there were good reasons for their not doing so, the Bolsheviks' genuine hostility to the Germans, Austrians and Turks, all established as conquerors and predators on historic Russian territory foremost among them. By the late summer of 1918, nevertheless, the Allies found themselves effectively at war with the Bolshevik government in Moscow, supporting counter-revolution in the south and in Siberia, and sustaining intervention forces of their own, British in North Russia, French in the Ukraine, Japanese and American on the Pacific Coast.

A war entirely subsidiary to the Great War ensued. In North Russia a mixed French-British-American force, under the command of the formidable and physically gigantic British General Ironside – a future Chief of the Imperial General Staff and alleged model for the fictional Richard Hannay of John Buchan's enormously popular adventure stories – made common cause with the local anti-Bolshevik Social Revolutionaries and pushed out a defensive perimeter 200 miles to the south of the White Sea; at Tulgas on the River Dvina, it sat out the winter of 1918–19, while the Bolsheviks organised forces against it.[47] Ironside meanwhile raised a local force of British-officered Russian troops, the Slavo-British Legion, received an Italian reinforcement, accepted the assistance of a Finnish contingent principally interested in annexing Russian territory, an aim from which it had to be deflected, and co-operated generally with the commanders of the British intervention forces in the Baltic. These included military missions to the Baltic-German militias in Latvia and Estonia – the most soldierly men he ever commanded, the future Field Marshal Alexander would say – and to the armies of the emergent states of Lithuania, Latvia and Estonia, as well as Rear Admiral Sir Walter Cowan's Baltic naval force.[48] Cowan's torpedo boats would, in the summer of 1919, sink two Russian battleships in Kronstadt harbour, the most important units of what remained of the new Soviet state's navy.[49] Meanwhile, in December 1918, the French landed troops in the Black Sea ports of Odessa and Sevastopol, units which included Greek and Polish contingents, attempted to raise local legions of Russians under French officers, established quarrelsome relations with the White forces and fell to fighting, unsuccessfully, against the Reds.[50] In the Far East both Japanese and American troops were landed at Vladivostok in August 1918, to consolidate a bridgehead for the evacuation of the Czech corps. A French supreme commander, Janin, next arrived to oversee operations, while the British unshipped large quantities of military stores to supply Admiral Kolchak's anti-Bolshevik army. The Japanese advanced towards Lake Baikal, the

Americans stayed put. Both contingents eventually left for home, while the Czechs, whom they had been sent to assist, finally struggled out of Russia in September 1920.[51] Allied intervention in the Russian Far East achieved nothing but the confirmation in Soviet eyes of the West's fundamentally anti-Bolshevik policy.

The reality of its policy was entirely contrary. On 22 July 1918, the British Prime Minister, David Lloyd George, told the War Cabinet that it was '"none of Britain's business what sort of government the Russians set up: a republic, a Bolshevik state or a monarchy". The indications are that President Wilson shared this view.'[52] It was a view that the French for a time shared also; until April, the dominant party in the French General Staff opposed offering support to the anti-Bolsheviks, the 'so-called patriotic groups', on the grounds that they favoured the German forces of occupation for class reasons, while the Bolsheviks, who had been 'duped by the Central Powers and [were now] perhaps aware of past errors', at least promised to continue the struggle.[53] France would later repudiate that position, to become the most sternly anti-Bolshevik of all the Allied powers. During the spring of 1918, however, it shared British and American hopes that the Bolsheviks could be used to reconstitute an Eastern Front on which military action would relieve the pressure in the west that threatened Allied defeat. That they also looked to the Czechs to reopen an Eastern offensive, and allowed themselves to be drawn progressively and piecemeal into complicity with the Whites, confuses an issue which Lenin and Stalin were later to represent in terms of outright Allied hostility to the Revolution from the start. In truth, the Allies, desperate for any diversion of German effort from their climactic offensive in France, did not become committedly anti-Bolshevik until the mid-summer of 1918 and then because the signs indicated, correctly, that the Bolsheviks had strayed from their own initially anti-German policy towards one of accepting German indulgence of their survival.

Until mid-summer the Germans, just as much as the Allies, had been puzzled to know how best to choose between Russia's warring parties for their own advantage. The army, which feared Red infection at home and the front, wanted the Bolsheviks 'liquidated'.[54] The Foreign Office, by contrast, though sharing the army's desire to keep Russia weak, and eventually to dismember it, argued that it was the Bolsheviks who had signed the Treaty of Brest-Litovsk, that the 'patriotic groups' rejected it and that it was in Germany's interest, therefore, to support the former at the expense of the latter. On 28

June the Kaiser, required to opt between pro- and anti-Bolshevik policies, accepted a Foreign Office recommendation that the Bolshevik government be assured that neither the German forces in the Baltic States nor their Finnish allies would move against Petrograd, which they were in a position to capture with ease, an assurance that permitted Lenin and Trotsky to transfer their only effective military formation, the Latvian Rifles, along the western stretch of the Trans-Siberian Railway to the Urals. There, at Kazan, at the end of July, they attacked the Czech Legion, and so began a counter-offensive that eventually unblocked the railway, pushed the Czechs eastward towards Vladivostok and brought supplies and reinforcements to the Red Armies fighting Kolchak's and Denikin's Whites in South Russia and Siberia.[55] The counter-offensive was to result in a Bolshevik victory in the civil war, a victory brought about not despite the Allies' eventual commitment to the Bolsheviks' enemies but because of Germany's positive decision to let Bolshevism survive.

THE CRISIS OF WAR IN THE WEST

While ignorant armies clashed at large over the vast spaces of the east, the garrisons of the narrow ground of the Western Front pressed closer for battle. The collapse of the Tsar's armies had re-created the strategic situation on which Schlieffen had predicated his plan for lightning victory over France: a strategic interval in which there would be no threat from Russia, leaving Germany free to bring a numerical superiority to bear on the axis of advance that led to Paris. The superiority was considerable. Having left forty second-rate infantry and three cavalry divisions in the east, to garrison the enormous territories conceded by the Bolsheviks at Brest-Litovsk, Ludendorff could deploy 192 divisions in the west, against 178 Allied.[56] They included most of the original élite of the army, the Guards, Jägers, Prussians, Swabians and the best of the Bavarians. The XIV Corps, for example, consisted of the 4th Guard Division, the 25th Division, composed of bodyguard regiments of small princely states, the 1st Division, from Prussia, and a wartime division, the 228th Reserve, formed of regiments from Brandenburg and the Prussian heartland.[57] All, by the fourth year of the war, contained a high proportion of replacements, and replacements of replacements, among their personnel; some infantry regiments had suffered over a hundred per cent

421

casualties, with individuals alone representing the cadres which had marched to war in 1914. As formations, nevertheless, they retained their *esprit de corps*, reinforced by the long string of victories won in the east. Only in the west had the German armies not yet overthrown the enemies they had faced; and, in the spring of 1918, the Kaiser's soldiers had been promised that the coming offensives would complete the record of triumph.

What the German infantry could not know, though they might guess, was that they constituted their country's last reserve of manpower. Britain and France were in no better case, both having reduced their infantry divisions from a strength of twelve to nine battalions in the previous year, and both lacking any further human resource from which to fill gaps in the ranks. They, however, had superior stocks of material – 4,500 against 3,670 German aircraft, 18,500 against 14,000 German guns, 800 against 10 German tanks – and, above all, they could look to the gathering millions of Americans to make good their inability to replace losses. Germany, by contrast, having embodied all its untrained men of military age not employed in absolutely essential civilian callings, could by January 1918 look only to the conscript class of 1900; and those youths would not become eligible for enlistment until the autumn. A double imperative thus pressed upon Hindenburg, Ludendorff and their soldiers in March 1918: to win the war before the New World appeared to redress the balance of the Old, but also to win before German manhood was exhausted by the ordeal of a final attack.

The choice of front for the final attack was limited, as it had always been for both sides, since the theatre of operations in the west had been entrenched at the end of the war of movement in 1914. The French had tried for a breakthrough in Artois and Champagne twice, in 1915, and then again in Champagne in 1917. The British had tried on the Somme in 1916 and in Flanders in 1917. The Germans had tried, in 1916, only at Verdun and then with limited objectives. For them, the era of limited objectives was over. They now had to destroy an army, the French or British, if they were to prevail, and the choice of front resolved itself into another effort at Verdun or a strike against the British. The options had been reviewed at the fateful conference at Mons on 11 November 1917. Colonel von der Schulenberg, Chief of Staff of the German Crown Prince's Army Group, there advocated a reprise of the offensive on its front, which included Verdun, on the grounds that a defeat of the British armies, however severe, would not deter Britain from continuing the war. If France were broken, how-ever – and the Verdun front offered the most promising locality for such an undertaking – the situation in the west would be transformed. Lieutenant Colonel Wetzell, Head of the Operations Section of the General Staff, concurred, and amplified Schulenberg's analysis: Verdun, he said, should be the place, for a victory there would shake French morale to its roots, prevent any chance of France mounting an offensive with American help and would expose the British to a subsequent German attack.

Ludendorff would have none of it. Having heard his subordinates out, he announced that German strength sufficed for only one great blow and laid down three conditions on which it must be based. Germany must strike as early as possible, 'before America can throw strong forces into the scale', which would mean the end of February or beginning of March. The object must be to 'beat the British'. He surveyed the sectors of the front on which such a blow might be launched and, discounting Flanders, announced that an attack 'near St Quentin appeared promising'.[58] That was the sector from which the great strategic withdrawal to the newly constructed Hindenburg Line had been made the previous spring. In front of it lay what the British called 'the old Somme battlefield' of 1916, a wasteland of shell holes and abandoned trenches. By attacking there, Ludendorff suggested, the assault divisions, in an operation to be codenamed Michael, could drive up the line of the River Somme towards the sea and 'roll up' the British front. There the matter was left. There were to be further conferences and more paper considerations of alternatives, including an attack in Flanders, codenamed George, another at Arras, code-named Mars and a third nearer Paris, codenamed Archangel, but on 21 January 1918, Ludendorff, after a final inspection of the armies, issued definite orders for Michael. The Kaiser was informed of the intention that day. Preliminary operational instructions were sent on 24 January and 8 February. On 10 March, the detailed plan was promulgated over Hindenburg's name: 'The Michael attack will take place on 21 March. Break into the first enemy positions at 9.40 a.m.'

Much tactical instruction accompanied the strategic directive. A Bavarian officer, Captain Hermann Geyer, had consolidated the army's thinking on the new concept of 'infiltration' – though the word was not one the German army used – and the obvious difficulties in his manual *The Attack in Position Warfare* of January 1918, by which Operation Michael was to be fought. It stressed rapid advance and disregard for security of the flanks.[59] 'The tactical breakthrough is not an objective in itself. Its purpose is to give the opportunity to apply the strongest form of attack, envelopment . . . infantry which looks to the right or the left soon comes to a stop . . . the fastest, not the slowest, must set the pace . . . the infantry must be warned against too great dependency on the creeping barrage.'[60] The specialised storm troops of the leading waves were above all to 'push on'. Ludendorff summed up Michael's object with a disavowal of the concept of a fixed strategic aim. 'We will punch a hole . . . For the rest, we shall see. We did it this way in Russia.'[61]

There were enough attack divisions which had served in Russia to bring to France some of the confidence won in a succession of victories over the Tsar's, Kerensky's and Lenin's armies. The British, however, were not Russians. Better equipped, better trained and so far un-defeated on the Western Front, they were unlikely to collapse simply because a hole was punched in their front. Ludendorff had, however, chosen better than he might have known in selecting the Somme as his principal assault zone. It was garrisoned by the Fifth Army, numerically almost the weakest of Haig's four armies, and one that had suffered heavily in the Passchendaele fighting and had not fully recovered. It was also commanded by a general, Hubert Gough, whose reputation was not for thoroughness, while the sector it occupied was the most difficult of all in the British zone to defend.

Gough, a cavalryman and a favourite of Douglas Haig, a fellow cavalryman, had played a leading part in the Passchendaele offensive and his army had suffered a major share of the casualties. Officers who served under him formed the opinion that lives were lost in the battles he organised because he failed to co-ordinate artillery support with infantry assaults, failed to limit his objectives to attainable ends, failed to curtail operations that had patently failed and failed to meet the standards of administrative efficiency which the commander of the neighbouring Second Army, Plumer, so estimably did. Lloyd George, during the winter of 1917, had tried to have Gough removed, but Haig's protection had spared him from dismissal. He now had to cope with two problems which exceeded his capacity to handle.

Neither was of his own making. The first concerned a major re-organisation of the army. At the beginning of 1918, the British, accepting a necessity recognised by the Germans in 1915 and the French in 1917, began to reduce the strength of its divisions from twelve battalions to nine. The change could be justified as a fulfilment of the trend to increase the proportion of artillery to infantry in each division, as it partly did, a recognition of the growing importance of heavy fire support as the war became one of guns rather than men. The underlying reason, however, was simply a shortage of soldiers. The War Cabinet had calculated that the British Expeditionary Force would require 615,000 men in 1918, simply to make good losses, but that only 100,000 were available from recruits at home, despite conscription.[62] The expedient accepted, besides that of dismounting some cavalry units, was to disband 145 battalions, and use their manpower as reinforcements for the remainder. Even so, nearly a quarter of the battalions had to leave the divisions in which they had served for years and find a new accommodation with unfamiliar commanders, supporting artillery batteries and engineer companies and neighbour battalions. It was particularly unfortunate that a high proportion of the disbanded and displaced battalions belonged to Gough's Fifth Army which, as the most recently formed, contained the largest number of the more junior war-raised units on whom the order to change divisions fell. Though reorganisation began in January, it was not completed until early March, and Gough's administrative failings then still left much work of integration to be done.

Gough had also had to position his army not only on a difficult battlefield but, in parts, on an unfamiliar one. As a help to the French, after the breakdown of so many of their formations in 1917, Haig had agreed to take over a portion of their line precisely in the sector chosen by Ludendorff for his great spring offensive. Gough had therefore to extend his right across the Somme, into the notoriously ill-maintained French trench system, while at the same time attempting to deepen and strengthen the extemporised defences dug by the British in front of the old Somme battlefield after the advance to the Hindenburg Line a year earlier. The task was onerous. Not only were the trenches behind the front line sketchy; the labour to improve his sector was lacking. The war in France was, quite as much as a shooting war, a digging war, and while his weakened divisions lacked the necessary hands in their infantry battalions, the specialist pioneer labour enlisted to supplement the work of the infantry was deficient also. In February, Fifth Army's labour force numbered only 18,000; by ruthless drafting from elsewhere, and by recruiting Chinese and Italian workers, the total was raised in early March to 40,000; but the majority of diggers were employed on roadwork.[63] Only a fifth of the

The German offensives, 1918

available hands were building defences, with the result that, while the first of the Fifth Army's three lines, the Forward, was complete, and the main, the Battle Zone, well provided with strongpoints and artillery positions, the third, or Brown Line, to which the defenders were to retire as an ultimate resort, was only 'spit-locked'. That meant that the surface had been excavated only to a foot's depth, that there were but occasional belts of wire and that machine-gun positions were indicated by notice boards.[64]

It was against these sketchy defences that the storm broke on the morning of 21 March. A compact mass of seventy-six first class German divisions fell upon twenty-eight British divisions, of unequal quality, the Germans advancing behind a surprise artillery bombardment across a front of fifty miles, on a morning of mist thickened by the use of gas, chlorine and phosgene, and lachrymatory shell. The gas was lethal, the lachrymatory an irritant designed to make the British infantry remove their respirators. 'It was impossible to see beyond a few yards outside as the misty fog was now thick and the cascade of screaming shells, explosions and vivid flashes everywhere was something one just endured', wrote Private A.H. Flindt, of the Royal Army Medical Corps, 'and waited for it to go – but it didn't.'[65] The barrage, intermixed with blistering mustard gas, went on for five hours, from 4.40 a.m. until 9.40 when, as Hindenburg's operation order of 10 March had laid down, the German storm troopers emerged from their trenches, passed through the gaps in their own wire, crossed no man's land and began to penetrate the positions of the dazed defenders opposite.

'Artillery was the great leveller', wrote Private T. Jacobs, of the 1st West Yorkshire Regiment, one of the regular battalions that had been in France from the beginning. 'Nobody could stand more than three hours of sustained shelling before they started feeling sleepy and numb. You're hammered after three hours and you're there for the picking when he comes over. It's a bit like being under an anaesthetic; you can't put a lot of resistance up . . . On the other fronts I had been on, there had been so much of our resistance that, whenever Gerry opened up, our artillery opened up and quietened him down but there was no retaliation this time. He had a free do at us.'[66]

Enough of the British defenders and their supporting artillery had survived the German bombardment, nevertheless, to offer scattered resistance as the Germans came forward. Firing largely blind by the 'Pulkowski' method, which depended on meteorological observation,

427

the German gunners had missed or overshot some key targets. As the Germans appeared out of no man's land, British guns and machine-gun nests sprang to life and surviving trench garrisons manned the parapet. 'I took up my position and I could see the Germans quite easily', wrote Private J. Jolly, of the 9th Norfolks, a Kitchener battalion, 'coming over a bank in large numbers about 200 to 300 yards away. They had already taken our front line [in the 6th Division Sector]. We opened fire and there appeared to be hundreds coming over that bank but they might just have been killed lying down. Their attack was certainly halted.'[67] Some way to the north of the Norfolks' position, a German NCO

> went on further against only feeble resistance but then the fog lifted and we were fired on by a machine-gun post. I got several bullets through my jacket but was not hit. We all took cover ... A platoon from another company joined me and between us we killed the six or seven men – every one of them – in the machine-gun post. I lost five or six men ... I looked across to the right and there were British prisoners going back ... about 120 – a company perhaps. They were stooping and hurrying back to avoid being hit. I think the English position had been covered by the nest that we had just wiped out and this much larger number of enemy decided they had better surrender.[68]

British machine-gunners in another post were luckier. 'I thought we had stopped them', remembered Private J. Parkinson,

> when I felt a bump in the back. I turned round and there was a German officer with a revolver in my back. 'Come along, Tommy. You've done enough.' I turned round then and said 'Thank you very much, Sir.' I know what I would have done if I had been held up by a machine gunner and had that revolver in my hand, I'd have finished him off. He must have been a real gentleman. It was twenty past ten. I know to the minute because I looked at my watch.[69]

By this time, only an hour after the German infantry had left their trenches for the assault, almost all the British positions in the Fifth Army's Forward Zone, twelve miles wide, had been overrun; only behind the obstacle of the ruined town of St Quentin was a stretch of line still held. It would soon fall as the Germans pressed on to the main battle zone, or Red Line. Much more strongly manned, the Red Line, attacked about noon, though in places earlier, put up a stronger resistance. Though it had been hit by the German preparatory bombardment, and then come under fire from the creeping barrage, artillery support for the German infantry naturally fell away as they entered their own beaten zone. The British artillery, which steadfastly refused to surrender some gun positions though outflanked to left and right, also helped to sustain the opposition the attackers met. A German corporal reported such an encounter.

> Suddenly, we were fired on by a battery with shrapnel at close range and had to throw ourselves to the ground. Closely packed, we found cover behind a low railway embankment . . . We had advanced seven to eight kilometres as the crow flies and now lay under a medium-calibre battery, under direct fire. The report from the guns and the explosion of the shells were simultaneous. A frontal attack against this made no sense . . . As suddenly as it had started, it stopped; we could breathe again. We rose up and were able to advance to the abandoned battery. The barrels of the guns were still hot. We saw some of the gunners running away.[70]

Much of the Red Line was lost to the British during the afternoon, either because the garrison ran away or was overwhelmed by the power of the attack. The worst loss of ground occurred south of St Quentin, at the point of junction with the French Sixth Army, which held the confluence of the Oise and Aisne rivers. As the British divisions in Gough's southernmost sector, the 36th (Ulster), the 14th, 18th and 58th Divisions, gave ground, the French were obliged to fall back also, opening a re-entrant that pointed towards Paris itself. In Gough's northern sector, where the Flesquières salient left by the battle for Cambrai in the previous November bulged into the German line, the Germans achieved a dangerous envelopment menacing the security of the British Third Army and threatening to undercut the British hold on Flanders. Since the aim of Operation Michael was to 'roll up' the British Expeditionary Force against the shore of the English Channel, it now promised to be achieving its object. In fact, the purpose of the German attack on each side of Flesquières was to cut off the salient, rather than capture it outright, thus adding to the bag of prisoners and opening a hole at the critical point of junction between Fifth and Third Armies through which a strong thrust north-eastward could be pushed.

As evening fell on 21 March, the BEF had suffered its first true defeat since trench warfare had begun three and a half years earlier. Along a front of nineteen miles, the whole forward position had been lost, except in two places held heroically by the South African Brigade and a brigade formed of three battalions of the Leicestershire Regiment, and much of the main position had been penetrated also. Guns had been lost in numbers, whole units had surrendered or fled to the rear and heavy casualties had been suffered by those that did stand and fight. In all, over 7,000 British infantrymen had been killed but 21,000 soldiers had been taken prisoner. The events of the day were the contrary of those of 1 July 1916, when 20,000 British soldiers had been killed but almost none had been taken prisoner and the high command and press alike had claimed a victory.

Day one of Operation Michael had undoubtedly been a German victory, although the total of German dead, over 10,000, exceeded that of the British, and the number of wounded – nearly 29,000 German against 10,000 British – greatly so. Even though some British battalions had given their all, an example being the 7th Sherwood Foresters, which lost 171 killed, including the commanding officer, they were the exception. The loss of ten infantry lieutenant colonels killed testifies to the desperate fight put up by some units; but it is also evidence of the degree of disorganisation that it required commanding officers to place themselves in the front line and, by setting an example to their stricken soldiers, pay the supreme sacrifice. Well-prepared units do not lose senior officers in such numbers, even in the circumstances of a whirlwind enemy offensive, unless there has been a collapse of morale at the lower level or a failure to provide support by higher authority. Both conditions were present in Fifth Army on 21 March. Many of the units, worn down by the attrition battles of 1917, were not in a fit state to defend their fronts, which were in any case patchily fortified, while Fifth Army's headquarters had no proper plan prepared to deal with a collapse should it begin to develop. 'I must confess', wrote an experienced infantryman in a retrospect of the aftermath, 'that the German breakthrough of 21 March 1918 should never have occurred. There was no cohesion of command, no determination, no will to fight, and no unity of companies or battalions.' The question must be whether the collapse, for collapse it was, belongs to the same psychological order of events as the collapse of the French army in the spring of 1917, the collapse of the Russian army after the Kerensky offensive and the collapse of the Italian army during Caporetto. All four armies, if the British are included, had by then

suffered over a hundred per cent casualties in their infantry complement, measured against the numbers with which they had gone to war,
and may simply have passed beyond the point of what was bearable by
flesh and blood.

If there is a difference to be perceived, it is in the extent of the psychological trauma and in its containment. The French army exhibited
signs of breakdown in over half its fighting formations and took a year
to recover. The Italian army, though it was chiefly the divisions on the
Isonzo front that gave way, suffered a general crisis, never really
recovered and had to be reinforced by large numbers of British and
French troops. The Russian army, under the strain of successive
defeats, two revolutions and the disintegration of the state system,
broke down altogether and eventually dissolved. The crisis of the
British Fifth Army was of a different and lesser order. Its defeat was
undoubtedly moral rather than material in character, and in that sense
resembled the defeat of Caporetto, but its malaise did not infect the
three other British armies, Third, Second or First; indeed, it was quite
swiftly contained within the Fifth Army itself which, only a week after
the German offensive's opening, had begun to recover and was fighting back. It had lost much ground and had been heavily re-inforced,
by other British, by French and by some American troops, yet it had
never ceased to function as an organisation, while many of its units
had sustained the will to resist, to hold ground and even to counter-
attack.

The worst days of the German offensive for the British, but also for
the Allies as a whole, were the third, fourth and fifth, 24–6 March,
days in which the danger grew of a separation of the British from the
French armies and of a progressive displacement of the whole British
line north-eastward towards the channel ports, precisely that 'rolling
up' which Ludendorff had laid down as Operation Michael's object.
The spectre of a breaking of the front infected the French high
command, just as it had done during the Marne campaign; but, while
in 1914 Joffre had used every measure at his disposal to keep in touch
with the BEF, now Pétain, commanding the French armies of the
north, took counsel of his fears. At eleven in the morning of 24 March,
he visited Haig at his headquarters to warn that he expected to be
attacked himself north of Verdun, could offer no more reinforcements
and now had as his principal concern the defence of Paris. When Haig
asked if he understood and accepted that the likely outcome of his
refusal to send further help was a separation of their two armies,

Pétain merely nodded his head.[71] Haig instantly realised that he had an inter-Allied crisis on his hands. Whereas, however, in similar circumstances in 1914, it was the British War Office which had taken steps to stiffen Sir John French's resolve, now Haig telephoned the War Office to ask for help in stiffening Pétain's. Two days later, at Doullens, near Amiens, directly in the line of the German axis of advance, an extempore Anglo-French conference was convened, chaired by the French President, Poincaré, and including Clemenceau, the Prime Minister, and Lord Milner, the British War Minister, as well as Pétain, Haig and Foch, as French Chief of Staff.

The meeting did not begin well. Haig outlined what had happened to the Fifth Army, explained that he had now put the portion of it south of the Somme under Pétain's control, as he had, but expressed his inability to do anything more in that sector. Pétain objected that the Fifth Army was 'broken' and untactfully compared Gough's troops to the Italians at Caporetto. There was an altercation between him and Henry Wilson, the Chief of the Imperial General Staff, ended by Pétain protesting that he had sent all the help he could and that the aim must now be to defend Amiens. Amiens was twenty miles beyond the furthest point yet reached by the Germans. At its mention, Foch, fireating as ever, burst out, 'we must fight in front of Amiens, we must fight where we are now . . . we must not now retire a single inch'. His intervention retrieved the situation. There were some hasty conversations in corners, after which it was suddenly agreed that Haig would serve under the command of Foch, who would be 'charged . . . with the co-ordination of the action of the British and French armies'.[72] The formula satisfied all parties, even Haig, who had resisted any dilution of his absolute independence of command ever since appointed to lead the BEF in December 1915. Foch's authority would be extended, on 3 April, to comprehend 'the direction of strategic operations', making him in effect Allied generalissimo.

His appointment came only just in time. The Germans by 5 April had advanced twenty miles on a front of fifty miles and stood within five miles of Amiens, which was defended by a screen of makeshift units, including engineers and railway troops, some American, fighting as infantry. The appointment of a single commander with absolute authority to allot reserves, French and British alike, wherever they were most needed, was essential in such a crisis. Nevertheless, the Germans were by this stage of their offensive in crisis also. Not only had the pace of their advance slowed, the advance itself had taken the wrong direction.

Yet sense of crisis was absent. The Kaiser was so delighted with the progress of the advance that on 23 March he had given German schoolchildren a 'victory' holiday and conferred on Hindenburg the Great Cross of the Iron Cross, last awarded to Blücher for the defeat of Napoleon in 1815. The map, nevertheless, by then already showed evidence of a crisis in development, and it was to grow with every passing day. Because the greatest success had been won at the outset on the extreme right of the British line, where it joined the French south of the Somme, it was in that sector that the German high command now decided to make the decisive effort, with the Second and Eighteenth Armies. The object was to be the separation of the British and French armies, while the Seventeenth was to follow behind and on the two leading armies' flank and the Sixth to prepare an advance north-westward towards the sea.[73] The order marked an abandonment of the strategy of a single, massive thrust, and the adoption of a three-pronged advance in which none of the prongs would be strong enough to achieve a breakthrough. As in 1914, during the advance on Paris, the German army was reacting to events, following the line of least resistance, rather than dominating and determining the outcome.

The accidents of military geography also began to work to the Germans' disadvantage. The nearer they approached Amiens, the more deeply did they become entangled in the obstacles of the old Somme battlefield, a wilderness of abandoned trenches, broken roads and shell-crater fields left behind by the movement of the front a year earlier. The Somme may not have won the war for the British in 1916 but the obstacle zone it left helped to ensure that in 1918 they did not lose it. Moreover, the British rear areas, stuffed with the luxuries enjoyed by the army of a nation which had escaped the years of blockade that in Germany had made the simplest necessities of life rare and expensive commodities, time and again tempted the advancing Germans to stop, plunder and satiate themselves. Colonel Albrecht von Thaer recorded that 'entire divisions totally gorged themselves on food and liquor' and had failed 'to press the vital attack forward'.[74]

Desolation and the temptation to loot may have been enemies as deadly to the Germans as the resistance of the enemy itself. On 4 April, however, the British added to their difficulties by launching a counterattack, mounted by the Australian Corps, outside Amiens, and next

433

day the German high command recognised that Operation Michael had run its course. 'OHL was forced to take the extremely hard decision to abandon the attack on Amiens for good . . . The enemy resistance was beyond our powers.' The Germans put their losses at a quarter of a million men, killed and wounded, about equal to those of the French and British combined, but the effect on the picked divisions assembled for the 'war-winning' Kaiser Battle went far beyond any numerical calculation of cost. 'More than ninety German divisions . . . were exhausted and demoralised . . . Many were down to 2,000 men.'[75] While the Allied losses included men of all categories, from combat infantry to line-of-communication troops, the German casualties had been suffered among an irreplaceable élite. The cause of the failure, moreover, reflected Major Wilhelm von Leeb, who would command one of Hitler's army groups in the Second World War, was that 'OHL has changed direction. It has made its decisions according to the size of territorial gain, rather than operational goals.'

Ludendorff's young staff officers, of whom Leeb was one and Thaer another, reproached him, as the fellowship of the Great General Staff allowed them to do, with Operation Michael's mismanagement. 'What is the purpose of your croaking?' he riposted. 'What do you want from me? Am I now to conclude peace at any price?'[76] That time of reckoning was not far distant, but, as Michael drew to its close, Ludendorff, refusing to admit a setback, immediately inaugurated the subordinate scheme, Operation George, against the British in Flanders. The objective, the channel coast behind Ypres, should have been easier to achieve than that of Operation Michael, for the sea lay only sixty miles beyond the point of assault; but the front before Ypres, on whose defences the BEF had laboured since October 1914, was perhaps stronger than any part of the Western Front, and the British were familiar with every nook and cranny of its trenches.

Mist again helped the Germans on 9 April by cloaking their preliminary moves and they also enjoyed a superiority in heavy artillery, the Bruchmüller battering train having been brought northward from the Somme for the preliminary bombardment. Weight of fire won an opening advantage. It frightened Haig enough for him to issue a message to Second and First Armies on 11 April which became famous as the 'Backs to the Wall' order. 'With our backs to the wall', it read, 'and believing in the justice of our cause, each one of us must fight on to the end . . . Every position must be held to the last man. There must be no retirement.' Retirement there was nonetheless, in part because Foch, now exerting to the full his power to allocate reserves, took the harsh but correct view that the British could survive without French help and must fight the battle out with their own reserves. The valiant little Belgian army took over a portion of the British line, the Royal Flying Corps operated energetically in close support, despite bad flying weather, and British machine gunners found plentiful targets as the German infantry pressed home their attacks almost in 1914 style. On 24 April, south of Ypres, the Germans succeeded in mounting one of their rare tank attacks of the war, but it was checked by the appearance of British tanks, superior both in number and quality, and repulsed. On 25 April the Germans succeeded in capturing one of the Flemish high points, Mount Kemmel, and on 29 April, another, the Scherpenberg, but those achievements marked the limit of their advance. On 29 April, Ludendorff accepted that, as on the Somme the month before, he had shot his bolt and must stop. The German official history recorded, 'The attack had not penetrated to the decisive heights of Cassel and the Mont des Cats, the possession of which would have compelled the [British] evacuation of the Ypres salient and the Yser position. No great strategic movement had become possible, and the Channel ports had not been reached. The second great offensive had not brought about the hoped-for decision.'[77]

The most noted event of the second German offensive had been the death in action on 21 April of the 'Red Baron', Manfred von Richthofen, leader of the Flying Circus and, with eighty victories in aerial combat, the highest ranking pilot ace in any of the war's air forces. Air operations were, however, marginal to the issue of defeat or victory even in 1918, when investment in air forces had begun to figure significantly among the allocation of national military resources. The true human significance of the 'Kaiser Battles' was thus far better represented by the balance sheet struck by the German army's medical reports in April. They established that between 21 March and 10 April, the three main assaulting armies 'had lost one-fifth of their original strength, or 303,450 men'. Worse was to come. The April offensive against the British in Flanders was eventually computed to have cost 120,000 men, out of a total strength of 800,000 in Fourth and Sixth Armies. A report from Sixth Army warned in mid-April that 'the troops will not attack, despite orders. The offensive has come to a halt.'[78]

Frustrated on the northern front, Ludendorff now decided to shift his effort against the French. From the nose of the salient created by the great advance of March, he might either have swung north-westward, as his original plan anticipated, or south-westward. Military logic was for the former option, which threatened the British rear area and the channel ports. The second, however, was favoured by the grain of the country, which offered an axis of advance down the valley of the Oise, and by the temptation of Paris, only seventy miles distant. Between it and the German armies stood the Chemin des Dames ridge, on which Nivelle's offensive had broken the previous May; but Nivelle had attacked in the old style, with wave after wave of infantry following the opening bombardment. Ludendorff trusted to his new style of attack to crack the French defences. He hoped, moreover, that a success would create the opportunity to renew the offensive in the north should he manage to draw enough of his enemies' reserves to the front outside Paris, which he had now brought directly under attack by the deployment of a long-range gun, known to the Allies as 'Big Bertha', which dropped shells into the city, psychologically if not objectively to considerable effect, from a range of seventy-five miles.

For this third offensive the largest concentration of artillery yet assembled was brought to the front, 6,000 guns supplied from an ammunition stock of two million shells.[79] All were fired off in a little over four hours on the morning of 27 May, against sixteen Allied divisions; three were British, exhausted in the battles of March and April, and brought down to the Chemin des Dames to rest. Immediately after the bombardment ceased, fifteen divisions of the German Sixth Army, with twenty-five more following, crossed a succession of water lines to reach the summit of the ridge, roll over it and continue down the reverse slope to the level ground beyond. The plan required them to halt, when open country was reached, as a preliminary to renewing the attack in the north, but the opportunity created was too attractive to relinquish. Ludendorff decided to exploit the gains of the first two days and during the next five days pressed his divisions forward as far as Soissons and Chateau-Thierry, until his outposts stood only fifty-six miles from the French capital. The Allies committed their reserves as slowly as they could, seeking to deny the Germans the satisfaction of a battle to the death, but even so were forced to engage three divisions on 28 May, five on 29 May, eight on 30 May, four on 31 May, five on 1 June and two more by 3 June. They included the 3rd and 2nd American Divisions, the latter including a brigade of the US Marine Corps, the most professional element of the doughboy army, and at Belleau Wood on 4 June and the days following the Marines added to their reputation for tenacity by steadfastly denying the Germans access to the road towards Rheims, the capture of which would have more than doubled the railway capacity on which they depended to feed their offensive. At an early stage of the battle in their sector it was suggested to a Marine officer by French troops retreating through their positions that he and his men should retreat also. 'Retreat?' answered Captain Lloyd Williams, in words which were to enter the mythology of the Corps, 'Hell, we just got here.'[80]

The Marine counter-attack at Belleau Wood was but one contribution, however, to a general response by French and British, as well as American troops, to the threat to Paris. Unknown to the Allies, the Germans had already decided to halt the third offensive on 3 June, in the face of mounting resistance, though also because once again the leading troops had overrun the supply columns which lagged far behind the advancing infantry and their supporting artillery. They had also lost another hundred thousand men and more, and, while French, British and American losses equalled theirs, the Allies retained the ability to replace casualties while they did not. The French, after a year of effective inactivity, were able to draw on a new annual class of conscripts and, though the strength of the British infantry, worn down by continuous fighting, was in absolute decline (it fell from 754,000 in July 1917 to 543,000 in June 1918) the Americans were now receiving 250,000 men a month in France and had twenty-five organised divisions in or behind the battle zone.[81] Fifty-five more were under organisation in the United States.

On 9 June Ludendorff renewed the offensive, in an attack on the River Matz, a tributary of the Oise, in an attempt to draw French reserves southward but also to widen the salient that now bulged westward between Paris and Flanders. He was still undecided whether to press his attack force against its upper edge, and strike against the British rear, his original intention, or against the lower and drive on the capital. The Matz, in any case a limited attack, was quickly broken off on 14 June when the French, with American assistance, counter-attacked and brought the initial advance to a halt. The German inability to sustain pressure was also hampered by the first outbreak of the so-called 'Spanish' influenza, in fact a worldwide epidemic originating in South Africa, which was to recur in the autumn with devastating effects in Europe but in June laid low nearly half a million German soldiers whose resistance, depressed by poor diet, was far lower than that of the well-fed Allied troops in the trenches opposite.

With his troop strength declining to a point where he could no longer count upon massing a superiority of numbers for attack, Ludendorff now had to make a critical choice between what was important but more difficult of achievement – the attack against the British in Flanders – and what was easier but of secondary significance, a drive towards Paris. He took nearly a month to make up his mind, a month in which the German leadership also met at Spa to review the progress of the war and the country's war aims. Shortage at home was now extreme, but there was nonetheless a discussion of introducing a 'full war economy'. Despite the near-desperate situation at the front, the Kaiser, government and high command all agreed, on 3 July, that, to complement the acquisition of territories in the east, the annexation of Luxembourg and the French iron and coal fields in Lorraine were the necessary and minimum terms for concluding the war in the west. On 13 July, the Reichstag, to express its confidence in the direction and progress of strategy, voted war credits for the twelfth time.[82] The Foreign Secretary, who had warned it that the war could not now be ended by 'military decision alone', was forced out of office on 8 July.[83]

Ludendorff remained wedded to military decision and on 15 July committed all the force he had left, fifty-two divisions, to an attack against the French. The temptation of Paris had proved irresistible. At first the offensive made excellent progress. The French, however, had had warning, from intelligence and observation experts, and on 18 July launched a heavy counter-stroke, mounted by the fiery Mangin with eighteen divisions in first line, at Villers-Cotterêts. It was the day Ludendorff travelled to Mons to discuss the transfer of troops to Flanders for his much-postponed offensive against the British. The French attack brought him hurrying back but there was little he could do to stem the flood. The French had five of the enormous American divisions, 28,000 strong, in their order of battle, and these fresh troops fought with a disregard for casualties scarcely seen on the Western Front since the beginning of the war. On the night of July 18/19 the German vanguards which had crossed the Marne three days earlier fell back across the river and the retreat continued in the days that followed. The fifth German offensive, and the battle called by the French the Second Marne, was over and could not be revived. Nor could the Flanders offensive against the British be undertaken. Merely to make good losses suffered in the attacks so far, the German high command calculated, required 200,000 replacements each month but, even by drawing on the next annual class of eighteen-year-olds, only 300,000 recruits stood available. The only other source was the hospitals, which returned 70,000 convalescents to the ranks each month, men whose fitness and will to fight was undependable. In six months, the strength of the army had fallen from 5.1 million to 4.2 million men and, even after every rear-echelon unit had been combed out, its fighting strength could not be increased. The number of divisions was, indeed, being reduced, as the weaker were broken up to feed the stronger.[84]

The army's discontent with its leadership was beginning to find a voice. Though Hindenburg remained a figurehead above reproach, Ludendorff's uncreative and repetitive strategy of frontal attacks now attracted criticism from within the General Staff. Lossberg, the great tactical expert, responded to the failure of the Second Battle of the Marne by arguing that the army should withdraw to the Siegfried Line of 1917, while on 20 July Major Niemann circulated a paper calling for negotiations with the Allies to be initiated at once. Ludendorff theatrically offered to resign but then recovered his nerve when the Allies did not move to exploit their success on the Marne. There was, he said, nothing to justify Lossberg's demands for a withdrawal and no sign that the Allies could break the German line.[85]

Had the material circumstances of the war been those of any of the previous years, Ludendorff's analysis might have been proved correct; but they were not. A German army unable to make good its losses was now confronted by a new enemy, the US Army, with four million fresh troops in action or training. More pertinently, its old enemies, the British and French, now had a new technical arm, their tank forces, with which to alter the terms of engagement. Germany's failure to match the Allies in tank development must be judged one of their worst military miscalculations of the war. Their own programme, undertaken too late and with little imagination, had resulted in the production of a monstrosity, the A7V, manned by a crew of twelve, in which soldiers of the pioneers ran the engine, infantrymen fired the machine guns and artillerymen operated the heavy gun. Moreover, industrial delays limited output to a few dozen, so that the German tank force chiefly depended on 170 tanks captured from the French and British.[86] They, by contrast, had by August 1918 several hundred each, the French fleet including a 13-ton Schneider-Creusot model mounting a 75-mm gun, while the British, besides a number of light 'whippet' tanks, possessed a solid mass of 500 medium Mark IV and Mark V machines, capable of moving at 5 mph over level ground and of concentrating intense cannon and machine-gun fire against targets of opportunity.

Ludendorff's belief during July that he retained the option of striking alternatively against the British or French was even more of a misconception than he might have imagined at worst. While his increasingly battle-worn infantry and horse-drawn artillery plodded forward over the worn battleground of the Marne, Foch and Haig were concentrating an enormous force of armour, 530 British tanks, 70 French, in front of Amiens, with the intention of breaking back into the old Somme battlefield through the extemporised defences constructed by the Germans after their advance in March and driving deep into their rear area. The blow was struck on 8 August, with the Canadian and the Australian Corps providing the infantry support for the tank assault. Haig had now come to depend increasingly on these two Dominion formations, which had been spared the blood-letting of 1916, to act as spearhead of his operations. Within four days most of the old Somme battlefield had been retaken and by the end of August the Allies had advanced as far as the outworks of the Hindenburg Line, from which they had been pushed back by the German offensive in March. Some of their progress was facilitated by deliberate German withdrawals, the enemy lacking both the strength and confidence to defend steadfastly outside the strong and prepared positions of 1917. On 6 September, indeed, Ludendorff was advised by Lossberg that the situation could only be retrieved by a retreat of nearly fifty miles to a line established on the Meuse. The advice was rejected, however, and during the rest of September the Germans consolidated their position in and forward of the Hindenburg Line.

Meanwhile the ever-stronger American army was taking an increasingly important part in operations. On 30 August, General John Pershing, who had reluctantly lent formations and even individual units piecemeal to the Allies, despite his determination to concentrate the American army as a single and potentially war-winning entity, achieved his purpose of bringing the First American Army into being. It was immediately deployed south of Verdun, opposite the tangled and waterlogged ground of the St. Mihiel Salient, which had been in German hands since 1914, and on 12 September launched the first all-American offensive of the war. The Germans opposite were preparing to abandon the Salient, in conformation with general orders to retire to the Hindenburg Line, but were nevertheless taken by surprise and subjected to a severe defeat. In a single day's fighting, the American I and IV Corps, attacking behind a barrage of 2,900 guns, drove the Germans from their positions, captured 466 guns and took 13,251 prisoners. The French, while paying tribute to the 'superb morale' of the Americans, ungraciously attributed their success to the fact that they had caught the Germans in the process of retiring. It was true that many Germans were all too ready to surrender but Pershing's army had nevertheless won an undoubted victory.[87]

Ludendorff paid a tribute the French would not. He attributed the growing malaise in his army and the sense of 'looming defeat' that afflicted it to 'the sheer number of Americans arriving daily at the front'. It was indeed immaterial whether the doughboys fought well or not. Though the professional opinion of veteran French and British officers that they were enthusiastic rather than efficient was correct, the critical issue was the effect of their arrival on the enemy. It was deeply depressing. After four years of a war in which they had destroyed the Tsar's army, trounced the Italians and Romanians, demoralised the French and, at the very least, denied the British clear-cut victory, they were now confronted with an army whose soldiers sprang, in uncountable numbers, as if from soil sown with dragons' teeth. Past hopes of victory had been predicated on calculable ratios of force to force. The intervention of the United States Army had robbed calculation of point. Nowhere among Germany's remaining resources could sufficient force be found to counter the millions America could bring across the Atlantic, and the consequent sense of the pointlessness of further effort rotted the resolution of the ordinary German soldier to do his duty.

It was in that mood that, during September, the German armies in the west fell back to their final line of resistance, the Hindenburg Line, most of which followed the line of the original Western Front marked out by the fighting of 1914, though enormously strengthened in subsequent years, particularly in the central sector fortified after the retirement for the Somme in the spring of 1917. On 26 September, in response to Foch's inspiring cry, 'Everyone to battle', the British, French, Belgian and American armies attacked with 123 divisions, with 57 divisions in reserve, against 197 German; but of those only 51 were classed by Allied intelligence as fully battleworthy.

Ludendorff had called 8 August, when the British and French tank armada had overwhelmed the front at Amiens, the 'black day of the German army'. It was 28 September, however, that was his own black day. Behind his expressionless and heavily physical façade, Ludendorff was a man of liquid emotions. 'You don't know Ludendorff', Bethmann Hollweg had told the chief of the Kaiser's naval cabinet earlier in the war. He was, the German Prime Minister said, 'only great at a time of success. If things go badly, he loses his nerve.'[88] The judgement was not wholly fair. Ludendorff had kept his nerve with decisive effect in the critical days of August 1914. Now, however, he lost it altogether, giving way to a paranoid rage 'against the Kaiser, the Reichstag, the navy and the home front'.[89] His staff shut the door of his office to stifle the noise of his rantings until he gradually regained an exhausted composure. At six o'clock he emerged to descend one floor of headquarters to Hindenburg's room. There he told the old field marshal that there was now no alternative but to seek an armistice. The position in the west was penetrated, the army would not fight, the civilian population had lost heart, the politicians wanted peace. Hindenburg silently took his right hand in both of his own and they parted 'like men who have buried their dearest hopes'.[90]

The domestic consequences were swift to follow. On 29 September, a day when Germany's ally, Bulgaria, opened negotiations with the French and British for an armistice on the Salonika front, the high command received the Kaiser, the Chancellor, von Hertling, and the Foreign Secretary, von Hintze, at headquarters in Spa to advise them that Germany must now make terms of its own. On 8 January 1918, President Wilson of the United States had presented Congress with fourteen points on which a peace honourable to all combatants and guaranteeing future world harmony could be made. It was on the basis of the Fourteen Points that the German leadership now decided to approach the Allies. Hintze proposed that any successful conclusion of negotiations, given the turmoil between the parliamentary parties within Germany, would require the establishment either of dictatorship or full democracy. The conference decided that only democratisation would persuade the Allies to concede the conditions for which the leadership still hoped – they included the retention of parts of Alsace-Lorraine and a German Poland – and accordingly accepted the resignation of Chancellor Hertling. In his place the Kaiser appointed, on 3 October, the moderate Prince Max of Baden, already known as an advocate of a negotiated peace and a major figure in the German Red Cross. He was also an opponent of Ludendorff and, as a first act, secured from Hindenburg a written admission that 'there was no further chance of forcing a peace on the enemy'.[91] That was prudent, for during early October Ludendorff began to recover his nerve. While Prince Max persuaded a wide range of parties to join his government, including the Majority Socialists, and while he secured for the Reichstag powers always denied it by the monarchy, including those of appointing the Minister of War and of making war and peace, Ludendorff began to talk of sustaining resistance and of rejecting President Wilson's conditions. Those were restated on 16 October, in terms which appeared to demand the abolition of the monarchy, as one of those 'arbitrary powers' menacing 'the peace of the world', to which the American President had declared himself an implacable enemy.

The army at the front, after its brief moral collapse in late September, when troops returning from the trenches had taunted those going up with cries of 'strike breakers', had indeed recovered something of its old spirit and was contesting the advance of the Allies towards the German frontier. In Flanders, where water obstacles were plentiful, the French were held up, to Foch's irritation, for some time. It was in these circumstances that Ludendorff composed a proclamation to the army on 24 October, which effectively defied the authority of the Chancellor and rejected the Wilson peace proposals, which it characterised as 'a demand for unconditional surrender. It is thus unacceptable to us soldiers. It proves that our enemy's desire for our destruction, which let loose the war in 1914, still exists undiminished. [It] can thus be nothing for us soldiers but a challenge to continue our resistance with all our strength.'[92]

An officer of the General Staff managed to suppress the proclamation before it was issued. One copy, by mistake, however, reached the headquarters in the east, *Ober Ost*, where the signal clerk, an Independent Socialist, conveyed it to the party in Berlin. By noon it had been published, setting the Reichstag in uproar. Prince Max, enraged by the insubordination – which, characteristically, Ludendorff had attempted to retract – confronted the Kaiser with the demand that he must now choose between Ludendorff and himself. When Ludendorff arrived in Berlin on 25 October, with Hindenburg – both had left headquarters against the Chancellor's specific instruction – he was told to report to Schloss Bellevue, where the

443

Kaiser was in residence, and there forced, on 26 October, to offer his resignation. It was accepted with the briefest of words and without thanks. Hindenburg's, also offered, was declined. When the two soldiers left the palace, Ludendorff refused to enter Hindenburg's car and made his way alone to the hotel where his wife was staying. Throwing himself into a chair, he sat silent for some time, then roused himself to predict 'In a fortnight we shall have no Empire and no Emperor left, you will see.'[93]

THE FALL OF EMPIRES

Ludendorff's forecast was exact to the day. By the time, however, that Wilhelm II abdicated, as he would on 9 November, two other empires, the Ottoman and the Habsburg, would have sued for peace also. The imminence of the Turkish collapse had been evident for some time. After the army's victories at Gallipoli and Kut, its vital energy had ebbed away. The continuing campaign in the Caucasus against the Russians had sapped its strength and chronic administrative inefficiency had deprived it of replacements. Though the number of divisions doubled during the war, from thirty-six to seventy, no more than forty existed at any one time and by 1918 all were weak, some scarcely as strong as a British brigade. The loyalty of the Arab divisions, moreover, was to be doubted after the Sherif of Mecca, Hussein, raised the standard of revolt in 1916. His Arab Army, operating against the flanks of the Turks in Arabia and Palestine, under the direction of the later famous liaison officer, Colonel T.E. Lawrence, distracted sizeable forces from the main battlefronts. The principal fighting was carried on, however, by the largely Indian army in Mesopotamia and, in Palestine, by an Egyptian-based British army which came to include large numbers of Australian and New Zealand cavalry.

Mesopotamia, south of Baghdad, the Turkish administrative centre, had been conquered by the British during 1917, and late in 1918 they had advanced to the oil centre of Mosul. The real focus of their effort against the Turks, however, was in Palestine, where they established a foothold on the other side of the Sinai desert at Gaza in 1917. Several attempts to break the Turks' Gaza line resulted in a Turkish evacuation of the position and the fall of Jerusalem on 9 December. During 1918 the British commander, Allenby, reorganised his forces and pushed his lines forward into northern Palestine where, by September, they opposed those of the Turks at

Megiddo, site of the first recorded battle in history. Allenby's breakthrough on 19–21 September brought about the collapse of Turkish resistance. On 30 October, five days after Ludendorff's dismissal, the Turkish government signed an armistice at Mudros, on the Aegean island of Lemnos, from which the Gallipoli expedition had been mounted forty-two months earlier.

Austria's nemesis came on the soil, if not wholly at the hands, of its despised enemy, Italy. After the triumph of Caporetto, which had driven the Italians down into the plains of the Po, so that at one moment even Venice seemed threatened, the Habsburg effort had petered out. The Italians reorganised and, rid of the pitiless dictatorship of Cadorna, gained heart. The real defence of their country, however, passed to the British and French, who had transferred sizeable contingents to the Italian front immediately after the Caporetto disaster and succeeded in sustaining a substantial force there, despite withdrawals to cope with the crisis in the Western Front, throughout 1918. On 24 June the Austrians, who had been able to build up their own numbers after the Russian collapse, attempted a double offensive out of the northern mountains and on the River Piave, the stop line of the Italian retreat from Caporetto. Both attacks were swiftly checked, that on the Piave by the assistance of an unseasonal flood which swept away the Austrian pontoon bridges. The intervention of nature was not an excuse accepted by the Habsburg high command for the failure. Conrad von Hötzendorf was removed from command and the young Emperor, Charles I, began to look for means to preserve his empire by political rather than military means. On 16 October, two weeks after he had already sent President Wilson word of his willingness to enter into an armistice, he issued a manifesto to his peoples that, in effect, transferred the state into a federation of nationalities.

The manifesto came too late. On 6 October his Serb, Croat and Slovene subjects had already formed a provisional government of the South Slavs or 'Yugoslavia'. On 7 October the Habsburg Poles joined with their former German- and Russian-ruled brothers to proclaim a free and independent Poland, on 28 October a Czecho-Slovak republic was proclaimed in Prague, while on 30 October the Emperor Charles's German subjects, the ultimate prop of his rule, claimed, in a constituent assembly, their freedom to determine foreign policy for a new German-Austrian state. Hungary, constitutionally an independent kingdom, declared itself so on 1 November. The other imperial nationalities, Ruthenes and Romanians, were making their own arrangements for their future. The uniformed representatives of all of them had already begun to abandon resistance and, in some cases, to cast away their arms and set off for home across the territories of the new states into which the empire had dissolved.[94] It was in these circumstances that Diaz, the Italian commander, launched an offensive, to be known as the battle of Vittorio Veneto, on 24 October. With extensive British and French help, the Italians succeeded in recrossing the River Piave, initiating an advance that culminated a week later on Austrian territory. The Austrians, with difficulty, opened armistice negotiations in the field on 1 November and instituted a ceasefire on 3 November. It was not recognised by the Italians until the following day. In the interval 300,000 prisoners fell into their hands.[95]

By the first week of November, therefore, the German empire stood alone as a combatant among the war's Central Powers. Under pressure from the French, British, Americans and Belgians, the army's resistance stiffened as it fell back across the battlefields of 1914 towards Belgium and the German frontier. There was hard fighting at the rivers and canals, casualties rose – among the penultimate fatalities was the British poet, Wilfred Owen, killed at the crossing of the River Sambre on 4 November – and the war, to the Allied soldiers battling at the front, seemed to threaten to prolong. Behind the lines, in Germany, however, resistance was crumbling. On 30 October the crews of the High Seas Fleet, ordered to sea for a final sortie to save its honour, broke into mutiny and refused to raise steam. Efforts to put down indiscipline resulted in the mutineers breaking into the armouries, seizing weapons and taking to the streets.[96] By 3 November, the day on which Austria accepted the armistice, the seaport of Kiel was in the hands of mutineers calling for revolution and next day the port admiral, Prince Henry of Prussia, the Kaiser's brother, had to flee the city in disguise.

The Kaiser had already left Berlin, on 29 October, for headquarters at Spa, in Belgium, to be closer to the army, on whose loyalty he still believed himself able to count, and to avoid the mounting pressure to abdicate. There was an apparent wisdom in his departure, for, at the beginning of the second week of November, power in the capital shifted irrevocably from the old imperial apparatus to the forces of revolution. The last achievements of Prince Max, as Chancellor, were to secure the appointment of a moderate general, Wilhelm Groener, as Ludendorff's successor and to insist that the delegation assembled to negotiate the armistice with the enemy would include civilian as well as military representatives. He thus assured that the conclusion of the armistice would be a joint military and political act, from which the soldiers could not subsequently extricate themselves by objecting to its political terms. This was his last contribution to Germany's future. On 9 November, with Berlin in turmoil and the moderate politicians threatened by street crowds orchestrated by Germany's Bolshevik leaders, Karl Liebknecht and Rosa Luxemburg, he transferred the office of chancellor to the Majority Socialist, Friedrich Ebert.[97]

On the same day the Kaiser, at Spa, confronted his own deposition from power. Unrealistic as ever, he had spent his ten days at headquarters fantasising about turning his army against his people, oblivious of the evidence that his soldiers now wanted only an end to the war and were, even at Spa itself, making common cause with the revolutionaries. Ebert, leader of the Majority Socialists, was anti-revolutionary, a patriot and even a monarchist. By 7 November, however, he knew that, unless he adopted the demands of the revolution growing in the streets, and they included abdication, his party would be discredited for good. That evening he warned Prince Max, 'The Kaiser must abdicate, otherwise we shall have the revolution.' Over the telephone to Spa, Max repeated the warning to the Kaiser, speaking to him, he said as if to soften the blow, as a relative as well as Chancellor: 'Your abdication has become necessary to save Germany from Civil War.'[98] The Kaiser refused to listen, once again threatened to use the army against the nation and ended by rejecting any thought of Prince Max resigning as Chancellor, a step Max himself knew was now inevitable. 'You sent out the armistice offer', Wilhelm II said, 'you will also have to accept the conditions', and rang off.

The German armistice delegation had already crossed enemy lines to meet the French representatives at Rethondes, in the Forest of Compiègne, outside Paris. Until the issues of the abdication and the Chancellorship had been settled, however, the delegates could not proceed. The terms of the armistice had been presented to them by Foch, and stark they were. They required the evacuation of all occupied territory, including Alsace-Lorraine, German since 1871, the military evacuation of the western bank of the Rhine and of three bridgeheads on the eastern bank at Mainz, Coblenz and Cologne; the surrender of enormous quantities of military equipment, and the internment in Allied hands of all submarines and the capital units of the High Seas Fleet; the repudiation of the treaties of Brest-Litovsk and Bucharest, under which the Germans occupied their conquered territories in the east; the payment of reparations for war damage; and, critically, acceptance of the continuation of the Allied blockade.[99] The continuation, as events would determine, eventually ensured Germany's compliance with peace terms even harsher than those of the Armistice to be imposed at the Versailles conference.

While the delegates at Rethondes waited to hear what power in Germany would permit them to put their signatures to the armistice document, two separate sets of events were unrolling in Berlin and at Spa. In Berlin on 9 November, Prince Max of Baden handed over the Chancellorship to Fritz Ebert. There was by then no alternative to the transfer of power. The streets were filled with revolutionary mobs, many of their members soldiers in uniform, while the leaders of the Majority Socialists' political enemies, Karl Liebknecht and Rosa Luxemburg, were already proclaiming a 'free Socialist republic', by which they meant a Bolshevik State. The last meeting between Max and Ebert was brief. 'Herr Ebert,' the Kaiser's brother-in-law announced, 'I commit the German Empire to your keeping.' The new Chancellor replied, 'I have lost two sons for this Empire.'[100] Many German parents could have said the same.

In Spa, on 9 November, the Emperor met the leaders of his army, the institution through which the Hohenzollern dynasty had risen to power, and to which it had always looked to sustain its dignity and authority. Wilhelm II still believed that, whatever disloyalties were being transacted by civilian politicians in Berlin, whatever affronts to order disturbed the streets, his subjects in field-grey remained true to their oath of military obedience. Even on 9 November he continued to delude himself that the army could be used against the people and the royal house preserved by turning German against German.[101] His generals knew otherwise. Hindenburg, the wooden titan, heard him out in silence. Groener, the workaday railway transport officer, son of a sergeant, who had replaced Ludendorff, found the sense to speak. He knew, from soundings taken among fifty regimental commanders, that the soldiers now wanted 'only one thing – an armistice at the earliest possible moment'. The price of that, to the House of Hohenzollern, was the Kaiser's abdication. The Kaiser heard him with continuing incredulity. What about, he asked, the *Fahneneide*, the oath on the regimental colours which bound every German soldier to die rather than disobey? Groener uttered the unutterable. 'Today', he said, 'the *Fahneneide* is only a form of words.'[102]

The fall of the House of Hohenzollern was swiftly concluded. Rejecting a suggestion that he should seek death in the trenches, as incompatible with his position as head of the German Lutheran Church, Wilhelm II departed by train to Holland on 10 November. On his arrival at the castle of Doorn, where he would spend long years of exile, long enough for Hitler to provide a guard of honour at the gates during the German occupation of the Netherlands, he requested 'a cup of good English tea'. On 28 November he signed the act of abdication. As his six sons had each sworn not to succeed him, the Hohenzollern dynasty thereby severed its connection with the headship of the German state and even with the crown of Prussia.

Germany was by then, in any case, effectively a republic, proclaimed on 9 November, though it would not acquire a president, in the person of Friedrich Ebert, until February 1919. Yet it was a republic without substance, lacking the essential constituent of any political entity, or an armed force to defend itself against its enemies. The last disciplined act of the old imperial army was to march back across the German frontiers with France and Belgium. Once on home territory, it demobilised itself. The soldiers discarded their uniforms and weapons and went home. That did not empty the German republic of armed men. As elsewhere in the changed political geography of central and eastern Europe – in the new republics of Poland, Finland, Estonia, Latvia and Lithuania, in the nominal monarchy of Hungary, in German-Austria – bodies of soldiers, loyal to orthodoxies old and new or to revolutionary ideologies, abounded. Nationalist orthodoxies would prevail in ethnically disparate Yugoslavia, in Czechoslovakia and in Poland, though that infant republic would have to fight for its borders, against German irregulars in the west and desperately against the Bolsheviks in the east. In Finland, in the Baltic states, in Hungary and in Germany itself, armed men menaced Red Revolution. It was put down in the east at the cost of civil strife. In Germany it threatened for a while to win by default, since constitutional republicanism could at first find no armed force to oppose it. Out of the wreck of the old imperial army, however, enough extemporised units were got together from men with no trade but soldiering – they bore such names as the Garde-Kavallerie-Schützen Division, the Freiwillige Landesjägerkorps, the Landeschützenkorps, the Freikorps Hülsen – to prevail in the battle of the streets in Berlin, Gotha, Halle, Dresden, Munich and many other German cities, to

449

repress German Bolshevism by brute force and to lay on the new republican government a permanent debt of gratitude to the improvised army's generals. Its regiments would form the nucleus of the 'hundred-thousand man army' that was all that was to be allowed to Germany by the peace conference of Versailles in 1919.[103]

While Germany's political future was being settled by civil war in the capital and the provinces, the armies of the Allies were advancing to take possession of the western Rhineland provinces and of the three bridgeheads across the river, at Mainz, Coblenz and Cologne, surrendered under the terms of the armistice. The soldiers of the armies of occupation, the French excepted, were quick to fraternise with the population. Enmity was swiftly overlaid by friendships, all the more readily as army rations made their way from cookhouses to family kitchens to feed people still subsisting on the skimpy wartime diet that the Allies' maintenance of blockade imposed. Hunger, even more than the threat of a full-scale invasion, was the measure that would eventually bring the German republic to sign the peace treaty on 23 June 1919. Two days earlier the High Seas Fleet, interned at the British anchorage at Scapa Flow, had been scuttled by its crews in final protest at the severity of the proffered terms.

There was historic irony in the Kaiser's naval officers choosing a watery grave for his magnificent battleships in a British harbour. Had he not embarked on a strategically unnecessary attempt to match Britain's maritime strength, fatal hostility between the two countries would have been avoided; so, too, in all possibility, might have been the neurotic climate of suspicion and insecurity from which the First World War was born. The unmarked graveyard of his squadrons inside the remotest islands of the British archipelago, guarding the exit from the narrow seas his fleet would have had to penetrate to achieve true oceanic status, remains as a memorial to selfish and ultimately pointless military ambition.

It is one of the many graveyards which are the Great War's chief heritage. The chronicle of its battles provides the dreariest literature in military history; no brave trumpets sound in memory for the drab millions who plodded to death on the featureless plains of Picardy and Poland; no litanies are sung for the leaders who coaxed them to slaughter. The legacy of the war's political outcome scarcely bears contemplation: Europe ruined as a centre of world civilisation, Christian kingdoms transformed through defeat into godless tyrannies, Bolshevik or Nazi, the superficial difference between their ideologies counting not at all in their cruelty to common and decent folk. All that was worst in the century which the First World War had opened, the deliberate starvation of peasant enemies of the people by provinces, the extermination of racial outcasts, the persecution of ideology's intellectual and cultural hate-objects, the massacre of ethnic minorities, the extinction of small national sovereignties, the destruction of parliaments and the elevation of commissars, gauleiters and warlords to power over voiceless millions, had its origins in the chaos it left behind. Of that, at the end of the century, little thankfully is left. Europe is once again, as it was in 1900, prosperous, peaceful and a power for good in the world.

The graveyards remain. Many of those who died in battle could never be laid to rest. Their bodies had been blown to pieces by shellfire and the fragments scattered beyond recognition. Many other bodies could not be recovered during the fighting and were then lost to view, entombed in crumbled shell holes or collapsed trenches or decomposing into the broken soil battle left behind. Few Russian or Turkish soldiers were ever decently interred and many German and Austrian soldiers killed on the shifting battlefields of the Eastern Front simply returned to earth. On the fixed battlegrounds of the west, the combatants made a better effort to observe the decencies. War cemeteries were organised from the outset, graves registration officers marked the plots and, when time permitted, chaplains and the dead men's comrades observed the solemnities. Even so, at the war's end, the remains of nearly half of those lost remained lost in actuality. Of the British Empire's million dead, most killed in France and Belgium, the bodies of over 500,000 were never to be found or, if found, not identified.[104] A similar proportion of the 1,700,000 French war dead had also disappeared. France buried or reburied the dead in a variety of ways, sometimes in individual graves, sometimes in collective ossuaries, as at Verdun. The Germans, working on foreign soil, and obliged to construct compact and inconspicuous cemeteries, often excavated enormous mass graves; that at Vladslo in Belgium, where the bodies of most of the volunteers killed in 1914 in the *Kindermord bei Ypern*, centres on a slab that covers the remains of over 20,000 young men.[105]

The British chose an entirely different and absolutely standard method of honouring the fallen. Each body was given a separate grave, recording name, age, rank, regiment and date and place of death; if unidentifiable, the headstone bore the words, composed by

451

Rudyard Kipling, himself a bereaved father, 'A Soldier of the Great War Known Unto God'. The names of those who had been lost altogether were inscribed on architectural monuments, the largest of which, at Thiepval, records the names of the 70,000 missing of the battle of the Somme. It was also decided that the cemeteries, large and small, should each be walled and planted as a classic English country garden, with mown grass between the headstones and roses and herbaceous plants at their feet. There was also to be a Cross of Sacrifice as a centrepoint of all but the smallest cemeteries and, in the larger, a symbolic altar, the Stone of Remembrance, bearing the inscription, also composed by Kipling, 'Their Name Liveth For Evermore'. Over six hundred cemeteries were eventually constructed and given into the care of the Imperial War Graves Commission which, working under a law of the French government deeding the ground as *sépultures perpétuelles*, recruited a body of over a thousand gardeners to care for them in perpetuity. All survive, still reverently tended by the Commission's gardeners, much visited by the British, sometimes by the great-grandchildren of those buried within, as poignant remembrance cards testify, but also by the curious of many nationalities. None fail to be moved by their extraordinary beauty. Eighty years of mowing and pruning have achieved the original intention of creating 'the appearance of a small park or garden', while the passage of time itself has conferred an ageless maturity. In spring, when the flowers blossom, the cemeteries are places of renewal and almost of hope, in autumn, when the leaves fall, of reflection and remembrance.

The ribbon of British cemeteries running from the North Sea to the Somme and beyond stands as an idealised memorial to all those whose extinction on the battlefields of the Great War is not commemorated. Their number is enormous. To the million dead of the British Empire and the 1,700,000 French dead, we must add 1,500,000 soldiers of the Habsburg Empire who did not return, two million Germans, 460,000 Italians, 1,700,000 Russians and many hundreds of thousands of Turks; their numbers were never counted.[106] As a proportion of those who volunteered or were conscripted, the death toll can be made to seem tolerable. It represents, for Germany, about 3.5 per cent of all who served. Calculated as a percentage of the youngest and fittest, the figures exceed by far what was emotionally bearable. Male mortality exceeded normal expectation, between 1914 and 1918, seven to eightfold in Britain, and tenfold in France, in which 17 per cent of

452

those who served were killed. Similar proportions were lost from the youngest age groups in Germany. 'Between 1870 and 1899, about 16 million boys were born; all but a few served in the army and some 13 per cent were killed.'[107] As in France and Britain, the figures, if calculated for the contingents most immediately liable for duty by reason of age, display an even heavier burden of loss. 'Year groups 1892–1895, men who were between 19 and 22 when war broke out, were reduced by 35–37 per cent.'[108]

One in three. Little wonder the post-war world spoke of a 'lost generation', that its parents were united by shared grief and that the survivors proceeded into the life that followed with a sense of inexplicable escape, often tinged by guilt, sometimes by rage and desire for revenge. Such thoughts were far from the minds of British and French veterans, who hoped only that the horrors of the trenches would not be repeated in their lifetime or that of their sons. They festered in the minds of many Germans, foremost in the mentality of the 'front fighter', Adolf Hitler, who in Munich in September 1922, threw down the threat of vengeance that would sow the seeds of a Second World War.

The Second World War was the continuation of the First, and indeed it is inexplicable except in terms of the rancours and instabilities left by the earlier conflict. The Kaiser's Germany, despite its enormous economic success, and the intellectual prestige achieved by its scholars throughout the world, had seethed with discontent, particularly over the disparity between its industrial and military power and its political standing among kingdoms and republics, Britain and France foremost, which enjoyed the reality rather than the empty title of empire. Its pre-war dissatisfactions paled beside those that overcame it in the aftermath of Versailles. Forced to disgorge the conquests of 1870–71 in Alsace and Lorraine and to surrender to an independent Poland the historic areas of German settlement in Silesia and West Prussia, humiliated by a compulsory disarmament that reduced its army to a tiny gendarmerie, dissolved its battlefleet altogether and abolished its air force, and blackmailed by the continuation of starvation through blockade into signing a humiliating peace treaty, republican Germany came to nurture grievances stronger by far than those that had distorted its international relations and domestic politics before 1914. The high-mindedness of the liberal democrat government of Weimar helped to palliate them not at all; its very political and diplomatic moderation, in the years when its economic mismanagement ruined the German middle class and its obeisance to French and British occupation and reparation policies narrowed national pride, fed the forces of extremism to which its principles stood in opposition. Throughout the 1920s, German liberal democracy floated above a turmoil of opposing currents, Marxist and National Socialist, that would eventually overwhelm it.

The liberation of the peoples of eastern Europe from the imperial rule of German-speaking dynasties, Hohenzollern or Habsburg, brought equally little tranquillity to the successor states they founded. None of them – Poland, Czechoslovakia, the Kingdom of the Serbs, Croats and Slovenes or, as it became known in 1929, Yugoslavia – emerged into independence with sufficient homogeneity to undertake a settled political life. Poland's independence was almost fatally compromised from the outset by its efforts to stake out a border at the extreme eastern limit of what was historically justifiable. In the war with Soviet Russia that followed, its armies escaped defeat by the barest margin. Their eventual and unexpected success, though an apparent national triumph, was to burden the new country with a collection of minorities, largely Ukrainian, that reduced the Polish proportion of the population to only 60 per cent. Its incorporation, moreover, of historic German land in the west and its envelopment of East Prussia, cradle of the German warrior class, would provide Hitler in 1939 with the pretext for a reprise of the aggression of 1914. Czechoslovakia's inheritance from the Habsburgs of another German minority in the Sudetenland equally robbed the new state of ethnic equilibrium, with fatal consequences for its integrity in 1938. Yugoslavia's unequal racial composition might have been brought into balance with good will; as events turned out, the determination of the Orthodox Christian Serbs to dominate, particularly over the Catholic Croats, undermined its coherence from an early date. Internal antipathies were to rob it of the power to resist Italian and German attack in 1941.

The two regional losers, Hungary and Bulgaria, were spared such disharmonies by loss of territory. Hungary's losses were so large, however, that it entered the post-war world with fierce grievances against the neighbours who had gained by the change of boundaries. Romania, the principal winner, over-generously compensated for its militarily disastrous intervention on the side of the Allies in 1916, inherited thereby a permanent source of discord with Hungary –

though also potentially with the Soviet Union – by acquiring minorities who amounted to more than a quarter of the population.

Greece, too, gained population, but at the cost of a disastrously ill-judged imperial campaign against the apparently moribund Turks. Persuaded that the moment of the 'Great Idea' – the reunion of the regions of historic Hellenic settlement, the guiding principle of Greek nationalism since the achievement of independence in 1832 – had at last come, Greece invaded Asia Minor in June 1919. A successful advance carried its troops almost to Ankara, the future capital of the future Turkish republic, until Kemal, the victor of Gallipoli, succeeded in energising a counter-offensive that in September 1922 overwhelmed the overstretched Greek army. At the Treaty of Lausanne that concluded the war in 1923, beaten Greece and victorious Turkey agreed to exchange the minorities on each other's soil, a process that extinguished the Greek presence in the coastal cities of the eastern Aegean, where Greeks had lived since the time of Homer and before, and brought over a million dispossessed refugees to join the four million Greeks of the mainland; many, so long separated had they been from the wellsprings of Greek culture, were Turkish-speaking. The poverty into which they entered and the griefs they brought with them were to fuel the class hatreds that burst into civil war in 1944–47.

A Balkan problem that had made the First World War dissolved, therefore, into new Balkan problems in its aftermath, problems that continued to the outbreak of the Second, problems that persist, indeed, to this day. Any one of the characteristically world-weary officials of Habsburg imperialism, if reincarnated today, might well ask what had changed. Much, of course, has changed in eastern Europe, which was the First World War's breeding ground, though chiefly as a result of the ruthless territorial and ethnic reorganisation of the region by Stalin in the wake of the Red Army's victories in 1945. The empires have at last gone, the Soviet Russian empire last of all, many of the minorities have gone, particularly from Poland and what are now the Czech Republic and Slovakia. Yet many of the minorities remain, above all in the countries where Stalin did not do his work, Romania, Hungary, and former Yugoslavia. Foreign authority demands of the Serbs authority to punish its political criminals, as the Habsburgs demanded of the Serbs in 1914. Foreign troops operate in the valleys of the Sava and the Drina rivers, just as they did in 1915. It is all very mysterious.

But then the First World War is a mystery. Its origins are mysterious. So is its course. Why did a prosperous continent, at the height of its success as a source and agent of global wealth and power and at one of the peaks of its intellectual and cultural achievement, choose to risk all it had won for itself and all it offered to the world in the lottery of a vicious and local internecine conflict? Why, when the hope of bringing the conflict to a quick and decisive conclusion was everywhere dashed to the ground within months of its outbreak, did the combatants decide nevertheless to persist in their military effort, to mobilise for total war and eventually to commit the totality of their young manhood to mutual and existentially pointless slaughter? Principle perhaps was at stake; but the principle of the sanctity of international treaty, which brought Britain into the war, scarcely merited the price eventually paid for its protection. Defence of the national territory was at stake also, the principle for which France fought at almost unbearable damage to its national well-being. Defence of the principle of mutual security agreement, underlying the declarations of Germany and Russia, was pursued to a point where security lost all meaning in the dissolution of state structures. Simple state interest, Austria's impulse and the oldest of all reasons for war-making, proved, as the pillars of imperialism collapsed about the Habsburgs, no interest at all.

Consequences, of course, cannot be foreseen. Experience can, by contrast, all too easily be projected into the future. The experience of the early warriors of 1914–18 – the probability of wounds or death, in circumstances of squalor and misery – swiftly acquired inevitability. There is mystery in that also. How did the anonymous millions, indistinguishably drab, undifferentially deprived of any scrap of the glories that by tradition made the life of the man-at-arms tolerable, find the resolution to sustain the struggle and to believe in its purpose? That they did is one of the undeniabilities of the Great War. Comradeship flourished in the earthwork cities of the Western and Eastern Fronts, bound strangers into the closest brotherhood, elevated the loyalties created within the ethos of temporary regimentality to the status of life-and-death blood ties. Men whom the trenches cast into intimacy entered into bonds of mutual dependency and sacrifice of self stronger than any of the friendships made in peace and better times. That is the ultimate mystery of the First World War. If we could understand its loves, as well as its hates, we would be nearer understanding the mystery of human life.

NOTES

CHAPTER ONE

1. A. Bullock, *Hitler*, London, 1952, p. 79
2. M. Gilbert, *The Holocaust*, London, 1987, p. 17
3. Personal Visits
4. J. Winter, *Sites of Memory, Sites of Mourning*, Cambridge, 1995, pp. 92–3
5. G. Ward and E. Gibson, *Courage Remembered*, London, 1989, pp. 89–90
6. R. Whalen, *Bitter Wounds*, German Victims of the Great War, Ithaca, 1984, p. 33
7. V. Ackermann, 'La vision allemande du soldat inconnu', in J-J Becker et al, *Guerres et cultures*, 1914–18, Paris, 1994, pp. 390–1
8. F. Thébaud, 'La guerre et le deuil chez les femmes françaises', in Becker, *Guerres*, pp. 114–15
9. Whalen, p. 41
10. B. Jelavich, *History of the Balkans*, 2, Cambridge, 1985, p. 121
11. M. Brock in R. Evans and H.P. von Strandmann, *The Coming of the First World War*, Oxford, 1988, p. 169
12. K. Baedeker, *Austria*, Leipzig, 1900, pp. 432–4
13. G. Best, *Humanity in Warfare*, London, 1980, p. 140
14. see M. Howard, 'Men Against Fire', in P. Paret, *Makers of Modern Strategy*, Princeton, 1986, pp. 510–26
15. see German, French and Russian military district maps, *Times History of the War*, I, London, 1914
16. J. Lucas, *Fighting Troops of the Austro-Hungarian Empire*, N.Y., 1987, p. 84
17. A. Gordon, *The Rules of the Game*, London, 1996, pp. 354–5

CHAPTER TWO

1. J. Keegan, *The Mask of Command*, London, 1987, pp. 40–2
2. see especially G. Parker, Chapter 5, in W. Murray, M. Knox and A. Bernstein, *The Making of Strategy*, Cambridge, 1994
3. P. Contamine, *War in the Middle Ages*, Oxford, 1984, p. 26
4. J. Thompson, *The Lifeblood of War*, London, 1991, Chapter 2.
5. M. Howard, *The Franco-Prussian War,* London, 1981, pp. 26–7
6. J. Hittle, *The Military Staff*, Harrisburg, 1961, Chapter 2
7. C. Hibbert, *The Destruction of Lord Raglan*, London, 1984, pp. 15–16
8. D. Porch, *The March to the Marne*, Cambridge, 1981, p. 331
9. H. Nicolson, *The Evolution of Diplomatic Method*, London, 1954, p. 75
10. S. Kern, *The Culture of Time and Space*, Cambridge, Mass., 1983, pp. 270–3
11. B. Sullivan, 'The Strategy of the Decisive Weight: Italy, 1882–1922' in Murray, Knox and Bernstein, p. 332
12. N. Stone, 'Moltke and Conrad' in P. Kennedy, *The War Plans of the Great Powers*, London, 1979, p. 234
13. J. McDermot, 'The Revolution in British Military Thinking from the Boer War to the Moroccan Crisis' in Kennedy, p. 105
14. L. Turner, 'The Significance of the Schlieffen Plan' in Kennedy, p. 200
15. A. J. P. Taylor, *The Struggle for Mastery in Europe*, Oxford, 1954, p. 317
16. G. Ritter, *The Schlieffen Plan*, London, 1958, p. 71
17. Ritter, pp. 22–5, 27–48, Maps 1, 2, 3, 6
18. G. Craig, *The Politics of the Prussian Army*, Princeton, 1955, pp. 278–9
19. H. Herwig, 'Strategic Uncertainties of a nation state: Prussia-Germany, 1871–1918', in Murray, Knox and Bernstein, p. 259
20. Herwig in Murray, Knox and Bernstein, p. 260
21. Ritter, p. 173
22. Ritter, p. 180
23. Ritter, p. 139
24. Ritter, p. 141
25. Ritter, p. 142
26. Ritter, p. 174
27. Ritter, p. 144

Notes

28. Ritter, p. 145
29. Ritter, p. 143
30. J. Edmonds, *Military Operations, France and Belgium, 1914*, I, London, 1928, Appendix 31
31. Edmonds, *1914*, I, Sketch 5
32. Ritter, pp. 141, 178
33. A. Bucholz, *Moltke, Schlieffen and Prussian War Planning*, N.Y., 1991, p. 267
34. A. Gat, *The Development of Military Thought*, 2, Oxford, 1992, pp. 153–7
35. Etat-major de L'armée, *Les armées françaises dans la grande guerre*, Paris, 1922, 1, i, annexes, p. 21
36. S. Williamson, 'Joffre Reshapes French Strategy' in Kennedy, p. 145
37. Gat, p. 155
38. Williamson in Kennedy, p. 147
39. Williamson in Kennedy, p. 147
40. Williamson in Kennedy, p. 135
41. L. Sayder, *The Ideology of the Offensive*, Ithaca, 1984, p. 182
42. B. Menning, *Bayonets Before Bullets: The Russian Imperial Army, 1861–1914*, Bloomington, 1992, p. 245
43. Menning, pp. 247–8
44. quoted N. Stone in Kennedy, p. 224
45. Stone in Kennedy, p. 228
46. Stone in Kennedy, p. 223
47. G. Tunstall, *Planning For War Against Russia and Serbia: Austro-Hungarian and German Military Strategies, 1871–1914*, N.Y., 1993, p. 138
48. D. Herrmann, *The Arming of Europe and the Making of the First World War*, Princeton, 1996, p. 156
49. J. Gooch, 'Italy During the First World War' in A. Millett and W. Murray, *Military Effectiveness*, I, Boston, 1988, p. 294
50. Herrmann, p. 176
51. Bucholz, p. 309
52. Bucholz, p. 285

CHAPTER THREE

1. C. Macartney, *The Habsburg Empire 1790–1918*, London, 1968, p. 806

2. V. Dedijer, *The Road to Sarajevo*, N.Y., 1996, pp. 374–5
3. Macartney p. 806
4. B. Jelavich, *History of the Balkans*, II, Cambridge, 1983, pp. 111–12
5. Macartney, p. 807
6. W. Jannon, *The Lions of July*, Novato, 1995, pp. 18–19
7. Jannon, p. 31
8. *The Annual Register, 1914,* London, 1915, p. 312
9. B. Tuchman, *August 1914*, London, 1962, p. 115
10. L. Albertini, *The Origins of the War of 1914*, II, London, 1953, p. 456
11. G. Tunstall, *Planning for War Against Russia and Serbia: Austro-Hungarian and German Military Strategies, 1871–1914*, N.Y., 1993, p. 83
12. Tunstall, p. 122
13. Albertini, II, p. 308
14. Turner in Kennedy, pp. 263–4
15. Turner in Kennedy, p. 264
16. Albertini, II, p. 538
17. Turner in Kennedy, p. 264
18. Turner in Kennedy, p. 265
19. J. Edmonds, *A Short History of World War One*, Oxford, 1951, pp. 130–3
20. Albertini, II, p. 491
21. Albertini, II, p. 555
22. Albertini, II, p. 557
23. Jannon, p. 220
24. Albertini, II, p. 674
25. Jannon, p. 239
26. Albertini, II, p. 572
27. Albertini, III, p. 31
28. Albertini, III, p. 40
29. Albertini, III, pp. 73–4
30. Albertini, III, pp. 69–70
31. Albertini, III, p. 183

CHAPTER FOUR

1. M. Paléologue, *An Ambassador's Memoirs*, I, London, 1923, p. 52

2. Bullock, *Hitler*, p. 45
3. L. Moyer, *Victory Must Be Ours*, London, 1995, pp. 72–3
4. A. Grasser, *Vingt jours de guerre aux temps héröiques*, Paris, 1918, pp. 35–6
5. R. Cobb, 'France and the Coming of War' in Evans and Strandmann, p. 133
6. F. Nagel, *Fritz*, Huntington, 1981, pp. 15–19
7. Bucholz, p. 163
8. Bucholz, p. 278
9. Cobb in Evans and Strandmann, p. 136
10. P. Vansittart, *Voices from the Great War*, London, 1981, p. 25
11. L. Macdonald, *1914: The Days of Hope*, London, 1987, p. 54
12. Macdonald, p. 55
13. E. Spears, *Liaison 1914*, London, 1968, p. 14
14. *Je serais soldat*, Paris, 1900
15. W. Bloem, *The Advance from Mons*, London, 1930, p. 56
16. E. Rommel, *Infantry Attacks*, London, 1990, p. 11
17. P. Haythornthwaite, *The World War One Sourcebook*, London, 1996, pp. 100–1
18. B. Tuchman, *August 1914*, London, 1962, pp. 166–7
19. R. Keyes, *Outrageous Fortune*, London, 1984, p. 7
20. S. Williamson, 'Joffre Reshapes French Strategy, 1911–13' in P. Kennedy, *The War Plans of the Great Powers*, 1880–1914, London, 1979, p. 137
21. Williamson in Kennedy, pp. 143–4
22. Albertini, III, p. 462
23. Albertini, III, p. 469
24. Tuchman, p. 105
25. M. Howard et al, *The Laws of War*, New Haven, 1994, p. 10
26. H. Gibson, *A Journal from Our Legation in Belgium*, N.Y.,1917, p. 91
27. Haythornthwaite, p. 150.
28. quoted Tuchman, p. 173
29. Intelligence Staff, American Expeditionary Force, *Histories of Two Hundred and Fifty-One German Divisions Which Participated in the War, 1914–18*, Washington, 1920, p. 23
30. M. Derez, 'The Flames of Louvain', in H. Cecil and P. Liddle, *Facing Armageddon*, London, 1996, pp. 619–20
31. M. Eksteins, *Rites of Spring: The Great War and the Birth of the Modern Age*, London, 1989, p. 93

32. Derez in Cecil and Liddle, p. 622
33. Derez in Cecil and Liddle, p. 622
34. *251 Divisions*, pp. 280–290
35. S. Tyng, *The Campaign of the Marne*, Oxford, 1935, p. 53
36. Quoted Tuchman, p. 173
37. Tyng, p. 54
38. D. Goodspeed, *Ludendorff*, London, 1966, p. 45
39. C. Duffy, in *Purnell's History of the First World War*, I, London, 1970, p. 137
40. quoted Duffy, *Purnell's*, p. 138
41. Duffy, *Purnell's*, p. 138
42. Goodspeed, p. 47
43. C. Duffy, *Frederick the Great*, London, 1985, p. 154
44. Etat-major de l'armée, *Les armées françaises dans la grande guerre*, Paris, 1922–39, I, i, annexes, 8
45. D. Johnson, *Battlefields of the World War*, N.Y., 1921, pp. 425–9
46. D. Porch, *The March to the Marne*, Cambridge, 1981, p. 178
47. *Les armées*, 10, ii, passim.
48. Porch, *March*, p. 177
49. *Les armées*, I, i, pp. 156–7
50. Tyng, pp. 68–9
51. Tyng, pp. 72–3
52. Tyng, p. 79
53. *Les armées*, I, i, p. 357
54. Reichsarchiv, *Der Weltkrieg*, Berlin, 1925–39, I, p. 310
55. *Weltkrieg*, I, pp. 303–4
56. *Weltkrieg*, I, p. 314
57. Tyng, p. 86
58. *Les armées*, 1, i, p. 425
59. Tyng, p. 101
60. Tyng, p. 102–3
61. see A. Horne, *To Lose a Battle*, London, 1969, p. 57
62. Tyng, p. 108
63. H. Contamine, *La revanche, 1871–1914*, Paris, 1957, p. 261
64. Tyng, p. 117
65. Edmonds, *Military Operations, France and Belgium 1914*, I, London, 1928, pp. 65–6
66. J. Terraine, *Mons*, London, 1960, p. 90
67. R. Kipling, 'On Greenhow Hill' in *Life's Handicap*, London, 1987, pp. 79–96

68. Bloem, p. 56
69. Bloem, p. 80
70. Bloem, p. 58
71. *Weltkrieg*, I, p. 500
72. Tyng, p. 117
73. Spears, *Liaison*, p. 192
74. quoted Spears, *Liaison*, pp. 526–7
75. Bloem, p. 110
76. Edmonds, *1914*, I, p. 494
77. Tyng, pp. 144–5
78. Edmonds, *1914,* I, p. 163
79. Spears, *Liaison*, pp. 228–32
80. Tyng, p. 156
81. Ritter, p. 141
82. D. Showalter, *Tannenberg*, Hamden, 1991, pp. 294–5
83. Tyng, p. 172
84. General von Kuhl, *Der Marnefeldzug*, Berlin, 1921, p. 121
85. R. Van Emden, *Tickled to Death to Go*, Staplehurst, 1996, pp. 59–60
86. Van Emden, pp. 60–61
87. Tuchman, p. 375
88. Tyng, p. 172
89. Contamine, *Revanche*, p. 261
90. *Les armées*, 10, ii, pp. 608 ff
91. Tuchman, pp. 339–43
92. Edmonds, *1914*, I, pp. 473–7
93. Spears, *Liaison*, pp. 366–7
94. *Weltkrieg* II, p. 279
95. Ritter, p. 189; Bucholz, p. 210
96. quoted Tyng, pp. 381–3
97. Tyng, p. 219
98. Tyng, p. 239
99. R. Holmes, *The Little Field Marshal*, London, 1981, p. 230
100. Holmes, p. 229
101. Spears, *Liaison*, p. 415
102. Tyng, p. 241
103. Edmonds, *1914*, I, p. 272
104. G. Aston, *Foch*, London, 1929, p. 122
105. W. Müller, *Die Sendung von Oberstleutnants Hentsch*, Berlin, 1922, p. 13

106. Müller, p. 14
107. Müller, p. 19
108. Müller, p. 22
109. Müller, p. 21
110. Tyng, p. 327
111. Porch, *March*, p. 202
112. Herrmann, p. 90
113. Terraine, *Mons*, p. 217
114. Johnson, pp. 292–3
115. Edmonds, *1914*, I, p. 326
116. Edmonds, *1914*, I, p. 378
117. quoted D. Mason, *Purnell's*, I, p. 296
118. Duffy, *Purnell's*, I, pp. 377–8
119. Edmonds, *1914*, I, p. 404
120. Duffy, *Purnell's*, I, pp. 380–1
121. Duffy, *Purnell's*, I, p. 380
122. Edmonds, *1914*, I, p. 380
123. L. Sellers, *The Hood Battalion*, London, 1995, pp. 24–5
124. C. Cruttwell, *A. History of the Great War*, Oxford, 1936, p. 100
125. S. Menezes, *Fidelity and Honour*, New Delhi, 1993, p. 247
126. Edmonds, *1914*, II, p. 268
127. M. Geyer, *Deutsche Rustungspolitik*, Frankfurt, 1984, pp. 83 ff
128. T. Nevin, *Ernst Jünger and Germany*, London, 1997, p. 43
129. Bullock, p. 48
130. Edmonds, *1914*, II, p. 124
131. Edmonds, *1914*, II, p. 259
132. Reichsarchiv, *Ypern*, Oldenburg, 1922, p. 133
133. Several personal visits
134. Nevin, p. 44
135. Macdonald, p. 418
136. *Ypern*, p. 204
137. *Ypern*, p. 206
138. Edmonds, *1914,* II, p. 324
139. *Ypern*, p. 216
140. J. Edmonds, *A Short History of World War I*, London, 1951, p. 75; G. Petrocini, *Histoire Militaire de la France*, III, Paris, 1991, p. 289; R. Wall and J. Winter, *The Upheaval of War*, London, 1988, pp. 16–18
141. Wall and Winter, p. 27
142. Wall and Winter, p. 25

143. Edmonds, *1914*, II, p. 223
144. P. Mason, *A Matter of Honour*, London, 1974, p. 417
145. Edmonds, *1914,* II, p. 406

CHAPTER FIVE

1. Wellington's *Despatches*, 30th June 1800
2. see Tunstall, Chapter 4; Bucholz, pp. 167, 176
3. Edmonds, *Short History*, map 2
4. N. Stone, *The Eastern Front 1914–17*, London, 1975, p. 48
5. Showalter, p. 536
6. Stone, p. 49
7. Stone, p. 44
8. D. Jones, 'Imperial Russia's Forces at War' in A. Millett and W. Murray, *Military Effectiveness*, I, Boston, 1988, p. 275
9. V. Buldakov et al, 'A Nation at War: the Russian Experience' in Cecil and Liddle, p. 542
10. Menning, p. 228
11. Jones in Millet and Murray, p. 273
12. Stone, p. 55
13. Stone, pp. 58–9
14. Stone, p. 59
15. Showalter, p. 147
16. Jones in Millett and Murray, p. 261; Showalter, p. 170
17. Showalter, p. 153
18. R. Asprey, *The German High Command at War*, London, 1991, p. 63
19. Stone, p. 62
20. Showalter, p. 170
21. Showalter, p. 230
22. Showalter, p. 289
23. Showalter, p. 324
24. Personal visit
25. Asprey, p. 80
26. Tunstall, pp. 95–6
27. J. Clinton Adams, *Flight in the Winter*, Princeton, 1942, pp. 13–14
28. Adams, p. 19
29. Adams, p. 27
30. G. Wawro, 'Morale in the Austro-Hungarian Army', in Cecil and Liddle, p. 400

31. Lucas, passim
32. Menning, p. 230
33. E. Glaise-Horstenau, *Österreich-Ungarns Letzter Krieg 1914–18*, Vienna, 1930, I, p. 74
34. Relation de l'état-major russe, *La Grande Guerre*, Paris, 1926, (tr. E. Chapouilly), p. 139
35. *Letzter Krieg*, I, Beilage 10.
36. *Letzter Krieg*, I, pp. 71–3
37. Stone, p. 88
38. Stone, p. 88
39. M. von Piettrich, *1914*, Vienna, 1934, p. 208
40. Relation de l'état-major russe (cited as *Relation*), p. 249
41. Stone, p. 90
42. G. Rothenburg, *The Army of Franz Joseph*, West Lafayette, 1976, p. 176
43. *Letzter Krieg*, I, p. 74
44. Stone, p. 90
45. Buldakov in Cecil and Liddle, p. 540
46. H. Dollinger, *Der Erste Weltkrieg*, Munich, 1924, pp. 98–9
47. Menning, pp. 228, 260
48. Rothenburg, p. 143
49. M. Howard, 'Men Against Fire', in Paret, p. 519
50. Menning, pp. 264–5
51. Menning, p. 250
52. Goodspeed, p. 99–102
53. *Relation*, 290
54. *Letzter Krieg*, I, Beilage 15
55. *Relation*, 436
56. *Relation*, 446–7
57. *Relation*, 462
58. *Relation*, 463
59. Stone, 104
60. Stone, 107
61. Personal visit, 1989
62. *Letzter Krieg*, I, 595–8
63. Jones in Millett and Murray, pp. 278–9
64. *Letzter Krieg*, I, Beilage 1
65. Rothenburg, p. 84
66. *Letzter Krieg*, I, pp. 141–2
67. Stone, p. 114

68. Rothenburg, p. 185
69. *Illustrated London News*, April 21, 1915
70. *251 Divisions*, p. 541 ff
71. Stone, p. 118
72. Stone, p. 117
73. S. Schama, *Landscape and Memory*, N.Y., 1996, pp. 65–6
74. *Letzter Krieg,* II, pp. 270–1

CHAPTER SIX

1. Stone, p. 135
2. C. Duffy, *The Fortress in the Age of Vauban*, London, 1985, p. 42
3. J. Keegan, *The Face of Battle*, London, 1976, p. 208
4. E. Solano, *Field Entrenchments*, London, 1915, p. 209
5. J. Dunn, *The War the Infantry Knew*, London, 1987, p. 77
6. Dunn, pp. 97–8
7. Dunn, pp. 111–12
8. Keegan, *Purnell's*, II, London, 1970, p. 579
9. G. C. Wynne, *If Germany Attacks*, London, 1940, p. 15
10. Wynne, p. 17
11. Keegan, *Purnell's*, II, p. 584
12. C. Messenger, *Trench Fighting*, London, 1972, p. 37
13. Johnson, p. 470
14. Keegan, *Purnell's*, II, pp. 576–87
15. Keegan, *Purnell's*, II, p. 583
16. Bucholz, pp. 285–6
17. Asprey, pp. 151–5
18. Holmes, p. 264
19. Edmonds, *1915,* I, p. 15
20. Edmonds, *1915,* I, pp. 59–65
21. Edmonds, *1915,* I, pp. 68–9
22. Edmonds, *1915,* I, p. 74
23. Wynne, p. 29
24. Wynne, p. 28
25. Wynne, pp. 30–31
26. Wynne, p. 40
27. D. Omissi, *The Sepoy and the Raj*, London, 1994, pp. 117–18
28. I. Hogg, *Purnell's*, II, pp. 609–11
29. W. Aggett, *The Bloody Eleventh*, III, London, 1995, p. 121

30. Edmonds, *1915,* I, p. 289
31. A. Bristow, *A Serious Disappointment*, 1995, p. 163
32. Wynne, p. 63
33. Wynne, p. 64
34. F. Forstner, *Das Reserve Infanterie Regiment 15*, Berlin, 1929, pp. 226–32
35. E. Spiers, 'The Scottish Soldier at War', in Cecil and Liddle, p. 326
36. Edmonds, *1915,* I, p. 143

CHAPTER SEVEN

1. G. Craig, *Germany 1866–1945*, Oxford, 1981, p. 119
2. T. Wise, *Purnell's*, I, pp. 321–9
3. L. Gann and P. Duignan, *The Rulers of German Africa*, London, 1977, p. 217
4. B. Farwell, *The Great War in Africa*, London, 1987, p. 71
5. Farwell, pp. 81–4
6. Farwell, p. 102
7. Gann and Duignan, p. 105
8. Farwell, p. 204
9. P. Halpern, *A Naval History of World War I*, Annapolis, 1994, p. 76
10. Halpern, p. 91
11. Halpern, pp. 94–5
12. J. Moore (ed), *Jane's Fighting Ships of World War I*, London, 1990, p. 237
13. R. Hough, *The Great War at Sea*, London, 1983, pp. 147–8
14. Halpern, p. 230
15. Jelavich, 2, p. 127
16. Halpern, p. 63
17. P. Mason, *A Matter of Honour*, London, 1974, p. 425
18. Omissi, p. 148
19. Menezes, p. 278
20. *Imperial Gazetteer of India*, IV, Oxford, 1907, pp. 109–11
21. M. Gilbert, *Winston Churchill*, II, London, 1967, p. 611
22. A. Palmer, *The Decline and Fall of the Ottoman Empire*, London, 1992, p. 226
23. Palmer, *Decline*, p. 230

24. M. Broxup (ed.), *The North Caucasus Barrier*, London, 1992, pp. 45 ff
25. B. Menning, 'The Army and Frontier in Russia' in *Transformations in Russian and Soviet Military History*, Colorado Springs, 1986, p. 34
26. K. Ahmed, *Kurdistan in the First World War*, London, 1994, pp. 88–9
27. Ahmed, p. 91
28. D. Muhlis, *Ottoman Military Organisation*, Istanbul, 1986, pp. 11–15
29. Halpern, p. 29
30. Taylor, *Struggle*, p. 532
31. J. Whittam, *The Politics of the Italian Army*, London, 1977, pp. 186–9
32. J. Edmonds, *Military Operations, Italy*, London, 1949, pp. 11–12
33. Ministerio della Guerra, *L'Escercito Italiano nella Grande Guerra*, I, Rome, 1927, pp. 168–70
34. Whittam, p. 194
35. Edmonds, *Italy*, p. 12
36. Edmonds, *Italy*, pp. 13–14
37. Stone, p. 145
38. Stone, p. 317, n.5
39. Edmonds, *France and Belgium, 1915*, I, p. 56
40. S. Bidwell and D. Graham, *Fire-Power*, London, 1982, p. 96
41. Stone, p. 145
42. Asprey, pp. 184–5
43. D. von Kalm, *Gorlice*, Berlin, 1930, p. 33
44. Goodspeed, pp. 132–3
45. Stone, p. 188
46. Stone, p. 187
47. Jones in Millett and Murray, pp. 278–9
48. G. Cassar, *The French and the Dardanelles*, London, 1971, pp. 35–40
49. *First Report of the Dardanelles Committee*, p. 15
50. R. Rhodes James, *Gallipoli*, London, 1965, p. 13
51. Rhodes James, p. 28
52. Rhodes James, p. 38
53. Rhodes James, p. 53
54. Cassar, p. 114

55. Rhodes James, p. 64
56. C. Pugsley, *Gallipoli. The New Zealand Story*, London, 1984, p. 30
57. Pugsley, p. 34
58. C. Aspinall-Oglander, *Gallipoli*, 2, London, 1929, p. 114
59. A. Livesey, *An Atlas of World War I*, London, 1994, p. 61
60. Aspinall-Oglander, Sketch 5A
61. Rhodes James, p. 61
62. Pugsley, p. 360
63. Adams, pp. 42–4
64. Adams, pp. 45–6
65. Cassar, p. 35
66. Cassar, pp. 226–35
67. A. Palmer, *The Gardeners of Salonika*, London, 1965, p. 55
68. Palmer, *Gardeners*, p. 62

CHAPTER EIGHT

1. M. Lewis, *The Navy of Britain*, London, 1948, pp. 112–39
2. J. Moore (ed.), *Jane's Fighting Ships of World War I*, London, 1990, pp. 35–49
3. A. Marder, *From the Dreadnought to Scapa Flow*, II, Oxford, 1965, pp. 238–9
4. Gordon, 355
5. Gordon, 355 and n.69, p. 664
6. H. Halpern, *A Naval History of World War I*, Annapolis, 1994, pp. 30–2
7. Halpern, pp. 36–7
8. J. Campbell, *Jutland*, London, 1986, pp. 373–4
9. Halpern, p. 299
10. Gordon, p. 21
11. Halpern, pp. 289–90
12. P. Kennedy, 'The Development of the German Naval Operations Plans against England, 1896–1914', in Kennedy, p. 171
13. Halpern, p. 38
14. Marder, II, p. 437
15. Halpern, p. 288
16. Halpern, p. 315
17. Halpern, p. 316

18. Marder, II, 445
19. J. Keegan, *Battle at Sea*, London, 1993, p. 129
20. Marder, III, pp. 175–6
21. Halpern, p. 327
22. Halpern, pp. 419–20
23. G. Rochet and G. Massobrio, *Breve Storia dell'Esercito Italiano, 1861–1943,* Turin, 1978, pp. 184–5
24. Stone, pp. 209–11
25. J. J. Becker, *The Great War and the French People*, London, 1985, pp. 22–3
26. *Les armées*, X, i, passim
27. C. Hughes, 'The New Armies', in I. Beckett and K. Simpson, *A Nation in Arms*, London, 1990, p. 105
28. Beckett and Simpson, appendix I, pp. 235–6
29. Asprey, pp. 218–19
30. I. Clarke, *Rumours of War*, Oxford, 1996, pp. 117–18
31. A. Horne, *The Price of Victory*, London, 1993, p. 43
32. Horne, *Price*, p. 97
33. Horne, *Price*, p. 149
34. Horne, *Price*, pp. 168–9
35. Cruttwell, p. 249
36. Horne, *Price*, pp. 252–66
37. Horne, *Price*, p. 284
38. *251 Divisions*, pp. 8–11
39. Asprey, pp. 111–12
40. Holmes, p. 256
41. Holmes, p. 314
42. Holmes, p. 308
43. G. De Groot, *Douglas Haig*, London, 1988, pp. 117–18
44. De Groot, p. 44
45. *251 Divisions*, passim
46. Beckett and Simpson, pp. 235–6
47. P. Griffith, *Battle Tactics of the Western Front*, London, 1994, p. 56
48. T. Travers, *The Killing Ground*, London, 1987, p. 144
49. M. Farndale, *A History of the Royal Artillery: The Western Front, 1914–18*, London, 1986, p. 144
50. Travers, p. 140
51. Travers, p. 140
52. Travers, p. 139

53. see, for example, the bibliographical references to T. Travers, P. Griffith and G. Sheffield in Cecil and Liddle, pp. 413 ff.
54. M. Browne, *The Imperial War Museum Book of the Somme*, London, 1996, p. 67
55. Keegan, *Face*, p. 245
56. Fourth Army Records, Public Record Office, WO158/233–6, July 2.
57. Wynne, p. 118
58. Wynne, p. 120
59. Clarke, p. 93
60. K. Macksey and J. Batchelor, *Tank*, London, 1971, pp. 14–25
61. Personal visit 1996; *The Daily Telegraph*, 29/6/96
62. Farwell, p. 293
63. see G. Robertson, *Chitral, The Story of a Minor Siege*, London, 1897
64. Asprey, pp. 207–8
65. Stone, pp. 229–30
66. Stone, p. 231
67. Asprey, p. 67
68. Stone, p. 68

CHAPTER NINE

1. R. Cobb, *French and Germans, Germans and French*, Oxford, 1983, pp. 3–35
2. J. Glubb, *Into Battle*, London, 1978, p. 153
3. see, passim, A. Clark, *The Donkeys*, London, 1961; L. Wolff, *In Flanders Fields*, London, 1958; N. Dixon, *On the Psychology of Military Incompetence*, London, 1976
4. J. Terraine, *Haig, The Educated Soldier*, London, 1963
5. quoted F. Davies and G. Maddocks, *Bloody Red Tabs*, London, 1995, p. 26
6. Davies and Maddocks, p. 23
7. P. Griffith, *Battle Tactics of the Western Front*, London, 1994, p. 171
8. Wynne, p. 125
9. Public Records Office, WO95/2366, 95/820, 153, 167/256/11
10. S. Bidwell and T. Graham, *Fire-Power*, London, 1982, pp. 141–3
11. Thébaud in J. J. Becker, *Guerres et Cultures*, p. 113

12. J. J. Becker, *The Great War and the French People*, Leamington Spa, 1985, p. 21
13. Becker, *Great War*, p. 227
14. R. Wall and J. Winter, *The Upheaval of War*, Cambridge, 1998, p. 30
15. L. Moyer, *Victory Must Be Ours*, London, 1995, p. 164
16. Wall and Winter, p. 117
17. Cruttwell, pp. 363–4
18. Moyer, pp. 165–71
19. T. Wilson, *The Myriad Faces of War*, London, 1986, p. 407
20. Becker, *Great War*, p. 324
21. Stone, p. 282
22. E. Spears, *Prelude to Victory*, London, 1939, p. 42
23. Wynne, p. 134
24. Wynne, pp. 166–7
25. Spears, *Prelude*, pp. 40–1
26. Wynne, p. 180
27. Wynne, p. 174
28. A. McKee, *Vimy Ridge*, London, 1966, p. 102
29. McKee, p. 116
30. Spears, *Prelude*, p. 331
31. Spears, *Prelude*, p. 41
32. Spears, *Prelude*, pp. 489–90
33. Spears, *Prelude*, p. 492
34. Spears, *Prelude*, p. 493
35. Spears, *Prelude*, p. 509
36. L. Smith, *Between Mutiny and Obedience: The Case of the French Fifth Infantry Division during World War I*, Princeton, 1994, p. 185
37. Becker, *Great War*, pp. 217–22
38. Becker, *Great War*, p. 219
39. M. Pedrocini, *Les mutineries de 1917*, Paris, 1967, Chapter 4
40. Smith, pp. 218–19
41. Smith, p. 197
42. Smith, p. 206–7
43. T. Ashworth, *Trench Warfare 1914–18: The Live and Let Live System*, London, 1980, pp. 15–16
44. Smith, pp. 225–6
45. Stone, p. 282
46. Becker, *Great War*, pp. 220–1

47. A. Wildman, *The End of the Russian Imperial Army*, N.Y., 1980, p. 109
48. Stone, pp. 284–5
49. Stone, pp. 299–300
50. O. Figes, *A People's Tragedy*, London, 1996, p. 378
51. Wildman, p. 128
52. Wildman, p. 149
53. quoted Figes, p. 315
54. R. Pipes, *The Russian Revolution*, London, 1990, p. 258
55. Pipes, pp. 321–2
56. Pipes, p. 329
57. Pipes, p. 328
58. Wildman, p. 335
59. Pipes, p. 393
60. Wynne, p. 294
61. Figes, p. 445
62. Pipes, p. 477
63. Pipes, p. 583
64. Buldakov in Cecil and Liddle, p. 542
65. Pipes, pp. 418–19
66. Buldakov in Cecil and Liddle, p. 542
67. J. Gooch, 'Italy During the First World War' in Millett and Williamson, p. 181
68. Whittam, p. 197
69. J. Gooch, 'Morale and Discipline in the Italian Army 1915–18' in Cecil and Liddle, p. 437
70. Gooch in Cecil and Liddle, p. 440
71. J. Keegan, 'An Army Downs Tools' (review of L. Smith, *Between Mutiny and Obedience*), *The Times Literary Supplement*, May 13 1994, pp. 3–4
72. Rochet and Massobrio, p. 185
73. C. Falls, *Caporetto*, London, 1966, p. 26
74. Falls, pp. 36–7
75. Falls, p. 40
76. Rommel, p. 177
77. Rommel, p. 221
78. Falls, p. 49
79. Gooch in Cecil and Liddle, p. 442
80. J. Pratt, *A History of United States Foreign Policy*, N.Y., 1959, pp. 477–82

81. Halpern, pp. 337–9
82. Asprey, p. 293
83. Halpern, p. 404
84. Halpern, p. 84
85. J. Terraine, *Business in Great Waters*, London, 1989, pp. 52–3
86. Terraine, *Great Waters*, p. 54
87. Terraine, *Great Waters*, p. 148
88. R. Blake, *The Private Papers of Douglas Haig*, London, 1952, p. 236
89. Woolf, p. 77
90. J. Terraine, *The Road to Passchendaele*, London, 1977, p. 156
91. Terraine, *Passchendaele*, p. 166
92. P. Oldham, *Pillboxes on the Western Front*, London, 1995, Chapter 6.
93. Wynne, pp. 288–9
94. Wynne, pp. 295–6
95. J. Edmonds, *Military Operations, France and Belgium, 1917*, II, London, 1948, p. 134
96. J. Morrow, *The Great War in the Air*, London, 1993, p. 202
97. Morrow, pp. 186–7
98. N. Steel and P. Hart, *Tumult in the Clouds*, London, 1997, pp. 25, 214
99. A. Kernan, *Crossing the Line*, N.Y., 1994, p. 108
100. Farndale, p. 203
101. Farndale, p. 204
102. Edmonds, *1917,* II, p. 148
103. E. Vaughan, *Some Desperate Glory*, London, 1981, pp. 219–32
104. Woolf, pp. 165–7
105. Wynne, pp. 307–8
106. Wynne, pp. 303–10
107. P. Griffith, *The British Army's Art of Attack 1916–18*, London, 1994, p. 89
108. De Groot, p. 341
109. De Groot, p. 343
110. D. Morton, *A Military History of Canada*, Toronto, 1992, p. 149
111. D. Morton, *When Your Number's Up*, London, 1993, p. 171
112. Edmonds, *Short History*, p. 252
113. Farndale, pp. 216–17
114. *251 Divisions*, p. 224

116. Travers, p. 22
117. Farndale, p. 223
118. Farndale, p. 224

CHAPTER TEN

1. M. Kitchen, *The Silent Dictatorship*, London, 1996, p. 123
2. M. E. S. Harries, *The Last Days of Innocence*, London, 1997, p. 89
3. Harries, p. 324
4. *251 Divisions*, p. 97
5. M. Middlebrook, *The Kaiser's Battle*, London, 1978, pp. 380–4
6. Middlebrook, *Kaiser*, p. 52
7. Middlebrook, *Kaiser*, p. 53
8. C. Falls, *The Great War*, London, 1959, p. 285
9. F. Fischer, *Germany's Aims in the First World War*, N.Y., 1967, p. 609
10. Fischer, p. 610
11. Kitchen, p. 248
12. Fischer, p. 450
13. Fischer, pp. 460–9
14. R. Luckett, *The White Generals*, N.Y., 1971, pp. 126–30
15. Luckett, p. 142
16. G. Mannerheim, *Memoirs*, N.Y., 1953, p. 176
17. Kitchen, p. 220
18. Fischer, p. 515
19. E. Mawdsley, *The Russian Civil War*, N.Y., 1989, p. 27
20. Mawdsley, pp. 286–7
21. Pipes, *Revolution*, p. 581
22. Pipes, *Revolution*, p. 581
23. Pipes, *Revolution*, p. 584
24. Mawdsley, p. 34
25. Pipes, *Revolution*, p. 584
26. Mawdsley, p. 26
27. Mawdsley, pp. 225–9
28. C. Ellis, *The British Intervention in Transcaspia, 1918–19*, London, 1963, p. 12
29. G. Uloth, *Riding to War*, privately printed, 1993, pp. 8–9
30. G. Bayliss, *Operations in Persia, 1914–19*, London, 1987, pp. 210–11

31. Ellis, p. 12
32. Ellis, pp. 57–65
33. Ellis, p. 12
34. Luckett, p. 196
35. Luckett, p. 197
36. Pipes, *Revolution*, p. 610
37. Mawdsley, p. 59
38. J. Bradley, *Allied Intervention in Russia*, London, 1968, p. 2
39. Bradley, pp. 11–14
40. Bradley, p. 181
41. Mawdsley, p. 20
42. Mawdsley, p. 21
43. Bradley, p. 18
44. Luckett, p. 163
45. Bradley, pp. 94–5
46. Mawdsley, p. 97
47. Luckett, pp. 198–208
48. N. Nicolson, *Alex*, London, 1963, pp. 57–66
49. G. Bennet, *Cowan's War*, London, 1964, p. 157
50. P. Kencz, *Civil War in South Russia*, N.Y., 1977, pp. 182–91
51. Bradley, pp. 106–31
52. Pipes, *Revolution*, p. 657
53. M. Carley, *Revolution and Intervention*, N.Y., 1983, p. 38
54. Pipes, *Revolution*, p. 657
55. Pipes, *Revolution*, p. 634
56. H. Herwig, *The First World War*, N.Y., 1997, pp. 400–1
57. Middlebrook, *Kaiser*, p. 382
58. J. Edmonds, *Military Operations, France and Belgium, 1918*, I, London, 1935, p. 139
59. Herwig, pp. 399–400
60. Edmonds, *1918*, I, p. 156
61. Herwig, p. 302
62. Edmonds, *1918*, I, p. 51
63. Edmonds, *1918*, I, p. 99
64. Edmonds, *1918*, I, p. 123
65. Middlebrook, *Kaiser*, p. 152
66. Middlebrook, *Kaiser*, p. 162
67. Middlebrook, *Kaiser*, p. 189
68. Middlebrook, *Kaiser*, pp. 191–2
69. Middlebrook, *Kaiser*, p. 192

70. Middlebrook, *Kaiser*, p. 238
71. Edmonds, *Short History*, p. 286
72. Edmonds, *Short History*, p. 542
73. Herwig, pp. 406–7
74. Herwig, p. 410
75. Herwig, p. 408
76. Hewig, p. 409
77. Edmonds, *Short History*, p. 305
78. Herwig, p. 404
79. Herwig, p. 415
80. Harries, p. 251
81. Edmonds, *Short History*, p. 323
82. Fischer, p. 622
83. Herwig, p. 416
84. Herwig, pp. 421–2
85. Kitchen, pp. 247–9
86. Herwig, p. 421
87. Harries, p. 345
88. Goodspeed, p. 208
89. Goodspeed, p. 211
90. Goodspeed, p. 211
91. R. Watt, *The Kings Depart*, London, 1968, p. 149
92. Goodspeed, p. 215
93. Goodspeed, pp. 216–17
94. Macartney, pp. 829–33
95. Macartney, p. 833
96. Watt, pp. 164–5
97. Watt, p. 195
98. Watt, p. 187
99. Cruttwell, pp. 595–6
100. Watt, p. 199
101. F. Carsten, *The Reichswehr and Politics, 1918–33,* Oxford, 1966, p. 8
102. Watt, p. 191
103. N. Jones, *Hitler's Heralds*, London, 1987, Appendix 4.
104. Ward and Gibson, p. 281
105. Winter, *Sites of Memory*, p. 108
106. Herwig, p. 439; Whalen, p. 40
107. J. Winter, *Upheaval*, pp. 16–27
108. Whalen, p. 41

BIBLIOGRAPHY

OFFICIAL HISTORIES

Neither Russia nor Turkey published official histories, the state structure of both empires having been devastated by the war and subsequent civil war. Nor is there an American official narrative history, though the United States government produced a number of volumes about specific aspects of the war. The most important official histories are the British, French, German, Austrian and Australian. The French history, though detailed, is desiccated in tone; the most useful volume is the tenth, divided into two parts, which contains the order of battle and records the movements and changes of command of divisions and higher formations. The Austrian official history also includes valuable orders of battle and provides a narrative less clinical than the French. The sixteen volumes of the German official history of operations on land was written in a detached general-staff style but is an indispensable record of the German army's activities; a companion series of informal battle narratives (e.g. Reichsarchiv, *Ypern, Gorlice*) is also useful. The British official series comprehends extended narratives of army operations in all theatres, a naval and an air force history, some technical volumes (medicine, transportation) and a subordinate and extremely detailed set of orders of battle, absolutely necessary to an understanding of Britain's part in the war. The Australian official historian, C. W. E. Bean, collected personal reminiscences from many participants. His series of volumes, as a result, has a human dimension none of the other official histories achieves, and anticipates in its approach that successfully adopted in the magnificent American official narrative of the Second World War. The titles of these official histories are as follows:

J. Edmonds, *Military Operations, France and Belgium, 1914–18*, London, 1925–48, and companion volumes on operations in Italy, Macedonia, Egypt and Palestine, the Dardanelles, Persia and East and

479

West Africa by other authors. The naval history, *Naval Operations*, London, 1920–31, was written by J. Corbett and H. Newbolt. The aviation volumes are those of W. Raleigh and H. Jones, *The War in the Air*, Oxford, 1922–37.

Etat-major de L'armée, *Les Armées françaises dans la grande guerre*, Paris, 1922–39

Reichsarchiv, *Der Weltkrieg*, Berlin, 1925–39

Bundesministerium für Landesverteidigung, *Österreich-Ungarns Letzter Krieg, 1914–18*, Vienna, 1930–8

C. W. E. Bean, *Australia in the War of 1914–18*, Sydney, 1921–43

General Histories

There are few satisfactory general histories of the war, perhaps because of the miseries and rancours it left behind. The losers preferred to forget, while even among the victors there was little enthusiasm for recalling the events which had literally decimated their populations. The British, who suffered proportionately least of the combatant great powers, produced the most successful general accounts. Theirs and others include:

J. Edmonds, *A Short History of World War I*, Oxford, 1951, a brief but comprehensive operational survey.

C. Falls, *The First World War*, London, 1960, incisive and compact.

M. Ferro, *The Great War 1914–18*, London, 1973, the first general history with a philosophical and cultural dimension.

A. J. P. Taylor, *The First World War: An Illustrated History*, London, 1963, characteristically succinct.

H. Herwig, *The First World War: Germany and Austria 1914–18*, London, 1997, is wider than its title suggests and surveys much modern scholarship.

Professor Hew Strachan's Oxford History, in press (two volumes), is expected to supplant C. M. R. F. Cruttwell, *A History of the Great War*, Oxford, 1934, dated but splendidly written.

Origins

The peremptory transition from an apparently profound peace to violent general war in a few mid-summer weeks in 1914 continues to defy attempts at explanation. Historians, after abandoning efforts to assign war guilt, turned first to an examination of causes, which

Bibliography

proved almost as contentious, eventually to an analysis of circumstances.

The bedrock of all discussion remains L. Albertini's *The Origins of the War of 1914* (3 volumes), Oxford, 1952–7, which provides a detailed chronology of the crisis and excerpts from the most important documents. A more recent and carefully balanced analysis of circumstances is provided by J. Joll, *1914: The Unspoken Assumptions*, London, 1984. Essential works on the unfolding of the crisis in each of the major combatant states are: I. Geiss, *Juli 1914*, Munich, 1965; J. Gooch, *Army, State and Society in Italy, 1870–1915*, N.Y., 1989; J. Keiger, *France and the Origins of the First World War*, N.Y., 1983; S. Williamson, *Austria-Hungary and the Origins of the First World War*, N.Y., 1991; and Z. Steiner, *Britain and the Origins of the First World War*, N.Y. 1977, which is particularly concerned with British official diplomacy. F. Fischer, in *Griff nach der Weltmacht*, Düsseldorf, 1961, and *Krieg der Illusionen*, Düsseldorf, 1969, controversially revived the issue of Germany's war guilt. Both, though causing outrage in Germany at the time of their publication, remain essential texts.

Two books on the mood of pre-war Europe are vital: M. Ekstein's *Rites of Spring*, Boston, 1989, and R. Wohl, *The Generation of 1914*, Cambridge, Mass., 1979.

War Plans

In *The Schlieffen Plan*, N.Y., 1959, G. Ritter dissected the texts of the German chief of staff which launched his army on its disastrous campaign the year after his death; it is perhaps the single most important book ever published on the First World War. Valuable commentaries are supplied by B. Tunstall, in *Planning for War Against Russia and Serbia*, N.Y., 1993, A. Bucholz, *Moltke, Schlieffen and Prussian War Planning*, N.Y., 1991, D. Herrmann, *The Arming of Europe and the Making of the First World War*, Princeton, 1996, and the essays in P. Kennedy, *The War Plans of the Great Powers*, London, 1979.

Conduct of the War

The strategy of the war, as distinct from planning for it, has generated little scholarship. Its tactics, on the other hand, have always stimulated investigation, perhaps because a successful tactical solution was

481

perceived to be the principal strategic necessity, particularly on the Western Front. In recent years a new generation of British, Australian and Canadian scholars have revived enquiry. Three leading writers are T. Travers' *The Killing Ground*, London, 1987 and *How the War Was Won*, London, 1992, P. Griffith, *Battle Tactics of the Western Front*, London, 1992 and *Forward into Battle*, Rambsbury, 1990 and H. Herwig *The First World War: Germany and Austria-Hungary 1914–18*, London, 1997. None achieves the incisiveness of the British ex-official historian, G. C. Wynne, who, in *If Germany Attacks*, London, 1940, produced an analysis of British and French adaptations of their methods of the offensive against entrenched positions and of the German response which has not been surpassed. A valuable insight into the nature of trench warfare on the 'inactive' sectors is supplied by T. Ashworth in *Trench Warfare: The Live and Let Live System*, London, 1980. Three important books on the war's generalship, casting much light on its strategy, are: R. Asprey, *The German High Command at War*, N.Y., 1991, M. Kitchen, *The Silent Dictatorship: The Politics of the German High Command under Hindenburg and Ludendorff*, London, 1976 and C. Barnett, *The Swordbearers*, London, 1963.

Armed Forces

There is a rich literature on the armed forces of the First World War, particularly on the British army. Among the best are: P. Simkins, *Kitchener's Army*, Manchester, 1986, a scholarly labour of love on the war's largest volunteer army, and I. Beckett and K. Simpson, *A Nation in Arms*, Manchester, 1985. Good books on the French army include D. Porch, *The March to the Marne*, Cambridge, 1981, L. Smith, *Between Mutiny and Obedience*, Princeton, 1994, and R. Challener, *The French Theory of the Nation in Arms*, N.Y., 1955; E. Weber, *Peasants into Frenchmen*, London, 1977, has illuminating passages in the acceptance of conscription by rural France before the war. G. Pedroncini, *Les mutineries de 1917*, Paris, 1967, is still definitive. B. Menning, *Bayonets Before Bullets: The Imperial Russian Army, 1861-1914*, Bloomington, 1994 is outstanding and is complemented by A. Wildman, *The End of the Russian Imperial Army*, Princeton, 1980. G. Rothenburg, *The Army of Franz Joseph*, West Lafayette, 1976, is the best book in English on the Austro-Hungarians but J. Lucas, *Fighting Troops of the Austro-Hungarian Army*, Speldhurst, 1987, is packed with useful detail. There is still no good book in English on the German army. A Millett and W. Williamson's *Military Effectiveness*, I, Boston, 1988, has excellent chapters on national armies. J. Gooch, *Army, State and Society in Italy, 1870–1915*, N.Y., 1989, is excellent and D. Omissi, *The Sepoy and the Raj*, London, 1994, on the Indian Army, is outstanding. Nothing comprehensive has yet been written in English on the Ottoman army of 1914–18.

There are several excellent studies of the German navy, including J. Steinberg, *Yesterday's Deterrent*, London, 1965, and H. Herwig, *Luxury Fleet*, London, 1980, and *The German Naval Officer Corps*, Oxford, 1973. On the Royal Navy, A Marder, *From the Dreadnought to Scapa Flow*, 5 vols, London, 1961–70, remains the classic authority. M. Vego, *Austro-Hungarian Naval Policy 1904–14*, London, 1996, is interesting on the preliminaries to the Austro-Italian naval war in the Adriatic.

The technical literature of air fighting is considerable but there are few books of worth on air forces. An interesting study is D. Winter, *The First of the Few: Fighter Pilots of the First World War*, London, 1982.

Battles and Campaigns

An early and now largely forgotten campaign history remains invaluable on the subject: S. Tyng, *The Campaign of the Marne*, Oxford, 1935. The best book on the contemporaneous battle in the east is D. Showalter, *Tannenberg*, Hamden, 1991. N. Stone, *The Eastern Front 1914–17*, N.Y., 1975, is indispensable. Important books on battles on the Western Front are: E. Spears, *Liaison 1914: A Narrative of the Great Retreat* and *Prelude to Victory*, London, 1939, on the Nivelle offensive; M. Middlebrook, *The First Day on the Somme*, London, 1971, and *The Kaiser's Battle*, London, 1978, on the opening of the German offensives of 1918; A. Horne, *The Price of Victory*, London, 1962, a classic account of Verdun; A. McKee, *Vimy Ridge*, London, 1962; and L. Wolff, *In Flanders Fields*, London, 1958, an impassioned account of Passchendaele. C. Falls, *Caporetto*, London, 1966, and A. Palmer, *The Gardeners of Salonika*, London, 1965, are the best studies of the Italian and Macedonian fronts in English. Gallipoli has produced an enormous literature, often of high quality. Good general books are: R. Rhodes James, *Gallipoli*, London, 1965, G. Cassar, *The French and the Dardanelles*, London,

1971, and A. Moorehead, *Gallipoli*, London, 1956, dated but highly readable. Useful books on the outer theatres of war are C. Falls, *Armageddon 1918*, London, 1964 (Palestine), A. Barker, *The Neglected War: Mesopotamia 1914–18*, London, 1967, and B. Farwell, *The Great War in Africa*, London, 1987. A compendium, *History of the First World War*, London, 1969–71, issued by Purnell in parts and edited by B. Pitt and P. Young, forming eight volumes, contains accounts of all the war's episodes, some by leading scholars. It is a valuable source, particularly for the more obscure campaigns (e.g. Tsingtao, the Caucasus). C. Ellis, *The Transcaspian Episode*, London, 1963, is a brilliant monograph on British intervention in South Russia in 1918. Allied intervention in Russia and on the military aspects of the Russian revolution and civil war are covered in J. Wheeler-Bennett, *Brest-Litovsk: The Forgotten Peace*, London, 1966, E. Mawdsley, *The Russian Civil War*, N.Y., 1989, R. Luckett, *The White Generals*, N.Y. 1971, J. Bradley, *Allied Intervention in Russia*, London, 1968, P. Kencz, *Civil War in South Russia*, N.Y., 1977 and M. Carley, *Revolution and Intervention*, N.Y. 1983.

Particular aspects of the naval war are well described in: J. Goldrick, *The King's Ships Were at Sea: The War in the North Sea, August, 1914 – February 1915*, Annapolis, 1984; P. Halpern, *The Naval War in the Mediterranean, 1914-18*, London, 1987, G. Bennet, *Coronel and the Falklands*, N.Y., 1962, and *Cowan's War: The Story of British Naval Operations in the Baltic, 1918-20*, London, 1964, and J. Terraine, *Business in Great Waters*, London, 1989, the best general account of the U-boat campaign. Among the enormous number of books on Jutland the following should be noted: N. Campbell, *Jutland: An Analysis of the Fighting*, London, 1986 and A. Gordon, *The Rules of the Game*, London, 1996.

Politics and Economics

Among notable books on the politics and economics of the war by academic writers are: V. Berghahn, *Germany and the Approach of War in 1914*, N.Y., 1973, G. Feldman, *Arms, Industry and Labor in Germany, 1914–18*, Princeton, 1966, D. French, *British Strategy and War Aims*, London, 1986, J. Galantai, *Hungary in the First World War*, Budapest, 1989, M. Geyer, *Deutsche Rüstungspolitik*, Frankfurt, 1984, P. Guinn, *British Strategy and Politics, 1914–18*, Oxford, 1965 and Z. Zeman, *The Break-up of the Habsburg Empire*, London, 1961.

Bibliography

Culture and Society

French scholars have recently made notable contributions to the social and cultural history of the war. They include J.-J. Becker and S. Audouin-Rouzeau, *Les sociétés européennes et la guerre de 1914-18*, Paris, 1990, J-J Becker et al, *Guerres et Cultures 1914–18*, Paris, 1994, J.-J. Becker, *La France en guerre, 1914–18*, Paris, 1988, and J.-J. Becker, *The Great War and the French People*, Leamington Spa, 1985. Becker's English collaborator, J. Winter, has edited, with W. Wall, *The Upheaval of War: Family, Work and Welfare in Europe, 1914–18*, Cambridge, 1988. His *Sites of Memory, Sites of Mourning: The Great War in European Cultural History*, Cambridge, 1995, is a moving essay on the efforts made by soldiers and civilian communities to bear, rationalise and commemorate the griefs the war caused. More literary, and now one of the most famous of all Great War books, is Paul Fussell, *The Great War and Modern Memory*, Oxford, 1975, a study of the English literature, particularly novels and memoirs. An older but still valuable French equivalent is J. Norton Cru, *Témoins*, new edition, Nancy, 1993. Two important books on the German experience are L. Moyer, *Victory Must Be Ours*, London, 1995, and R. Whalen, *Bitter Wounds: German Victims of the Great War*, Ithaca, 1984. In *The Myriad Faces of War*, Cambridge, 1986, Trevor Wilson has constructed a multi-faceted portrait of the British war experience. An interesting American perspective is E. Leed, *No Man's Land: Combat and Identity in World War I*, Cambridge, 1979.

Biography

The military leaders of the First World War have found few retrospective admirers. This increasingly seems unfair. They were men presented by an almost insuperable problem – how to break a strong fortified front with weak, indeed inadequate means – and none was any much worse a general than another. An interesting collective portrait is presented by Correlli Barnett in *The Swordbearers*, London, 1963; his subjects are Moltke the Younger, Admiral Sir John Jellicoe, Commander of the Grand Fleet, Pétain and Ludendorff. Basil Liddell Hart's sympathetic biography of *Foch: Man of Orleans*, 1931, stands the test of time. So does J. Wheeler-Bennett's Life of *Hindenburg: the Wooden Titan*, London, 1936. D. Goodspeed is excellent on *Ludendorff*, London, 1966. Haig remains an enigma, an efficient military technician deficient in human feeling. John Terraine supplies a partisan defence of his achievements in *Haig: the Educated Soldier*, London, 1963; a more sceptical biography, emphasising the less rational side of his character, is by G. De Groot, *Douglas Haig*, London, 1988; also to be noted is *Haig's Command* by D. Winter, London, 1991. *The Private Papers of Douglas Haig*, edited by R. Blake, 1952, is indispensable. So, too, is Philip Magnus on *Kitchener*, N.Y. 1959. D. Smythe, *Pershing*, Bloomington, 1986, provides the best biography of the General of the (American) Armies. R. Holmes has written an excellent biography of Sir John French in *The Little Field Marshal*, London, 1981. Good biographies of British admirals are provided by R. Mackay, *Fisher of Kilverstone*, Oxford, 1973, A. Temple Patterson, *Jellicoe*, London, 1969, and S. Roskill, *Earl Beatty*, London, 1980.

INDEX

Index

495

The World at War, 1914